AUTOMOTIVE ENGINE PERFORMANCE

THIRD EDITION

Boston   Columbus   Indianapolis   New York   San Francisco   Upper Saddle River
Amsterdam   Cape Town   Dubai   London   Madrid   Milan   Munich   Paris   Montreal   Toronto
Delhi   Mexico City   Sao Paulo   Sydney   Hong Kong   Seoul   Singapore   Taipei   Tokyo

Editor in Chief: Vernon Anthony
Acquisitions Editor: Wyatt Morris
Editorial Assistant: Christopher Reed
Director of Marketing: David Gesell
Marketing Manager: Kara Clark
Marketing Assistant: Les Roberts
Senior Managing Editor: JoEllen Gohr
Project Manager: Jessica H. Sykes
Senior Operations Supervisor: Pat Tonneman
Operations Specialist: Laura Weaver
Art Director: Candace Rowley
Text and Cover Designer: Anne DeMarinis

Cover Art: Shutterstock
Media Editor: Michelle Churma
Lead Media Project Manager: Karen Bretz
Full-Service Project Management: Kelli Jauron/ S4Carlisle Publishing Services
Composition: S4Carlisle Publishing Services
Printer/Binder: Courier/Kendallville
Cover Printer: Lehigh-Phoenix Color/Hagerstown
Text Font: Helvetica Neue

Prentice Hall
is an imprint of

www.pearsonhighered.com

ISBN 10:   0-13-508504-7
ISBN 13: 978-0-13-508504-2

PREFACE

PROFESSIONAL TECHNICIAN SERIES Part of Pearson Automotive's Professional Technician Series, the third edition of *Automotive Engine Performance* represents the future of automotive textbooks. The series is a full-color, media-integrated solution for today's students and instructors. The series includes textbooks that cover all eight areas of ASE certification, plus additional titles covering common courses.

Current revisions are written by a team of very experienced writers and teachers. The series is also peer reviewed for technical accuracy.

UPDATES TO THE THIRD EDITION

- Ten new chapters including:
  - Gasoline
  - Alternative Fuels
  - Diesel and Biodiesel Fuels
  - Electronic Throttle Control Systems
  - Variable Valve Timing Systems
- Dramatic new full-color design.
- Over 50 new color photos and line drawings have been added to this edition.
- Content has been streamlined for easier reading and comprehension.
- Text is fully-integrated with MyAutomotiveKit, an online supplement for homework, quizzing, testing, multimedia activities, and videos.
- Unlike other textbooks, this book is written so that the theory, construction, diagnosis, and service of a particular component or system are presented in one location. There is no need to search through the entire book for other references to the same topic.

ASE AND NATEF CORRELATED

NATEF certified programs need to demonstrate that they use course material that covers NATEF and ASE tasks. All Professional Technician textbooks have been correlated to the appropriate ASE and NATEF task lists. These correlations can be found in two locations:

- As an appendix to each book.
- At the beginning of each chapter in the Instructor's Manual.

A COMPLETE INSTRUCTOR AND STUDENT SUPPLEMENTS PACKAGE

All Professional Technician textbooks are accompanied by a full set of instructor and student supplements. Please see page vi for a detailed list of supplements.

A FOCUS ON DIAGNOSIS AND PROBLEM SOLVING

The Professional Technician Series has been developed to satisfy the need for a greater emphasis on problem diagnosis. Automotive instructors and service managers agree that students and beginning technicians need more training in diagnostic procedures and skill development. To meet this need and demonstrate how real-world problems are solved, "Real World Fix" features are included throughout and highlight how real-life problems are diagnosed and repaired.

The following pages highlight the unique core features that set the Professional Technician Series book apart from other automotive textbooks.

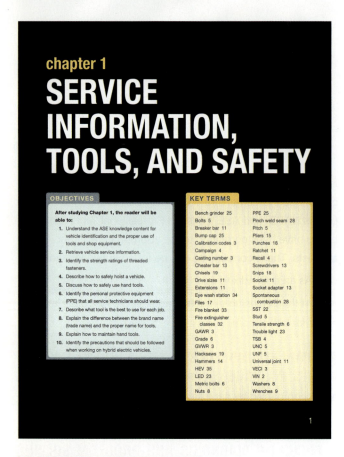

chapter 1
SERVICE INFORMATION, TOOLS, AND SAFETY

OBJECTIVES

After studying Chapter 1, the reader will be able to:

1. Understand the ASE knowledge content for vehicle identification and the proper use of tools and shop equipment.
2. Retrieve vehicle service information.
3. Identify the strength ratings of threaded fasteners.
4. Describe how to safely hoist a vehicle.
5. Discuss how to safely use hand tools.
6. Identify the personal protective equipment (PPE) that all service technicians should wear.
7. Describe what tool is the best to use for each job.
8. Explain the difference between the brand name (trade name) and the proper name for tools.
9. Explain how to maintain hand tools.
10. Identify the precautions that should be followed when working on hybrid electric vehicles.

KEY TERMS

Bench grinder 25	PPE 25
Bolts 5	Pinch weld seam 28
Breaker bar 11	Pitch 5
Bump cap 25	Pliers 15
Calibration codes 3	Punches 16
Campaign 4	Ratchet 11
Casting number 3	Recall 4
Cheater bar 13	Screwdrivers 13
Chisels 19	Snips 18
Drive sizes 11	Socket 11
Extensions 11	Socket adapter 13
Eye wash station 34	Spontaneous
Files 17	combustion 28
Fire blanket 33	SST 22
Fire extinguisher	Stud 5
classes 32	Tensile strength 6
GAWR 3	Trouble light 23
Grade 6	TSB 4
GVWR 3	UNC 5
Hacksaws 19	UNF 5
Hammers 14	Universal joint 11
HEV 35	VECI 3
LED 23	VIN 2
Metric bolts 6	Washers 8
Nuts 8	Wrenches 9

1

OBJECTIVES AND KEY TERMS appear at the beginning of each chapter to help students and instructors focus on the most important material in each chapter. The chapter objectives are based on specific ASE and NATEF tasks.

SAFETY TIP

Shop Cloth Disposal

Always dispose of oily shop cloths in an enclosed container to prevent a fire. ● **SEE FIGURE 1–69**. Whenever oily cloths are thrown together on the floor or workbench, a chemical reaction can occur, which can ignite the cloth even without an open flame. This process of ignition without an open flame is called **spontaneous combustion.**

SAFETY TIPS alert students to possible hazards on the job and how to avoid them.

REAL WORLD FIX

Three Brake Jobs in 40,000 Miles

A service technician was asked to replace the front disc brake pads on a Pontiac Grand Am because the sensors were touching the rotors and making a squealing sound. This was the third time that the front brakes needed to be replaced. Previous brake repairs had been limited to replacement of the front disc brake pads only.

When the caliper was removed and the pads inspected, it was discovered that a part of one pad had broken and a piece of the lining was missing. ● **SEE FIGURE 13–15.**

REAL WORLD FIXES presents students with actual automotive scenarios and shows how these common (and sometimes uncommon) problems were diagnosed and repaired.

TECH TIP

It Just Takes a Second

Whenever removing any automotive component, it is wise to screw the bolts back into the holes a couple of threads by hand. This ensures that the right bolt will be used in its original location when the component or part is put back on the vehicle.

TECH TIPS feature real-world advice and "tricks of the trade" from ASE-certified master technicians.

FREQUENTLY ASKED QUESTION

How Many Types of Screw Heads Are Used in Automotive Applications?

There are many, including Torx, hex (also called Allen), plus many others used in custom vans and motor homes. ● **SEE FIGURE 1–9**.

FREQUENTLY ASKED QUESTIONS are based on the author's own experience and provide answers to many of the most common questions asked by students and beginning service technicians.

NOTE: Most of these "locking nuts" are grouped together and are commonly referred to as *prevailing torque nuts*. This means that the nut will hold its tightness or torque and not loosen with movement or vibration.

NOTES provide students with additional technical information to give them a greater understanding of a specific task or procedure.

CAUTION: *Never* use hardware store (nongraded) bolts, studs, or nuts on any vehicle steering, suspension, or brake component. Always use the exact size and grade of hardware that is specified and used by the vehicle manufacturer.

CAUTIONS alert students about potential damage to the vehicle that can occur during a specific task or service procedure.

> ☠ **WARNING**
>
> Do not use incandescent trouble lights around gasoline or other flammable liquids. The liquids can cause the bulb to break and the hot filament can ignite the flammable liquid which can cause personal injury or even death.

WARNINGS alert students to potential dangers to themselves during a specific task or service procedure.

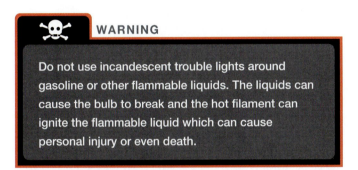

THE SUMMARY, REVIEW QUESTIONS, AND CHAPTER QUIZ at the end of each chapter help students review the material presented in the chapter and test themselves to see how much they've learned.

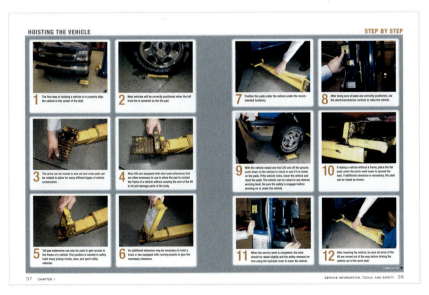

STEP-BY-STEP photo sequences show in detail the steps involved in performing a specific task or service procedure.

SUPPLEMENTS

INSTRUCTOR SUPPLEMENTS The instructor supplement package has been completely revamped to reflect the needs of today's instructors. The all new **Annotated Instructor's Guide (ISBN 0-13-509390-2)** is the cornerstone of the package and includes:

- Chapter Openers that list
  — NATEF/ASE tasks covered in the chapter
  — all key terms
  — all Chapter Objectives

- The entire text (matching page numbers) with margin notes. These notes include:
  — Tips for in-class demonstrations
  — Suggested hands-on activities
  — Cross-curricular activities
  — Internet search tips
  — Assessments
  — Safety tips
  — Classroom discussion questions

- A guide to using MyAutomotiveKit in the course

Also, in every Professional Technician Series Annotated Instructor's Guide there is an **Instructor's CD** that contains:

- PowerPoint presentations*
- Image Library containing every image in the book for use in class or customized PowerPoints*
- Test Generator software and test bank*
- Chapter Quizzes
- Chapter Review Questions
- English and Spanish Glossaries*
- NATEF Correlated Task Sheets* (also available as a printed supplement [ISBN 0-13-509350-3])
- NATEF/ASE Correlation Charts

* All these are available for download from www.pearsonhighered.com.

MYAUTOMOTIVEKIT An offshoot of the extremely popular MyAutomotive Lab, these online kits can be used with all Professional Technician Series textbooks for quizzing, testing, homework, and multimedia activities. All assignments are automatically graded and entered into a gradebook for the course. In addition to assessment materials, MyAutomotiveKit includes:

- **Interactive Animations**
- Two- to five-minute **video clips** showing procedures
- A **3D virtual garage** that simulates the shop experience in the real world by focusing on customer complaints, conducting tests to determine the problem with the vehicle, and submitting a written work order to the instructor
- All materials are broken down by chapter for easy navigation and use

To get instructor access to MyAutomotiveKit, please visit

www.myautomotivekit.com

STUDENT SUPPLEMENTS NO MORE CDs!!

As a result of extensive student input, Pearson is no longer binding CDs into automotive students' textbooks. Today's student has more access to the Internet than ever so all supplemental materials are downloadable at the following site for no additional charge:

www.pearsoned.com/autostudent

On the site, students will find:

- PowerPoint presentations
- Chapter review questions and quizzes
- English and Spanish Glossaries
- A full Spanish translation of the text
- Links to MyAutomotiveKit

MYAUTOMOTIVEKIT FOR THE STUDENT For the student, **MyAutomotiveKit** is a one-stop shop for homework, quizzes, tests, and a new way of learning. Key concepts are reinforced through media. Students will find part identification activities, word search games, interactive animations, and a 3D virtual garage for help with diagnosis.

ACKNOWLEDGMENTS

A large number of people and organizations have cooperated in providing the reference material and technical information used in this text. The author wishes to express sincere thanks to the following individuals and organizations for their special contributions:

Richard Krieger

James (Mike) Watson, Watson Automotive LLC

Bill Fulton, Ohio Automotive Technology

Jim Morton, Automotive Training Center (ATC)

Jim Linder, Linder Technical Services, Inc.

John Thornton, Autotrain

Dave Scaler, Mechanic's Education Association

TECHNICAL AND CONTENT REVIEWERS The following people reviewed the manuscript before production and checked it for technical accuracy and clarity of presentation. Their suggestions and recommendations were included in the final draft of the manuscript. Their input helped make this textbook clear and technically accurate while maintaining the easy-to-read style that has made other books from the same author so popular.

Jim Anderson
Greenville High School

Victor Bridges
Umpqua Community College

Dr. Roger Donovan
Illinois Central College

A. C. Durdin
Moraine Park Technical College

Herbert Ellinger
Western Michigan University

Al Engledahl
College of Dupage

Larry Hagelberger
Upper Valley Joint Vocational School

Oldrick Hajzler
Red River College

Betsy Hoffman
Vermont Technical College

Steven T. Lee
Lincoln Technical Institute

Carlton H. Mabe, Sr.
Virginia Western Community College

Roy Marks
Owens Community College

Tony Martin
University of Alaska Southeast

Kerry Meier
San Juan College

Fritz Peacock
Indiana Vocational Technical College

Dennis Peter
NAIT (Canada)

Kenneth Redick
Hudson Valley Community College

Mitchell Walker
St. Louis Community College at Forest Park

Jennifer Wise
Sinclair Community College

Special thanks to instructional designer **Alexis I. Skriloff James.**

PHOTO SEQUENCES The author wishes to thank Blaine Heeter, Mike Garblik, and Chuck Taylor of Sinclair Community College in Dayton, Ohio, and James (Mike) Watson who helped with many of the photos.

Most of all, I wish to thank Michelle Halderman for her assistance in all phases of manuscript preparation.

—James D. Halderman

ABOUT THE AUTHOR

JIM HALDERMAN brings a world of experience, knowledge, and talent to his work. His automotive service experience includes working as a flat-rate technician, a business owner, and a professor of automotive technology at a leading U.S. community college for more than 20 years.

He has a Bachelor of Science Degree from Ohio Northern University and a Masters Degree in Education from Miami University in Oxford, Ohio. Jim also holds a U.S. Patent for an electronic transmission control device. He is an ASE certified Master Automotive Technician and Advanced Engine Performance (L1) ASE certified.

Jim is the author of many automotive textbooks all published by Prentice Hall.

Jim has presented numerous technical seminars to national audiences including the California Automotive Teachers (CAT) and the Illinois College Automotive Instructor Association (ICAIA). He is also a member and presenter at the North American Council of Automotive Teachers (NACAT). Jim was also named Regional Teacher of the Year by General Motors Corporation and an outstanding alumnus of Ohio Northern University.

Jim and his wife, Michelle, live in Dayton, Ohio. They have two children. You can reach Jim at

jim@jameshalderman.com

BRIEF CONTENTS

CONTENTS

chapter 14
IN-VEHICLE ENGINE SERVICE   221

chapter 15
ADVANCED STARTING AND CHARGING SYSTEMS DIAGNOSIS   232

chapter 16
IGNITION SYSTEM COMPONENTS AND OPERATION   259

After studying Chapter 1, the reader will be able to:

1. Understand the ASE knowledge content for vehicle identification and the proper use of tools and shop equipment.
2. Retrieve vehicle service information.
3. Identify the strength ratings of threaded fasteners.
4. Describe how to safely hoist a vehicle.
5. Discuss how to safely use hand tools.
6. Identify the personal protective equipment (PPE) that all service technicians should wear.
7. Describe what tool is the best to use for each job.
8. Explain the difference between the brand name (trade name) and the proper name for tools.
9. Explain how to maintain hand tools.
10. Identify the precautions that should be followed when working on hybrid electric vehicles.

Bench grinder 25
Bolts 5
Breaker bar 11
Bump cap 25
Calibration codes 3
Campaign 4
Casting number 3
Cheater bar 13
Chisels 19
Drive sizes 11
Extensions 11
Eye wash station 34
Files 17
Fire blanket 33
Fire extinguisher classes 32
GAWR 3
Grade 6
GVWR 3
Hacksaws 19
Hammers 14
HEV 35
LED 23
Metric bolts 6
Nuts 8

PPE 25
Pinch weld seam 28
Pitch 5
Pliers 15
Punches 18
Ratchet 11
Recall 4
Screwdrivers 13
Snips 18
Socket 11
Socket adapter 13
Spontaneous combustion 28
SST 22
Stud 5
Tensile strength 6
Trouble light 23
TSB 4
UNC 5
UNF 5
Universal joint 11
VECI 3
VIN 2
Washers 8
Wrenches 9

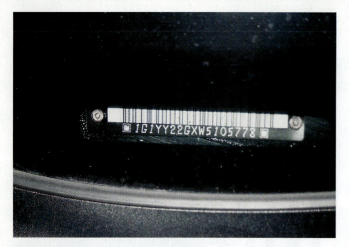

FIGURE 1–1 Typical vehicle identification number (VIN) as viewed through the windshield.

FIGURE 1–2 The vehicle emissions control information (VECI) sticker is placed under the hood.

VEHICLE IDENTIFICATION

MAKE, MODEL, AND YEAR All service work requires that the vehicle and its components be properly identified. The most common identification is the make, model, and year of the vehicle.

Make: e.g., Chevrolet

Model: e.g., Impala

Year: e.g., 2008

VEHICLE IDENTIFICATION NUMBER The year of the vehicle is often difficult to determine exactly. A model may be introduced as the next year's model as soon as January of the previous year. Typically, a new model year starts in September or October of the year prior to the actual new year, but not always. This is why the **vehicle identification number**, usually abbreviated **VIN**, is so important. ● SEE FIGURE 1–1.

Since 1981, all vehicle manufacturers have used a VIN that is 17 characters long. Although every vehicle manufacturer assigns various letters or numbers within these 17 characters, there are some constants, including:

- The first number or letter designates the country of origin. ● **SEE CHART 1–1.**
- The fourth or fifth character is the car line/series.
- The sixth character is the body style.
- The seventh character is the restraint system.
- The eighth character is often the engine code. (Some engines cannot be determined by the VIN number.)
- The tenth character represents the year on all vehicles. ● **SEE CHART 1–2.**

1 = United States	J = Japan	W = Germany
2 = Canada	K = Korea	X = Russia
3 = Mexico	L = China	Y = Sweden
4 = United States	R = Taiwan	Z = Italy
5 = United States	S = England	
6 = Australia	T = Czechoslovakia	
8 = Argentina	U = Romania	
9 = Brazil	V = France	

CHART 1–1

The first number or letter in the VIN identifies the country where the vehicle was made.

A = 1980/2010	L = 1990/2020	Y = 2000/2030
B = 1981/2011	M = 1991/2021	1 = 2001/2031
C = 1982/2012	N = 1992/2022	2 = 2002/2032
D = 1983/2013	P = 1993/2023	3 = 2003/2033
E = 1984/2014	R = 1994/2024	4 = 2004/2034
F = 1985/2015	S = 1995/2025	5 = 2005/2035
G = 1986/2016	T = 1996/2026	6 = 2006/2036
H = 1987/2017	V = 1997/2027	7 = 2007/2037
J = 1988/2018	W = 1998/2028	8 = 2008/2038
K = 1989/2019	X = 1999/2029	9 = 2009/2039

CHART 1–2

The pattern repeats every 30 years for the year of manufacture.

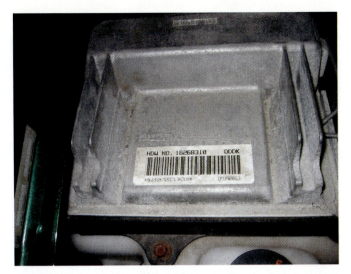

FIGURE 1–3 A typical calibration code sticker on the case of a controller. The information on the sticker is often needed when ordering parts or a replacement controller.

FIGURE 1–4 Casting numbers on major components can be either cast or stamped.

VEHICLE SAFETY CERTIFICATION LABEL A vehicle safety certification label is attached to the left side pillar post on the rearward-facing section of the left front door. This label indicates the month and year of manufacture as well as the **gross vehicle weight rating (GVWR)**, the **gross axle weight rating (GAWR)**, and the vehicle identification number (VIN).

VECI LABEL The **vehicle emissions control information (VECI)** label under the hood of the vehicle shows informative settings and emission hose routing information. ● SEE FIGURE 1–2.

The VECI label (sticker) can be located on the bottom side of the hood, the radiator fan shroud, the radiator core support, or on the strut towers. The VECI label usually includes the following information:

- Engine identification
- Emissions standard that the vehicle meets
- Vacuum hose routing diagram
- Base ignition timing (if adjustable)
- Spark plug type and gap
- Valve lash
- Emission calibration code

CALIBRATION CODES **Calibration codes** are usually located on Powertrain Control Modules (PCMs) or other controllers. Whenever diagnosing an engine operating fault, it is often necessary to use the calibration code to be sure that the vehicle is the subject of a technical service bulletin or other service procedure. ● SEE FIGURE 1–3.

CASTING NUMBERS When an engine part such as a block is cast, a number is put into the mold to identify the casting. ● SEE FIGURE 1–4. These **casting numbers** can be used to identify the part and check dimensions such as the cubic inch displacement and other information, such as the year of manufacture. Sometimes changes are made to the mold, yet the casting number is not changed. Most often the casting number is the best piece of identifying information that the service technician can use for identifying an engine.

FIGURE 1–5 Electronic service information is available from aftermarket sources such as All-Data and Mitchell-on-Demand, as well as on websites hosted by vehicle manufacturers.

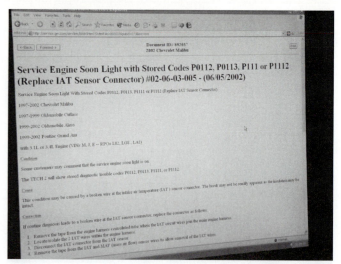

FIGURE 1–6 Technical service bulletins (TSB) are issued by vehicle manufacturers when a fault occurs that affects many vehicles with the same problem. The TSB then provides the fix for the problem including any parts needed and detailed instructions.

SERVICE INFORMATION

SERVICE MANUALS Service information is used by the service technician to determine specifications and service procedures, and any needed special tools.

Factory and aftermarket service manuals contain specifications and service procedures. While factory service manuals cover just one year and one or more models of the same vehicle, most aftermarket service manufacturers cover multiple years and/or models in one manual. Included in most service manuals are the following:

- Capacities and recommended specifications for all fluids
- Specifications including engine and routine maintenance items
- Testing procedures
- Service procedures including the use of special tools when needed

ELECTRONIC SERVICE INFORMATION Electronic service information is available mostly by subscription and provides access to an Internet site where service manual-type information is available. ● **SEE FIGURE 1–5**. Most vehicle manufacturers also offer electronic service information to their dealers and to most schools and colleges that offer corporate training programs.

TECHNICAL SERVICE BULLETINS **Technical service bulletins**, often abbreviated **TSB**, sometimes called *technical service information bulletins (TSIB)* are issued by the vehicle

manufacturer to notify service technicians of a problem and include the necessary corrective action. Technical service bulletins are designed for dealership technicians but are republished by aftermarket companies and made available along with other service information to shops and vehicle repair facilities. ● **SEE FIGURE 1–6**.

INTERNET The Internet has opened the field for information exchange and access to technical advice. One of the most useful websites is the International Automotive Technician's Network at **www.iatn.net**. This is a free site but service technicians must register to join. If a small monthly sponsor fee is paid, the shop or service technician can gain access to the archives, which include thousands of successful repairs in the searchable database.

RECALLS AND CAMPAIGNS A **recall** or **campaign** is issued by a vehicle manufacturer and a notice is sent to all owners in the event of a safety-related fault or concern. While these faults may be repaired by shops, it is generally handled by a local dealer. Items that have created recalls in the past have included potential fuel system leakage problems, exhaust leakage, or electrical malfunctions that could cause a possible fire or the engine to stall. Unlike technical service bulletins whose cost is only covered when the vehicle is within the warranty period, a recall or campaign is always done at no cost to the vehicle owner.

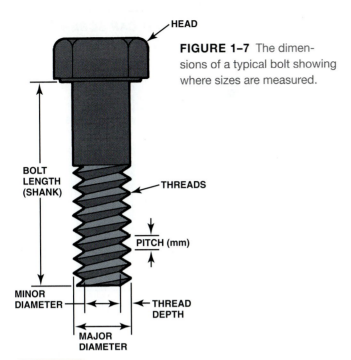

FIGURE 1–7 The dimensions of a typical bolt showing where sizes are measured.

HEAD

BOLT LENGTH (SHANK)

THREADS

PITCH (mm)

MINOR DIAMETER

THREAD DEPTH

MAJOR DIAMETER

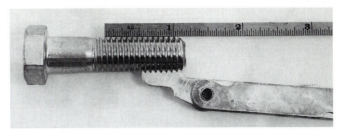

FIGURE 1–8 Thread pitch gauge used to measure the pitch of the thread. This bolt has 13 threads to the inch.

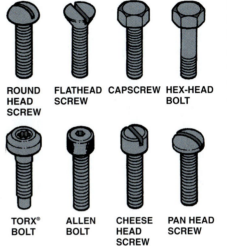

FIGURE 1–9 Bolts and screws have many different heads which determine what tool is needed.

ROUND HEAD SCREW

FLATHEAD SCREW

CAPSCREW

HEX-HEAD BOLT

TORX® BOLT

ALLEN BOLT

CHEESE HEAD SCREW

PAN HEAD SCREW

? FREQUENTLY ASKED QUESTION

What Should Be Included on a Work Order?

A work order is a legal document that should include the following information:

1. Customer information
2. Identification of the vehicle including the VIN
3. Related service history information
4. The "three Cs":
   - Customer concern (complaint)
   - Cause of the concern
   - Correction or repairs that were required to return the vehicle to proper operation.

THREADED FASTENERS

BOLTS AND THREADS   Most of the threaded fasteners used on vehicles are **bolts**. Bolts are called *cap screws* when they are threaded into a casting. Automotive service technicians usually refer to these fasteners as *bolts*, regardless of how they are used. In this chapter, they are called bolts. Sometimes, studs are used for threaded fasteners. A **stud** is a short rod with threads on both ends. Often, a stud will have coarse threads on one end and fine threads on the other end. The end of the stud with coarse threads is screwed into the casting. A nut is used on the opposite end to hold the parts together.

The fastener threads *must* match the threads in the casting or nut. The threads may be measured either in fractions of

an inch (called fractional) or in metric units. The size is measured across the outside of the threads, called the *crest* of the thread. ● SEE FIGURE 1–7.

FRACTIONAL BOLTS   Fractional threads are either coarse or fine. The coarse threads are called **unified national coarse (UNC)**, and the fine threads are called **unified national fine (UNF)**. Standard combinations of sizes and number of threads per inch (called **pitch**) are used. Pitch can be measured with a thread pitch gauge as shown in ● **FIGURE 1–8**. Bolts are identified by their diameter and length as measured from below the head, and not by the size of the head or the size of the wrench used to remove or install the bolt.

Fractional thread sizes are specified by the diameter in fractions of an inch and the number of threads per inch. Typical UNC thread sizes would be 5/16-18 and 1/2-13. Similar UNF thread sizes would be 5/16-24 and 1/2-20. ● SEE CHART 1–3.

? FREQUENTLY ASKED QUESTION

How Many Types of Screw Heads Are Used in Automotive Applications?

There are many, including Torx, hex (also called Allen), plus many others used in custom vans and motor homes. ● SEE FIGURE 1–9.

SIZE	THREADS PER INCH NC UNC	THREADS PER INCH NF UNF	OUTSIDE DIAMETER INCHES
0	..	80	0.0600
1	64	..	0.0730
1	..	72	0.0730
2	56	..	0.0860
2	..	64	0.0860
3	48	..	0.0990
3	..	56	0.0990
4	40	..	0.1120
4	..	48	0.1120
5	40	..	0.1250
5	..	44	0.1250
6	32	..	0.1380
6	..	40	0.1380
8	32	..	0.1640
8	..	36	0.1640
10	24	..	0.1900
10	..	32	0.1900
12	24	..	0.2160
12	..	28	0.2160
1/4	20	..	0.2500
1/4	..	28	0.2500
5/16	18	..	0.3125
5/16	..	24	0.3125
3/8	16	..	0.3750
3/8	..	24	0.3750
7/16	14	..	0.4375
7/16	..	20	0.4375
1/2	13	..	0.5000
1/2	..	20	0.5000
9/16	12	..	0.5625
9/16	..	18	0.5625
5/8	11	..	0.6250
5/8	..	18	0.6250
3/4	10	..	0.7500
3/4	..	16	0.7500
7/8	9	..	0.8750
7/8	..	14	0.8750
1	8	..	1.0000
1	..	12	1.0000
1 1/8	7	..	1.1250
1 1/8	..	12	1.1250
1 1/4	7	..	1.2500
1 1/4	..	12	1.2500
1 3/8	6	..	1.3750
1 3/8	..	12	1.3750
1 1/2	6	..	1.5000
1 1/2	..	12	1.5000
1 3/4	5	..	1.7500
2	4 1/2	..	2.0000
2 1/4	4 1/2	..	2.2500
2 1/2	4	..	2.5000
2 3/4	4	..	2.7500
3	4	..	3.0000
3 1/4	4	..	3.2500
3 1/2	4	..	3.5000
3 3/4	4	..	3.7500
4	4	..	4.0000

CHART 1–3

American standard is one method of sizing fasteners.

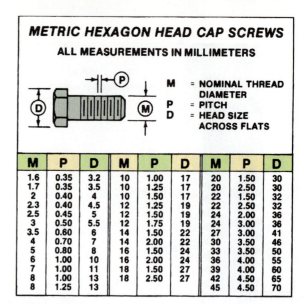

METRIC HEXAGON HEAD CAP SCREWS

ALL MEASUREMENTS IN MILLIMETERS

M = NOMINAL THREAD DIAMETER
P = PITCH
D = HEAD SIZE ACROSS FLATS

M	P	D	M	P	D	M	P	D
1.6	0.35	3.2	10	1.00	17	20	1.50	30
1.7	0.35	3.5	10	1.25	17	20	2.50	30
2	0.40	4	10	1.50	17	22	1.50	32
2.3	0.40	4.5	12	1.25	19	22	2.50	32
2.5	0.45	5	12	1.50	19	24	2.00	36
3	0.50	5.5	12	1.75	19	24	3.00	36
3.5	0.60	6	14	1.50	22	27	3.00	41
4	0.70	7	14	2.00	22	30	3.50	46
5	0.80	8	16	1.50	24	33	3.50	50
6	1.00	10	16	2.00	24	36	4.00	55
7	1.00	11	18	1.50	27	39	4.00	60
8	1.00	13	18	2.50	27	42	4.50	65
8	1.25	13				45	4.50	70

FIGURE 1–10 The metric system specifies fasteners by diameter, length, and pitch.

THREADED FASTENERS (CONTINUED)

METRIC BOLTS   The size of a **metric bolt** is specified by the letter *M* followed by the diameter in millimeters (mm) across the outside (crest) of the threads. Typical metric sizes would be M8 and M12. Fine metric threads are specified by the thread diameter followed by X and the distance between the threads measured in millimeters (M8 X 1.5). ● **SEE FIGURE 1–10.**

GRADES OF BOLTS   Bolts are made from many different types of steel, and for this reason some are stronger than others. The strength or classification of a bolt is called the **grade**. The bolt heads are marked to indicate their grade strength.

The actual grade of bolts is two more than the number of lines on the bolt head. Metric bolts have a decimal number to indicate the grade. More lines or a higher grade number indicate a stronger bolt. In some cases, nuts and machine screws have similar grade markings. Higher grade bolts usually have threads that are rolled rather than cut, which also makes them stronger. ● **SEE FIGURE 1–11.**

CAUTION: *Never* **use hardware store (nongraded) bolts, studs, or nuts on any vehicle steering, suspension, or brake component. Always use the exact size and grade of hardware that is specified and used by the vehicle manufacturer.**

TENSILE STRENGTH OF FASTENERS   Graded fasteners have a higher tensile strength than nongraded fasteners. **Tensile strength** is the maximum stress used under tension

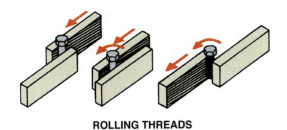

ROLLING THREADS

FIGURE 1–11 Stronger threads are created by cold-rolling a heat-treated bolt blank instead of cutting the threads, using a die.

				METRIC CLASS
4.6	8.8	9.8	10.9	
60,000	120,000	130,000	150,000	APPROXIMATE MAXIMUM POUND FORCE PER SQUARE INCH

FIGURE 1–12 Metric bolt (cap screw) grade markings and approximate tensile strength.

SAE BOLT DESIGNATIONS

SAE GRADE NO.	SIZE RANGE	TENSILE STRENGTH, PSI	MATERIAL	HEAD MARKING
1	1/4 through 1 1/2	60,000	Low or medium carbon steel	
2	1/4 through 3/4	74,000		
	7/8 through 1 1/2	60,000		
5	1/4 through 1	120,000	Medium carbon steel, quenched and tempered	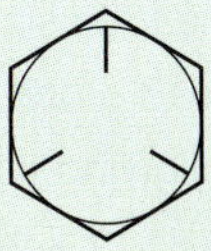
	1-1/8 through 1 1/2	105,000		
5.2	1/4 through 1	120,000	Low carbon martensite steel,* quenched and tempered	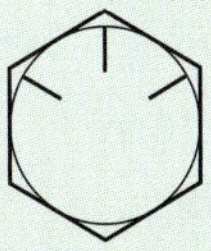
7	1/4 through 1 1/2	133,000	Medium carbon alloy steel, quenched and tempered	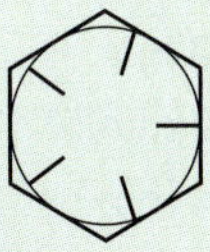
8	1/4 through 1 1/2	150,000	Medium carbon alloy steel, quenched and tempered	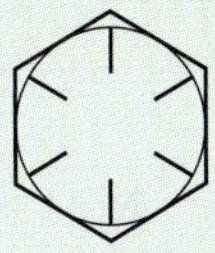
8.2	1/4 through 1	150,000	Low carbon martensite steel,* quenched and tempered	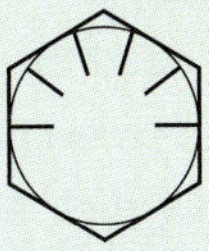

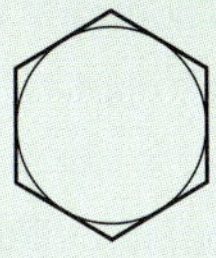

CHART 1–4

The tensile strength rating system as specified by the Society of Automotive Engineers (SAE).

(lengthwise force) without causing failure of the fastener. Tensile strength is specified in pounds per square inch (psi).

The strength and type of steel used in a bolt is supposed to be indicated by a raised mark on the head of the bolt. The type of mark depends on the standard to which the bolt was manufactured. Most often, bolts used in machinery are made to

SAE Standard J429. ● **SEE CHART 1–4** that shows the grade and specified tensile strength.

Metric bolt tensile strength property class is shown on the head of the bolt as a number, such as 4.6, 8.8, 9.8, and 10.9; the higher the number, the stronger the bolt. ● **SEE FIGURE 1–12.**

HEX NUT **JAM NUT** **NYLON LOCK NUT** **CASTLE NUT** **ACORN NUT**

FIGURE 1–13 Nuts come in a variety of styles, including locking (prevailing torque) types, such as the distorted thread and nylon insert type.

FLAT WASHER **LOCK WASHER** **STAR WASHER** **STAR WASHER**

FIGURE 1–14 Washers come in a variety of styles, including flat and serrated used to help prevent a fastener from loosening.

THREADED FASTENERS (CONTINUED)

 TECH TIP

A 1/2-Inch Wrench Does Not Fit a 1/2-Inch Bolt

A common mistake made by persons new to the automotive field is to think that the size of a bolt or nut is the size of the head. The size of the bolt or nut (outside diameter of the threads) is usually smaller than the size of the wrench or socket that fits the head of the bolt or nut. Examples are given in the following table:

Wrench Size	Thread Size
7/16 in.	1/4 in.
1/2 in.	5/16 in.
9/16 in.	3/8 in.
5/8 in.	7/16 in.
3/4 in.	1/2 in.
10 mm	6 mm
12 mm or 13 mm*	8 mm
14 mm or 17 mm*	10 mm

* European (Système International d'Unités-SI) metric.

 **TECH TIP**

It Just Takes a Second

Whenever removing any automotive component, it is wise to screw the bolts back into the holes a couple of threads by hand. This ensures that the right bolt will be used in its original location when the component or part is put back on the vehicle. Often, the same diameter of fastener is used on a component, but the length of the bolt may vary. Spending just a couple of seconds to put the bolts and nuts back where they belong when the part is removed can save a lot of time when the part is being reinstalled. Besides making certain that the right fastener is being installed in the right place, this method helps prevent bolts and nuts from getting lost or kicked away. How much time have you wasted looking for that lost bolt or nut?

NUTS Nuts are the female part of a threaded fastener. Most nuts used on cap screws have the same hex size as the cap screw head. Some inexpensive nuts use a hex size larger than the cap screw head. Metric nuts are often marked with dimples to show their strength. More dimples indicate stronger nuts. Some nuts and cap screws use interference fit threads to keep them from accidentally loosening. This means that the shape of the nut is slightly distorted or that a section of the threads is deformed. Nuts can also be kept from loosening with a nylon washer fastened in the nut or with a nylon patch or strip on the threads. ● **SEE FIGURE 1–13.**

NOTE: Most of these "locking nuts" are grouped together and are commonly referred to as *prevailing torque nuts*. This means that the nut will hold its tightness or torque and not loosen with movement or vibration. Most prevailing torque nuts should be replaced whenever removed to ensure that the nut will not loosen during service. Always follow the manufacturer's recommendations. Anaerobic sealers, such as Loctite, are used on the threads where the nut or cap screw must be both locked and sealed.

WASHERS Washers are often used under cap screw heads and under nuts. ● **SEE FIGURE 1–14.** Plain flat washers are used to provide an even clamping load around the fastener. Lock washers are added to prevent accidental loosening. In some accessories, the washers are locked onto the nut to provide easy assembly.

FIGURE 1–15 A forged wrench after it has been forged but before the flashing, which is the extra material around the wrench, has been removed.

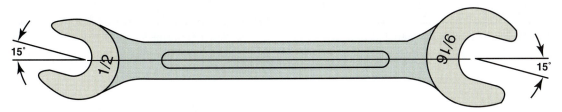

FIGURE 1–16 A typical open-end wrench. The size is different on each end and notice that the head is angled 15 degrees at the end.

HAND TOOLS

WRENCHES   Wrenches are the most used hand tool by service technicians. **Wrenches** are used to grasp and rotate threaded fasteners. Most wrenches are constructed of forged alloy steel, usually chrome-vanadium steel. ● **SEE FIGURE 1–15**.

After the wrench is formed, the wrench is hardened, and then tempered to reduce brittleness, and then chrome plated. There are several types of wrenches.

OPEN-END WRENCH.   An open-end wrench is usually used to loosen or tighten bolts or nuts that do not require a lot of torque. Because of the *open* end, this type of wrench can be easily placed on a bolt or nut with an angle of 15 degrees, which allows the wrench to be flipped over and used again to continue to rotate the fastener. The major disadvantage of an open-end wrench is the lack of torque that can be applied due to the fact that the open jaws of the wrench only contact two flat surfaces of the fastener. An open-end wrench has two different sizes; one at each end. ● **SEE FIGURE 1–16**.

BOX-END WRENCH.   A *box-end wrench*, also called a *closed-end wrench*, is placed over the top of the fastener and grips the points of the fastener. A box-end wrench is angled 15 degrees to allow it to clear nearby objects.

Therefore, a box-end wrench should be used to loosen or to tighten fasteners because it grasps around the entire head of the fastener. A box-end wrench has two different sizes; one at each end. ● **SEE FIGURE 1–17**.

Most service technicians purchase *combination wrenches*, which have the open end at one end and the same size box end on the other end. ● **SEE FIGURE 1–18**.

A combination wrench allows the technician to loosen or tighten a fastener using the box end of the wrench, turn it around, and use the open end to increase the speed of rotating the fastener.

ADJUSTABLE WRENCH.   An *adjustable wrench* is often used where the exact size wrench is not available or when a large nut, such as a wheel spindle nut, needs to be rotated but not tightened. An adjustable wrench should not be used to loosen or tighten fasteners because the torque applied to the wrench can cause the movable jaws to loosen their grip on the fastener, causing it to become rounded. ● **SEE FIGURE 1–19**.

LINE WRENCHES.   Line wrenches are also called *flare-nut wrenches*, *fitting wrenches*, or *tube-nut wrenches* and are designed to grip almost all the way around a nut used to retain a

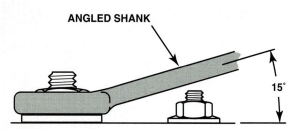

FIGURE 1–17 The end of a box-end wrench is angled 15 degrees to allow clearance for nearby objects or other fasteners.

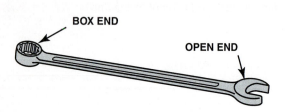

FIGURE 1–18 A combination wrench has an open end at one end and a box end at the other end.

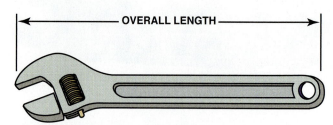

FIGURE 1–19 An adjustable wrench. Adjustable wrenches are sized by the overall length of the wrench and not by how far the jaws open. Common sizes of adjustable wrenches include 8, 10, and 12 inch.

FIGURE 1–20 The end of a typical line wrench, which shows that it is capable of grasping most of the head of the fitting.

HAND TOOLS (CONTINUED)

 **TECH TIP**

Hide Those from the Boss

An apprentice technician started working for a shop and put his top tool box on a workbench. Another technician observed that, along with a complete set of good-quality tools, the box contained several adjustable wrenches. The more experienced technician said, "Hide those from the boss." The boss does not want any service technician to use adjustable wrenches. If any adjustable wrench is used on a bolt or nut, the movable jaw often moves or loosens and starts to round the head of the fastener. If the head of the bolt or nut becomes rounded, it becomes that much more difficult to remove.

fuel or refrigerant line, and yet, be able to be installed over the line. ● **SEE FIGURE 1–20**.

SAFE USE OF WRENCHES Wrenches should be inspected before use to be sure they are not cracked, bent, or damaged. All wrenches should be cleaned after use before being returned to the tool box. Always use the correct size of wrench for the fastener being loosened or tightened to help prevent the rounding of the flats of the fastener. When attempting to loosen a fastener, pull a wrench—do not push a wrench. If a wrench is pushed, your knuckles can be hurt when forced into another object if the fastener breaks loose or if the wrench slips. Always keep wrenches and all hand tools clean to help prevent rust and to allow for a better, firmer grip. Never expose any tool to excessive heat. High temperatures can reduce the strength ("draw the temper") of metal tools.

Never use a hammer on any wrench unless you are using a special "staking face" wrench designed to be used with a hammer. Replace any tools that are damaged or worn.

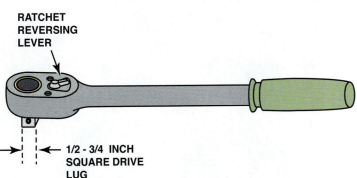

FIGURE 1–21 A typical ratchet used to rotate a socket. A ratchet makes a ratcheting noise when it is being rotated in the opposite direction from loosening or tightening. A knob or lever on the ratchet allows the user to switch directions.

FIGURE 1–22 A typical flex handle used to rotate a socket, also called a breaker bar because it usually has a longer handle than a ratchet and therefore, can be used to apply more torque to a fastener than a ratchet.

FIGURE 1–23 The most commonly used socket drive sizes include 1/4-inch, 3/8-inch, and 1/2-inch drive.

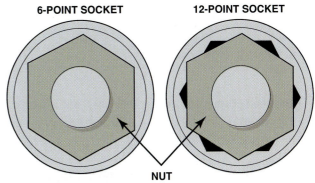

FIGURE 1–24 A 6-point socket fits the head of a bolt or nut on all sides. A 12-point socket can round off the head of a bolt or nut if a lot of force is applied.

RATCHETS, SOCKETS, AND EXTENSIONS

A **socket** fits over the fastener and grips the points and/or flats of the bolt or nut. The socket is rotated (driven) using either a long bar called a **breaker bar** (flex handle) or a ratchet. ● SEE FIGURES 1–21 and 1–22.

A **ratchet** is a tool that turns the socket in only one direction and allows the rotating of the ratchet handle back and forth in a narrow space. Socket **extensions** and **universal joints** are also used with sockets to allow access to fasteners in restricted locations.

DRIVE SIZE. Sockets are available in various **drive sizes**, including 1/4 inch, 3/8 inch, and 1/2 inch sizes for most automotive use. ● SEE FIGURES 1–23 AND 1–24.

TECH TIP

Right to Tighten

It is sometimes confusing which way to rotate a wrench or screwdriver, especially when the head of the fastener is pointing away from you. To help visualize while looking at the fastener, say "righty tighty, lefty loosey."

Many heavy-duty truck and/or industrial applications use 3/4 in. and 1 in. sizes. The drive size is the distance of each side of the square drive. Sockets and ratchets of the same size are designed to work together.

REGULAR AND DEEP WELL. Sockets are available in regular length for use in most applications or in a deep well design that allows for access to a fastener that uses a long stud or other similar conditions. ● SEE FIGURE 1–25.

TORQUE WRENCHES

Torque wrenches are socket turning handles that are designed to apply a known amount of force to the fastener. There are two basic types of torque wrenches including:

1. **Clicker type.** This type of torque wrench is first set to the specified torque and then it "clicks" when the set torque value has been reached. When force is removed from the torque wrench handle, another click is heard. The setting on a clicker-type torque wrench should be set back to zero after use and checked for proper calibration regularly. ● SEE FIGURE 1–26.

2. **Beam-type.** This type of torque wrench is used to measure torque, but instead of presenting the value, the actual torque is displayed on the dial of the wrench as the fastener is being

DEEP SOCKET

REGULAR SOCKET

FIGURE 1–25 Allows access to the nut that has a stud plus other locations needing great depth, such as spark plugs.

FIGURE 1–26 Using a clicker-type torque wrench to tighten connecting rod nuts on an engine.

HAND TOOLS (CONTINUED)

tightened. Beam-type torque wrenches are available in 1/4 in., 3/8 in., and 1/2 in. drives and both English and metric units. ● **SEE FIGURE 1–27.**

SAFE USE OF SOCKETS AND RATCHETS Always use the proper size socket that correctly fits the bolt or nut. All sockets and ratchets should be cleaned after use before being placed back into the tool box. Sockets are available in short and deep well designs. Never expose any tool to excessive heat. High temperatures can reduce the strength ("draw the temper") of metal tools.

Never use a hammer on a socket handle unless you are using a special "staking face" wrench designed to be used with a hammer. Replace any tools that are damaged or worn.

Also select the appropriate drive size. For example, for small work, such as on the dash, select a 1/4-in. drive. For most general service work, use a 3/8-in. drive and for suspension and steering and other large fasteners, select a 1/2-in. drive. When loosening a fastener, always pull the ratchet toward you rather than push it outward.

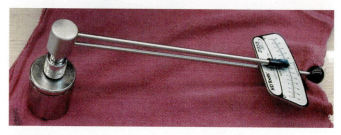

FIGURE 1–27 A beam-type torque wrench that displays the torque reading on the face of the dial. The beam display is read as the beam deflects, which is in proportion to the amount of torque applied to the fastener.

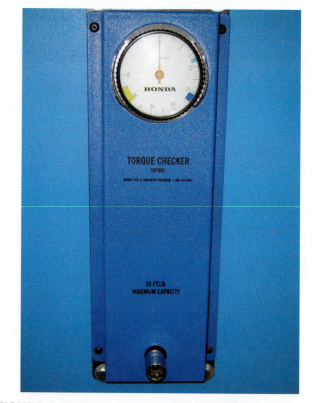

FIGURE 1–28 Torque wrench calibration checker.

TECH TIP

Check Torque Wrench Calibration Regularly

Torque wrenches should be checked regularly. For example, Honda has a torque wrench calibration setup at each of their training centers. It is expected that a torque wrench be checked for accuracy before every use. Most experts recommend that torque wrenches be checked and adjusted as needed at least every year and more often if possible.
● **SEE FIGURE 1–28.**

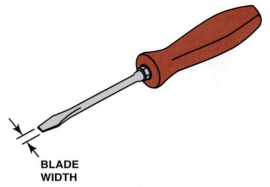

BLADE WIDTH

FIGURE 1–29 A flat-tip (straight-blade) screwdriver. The width of the blade should match the width of the slot in the fastener being loosened or tightened.

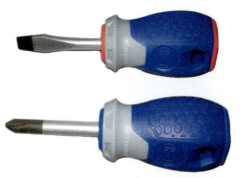

FIGURE 1–30 Two stubby screwdrivers that are used to access screws that have limited space above. A straight blade is on top and a #2 Phillips screwdriver is on the bottom.

TECH TIP

Use Socket Adapters with Caution

A **socket adapter** allows the use of one size of socket and another drive size ratchet or breaker bar. Socket adapters are available and can be used for different drive size sockets on a ratchet. Combinations include:

- 1/4-in. drive—3/8-in. sockets
- 3/8-in. drive—1/4-in. sockets
- 3/8-in. drive—1/2-in. sockets
- 1/2-in. drive—3/8-in. sockets

Using a larger drive ratchet or breaker bar on a smaller size socket can cause the application of too much force to the socket, which could crack or shatter. Using a smaller size drive tool on a larger socket will usually not cause any harm, but would greatly reduce the amount of torque that can be applied to the bolt or nut.

SCREWDRIVERS

STRAIGHT-BLADE SCREWDRIVER. Many smaller fasteners are removed and installed by using a **screwdriver**. Screwdrivers are available in many sizes and tip shapes. The most commonly used screwdriver is called a *straight blade* or *flat tip.*

Flat-tip screwdrivers are sized by the width of the blade and this width should match the width of the slot in the screw. ● **SEE FIGURE 1–29**.

TECH TIP

Avoid Using "Cheater Bars"

Whenever a fastener is difficult to remove, some technicians will insert the handle of a ratchet or a breaker bar into a length of steel pipe sometimes called a **cheater bar.** The extra length of the pipe allows the technician to exert more torque than can be applied using the drive handle alone. However, the extra torque can easily overload the socket and ratchet, causing them to break or shatter, which could cause personal injury.

CAUTION: Do not use a screwdriver as a pry tool or as a chisel. Screwdrivers are hardened steel only at the tip and are not designed to be pounded on or used for prying because they could bend easily. Always use the proper tool for each application.

PHILLIPS SCREWDRIVER. Another type of commonly used screwdriver is called a Phillips screwdriver, named for Henry F. Phillips, who invented the crosshead screw in 1934. Due to the shape of the crosshead screw and screwdriver, a Phillips screw can be driven with more torque than can be achieved with a slotted screw.

A Phillips head screwdriver is specified by the length of the handle and the size of the point at the tip. A #1 tip has a sharp point, a #2 tip is the most commonly used, and a #3 tip is blunt and is only used for larger sizes of Phillips head fasteners. For example, a #2 × 3 in. Phillips screwdriver would typically measure 6 in. from the tip of the blade to the end of the handle (3 in. long handle and 3 in. long blade) with a #2 tip.

Both straight-blade and Phillips screwdrivers are available with a short blade and handle for access to fasteners with limited room. ● **SEE FIGURE 1–30**.

FIGURE 1–31 An offset screwdriver is used to install or remove fasteners that do not have enough space above to use a conventional screwdriver.

FIGURE 1–32 An impact screwdriver used to remove slotted or Phillips head fasteners that cannot be broken loose using a standard screwdriver.

HAND TOOLS (CONTINUED)

OFFSET SCREWDRIVERS. Offset screwdrivers are used in places where a conventional screwdriver cannot fit. An offset screwdriver is bent at the ends and is used similar to a wrench. Most offset screwdrivers have a straight blade at one end and a Phillips end at the opposite end. ● **SEE FIGURE 1–31**.

IMPACT SCREWDRIVER. An *impact screwdriver* is used to break loose or tighten a screw. A hammer is used to strike the end after the screwdriver holder is placed in the head of the screw and rotated in the desired direction. The force from the hammer blow does two things: It applies a force downward holding the tip of the screwdriver in the slot and then applies a twisting force to loosen (or tighten) the screw. ● **SEE FIGURE 1–32**.

SAFE USE OF SCREWDRIVERS
Always use the proper type and size screwdriver that matches the fastener. Try to avoid pressing down on a screwdriver because if it slips, the screwdriver tip could go into your hand, causing serious personal injury. All screwdrivers should be cleaned after use. Do not use a screwdriver as a prybar; always use the correct tool for the job.

HAMMERS AND MALLETS
Hammers and mallets are used to force objects together or apart. The shape of the back part of the hammer head (called the *peen*) usually determines the name. For example, a ball-peen hammer has a rounded end like a ball and it is used to straighten oil pans and valve covers, using the hammer head, and for shaping metal, using the ball peen. ● **SEE FIGURE 1–33**.

NOTE: A claw hammer has a claw used to remove nails and is not used for automotive service.

A hammer is usually sized by the weight of the head of the hammer and the length of the handle. For example, a commonly used ball-peen hammer has an 8-ounce head with an 11-inch handle.

> **? FREQUENTLY ASKED QUESTION**
>
> **What Is a Robertson Screwdriver?**
>
> A Canadian named P. L. Robertson invented the Robertson screw and screwdriver in 1908, which uses a square-shaped tip with a slight taper. The Robertson screwdriver uses color-coded handles because different size screws required different tip sizes. The color and sizes include:
>
> - Orange (#00)—Number 1 and 2 screws
> - Yellow (#0)—Number 3 and 4 screws
> - Green (#1)—Number 5, 6, and 7 screws
> - Red (#2)—Number 8, 9, and 10 screws
> - Black (#3)—Number 12 and larger screws
>
> The Robertson screws are rarely found in the United States but are common in Canada.

FIGURE 1–33 A typical ball-peen hammer.

FIGURE 1–34 A rubber mallet used to deliver a force to an object without harming the surface.

FIGURE 1–35 A dead-blow hammer that was left outside in freezing weather. The plastic covering was damaged, which destroyed this hammer. The lead shot is encased in the metal housing and then covered.

MALLETS. *Mallets* are a type of hammer with a large striking surface, which allows the technician to exert force over a larger area than a hammer, so as not to harm the part or component. Mallets are made from a variety of materials including rubber, plastic, or wood. ● SEE FIGURE 1–34.

DEAD-BLOW HAMMER. A shot-filled plastic hammer is called a *dead-blow hammer*. The small lead balls (shot) inside a plastic head prevent the hammer from bouncing off of the object when struck. ● SEE FIGURE 1–35.

SAFE USE OF HAMMERS AND MALLETS
All mallets and hammers should be cleaned after use and not exposed to extreme temperatures. Never use a hammer or mallet that is damaged in any way and always use caution to avoid doing damage to the components and the surrounding area. Always follow the hammer manufacturer's recommended procedures and practices.

PLIERS

SLIP-JOINT PLIERS. A **pliers** is capable of holding, twisting, bending, and cutting objects and is an extremely useful classification of tools. The common household type of pliers is called the *slip-joint pliers*. There are two different positions where the junction of the handles meets to achieve a wide range of sizes of objects that can be gripped. ● SEE FIGURE 1–36.

MULTIGROOVE ADJUSTABLE PLIERS. For gripping larger objects, a set of *multigroove adjustable pliers* is a commonly used

🔧 **TECH TIP**

Pound with Something Softer

If you must pound on something, be sure to use a tool that is softer than what you are about to pound on to avoid damage. Examples are given in the following table.

The Material Being Pounded	What to Pound with
Steel or cast iron	Brass or aluminum hammer or punch
Aluminum	Plastic or rawhide mallet or plastic-covered dead-blow hammer
Plastic	Rawhide mallet or plastic dead-blow hammer

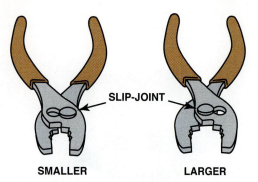

SLIP-JOINT

SMALLER   LARGER

FIGURE 1–36 Typical slip-joint pliers is a common household pliers. The slip joint allows the jaws to be opened to two different settings.

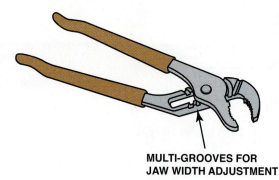

MULTI-GROOVES FOR
JAW WIDTH ADJUSTMENT

FIGURE 1–37 Multigroove adjustable pliers is known by many names, including the trade name "Channel Locks.®"

FIGURE 1–38 Linesman's pliers are very useful because it can help perform many automotive service jobs.

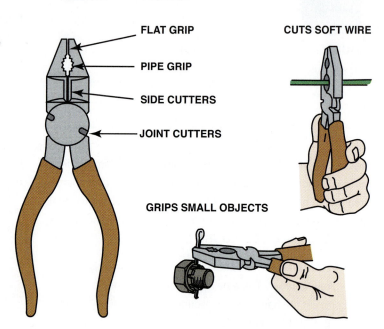

FLAT GRIP

PIPE GRIP

SIDE CUTTERS

JOINT CUTTERS

CUTS SOFT WIRE

GRIPS SMALL OBJECTS

HAND TOOLS (CONTINUED)

tool of choice by many service technicians. Originally designed to remove the various size nuts holding rope seals used in water pumps, the name *water pump pliers* is also used. These types of pliers are commonly called by their trade name *Channel Locks®*. ● **SEE FIGURE 1–37**.

LINESMAN'S PLIERS. *Linesman's pliers* is a hand tool specifically designed for cutting, bending, and twisting wire. While commonly used by construction workers and electricians, linesman's pliers is a very useful tool for the service technician who deals with wiring. The center parts of the jaws are designed to grasp round objects such as pipe or tubing without slipping. ● **SEE FIGURE 1–38**.

DIAGONAL PLIERS. *Diagonal pliers* is designed to cut only. The cutting jaws are set at an angle to make it easier to cut wires. Diagonal pliers are also called *side cuts* or *dikes*. These pliers are constructed of hardened steel and they are used mostly for cutting wire. ● **SEE FIGURE 1–39**.

NEEDLE-NOSE PLIERS. *Needle-nose pliers* are designed to grip small objects or objects in tight locations. Needle-nose pliers have long, pointed jaws, which allow the tips to reach into narrow openings or groups of small objects. ● **SEE FIGURE 1–40**.

Most needle-nose pliers have a wire cutter located at the base of the jaws near the pivot. There are several variations of needle nose pliers, including right angle jaws or slightly angled to allow access to certain cramped areas.

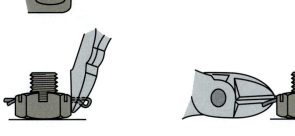

CUTTING WIRES CLOSE TO TERMINALS

PULLING OUT AND SPREADING COTTER PIN

FIGURE 1–39 Diagonal-cut pliers is another common tool that has many names.

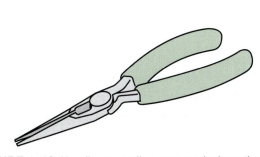

FIGURE 1–40 Needle-nose pliers are used where there is limited access to a wire or pin that needs to be installed or removed.

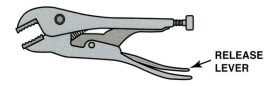

RELEASE LEVER

FIGURE 1–41 Locking pliers are best known by their trade name Vise Grips.®

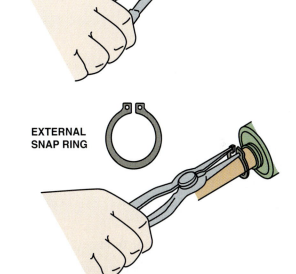

INTERNAL SNAP RING

EXTERNAL SNAP RING

FIGURE 1–42 Snap-ring pliers are also called lock ring pliers and most are designed to remove internal and external snap rings (lock rings).

LOCKING PLIERS. *Locking pliers* are adjustable pliers that can be locked to hold objects from moving. Most locking pliers also have wire cutters built into the jaws near the pivot point. Locking pliers come in a variety of styles and sizes and are commonly referred to by the trade name *Vise Grips*®. The size is the length of the pliers, not how far the jaws open. ● **SEE FIGURE 1–41.**

SNAP-RING PLIERS. *Snap-ring pliers* is used to remove and install snap-rings. Many snap-ring pliers are designed to be able to remove and install both inward, as well as outward, expanding snap rings. Some snap-ring pliers can be equipped with serrated-tipped jaws for grasping the opening in the snap ring, while others are equipped with points, which are inserted into the holes in the snap ring. ● **SEE FIGURE 1–42.**

SAFE USE OF PLIERS   Pliers should not be used to remove any bolt or other fastener. Pliers should only be used when specified for use by the vehicle manufacturer.

FILES   Files are used to smooth metal and are constructed of hardened steel with diagonal rows of teeth. Files are available with a single row of teeth called a *single cut file*, as well as two rows of teeth cut at an opposite angle called a *double cut file*. Files are available in a variety of shapes and sizes from small flat files, half-round files, and triangular files. ● **SEE FIGURE 1–43.**

SAFE USE OF FILES   Always use a file with a handle. Because files only cut when moved forward, a handle must be attached to prevent possible personal injury. After making a

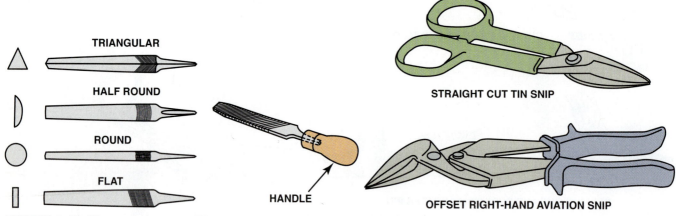

FIGURE 1–43 Files come in many different shapes and sizes. Never use a file without a handle.

FIGURE 1–44 Tin snips are used to cut thin sheets of metal or carpet.

HAND TOOLS (CONTINUED)

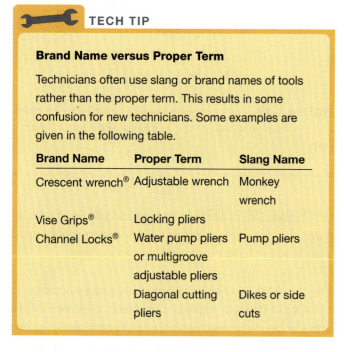

TECH TIP

Brand Name versus Proper Term

Technicians often use slang or brand names of tools rather than the proper term. This results in some confusion for new technicians. Some examples are given in the following table.

Brand Name	Proper Term	Slang Name
Crescent wrench®	Adjustable wrench	Monkey wrench
Vise Grips®	Locking pliers	
Channel Locks®	Water pump pliers or multigroove adjustable pliers	Pump pliers
	Diagonal cutting pliers	Dikes or side cuts

forward strike, lift the file and return the file to the starting position; avoid dragging the file backward.

SNIPS   Service technicians are often asked to fabricate sheet metal brackets or heat shields and need to use one or more types of cutters available called **snips**. *Tin snips* are the simplest and are designed to make straight cuts in a variety of materials, such as sheet steel, aluminum, or even fabric. A variation of the tin snips is called *aviation tin snips*. There are three designs of aviation snips including one designed to cut straight (called a *straight cut aviation snip*), one designed to cut left (called an *offset left aviation snip*), and one designed to cut right (called an *offset right aviation snip*). ● **SEE FIGURE 1–44**.

UTILITY KNIFE   A *utility knife* uses a replaceable blade and is used to cut a variety of materials such as carpet, plastic, wood, and paper products, such as cardboard. ● **SEE FIGURE 1–45**.

SAFE USE OF CUTTERS   Whenever using cutters, always wear eye protection or a face shield to guard against the possibility of metal pieces being ejected during the cut. Always follow recommended procedures.

PUNCHES   A **punch** is a small diameter steel rod that has a smaller diameter ground at one end. A punch is used to drive a pin out that is used to retain two components. Punches come in a variety of sizes, which are measured across the diameter of the machined end. Sizes include 1/16″, 1/8″, 3/16″, and 1/4″. ● **SEE FIGURE 1–46**.

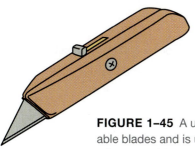

FIGURE 1–45 A utility knife uses replaceable blades and is used to cut carpet and other materials.

PIN

FIGURE 1–46 A punch used to drive pins from assembled components. This type of punch is also called a pin punch.

FIGURE 1–47 Warning stamped on the side of a punch warning that goggles should be worn when using this tool. Always follow safety warnings.

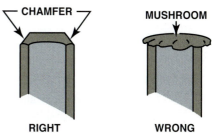

CHAMFER   MUSHROOM

RIGHT   WRONG

FIGURE 1–48 Use a grinder or a file to remove the mushroom material on the end of a punch or chisel.

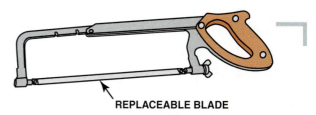

REPLACEABLE BLADE

FIGURE 1–49 A typical hacksaw that is used to cut metal. If cutting sheet metal or thin objects, a blade with more teeth should be used.

CHISELS   A **chisel** has a straight, sharp cutting end that is used for cutting off rivets or to separate two pieces of an assembly. The most common design of chisel used for automotive service work is called a *cold chisel*.

SAFE USE OF PUNCHES AND CHISELS

Always wear eye protection when using a punch or a chisel because the hardened steel is brittle and parts of the punch could fly off and cause serious personal injury. See the warning stamped on the side of this automotive punch in ● **FIGURE 1–47**.

The tops of punches and chisels can become rounded off from use, which is called "mushroomed." This material must be ground off to help avoid the possibility of the overhanging material being loosened and becoming airborne during use. ● **SEE FIGURE 1–48.**

HACKSAWS   A **hacksaw** is used to cut metals, such as steel, aluminum, brass, or copper. The cutting blade of a hacksaw is replaceable and the sharpness and number of teeth can be varied to meet the needs of the job. Use 14 or 18 teeth per inch (TPI) for cutting plaster or soft metals, such as aluminum and copper. Use 24 or 32 teeth per inch for steel or pipe. Hacksaw blades should be installed with the teeth pointing away from the handle. This means that a hacksaw only cuts while the blade is pushed in the forward direction. ● **SEE FIGURE 1–49**.

SAFE USE OF HACKSAWS

Check that the hacksaw is equipped with the correct blade for the job and that the teeth are pointed away from the handle. When using a hacksaw, move the hacksaw slowly away from you, then lift slightly and return for another cut.

BASIC HAND TOOL LIST

The following is a typical list of hand tools every automotive technician should possess. Specialty tools are not included.

Safety glasses

Tool chest

1/4-in. drive socket set (1/4 in. to 9/16 in. standard and deep sockets; 6 mm to 15 mm standard and deep sockets)

1/4-in. drive ratchet

1/4-in. drive 2-in. extension

1/4-in. drive 6-in. extension

1/4-in. drive handle

3/8-in. drive socket set (3/8 in. to 7/8 in. standard and deep sockets; 10 mm to 19 mm standard and deep sockets)

3/8-in. drive Torx set (T40, T45, T50, and T55)

3/8-in. drive 13/16-in. plug socket

3/8-in. drive 5/8-in. plug socket

3/8-in. drive ratchet

3/8-in. drive 1 1/2-in. extension

3/8-in. drive 3-in. extension

3/8-in. drive 6-in. extension

3/8-in. drive 18-in. extension

3/8-in. drive universal

1/2-in. drive socket set (1/2 in. to 1 in. standard and deep sockets)

1/2-in. drive ratchet

1/2-in. drive breaker bar

1/2-in. drive 5-in. extension

1/2-in. drive 10-in. extension

3/8-in. to 1/4-in. adapter

1/2-in. to 3/8-in. adapter

3/8-in. to 1/2-in. adapter

Crowfoot set (fractional in.)

Crowfoot set (metric)

3/8- through 1-in. combination wrench set

10 mm through 19 mm combination wrench set

1/16-in. through 1/4-in. hex wrench set

2 mm through 12 mm hex wrench set

3/8-in. hex socket

13 mm to 14 mm flare-nut wrench

15 mm to 17 mm flare-nut wrench

5/16-in. to 3/8-in. flare-nut wrench

7/16-in. to 1/2-in. flare-nut wrench

1/2-in. to 9/16-in. flare-nut wrench

Diagonal pliers

Needle pliers

Adjustable-jaw pliers

Locking pliers

Snap-ring pliers

Stripping or crimping pliers

Ball-peen hammer

Rubber hammer

Dead-blow hammer

Five-piece standard screwdriver set

Four-piece Phillips screwdriver set

#15 Torx screwdriver

#20 Torx screwdriver

Center punch

Pin punches (assorted sizes)

Chisel

Utility knife

Valve core tool

Filter wrench (large filters)

Filter wrench (smaller filters)

Test light

Feeler gauge

Scraper

Pinch bar

Magnet

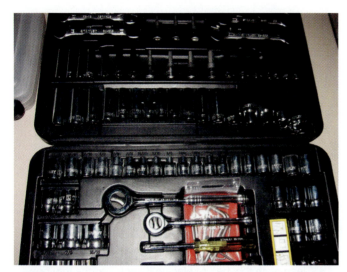

FIGURE 1–50 A typical beginning technician tool set that includes the basic tools to get started.

FIGURE 1–51 A typical large tool box, showing just one of many drawers.

FIGURE 1–52 A typical 12-volt test light.

TOOL SETS AND ACCESSORIES

A beginning service technician may wish to start with a small set of tools before purchasing an expensive tool set. ● **SEE FIGURES 1–50** and **1–51**.

TECH TIP

Need to Borrow a Tool More Than Twice? Buy It!

Most service technicians agree that it is okay for a beginning technician to borrow a tool occasionally. However, if a tool has to be borrowed more than twice, then be sure to purchase it as soon as possible. Also, whenever a tool is borrowed, be sure that you clean the tool and let the technician you borrowed the tool from know that you are returning the tool. These actions will help in any future dealings with other technicians.

ELECTRICAL HAND TOOLS

TEST LIGHT A test light is used to test for electricity. A typical automotive test light consists of a clear plastic screwdriver-like handle that contains a lightbulb. A wire is attached to one terminal of the bulb, which the technician connects to a clean metal part of the vehicle. The other end of the bulb is attached to a point that can be used to test for electricity at a connector or wire. When there is power at the point and a good connection at the other end, the lightbulb lights. ● **SEE FIGURE 1–52**.

SOLDERING GUNS

ELECTRIC SOLDERING GUN. This type of soldering gun is usually powered by 110-volt AC and often has two power settings expressed in watts. A typical electric soldering gun will produce from 85 to 300 watts of heat at the tip, which is more than adequate for soldering.

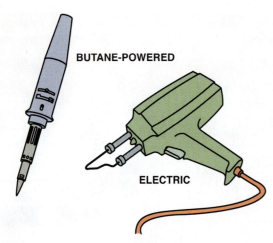

BUTANE-POWERED

ELECTRIC

FIGURE 1–53 An electric and butane-powered soldering guns used to make electrical repairs. Soldering guns are sold by the wattage rating. The higher the wattage, the greater amount of heat created. Most solder guns used for automotive electrical work usually fall within the 60- to 160-watt range.

ELECTRICAL HAND TOOLS (CONTINUED)

ELECTRIC SOLDERING PENCIL. This type of soldering iron is less expensive and creates less heat than an electric soldering gun. A typical electric soldering pencil (iron) creates 30 to 60 watts of heat and is suitable for soldering smaller wires and connections.

BUTANE-POWERED SOLDERING IRON. A butane-powered soldering iron is portable and very useful for automotive service work because an electrical cord is not needed. Most butane-powered soldering irons produce about 60 watts of heat, which is enough for most automotive soldering. ● **SEE FIGURE 1–53**.

ELECTRICAL WORK HAND TOOLS
In addition to a soldering iron, most service technicians who do electrical-related work should have the following:

- Wire cutters
- Wire strippers
- Wire crimpers
- Heat gun for heat shrink tubing

DIGITAL METER
A digital meter is a necessary tool for any electrical diagnosis and troubleshooting. A digital multimeter, abbreviated DMM, is usually capable of measuring the following units of electricity:

- DC volts
- AC volts
- Ohms
- Amperes

HAND TOOL MAINTENANCE

Most hand tools are constructed of rust-resistant metals but they can still rust or corrode if not properly maintained. For best results and long tool life, the following steps should be taken:

- Clean each tool before placing it back into the tool box.
- Keep tools separated. Moisture on metal tools will start to rust more readily if the tools are in contact with another metal tool.
- Line the drawers of the tool box with a material that will prevent the tools from moving as the drawers are opened and closed. This helps to quickly locate the proper tool and size.
- Release the tension on all "clicker-type" torque wrenches.
- Keep the tool box secure.

? FREQUENTLY ASKED QUESTION

What Is an "SST"?

Vehicle manufacturers often specify a **special service tool (SST)** to properly disassemble and assemble components, such as transmissions and other components. These tools are also called special tools and are available from the vehicle manufacturer or their tool supplier, such as Kent-Moore and Miller tools. Many service technicians do not have access to special service tools so they use generic versions that are available from aftermarket sources.

FIGURE 1–54 A fluorescent trouble light operates cooler and is safer to use in the shop because it is protected against accidental breakage where gasoline or other flammable liquids would happen to come in contact with the light.

FIGURE 1–55 A typical 1/2-in. drive air impact wrench. The direction of rotation can be changed to loosen or tighten a fastener.

TROUBLE LIGHTS

INCANDESCENT *Incandescent lights* use a filament that produces light when electric current flows through the bulb. This was the standard **trouble light**, also called a *work light* for many years until safety issues caused most shops to switch to safer fluorescent or LED lights. If incandescent lightbulbs are used, try to locate bulbs that are rated "rough service," which is designed to withstand shock and vibration more than conventional lightbulbs.

FIGURE 1–56 A typical battery-powered 3/8-in. drive impact wrench.

☠ **WARNING**

Do not use incandescent trouble lights around gasoline or other flammable liquids. The liquids can cause the bulb to break and the hot filament can ignite the flammable liquid which can cause personal injury or even death.

LED TROUBLE LIGHT Light-emitting diode (LED) trouble lights are excellent to use because they are shock resistant, long lasting, and do not represent a fire hazard. Some trouble lights are battery powered and therefore can be used in places where an attached electrical cord could present problems.

AIR AND ELECTRICALLY OPERATED TOOLS

FLUORESCENT A trouble light is an essential piece of shop equipment, and for safety, should be fluorescent rather than incandescent. Incandescent lightbulbs can scatter or break if gasoline were to be splashed onto the bulb creating a serious fire hazard. Fluorescent light tubes are not as likely to be broken and are usually protected by a clear plastic enclosure. Trouble lights are usually attached to a retractor, which can hold 20 to 50 feet of electrical cord. ● **SEE FIGURE 1–54.**

IMPACT WRENCH An impact wrench, either air or electrically powered, is a tool that is used to remove and install fasteners. The air-operated 1/2-in. drive impact wrench is the most commonly used unit. ● **SEE FIGURE 1–55.**

    Electrically powered impact wrenches commonly include:

- Battery-powered units. ● **SEE FIGURE 1–56.**
- 110-volt AC-powered units. This type of impact is very useful, especially if compressed air is not readily available.

FIGURE 1–57 A black impact socket. Always use an impact-type socket whenever using an impact wrench to avoid the possibility of shattering the socket which could cause personal injury.

AIR AND ELECTRICITY OPERATED TOOLS (CONTINUED)

FIGURE 1–58 An air ratchet is a very useful tool that allows fast removal and installation of fasteners, especially in areas that are difficult to reach or do not have room enough to move a hand ratchet or wrench.

> ☠ **WARNING**
>
> Always use impact sockets with impact wrenches, and always wear eye protection in case the socket or fastener shatters. Impact sockets are thicker walled and constructed with premium alloy steel. They are hardened with a black oxide finish to help prevent corrosion and distinguish them from regular sockets. ● SEE FIGURE 1–57.

FIGURE 1–59 This typical die grinder surface preparation kit includes the air-operated die grinder as well as a variety of sanding disks for smoothing surfaces or removing rust.

AIR RATCHET   An air ratchet is used to remove and install fasteners that would normally be removed or installed using a ratchet and a socket. ● **SEE FIGURE 1–58**.

DIE GRINDER   A die grinder is a commonly used air-powered tool which can also be used to sand or remove gaskets and rust. ● **SEE FIGURE 1–59**.

BENCH- OR PEDESTAL-MOUNTED GRINDER   These high-powered grinders can be equipped with a wire brush wheel and/or a stone wheel.

- **Wire brush wheel**—This type is used to clean threads of bolts as well as to remove gaskets from sheet metal engine parts.
- **Stone wheel**—This type is used to grind metal or to remove the mushroom from the top of punches or chisels. ● **SEE FIGURE 1–60**.

FIGURE 1–60 A typical pedestal grinder with a wire wheel on the left side and a stone wheel on the right side. Even though this machine is equipped with guards, safety glasses or a face shield should always be worn whenever using a grinder or wire wheel.

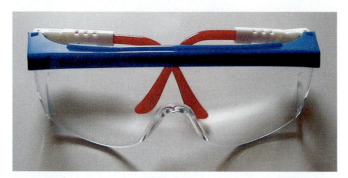

FIGURE 1–61 Safety glasses should be worn at all times when working on or around any vehicle or servicing any components.

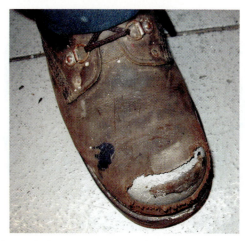

FIGURE 1–62 Steel-toed shoes are a worthwhile investment to help prevent foot injury due to falling objects. Even these well-worn shoes can protect the feet of this service technician.

Air and Electrically Operated Tools (CONTINUED)

> ☠ **WARNING**
>
> Always wear a face shield when using a wire wheel or a grinder.

Most **bench grinders** are equipped with a grinder wheel (stone) on one end and a wire brush wheel on the other end. A bench grinder is a very useful piece of shop equipment and the wire wheel end can be used for the following:

- Cleaning threads of bolts
- Cleaning gaskets from sheet metal parts, such as steel valve covers

CAUTION: Only use a steel wire brush on steel or iron components. If a steel wire brush is used on aluminum or copper-based metal parts, it can remove metal from the part.

The grinding stone end of the bench grinder can be used for the following:

- Sharpening blades and drill bits
- Grinding off the heads of rivets or parts
- Sharpening sheet metal parts for custom fitting

PERSONAL PROTECTIVE EQUIPMENT

Service technicians should wear **personal protective equipment (PPE)** to prevent personal injury. The personal protection devices include the following:

SAFETY GLASSES Wear safety glasses at all times while servicing any vehicle and be sure that they meet standard ANSI Z87.1. ● SEE FIGURE 1–61.

STEEL-TOED SAFETY SHOES ● SEE FIGURE 1–62. If steel-toed safety shoes are not available, then leather-topped shoes offer more protection than canvas or cloth.

BUMP CAP Service technicians working under a vehicle should wear a **bump cap** to protect the head against under-vehicle objects and the pads of the lift. ● SEE FIGURE 1–63.

HEARING PROTECTION Hearing protection should be worn if the sound around you requires that you raise your voice (sound level higher than 90 dB). For example, a typical lawn-mower produces noise at a level of about 110 dB. This means that everyone who uses a lawnmower or other lawn or garden equipment should wear ear protection.

GLOVES Many technicians wear gloves not only to help keep their hands clean but also to help protect their skin from the effects of dirty engine oil and other possibly hazardous materials.

FIGURE 1–63 One version of a bump cap is a molded plastic insert that is worn inside a regular cloth cap.

PERSONAL PROTECTIVE EQUIPMENT (CONTINUED)

Several types of gloves and their characteristics include:

- **Latex surgical gloves.** These gloves are relatively inexpensive, but tend to stretch, swell, and weaken when exposed to gas, oil, or solvents.

- **Vinyl gloves.** These gloves are also inexpensive and are not affected by gas, oil, or solvents.

- **Polyurethane gloves.** These gloves are more expensive, yet very strong. Even though these gloves are also not affected by gas, oil, or solvents, they do tend to be slippery.

- **Nitrile gloves.** These gloves are exactly like latex gloves, but are not affected by gas, oil, or solvents, yet they tend to be expensive.

- **Mechanic's gloves.** These gloves are usually made of synthetic leather and spandex and provide thermo protection, as well as protection from dirt and grime.

● **SEE FIGURE 1–64.**

FIGURE 1–64 Protective gloves are available in several sizes and materials.

SAFETY PRECAUTIONS

Besides wearing personal safety equipment, there are also many actions that should be performed to keep safe in the shop. These actions include:

- Remove jewelry that may get caught on something or act as a conductor to an exposed electrical circuit. ● **SEE FIGURE 1–65.**

- Take care of your hands. Keep your hands clean by washing with soap and hot water that is at least 110°F (43°C).

- Avoid loose or dangling clothing.

- When lifting any object, get a secure grip with solid footing. Keep the load close to your body to minimize the strain. Lift with your legs and arms, not your back.

- Do not twist your body when carrying a load. Instead, pivot your feet to help prevent strain on the spine.

- Ask for help when moving or lifting heavy objects.

- Push a heavy object rather than pull it. (This is opposite to the way you should work with tools—never push a wrench! If you do and a bolt or nut loosens, your entire weight is used to propel your hand(s) forward. This usually results in cuts, bruises, or other painful injury.)

- Always connect an exhaust hose to the tailpipe of any running vehicle to help prevent the buildup of carbon monoxide inside a closed garage space. ● **SEE FIGURE 1–66.**

- When standing, keep objects, parts, and tools with which you are working between chest height and waist height. If seated, work at tasks that are at elbow height.

- Always be sure the hood is securely held open.

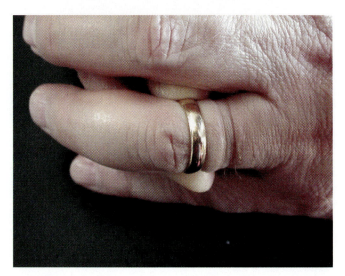

FIGURE 1–65 Remove all jewelry before performing service work on any vehicle.

FIGURE 1–66 Always connect an exhaust hose to the tailpipe of a vehicle to be run inside a building.

FIGURE 1–67 A binder clip being used to keep a fender cover from falling off.

FIGURE 1–68 Covering the interior as soon as the vehicle comes in for service helps improve customer satisfaction.

VEHICLE PROTECTION

FENDER COVERS Whenever working under the hood of any vehicle be sure to use fender covers. They not only help protect the vehicle from possible damage but they also provide a clean surface to place parts and tools. The major problem with using fender covers is that they tend to move and often fall off the vehicle. To help prevent the fender covers from falling off secure them to a lip of the fender using a *binder clip* available at most office supply stores. ● **SEE FIGURE 1–67.**

INTERIOR PROTECTION Always protect the interior of the vehicle from accidental damage or dirt and grease by covering the seat, steering wheel, and floor with a protective covering. ● **SEE FIGURE 1–68.**

 SAFETY TIP

Shop Cloth Disposal

Always dispose of oily shop cloths in an enclosed container to prevent a fire. ● **SEE FIGURE 1–69.** Whenever oily cloths are thrown together on the floor or workbench, a chemical reaction can occur, which can ignite the cloth even without an open flame. This process of ignition without an open flame is called **spontaneous combustion.**

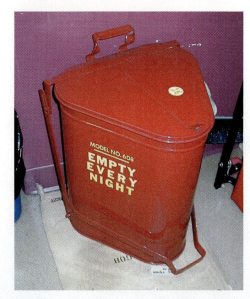

FIGURE 1–69 All oily shop cloths should be stored in a metal container equipped with a lid to help prevent spontaneous combustion.

SAFETY LIFTING (HOISTING) A VEHICLE

Many chassis and underbody service procedures require that the vehicle be hoisted or lifted off the ground. The simplest methods involve the use of drive-on ramps or a floor jack and safety (jack) stands, whereas in-ground or surface-mounted lifts provide greater access.

Setting the pads is a critical part of this hoisting procedure. All vehicle service information including service, shop and owner's manuals, include recommended locations to be used when hoisting (lifting) a vehicle. Newer vehicles have a triangle decal on the driver's door indicating the recommended lift points. The recommended standards for the lift points and lifting procedures are found in SAE Standard JRP-2184. ● **SEE FIGURE 1–70.**

These recommendations typically include the following points:

1. The vehicle should be centered on the lift or hoist so as not to overload one side or put too much force either forward or rearward. ● **SEE FIGURE 1–71.**

2. The pads of the lift should be spread as far apart as possible to provide a stable platform.

3. Each pad should be placed under a portion of the vehicle that is strong and capable of supporting the weight of the vehicle.

   a. Pinch welds at the bottom edge of the body are generally considered to be strong.

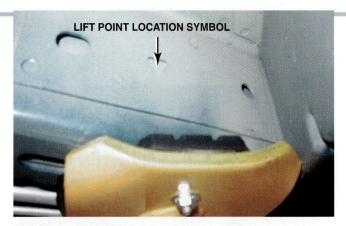

LIFT POINT LOCATION SYMBOL

FIGURE 1–70 Most newer vehicles have a triangle symbol indicating the recommended hoisting lift location.

CAUTION: Even though pinch weld seams are the recommended location for hoisting many vehicles with unitized bodies (unit-body), care should be taken not to place the pad(s) too far forward or rearward. Incorrect placement of the vehicle on the lift could cause the vehicle to be imbalanced, and the vehicle could fall. This is exactly what happened to the vehicle in ● FIGURE 1–72.

   b. Boxed areas of the body are the best places to position the pads on a vehicle without a frame. Be careful to note whether the arms of the lift might come into contact with other parts of the vehicle before the pad

(a)

(b)

FIGURE 1–71 (a) Tall safety stands can be used to provide additional support for the vehicle while on the hoist.
(b) A block of wood should be used to avoid the possibility of doing damage to components supported by the stand.

FIGURE 1–72 This training vehicle fell from the hoist because the pads were not set correctly. No one was hurt but the vehicle was damaged.

touches the intended location. Commonly damaged areas include the following:

(1) Rocker panel moldings

(2) Exhaust system (including catalytic converter)

(3) Tires or body panels (● **SEE FIGURES 1–73** and **1–74.**)

4. The vehicle should be raised about a foot (30 centimeters [cm]) off the floor, then stopped and shaken to check for stability. If the vehicle seems to be stable when checked at a short distance from the floor, continue raising the vehicle and continue to view the vehicle until it has reached the desired height. The hoist should be lowered onto the mechanical locks, and then raised off of the locks before lowering.

CAUTION: Do not look away from the vehicle while it is being raised (or lowered) on a hoist. Often one side or one end of the hoist can stop or fail, resulting in the vehicle being slanted enough to slip or fall, creating physical damage not only to the vehicle and/or hoist but also to the technician or others who may be nearby.

HINT: Most hoists can be safely placed at any desired height. For ease while working, the area in which you are working should be at chest level. When working on brakes or suspension components, it is not necessary to work on them down near the floor or over your head. Raise the hoist so that the components are at chest level.

5. Before lowering the hoist, the safety latch(es) must be released and the direction of the controls reversed. The speed downward is often adjusted to be as slow as possible for additional safety.

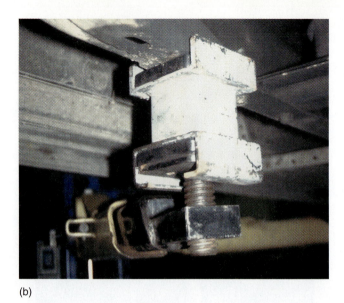

(a)

(b)

FIGURE 1–73 (a) An assortment of hoist pad adapters that are often needed to safely hoist many pickup trucks, vans, and sport utility vehicles (SUVs). (b) A view from underneath a Chevrolet pickup truck showing how the pad extensions are used to attach the hoist lifting pad to contact the frame.

(a)

(b)

FIGURE 1–74 (a) The pad arm is just contacting the rocker panel of the vehicle. (b) The pad arm has dented the rocker panel on this vehicle because the pad was set too far inward underneath the vehicle.

JACKS AND SAFETY STANDS

Floor jacks properly rated for the weight of the vehicle being raised are a common vehicle lifting tool. Floor jacks are portable and relatively inexpensive and must be used with safety (jack) stands. The floor jack is used to raise the vehicle off the ground and safety stands should be placed under the frame on the body of the vehicle. The weight of the vehicle should never be kept on the hydraulic floor jack because a failure of the jack could cause the vehicle to fall. ● **SEE FIGURE 1–75.** The jack is then slowly released to allow the vehicle weight to be supported on the safety stands. If the front or rear of the vehicle is being raised, the opposite end of the vehicle must be blocked.

CAUTION: **Safety stands should be rated higher than the weight they support.**

(a)

(b)

FIGURE 1–75 (a) A typical 3-ton (6,000-pound) capacity hydraulic jack. (b) Whenever a vehicle is raised off the ground, a safety stand should be placed under the frame, axle, or body to support the weight of the vehicle.

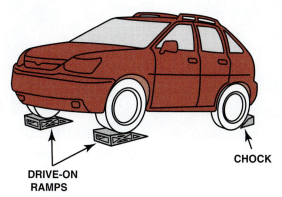

CHOCK

DRIVE-ON RAMPS

FIGURE 1–76 Drive-on-type ramps are dangerous to use. The wheels on the ground level must be chocked (blocked) to prevent accidental movement down the ramp.

DRIVE-ON RAMPS

Ramps are an inexpensive way to raise the front or rear of a vehicle. ● **SEE FIGURE 1–76**. Ramps are easy to store, but they can be dangerous because they can "kick out" when driving the vehicle onto the ramps.

CAUTION: Professional repair shops do not use ramps because they are dangerous to use. Use only with extreme care.

ELECTRICAL CORD SAFETY

Use correctly grounded three-prong sockets and extension cords to operate power tools. Some tools use only two-prong plugs. Make sure these are double insulated and repair or replace any electrical cords that are cut or damaged to prevent the possibility of an electrical shock. When not in use, keep electrical cords off the floor to prevent tripping over them. Tape the cords down if they are placed in high foot traffic areas.

JUMP STARTING AND BATTERY SAFETY

To jump start another vehicle with a dead battery, connect good-quality copper jumper cables as indicated in ● **FIGURE 1–77** or a jump box. The last connection made should always be on the engine block or an engine bracket as far from the battery as possible. It is normal for a spark to be created when the jumper cables finally complete the jumping circuit, and this spark could cause an explosion of the gases around the battery. Many newer vehicles have special ground connections built away from the

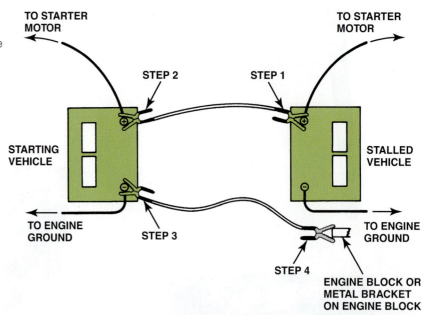

FIGURE 1–77 Jumper cable usage guide. Follow the same connections if using a portable jump box.

TO STARTER MOTOR

TO STARTER MOTOR

STEP 2

STEP 1

STARTING VEHICLE

STALLED VEHICLE

TO ENGINE GROUND

STEP 3

TO ENGINE GROUND

STEP 4

ENGINE BLOCK OR METAL BRACKET ON ENGINE BLOCK

JUMP STARTING AND BATTERY SAFETY (CONTINUED)

battery just for the purpose of jump starting. Check the owner's manual or service information for the exact location.

Batteries contain acid and should be handled with care to avoid tipping them greater than a 45-degree angle. Always remove jewelry when working around a battery to avoid the possibility of electrical shock or burns, which can occur when the metal comes in contact with a 12-volt circuit and ground, such as the body of the vehicle.

 **SAFETY TIP**

Air Hose Safety

Improper use of an air nozzle can cause blindness or deafness. Compressed air must be reduced to less than 30 psi (206 kPa). ● **SEE FIGURE 1–78**. If an air nozzle is used to dry and clean parts, make sure the airstream is directed away from anyone else in the immediate area. Coil and store air hoses when they are not in use.

FIGURE 1–78 The air pressure going to the nozzle should be reduced to 30 psi or less to help prevent personal injury.

FIRE EXTINGUISHERS

There are four **fire extinguisher classes**. Each class should be used on specific fires only:

- **Class A** is designed for use on general combustibles, such as cloth, paper, and wood.
- **Class B** is designed for use on flammable liquids and greases, including gasoline, oil, thinners, and solvents.
- **Class C** is used only on electrical fires.
- **Class D** is effective only on combustible metals such as powdered aluminum, sodium, or magnesium.

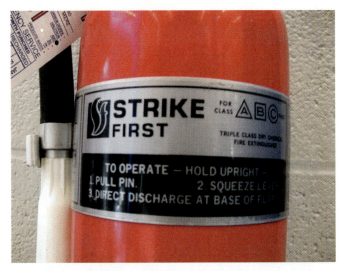

FIGURE 1–79 A typical fire extinguisher designed to be used on type A, B, or C fires.

FIGURE 1–80 A CO_2 fire extinguisher being used on a fire set in an open drum during a demonstration at a fire training center.

The class rating is clearly marked on the side of every fire extinguisher. Many extinguishers are good for multiple types of fires. ● **SEE FIGURE 1–79**.

When using a fire extinguisher, remember the word "PASS."

P = Pull the safety pin.

A = Aim the nozzle of the extinguisher at the base of the fire.

S = Squeeze the lever to actuate the extinguisher.

S = Sweep the nozzle from side-to-side.

● **SEE FIGURE 1–80**.

TYPES OF FIRE EXTINGUISHERS   Types of fire extinguishers include the following.

- **Water.** A water fire extinguisher, usually in a pressurized container, is good to use on Class A fires by reducing the temperature to the point where a fire cannot be sustained.

- **Carbon dioxide (CO_2).** A carbon dioxide fire extinguisher is good for almost any type of fire, especially Class B or Class C materials. A CO_2 fire extinguisher works by removing the oxygen from the fire and the cold CO_2 also helps reduce the temperature of the fire.

- **Dry chemical (yellow).** A dry chemical fire extinguisher is good for Class A, B, or C fires by coating the flammable materials, which eliminates the oxygen from the fire. A dry chemical fire extinguisher tends to be very corrosive and will cause damage to electronic devices.

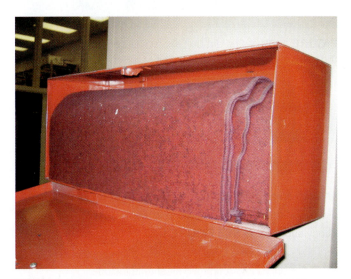

FIGURE 1–81 A treated wool blanket is kept in an easy-to-open wall-mounted holder and should be placed in a central location in the shop.

FIRE BLANKETS

Fire blankets are required to be available in the shop areas. If a person is on fire, a fire blanket should be removed from its storage bag and thrown over and around the victim to smother the fire. ● **SEE FIGURE 1–81** showing a typical fire blanket.

FIGURE 1–82 A first aid box should be centrally located in the shop and kept stocked with the recommended supplies.

FIGURE 1–83 A typical eye wash station. Often a thorough flushing of the eyes with water is the first and often the best treatment in the event of eye contamination.

FIRST AID AND EYE WASH STATIONS

All shop areas must be equipped with a first aid kit and an eye wash station centrally located and kept stocked with emergency supplies. ● **SEE FIGURE 1–82**.

FIRST AID KIT A first aid kit should include:

- Bandages (variety)
- Gauze pads
- Roll gauze
- Iodine swab sticks
- Antibiotic ointment
- Hydrocortisone cream
- Burn gel packets
- Eye wash solution
- Scissors
- Tweezers
- Gloves
- First aid guide

Every shop should have a person trained in first aid. If there is an accident, call for help immediately.

EYE WASH STATION An **eye wash station** should be centrally located and used whenever any liquid or chemical gets into the eyes. If such an emergency does occur, keep eyes in a constant stream of water and call for professional assistance. ● **SEE FIGURE 1–83**.

 SAFETY TIP

Infection Control Precautions

Working on a vehicle can result in personal injury including the possibility of being cut or hurt enough to cause bleeding. Some infections such as hepatitis B, HIV (which can cause acquired immunodeficiency syndrome, or AIDS), hepatitis C virus, and others are transmitted in the blood. These infections are commonly called blood-borne pathogens. Report any injury that involves blood to your supervisor and take the necessary precautions to avoid coming in contact with blood from another person.

FIGURE 1–84 A warning label on a Honda hybrid warns that a person can be killed due to the high-voltage circuits under the cover.

FIGURE 1–85 The high-voltage disconnect switch is in the trunk area on a Toyota Prius. Insulated rubber lineman's gloves should be worn when removing this plug. (Courtesy of Tony Martin)

HYBRID ELECTRIC VEHICLE SAFETY ISSUES

Hybrid electric vehicles (HEVs) use a high-voltage battery pack and an electric motor(s) to help propel the vehicle. ● **SEE FIGURE 1–84** for an example of a typical warning label on a hybrid electric vehicle. The gasoline or diesel engine also is equipped with a generator or a combination starter and an integrated starter generator (ISG) or integrated starter alternator (ISA). To safely work around a hybrid electric vehicle, the high-voltage (HV) battery and circuits should be shut off following these steps:

STEP 1 Turn off the ignition key (if equipped) and remove the key from the ignition switch. (This will shut off all high-voltage circuits if the relay[s] is [are] working correctly.)

STEP 2 Disconnect the high-voltage circuits.

> ☠ **WARNING**
>
> Some vehicle manufacturers specify that insulated rubber *lineman's gloves* be used whenever working around the high-voltage circuits to prevent the danger of electrical shock.

TOYOTA PRIUS The cutoff switch is located in the trunk. To gain access, remove three clips holding the upper left portion of the trunk side cover. To disconnect the high-voltage system, pull the orange handled plug while wearing insulated rubber lineman's gloves. ● **SEE FIGURE 1–85**.

FORD ESCAPE/MERCURY MARINER Ford and Mercury specify that the following steps should be included when working with the high-voltage (HV) systems of a hybrid vehicle:

- Four orange cones are to be placed at the four corners of the vehicle to create a buffer zone.

- High-voltage insulated gloves are to be worn with an outer leather glove to protect the inner rubber glove from possible damage.

- The service technician should also wear a face shield and a fiberglass hook should be in the area and used to move a technician in the event of electrocution.

The high-voltage shut-off switch is located in the rear of the vehicle under the right side carpet. ● **SEE FIGURE 1–86**. Rotate the handle to the "service shipping" position, lift it out to

FIGURE 1–86 The high-voltage shut-off switch on a Ford Escape hybrid. The switch is located under the carpet at the rear of the vehicle.

FIGURE 1–87 The shut-off switch on a GM parallel hybrid truck is green because this system uses 42 volts instead of higher, and possibly fatal, voltages used in other hybrid vehicles.

JUMP STARTING AND BATTERY SAFETY (CONTINUED)

disable the high-voltage circuit, and wait 5 minutes before removing high-voltage cables.

HONDA CIVIC To totally disable the high-voltage system on a Honda Civic, remove the main fuse (labeled number 1) from the driver's side underhood fuse panel. This should be all that is necessary to shut off the high-voltage circuit. If this is not possible, then remove the rear seat cushion and seat back. Remove the metal switch cover labeled "up" and remove the red locking cover. Move the "battery module switch" down to disable the high-voltage system.

CHEVROLET SILVERADO/GMC SIERRA PICKUP TRUCK The high-voltage shut-off switch is located under the rear passenger seat. Remove the cover marked "energy storage box" and turn the green service disconnect switch to the horizontal position to turn off the high-voltage circuits.
● **SEE FIGURE 1–87.**

WARNING

Do not touch any orange wiring or component without following the vehicle manufacturer's procedures and wearing the specified personal protective equipment.

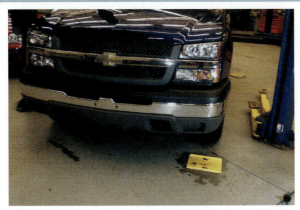

1 The first step in hoisting a vehicle is to properly align the vehicle in the center of the stall.

2 Most vehicles will be correctly positioned when the left front tire is centered on the tire pad.

3 The arms can be moved in and out and most pads can be rotated to allow for many different types of vehicle construction.

4 Most lifts are equipped with short pad extensions that are often necessary to use to allow the pad to contact the frame of a vehicle without causing the arm of the lift to hit and damage parts of the body.

5 Tall pad extensions can also be used to gain access to the frame of a vehicle. This position is needed to safely hoist many pickup trucks, vans, and sport utility vehicles.

6 An additional extension may be necessary to hoist a truck or van equipped with running boards to give the necessary clearance.

CONTINUED ▶

7 Position the pads under the vehicle under the recommended locations.

8 After being sure all pads are correctly positioned, use the electromechanical controls to raise the vehicle.

9 With the vehicle raised one foot (30 cm) off the ground, push down on the vehicle to check to see if it is stable on the pads. If the vehicle rocks, lower the vehicle and reset the pads. The vehicle can be raised to any desired working level. Be sure the safety is engaged before working on or under the vehicle.

10 If raising a vehicle without a frame, place the flat pads under the pinch weld seam to spread the load. If additional clearance is necessary, the pads can be raised as shown.

11 When the service work is completed, the hoist should be raised slightly and the safety released before using the hydraulic lever to lower the vehicle.

12 After lowering the vehicle, be sure all arms of the lift are moved out of the way before driving the vehicle out of the work stall.

SUMMARY

1. Bolts, studs, and nuts are commonly used as fasteners in the chassis. The sizes for fractional and metric threads are different and are not interchangeable. The grade is the rating of the strength of a fastener.

2. Whenever a vehicle is raised above the ground, it must be supported at a substantial section of the body or frame.

3. Wrenches are available in open end, box end, and combination open and box end.

4. An adjustable wrench should only be used where the proper size is not available.

5. Line wrenches are also called flare-nut wrenches, fitting wrenches, or tube-nut wrenches and are used to remove fuel or refrigerant lines.

6. Sockets are rotated by a ratchet or breaker bar, also called a flex handle.

7. Torque wrenches measure the amount of torque applied to a fastener.

8. Screwdriver types include straight blade (flat tip) and Phillips.

9. Hammers and mallets come in a variety of sizes and weights.

10. Pliers are a useful tool and are available in many different types, including slip-joint, multigroove, linesman's, diagonal, needle-nose, and locking pliers.

11. Other common hand tools include snap-ring pliers, files, cutters, punches, chisels, and hacksaws.

12. Hybrid electric vehicles should be de-powered if any of the high-voltage components are going to be serviced.

REVIEW QUESTIONS

1. List three precautions that must be taken whenever hoisting (lifting) a vehicle.

2. Describe how to determine the grade of a fastener, including how the markings differ between fractional and metric bolts.

3. List four items that are personal protective equipment (PPE).

4. List the types of fire extinguishers and their usage.

5. Why are wrenches offset 15 degrees?

6. What are the other names for a line wrench?

7. What are the standard automotive drive sizes for sockets?

8. Which type of screwdriver requires the use of a hammer or mallet?

9. What is inside a dead-blow hammer?

10. What type of cutter is available in left and right cutters?

CHAPTER QUIZ

1. The correct location for the pads when hoisting or jacking the vehicle can often be found in the _____.
   a. Service manual
   b. Shop manual
   c. Owner's manual
   d. All of the above

2. For the best working position, the work should be _____.
   a. At neck or head level
   b. At knee or ankle level
   c. Overhead by about 1 foot
   d. At chest or elbow level

3. A high-strength bolt is identified by _____.
   a. A UNC symbol
   b. Lines on the head
   c. Strength letter codes
   d. The coarse threads

4. A fastener that uses threads on both ends is called a _____.
   a. Cap screw
   b. Stud
   c. Machine screw
   d. Crest fastener

5. When working with hand tools, always _____.
   a. Push the wrench—don't pull toward you
   b. Pull a wrench—don't push a wrench away from you

6. The proper term for Channel Locks is _____.
   a. Vise Grips
   b. Crescent wrench
   c. Locking pliers
   d. Multigroove adjustable pliers

7. The proper term for Vise Grips is _____.
   a. Locking pliers
   b. Slip-joint pliers
   c. Side cuts
   d. Multigroove adjustable pliers

8. Two technicians are discussing torque wrenches. Technician A says that a torque wrench is capable of tightening a fastener with more torque than a conventional breaker bar or ratchet. Technician B says that a torque wrench should be calibrated regularly for the most accurate results. Which technician is correct?
   a. Technician A only
   b. Technician B only
   c. Both Technicians A and B
   d. Neither Technician A nor B

9. What type of screwdriver should be used if there is very limited space above the head of the fastener?
   a. Offset screwdriver
   b. Stubby screwdriver
   c. Impact screwdriver
   d. Robertson screwdriver

10. What type of hammer is plastic coated, has a metal casing inside, and is filled with small lead balls?
    a. Dead-blow hammer
    b. Soft-blow hammer
    c. Sledgehammer
    d. Plastic hammer

After studying Chapter 2, the reader will be able to:

1. Prepare for the ASE assumed knowledge content required by all service technicians to adhere to environmentally appropriate actions and behavior.

2. Define the Occupational Safety and Health Act (OSHA).

3. Explain the term material safety data sheet (MSDS).

4. Identify hazardous waste materials in accordance with state and federal regulations and follow proper safety precautions while handling hazardous waste materials.

5. Define the steps required to safely handle and store automotive chemicals and waste.

Aboveground storage tank (AGST) 45
Asbestosis 43
BCI 48
CAA 42
CFR 41
EPA 41
Hazardous waste material 41
HEPA vacuum 43
Mercury 50
MSDS 42
OSHA 41
RCRA 42
Right-to-know laws 41
Solvent 43
Underground storage tank (UST) 45
Used oil 44
WHMIS 42

HAZARDOUS WASTE

DEFINITION OF HAZARDOUS WASTE
Hazardous waste materials are chemicals, or components, that the shop no longer needs that pose a danger to the environment and people if they are disposed of in ordinary garbage cans or sewers. However, no material is considered hazardous waste until the shop has finished using it and is ready to dispose of it.

PERSONAL PROTECTIVE EQUIPMENT (PPE)
When handling hazardous waste material, one must always wear the proper protective clothing and equipment detailed in the right-to-know laws. This includes respirator equipment. All recommended procedures must be followed accurately. Personal injury may result from improper clothing, equipment, and procedures when handling hazardous materials.

FEDERAL AND STATE LAWS

OCCUPATIONAL SAFETY AND HEALTH ACT
The United States Congress passed the **Occupational Safety and Health Act (OSHA)** in 1970. This legislation was designed to assist and encourage the citizens of the United States in their efforts to assure:

- Safe and healthful working conditions by providing research, information, education, and training in the field of occupational safety and health.
- Safe and healthful working conditions for working men and women by authorizing enforcement of the standards developed under the Act.

Because about 25% of workers are exposed to health and safety hazards on the job, the OSHA standards are necessary to monitor, control, and educate workers regarding health and safety in the workplace.

EPA
The **Environmental Protection Agency (EPA)** publishes a list of hazardous materials that is included in the **Code of Federal Regulations (CFR)**. The EPA considers waste hazardous if it is included on the EPA list of hazardous materials, or it has one or more of the following characteristics:

- **Reactive**—Any material that reacts violently with water or other chemicals is considered hazardous.
- **Corrosive**—If a material burns the skin, or dissolves metals and other materials, a technician should consider it hazardous. A pH scale is used, with the number 7 indicating neutral. Pure water has a pH of 7. Lower numbers indicate an acidic solution and higher numbers indicate a caustic solution. If a material releases cyanide gas, hydrogen sulfide gas, or similar gases when exposed to low pH acid solutions, it is considered hazardous.

- **Toxic**—Materials are hazardous if they leak one or more of eight different heavy metals in concentrations greater than 100 times the primary drinking water standard.
- **Ignitable**—A liquid is hazardous if it has a flash point below 140°F (60°C), and a solid is hazardous if it ignites spontaneously.
- **Radioactive**—Any substance that emits measurable levels of radiation is radioactive. When individuals bring containers of a highly radioactive substance into the shop environment, qualified personnel with the appropriate equipment must test them.

 WARNING

> Hazardous waste disposal laws include serious penalties for anyone responsible for breaking these laws.

RIGHT-TO-KNOW LAWS
The **right-to-know laws** state that employees have a right to know when the materials they use at work are hazardous. The right-to-know laws started with the Hazard Communication Standard published by the Occupational Safety and Health Administration (OSHA) in 1983. Originally, this document was intended for chemical companies and manufacturers that required employees to handle hazardous materials in their work situation but the federal courts have decided to apply these laws to all companies, including automotive service shops. Under the right-to-know laws, the employer has responsibilities regarding the handling of hazardous materials by their employees. All employees must be trained about the types of hazardous materials they will

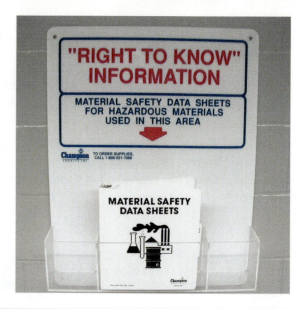

FIGURE 2–1 Material safety data sheets (MSDS) should be readily available for use by anyone in the area who may come into contact with hazardous materials.

encounter in the workplace. The employees must be informed about their rights under legislation regarding the handling of hazardous materials.

MATERIAL SAFETY DATA SHEETS (MSDS). All hazardous materials must be properly labeled, and information about each hazardous material must be posted on **material safety data sheets (MSDS)** available from the manufacturer. In Canada, MSDS information is called **Workplace Hazardous Materials Information Systems (WHMIS)**.

The employer has a responsibility to place MSDS information where they are easily accessible by all employees. The MSDS information provide the following information about the hazardous material: chemical name, physical characteristics, protective handling equipment, explosion/fire hazards, incompatible materials, health hazards, medical conditions aggravated by exposure, emergency and first-aid procedures, safe handling, and spill/leak procedures.

The employer also has a responsibility to make sure that all hazardous materials are properly labeled. The label information must include health, fire, and reactivity hazards posed by the material, as well as the protective equipment necessary to handle the material. The manufacturer must supply all warning and precautionary information about hazardous materials. This information must be read and understood by the employee before handling the material. ● **SEE FIGURE 2–1.**

RESOURCE CONSERVATION AND RECOVERY ACT (RCRA)
Federal and state laws control the disposal of hazardous waste materials and every shop employee must be familiar with these laws. Hazardous waste disposal laws include the **Resource Conservation and Recovery Act (RCRA)**. This law states that hazardous material users are responsible for hazardous materials from the time they become a waste until the proper waste disposal is completed. Many shops hire an independent hazardous waste hauler to dispose of hazardous waste material. The shop owner, or manager, should have a written contract with the hazardous waste hauler. Rather than have hazardous waste material hauled to an approved hazardous waste disposal site, a shop may choose to recycle the material in the shop. Therefore, the user must store hazardous waste material properly and safely, and be responsible for the transportation of this material until it arrives at an approved hazardous waste disposal site, where it can be processed according to the law. The RCRA controls the following types of automotive waste:

- Paint and body repair products waste
- Solvents for parts and equipment cleaning
- Batteries and battery acid
- Mild acids used for metal cleaning and preparation
- Waste oil, and engine coolants or antifreeze
- Air-conditioning refrigerants and oils
- Engine oil filters

CLEAN AIR ACT Air-conditioning (A/C) systems and refrigerant are regulated by the **Clean Air Act (CAA)**, Title VI, Section 609. Technician certification and service equipment is also regulated. Any technician working on automotive A/C systems must be certified. A/C refrigerants must not be released or vented into the atmosphere, and used refrigerants must be recovered.

ASBESTOS HAZARDS

Friction materials such as brake and clutch linings often contain asbestos. While asbestos has been eliminated from most original equipment friction materials, the automotive service technician cannot know whether or not the vehicle being serviced is or is not equipped with friction materials containing asbestos. It is important that all friction materials be handled as if they do contain asbestos.

Asbestos exposure can cause scar tissue to form in the lungs. This condition is called **asbestosis**. It gradually causes increasing shortness of breath, and the scarring to the lungs is permanent.

Even low exposures to asbestos can cause *mesothelioma*, a type of fatal cancer of the lining of the chest or abdominal cavity. Asbestos exposure can also increase the risk of *lung cancer* as well as cancer of the voice box, stomach, and large intestine. It usually takes 15 to 30 years or more for cancer or asbestos lung scarring to show up after exposure. Scientists call this the *latency period*.

Government agencies recommend that asbestos exposure should be eliminated or controlled to the lowest level possible. These agencies have developed recommendations and standards that the automotive service technician and equipment manufacturer should follow. These U.S. federal agencies include the National Institute for Occupational Safety and Health (NIOSH), Occupational Safety and Health Administration (OSHA), and Environmental Protection Agency (EPA).

ASBESTOS OSHA STANDARDS
The Occupational Safety and Health Administration (OSHA) has established three levels of asbestos exposure. Any vehicle service establishment that does either brake or clutch work must limit employee exposure to asbestos to less than 0.2 fibers per cubic centimeter (cc) as determined by an air sample.

If the level of exposure to employees is greater than specified, corrective measures must be performed and a large fine may be imposed.

NOTE: Research has found that worn asbestos fibers such as those from automotive brakes or clutches may not be as hazardous as first believed. Worn asbestos fibers do not have sharp flared ends that can latch onto tissue, but rather are worn down to a dust form that resembles talc. Grinding or sawing operations on unworn brake shoes or clutch discs *will* contain *harmful* asbestos fibers. To limit health damage, always use proper handling procedures while working around any component that may contain asbestos.

ASBESTOS EPA REGULATIONS
The federal Environmental Protection Agency (EPA) has established procedures for the removal and disposal of asbestos. The EPA procedures require that products containing asbestos be "wetted" to prevent the asbestos fibers from becoming airborne. According to the EPA, asbestos-containing materials can be disposed of as regular waste. Only when asbestos becomes airborne is it considered to be hazardous.

ASBESTOS HANDLING GUIDELINES
The air in the shop area can be tested by a testing laboratory, but this can be expensive. Tests have determined that asbestos levels can easily be kept below the recommended levels by using a liquid, like water, or a special vacuum.

NOTE: Even though asbestos is being removed from brake and clutch lining materials, the service technician cannot tell whether or not the old brake pads, shoes, or clutch discs contain asbestos. Therefore, to be safe, the technician should assume that all brake pads, shoes, or clutch discs contain asbestos.

HEPA VACUUM. A special **high-efficiency particulate air (HEPA) vacuum** system has been proven to be effective in keeping asbestos exposure levels below 0.1 fibers per cubic centimeter.

SOLVENT SPRAY. Many technicians use an aerosol can of brake cleaning solvent to wet the brake dust and prevent it from becoming airborne. A **solvent** is a liquid that is used to dissolve dirt, grime, or solid particles. Commercial brake cleaners are available that use a concentrated cleaner that is mixed with water. ● **SEE FIGURE 2–2.** The waste liquid is filtered, and when dry, the filter can be disposed of as solid waste.

☠ WARNING

Never use compressed air to blow brake dust. The fine talclike brake dust can create a health hazard even if asbestos is not present or is present in dust rather than fiber form.

FIGURE 2–2 All brakes should be moistened with water or solvent to help prevent brake dust from becoming airborne.

DISPOSAL OF BRAKE DUST AND BRAKE SHOES. The hazard of asbestos occurs when asbestos fibers are airborne. Once the asbestos has been wetted down, it is then considered to be solid waste, rather than hazardous waste. Old brake shoes and pads should be enclosed, preferably in a plastic bag, to help prevent any of the brake material from becoming airborne. *Always follow current federal and local laws concerning disposal of all waste.*

USED BRAKE FLUID

Most brake fluid is made from polyglycol, is water soluble, and can be considered hazardous if it has absorbed metals from the brake system.

STORAGE AND DISPOSAL OF BRAKE FLUID

- Collect brake fluid in a container clearly marked to indicate that it is designated for that purpose.
- If the waste brake fluid is hazardous, be sure to manage it appropriately and use only an authorized waste receiver for its disposal.
- If the waste brake fluid is nonhazardous (such as old, but unused), determine from your local solid waste collection provider what should be done for its proper disposal.
- Do not mix brake fluid with used engine oil.
- Do not pour brake fluid down drains or onto the ground.
- Recycle brake fluid through a registered recycler.

USED OIL

Used oil is any petroleum-based or synthetic oil that has been used. During normal use, impurities such as dirt, metal scrapings, water, or chemicals can get mixed in with the oil. Eventually, this used oil must be replaced with virgin or re-refined oil. The EPA's used oil management standards include a three-pronged approach to determine if a substance meets the definition of *used oil*. To meet the EPA's definition of used oil, a substance must meet each of the following three criteria.

- **Origin.** The first criterion for identifying used oil is based on the oil's origin. Used oil must have been refined from crude oil or made from synthetic materials. Animal and vegetable oils are excluded from the EPA's definition of used oil.
- **Use.** The second criterion is based on whether and how the oil is used. Oils used as lubricants, hydraulic fluids, heat transfer fluids, and for other similar purposes are considered used oil. The EPA's definition also excludes products used as cleaning agents, as well as certain petroleum-derived products like antifreeze and kerosene.
- **Contaminants.** The third criterion is based on whether or not the oil is contaminated with either physical or chemical impurities. In other words, to meet the EPA's definition, used oil must become contaminated as a result of being used. This aspect of the EPA's definition includes residues and contaminants generated from handling, storing, and processing used oil.

FIGURE 2–3 A typical above-ground oil storage tank.

NOTE: The release of only one gallon of used oil (a typical oil change) can make a million gallons of fresh water undrinkable.

If used oil is dumped down the drain and enters a sewage treatment plant, concentrations as small as 50 to 100 PPM (parts per million) in the waste water can foul sewage treatment processes. Never mix a listed hazardous waste, gasoline, waste water, halogenated solvent, antifreeze, or an unknown waste material with used oil. Adding any of these substances will cause the used oil to become contaminated, which classifies it as hazardous waste.

STORAGE AND DISPOSAL OF USED OIL
Once oil has been used, it can be collected, recycled, and used over and over again. An estimated 380 million gallons of used oil are recycled each year. Recycled used oil can sometimes be used again for the same job or can take on a completely different task. For example, used engine oil can be re-refined and sold at the store as engine oil or processed for furnace fuel oil. After collecting used oil in an appropriate container such as a 55-gallon steel drum, The material must be disposed of in one of two ways:

- Shipped offsite for recycling
- Burned in an onsite or offsite EPA-approved heater for energy recovery

Used oil must be stored in compliance with an existing **underground storage tank (UST)** or an **aboveground storage tank (AGST)** standard, or kept in separate containers. ● SEE

FIGURE 2–3. Containers are portable receptacles, such as a 55-gallon steel drum.

KEEP USED OIL STORAGE DRUMS IN GOOD CONDITION. This means that they should be covered, secured from vandals, properly labeled, and maintained in compliance with local fire codes. Frequent inspections for leaks, corrosion, and spillage are an essential part of container maintenance.

NEVER STORE USED OIL IN ANYTHING OTHER THAN TANKS AND STORAGE CONTAINERS. Used oil may also be stored in units that are permitted to store regulated hazardous waste.

USED OIL FILTER DISPOSAL REGULATIONS. Used oil filters contain used engine oil that may be hazardous. Before an oil filter is placed into the trash or sent to be recycled, it must be drained using one of the following hot-draining methods approved by the EPA.

- Puncture the filter antidrainback valve or filter dome end and hot-drain for at least 12 hours
- Hot-drain and crushing
- Dismantling and hot draining
- Any other hot-draining method, which will remove all the used oil from the filter

After the oil has been drained from the oil filter, the filter housing can be disposed of in any of the following ways:

- Sent for recycling
- Picked up by a service contract company
- Disposed of in regular trash

FIGURE 2–4 Washing hands and removing jewelry are two important safety habits all service technicians should practice.

FIGURE 2–5 Typical fireproof flammable storage cabinet.

SOLVENTS

The major sources of chemical danger are liquid and aerosol brake cleaning fluids that contain chlorinated hydrocarbon solvents. Several other chemicals that do not deplete the ozone, such as heptane, hexane, and xylene, are now being used in nonchlorinated brake cleaning solvents. Some manufacturers are also producing solvents they describe as environmentally responsible, which are biodegradable and noncarcinogenic (non-cancer-causing).

There is no specific standard for physical contact with chlorinated hydrocarbon solvents or the chemicals replacing them. All contact should be avoided whenever possible. The law requires an employer to provide appropriate protective equipment and ensure proper work practices by an employee handling these chemicals.

EFFECTS OF CHEMICAL POISONING The effects of exposure to chlorinated hydrocarbon and other types of solvents can take many forms. Short-term exposure at low levels can cause symptoms such as:

- Headache
- Nausea
- Drowsiness
- Dizziness
- Lack of coordination
- Unconsciousness

It may also cause irritation of the eyes, nose, and throat, and flushing of the face and neck. Short-term exposure to higher concentrations can cause liver damage with symptoms

SAFETY TIP

Hand Safety

Service technicians should wash their hands with soap and water after handling engine oil or differential or transmission fluids, or wear protective rubber gloves. Another safety hint is that the service technician should not wear watches, rings, or other jewelry that could come in contact with electrical or moving parts of a vehicle. ● **SEE FIGURE 2–4.**

such as yellow jaundice or dark urine. Liver damage may not become evident until several weeks after the exposure.

HAZARDOUS SOLVENTS AND REGULATORY STATUS

Most solvents are classified as hazardous wastes. Other characteristics of solvents include the following:

- Solvents with flash points below 60°C are considered flammable and, like gasoline, are federally regulated by the Department of Transportation (DOT).
- Solvents and oils with flash points above 60°C are considered combustible and, like engine oil, are also regulated by the DOT. All flammable items must be stored in a fireproof container. ● **SEE FIGURE 2–5.**

It is the responsibility of the repair shop to determine if its spent solvent is hazardous waste. Solvent reclaimers are available that clean and restore the solvent so it lasts indefinitely.

FIGURE 2–6 Using a water-based cleaning system helps reduce the hazards from using strong chemicals.

FIGURE 2–7 Used antifreeze coolant should be kept separate and stored in a leakproof container until it can be recycled or disposed of according to federal, state, and local laws. Note that the storage barrel is placed inside another container to catch any coolant that may spill out of the inside barrel.

 FREQUENTLY ASKED QUESTION

How can you tell if a solvent is hazardous?

If a solvent or any of the ingredients of a product contains "fluor" or "chlor" then it is likely to be hazardous. Check the instructions on the label for proper use and disposal procedures.

USED SOLVENTS Used or spent solvents are liquid materials that have been generated as waste and may contain xylene, methanol, ethyl ether, and methyl isobutyl ketone (MIBK). These materials must be stored in OSHA-approved safety containers with the lids or caps closed tightly. Additional requirements include the following:

- Containers should be clearly labeled "Hazardous Waste" and the date the material was first placed into the storage receptacle should be noted.

- Labeling is not required for solvents being used in a parts washer.

- Used solvents will not be counted toward a facility's monthly output of hazardous waste if the vendor under contract removes the material.

- Used solvents may be disposed of by recycling with a local vendor, such as SafetyKleen®, to have the used solvent removed according to specific terms in the vendor agreement.

- Use aqueous-based (nonsolvent) cleaning systems to help avoid the problems associated with chemical solvents. ● **SEE FIGURE 2–6.**

COOLANT DISPOSAL

Coolant is a mixture of antifreeze and water. New antifreeze is not considered to be hazardous even though it can cause death if ingested. Used antifreeze may be hazardous due to dissolved metals from the engine and other components of the cooling system. These metals can include iron, steel, aluminum, copper, brass, and lead (from older radiators and heater cores). Coolant should be disposed of in one of the following ways:

- Coolant should be recycled either onsite or offsite.

- Used coolant should be stored in a sealed and labeled container. ● **SEE FIGURE 2–7.**

- Used coolant can often be disposed of into municipal sewers with a permit. Check with local authorities and obtain a permit before discharging used coolant into sanitary sewers.

LEAD–ACID BATTERY WASTE

About 70 million spent lead–acid batteries are generated each year in the United States alone. Lead is classified as a toxic metal and the acid used in lead–acid batteries is highly corrosive. The vast majority (95% to 98%) of these batteries are recycled through lead reclamation operations and secondary lead smelters for use in the manufacture of new batteries.

BATTERY DISPOSAL Used lead–acid batteries must be reclaimed or recycled in order to be exempt from hazardous waste regulations. Leaking batteries must be stored and transported as hazardous waste. Some states have more strict regulations, which require special handling procedures and transportation. According to the **Battery Council International (BCI)**, battery laws usually include the following rules:

1. Lead–acid battery disposal is prohibited in landfills or incinerators. Batteries are required to be delivered to a battery retailer, wholesaler, recycling center, or lead smelter.

2. All retailers of automotive batteries are required to post a sign that displays the universal recycling symbol and indicates the retailer's specific requirements for accepting used batteries.

3. Battery electrolyte contains sulfuric acid, which is a very corrosive substance capable of causing serious personal injury, such as skin burns and eye damage. In addition, the battery plates contain lead, which is highly poisonous. For this reason, disposing of batteries improperly can cause environmental contamination and lead to severe health problems.

BATTERY HANDLING AND STORAGE Batteries, whether new or used, should be kept indoors if possible. The storage location should be an area specifically designated for battery storage and must be well ventilated (to the outside). If outdoor storage is the only alternative, a sheltered and secured area with acid-resistant secondary containment is strongly recommended. It is also advisable that acid-resistant secondary containment be used for indoor storage. In addition, batteries should be placed on acid-resistant pallets and never stacked.

FUEL SAFETY AND STORAGE

Gasoline is a very explosive liquid. The expanding vapors that come from gasoline are extremely dangerous. These vapors are present even in cold temperatures. Vapors formed in gasoline tanks on many vehicles are controlled, but vapors from gasoline storage may escape from the can, resulting in a hazardous situation. Therefore, place gasoline storage containers in a well-ventilated space. Although diesel fuel is not as volatile as gasoline, the same basic rules apply to diesel fuel and gasoline storage. These rules include the following:

1. Use storage cans that have a flash-arresting screen at the outlet. These screens prevent external ignition sources from igniting the gasoline within the can when someone pours the gasoline or diesel fuel.

2. Use only a red approved gasoline container to allow for proper hazardous substance identification. ● **SEE FIGURE 2–8.**

3. Do not fill gasoline containers completely full. Always leave the level of gasoline at least one inch from the top of the container. This action allows expansion of the gasoline at higher temperatures. If gasoline containers are completely full, the gasoline will expand when the temperature increases. This expansion forces gasoline from the can and creates a dangerous spill. If gasoline or diesel fuel containers must be stored, place them in a designated storage locker or facility.

4. Never leave gasoline containers open, except while filling or pouring gasoline from the container.

5. Never use gasoline as a cleaning agent.

6. Always connect a ground strap to containers when filling or transferring fuel or other flammable products from one container to another to prevent static electricity that could result in explosion and fire. These ground wires prevent the buildup of a static electric charge, which could result in a spark and disastrous explosion.

FIGURE 2–8 This red gasoline container holds about 30 gallons of gasoline and is used to fill vehicles used for training.

AIRBAG HANDLING

Airbag modules are pyrotechnic devices that can be ignited if exposed to an electrical charge or if the body of the vehicle is subjected to a shock. Airbag safety should include the following precautions:

1. Disarm the airbag(s) if you will be working in the area where a discharged bag could make contact with any part of your body. Consult service information for the exact procedure to follow for the vehicle being serviced. The usual procedure is to deploy the airbag using a 12-volt power supply, such as a jump start box, using long wires to connect to the module to ensure a safe deployment.

2. Do not expose an airbag to extreme heat or fire.

3. Always carry an airbag pointing away from your body.

4. Place an airbag module facing upward.

5. Always follow the manufacturer's recommended procedure for airbag disposal or recycling, including the proper packaging to use during shipment.

6. Wear protective gloves if handling a deployed airbag.

7. Always wash your hands or body well if exposed to a deployed airbag. The chemicals involved can cause skin irritation and possible rash development.

USED TIRE DISPOSAL

Used tires are an environmental concern because of several reasons, including the following:

1. In a landfill, they tend to "float" up through the other trash and rise to the surface.

2. The inside of tires traps and holds rainwater, which is a breeding ground for mosquitoes. Mosquito-borne diseases include encephalitis and dengue fever.

3. Used tires present a fire hazard and, when burned, create a large amount of black smoke that contaminates the air.

Used tires should be disposed of in one of the following ways:

1. Used tires can be reused until the end of their useful life.

2. Tires can be retreaded.

3. Tires can be recycled or shredded for use in asphalt.

4. Derimmed tires can be sent to a landfill (most landfill operators will shred the tires because it is illegal in many states to landfill whole tires).

5. Tires can be burned in cement kilns or other power plants where the smoke can be controlled.

6. A registered scrap tire handler should be used to transport tires for disposal or recycling.

FIGURE 2–9 Air-conditioning refrigerant oil must be kept separated from other oils because it contains traces of refrigerant and must be treated as hazardous waste.

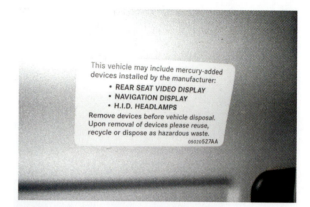

FIGURE 2–10 Placard near driver's door, including what devices in the vehicle contain mercury.

AIR-CONDITIONING REFRIGERANT OIL DISPOSAL

Air-conditioning refrigerant oil contains dissolved refrigerant and is therefore considered to be hazardous waste. This oil must be kept separated from other waste oil or the entire amount of oil must be treated as hazardous. Used refrigerant oil must be sent to a licensed hazardous waste disposal company for recycling or disposal. **SEE FIGURE 2–9.**

WASTE CHART   All automotive service facilities create some waste and while most of it is handled properly, it is important that all hazardous and nonhazardous waste be accounted for and properly disposed.  **SEE CHART 2–1** for a list of typical wastes generated at automotive shops, plus a checklist for keeping track of how these wastes are handled.

> ### TECH TIP
>
> **Remove Components that Contain Mercury**
>
> Some vehicles have a placard near the driver's side door that lists the components that contain the heavy metal, mercury. **Mercury** can be absorbed through the skin and is a heavy metal that once absorbed by the body does not leave. ● **SEE FIGURE 2–10.**
>
> These components should be removed from the vehicle before the rest of the body is sent to be recycled to help prevent releasing mercury into the environment.

> ### TECH TIP
>
> **What Every Technician Should Know**
>
> The Hazardous Materials Identification Guide (HMIG) is the standard labeling for all materials. The service technician should be aware of the meaning of the label. ● **SEE FIGURE 2–11.**

WASTE STREAM	TYPICAL CATEGORY IF NOT MIXED WITH OTHER HAZARDOUS WASTE	IF DISPOSED IN LANDFILL AND NOT MIXED WITH A HAZARDOUS WASTE	IF RECYCLED
Used oil	Used oil	Hazardous waste	Used oil
Used oil filters	Nonhazardous solid waste, if completely drained	Nonhazardous solid waste, if completely drained	Used oil, if not drained
Used transmission fluid	Used oil	Hazardous waste	Used oil
Used brake fluid	Used oil	Hazardous waste	Used oil
Used antifreeze	Depends on characterization	Depends on characterization	Depends on characterization
Used solvents	Hazardous waste	Hazardous waste	Hazardous waste
Used citric solvents	Nonhazardous solid waste	Nonhazardous solid waste	Hazardous waste
Lead–acid automotive batteries	Not a solid waste if returned to supplier	Hazardous waste	Hazardous waste
Shop rags used for oil	Used oil	Depends on used oil characterization	Used oil
Shop rags used for solvent or gasoline spills	Hazardous waste	Hazardous waste	Hazardous waste
Oil spill absorbent material	Used oil	Depends on used oil characterization	Used oil
Spill material for solvent and gasoline	Hazardous waste	Hazardous waste	Hazardous waste
Catalytic converter	Not a solid waste if returned to supplier	Nonhazardous solid waste	Nonhazardous solid waste
Spilled or unused fuels	Hazardous waste	Hazardous waste	Hazardous waste
Spilled or unusable paints and thinners	Hazardous waste	Hazardous waste	Hazardous waste
Used tires	Nonhazardous solid waste	Nonhazardous solid waste	Nonhazardous solid waste

CHART 2–1

Typical Wastes Generated at Auto Repair Shops and Typical Category (Hazardous or Nonhazardous) by Disposal Method

Hazardous Materials Identification Guide (HMIG)

TYPE HAZARD		DEGREE	
○	HEALTH	4 - Extreme
○	FLAMMABILITY	3 - Serious
○	REACTIVITY	2 - Moderate
○	PROTECTIVE EQUIPMENT	1 - Slight
		0 - Minimal

HAZARD RATING AND PROTECTIVE EQUIPMENT

Health		Flammable		Reactive	
Type of Possible Injury		Susceptibility of materials to burn		Susceptibility of materials to release energy	
4	Highly Toxic. May be fatal on short-term exposure. Special protective equipment required.	4	Extremely flammable gas or liquid. Flash Point below 73°F.	4	Extreme. Explosive at room temperature.
3	Toxic. Avoid inhalation or skin contact.	3	Flammable. Flash Point 73°F to 100°F.	3	Serious. May explode if shocked, heated under confinement or mixed w/ water.
2	Moderately Toxic. May be harmful if inhaled or absorbed.	2	Combustible. Requires moderate heating to ignite. Flash Point 100°F to 200°F.	2	Moderate. Unstable, may react with water.
1	Slightly Toxic. May cause slight irritation.	1	Slightly Combustible. Requires strong heating to ignite.	1	Slight. May react if heated or mixed with water.
0	Minimal. All chemicals have a slight degree of toxicity.	0	Minimal. Will not burn under normal conditions.	0	Minimal. Normally stable, does not react with water.

Protective Equipment

A	Safety Glasses	E	Safety Glasses + Gloves + Dust Respirator	I	Safety Glasses + Gloves + Combination Dust & Vapor Respirator
B	Safety Glasses + Gloves	F	Safety Glasses + Gloves + Apron + Dust Respirator	J	Chemical Goggles + Gloves + Apron + Combination Dust & Vapor Respirator
C	Safety Glasses + Gloves + Apron	G	Safety Glasses + Gloves + Vapor Respirator	K	Apron + Gloves + Full Protection Suit + Boots
D	Faceshield + Gloves + Apron	H	Chemical Goggles + Gloves + Apron + Vapor Respirator	X	Ask your supervisor for guidance.

SUMMARY

1. Hazardous materials include common automotive chemicals, liquids, and lubricants, especially those whose ingredients contain *chlor* or *fluor* in their name.

2. Right-to-know laws require that all workers have access to material safety data sheets (MSDS).

3. Asbestos fibers should be avoided and removed according to current laws and regulations.

4. Used engine oil contains metals worn from parts and should be handled and disposed of properly.

5. Solvents represent a serious health risk and should be avoided as much as possible.

6. Coolant should be disposed of properly or recycled.

7. Batteries are considered to be hazardous waste and should be discarded to a recycling facility.

REVIEW QUESTIONS

1. List five common automotive chemicals or products that may be considered hazardous materials.

2. List five precautions to which every technician should adhere when working with automotive products and chemicals.

CHAPTER QUIZ

1. Hazardous materials include all of the following *except* _____.
   - a. Engine oil
   - b. Asbestos
   - c. Water
   - d. Brake cleaner

2. To determine if a product or substance being used is hazardous, consult _____.
   - a. A dictionary
   - b. An MSDS
   - c. SAE standards
   - d. EPA guidelines

3. Exposure to asbestos dust can cause what condition?
   - a. Asbestosis
   - b. Mesothelioma
   - c. Lung cancer
   - d. All of the above are possible

4. Wetted asbestos dust is considered to be _____.
   - a. Solid waste
   - b. Hazardous waste
   - c. Toxic
   - d. Poisonous

5. An oil filter should be hot drained for how long before disposing of the filter?
   - a. 30 to 60 minutes
   - b. 4 hours
   - c. 8 hours
   - d. 12 hours

6. Used engine oil should be disposed of by all *except* the following methods.
   - a. Disposed of in regular trash
   - b. Shipped offsite for recycling
   - c. Burned onsite in a waste oil-approved heater
   - d. Burned offsite in a waste oil-approved heater

7. All of the following are the proper ways to dispose of a drained oil filter *except* _____.
   - a. Sent for recycling
   - b. Picked up by a service contract company
   - c. Disposed of in regular trash
   - d. Considered to be hazardous waste and disposed of accordingly

8. Which act or organization regulates air-conditioning refrigerant?
   - a. Clean Air Act (CAA)
   - b. MSDS
   - c. WHMIS
   - d. Code of Federal Regulations (CFR)

9. Gasoline should be stored in approved containers that include what color(s)?
   - a. A red container with yellow lettering
   - b. A red container
   - c. A yellow container
   - d. A yellow container with red lettering

10. What automotive devices may contain mercury?
   - a. Rear seat video displays
   - b. Navigation displays
   - c. HID headlights
   - d. All of the above

GASOLINE ENGINE OPERATION, PARTS, AND SPECIFICATIONS

After studying Chapter 3, the reader will be able to:

1. Prepare for Engine Repair (A1) ASE certification test content area "A" (General Engine Diagnosis).
2. Explain how a four-stroke cycle gasoline engine operates.
3. List the various characteristics by which vehicle engines are classified.
4. Discuss how a compression ratio is calculated.
5. Explain how engine size is determined.
6. Describe how turbocharging or supercharging increases engine power.

Block 55
Bore 63
Boxer 59
Cam-in-block design 60
Camshaft 60
Combustion 55
Combustion chamber 55
Compression ratio (CR) 65
Connecting rod 57
Crankshaft 57
Cycle 59
Cylinder 57
Displacement 63
Double overhead camshaft (DOHC) 60
Exhaust valve 57
External combustion engine 55
Four-stroke cycle 59

Intake valve 57
Internal combustion engine 55
Mechanical force 55
Mechanical power 55
Naturally aspirated 61
Nonprincipal end 62
Oil galleries 56
Pancake 59
Piston stroke 59
Principal end 62
Pushrod engine 60
Rotary engine 61
Single overhead camshaft (SOHC) 60
Stroke 63
Supercharger 61
Top dead center (TDC) 57
Turbocharger 61
Wankel engine 61

FIGURE 3–1 The rotating assembly for a V-8 engine that has eight pistons and connecting rods and one crankshaft.

FIGURE 3–2 A cylinder head with four valves per cylinder, two intake valves (larger) and two exhaust valves (smaller) per cylinder.

ENERGY AND POWER

Energy is used to produce power. The chemical energy in fuel is converted to heat by the burning of the fuel at a controlled rate. This process is called **combustion**. If engine combustion occurs within the power chamber, the engine is called an **internal combustion engine**.

NOTE: An external combustion engine is an engine that burns fuel outside of the engine itself, such as a steam engine.

Engines used in automobiles are internal combustion heat engines. They convert the chemical energy of the gasoline into heat within a power chamber that is called a **combustion chamber**. Heat energy released in the combustion chamber raises the temperature of the combustion gases within the chamber. The increase in gas temperature causes the pressure of the gases to increase. The pressure developed within the combustion chamber is applied to the head of a piston or to a turbine wheel to produce a usable **mechanical force**, which is then converted into useful **mechanical power**.

ENGINE CONSTRUCTION OVERVIEW

BLOCK   All automotive and truck engines are constructed using a solid frame, called a **block**. A block is constructed of cast iron or aluminum and provides the foundation for most of the engine components and systems. The block is cast and then machined to very close tolerances to allow other parts to be installed.

ROTATING ASSEMBLY   Pistons are installed in the block and move up and down during engine operation. Pistons are connected to *connecting rods*, which connect the pistons to the crankshaft. The crankshaft converts the up-and-down motion of the piston to rotary motion, which is then transmitted to the drive wheels and propels the vehicle. ● **SEE FIGURE 3–1.**

CYLINDER HEADS   All engines use a cylinder head to seal the top of the cylinders, which are in the engine block. The cylinder head also contains valves that allow air and fuel into the cylinder, called intake valves and exhaust valves, which open after combustion to allow the hot gases left over to escape from the engine. Cylinder heads are constructed of cast iron or aluminum and are then machined for the valves and other valve-related components. Cooling passages are formed during the casting process and coolant is circulated around the combustion chamber to keep temperatures controlled. ● **SEE FIGURE 3–2.**

FIGURE 3–3 The coolant temperature is controlled by the thermostat which opens and allows coolant to flow to the radiator when the temperature reaches the rating temperature of the thermostat.

ENGINE CONSTRUCTION OVERVIEW (CONTINUED)

INTAKE AND EXHAUST MANIFOLDS Air and fuel enters the engine through an intake manifold and exits the engine through the exhaust manifold. Intake manifolds operate cooler than exhaust manifolds and are therefore constructed of nylon reinforced plastic or aluminum. Exhaust manifolds must be able to withstand hot exhaust gases and therefore most are constructed from cast iron.

COOLING SYSTEM All engines must have a cooling system to control engine temperatures. While some older engines were air cooled, all current production passenger vehicle engines are cooled by circulating antifreeze coolant through passages in the block and cylinder head. The coolant picks up the heat from the engine and after the thermostat opens, the water pump circulates the coolant through the radiator where the excess heat is released to the outside air, cooling the coolant. The coolant is continuously circulated through the cooling system and the temperature is controlled by the thermostat. ● **SEE FIGURE 3–3**.

LUBRICATION SYSTEM All engines contain moving and sliding parts that must be kept lubricated to reduce wear and friction. The oil pan, bolted to the bottom of the engine block, holds 4 to 7 quarts (liters) of oil. An oil pump, which is driven by the engine, forces the oil through the oil filter and then into passages in the crankshaft and block. These passages are called **oil galleries**. The oil is also forced up to the valves and then falls down through openings in the cylinder head and block back into the oil pan. ● **SEE FIGURE 3–4**.

FUEL SYSTEM AND IGNITION SYSTEM All engines require fuel and an ignition system to ignite the fuel–air mixture in the cylinders. The fuel system includes the following components:

- Fuel tank where fuel is stored
- Fuel filter and lines
- Fuel injectors, which spray fuel into the intake manifold or directly into the cylinder, depending on the type of system used

The ignition system is designed to take 12 volts from the battery and convert it to 5,000 to 40,000 volts needed to jump the gap of a spark plug. Spark plugs are threaded into the cylinder head of each cylinder, and when the spark occurs, it ignites the air–fuel mixture in the cylinder creating pressure and forcing the piston down in the cylinder. The components included on the ignition system include:

- Spark plugs
- Ignition coils
- Ignition control module (ICM)
- Associated wiring

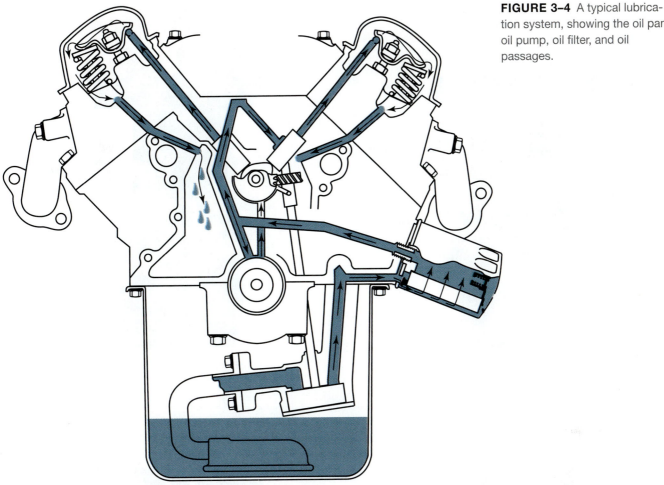

FOUR-STROKE CYCLE OPERATION

Most automotive engines use the four-stroke cycle of events, begun by the starter motor which rotates the engine. The four-stroke cycle is repeated for each cylinder of the engine. ● SEE FIGURE 3–5.

- **Intake stroke.** The **intake valve** is open and the piston inside the cylinder travels downward, drawing a mixture of air and fuel into the cylinder.

- **Compression stroke.** As the engine continues to rotate, the intake valve closes and the piston moves upward in the cylinder, compressing the air–fuel mixture.

- **Power stroke.** When the piston gets near the top of the cylinder (called **top dead center [TDC]**), the spark at the spark plug ignites the air–fuel mixture, which forces the piston downward.

- **Exhaust stroke.** The engine continues to rotate, and the piston again moves upward in the cylinder. The exhaust

valve opens, and the piston forces the residual burned gases out of the **exhaust valve** and into the exhaust manifold and exhaust system.

This sequence repeats as the engine rotates. To stop the engine, the electricity to the ignition system is shut off by the ignition switch.

A piston that moves up and down, or reciprocates, in a **cylinder** can be seen in this illustration. The piston is attached to a **crankshaft** with a **connecting rod**. This arrangement allows the piston to reciprocate (move up and down) in the cylinder as the crankshaft rotates. ● SEE FIGURE 3–6.

The combustion pressure developed in the combustion chamber at the correct time will push the piston downward to rotate the crankshaft.

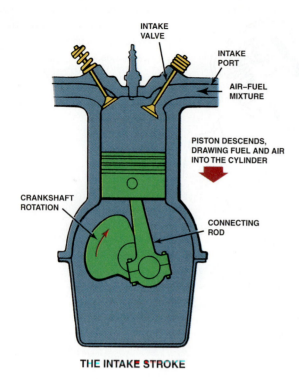

INTAKE VALVE
INTAKE PORT
AIR–FUEL MIXTURE

PISTON DESCENDS, DRAWING FUEL AND AIR INTO THE CYLINDER

CRANKSHAFT ROTATION
CONNECTING ROD

THE INTAKE STROKE

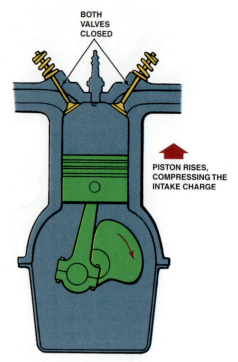

BOTH VALVES CLOSED

PISTON RISES, COMPRESSING THE INTAKE CHARGE

THE COMPRESSION STROKE

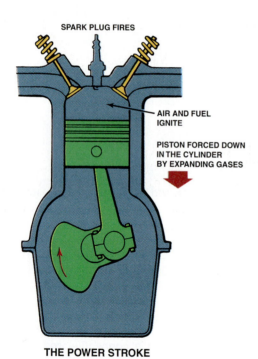

SPARK PLUG FIRES

AIR AND FUEL IGNITE

PISTON FORCED DOWN IN THE CYLINDER BY EXPANDING GASES

THE POWER STROKE

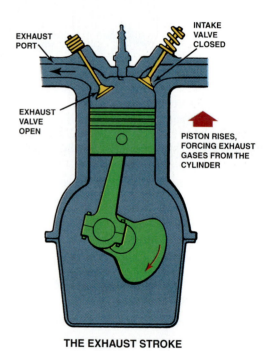

EXHAUST PORT
INTAKE VALVE CLOSED

EXHAUST VALVE OPEN

PISTON RISES, FORCING EXHAUST GASES FROM THE CYLINDER

THE EXHAUST STROKE

FIGURE 3–5 The downward movement of the piston draws the air–fuel mixture into the cylinder through the intake valve on the intake stroke. On the compression stroke, the mixture is compressed by the upward movement of the piston with both valves closed. Ignition occurs at the beginning of the power stroke, and combustion drives the piston downward to produce power. On the exhaust stroke, the upward-moving piston forces the burned gases out the open exhaust valve.

FIGURE 3–6 Cutaway of an engine showing the cylinder, piston, connecting rod, and crankshaft.

THE 720° CYCLE

Each cycle of events requires that the engine crankshaft make two complete revolutions or 720° (360° × 2 = 720°). The greater the number of cylinders, the closer together the power strokes occur. To find the angle between cylinders of an engine, divide the number of cylinders into 720°.

Angle with three cylinders = 720°/3 = 240°

Angle with four cylinders = 720°/4 = 180°

Angle with five cylinders = 720°/5 = 144°

Angle with six cylinders = 720°/6 = 120°

Angle with eight cylinders = 720°/8 = 90°

Angle with ten cylinders = 720°/10 = 72°

This means that in a four-cylinder engine, a power stroke occurs at every 180° of the crankshaft rotation (every 1/2 rotation). A V-8 is a much smoother operating engine because a power stroke occurs twice as often (every 90° of crankshaft rotation).

Engine cycles are identified by the number of piston strokes required to complete the cycle. A **piston stroke** is a one-way piston movement between the top and bottom of the cylinder. During one stroke, the crankshaft revolves 180° (1/2 revolution). A **cycle** is a complete series of events that continually repeat. Most automobile engines use a **four-stroke cycle**.

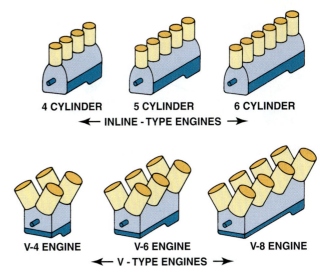

FIGURE 3–7 Automotive engine cylinder arrangements.

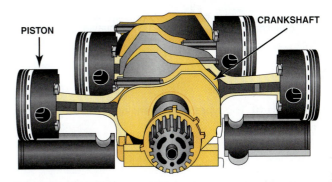

FIGURE 3–8 A horizontally opposed engine design helps to lower the vehicle's center of gravity.

ENGINE CLASSIFICATION AND CONSTRUCTION

Engines are classified by several characteristics including:

- **Number of strokes.** Most automotive engines use the four-stroke cycle.

- **Cylinder arrangement.** An engine with more cylinders is smoother operating because the power pulses produced by the power strokes are more closely spaced. An inline engine places all cylinders in a straight line. Four-, five-, and six-cylinder engines are commonly manufactured inline engines. A V-type engine, such as a V-6 or V-8, has the number of cylinders split and built into a V-shape. ● SEE FIGURE 3–7. Horizontally opposed four- and six-cylinder engines have two banks of cylinders that are horizontal, resulting in a low engine. This style of engine is used in Porsche and Subaru engines and is often called the **boxer** or **pancake** engine design. ● SEE FIGURE 3–8.

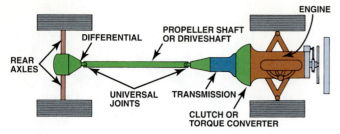

FIGURE 3–9 A longitudinally mounted engine drives the rear wheels through a transmission, driveshaft, and differential assembly.

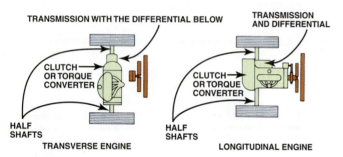

FIGURE 3–10 Two types of front-engine, front-wheel drive.

FIGURE 3–11 Cutaway of a V-8 engine showing the lifters, pushrods, roller rocker arms, and valves.

ENGINE CLASSIFICATION AND CONSTRUCTION (CONTINUED)

- **Longitudinal or transverse mounting.** Engines may be mounted either parallel with the length of the vehicle (longitudinally) or crosswise (transversely). ● **SEE FIGURES 3–9 AND 3–10.** The same engine may be mounted in various vehicles in either direction.

  NOTE: Although it might be possible to mount an engine in different vehicles both longitudinally and transversely, the engine component parts may *not* be interchangeable. Differences can include different engine blocks and crankshafts, as well as different water pumps.

- **Valve and camshaft number and location.** The number of valves and the number and location of camshafts are a major factor in engine operation. A typical older-model engine uses one intake valve and one exhaust valve per cylinder. Many newer engines use two intake and two exhaust valves per cylinder. The valves are opened by a **camshaft**. For high-speed engine operation, the camshaft should be overhead (over the valves). Some engines use one camshaft for the intake valves and a separate camshaft for the exhaust valves. When the camshaft is located in the block, the valves are operated by lifters, pushrods, and rocker arms. ● **SEE FIGURE 3–11.** This type of engine is called a **pushrod engine** or **cam-in-block design.** An overhead camshaft engine has the camshaft above the valves in the cylinder head. When one overhead camshaft is used, the design is called a **single overhead camshaft (SOHC)** design. When two overhead camshafts are used, the design is called a **double overhead camshaft (DOHC)** design. See ● **SEE FIGURES 3–12 and 3–13.**

  NOTE: A V-type engine uses two banks or rows of cylinders. An SOHC design therefore uses two camshafts, but only one camshaft per bank (row) of cylinders. A DOHC V-6, therefore, has four camshafts, two for each bank.

- **Type of fuel.** Most engines operate on gasoline, whereas some engines are designed to operate on methanol, natural gas, propane, or diesel fuel.

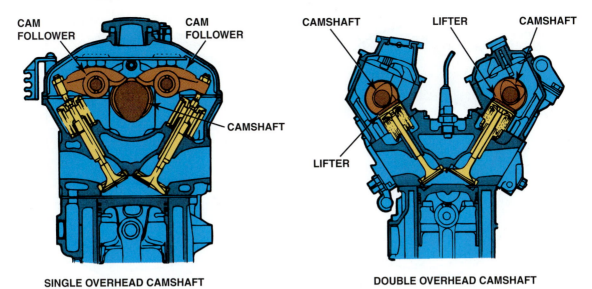

SINGLE OVERHEAD CAMSHAFT

DOUBLE OVERHEAD CAMSHAFT

FIGURE 3–12 SOHC engines usually require additional components such as a rocker arm to operate all of the valves. DOHC engines often operate the valves directly.

FIGURE 3–13 A dual overhead camshaft (DOHC) V-8 engine with the cam cover removed.

- **Cooling method.** Most engines are liquid cooled, but some older models were air cooled.

- **Type of induction pressure.** If atmospheric air pressure is used to force the air–fuel mixture into the cylinders, the engine is called **naturally aspirated**. Some engines use a **turbocharger** or **supercharger** to force the air–fuel mixture into the cylinder for even greater power.

? **FREQUENTLY ASKED QUESTION**

What Is a Rotary Engine?

A successful alternative engine design is the **rotary engine,** also called the **Wankel engine** after its inventor. The Mazda RX-7 and RX-8 represents the only long-term use of the rotary engine. The rotating combustion chamber engine runs very smoothly, and it produces high power for its size and weight.

The basic rotating combustion chamber engine has a triangular-shaped rotor turning in a housing. The housing is in the shape of a geometric figure called a two-lobed epitrochoid. A seal on each corner, or apex, of the rotor is in constant contact with the housing, so the rotor must turn with an eccentric motion. This means that the center of the rotor moves around the center of the engine. The eccentric motion can be seen in ● **FIGURE 3–14**.

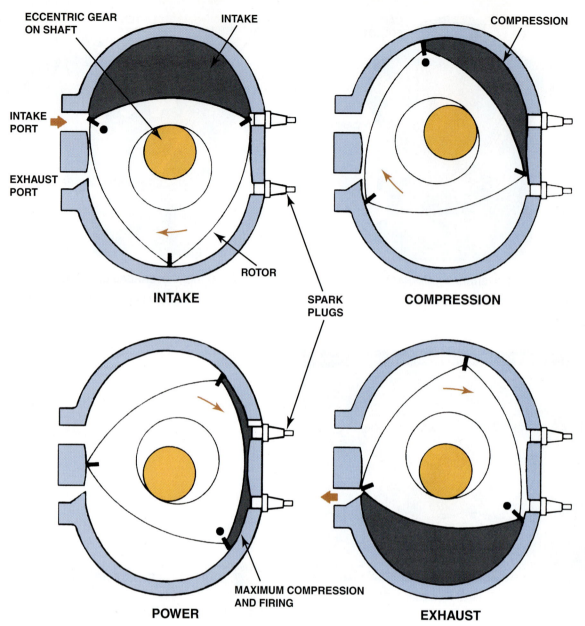

FIGURE 3–14 Rotary engine operates on the four-stroke cycle but uses a rotor instead of a piston and crankshaft to achieve intake, compression, power, and exhaust stroke.

ENGINE ROTATION DIRECTION

The SAE standard for automotive engine rotation is counter-clockwise (CCW) as viewed from the flywheel end (clockwise as viewed from the front of the engine). The flywheel end of the engine is the end to which the power is applied to drive the vehicle. This is called the **principal end** of the engine. The **nonprincipal end** of the engine is opposite the principal end and is generally referred to as the *front* of the engine, where the accessory belts are used. ● **SEE FIGURE 3–15**.

In most rear-wheel-drive vehicles, therefore, the engine is mounted longitudinally with the principal end at the rear of the engine. Most transversely mounted engines also adhere to the same standard for direction of rotation. Many Honda engines and some marine applications may differ from this standard.

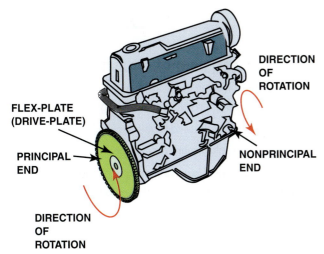

FIGURE 3–15 Inline four-cylinder engine showing principal and nonprincipal ends. Normal direction of rotation is clockwise (CW) as viewed from the front or accessory belt end (nonprincipal end).

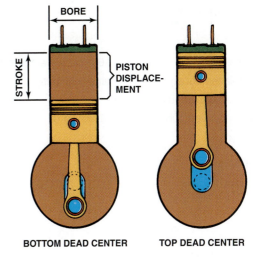

FIGURE 3–16 The bore and stroke of pistons are used to calculate an engine's displacement.

BORE

The diameter of a cylinder is called the **bore**. The larger the bore, the greater the area on which the gases have to work. Pressure is measured in units, such as pounds per square inch (PSI). The greater the area (in square inches), the higher the force exerted by the pistons to rotate the crankshaft. ● **SEE FIGURE 3–16.**

? FREQUENTLY ASKED QUESTION

Where Does an Engine Stop?

When the ignition system is turned off, the firing of the spark plugs stops and the engine will rotate until it stops due to the inertia of the rotating parts. The greatest resistance that occurs in the engine happens during the compression stroke. It has been determined that an engine usually stops when one of the cylinders is about 70 degrees before top dead center (BTDC) on the compression stroke with a variation of plus or minus 10 degrees.

This explains why technicians discover that the starter ring gear is worn at two locations on a four-cylinder engine. The engine stops at one of the two possible places depending on which cylinder is on the compression stroke.

STROKE

The distance the piston travels down in the cylinder is called the **stroke**. The longer this distance is, the greater the amount of air–fuel mixture that can be drawn into the cylinder. The more air–fuel mixture inside the cylinder, the more force will result when the mixture is ignited.

ENGINE DISPLACEMENT

Engine size is described as displacement. **Displacement** is the cubic inch (cu. in.) or cubic centimeter (cc) volume displaced or swept by all of the pistons. A liter (L) is equal to 1,000 cubic centimeters; therefore, most engines today are identified by their displacement in liters.

> 1 L = 1,000 cc
>
> 1 L = 61 cu. in.
>
> 1 cu. in. = 16.4 cc

The formula to calculate the displacement of an engine is basically the formula for determining the volume of a cylinder multiplied by the number of cylinders. However, because the formula has been publicized in many different forms, it seems somewhat confusing. Regardless of the method used, the results will be the same. The easiest and most commonly used formula is

bore × bore × stroke × 0.7854 × number of cylinders

For example, take a 6-cylinder engine where, bore = 4.000 in., stroke = 3.000 in. Applying the formula,

4.000 in. × 4.000 in. × 3.000 in. × 0.7854 × 6 = 226 cu. in.

Because 1 cubic inch equals 16.4 cubic centimeters, this engine displacement equals 3,706 cubic centimeters or, rounded to 3,700 cubic centimeters, 3.7 liters.

How to convert cubic inches to liters: 61.02 cubic inches = 1 liter

Example:

From liter to cubic inch—5.0 L × 61.02 = 305 CID
From cubic inch to liter—305 ÷ 61.02 = 5.0 L

 **TECH TIP**

All 3.8-Liter Engines Are Not the Same!

Most engine sizes are currently identified by displacement in liters. However, not all 3.8-liter engines are the same. See, for example, the following table:

Engine	Displacement
Chevrolet-built 3.8-L, V-6	229 cu. in.
Buick-built 3.8-L, V-6 (also called 3,800 cc)	231 cu. in.
Ford-built 3.8-L, V-6	232 cu. in.

The exact conversion from liters (or cubic centimeters) to cubic inches is 231.9 cubic inches. However, due to rounding of exact cubic-inch displacement and rounding of the exact cubic-centimeter volume, several entirely different engines can be marketed with the exact same liter designation. To reduce confusion and reduce the possibility of ordering incorrect parts, the vehicle identification number (VIN) should be noted for the vehicle being serviced. The VIN should be visible through the windshield on all vehicles. Since 1980, the *engine* identification number or letter is usually the eighth digit or letter from the left.

Smaller, 4-cylinder engines can also cause confusion because many vehicle manufacturers use engines from both overseas and domestic manufacturers. Always refer to service manual information to be assured of correct engine identification.

ENGINE SIZE VERSUS HORSEPOWER The larger the engine, the more power the engine is capable of producing. Several sayings are often quoted about engine size:

"There is no substitute for cubic inches."

"There is no replacement for displacement."

Although a large engine generally uses more fuel, making an engine larger is often the easiest way to increase power.

Engine Size Conversion Chart
Liters to Cubic Inches

Liters	Cubic Inches	Liters	Cubic Inches
1.0	61	4.3	260/262/265
1.3	79	4.4	267
1.4	85	4.5	273
1.5	91	4.6	280/281
1.6	97/98	4.8	292
1.7	105	4.9	300/301
1.8	107/110/112	5.0	302/304/305/307
1.9	116	5.2	318
2.0	121/122	5.3	327
2.1	128	5.4	330
2.2	132/133/134/135	5.7	350
2.3	138/140	5.8	351
2.4	149	5.9	360
2.5	150/153	6.0	366/368
2.6	156/159	6.1	370
2.8	171/173	6.2	381
2.9	177	6.4	389/390/391
3.0	181/182/183	6.5	396
3.1	191	6.6	400
3.2	196	6.9	420
3.3	200/201	7.0	425/427/428/429
3.4	204	7.2	440
3.5	215	7.3	445
3.7	225	7.4	454
3.8	229/231/232	7.5	460
3.9	239/240	7.8	475/477
4.0	241/244	8.0	488
4.1	250/252	8.4	510
4.2	255/258	8.8	534

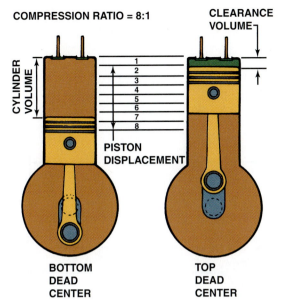

FIGURE 3–17 Compression ratio is the ratio of the total cylinder volume (when the piston is at the bottom of its stroke) to the clearance volume (when the piston is at the top of its stroke).

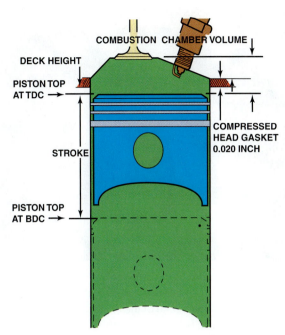

FIGURE 3–18 Combustion chamber volume is the volume above the piston with the piston at top dead center.

COMPRESSION RATIO

The compression ratio of an engine is an important consideration when rebuilding or repairing an engine. **Compression ratio (CR)** is the ratio of the volume in the cylinder above the piston when the piston is at the bottom of the stroke to the volume in the cylinder above the piston when the piston is at the top of the stroke. ● SEE FIGURE 3–17.

If Compression Is Lower	If Compression Is Higher
Lower power	Higher power possible
Poorer fuel economy	Better fuel economy
Easier engine cranking	Harder to crank engine, especially when hot
More advanced ignition timing possible without spark knock (detonation)	Less ignition timing required to prevent spark knock (detonation)

$$CR = \frac{\text{Volume in cylinder with piston at bottom of cylinder}}{\text{Volume in cylinder with piston at top center}}$$

● SEE FIGURE 3–18.

For example: What is the compression ratio of an engine with 50.3-cu. in. displacement in one cylinder and a combustion chamber volume of 6.7 cu. in.?

$$CR = \frac{50.3 + 6.7 \text{ cu. in.}}{6.7 \text{ cu. in.}} = \frac{57.0}{} = 8.5$$

FIGURE 3–19 The distance between the centerline of the main bearing journal and the centerline of the connecting rod journal determines the stroke of the engine. This photo is a little unusual because this is from a V-6 with a splayed crankshaft used to even out the impulses on a 90°, V-6 engine design.

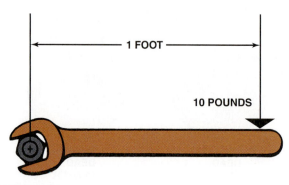

FIGURE 3–20 Torque is a twisting force equal to the distance from the pivot point times the force applied expressed in units called pound-feet (lb-ft) or Newton-meters (N-m).

THE CRANKSHAFT DETERMINES THE STROKE

The stroke of an engine is the distance the piston travels from top dead center (TDC) to bottom dead center (BDC). This distance is determined by the throw of the crankshaft. The throw is the distance from the centerline of the crankshaft to the centerline of the crankshaft rod journal. The throw is one-half of the stroke. ● SEE FIGURE 3–19 for an example of a crankshaft as installed in a GM V-6 engine.

If the crankshaft is replaced with one with a greater stroke, the pistons will be pushed up over the height of the top of the block (deck). The solution to this problem is to install replacement pistons with the piston pin relocated higher on the piston. Another alternative is to replace the connecting rod with a shorter one to prevent the piston from traveling too far up in the cylinder. Changing the connecting rod length does *not* change the stroke of an engine. Changing the connecting rod only changes the position of the piston in the cylinder.

TORQUE

Torque is the term used to describe a rotating force that may or may not result in motion. Torque is measured as the amount of force multiplied by the length of the lever through which it acts. If a one-foot-long wrench is used to apply 10 pounds of force to the end of the wrench to turn a bolt, then you are exerting 10 pound-feet of torque. ● SEE FIGURE 3–20.

The metric unit for torque is Newton-meters because Newton is the metric unit for force and the distance is expressed in meters.

one pound-foot = 1.3558 Newton-meters

one Newton-meter = 0.7376 pound-foot

POWER

The term power means the rate of doing work. Power equals work divided by time. Work is achieved when a certain amount of mass (weight) is moved a certain distance by a force. It does not make a difference in the amount of work accomplished if the object is moved in 10 seconds or 10 minutes, but it does affect the amount of power needed. Power is expressed in units of foot-pounds per minute.

HORSEPOWER AND ALTITUDE

Because the density of the air is lower at high altitude, the power that a normal engine can develop is greatly reduced at high altitude. According to SAE conversion factors, a non-supercharged or nonturbocharged engine loses about 3% of its power for every 1,000 feet (300 meters [m]) of altitude.

Therefore, an engine that develops 150 brake horsepower at sea level will only produce about 85 brake horsepower at the top of Pike's Peak in Colorado at 14,110 feet (4,300 meters). Supercharged and turbocharged engines are not as greatly affected by altitude as normally aspirated engines. Normally aspirated, remember, means engines that breathe air at normal atmospheric pressure.

 **TECH TIP**

Quick-and-Easy Engine Efficiency Check

A good, efficient engine is able to produce a lot of power from little displacement. A common rule of thumb is that an engine is efficient if it can produce *1 horsepower per cubic inch* of displacement. Many engines today are capable of this feat, such as the following:

Ford	4.6-L V-8 (281 cu. in.)	305 hp
Chevrolet	3.4-L V-6 (207 cu. in.)	210 hp
Chrysler	3.5-L V-6 (214 cu. in.)	214 hp
Acura	3.2-L V-6 (195 cu. in.)	270 hp

An engine is very powerful for its size if it can produce *100 hp per liter*. This efficiency goal is harder to accomplish. Most factory stock engines that can achieve this feat are supercharged or turbocharged.

SUMMARY

1. The four strokes of the four-stroke cycle are intake, compression, power, and exhaust.
2. Engines are classified by number and arrangement of cylinders and by number and location of valves and camshafts, as well as by type of mounting, fuel used, cooling method, and induction pressure.
3. Most engines rotate clockwise as viewed from the front (accessory) end of the engine. The SAE standard is counterclockwise as viewed from the principal (flywheel) end of the engine.
4. Engine size is called displacement and represents the volume displaced or swept by all of the pistons.

REVIEW QUESTIONS

1. Name the strokes of a four-stroke cycle.
2. If an engine at sea level produces 100 horsepower, how many horsepower would it develop at 6,000 feet of altitude?

1. All overhead valve engines _____.
   a. Use an overhead camshaft
   b. Have the overhead valves in the head
   c. Operate by the rotary cycle
   d. Use the camshaft to close the valves

2. An SOHC V-8 engine has how many camshafts?
   a. One
   b. Two
   c. Three
   d. Four

3. The coolant flow through the radiator is controlled by the _____.
   a. Size of the passages in the block
   b. Thermostat
   c. Cooling fan(s)
   d. Water pump

4. Torque is expressed in units of _____.
   a. Pound-feet
   b. Foot-pounds
   c. Foot-pounds per minute
   d. Pound-feet per second

5. Horsepower is expressed in units of _____.
   a. Pound-feet
   b. Foot-pounds
   c. Foot-pounds per minute
   d. Pound-feet per second

6. A normally aspirated automobile engine loses about _____ power per 1,000 feet of altitude.
   a. 1%
   b. 3%
   c. 5%
   d. 6%

7. One cylinder of an automotive four-stroke cycle engine completes a cycle every _____.
   a. 90°
   b. 180°
   c. 360°
   d. 720°

8. How many rotations of the crankshaft are required to complete each stroke of a four-stroke cycle engine?
   a. One-fourth
   b. One-half
   c. One
   d. Two

9. A rotating force is called _____.
   a. Horsepower
   b. Torque
   c. Combustion pressure
   d. Eccentric movement

10. Technician A says that a crankshaft determines the stroke of an engine. Technician B says that the length of the connecting rod determines the stroke of an engine. Which technician is correct?
    a. Technician A only
    b. Technician B only
    c. Both Technicians A and B
    d. Neither Technician A nor B

OPERATION AND DIAGNOSIS

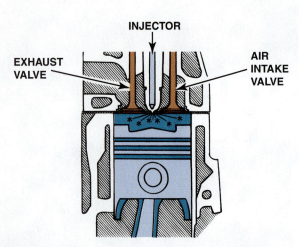

FIGURE 4–1 Diesel combustion occurs when fuel is injected into the hot, highly compressed air in the cylinder.

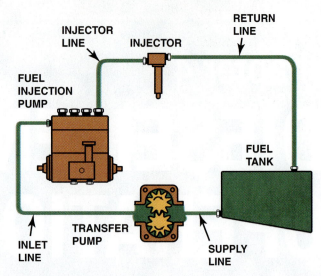

FIGURE 4–2 A typical injector-pump-type automotive diesel fuel injection system.

DIESEL ENGINES

In 1892, a German engineer named Rudolf Diesel perfected the compression-ignition engine that bears his name. The diesel engine uses heat created by compression to ignite the fuel, so it requires no spark ignition system.

The diesel engine requires compression ratios of 16:1 and higher. Incoming air is compressed until its temperature reaches about 1000°F (540°C). This is called **heat of compression**. As the piston reaches the top of its compression stroke, fuel is injected into the cylinder, where it is ignited by the hot air. ● **SEE FIGURE 4–1.**

As the fuel burns, it expands and produces power. Because of the very high compression and torque output of a diesel engine, it is made heavier and stronger than the same size gasoline-powered engine.

A common diesel engine uses a fuel system precision **injection pump** and individual fuel injectors. The pump delivers fuel to the injectors at a high pressure and at timed intervals. Each injector sprays fuel into the combustion chamber at the precise moment required for efficient combustion. ● **SEE FIGURE 4–2.**

In a diesel engine, air is not controlled by a throttle as in a gasoline engine. Instead, the amount of fuel injected is varied to control power and speed. The air–fuel mixture of a diesel can vary from as lean as 85:1 at idle to as rich as 20:1 at full load. This higher air–fuel ratio and the increased compression pressures make the diesel more fuel-efficient than a gasoline engine in part because diesel engines do not suffer from throttling losses. Throttling losses involve the power needed in a gasoline engine to draw air past a closed or partially closed throttle.

In a gasoline engine, the speed and power are controlled by the throttle valve, which controls the amount of air entering the engine. Adding more fuel to the cylinders of a gasoline engine without adding more air (oxygen) will not increase the speed or power of the engine. In a diesel engine, speed and power are not controlled by the amount of air entering the cylinders because the engine air intake is always wide open. Therefore, the engine always has enough oxygen to burn the fuel in the cylinder and will increase speed (and power) when additional fuel is supplied.

Diesel engines are built in both two-stroke and four-stroke versions. The most common two-stroke diesels were the truck and industrial engines made by Detroit Diesel. In these engines, air intake is through ports in the cylinder wall. Exhaust is through poppet valves in the head. A blower pushes air into the air box surrounding liner ports to supply air for combustion and to blow the exhaust gases out of the exhaust valves.

INDIRECT AND DIRECT INJECTION In an **indirect injection** (abbreviated **IDI**) diesel engine, fuel is injected into a small prechamber, which is connected to the cylinder by a narrow opening. The initial combustion takes place in this

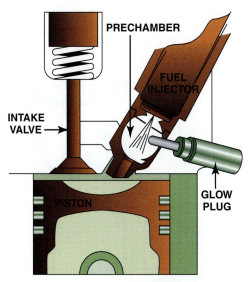

FIGURE 4–3 An indirect injection diesel engine uses a prechamber and a glow plug.

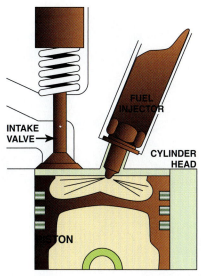

FIGURE 4–4 A direct injection diesel engine injects the fuel directly into the combustion chamber. Many designs do not use a glow plug.

prechamber. This has the effect of slowing the rate of combustion, which tends to reduce noise. ● **SEE FIGURE 4–3.**

All indirect diesel injection engines require the use of a glow plug.

In a **direct injection** (abbreviated **DI**) diesel engine, fuel is injected directly into the cylinder. The piston incorporates a depression where initial combustion takes place. Direct injection diesel engines are generally more efficient than indirect injection engines, but have a tendency to produce greater amounts of noise. ● **SEE FIGURE 4–4.**

While some direct injection diesel engines use glow plugs to help cold starting and to reduce emissions, some direct injection diesel engines do not use glow plugs.

DIESEL FUEL IGNITION Ignition occurs in a diesel engine by injecting fuel into the air charge, which has been heated by compression to a temperature greater than the ignition point of the fuel or about 1000°F (538°C). The chemical reaction of burning the fuel liberates heat, which causes the gases to expand,

forcing the piston to rotate the crankshaft. A four-stroke diesel engine requires two rotations of the crankshaft to complete one cycle. On the intake stroke, the piston passes TDC, the intake valve(s) open, the fresh air is admitted into the cylinder, and the exhaust valve is still open for a few degrees to allow all of the exhaust gases to escape. On the compression stroke, after the piston passes BDC, the intake valve closes and the piston travels up to TDC (completion of the first crankshaft rotation). On the power stroke, the piston nears TDC on the compression stroke, the diesel fuel is injected by the injectors, and the fuel starts to burn, further heating the gases in the cylinder. During this power stroke, the piston passes TDC and the expanding gases force the piston down, rotating the crankshaft. On the exhaust stroke, as the piston passes BDC, the exhaust valves open and the exhaust gases start to flow out of the cylinder. This continues as the piston travels up to TDC, pumping the spent gases out of the cylinder. At TDC, the second crankshaft rotation is complete.

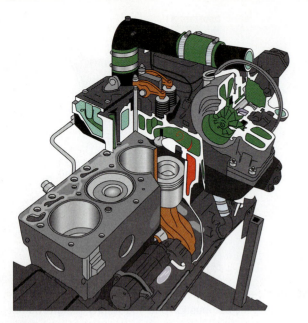

FIGURE 4–5 The common rail on a Cummins diesel engine. A high-pressure pump (up to 30,000 PSI) is used to supply diesel fuel to this common rail, which has cubes running to each injector. Note the thick cylinder walls and heavy-duty construction.

FIGURE 4–6 A rod/piston assembly from a 5.9-liter Cummins diesel engine used in a Dodge pickup truck.

THREE PHASES OF COMBUSTION

There are three distinct phases or parts to the combustion in a diesel engine.

1. **Ignition delay.** Near the end of the compression stroke, fuel injection begins, but ignition does not begin immediately. This period is called delay.

2. **Rapid combustion.** This phase of combustion occurs when the fuel first starts to burn, creating a sudden rise in cylinder pressure. It is this rise in combustion chamber pressure that causes the characteristic diesel engine knock.

3. **Controlled combustion.** After the rapid combustion occurs, the rest of the fuel in the combustion chamber begins to burn and injection continues. This is an area near the injector that contains fuel surrounded by air. This fuel burns as it mixes with the air.

DIESEL ENGINE CONSTRUCTION

Diesel engines must be constructed heavier than gasoline engines because of the tremendous pressures that are created in the cylinders during operation. The torque output of a diesel engine is often double or more than the same size gasoline powered engines. See the comparison chart.

System or Component	Diesel Engine	Gasoline Engine
Block	Cast iron and heavy ● SEE FIGURE 4–5.	Cast iron or aluminum and as light as possible
Cylinder head	Cast iron or aluminum	Cast iron or aluminum
Compression ratio	17:1 to 25:1	8:1 to 12:1
Peak engine speed	2000 to 2500 RPM	5000 to 8000 RPM
Pistons and connecting rods	Aluminum with combustion pockets and heavy-duty rods ● SEE FIGURE 4–6.	Aluminum, usually flat top or with valve relief but no combustion pockets

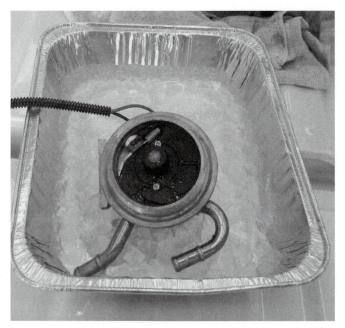

FIGURE 4–7 Using an ice bath to test the fuel temperature sensor.

FIGURE 4–8 A typical distributor-type diesel injection pump showing the pump, lines, and fuel filter.

FUEL TANK AND LIFT PUMP

A fuel tank used on a vehicle equipped with a diesel engine differs from the one used with a gasoline engine in several ways, including:

- A larger filler neck for diesel fuel. Gasoline filler necks are smaller for the unleaded gasoline nozzle.

- No evaporative emission control devices or charcoal (carbon) canister. Diesel fuel is not as volatile as gasoline and, therefore, diesel vehicles do not have evaporative emission control devices.

The diesel fuel is drawn from the fuel tank by a **lift pump** and delivers the fuel to the injection pump. Between the fuel tank and the lift pump is a **water–fuel separator.** Water is heavier than diesel fuel and sinks to the bottom of the separator. Part of normal routine maintenance on a vehicle equipped with a diesel engine is to drain the water from the water–fuel separator. A float is usually used inside the separator, which is connected to a warning light on the dash that lights if the water reaches a level where it needs to be drained.

NOTE: Water can cause corrosive damage as well as wear to diesel engine parts because water is not a good lubricant. Water cannot be atomized by a diesel fuel injector nozzle and will often "blow out" the nozzle tip.

Many diesel engines also use a fuel temperature sensor. The computer uses this information to adjust fuel delivery based on the density of the fuel. ● SEE FIGURE 4–7.

INJECTION PUMP

A diesel engine injection pump is used to increase the pressure of the diesel fuel from very low values from the lift pump to the extremely high pressures needed for injection.

Injection pumps are usually driven by a gear off the camshaft at the front of the engine. As the injection pump shaft rotates, the diesel fuel is fed from a fill port to a high-pressure chamber. If a distributor-type injection pump is used, the fuel is forced out of the injection port to the correct injector nozzle through the high-pressure line. ● SEE FIGURE 4–8.

NOTE: Because of the very tight tolerances in a diesel engine, the smallest amount of dirt can cause excessive damage to the engine and to the fuel injection system.

DISTRIBUTOR INJECTION PUMP A distributor diesel injection pump is a high-pressure pump assembly with lines leading to each individual injector. The high-pressure lines between the distributor and the injectors must be the exact same length to ensure proper injection timing. The injection pump itself creates the injection advance needed for engine speeds above idle and the fuel is discharged into the lines. The high-pressure fuel causes the injectors to open. Due to the internal friction of the lines, there is a slight delay before fuel pressure opens the injector nozzle. ● SEE FIGURE 4–9.

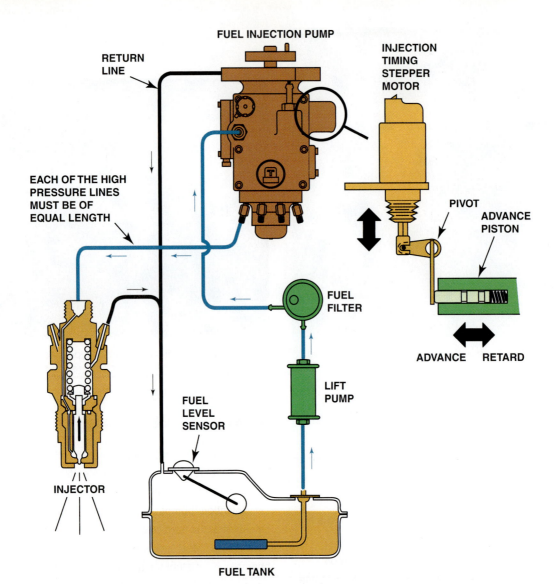

FIGURE 4–9 A schematic of a Stanadyne diesel fuel injection pump assembly showing all of the related components.

INJECTION PUMP (CONTINUED)

NOTE: The lines expand some during an injection event. This is how timing checks are performed. The pulsing of the injector line is picked up by a probe used to detect the injection event similar to a timing light used to detect a spark on a gasoline engine.

HIGH-PRESSURE COMMON RAIL Newer diesel engines use a fuel delivery system referred to as a **high-pressure common rail (HPCR)** design. Diesel fuel under high pressure, over 20,000 psi (138,000 kPa), is applied to the injectors, which are opened by a solenoid controlled by the computer. Because the injectors are computer controlled, the combustion process can be precisely controlled to provide maximum engine efficiency with the lowest possible noise and exhaust emissions. ● **SEE FIGURE 4–10.**

HEUI SYSTEM

Ford 7.3- and 6.0-liter diesels use a system Ford calls a **Hydraulic Electronic Unit Injection** system, or **HEUI** system. The components that replace the traditional mechanical injection pump include a high-pressure oil pump and reservoir, pressure regulator for the oil, and passages in the cylinder head for flow of fuel to the injectors.

Fuel is drawn from the tank by the tandem fuel pump, which circulates fuel at low pressure through the fuel filter/water separator/fuel heater bowl and then fuel is directed back to the fuel pump where fuel is pumped at high pressure into the cylinder head fuel galleries. The injectors, which are hydraulically actuated by the oil pressure from the high-pressure oil pump, are then fired by the Powertrain Control Module (PCM). The control system for

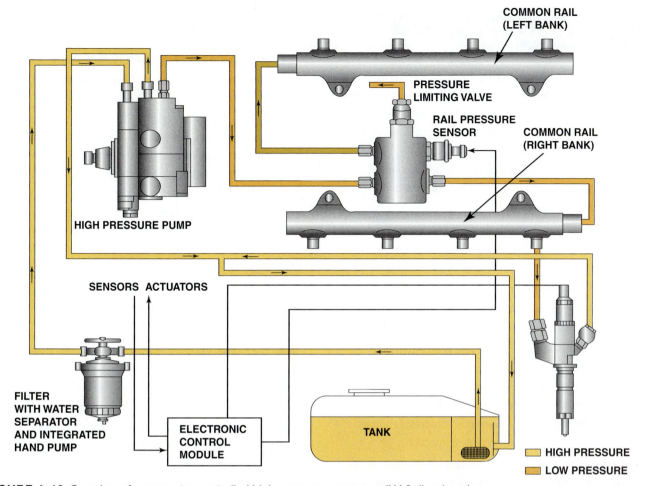

FIGURE 4–10 Overview of a computer-controlled high-pressure common rail V-8 diesel engine.

the fuel injectors is the PCM and the injectors are fired based on various inputs received by the PCM. ● **SEE FIGURE 4–11**.

HEUI injectors rely on O-rings to keep fuel and oil from mixing or escaping, causing performance problems or engine damage. HEUI injectors use five O-rings. The three external O-rings should be replaced with updated O-rings if they fail. The two internal O-rings are not replaceable and if these fail, the injector or injectors must be replaced. The most common symptoms of injector O-ring trouble include:

- Oil getting in the fuel
- The fuel filter element turning black
- Long cranking times before starting

FIGURE 4–11 A HEUI injector from a Ford PowerStroke diesel engine. The grooves indicate the location of the O-rings.

- Sluggish performance
- Reduction in power
- Increased oil consumption often accompanies O-ring problems or any fault that lets fuel in the oil

DIESEL INJECTOR NOZZLES

Diesel injector nozzles are spring-loaded closed valves that spray fuel directly into the combustion chamber or precombustion chamber. Injector nozzles are threaded into the cylinder head, one for each cylinder, and are replaceable as an assembly.

The top of the injector nozzle has many holes to deliver an atomized spray of diesel fuel into the cylinder. Parts of a diesel injector nozzle include:

- **Heat shield.** This is the outer shell of the injector nozzle and has external threads where it seals in the cylinder head.

- **Injector body.** This is the inner part of the nozzle and contains the injector needle valve and spring, and threads into the outer heat shield.

- **Diesel injector needle valve.** This precision machined valve and the tip of the needle seal against the injector body when it is closed. When the valve is open, diesel fuel is sprayed into the combustion chamber. This passage is controlled by a solenoid on diesel engines equipped with computer-controlled injection.

- **Injector pressure chamber.** The pressure chamber is a machined cavity in the injector body around the tip of the injector needle. Injection pump pressure forces fuel into this chamber, forcing the needle valve open.

TECH TIP

Change Oil Regularly in a Ford Diesel Engine

Ford 7.3- and 6.0-liter diesel engines pump unfiltered oil from the sump to the high-pressure oil pump and then to the injectors. This means that not changing oil regularly can contribute to accumulation of dirt in the engine and will subject the fuel injectors to wear and potential damage as particles suspended in the oil get forced into the injectors.

TECH TIP

Never Allow a Diesel Engine to Run Out of Fuel

If a gasoline-powered vehicle runs out of gasoline, it is an inconvenience and a possible additional expense to get some gasoline. However, if a vehicle equipped with a diesel engine runs out of fuel, it can be a major concern.

Besides adding diesel fuel to the tank, the other problem is getting all of the air out of the pump, lines, and injectors so the engine will operate correctly.

The procedure usually involves cranking the engine long enough to get liquid diesel fuel back into the system, but at the same time keeping cranking time short enough to avoid overheating the starter. Consult service information for the exact service procedure if the diesel engine is run out of fuel.

NOTE: Some diesel engines such as the first generation General Motors Duramax V-8 are equipped with a priming pump located under the hood on top of the fuel filter. Pushing down and releasing the priming pump with a vent valve open will purge any trapped air from the system. Always follow the vehicle manufacturer's instructions.

DIESEL INJECTOR NOZZLE OPERATION

The electric solenoid attached to the injector nozzle is computer controlled and opens to allow fuel to flow into the injector pressure chamber. ● **SEE FIGURE 4–12**.

The diesel injector nozzle is mechanically opened by the high-pressure fuel delivered to the nozzle by the injector pump. The fuel flows down through a fuel passage in the injector body and into the pressure chamber. The high fuel pressure in the pressure chamber forces the needle valve upward, compressing the needle valve return spring and forcing the needle valve open. When the needle valve opens, diesel fuel is discharged into the combustion chamber in a hollow cone spray pattern.

Any fuel that leaks past the needle valve returns to the fuel tank through a return passage and line.

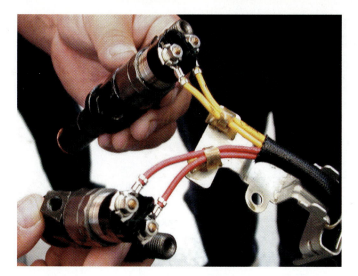

FIGURE 4–12 Typical computer-controlled diesel engine fuel injectors.

GLOW PLUGS

Glow plugs are always used in diesel engines equipped with a precombustion chamber and may be used in direct injection diesel engines to aid starting. A **glow plug** is a heating element that uses 12 volts from the battery and aids in the starting of a cold engine. As the temperature of the glow plug increases, the resistance of the heating element inside increases, thereby reducing the current in amperes needed by the glow plugs.

Most glow plugs used in newer vehicles are controlled by the Powertrain Control Module (PCM), which monitors coolant temperature and intake air temperature. The glow plugs are turned on or pulsed on or off depending on the temperature of the engine. The PCM will also keep the glow plug turned on after the engine starts to reduce white exhaust smoke (unburned fuel) and to improve idle quality after starting. ● **SEE FIGURE 4–13**.

The "wait to start" lamp will light when the engine and the outside temperature is low to allow time for the glow plugs to get hot. The "wait to start" lamp will not come on when the glow plugs are operating after the engine starts.

NOTE: The glow plugs are removed to test cylinder compression using a special high-pressure reading gauge.

? FREQUENTLY ASKED QUESTION

What Are Diesel Engine Advantages and Disadvantages?

A diesel engine has several advantages compared to a similar size gasoline-powered engine including:

1. More torque output
2. Greater fuel economy
3. Long service life

A diesel engine has several disadvantages compared to a similar size gasoline-powered engine including:

1. Engine noise, especially when cold and/or at idle speed
2. Exhaust smell
3. Cold weather startability
4. A vacuum pump is needed to supply the vacuum needs of the heat, ventilation, and air conditioning system
5. Heavier than a gasoline engine.
   ● **SEE FIGURE 4–14.**
6. Fuel availability

ENGINE-DRIVEN VACUUM PUMP

Because a diesel engine is unthrottled, it creates very little vacuum in the intake manifold. Several engine and vehicle components operate using vacuum, such as the exhaust gas recirculation (EGR) valve and the heating and ventilation blend and air doors. Most diesels used in cars and light trucks are equipped with an engine-driven vacuum pump to supply the vacuum for these components.

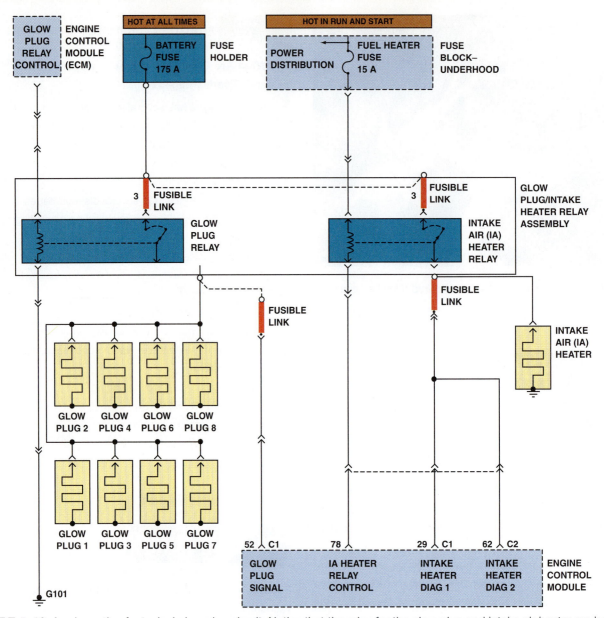

FIGURE 4–13 A schematic of a typical glow plug circuit. Notice that the relay for the glow plug and intake air heater are both computer controlled.

FIGURE 4–14 Roller lifter from a GM Duramax 6.6-liter V-8 diesel engine. Notice the size of this lifter compared to a roller lifter used in a gasoline engine.

DIESEL FUEL

Diesel fuel must meet an entirely different set of standards than gasoline. The fuel in a diesel engine is not ignited with a spark, but is ignited by the heat generated by high compression. The pressure of compression (400 to 700 PSI or 2,800 to 4,800 kPa) generates temperatures of 1200° to 1600°F (700° to 900°C), which speeds the preflame reaction to start the ignition of fuel injected into the cylinder.

All diesel fuel must be clean, be able to flow at low temperatures, and be of the proper cetane rating.

- **Cleanliness.** It is imperative that the fuel used in a diesel engine be clean and free from water. Unlike the case with gasoline engines, the fuel is the lubricant and coolant for the diesel injector pump and injectors. Good-quality diesel fuel contains additives such as oxidation inhibitors, detergents, dispersants, rust preventatives, and metal deactivators.

- **Low-temperature fluidity.** Diesel fuel must be able to flow freely at all expected ambient temperatures. One specification for diesel fuel is its "pour point," which is the temperature below which the fuel would stop flowing. **Cloud point** is another concern with diesel fuel at lower temperatures. Cloud point is the low-temperature point at which the waxes present in most diesel fuel tend to form wax crystals that clog the fuel filter. Most diesel fuel suppliers distribute fuel with the proper pour point and cloud point for the climate conditions of the area.

- **Cetane number.** The cetane number for diesel fuel is the opposite of the octane number for gasoline. The **cetane number** is a measure of the ease with which the fuel can be ignited. The cetane rating of the fuel determines, to a great extent, its ability to start the engine at low temperatures and to provide smooth warm-up and even combustion. The cetane rating of diesel fuel should be between 45 and 50. The higher the cetane rating, the more easily the fuel is ignited, whereas the higher the octane rating, the more slowly the fuel burns.

Other diesel fuel specifications include its flash point, sulfur content, and classification. The **flash point** is the temperature at which the vapors on the surface of the fuel will ignite if exposed to an open flame. The flash point does *not* affect diesel engine operation. However, a lower than normal flash point could indicate contamination of the diesel fuel with gasoline or a similar substance.

The sulfur content of diesel fuel is very important to the life of the engine. Since 2007, all diesel fuel has to have less than 15 parts per million (PPM) of sulfur and is called ultra low sulfur diesel (ULSD). This is way down from the previous limit for low sulfur diesel of 500 PPM. Sulfur in the fuel creates sulfuric acid during the combustion process, which can damage engine components and cause piston ring wear. Federal regulations are getting extremely tight on sulfur content. High-sulfur fuel contributes to acid rain.

ASTM also classifies diesel fuel by volatility (boiling range) into the following grades:

GRADE #1   This grade of diesel fuel has the lowest boiling point and the lowest cloud and pour points; it also has a lower BTU content—less heat per pound of fuel. As a result, grade #1 is suitable for use during low-temperature (winter) operation. Grade #1 produces less heat per pound of fuel compared to grade #2 and may be specified for use in diesel engines involved in frequent changes in load and speed, such as those found in city buses and delivery trucks.

GRADE #2   This grade has a higher boiling range, cloud point, and pour point as compared with grade #1. It is usually specified where constant speed and high loads are encountered, such as in long-haul trucking and automotive diesel applications.

FIGURE 4–15 A hydrometer is used to measure the API specific gravity of diesel fuel. The unit of measure is usually the American Petroleum Institute (API) scale.

API Gravity Comparison Chart			
	Values for API Scale Oil		
API Gravity Scale	Specific Gravity S	Weight Density, lb/ft P	Pounds per Gallon
0			
2			
4			
6			
8			
10	1.0000	62.36	8.337
12	0.9861	61.50	8.221
14	0.9725	60.65	8.108
16	0.9593	59.83	7.998
18	0.9465	59.03	7.891
20	0.9340	58.25	7.787
22	0.9218	57.87	7.736
24	0.9100	56.75	7.587
26	0.8984	56.03	7.490
28	0.8871	55.32	7.396
30	0.8762	54.64	7.305
32	0.8654	53.97	7.215
34	0.8550	53.32	7.128
36	0.8448	52.69	7.043
38	0.8348	51.06	6.960
40	0.8251	51.46	6.879
42	0.8155	50.86	6.799
44	0.8030	50.28	6.722
46	0.7972	49.72	6.646
48	0.7883	49.16	6.572
50	0.7796	48.62	6.499
52	0.7711	48.09	6.429
54	0.7628	47.57	6.359
56	0.7547	47.07	6.292
58	0.7467	46.57	6.225
60	0.7389	46.08	6.160
62	0.7313	45.61	6.097
64	0.7238	45.14	6.034
66	0.7165	44.68	5.973
68	0.7093	44.23	5.913
70	0.7022	43.79	5.854
72	0.6953	43.36	5.797
74	0.6886	42.94	5.741
76	0.6819	42.53	5.685
78	0.6754	41.72	5.631
80	0.6690	41.32	5.577
82	0.6628	41.13	5.526
84	0.6566	40.95	5.474
86	0.6506	40.57	5.424
88	0.6446	40.20	5.374
90	0.6388	39.84	5.326
92	0.6331	39.48	5.278
94	0.6275	39.13	5.231
96	0.6220	38.79	5.186
98	0.6116	38.45	5.141
100	0.6112	38.12	5.096

DIESEL FUEL SPECIFIC GRAVITY TESTING

The density of diesel fuel should be tested whenever there is a driveability concern. The density or specific gravity of diesel fuel is measured in units of **API gravity**. API gravity is an arbitrary scale expressing the gravity or density of liquid petroleum products devised jointly by the American Petroleum Institute and the National Bureau of Standards. The measuring scale is calibrated in terms of degrees API. Oil with the least-specific gravity has the highest API gravity. The formula for determining API gravity is as follows:

Degrees API gravity = (141.5/specific gravity at 60°F) − 131.5

The normal API gravity for #1 diesel fuel is 39 to 44 (typically 40). The normal API gravity for #2 diesel fuel is 30 to 39 (typically 35). A hydrometer calibrated in API gravity units should be used to test diesel fuel. ● **SEE FIGURE 4–15**.

DIESEL FUEL HEATERS

Diesel fuel heaters help prevent power loss and stalling in cold weather. The heater is placed in the fuel line between the tank and the primary filter. Some coolant heaters are thermostatically controlled, which allows fuel to bypass the heater once it has reached operating temperature.

FIGURE 4–16 A wire wound electrical heater is used to warm the intake air on some diesel engines.

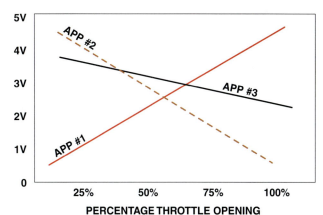

FIGURE 4–17 A typical accelerator pedal position (APP) sensor uses three different sensors in one package with each creating a different voltage as the accelerator is moved.

❓ FREQUENTLY ASKED QUESTION

How Can You Tell If Gasoline Has Been Added to the Diesel Fuel by Mistake?

If gasoline has been accidentally added to diesel fuel and is burned in a diesel engine, the result can be very damaging to the engine. The gasoline can ignite faster than diesel fuel, which would tend to increase the temperature of combustion. This high temperature can harm injectors and glow plugs, as well as pistons, head gaskets, and other major diesel engine components. If contaminated fuel is suspected, first smell the fuel at the filler neck. If the fuel smells like gasoline, then the tank should be drained and refilled with diesel fuel. If the smell test does not indicate a gasoline (or any rancid smell), then test a sample for proper API gravity.

NOTE: Diesel fuel designed for on-road use should be green in color. Red diesel fuel should only be found in off-road or farm equipment.

HEATED INTAKE AIR

Some diesels, such as the General Motors 6.6-liter Duramax V-8, use an electrical heater wire to warm the intake air to help in cold weather starting and running. ● **SEE FIGURE 4–16.**

ACCELERATOR PEDAL POSITION SENSOR

Some light truck diesel engines are equipped with an electronic throttle to control the amount of fuel injected into the engine. Because a diesel engine does not use a throttle in the air intake, the only way to control engine speed is by controlling the amount of fuel being injected into the cylinders. Instead of a mechanical link from the accelerator pedal to the diesel injection pump, a throttle-by-wire system uses an accelerator pedal position sensor. To ensure safety, it consists of three separate sensors that change in voltage as the accelerator pedal is depressed. ● **SEE FIGURE 4–17.**

The computer checks for errors by comparing the voltage output of each of the three sensors inside the APP and compares them to what they should be if there are no faults. If an error is detected, the engine and vehicle speed are often reduced.

SOOT OR PARTICULATE MATTER

Soot particles may come directly from the exhaust tailpipe or they can also form when emissions of nitrogen oxide and various sulfur oxides chemically react with other pollutants suspended in the atmosphere. Such reactions result in the formation of ground-level ozone, commonly known as smog. Smog is the most visible form of what is generally referred to as particulate matter. Particulate matter refers to tiny particles of solid or semisolid material suspended in the atmosphere. This includes particles between 0.1 micron and 50 microns in diameter. The heavier particles, larger than 50 microns, typically tend to settle out quickly due to gravity. Particulates are generally categorized as follows:

- **TSP, Total Suspended Particulate**—Refers to all particles between 0.1 and 50 microns. Up until 1987, the EPA standard for particulates was based on levels of TSP.

- **PM10**—Particulate matter of 10 microns or less (approximately 1/6 the diameter of a human hair). EPA has a standard for particles based on levels of PM10.

- **PM2.5**—Particulate matter of 2.5 microns or less (approximately 1/20 the diameter of a human hair), also called "fine" particles. In July 1997, the EPA approved a standard for PM2.5.

In general, soot particles produced by diesel combustion fall into the categories of fine, that is, less than 2.5 microns and ultrafine, less than 0.1 micron. Ultrafine particles make up about 80% to 95% of soot.

DIESEL OXIDATION CATALYST (DOC)

Diesel oxidation catalyst (DOC) consists of a flow-through honeycomb-style substrate structure that is washcoated with a layer of catalyst materials, similar to those used in a gasoline engine catalytic converter. These materials include the precious metals platinum and palladium, as well as other base metals catalysts. Catalysts chemically react with exhaust gas to convert harmful nitrogen oxide into nitrogen dioxide, and to oxidize absorbed hydrocarbons. The chemical reaction acts as a combustor for the unburned fuel that is characteristic of diesel compression ignition. The main function of the DOC is to start a regeneration event by converting the fuel-rich exhaust gases to heat.

The DOC also reduces carbon monoxide, hydrocarbons, plus odor-causing compounds such as aldehydes and sulfur, and the soluble organic fraction of particulate matter. During a regeneration event, the Catalyst System Efficiency test will run. The engine control module (ECM) monitors this efficiency of the DOC by determining if the exhaust gas temperature sensor (EGT Sensor 1) reaches a predetermined temperature during a regeneration event.

? **FREQUENTLY ASKED QUESTION**

What Is the Big Deal for the Need to Control Very Small Soot Particles?

For many years soot or particulate matter (PM) was thought to be less of a health concern than exhaust emissions from gasoline engines. It was felt that the soot could simply fall to the ground without causing any noticeable harm to people or the environment. However, it was discovered that the small soot particulates when breathed in are not expelled from the lungs like larger particles but instead get trapped in the deep areas of the lungs where they accumulate.

DIESEL EXHAUST PARTICULATE FILTER (DPF)

The heated exhaust gas from the DOC flows into the diesel particulate filter (DPF), which captures diesel exhaust gas particulates (soot) to prevent them from being released into the atmosphere. This is done by forcing the exhaust through a porous cell which has a silicon carbide substrate with honeycomb-cell-type channels that trap the soot. The channels are washcoated with catalyst materials similar to those in the DOC filter. The main difference between the DPF and a typical catalyst filter is that the entrance to every other cell channel in the DPF substrate is blocked at one end. So instead of flowing directly through the channels, the exhaust gas is forced through the porous walls of the blocked channels and exits through the adjacent open-ended channels. This type of filter is also referred to as a "wall-flow" filter.

Soot particulates in the gas remain trapped on the DPF channel walls where, over time, the trapped particulate matter will begin to clog the filter. The filter must therefore be purged periodically to remove accumulated soot particles. The process of purging soot from the DPF is described as **regeneration**. ● **SEE FIGURE 4–18**.

EXHAUST GAS TEMPERATURE SENSORS   There are two exhaust gas temperature sensors that function in much the same way as engine temperature sensors. EGT Sensor 1 is positioned between the DOC and the DPF where it can measure the temperature of the exhaust gas entering the DPF. EGT

FIGURE 4–18 A diesel exhaust particulate filter on a Cummins 6.7-liter diesel engine.

FIGURE 4–19 A differential pressure sensor showing the two hoses from the diesel exhaust particulate filter.

Sensor 2 measures the temperature of the exhaust gas stream immediately after it exits the DPF.

The engine control module (ECM) monitors the signals from the EGT sensors as part of its calibrations to control DPF regeneration. The ECM supplies biased 5 volts to the signal circuit and a ground on the low reference circuit to EGT Sensor 1. When the EGT Sensor 1 is cold, the sensor resistance is high. As the temperature increases, the sensor resistance decreases. With high sensor resistance, the ECM detects a high voltage on the signal circuit. With lower sensor resistance, the ECM detects a lower voltage on the signal circuit. Proper exhaust gas temperatures at the inlet of the DPF are crucial for proper operation and for starting the regeneration process. Too high a temperature at the DPF will cause the DPF substrate to melt or crack. Regeneration will be terminated at temperatures above 1470°F (800°C). With too low a temperature, self-regeneration will not fully complete the soot-burning process.

DPF DIFFERENTIAL PRESSURE SENSOR (DPS)
The DPF **differential pressure sensor (DPS)** has two pressure sample lines:

- One line is attached before the DPF, labeled P1
- The other is located after the DPF, labeled P2

The exact location of the DPS varies by vehicle model type (medium duty, pickup or van). By measuring P1 exhaust supply pressure from the DOC, and P2, post DPF pressure, the ECM can determine differential pressure, also referred to as "delta"

pressure, across the DPF. Data from the DPF differential pressure sensor is used by the ECM to calibrate for controlling DPF exhaust system operation. ● **SEE FIGURE 4–19.**

DIESEL PARTICULATE FILTER REGENERATION
Soot particulates in the gas remain trapped on the DPF channel walls where, over time, the buildup of trapped particulate matter will begin to clog the filter. The filter must therefore be purged periodically to remove accumulated soot particles. The process of purging soot from the DPF by incineration is described as regeneration. When the temperature of the exhaust gas is increased sufficiently, the heat incinerates the soot particles trapped in the

filter, leaving only residual ash from the engine's combustion of lubrication oil. The filter is effectively renewed.

The primary reason for soot removal is to prevent the buildup of exhaust back pressure. Excessive back pressure increases fuel consumption, reduces power output, and can potentially cause engine damage. There are a number of operational factors that can trigger the diesel engine control module to initiate a DPF regeneration sequence. The ECM monitors:

- Distance since last DPF regeneration
- Fuel used since last DPF regeneration
- Engine run time since last DPF regeneration
- Exhaust differential pressure across the DPF

DPF REGENERATION PROCESS
A number of engine components are required to function together for the regeneration process to be performed. ECM controls that impact DPF regeneration include late post-injections, engine speed, and adjusting fuel pressure. Adding late post-injection pulses provides the engine with additional fuel to be oxidized in the DOC which increases exhaust temperatures entering the DPF to about 900°F (500°C) and higher. The intake air valve acts as a restrictor that reduces air entry to the engine which increases engine operating temperature. The intake air heater may also be activated to warm intake air during regeneration.

The variable vane turbocharger also plays a role in achieving regeneration temperatures by reducing or increasing boost depending on engine load.

TYPES OF DPF REGENERATION
DPF regeneration can be initiated in a number of ways, depending on the vehicle application and operating circumstances. The two main regeneration types are:

- Passive
- Active

PASSIVE REGENERATION. During normal vehicle operation when driving conditions produce sufficient load and exhaust temperatures, passive DPF regeneration may occur. This passive regeneration occurs without input from the ECM or the driver. A passive regeneration may typically occur while the vehicle is being driven at highway speed or towing a trailer.

ACTIVE REGENERATION. Active regeneration is commanded by the ECM when it determines that the DPF requires it to remove excess soot buildup and conditions for filter regeneration have been met. Active regeneration is usually not noticeable to the

FREQUENTLY ASKED QUESTION

Will the Post-Injection Pulses Reduce Fuel Economy?

Maybe. Due to the added fuel injection pulses and late fuel injection timing, an increase in fuel consumption may be noticed on the Driver Information Center (DIC) during the regeneration time period. A drop in overall fuel economy should not be noticeable.

driver. The vehicle needs to be driven at speeds above 30 mph for approximately 20 to 30 minutes to complete a full regeneration. During regeneration, the exhaust gases reach temperatures above 1000°F (550°C). If a regeneration event is interrupted for any reason, it will continue where it left off (including the next drive cycle) when the conditions are met for regeneration. Active regeneration is for the most part transparent to the customer. There are times when regeneration is required, but the operating conditions do not meet the ECM's requirements, such as on a delivery vehicle that is driven on frequent short trips or subjected to extended idling conditions. In such cases, the ECM turns on a "regeneration required" indicator to notify the vehicle operator that the filter requires cleaning.

DPF SERVICE REGENERATION
Another active regeneration method, the "DPF Service Regeneration" is a useful tool for the dealership technician. The procedure would typically be used to clean the DPF when vehicle operating conditions did not allow the DPF to regenerate normally while the vehicle is driven. A service regeneration procedure can also be run in order to clean the DPF when there is an unknown amount of soot present. This might result from engine or engine control errors caused by a Charge Air Cooler leak or low compression. In these cases, a DTC P2463 would normally set, and the DPF would have 80 grams or less of accumulated soot. If over 100 grams of soot are present, P244B sets and a service light comes on to warn the driver.

CONDITIONS FOR RUNNING A DPF SERVICE REGENERATION
A service regeneration cannot be initiated if there are active diagnostic trouble codes (DTCs) present. Other conditions that the ECM checks are as follows:

- The battery voltage is greater than 10 volts.
- The engine speed is between 600 and 1250 RPM.

- The brake pedal is in the released position.

- The accelerator pedal is in the released position.

- The transmission must be in park or neutral.

- The engine coolant temperature (ECT) is between 158°F (70°C) and 239°F (115°C).

- The vehicle's fuel tank level must be between 15% and 85% capacity. For safety, refueling should never be performed during the regeneration process.

- The exhaust gas temperature (EGT Sensors 1 and 2) must be less than 752°F (400°C).

CAUTION: To avoid extremely elevated exhaust temperatures, inspect the exhaust cooler vent located at the tailpipe and remove any debris or mud that would impede its operation.

1. **DO NOT connect any shop exhaust removal hoses to the vehicle's tailpipe.**

2. **Park the vehicle outdoors and keep people, other vehicles, and combustible material a safe distance away from the vehicle during Service Regeneration.**

3. **Do not leave the vehicle unattended during Service Regeneration.**

☠ **WARNING**

Tailpipe outlet exhaust temperature will be greater than 572°F (300°C) during service regeneration. To help prevent personal injury or property damage from fire or burns, keep vehicle exhaust away from any object and people.

ASH LOADING

Regeneration will not burn off ash. Only the particulate matter (PM) is burned off during regeneration. Ash is a noncombustible by-product from normal oil consumption. Ash accumulation in the DPF will eventually cause a restriction in the particulate filter. To service an ash loaded DPF, the DPF will need to be removed from the vehicle and cleaned or replaced. Low ash content engine oil (API CJ-4) is required for vehicles with the DPF system. The CJ-4 rated oil is limited to 1% ash content.

DIESEL EXHAUST SMOKE DIAGNOSIS

While some exhaust smoke is considered normal operation for many diesel engines, especially older units, the cause of excessive exhaust smoke should be diagnosed and repaired.

BLACK SMOKE Black exhaust smoke is caused by incomplete combustion because of a lack of air or a fault in the injection system that could cause an excessive amount of fuel in the cylinders. Items that should be checked include the following:

- Check the fuel specific gravity (API gravity).

- Perform an injector balance test to locate faulty injectors using a scan tool.

- Check for proper operation of the engine coolant temperature (ECT) sensor.

- Check for proper operation of the fuel rail pressure (FRP) sensor.

- Check for restrictions in the intake or turbocharger.

- Check to see if the engine is using oil.

WHITE SMOKE White exhaust smoke occurs most often during cold engine starts because the smoke is usually condensed fuel droplets. White exhaust smoke is also an indication of cylinder misfire on a warm engine. The most common causes of white exhaust smoke include:

- Inoperative glow plugs

- Low engine compression

- Incorrect injector spray pattern

- A coolant leak into the combustion chamber

GRAY OR BLUE SMOKE Blue exhaust smoke is usually due to oil consumption caused by worn piston rings, scored cylinder walls, or defective valve stem seals. Gray or blue smoke can also be caused by a defective injector(s).

FIGURE 4–20 A scan tool is used to retrieve diagnostic trouble codes and to perform injector balance tests.

FIGURE 4–21 A compression gauge designed for the higher compression rate of a diesel engine should be used when checking the compression.

SCAN TOOL DIAGNOSIS

Diesel engines since the late 1980s have been computer controlled and are equipped with sensors and activators to control functions that were previously mechanically controlled. All light truck diesels since 1996 have also adhered to onboard diagnostic systems (second generation [OBD-II]). The use of a scan tool to check for diagnostic trouble codes (DTCs) and to monitor engine operation is one of the first diagnostic steps. ● SEE FIGURE 4–20.

COMPRESSION TESTING

A compression test is fundamental for determining the mechanical condition of a diesel engine. Worn piston rings can cause low power and excessive exhaust smoke. A diesel engine should produce at least 300 PSI (2,068 kPa) of compression pressure and all cylinders should be within 50 PSI (345 kPa) of each other. ● SEE FIGURE 4–21.

GLOW PLUG RESISTANCE BALANCE TEST

Glow plugs increase in resistance as their temperature increases. All glow plugs should have about the same resistance when checked with an ohmmeter. A similar test of the resistance of the glow plugs can be used to detect a weak cylinder. This test is particularly helpful on a diesel engine that is not computer controlled. To test for even cylinder balance using glow plug resistance, perform the following on a warm engine.

1. Unplug, measure, and record the resistance of all of the glow plugs.
2. With the wires still removed from the glow plugs, start the engine.
3. Allow the engine to run for several minutes to allow the combustion inside the cylinder to warm the glow plugs.
4. Measure the plugs and record the resistance of all of the glow plugs.
5. The resistance of all of the glow plugs should be higher than at the beginning of the test. A glow plug that is in a cylinder that is not firing correctly will not increase in resistance as much as the others.
6. Another test is to measure exhaust manifold temperature at each exhaust port. Misfiring cylinders will run cold. This can be done with a contact or noncontact thermometer.

FIGURE 4–22 A typical pop tester used to check the spray pattern of a diesel engine injector.

INJECTOR POP TESTING

A **pop tester** is a device used for checking a diesel injector nozzle for proper spray pattern. The handle is depressed and pop off pressure is displayed on the gauge. ● **SEE FIGURE 4–22**.

The spray pattern should be a hollow cone. This will vary depending on design. The nozzle should also be tested for leakage—dripping of the nozzle while under pressure. If the spray pattern is not correct, cleaning, repairing, or replacing of the injector nozzle may be necessary.

DIESEL EMISSION TESTING

The most commonly used diesel exhaust emission test used in state or local testing programs is called the **opacity** test. Opacity means the percentage of light that is blocked by the exhaust smoke.

- A 0% opacity means that the exhaust has no visible smoke and does not block light from a beam projected through the exhaust smoke.

- A 100% opacity means that the exhaust is so dark that it completely blocks light from a beam projected through the exhaust smoke.

- A 50% opacity means that the exhaust blocks half of the light from a beam projected through the exhaust smoke.

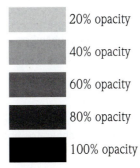

20% opacity

40% opacity

60% opacity

80% opacity

100% opacity

Do Not Switch Injectors

In the past, it was common practice to switch diesel fuel injectors from one cylinder to another when diagnosing a dead cylinder problem. However, most high-pressure common rail systems used in new diesels use precisely calibrated injectors that should not be mixed up during service. Each injector has its own calibration number. ● **SEE FIGURE 4–23.**

FIGURE 4–23 The letters on the side of this injector on a Cummins 6.7-liter diesel indicate the calibration number for the injector.

DIESEL EMISSION TESTING (CONTINUED)

SNAP ACCELERATION TEST In a snap acceleration test, the vehicle is held stationary with wheel chocks and brakes released as the engine is rapidly accelerated to high idle with the transmission in neutral while smoke emissions are measured. This test is conducted a minimum of six times and the three most consistent measurements are averaged together for a final score.

ROLLING ACCELERATION TEST Vehicles with a manual transmission are rapidly accelerated in low gear from an idle speed to a maximum governed RPM while the smoke emissions are measured.

STALL ACCELERATION TEST Vehicles with automatic transmissions are held in a stationary position with the parking brake and service brakes applied while the transmission is placed in "drive." The accelerator is depressed and held momentarily while smoke emissions are measured.

The standards for diesels vary according to the type of vehicle and other factors, but usually include a 40% opacity or less.

SUMMARY

1. A diesel engine uses heat of compression to ignite the diesel fuel when it is injected into the compressed air in the combustion chamber.

2. There are two basic designs of combustion chambers used in diesel engines. Indirect injection (IDI) uses a pre-combustion chamber whereas a direct injection (DI) occurs directly into the combustion chamber.

3. The three phases of diesel combustion include:
   a. Ignition delay
   b. Rapid combustion
   c. Controlled combustion

4. The typical diesel engine fuel system consists of the fuel tank, lift pump, water–fuel separator, and fuel filter.

5. The engine-driven injection pump supplies high-pressure diesel fuel to the injectors.

6. The two most common types of fuel injection used in automotive diesel engines are:
   a. Distributor-type injection pump
   b. Common rail design where all of the injectors are fed from the same fuel supply from a rail under high pressure

7. Injector nozzles are either opened by the high-pressure pulse from the distributor pump or electrically by the computer on a common rail design.

8. Glow plugs are used to help start a cold diesel engine and help prevent excessive white smoke during warm-up.

9. The higher the cetane rating of diesel fuel, the more easily the fuel is ignited.

10. Most automotive diesel engines are designed to operate on grade #2 diesel fuel in moderate weather conditions.

11. The API specific gravity of diesel fuel should be 30 to 39 with a typical reading of 35 for #2 diesel fuel.

12. Diesel engines can be tested using a scan tool, as well as measuring the glow plug resistance or compression reading to determine a weak or nonfunctioning cylinder.

REVIEW QUESTIONS

1. What is the difference between direct injection and indirect injection?

2. What are the three phases of diesel ignition?

3. What are the most commonly used types of automotive diesel injection systems?

4. Why are glow plugs kept working after the engine starts?

5. What is the advantage of using diesel fuel with a high cetane rating?

6. How is the specific gravity of diesel fuel tested?

CHAPTER QUIZ

1. How is diesel fuel ignited in a warm diesel engine?
   a. Glow plugs
   b. Heat of compression
   c. Spark plugs
   d. Distributorless ignition system

2. Which type of diesel injection produces less noise?
   a. Indirect injection (IDI)
   b. Common rail
   c. Direct injection
   d. Distributor injection

3. Which diesel injection system requires the use of a glow plug?
   a. Indirect injection (IDI)
   b. High-pressure common rail
   c. Direct injection
   d. Distributor injection

4. The three phases of diesel ignition include _____.
   a. Glow plug ignition, fast burn, slow burn
   b. Slow burn, fast burn, slow burn
   c. Ignition delay, rapid combustion, controlled combustion
   d. Glow plug ignition, ignition delay, controlled combustion

5. What fuel system component is used in a vehicle equipped with a diesel engine that is not usually used on the same vehicle when it is equipped with a gasoline engine?
   a. Fuel filter
   b. Fuel supply line
   c. Fuel return line
   d. Water–fuel separator

6. The diesel injection pump is usually driven by a _____.
   a. Gear off the camshaft
   b. Belt off the crankshaft
   c. Shaft drive off of the crankshaft
   d. Chain drive off of the camshaft

7. Which diesel system supplies high-pressure diesel fuel to all of the injectors all of the time?
   a. Distributor
   b. Inline
   c. High-pressure common rail
   d. Rotary

8. Glow plugs should have high resistance when _____ and lower resistance when _____.
   a. Cold/warm
   b. Warm/cold
   c. Wet/dry
   d. Dry/wet

9. Technician A says that glow plugs are used to help start a diesel engine and are shut off as soon as the engine starts. Technician B says that the glow plugs are turned off as soon as a flame is detected in the combustion chamber. Which technician is correct?
   a. Technician A only
   b. Technician B only
   c. Both Technicians A and B
   d. Neither Technician A nor B

10. What part should be removed to test cylinder compression on a diesel engine?
    a. An injector
    b. An intake valve rocker arm and stud
    c. An exhaust valve
    d. A glow plug

GASOLINE

DEFINITION **Gasoline** is a term used to describe a complex mixture of various hydrocarbons refined from crude petroleum oil for use as a fuel in engines. Gasoline and air burns in the cylinder of the engine and produces heat and pressure which is transferred to rotary motion inside the engine and eventually powers the drive wheels of a vehicle. When combustion occurs, carbon dioxide and water are produced if the process is perfect and all of the air and all of the fuel are consumed in the process.

CHEMICAL COMPOSITION Gasoline is a combination of hydrocarbon molecules that have between five and 12 carbon atoms. The names of these various hydrocarbons are based on the number of carbon atoms and include:

- **Methane**—one carbon atom
- **Ethane**—two carbon atoms
- **Propane**—three carbon atoms
- **Butane**—four carbon atoms
- **Pentane**—five carbon atoms
- **Hexane**—six carbon atoms
- **Heptane**—seven carbon atoms (Used to test octane rating—has an octane rating of zero)
- **Octane**—eight carbon atoms (A type of octane is used as a basis for antiknock rating)

REFINING

TYPES OF CRUDE OIL Refining is a complex combination of interdependent processing units that can separate crude oil into useful products such as gasoline and diesel fuel. As it comes out of the ground, **petroleum** (meaning "rock oil") crude can be as thin and light colored as apple cider or as thick and black as melted tar. A barrel of crude oil is 42 gallons, not 55 gallons as commonly used for industrial barrels. Typical terms used to describe the type of crude oil include:

- Thin crude oil has a high American Petroleum Institute (API) gravity, and therefore, is called *high-gravity* crude.
- Thick crude oil is called *low-gravity* crude. High-gravity-type crude contains more natural gasoline and its lower sulfur and nitrogen content makes it easier to refine.
- Low-sulfur crude oil is also known as "sweet" crude.
- High-sulfur crude oil is also known as "sour" crude.

DISTILLATION In the late 1800s, crude was separated into different products by boiling, in a process called **distillation**. Distillation works because crude oil is composed of hydrocarbons with a broad range of boiling points.

In a distillation column, the vapor of the lowest-boiling hydrocarbons, propane and butane, rises to the top. The straight-run gasoline (also called naphtha), kerosene, and diesel fuel cuts are drawn off at successively lower positions in the column.

CRACKING **Cracking** is the process where hydrocarbons with higher boiling points could be broken down (cracked) into lower-boiling hydrocarbons by treating them to very high temperatures. This process, called *thermal cracking*, was used to increase gasoline production starting in 1913.

Instead of high heat, today cracking is performed using a catalyst and is called **catalytic cracking**. A catalyst is a material that speeds up or otherwise facilitates a chemical reaction without undergoing a permanent chemical change itself. Catalytic cracking produces gasoline of higher quality than thermal cracking.

Hydrocracking is similar to catalytic cracking in that it uses a catalyst, but the catalyst is in a hydrogen atmosphere. Hydrocracking can break down hydrocarbons that are resistant to catalytic cracking alone, and it is used to produce diesel fuel rather than gasoline.

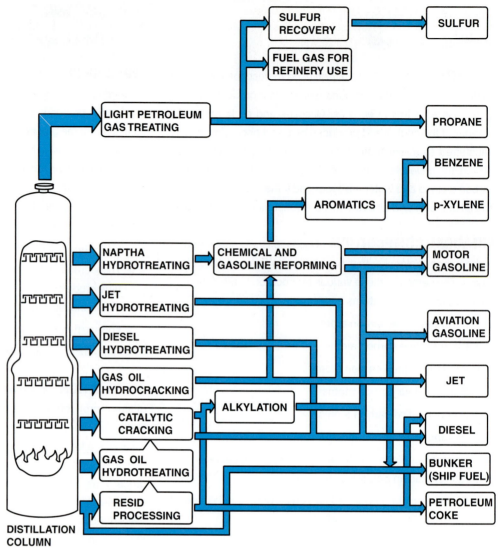

FIGURE 5–1 The crude oil refining process showing most of the major steps and processes.

REFINING (CONTINUED)

Other types of refining processes include:

- Reforming
- Alkylation
- Isomerization
- Hydrotreating
- Desulfurization

● **SEE FIGURE 5–1**.

SHIPPING The gasoline is transported to regional storage facilities by tank railway car or by pipeline. In the pipeline method, all gasoline from many refiners is often sent through the same pipeline and can become mixed. All gasoline is said to be **fungible**, meaning that it is capable of being interchanged because each grade is created to specification so there is no reason to keep the different gasoline brands separated except for grade. Regular grade, mid-grade, and premium grades are separated in the pipeline and the additives are added at the regional storage facilities and then shipped by truck to individual gas stations.

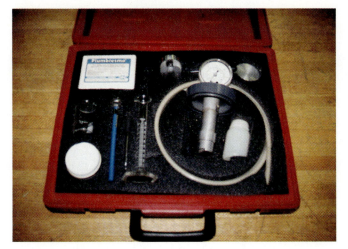

FIGURE 5–2 A gasoline testing kit, including an insulated container where water at 100°F is used to heat a container holding a small sample of gasoline. The reading on the pressure gauge is the Reid vapor pressure (RVP).

VOLATILITY

DEFINITION OF VOLATILITY Volatility describes how easily the gasoline evaporates (forms a vapor). The definition of volatility assumes that the vapors will remain in the fuel tank or fuel line and will cause a certain pressure based on the temperature of the fuel.

REID VAPOR PRESSURE (RVP) Reid vapor pressure **(RVP)** is the pressure of the vapor above the fuel when the fuel is at 100°F (38°C). Increased vapor pressure permits the engine to start in cold weather. Gasoline without air will not burn. Gasoline must be vaporized (mixed with air) to burn in an engine. ● **SEE FIGURE 5–2.**

SEASONAL BLENDING Cold temperatures reduce the normal vaporization of gasoline; therefore, winter-blended gasoline is specially formulated to vaporize at lower temperatures for proper starting and driveability at low ambient temperatures. The **American Society for Testing and Materials (ASTM)** standards for winter-blend gasoline allow volatility of up to 15 pounds per square inch (PSI) RVP.

At warm ambient temperatures, gasoline vaporizes easily. However, the fuel system (fuel pump, carburetor, fuel-injector nozzles, etc.) is designed to operate with liquid gasoline. The volatility of summer-grade gasoline should be about 7.0 PSI RVP. According to ASTM standards, the maximum RVP should be 10.5 PSI for summer-blend gasoline.

DISTILLATION CURVE Besides Reid vapor pressure, another method of classifying gasoline volatility is the **distillation curve**. A curve on a graph is created by plotting the temperature at which the various percentage of the fuel evaporates. A typical distillation curve is shown in ● **FIGURE 5–3.**

DRIVEABILITY INDEX A distillation curve shows how much of a gasoline evaporates at what temperature range. To predict cold-weather driveability, an index was created called the **driveability index**, also called the *distillation index*, and abbreviated **DI.**

The DI was developed using the temperature for the evaporated percentage of 10% (labeled T10), 50% (labeled T50), and 90% (labeled T90). The formula for DI is:

$$DI = 1.5 \times T10 + 3 \times T50 + T90$$

The total DI is a temperature and usually ranges from 1000°F to 1200°F. The lower values of DI generally result in good cold-start and warm-up performance. A high DI number is less volatile than a low DI number.

NOTE: Most premium-grade gasoline has a higher (worse) DI than regular-grade or midgrade gasoline, which could cause poor cold-weather driveability. Vehicles designed to operate on premium-grade gasoline are programmed to handle the higher DI, but engines designed to operate on regular-grade gasoline may not be able to provide acceptable cold-weather driveability.

VOLATILITY-RELATED PROBLEMS At higher temperatures, liquid gasoline can easily vaporize, which can cause **vapor lock**. Vapor lock is a *lean* condition caused by vaporized

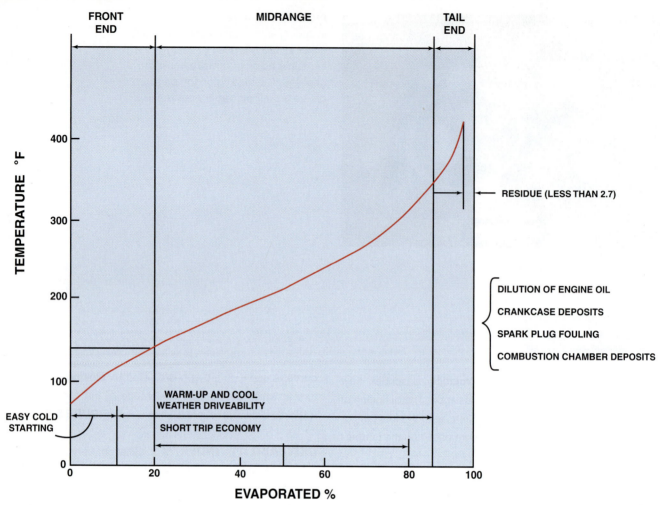

FIGURE 5–3 A typical distillation curve. Heavier molecules evaporate at higher temperatures and contain more heat energy for power, whereas the lighter molecules evaporate easier for starting.

VOLATILITY (CONTINUED)

fuel in the fuel system. This vaporized fuel takes up space normally occupied by liquid fuel. Bubbles that form in the fuel cause vapor lock, preventing proper operation of the fuel-injection system.

Heat causes some fuel to evaporate, thereby causing bubbles. Sharp bends cause the fuel to be restricted at the bend. When the fuel flows past the bend, the fuel can expand to fill the space after the bend. This expansion drops the pressure, and bubbles form in the fuel lines. When the fuel is full of bubbles, the engine is not being supplied with enough fuel and the engine runs lean. A lean engine will stumble during acceleration, will run rough, and may stall. Warm weather and alcohol-blended fuels both tend to increase vapor lock and engine performance problems.

If winter-blend gasoline (or high-RVP fuel) is used in an engine during warm weather, the following problems may occur:

1. Rough idle
2. Stalling
3. Hesitation on acceleration
4. Surging

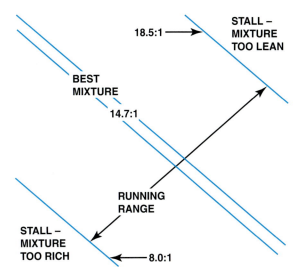

FREQUENTLY ASKED QUESTION

Why Do I Get Lower Gas Mileage in the Winter?

Several factors cause the engine to use more fuel in the winter than in the summer, including:

- Gasoline that is blended for use in cold climates is designed for ease of starting and contains fewer heavy molecules, which contribute to fuel economy. The heat content of winter gasoline is lower than summer-blended gasoline.

- In cold temperatures, all lubricants are stiff, causing more resistance. These lubricants include the engine oil, as well as the transmission and differential gear lubricants.

- Heat from the engine is radiated into the outside air more rapidly when the temperature is cold, resulting in longer run time until the engine has reached normal operating temperature.

- Road conditions, such as ice and snow, can cause tire slippage or additional drag on the vehicle.

FIGURE 5–4 An engine will not run if the air–fuel mixture is either too rich or too lean.

GASOLINE COMBUSTION PROCESS

CHEMICAL REACTIONS The combustion process involves the chemical combination of oxygen (O_2) from the air (about 21% of the atmosphere) with the hydrogen and carbon from the fuel. In a gasoline engine, a spark starts the combustion process, which takes about 3 ms (0.003 sec) to be completed inside the cylinder of an engine. The chemical reaction that takes place can be summarized as follows: hydrogen (H) plus carbon (C) plus oxygen (O_2) plus nitrogen (N) plus spark equals heat plus water (H_2O) plus carbon monoxide (CO) (if incomplete combustion) plus carbon dioxide (CO_2) plus hydrocarbons (HC) plus oxides of nitrogen (NO_X) plus many other chemicals. In an equation format it looks like this:

$$H + C + O_2 + N + Spark = Heat + CO_2 + HC + NO_x$$

HEAT ENERGY The heat produced by the combustion process is measured in **British thermal units (BTUs)**. One BTU is the amount of heat required to raise one pound of water one Fahrenheit degree. The metric unit of heat is the *calorie* (cal). One calorie is the amount of heat required to raise the temperature of one gram (g) of water one Celsius degree.

Gasoline—About 130,000 BTUs per gallon

AIR–FUEL RATIOS Fuel burns best when the intake system turns it into a fine spray and mixes it with air before sending it into the cylinders. In fuel-injected engines, the fuel becomes a spray and mixes with the air in the intake manifold. There is a direct relationship between engine airflow and fuel requirements; this is called the **air–fuel ratio**.

The air–fuel ratio is the proportion by weight of air and gasoline that the injection system mixes as needed for engine combustion. The mixtures, with which an engine can operate without stalling, range from 8 to 1 to 18.5 to 1. ● **SEE FIGURE 5–4**.

These ratios are usually stated by weight, such as:

- 8 parts of air by weight combined with 1 part of gasoline by weight (8:1), which is the richest mixture that an engine can tolerate and still fire reliably.

- 18.5 parts of air mixed with 1 part of gasoline (18.5:1), which is the leanest practical ratio. Richer or leaner air–fuel ratios cause the engine to misfire badly or not run at all.

STOICHIOMETRIC AIR–FUEL RATIO The ideal mixture or ratio at which all of the fuel combines with all of the oxygen in the air and burns completely is called the **stoichiometric** ratio, a chemically perfect combination. In theory, this ratio for gasoline is an air–fuel mixture of 14.7 to 1. ● **SEE FIGURE 5–5**.

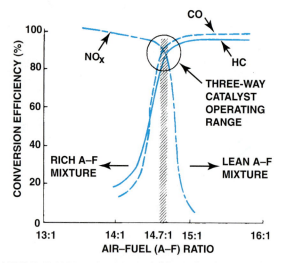

FIGURE 5–5 With a three-way catalytic converter, emission control is most efficient with an air–fuel ratio between 4.65 to 1 and 14.75 to 1.

GASOLINE COMBUSTION PROCESS (CONTINUED)

In reality, the exact ratio at which perfect mixture and combustion occurs depends on the molecular structure of gasoline, which can vary. The stoichiometric ratio is a compromise between maximum power and maximum economy.

NORMAL AND ABNORMAL COMBUSTION

The **octane rating** of gasoline is the measure of its antiknock properties. *Engine knock* (also called **detonation**, **spark knock**, or **ping**) is a metallic noise an engine makes, usually during acceleration, resulting from abnormal or uncontrolled combustion inside the cylinder.

Normal combustion occurs smoothly and progresses across the combustion chamber from the point of ignition. ● SEE FIGURE 5–6.

Normal flame-front combustion travels between 45 and 90 mph (72 and 145 km/h). The speed of the flame front depends on air–fuel ratio, combustion chamber design (determining amount of turbulence), and temperature.

During periods of spark knock (detonation), the combustion speed increases by up to 10 times to near the speed of sound. The increased combustion speed also causes increased temperatures and pressures, which can damage pistons, gaskets, and cylinder heads. ● SEE FIGURE 5–7.

One of the first additives used in gasoline was **tetraethyl lead (TEL)**. TEL was added to gasoline in the early 1920s to reduce the tendency to knock. It was often called ethyl or high-test gasoline.

OCTANE RATING

The antiknock standard or basis of comparison was the knock-resistant hydrocarbon isooctane, chemically called trimethylpentane (C_8H_{18}), also known as 2-2-4 trimethylpentane. If a gasoline tested had the exact same antiknock characteristics as isooctane, it was rated as 100-octane gasoline. If the gasoline tested had only 85% of the antiknock properties of isooctane, it was rated as 85 octane. Remember, octane rating is only a comparison test.

The two basic methods used to rate gasoline for antiknock properties (octane rating) are the *research method* and the *motor method*. Each uses a model of the special cooperative fuel research (CFR) single-cylinder engine. The research method and the motor method vary as to temperature of air, spark advance, and other parameters. The research method typically results in readings that are 6 to 10 points higher than those of the motor method. For example, a fuel with a research octane number (RON) of 93 might have a motor octane number (MON) of 85.

The octane rating posted on pumps in the United States is the average of the two methods and is referred to as (R + M) ÷ 2, meaning that, for the fuel used in the previous example, the rating posted on the pumps would be

$$\frac{RON + MON}{2} = \frac{93 + 85}{2} = 89$$

The pump octane is called the **antiknock index (AKI)**.

GASOLINE GRADES AND OCTANE NUMBER
The posted octane rating on gasoline pumps is the rating achieved by the average of the research and the motor methods. ● SEE FIGURE 5–8.

Except in high-altitude areas, the grades and octane ratings are as follows:

Grades	Octane rating
Regular	87
Midgrade (also called Plus)	89
Premium	91 or higher

? **FREQUENTLY ASKED QUESTION**

What Grade of Gasoline Does the EPA Use When Testing Engines?

Due to the various grades and additives used in commercial fuel, the government (EPA) uses a liquid called indolene. Indolene has a research octane number of 96.5 and a motor method octane rating of 88, which results in an R + M ÷ 2 rating of 92.25.

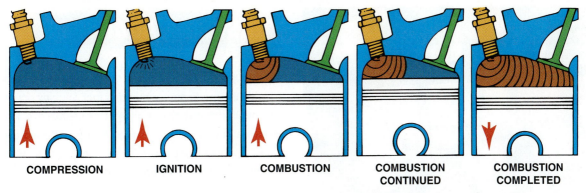

| COMPRESSION | IGNITION | COMBUSTION | COMBUSTION CONTINUED | COMBUSTION COMPLETED |

FIGURE 5–6 Normal combustion is a smooth, controlled burning of the air–fuel mixture.

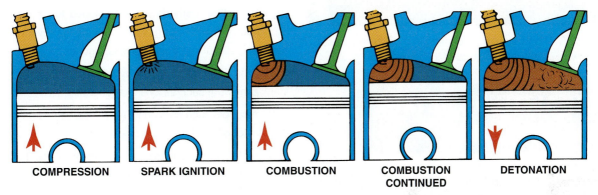

| COMPRESSION | SPARK IGNITION | COMBUSTION | COMBUSTION CONTINUED | DETONATION |

FIGURE 5–7 Detonation is a secondary ignition of the air–fuel mixture. It is also called spark knock or pinging.

TECH TIP

Horsepower and Fuel Flow

To produce 1 hp, the engine must be supplied with 0.50 lb of fuel per hour (lb/hr). Fuel injectors are rated in pounds per hour. For example, a V-8 engine equipped with 25 lb/hr fuel injectors could produce 50 hp per cylinder (per injector) or 400 hp. Even if the cylinder head or block is modified to produce more horsepower, the limiting factor may be the injector flow rate.

The following are flow rates and resulting horsepower for a V-8 engine:

30 lb/hr: 60 hp per cylinder or 480 hp
35 lb/hr: 70 hp per cylinder or 560 hp
40 lb/hr: 80 hp per cylinder or 640 hp

Of course, injector flow rate is only one of many variables that affect power output. Installing larger injectors without other major engine modification could decrease engine output and drastically increase exhaust emissions.

FIGURE 5–8 A pump showing regular with a pump octane of 87, plus rated at 89, and premium rated at 93. These ratings can vary with brand as well as in different parts of the country.

FIGURE 5–9 The posted octane rating in most high-altitude areas shows regular at 85 instead of the usual 87.

HIGH-ALTITUDE OCTANE REQUIREMENTS

As the altitude increases, atmospheric pressure drops. The air is less dense because a pound of air takes more volume. The octane rating of fuel does not need to be as high because the engine cannot take in as much air. This process will reduce the combustion (compression) pressures inside the engine. In mountainous areas, gasoline (R + M) ÷ 2 octane ratings are two or more numbers lower than normal (according to the SAE, about one octane number lower per 1,000 ft or 300 m in altitude). ● SEE FIGURE 5–9.

A secondary reason for the lowered octane requirement of engines running at higher altitudes is the normal enrichment of the air–fuel ratio and lower engine vacuum with the decreased air density. Some problems, therefore, may occur when driving out of high-altitude areas into lower-altitude areas where the octane rating must be higher. Most computerized engine control systems can compensate for changes in altitude and modify air–fuel ratio and ignition timing for best operation.

Because the combustion burn rate slows at high altitude, the ignition (spark) timing can be advanced to improve power. The amount of timing advance can be about 1 degree per 1,000 ft over 5,000 ft. Therefore, if driving at 8,000 ft of altitude, the ignition timing can be advanced 3 degrees.

High altitude also allows fuel to evaporate more easily. The volatility of fuel should be reduced at higher altitudes to prevent vapor from forming in sections of the fuel system, which can cause driveability and stalling problems. The extra heat generated in climbing to higher altitudes plus the lower atmospheric pressure at higher altitudes combine to cause vapor lock problems as the vehicle goes to higher altitudes.

GASOLINE ADDITIVES

DYE Dye is usually added to gasoline at the distributor to help identify the grade and/or brand of fuel. In many countries, fuels are required to be colored using a fuel-soluble dye. In the United States and Canada, diesel fuel used for off-road use and not taxed is required to be dyed red for identification. Gasoline sold for off-road use in Canada is dyed purple.

OCTANE IMPROVER ADDITIVES When gasoline companies, under federal EPA regulations, removed tetraethyl lead from gasoline, other methods were developed to help maintain the antiknock properties of gasoline. Octane improvers (enhancers) can be grouped into three broad categories:

1. Aromatic hydrocarbons (hydrocarbons containing the benzene ring) such as xylene and toluene

2. Alcohols such as ethanol (ethyl alcohol), methanol (methyl alcohol), and tertiary butyl alcohol (TBA)

3. Metallic compounds such as methylcyclopentadienyl manganese tricarbonyl (MMT)

NOTE: MMT has been proven to be harmful to catalytic converters and can cause spark plug fouling. However, MMT is currently one of the active ingredients commonly found in octane improvers available to the public and in some gasoline sold in Canada. If an octane boost additive has been used that contains MMT, the spark plug porcelain will be rust colored around the tip.

Propane and butane, which are volatile by-products of the refinery process, are also often added to gasoline as octane improvers. The increase in volatility caused by the added propane and butane often leads to hot-weather driveability problems.

OXYGENATED FUEL ADDITIVES Oxygenated fuels contain oxygen in the molecule of the fuel itself. Examples of oxygenated fuels include methanol, ethanol, methyl tertiary butyl ether (MTBE), tertiary-amyl methyl ether (TAME), and ethyl tertiary butyl ether (ETBE).

Oxygenated fuels are commonly used in high-altitude areas to reduce carbon monoxide (CO) emissions. The extra oxygen in the fuel itself is used to convert harmful CO into carbon dioxide (CO_2). The extra oxygen in the fuel helps ensure that there is enough oxygen to convert all CO into CO_2 during the combustion process in the engine or catalytic converter.

FIGURE 5–10 This fuel tank indicates that the gasoline is blended with 10% ethanol (ethyl alcohol) and can be used in any gasoline vehicle. E85 contains 85% ethanol and can only be used in vehicles specifically designed to use it.

FIGURE 5–11 A container with gasoline containing alcohol. Notice the separation line where the alcohol–water mixture separated from the gasoline and sank to the bottom.

? **FREQUENTLY ASKED QUESTION**

Can Regular-Grade Gasoline Be Used If Premium Is the Recommended Grade?

Maybe. It is usually possible to use regular-grade or midgrade (plus) gasoline in most newer vehicles without danger of damage to the engine. Most vehicles built since the 1990s are equipped with at least one knock sensor. If a lower octane gasoline than specified is used, the engine ignition timing setting will usually cause the engine to spark knock, also called detonation or ping. This spark knock is detected by the knock sensor(s), which sends a signal to the computer. The computer then retards the ignition timing until the spark knock stops.

NOTE: Some scan tools will show the "estimated octane rating" of the fuel being used, which is based on knock sensor activity.

As a result of this spark timing retardation, the engine torque is reduced. While this reduction in power is seldom noticed, it will reduce fuel economy, often by 4 to 5 miles per gallon. If premium gasoline is then used, the PCM will gradually permit the engine to operate at the more advanced ignition timing setting. Therefore, it may take several tanks of premium gasoline to restore normal fuel economy. For best overall performance, use the grade of gasoline recommended by the vehicle manufacturer.

METHYL TERTIARY BUTYL ETHER (MTBE). MTBE is manufactured by means of the chemical reaction of methanol and isobutylene. Unlike methanol, MTBE does not increase the volatility of the fuel, and is not as sensitive to water as are other alcohols. The maximum allowable volume level, according to the EPA, is 15% but is currently being phased out due to health concerns, as well as MTBE contamination of drinking water if spilled from storage tanks.

TERTIARY-AMYL METHYL ETHER. Tertiary-amyl methyl ether (TAME) contains an oxygen atom bonded to two carbon atoms and is added to gasoline to provide oxygen to the fuel. It is slightly soluble in water, very soluble in ethers and alcohol, and soluble in most organic solvents including hydrocarbons.

ETHYL TERTIARY BUTYL ETHER. ETBE is derived from ethanol. The maximum allowable volume level is 17.2%. The use of ETBE is the cause of much of the odor from the exhaust of vehicles using reformulated gasoline.

ETHANOL. Ethanol, also called *ethyl alcohol* is drinkable alcohol and is usually made from grain. Adding 10% ethanol (ethyl alcohol or grain alcohol) increases the (R + M) ÷ 2 octane rating by three points. The alcohol added to the base gasoline, however, also raises the volatility of the fuel about 0.5 PSI. Most automobile manufacturers permit up to 10% ethanol if driveability problems are not experienced.

The oxygen content of a 10% blend of ethanol in gasoline, called E10, is 3.5% oxygen by weight. ● **SEE FIGURE 5–10.**

Keeping the fuel tank full reduces the amount of air and moisture in the tank. ● **SEE FIGURE 5–11.**

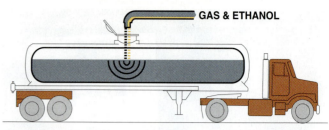
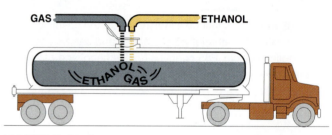

FIGURE 5–13 Sequential blending uses a computer to calculate the correct ratio as well as the prescribed order in which the products are loaded.

GASOLINE BLENDING

Gasoline additives, such as ethanol and dyes, are usually added to the fuel at the distributor. Adding ethanol to gasoline is a way to add oxygen to the fuel itself. Gasoline containing an addition that has oxygen is called *oxygenated fuel*. There are three basic methods used to blend ethanol with gasoline to create E10 (10% ethanol, 90% gasoline).

1. **In-line blending**—Gasoline and ethanol are mixed in a storage tank or in the tank of a transport truck while it is being filled. Because the quantities of each can be accurately measured, this method is most likely to produce a well-mixed blend of ethanol and gasoline. ● SEE FIGURE 5–12.

2. **Sequential blending**—This method is usually performed at the wholesale terminal and involves adding a measured amount of ethanol to a tank truck followed by a measured amount of gasoline. ● SEE FIGURE 5–13.

3. **Splash blending**—Splash blending can be done at the retail outlet or distributor and involves separate purchases of ethanol and gasoline. In a typical case, a distributor can purchase gasoline, and then drive to another supplier and purchase ethanol. The ethanol is then added (splashed) into the tank of gasoline. This method is the least-accurate method of blending and can result in ethanol concentration for E10 that should be 10% to range from 5% to over 20% in some cases. ● SEE FIGURE 5–14.

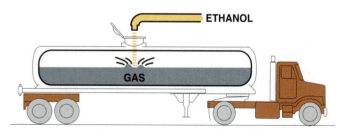

FIGURE 5–14 Splash blending occurs when the ethanol is added to a tanker with gasoline and is mixed as the truck travels to the retail outlet.

REFORMULATED GASOLINE

Reformulated gasoline (RFG) is manufactured to help reduce emissions. The gasoline refiners reformulate gasoline by using additives that contain at least 2% oxygen by weight and reducing the additive benzene to a maximum of 1% by volume. Two other major changes done at the refineries are as follows:

1. **Reduce light compounds.** Refineries eliminate butane, pentane, and propane, which have a low boiling point and evaporate easily. These unburned hydrocarbons are released into the atmosphere during refueling and through the fuel tank vent system, contributing to smog formation. Therefore, reducing the light compounds from gasoline helps reduce evaporative emissions.

2. **Reduce heavy compounds.** Refineries eliminate heavy compounds with high boiling points such as aromatics and olefins. The purpose of this reduction is to reduce the amount of unburned hydrocarbons that enter the catalytic converter, which makes the converter more efficient, thereby reducing emissions.

Because many of the heavy compounds are eliminated, a drop in fuel economy of about 1 mpg has been reported in areas where reformulated gasoline is being used. Formaldehyde is formed when RFG is burned, and the vehicle exhaust has a unique smell when reformulated gasoline is used.

 FREQUENTLY ASKED QUESTION

Is Water Heavier Than Gasoline?

Yes. Water weighs about 7 pounds per gallon whereas gasoline weighs about 6 pounds per gallon. The density as measured by specific gravity includes:

Water = 1.000 (the baseline for specific gravity)

Gasoline = 0.730 to 0.760

This means that any water that gets into the fuel tank will sink to the bottom.

TESTING GASOLINE FOR ALCOHOL CONTENT

Take the following steps when testing gasoline for alcohol content.

 WARNING

Do not smoke or run the test around sources of ignition!

1. Pour suspect gasoline into a graduated cylinder.
2. Carefully fill the graduated cylinder to the 90-mL mark.
3. Add 10 mL of water to the graduated cylinder by counting the number of drops from an eyedropper.
4. Put the stopper in the cylinder and shake vigorously for 1 minute. Relieve built-up pressure by occasionally removing the stopper. Alcohol dissolves in water and will drop to the bottom of the cylinder.
5. Place the cylinder on a flat surface and let it stand for 2 minutes.
6. Take a reading near the bottom of the cylinder at the boundary between the two liquids.
7. For percent of alcohol in gasoline, subtract 10 from the reading and multiply by 10.

For example,

The reading is 20 mL: 20 − 10 = 10% alcohol

If the increase in volume is 0.2% or less, it may be assumed that the test gasoline contains no alcohol. ● **SEE FIGURE 5–15**. Alcohol content can also be checked using an electronic tester. See the step-by-step sequence at the end of the chapter.

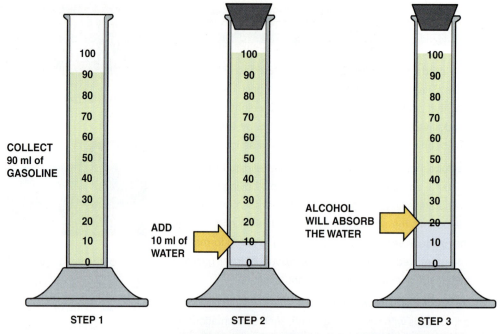

FIGURE 5–15 Checking gasoline for alcohol involves using a graduated cylinder and adding water to check if the alcohol absorbs the water.

COLLECT 90 ml of GASOLINE

STEP 1

ADD 10 ml of WATER

STEP 2

ALCOHOL WILL ABSORB THE WATER

STEP 3

FIGURE 5–16 The gas cap on a Ford vehicle notes that BP fuel is recommended.

 FREQUENTLY ASKED QUESTION

How Does Alcohol Content in the Gasoline Affect Engine Operation?

In most cases, the use of gasoline containing 10% or less of ethanol (ethyl alcohol) has little or no effect on engine operation. However, because the addition of 10% ethanol raises the volatility of the fuel slightly, occasional rough idle or stalling may be noticed, especially during warm weather. The rough idle and stalling may also be noticeable after the engine is started, driven, then stopped for a short time. Engine heat can vaporize the alcohol-enhanced fuel causing bubbles to form in the fuel system. These bubbles in the fuel prevent the proper operation of the fuel injection system and result in a hesitation during acceleration, rough idle, or in severe cases repeated stalling until all the bubbles have been forced through the fuel system, replaced by cooler fuel from the fuel tank.

 FREQUENTLY ASKED QUESTION

What Is "Top-Tier" Gasoline?

Top-tier gasoline is gasoline that has specific standards for quality, including enough detergent to keep all intake valves clean. Four automobile manufacturers, including BMW, General Motors, Honda, and Toyota, developed the standards. Top-tier gasoline exceeds the quality standards developed by the **World Wide Fuel Charter (WWFC)** that was established in 2002 by vehicle and engine manufacturers. The gasoline companies that agreed to make fuel that matches or exceeds the standards as a top-tier fuel include ChevronTexaco and ConocoPhillips. Ford has specified that BP fuel, sold in many parts of the country, is the recommended fuel to use in Ford vehicles. ● **SEE FIGURE 5–16.**

GENERAL GASOLINE RECOMMENDATIONS

The fuel used by an engine is a major expense in the operation cost of the vehicle. The proper operation of the engine depends on clean fuel of the proper octane rating and vapor pressure for the atmospheric conditions.

To help ensure proper engine operation and keep fuel costs to a minimum, follow these guidelines:

1. Purchase fuel from a busy station to help ensure that it is fresh and less likely to be contaminated with water or moisture.

2. Keep the fuel tank above one-quarter full, especially during seasons in which the temperature rises and falls by more than 20°F between daytime highs and nighttime lows. This helps to reduce condensed moisture in the fuel tank and could prevent gas line freeze-up in cold weather.

   NOTE: Gas line freeze-up occurs when the water in the gasoline freezes and forms an ice blockage in the fuel line.

3. Do not purchase fuel with a higher octane rating than is necessary. Try using premium high-octane fuel to check for operating differences. Most newer engines are equipped with a detonation (knock) sensor that signals the vehicle computer to retard the ignition timing when spark knock occurs. Therefore, an operating difference may not be noticeable to the driver when using a low-octane fuel, except for a decrease in power and fuel economy. In other words, the engine with a knock sensor will tend to operate knock free on regular fuel, even if premium, higher-octane fuel is specified. Using premium fuel may result in more power and greater fuel economy. The increase in fuel economy, however, would have to be substantial to justify the increased cost of high-octane premium fuel. Some drivers find a good compromise by using midgrade (plus) fuel to benefit from the engine power and fuel economy gains without the cost of using premium fuel all the time.

4. Avoid using gasoline with alcohol in warm weather, even though many alcohol blends do not affect engine driveability. If warm-engine stumble, stalling, or rough idle occurs, change brands of gasoline.

5. Do not purchase fuel from a retail outlet when a tanker truck is filling the underground tanks. During the refilling procedure, dirt, rust, and water may be stirred up in the

FIGURE 5–17 Many gasoline service stations have signs posted warning customers to place plastic fuel containers on the ground while filling. If placed in a trunk or pickup truck bed equipped with a plastic liner, static electricity could build up during fueling and discharge from the container to the metal nozzle, creating a spark and possible explosion. Some service stations have warning signs not to use cell phones while fueling to help avoid the possibility of an accidental spark creating a fire hazard.

underground tanks. This undesirable material may be pumped into your vehicle's fuel tank.

6. Do not overfill the gas tank. After the nozzle clicks off, add just enough fuel to round up to the next dime. Adding additional gasoline will cause the excess to be drawn into the charcoal canister. This can lead to engine flooding and excessive exhaust emissions.

7. Be careful when filling gasoline containers. Always fill a gas can on the ground to help prevent the possibility of static electricity buildup during the refueling process. ● SEE FIGURE 5–17.

TECH TIP

The Sniff Test

Problems can occur with stale gasoline from which the lighter parts of the gasoline have evaporated. Stale gasoline usually results in a no-start situation. If stale gasoline is suspected, sniff it. If it smells rancid, replace it with fresh gasoline.

NOTE: If storing a vehicle, boat, or lawnmower over the winter, put some gasoline stabilizer into the gasoline to reduce the evaporation and separation that can occur during storage. Gasoline stabilizer is frequently available at lawnmower repair shops or marinas.

FREQUENTLY ASKED QUESTION

Why Should I Keep the Fuel Gauge Above One-Quarter Tank?

The fuel pickup inside the fuel tank can help keep water from being drawn into the fuel system unless water is all that is left at the bottom of the tank. Over time, moisture in the air inside the fuel tank can condense, causing liquid water to drop to the bottom of the fuel tank (water is heavier than gasoline—about 8 lb per gallon for water and about 6 lb per gallon for gasoline). If alcohol-blended gasoline is used, the alcohol can absorb the water and the alcohol–water combination can be burned inside the engine. However, when water combines with alcohol, a separation layer occurs between the gasoline at the top of the tank and the alcohol–water combination at the bottom. When the fuel level is low, the fuel pump will draw from this concentrated level of alcohol and water. Because alcohol and water do not burn as well as pure gasoline, severe driveability problems can occur such as stalling, rough idle, hard starting, and missing.

TECH TIP

Do Not Overfill the Fuel Tank

Gasoline fuel tanks have an expansion volume area at the top. The volume of this expansion area is equal to 10% to 15% of the volume of the tank. This area is normally not filled with gasoline, but rather is designed to provide a place for the gasoline to expand into, if the vehicle is parked in the hot sun and the gasoline expands. This prevents raw gasoline from escaping from the fuel system. A small restriction is usually present to control the amount of air and vapors that can escape the tank and flow to the charcoal canister.

This volume area could be filled with gasoline if the fuel is slowly pumped into the tank. Since it can hold an extra 10% (2 gallons in a 20-gallon tank), some people deliberately try to fill the tank completely. When this expansion volume is filled, liquid fuel (rather than vapors) can be drawn into the charcoal canister. When the purge valve opens, liquid fuel can be drawn into the engine, causing an excessively rich air–fuel mixture. Not only can this liquid fuel harm vapor recovery parts, but overfilling the gas tank could also cause the vehicle to fail an exhaust emission test, particularly during an enhanced test when the tank could be purged while on the rollers.

1 A fuel composition tester (SPX Kent-Moore J-44175) is the recommended tool, by General Motors, to use to test the alcohol content of gasoline.

2 This battery-powered tester uses light-emitting diodes (LEDs), meter lead terminals, and two small openings for the fuel sample.

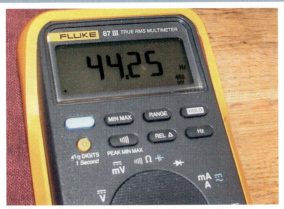

3 The first step is to verify the proper operation of the tester by measuring the air frequency by selecting AC hertz on the meter. The air frequency should be between 35 Hz and 48 Hz.

4 After verifying that the tester is capable of correctly reading the air frequency, gasoline is poured into the testing cell of the tool.

5 Record the AC frequency as shown on the meter and subtract 50 from the reading. (e.g., 60.50 − 50.00 = 10.5). This number (10.5) is the percentage of alcohol in the gasoline sample.

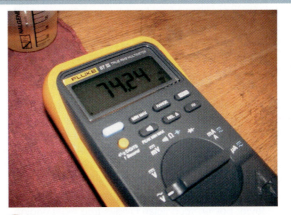

6 Adding additional amounts of ethyl alcohol (ethanol) increases the frequency reading.

SUMMARY

1. Gasoline is a complex blend of hydrocarbons. Gasoline is blended for seasonal usage to achieve the correct volatility for easy starting and maximum fuel economy under all driving conditions.

2. Winter-blend fuel used in a vehicle during warm weather can cause a rough idle and stalling because of its higher Reid vapor pressure (RVP).

3. Abnormal combustion (also called detonation or spark knock) increases both the temperature and the pressure inside the combustion chamber.

4. Most regular-grade gasoline today, using the (R + M) ÷ 2 rating method, is 87 octane; midgrade (plus) is 89; and premium grade is 91 or higher.

5. Oxygenated fuels contain oxygen to lower CO exhaust emissions.

6. Gasoline should always be purchased from a busy station, and the tank should not be overfilled.

REVIEW QUESTIONS

1. What is the difference between summer-blend and winter-blend gasoline?

2. What is Reid vapor pressure?

3. What is vapor lock?

4. What does the (R + M) ÷ 2 gasoline pump octane rating indicate?

5. What are the octane improvers that may be used during the refining process?

6. What is stoichiometric?

CHAPTER QUIZ

1. Winter-blend gasoline _____.
   a. Vaporizes more easily than summer-blend gasoline
   b. Has a higher RVP
   c. Can cause engine driveability problems if used during warm weather
   d. All of the above

2. Vapor lock can occur _____.
   a. As a result of excessive heat near fuel lines
   b. If a fuel line is restricted
   c. During both a and b
   d. During neither a nor b

3. Technician A says that spark knock, ping, and detonation are different names for abnormal combustion. Technician B says that any abnormal combustion raises the temperature and pressure inside the combustion chamber and can cause severe engine damage. Which technician is correct?
   a. Technician A only
   b. Technician B only
   c. Both Technicians A and B
   d. Neither Technician A nor B

4. Technician A says that the research octane number is higher than the motor octane number. Technician B says that the octane rating posted on fuel pumps is an average of the two ratings. Which technician is correct?
   a. Technician A only
   b. Technician B only
   c. Both Technicians A and B
   d. Neither Technician A nor B

5. Technician A says that in going to high altitudes, engines produce lower power. Technician B says that most engine control systems can compensate the air–fuel mixture for changes in altitude. Which technician is correct?
   a. Technician A only
   b. Technician B only
   c. Both Technicians A and B
   d. Neither Technician A nor B

6. Which method of blending ethanol with gasoline is the most accurate?
   a. In-line
   b. Sequential
   c. Splash
   d. All of the above are equally accurate methods

7. What can be used to measure the alcohol content in gasoline?
   a. graduated cylinder
   b. electronic tester
   c. scan tool
   d. either a or b

8. To avoid problems with the variation of gasoline, all government testing uses _____ as a fuel during testing procedures.
   a. MTBE (methyl tertiary butyl ether)
   b. Indolene
   c. Xylene
   d. TBA (tertiary butyl alcohol)

9. Avoid topping off the fuel tank because _____.
   a. It can saturate the charcoal canister
   b. The extra fuel simply spills onto the ground
   c. The extra fuel increases vehicle weight and reduces performance
   d. The extra fuel goes into the expansion area of the tank and is not used by the engine

10. Using ethanol-enhanced or reformulated gasoline can result in reduced fuel economy.
    a. True
    b. False

ALTERNATIVE FUELS

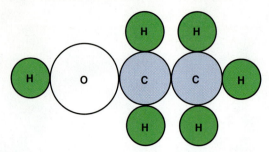

FIGURE 6–1 The ethanol molecule showing two carbon atoms, six hydrogen atoms, and one oxygen atom.

ETHANOL

ETHANOL TERMINOLOGY **Ethanol** is also called **ethyl alcohol** or **grain alcohol**, because it is usually made from grain and is the type of alcohol found in alcoholic drinks such as beer, wine, and distilled spirits like whiskey. Ethanol is composed of two carbon atoms and six hydrogen atoms with one added oxygen atom. ● **SEE FIGURE 6–1**.

ETHANOL PRODUCTION Conventional ethanol is derived from grains, such as corn, wheat, or soybeans. Corn, for example, is converted to ethanol in either a dry or wet milling process. In dry milling operations, liquefied cornstarch is produced by heating cornmeal with water and enzymes. A second enzyme converts the liquefied starch to sugars, which are fermented by yeast into ethanol and carbon dioxide. Wet milling operations separate the fiber, germ (oil), and protein from the starch before it is fermented into ethanol.

The majority of the ethanol in the United States is made from:

- Corn
- Grain
- Sorghum
- Wheat
- Barley
- Potatoes

In Brazil, the world's largest ethanol producer, it is made from sugarcane. Ethanol can be made by the dry mill process in which the starch portion of the corn is fermented into sugar and then distilled into alcohol.

The major steps in the dry mill process include:

1. **Milling.** The feedstock passes through a hammer mill that turns it into a fine powder called *meal*.

2. **Liquefaction.** The meal is mixed with water and then passed through cookers where the starch is liquefied. Heat is applied at this stage to enable liquefaction. Cookers use a high-temperature stage of about 250°F to 300°F (120°C to 150°C) to reduce bacteria levels and then a lower temperature of about 200°F (95°C) for a holding period.

3. **Saccharification.** The mash from the cookers is cooled and a secondary enzyme is added to convert the liquefied starch to fermentable sugars (dextrose).

4. **Fermentation.** Yeast is added to the mash to ferment the sugars to ethanol and carbon dioxide.

5. **Distillation.** The fermented mash, now called beer, contains about 10% alcohol plus all the nonfermentable solids from the corn and yeast cells. The mash is pumped to the continuous-flow, distillation system where the alcohol is removed from the solids and the water. The alcohol leaves the top of the final column at about 96% strength, and the residue mash, called *silage*, is transferred from the base of the column to the co-product processing area.

6. **Dehydration.** The alcohol from the top of the column passes through a dehydration system where the remaining water will be removed. The alcohol product at this stage is called **anhydrous ethanol** (pure, no more than 0.5% water).

7. **Denaturing.** Ethanol that will be used for fuel must be denatured, or made unfit for human consumption, with a small amount of gasoline (2% to 5%), methanol, or denatonium benzoate. This is done at the ethanol plant.

CELLULOSE ETHANOL

TERMINOLOGY   **Cellulose ethanol** can be produced from a wide variety of cellulose biomass feedstock, including:

- Agricultural plant wastes (corn stalks, cereal straws)
- Plant wastes from industrial processes (sawdust, paper pulp)
- Energy crops grown specifically for fuel production.

These nongrain products are often referred to as **cellulosic biomass**. Cellulosic biomass is composed of cellulose and lignin, with smaller amounts of proteins, lipids (fats, waxes, and oils), and ash. About two-thirds of cellulosic materials are present as cellulose, with lignin making up the bulk of the remaining dry mass.

REFINING CELLULOSE BIOMASS   As with grains, processing cellulose biomass involves extracting fermentable sugars from the feedstock. But the sugars in cellulose are locked in complex carbohydrates called polysaccharides (long chains of simple sugars). Separating these complex structures into fermentable sugars is needed to achieve the efficient and economic production of cellulose ethanol.

Two processing options are employed to produce fermentable sugars from cellulose biomass:

- Acid hydrolysis is used to break down the complex carbohydrates into simple sugars.
- Enzymes are employed to convert the cellulose biomass to fermentable sugars. The final step involves microbial fermentation, yielding ethanol and carbon dioxide.

NOTE: Cellulose ethanol production substitutes biomass for fossil fuels. The greenhouse gases produced by the combustion of biomass are offset by the CO_2 absorbed by the biomass as it grows in the field.

? FREQUENTLY ASKED QUESTION

What Is Switchgrass?

Switchgrass (*Panicum virgatum*) can be used to make ethanol and is a summer perennial grass that is native to North America. It is a natural component of the tall-grass prairie, which covered most of the Great Plains, but was also found on the prairie soils in the Black Belt of Alabama and Mississippi. Switchgrass is resistant to many pests and plant diseases, and is capable of producing high yields with very low applications of fertilizer. This means that the need for agricultural chemicals to grow switchgrass is relatively low. Switchgrass is also very tolerant of poor soils, flooding, and drought, which are widespread agricultural problems in the southeast.

There are two main types of switchgrass:

- **Upland types**—usually grow 5 to 6 feet tall
- **Lowland types**—grow up to 12 feet tall and are typically found on heavy soils in bottomland sites

Better energy efficiency is gained because less energy is used to produce ethanol from switchgrass.

E85

WHAT IS E85?   Vehicle manufacturers have available vehicles that are capable of operating on gasoline plus ethanol or a combination of gasoline and ethanol called **E85**. E85 is composed of 85% ethanol and 15% gasoline.

Pure ethanol has an octane rating of about 113. E85, which contains 35% oxygen by weight, has an octane rating of about 100 to 105. This compares to a regular unleaded gasoline which has a rating of 87. ● **SEE FIGURE 6–2**.

NOTE: The octane rating of E85 depends on the exact percent of ethanol used, which can vary from 81% to 85%. It also depends on the octane rating of the gasoline used to make E85.

HEAT ENERGY OF E85   E85 has less heat energy than gasoline.

FIGURE 6–2 Some retail stations offer a variety of fuel choices, such as this station in Ohio where E10 and E85 are available.

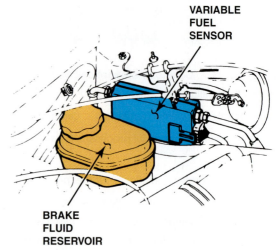

FIGURE 6–3 The location of the variable fuel sensor can vary, depending on the make and model of vehicle, but it is always in the fuel line between the fuel tank and the fuel injectors.

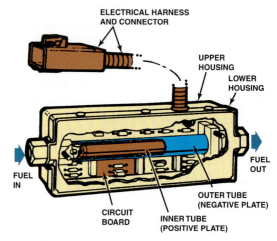

FIGURE 6–4 A cutaway view of a typical variable fuel sensor.

E85 (CONTINUED)

Gasoline = 114,000 BTUs per gallon

E85 = 87,000 BTUs per gallon

This means that the fuel economy is reduced by 20% to 30% if E85 is used instead of gasoline.

Example: A Chevrolet Tahoe 5.3-liter V-8 with an automatic transmission has an EPA rating of 15 mpg in the city and 20 mpg on the highway when using gasoline. If this same vehicle was fueled with E85, the EPA fuel economy rating drops to 11 mpg in the city and 15 mpg on the highway.

ALTERNATIVE-FUEL VEHICLES

The 15% gasoline in this blend helps the engine start, especially in cold weather. Vehicles equipped with this capability are commonly referred to as **alternative-fuel vehicles (AFVs)**, **Flex Fuels**, and **flexible fuel vehicles**, or **FFVs**. Using E85 in a flex-fuel vehicle can result in a power increase of about 5%. For example, an engine rated at 200 hp using gasoline or E10 could produce 210 hp if using E85.

NOTE: E85 may test as containing less than 85% ethanol if tested in cold climates because it is often blended according to outside temperature. A lower percentage of ethanol with a slightly higher percentage of gasoline helps engines start in cold climates.

These vehicles are equipped with an electronic sensor in the fuel supply line that detects the presence and percentage of ethanol. The PCM then adjusts the fuel injector on-time and ignition timing to match the needs of the fuel being used.

E85 contains less heat energy, and therefore will use more fuel, but the benefits include a lower cost of the fuel and the environmental benefit associated with using an oxygenated fuel.

General Motors, Ford, Chrysler, Mazda, and Honda are a few of the manufacturers offering E85 compatible vehicles. E85 vehicles use fuel system parts designed to withstand the additional alcohol content, modified driveability programs that adjust fuel delivery and timing to compensate for the various percentages of ethanol fuel, and a **fuel compensation sensor** that measures both the percentage of ethanol blend and the temperature of the fuel. This sensor is also called a **variable fuel sensor**. ● **SEE FIGURES 6–3 AND 6–4.**

FIGURE 6–5 A pump for E85 (85% ethanol and 15% gasoline). E85 is available in more locations every year.

TECH TIP

Purchase a Flex-Fuel Vehicle

If purchasing a new or used vehicle, try to find a flex-fuel vehicle. Even though you may not want to use E85, a flex-fuel vehicle has a more robust fuel system than a conventional fuel system designed for gasoline or E10. The enhanced fuel system components and materials usually include:

- Stainless steel fuel rail
- Graphite commutator bars instead of copper in the fuel pump motor (ethanol can oxidize into acetic acid, which can corrode copper)
- Diamond-like carbon (DLC) corrosion-resistant fuel injectors
- Alcohol-resistant O-rings and hoses

The cost of a flex-fuel vehicle compared with the same vehicle designed to operate on gasoline is a no-cost or a low-cost option.

FREQUENTLY ASKED QUESTION

How Does a Sensorless Flex-Fuel System Work?

Many General Motors flex-fuel vehicles do not use a fuel compensation sensor and instead use the oxygen sensor to detect the presence of the lean mixture and the extra oxygen in the fuel.

The Powertrain Control Module (PCM) then adjusts the injector pulse-width and the ignition timing to optimize engine operation to the use of E85. This type of vehicle is called a *virtual flexible fuel vehicle*, abbreviated **V-FFV**. The virtual flexible fuel vehicle can operate on pure gasoline or blends up to 85% ethanol.

E85 FUEL SYSTEM REQUIREMENTS   Most E85 vehicles are very similar to non-E85 vehicles. Fuel system components may be redesigned to withstand the effects of higher concentrations of ethanol. In addition, since the stoichiometric point for ethanol is 9:1 instead of 14.7:1 as for gasoline, the air–fuel mixture has to be adjusted for the percentage of ethanol present in the fuel tank. In order to determine this percentage of ethanol in the fuel tank, a compensation sensor is used. The fuel compensation sensor is the only additional piece of hardware required on some E85 vehicles. The fuel compensation sensor provides both the ethanol percentage and the fuel temperature to the PCM. The PCM uses this information to adjust both the ignition timing and the quantity of fuel delivered to the engine. The fuel compensation sensor uses a microprocessor to measure both the ethanol percentage and the fuel temperature.

This information is sent to the PCM on the signal circuit. The compensation sensor produces a square wave frequency and pulse width signal. The normal frequency range of the fuel compensation sensor is 50 hertz, which represents 0% ethanol and 150 hertz, which represents 100% ethanol. The pulse width of the signal varies from 1 millisecond to 5 milliseconds. One millisecond would represent a fuel temperature of −40°F (−40°C), and 5 milliseconds would represent a fuel temperature of 257°F (125°C). Since the PCM knows both the fuel temperature and the ethanol percentage of the fuel, it can adjust fuel quantity and ignition timing for optimum performance and emissions.

The benefits of E85 vehicles are less pollution, less CO_2 production, and less dependence on oil. ● **SEE FIGURE 6–5.**

Ethanol-fueled vehicles generally produce the same pollutants as gasoline vehicles; however, they produce less CO and CO_2 emissions. While CO_2 is not considered a pollutant, it is thought to lead to global warming and is called a greenhouse gas.

FLEX-FUEL VEHICLE IDENTIFICATION Flexible fuel

vehicles (FFVs) can be identified by:

- Emblems on the side, front, and/or rear of the vehicle
- Yellow fuel cap showing E85/gasoline (● **SEE FIGURE 6–6**)
- Vehicle emission control information (VECI) label under the hood (● **SEE FIGURE 6–7**)
- Vehicle identification number (VIN)

Vehicles that are flexible fuel include:

Chrysler

2004+
- 4.7L Dodge Ram Pickup 1500 Series
- 2.7L Dodge Stratus Sedan
- 2.7L Chrysler Sebring Sedan
- 3.3L Caravan and Grand Caravan SE

2003–2004
- 2.7L Dodge Stratus Sedan
- 2.7L Chrysler Sebring Sedan

2003
- 3.3L Dodge Cargo Minivan

2000–2003
- 3.3L Chrysler Voyager Minivan
- 3.3L Dodge Caravan Minivan 3.3L Chrysler Town and Country Minivan

1998–1999
- 3.3L Dodge Caravan Minivan
- 3.3L Plymouth Voyager Minivan
- 3.3L Chrysler Town & Country Minivan

Ford Motor Company

*Ford offers the flex fuel capability as an option on select vehicles—see the owner's manual.

2004+
- 4.0L Explorer Sport Trac
- 4.0L Explorer (4-door)
- 3.0L Taurus Sedan and Wagon

2002–2004
- 4.0L Explorer (4-door)
- 3.0L Taurus Sedan and Wagon

2002–2003
- 3.0L Supercab Ranger Pickup 2WD

2001
- 3.0L Supercab Ranger Pickup 2WD
- 3.0L Taurus LX, SE, and SES Sedan

1999–2000
- 3.0L Ranger Pickup 4WD and 2WD

General Motors

*Select vehicles only—see your owner's manual.

2005+
- 5.3L Vortec-Engine Avalanche
- 5.3L Vortec-Engine Police Package Tahoe

2003–2005
- 5.3L V8 Chevy Silverado* and GMC Sierra* Half-Ton Pickups 2WD and 4WD
- 5.3L Vortec-Engine Suburban, Tahoe, Yukon, and Yukon XL

2002
- 5.3L V8 Chevy Silverado* and GMC Sierra* Half-Ton Pickups 2WD and 4WD
- 5.3L Vortec-Engine Suburban, Tahoe, Yukon, and Yukon XL
- 2.2L Chevy S10 Pickup 2WD
- 2.2L Sonoma GMC Pickup 2WD

2000–2001
- 2.2L Chevy S10 Pickup 2WD
- 2.2L GMC Sonoma Pickup 2WD

Isuzu

2000–2001
- 2.2L Hombre Pickup 2WD

Mazda

1999–2003
- 3.0L Selected B3000 Pickups

Mercedes-Benz

2005+
- 2.6L C240 Luxury Sedan and Wagon

2003
- 3.2L C320 Sport Sedan and Wagon

Mercury

2002–2004
- 4.0L Selected Mountaineers

2000–2004
- 3.0L Selected Sables

Nissan

2005+
- 5.6L DOHC V8 Engine

*Select vehicles only—see the owner's manual or VECI sticker under the hood.

FIGURE 6–6 A flex-fuel vehicle often has a yellow gas cap, which is labeled E85/gasoline.

FIGURE 6–7 A vehicle emission control information (VECI) sticker on a flexible fuel vehicle indicating that it can use ethanol from 0 to 85%.

TECH TIP

Avoid Resetting Fuel Compensation

Starting in 2006, General Motors vehicles designed to operate on E85 do not use a fuel compensation sensor, but instead use the oxygen sensor and refueling information to calculate the percentage of ethanol in the fuel. The PCM uses the fuel level sensor to sense that fuel has been added and starts to determine the resulting ethanol content by using the oxygen sensor. However, if a service technician were to reset fuel compensation by clearing long-term fuel trim, the PCM starts the calculation based on base fuel, which is gasoline with less than or equal to 10% ethanol (E10). If the fuel tank has E85, then the fuel compensation cannot be determined unless the tank is drained and refilled with base fuel. Therefore, avoid resetting the fuel compensation setting unless it is known that the fuel tank contains gasoline or E10 only.

HOW TO READ A VEHICLE IDENTIFICATION NUMBER

The vehicle identification number (VIN) is required by federal regulation to contain specific information about the vehicle. The following chart shows the character in the eighth position of the VIN number from Ford Motor Company, General Motors, and Chrysler that designates their vehicles as flexible fuel vehicles.

Ford Motor Company

Vehicle	8th Character
Ford Crown Victoria	V
Ford F-150	V
Ford Explorer	K
Ford Ranger	V
Ford Taurus	2
Lincoln Town Car	V
Mercury Mountaineer	K
Mercury Sable	2
Mercury Grand Marquis	V

General Motors

Vehicle	8th Character
Chevrolet Avalanche	Z
Chevrolet Impala	K
Chevrolet Monte Carlo	K
Chevrolet S-10 Pickup	5
Chevrolet Sierra	Z
Chevrolet Suburban	Z
Chevrolet Tahoe	Z
GMC Yukon and Yukon XL	Z
GMC Silverado	Z
GMC Sonoma	5

ALTERNATIVE-FUEL VEHICLES (CONTINUED)

Chrysler

Vehicle	8th Character
Chrysler Sebring	T
Chrysler Town & Country	E, G or 3
Dodge Caravan	E, G or 3
Dodge Cargo Minivan	E, G or 3
Dodge Durango	P
Dodge Ram	P
Dodge Stratus	T
Plymouth Voyager	E, G or 3

Mazda

Vehicle	8th Character
B3000 Pickup	V

Nissan

Vehicle	4th Character
Titan	B

Mercedes Benz

Check owner's manual or the VECI sticker under the hood.

NOTE: For additional information on E85 and for the location of E85 stations in your area, go to www.e85fuel.com.

 FREQUENTLY ASKED QUESTION

How Long Can Oxygenated Fuel Be Stored Before All of the Oxygen Escapes?

The oxygen in oxygenated fuels, such as E10 and E85, is not in a gaseous state like the CO_2 in soft drinks. The oxygen is part of the molecule of ethanol or other oxygenates and does not bubble out of the fuel. Oxygenated fuels, just like any fuel, have a shelf life of about 90 days.

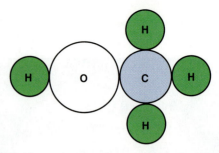

FIGURE 6–8 The molecular structure of methanol showing the one carbon atom, four hydrogen atoms, and one oxygen atom.

METHANOL

METHANOL TERMINOLOGY **Methanol**, also known as *methyl alcohol*, *wood alcohol*, or *methyl hydrate,* is a chemical compound formula that includes one carbon atom and four hydrogen atoms and one oxygen. ● **SEE FIGURE 6–8**.

Methanol is a light, volatile, colorless, tasteless, flammable, poisonous liquid with a very faint odor. It is used as an antifreeze, a solvent, and a fuel. It is also used to denature ethanol. Methanol burns in air, forming CO_2 (carbon dioxide) and H_2O (water). A methanol flame is almost colorless. Because of its poisonous properties, methanol is also used to denature ethanol. Methanol is often called wood alcohol because it was once produced chiefly as a by-product of the destructive distillation of wood. ● **SEE FIGURE 6–9**.

PRODUCTION OF METHANOL The biggest source of methanol in the United States is coal. Using a simple reaction between coal and steam, a gas mixture called **syn-gas** (*synthesis gas*) is formed. The components of this mixture are carbon monoxide and hydrogen, which, through an additional chemical reaction, are converted to methanol.

Natural gas can also be used to create methanol and is reformed or converted to synthesis gas, which is later made into methanol.

Biomass can be converted to synthesis gas by a process called partial oxidation, and later converted to methanol. **Biomass** is organic material, such as:

- Urban wood wastes
- Primary mill residues
- Forest residues
- Agricultural residues
- Dedicated energy crops (e.g., sugarcane and sugar beets) that can be made into fuel

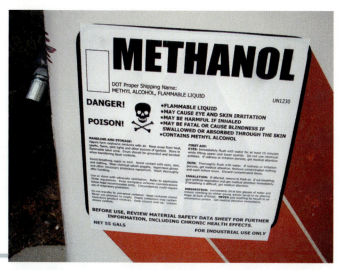

FIGURE 6–9 Sign on methanol pump shows that methyl alcohol is a poison and can cause skin irritation and other personal injury. Methanol is used in industry as well as being a fuel.

FIGURE 6–10 Propane fuel storage tank in the trunk of a Ford taxi.

Electricity can be used to convert water into hydrogen, which is then reacted with carbon dioxide to produce methanol.

Methanol is toxic and can cause blindness and death. It can enter the body by ingestion, inhalation, or absorption through the skin. Dangerous doses will build up if a person is regularly exposed to fumes or handles liquid without skin protection. If methanol has been ingested, a doctor should be contacted immediately. The usual fatal dose is 4 fl oz (100 to 125 mL).

M85 Some flexible fuel vehicles are designed to operate on 85% methanol and 15% gasoline called **M85**. Methanol is very corrosive and requires that the fuel system components be constructed of stainless steel and other alcohol-resistant rubber and plastic components. The heat content of M85 is about 60% of that of gasoline.

PROPANE

Propane is the most widely used of all of the alternative fuels. Propane is normally a gas but is easily compressed into a liquid and stored in inexpensive containers. When sold as a fuel, it is also known as **liquefied petroleum gas (LPG)** or **LP-gas** because the propane is often mixed with about 10% of other gases such as butane, propylene, butylenes, and mercaptan to give the colorless and odorless propane a smell. Propane is nontoxic, but if inhaled can cause asphyxiation through lack of oxygen. Propane is heavier than air and lays near the floor if released into the atmosphere. Propane is commonly used in forklifts and other equipment used inside warehouses and factories because the exhaust from the engine using propane is not harmful. Propane is a by-product of petroleum refining of natural gas. In order to liquefy the fuel, it is stored in strong tanks at about 300 PSI (2,000 kPa). The heating value of propane is less than that of gasoline; therefore, more is required, which reduces the fuel economy. ● **SEE FIGURE 6–10**.

FIGURE 6–11 The blue sticker on the rear of this vehicle indicates that it is designed to use compressed natural gas.

FIGURE 6–12 A CNG storage tank from a Honda Civic GX shown with the fixture used to support it while it is being removed or installed in the vehicle. Honda specifies that three technicians be used to remove or install the tank through the rear door of the vehicle due to the size and weight of the tank.

COMPRESSED NATURAL GAS (CNG)

CNG VEHICLE DESIGN Another alternative fuel that is often used in fleet vehicles is **compressed natural gas**, or **CNG**, and vehicles using this fuel are often referred to as **natural gas vehicles (NGVs)**. Look for the blue CNG label on vehicles designed to operate on compressed natural gas. ● **SEE FIGURE 6–11**.

Natural gas has to be compressed to about 3,000 PSI (20,000 kPa) or more, so that the weight and the cost of the storage container is a major factor when it comes to preparing a vehicle to run on CNG. The tanks needed for CNG are typically constructed of 0.5-inch-thick (3 mm) aluminum reinforced with fiberglass. ● **SEE FIGURE 6–12**. The octane rating of CNG is about 130 and the cost per gallon is about half of the cost of gasoline. However, the heat value of CNG is also less, and therefore more is required to produce the same power and the miles per gallon is less.

CNG COMPOSITION Compressed natural gas is made up of a blend of:

- Methane
- Propane
- Ethane
- N-butane
- Carbon dioxide
- Nitrogen

Once it is processed, it is at least 93% methane. Natural gas is nontoxic, odorless, and colorless in its natural state. It is odorized during processing, using ethyl mercaptan ("skunk"), to allow for easy leak detection. Natural gas is lighter than air and will rise when released into the air. Since CNG is already a vapor, it does not need heat to vaporize before it will burn, which improves cold start-up and results in lower emissions during cold operation. However, because it is already in a gaseous state, it does displace some of the air charge in the intake manifold. This leads to about a 10% reduction in engine power as compared to an engine operating on gasoline. Natural gas also burns slower than gasoline; therefore, the ignition timing must be advanced more when the vehicle operates on natural gas. The stoichiometric ratio, the point at which all the air and fuel is used or burned is 16.5:1 compared to 14.7:1 for gasoline. This means that more air is required to burn one pound of natural gas than is required to burn one pound of gasoline. ● **SEE FIGURE 6–13**.

The CNG engine is designed to include:

- Increased compression ratio
- Strong pistons and connecting rods
- Heat-resistant valves
- Fuel injectors designed for gaseous fuel instead of liquid fuel

What Is the Amount of CNG Equal to in Gasoline?

To achieve the amount of energy of one gallon of gasoline, 122 cubic feet of compressed natural gas (CNG) is needed. While the octane rating of CNG is much higher than gasoline (130 octane), using CNG instead of gasoline in the same engine would result in a reduction 10% to 20% of power due to the lower heat energy that is released when CNG is burned in the engine.

FIGURE 6–13 The fuel injectors used on this Honda Civic GX CNG engine are designed to flow gaseous fuel instead of liquid fuel and cannot be interchanged with any other type of injector.

FIGURE 6–14 This CNG pump is capable of supplying compressed natural gas at either 3,000 PSI or 3,600 PSI. The price per gallon is higher for the higher pressure.

CNG FUEL SYSTEMS When completely filled, the CNG tank has 3,600 PSI of pressure in the tank. When the ignition is turned on, the alternate fuel electronic control unit activates the high-pressure lock-off, which allows high-pressure gas to pass to the high-pressure regulator. The high-pressure regulator reduces the high-pressure CNG to approximately 170 PSI and sends it to the low-pressure lock-off. The low-pressure lock-off is also controlled by the alternate fuel electronic control unit and is activated at the same time that the high-pressure lock-off is activated. From the low-pressure lock-off, the CNG is directed to the low-pressure regulator. This is a two-stage regulator that first reduces the pressure to approximately 4 to 6 PSI in the first stage and then to 4.5 to 7 inches of water in the second stage. Twenty-eight inches of water is equal to 1 PSI, therefore, the final pressure of the natural gas entering the engine is very low. From here, the low-pressure gas is delivered to the gas mass sensor/mixture control valve. This valve controls the air–fuel mixture. The CNG gas distributor adapter then delivers the gas to the intake stream.

CNG vehicles are designed for fleet use that usually have their own refueling capabilities. One of the drawbacks to using CNG is the time that it takes to refuel a vehicle. The ideal method of refueling is the slow fill method. The slow filling method compresses the natural gas as the tank is being fueled. This method ensures that the tank will receive a full charge of

CNG; however, this method can take three to five hours to accomplish. If more than one vehicle needs filling, the facility will need multiple CNG compressors to refuel the vehicles.

There are three commonly used CNG refilling station pressures:

P24—2,400 PSI

P30—3,000 PSI

P36—3,600 PSI

Try to find and use a station with the highest refilling pressure. Filling at lower pressures will result in less compressed natural gas being installed in the storage tank, thereby reducing the driving range. ● **SEE FIGURE 6–14.**

The fast fill method uses CNG that is already compressed. However, as the CNG tank is filled rapidly, the internal temperature of the tank will rise, which causes a rise in tank pressure. Once the temperature drops in the CNG tank, the pressure in the tank also drops, resulting in an incomplete charge in the CNG tank. This refueling method may take only about five minutes; however, it will result in an incomplete charge to the CNG tank, reducing the driving range.

LIQUEFIED NATURAL GAS (LNG)

Natural gas can be turned into a liquid if cooled to below −260°F (−127°C). The natural gas condenses into a liquid at normal atmospheric pressure and the volume is reduced by about 600 times. This means that the natural gas can be more efficiently transported over long distances where no pipelines are present when liquefied.

Because the temperature of liquefied natural gas (LNG) must be kept low, it is only practical for use in short haul trucks where they can be refueled from a central location.

P-SERIES FUELS

P-series alternative fuel is patented by Princeton University and is a non-petroleum- or natural gas-based fuel suitable for use in flexible fuel vehicles or any vehicle designed to operate on E85 (85% ethanol, 15% gasoline). P-series fuel is recognized by the United States Department of Energy as being an alternative fuel, but is not yet available to the public. P-series fuels are blends of the following:

- Ethanol (ethyl alcohol)
- Methyltetrahydrofuron, abbreviated MTHF
- Natural gas liquids, such as pentanes
- Butane

COMPOSITION OF P-SERIES FUELS (BY VOLUME)

COMPONENT	REGULAR GRADE	PREMIUM GRADE	COLD WEATHER
Pentanes plus	32.5%	27.5%	16.0%
MTHF	32.5%	17.5%	26.0%
Ethanol	35.0%	55.0%	47.0%
Butane	0.0%	0.0%	11.0%

CHART 6–1

P-series fuel varies in composition, depending on the octane rating and temperature.

? FREQUENTLY ASKED QUESTION

What Is a Tri-Fuel Vehicle?

In Brazil, most vehicles are designed to operate on ethanol or gasoline or any combination of the two. In this South American country, ethanol is made from sugarcane, is commonly available, and is lower in price than gasoline. Compressed natural gas (CNG) is also being made available so many vehicle manufacturers in Brazil, such as General Motors and Ford, are equipping vehicles to be capable of using gasoline, ethanol, or CNG. These vehicles are called tri-fuel vehicles.

The ethanol and MTHF are produced from renewable feedstocks, such as corn, waste paper, biomass, agricultural waste, and wood waste (scraps and sawdust). The components used in P-type fuel can be varied to produce regular grade, premium grade, or fuel suitable for cold climates. ● SEE CHART 6–1 for the percentages of the ingredients based on fuel grade.

● SEE CHART 6–2 for a comparison of the most frequently used alternative fuels.

Alternative Fuel Comparison Chart

CHARACTERISTIC	PROPANE	CNG	METHANOL	ETHANOL	REGULAR UNLEADED GAS
Octane	104	130	100	100	87–93
BTU per gallon	91,000	N.A.	70,000	83,000	114,000–125,000
Gallon equivalent	1.15	122 cubic feet— 1 gallon of gasoline	1.8	1.5	1
On-board fuel storage	Liquid	Gas	Liquid	Liquid	Liquid
Miles/gallon as compared to gas	85%	N.A.	55%	70%	100%
Relative tank size required to yield driving range equivalent to gas	Tank is 1.25 times larger	Tank is 3.5 times larger	Tank is 1.8 times larger	Tank is 1.5 times larger	
Pressure	200 PSI	3,000–3,600 PSI	N.A.	N.A.	N.A.
Cold weather capability	Good	Good	Poor	Poor	Good
Vehicle power	5–10% power loss	10–20% power loss	4% power increase	5% power increase	Standard
Toxicity	Nontoxic	Nontoxic	Highly toxic	Toxic	Toxic
Corrosiveness	Noncorrosive	Noncorrosive	Corrosive	Corrosive	Minimally corrosive
Source	Natural gas/ petroleum refining	Natural gas/ crude oil	Natural gas/coal	Sugar and starch crops/biomass	Crude oil

CHART 6–2

The characteristics of alternative fuels compared to regular unleaded gasoline shows that all have advantages and disadvantages.

SYNTHETIC FUELS

Synthetic fuels can be made from a variety of products, using several different processes. Synthetic fuel must, however, make these alternatives practical only when conventional petroleum products are either very expensive or not available.

FISCHER-TROPSCH Synthetic fuels were first developed using the **Fischer-Tropsch** method and have been in use since the 1920s to convert coal, natural gas, and other fossil fuel products into a fuel that is high in quality and clean-burning. The process for producing Fischer-Tropsch fuels was patented by two German scientists, Franz Fischer and Hans Tropsch, during World War I. The Fischer-Tropsch method uses carbon monoxide and hydrogen (the same synthesis gas used to produce hydrogen fuel) to convert coal and other hydrocarbons to liquid fuels in a process similar to hydrogenation, another method for hydrocarbon conversion. The process using natural gas, also called **gas-to-liquid (GTL)** technology, uses a catalyst, usually iron or cobalt, and incorporates steam re-forming to give off the by-products of carbon dioxide, hydrogen, and carbon monoxide. ● **SEE FIGURE 6–15**.

Whereas traditional fuels emit environmentally harmful particulates and chemicals, namely sulfur compounds, Fischer-Tropsch fuels combust with no soot or odors and emit only low levels of toxins. Fischer-Tropsch fuels can also be blended with traditional transportation fuels with little equipment modification, as they use the same engine and equipment technology as traditional fuels.

The fuels contain a very low sulfur and aromatic content and they produce virtually no particulate emissions. Researchers also expect reductions in hydrocarbon and carbon monoxide emissions. Fischer-Tropsch fuels do not differ in fuel performance from gasoline and diesel. At present, Fischer-Tropsch fuels are very expensive to produce on a large scale, although research is under way to lower processing costs. Diesel fuel created using the Fischer-Tropsch diesel (**FTD**) process is often called *GTL diesel*. GTL diesel can also be combined with petroleum diesel to produce a GTL blend. This fuel product is currently being sold in Europe and plans are in place to introduce it in North America.

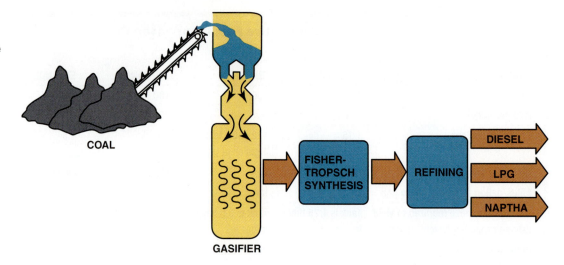

FIGURE 6–15 A Fischer-Tropsch processing plant is able to produce a variety of fuels from coal.

COAL

GASIFIER

FISHER-TROPSCH SYNTHESIS

REFINING

DIESEL

LPG

NAPTHA

COAL TO LIQUID (CTL)   Coal is very abundant in the United States and coal can be converted to a liquid fuel through a process called **coal to liquid (CTL)**. The huge cost is the main obstacle to these plants. The need to invest $1.4 billion per plant before it can make product is the reason no one has built a CTL plant yet in the United States. Investors need to be convinced that the cost of oil is going to remain high in order to get them to commit this kind of money.

A large plant might be able to produce 120,000 barrels of liquid fuel a day and would consume about 50,000 tons of coal per day. However, such a plant would create about 6,000 tons of CO_2 per day. These CO_2 emissions, which could contribute to global warming, and the cost involved make CTL a technology that is not likely to expand.

Two procedures can be used to convert coal-to-liquid fuel:

1. **Direct**—In the direct method, coal is broken down to create liquid products. First the coal is reacted with hydrogen (H_2) at high temperatures and pressure with a catalyst. This process creates a synthetic crude, called **syncrude**, which is then refined to produce gasoline or diesel fuel.

2. **Indirect**—In the indirect method, coal is first turned into a gas and the molecules are reassembled to create the desired product. This process involves turning coal into a gas called syn-gas. The syngas is then converted into liquid, using the Fischer-Tropsch (FT) process.

Russia has been using CTL by injecting air into the underground coal seams. Ignition is provided and the resulting gases are trapped and converted to liquid gasoline and diesel fuel through the Fischer-Tropsch process. This underground method is called **underground coal gasification (UCG)**.

METHANOL TO GASOLINE   Exxon Mobil has developed a process for converting methanol (methyl alcohol) into gasoline in a process called **methanol-to-gasoline (MTG)**. The MTG process was discovered by accident when a gasoline additive made from methanol was being created. The process instead created olefins (alkenes), paraffins (alkenes), and aromatic compounds, which in combination are known as gasoline. The process uses a catalyst and is currently being produced in New Zealand.

FUTURE OF SYNTHETIC FUELS   Producing gasoline and diesel fuels by other methods besides refining from crude oil has usually been more expensive. With the increasing cost of crude oil, alternative methods are now becoming economically feasible. Whether or not the diesel fuel or gasoline is created from coal, natural gas, or methanol, or created by refining crude oil, the transportation and service pumps are already in place. Compared to using compressed natural gas or other similar alternative fuels, synthetic fuels represent the lowest cost.

SAFETY PROCEDURES WHEN WORKING WITH ALTERNATIVE FUELS

All fuels are flammable and many are explosive under certain conditions. Whenever working around compressed gases of any kind (CNG, LNG, propane, or LPG), always wear personal protective equipment (PPE), including at least the following items:

1. Safety glasses and/or face shield.

2. Protective gloves.

3. Long-sleeved shirt and pants to help protect bare skin from the freezing effects of gases under pressure in the event that the pressure is lost.

4. If any fuel gets on the skin, the area should be washed immediately.

5. If fuel spills on clothing, change into clean clothing as soon as possible.

6. If fuel spills on a painted surface, flush the surface with water and air dry. If simply wiped off with a dry cloth, the paint surface could be permanently damaged.

7. As with any fuel-burning vehicle, always vent the exhaust to the outside. If methanol fuel is used, the exhaust contains *formaldehyde*, which has a sharp odor and can cause severe burning of the eyes, nose, and throat.

 **WARNING**

Do not smoke or have an open flame in the area when working around or refueling any vehicle.

SUMMARY

1. Flexible fuel vehicles (FFVs) are designed to operate on gasoline or gasoline-ethanol blends up to 85% ethanol (E85).

2. Ethanol can be made from grain, such as corn, or from cellulosic biomass, such as switchgrass.

3. E85 has fewer BTUs of energy per gallon compared with gasoline and will therefore provide lower fuel economy.

4. Older flexible fuel vehicles used a fuel compensation sensor but newer models use the oxygen sensor to calculate the percentage of ethanol in the fuel being burned.

5. Methanol is also called methyl alcohol or wood alcohol and, while it can be made from wood, it is mostly made from natural gas.

6. Propane is the most widely used alternative fuel. Propane is also called liquefied petroleum gas (LPG).

7. Compressed natural gas (CNG) is available for refilling in several pressures, including 2,400 PSI, 3,000 PSI, and 3,600 PSI.

8. P-series fuel is recognized by the United States Department of Energy as being an alternative fuel. P-series fuel is a non-petroleum-based fuel suitable for use in a flexible fuel vehicle. However, P-series fuel is not commercially available.

9. Synthetic fuels are usually made using the Fischer-Tropsch method to convert coal or natural gas into gasoline and diesel fuel.

10. Safety procedures when working around alternative fuel include wearing the necessary personal protective equipment (PPE), including safety glasses and protective gloves.

REVIEW QUESTIONS

1. Ethanol is also known by what other terms?

2. The majority of ethanol in the United States is made from what farm products?

3. How is a flexible fuel vehicle identified?

4. Methanol is also known by what other terms?

5. What other gases are often mixed with propane?

6. Why is it desirable to fill a compressed natural gas (CNG) vehicle with the highest pressure available?

7. P-series fuel is made of what products?

8. The Fischer-Tropsch method can be used to change what into gasoline?

1. Ethanol can be produced from what products?
   a. Switchgrass
   c. Sugarcane
   b. Corn
   d. Any of the above

2. E85 means that the fuel is made from _____.
   a. 85% gasoline, 15% ethanol
   b. 85% ethanol, 15% gasoline
   c. Ethanol that has 15% water
   d. Pure ethyl alcohol

3. A flex-fuel vehicle can be identified by _____.
   a. Emblems on the side, front, and/or rear of the vehicle
   b. VECI
   c. VIN
   d. Any of the above

4. Methanol is also called _____.
   a. Methyl alcohol
   c. Methyl hydrate
   b. Wood alcohol
   d. All of the above

5. Which alcohol is dangerous (toxic)?
   a. Methanol
   c. Both ethanol and methanol
   b. Ethanol
   d. Neither ethanol nor methanol

6. Which is the most widely used alternative fuel?
   a. E85
   c. CNG
   b. Propane
   d. M85

7. Liquefied petroleum gas (LPG) is also called _____.
   a. E85
   c. Propane
   b. M85
   d. P-series fuel

8. How much compressed natural gas (CNG) does it require to achieve the energy of one gallon of gasoline?
   a. 130 cubic feet
   c. 105 cubic feet
   b. 122 cubic feet
   d. 91 cubic feet

9. When refueling a CNG vehicle, why is it recommended that the tank be filled to a high pressure?
   a. The range of the vehicle is increased
   b. The cost of the fuel is lower
   c. Less of the fuel is lost to evaporation
   d. Both a and c

10. Producing liquid fuel from coal or natural gas usually uses which process?
    a. Syncrude
    c. Fischer-Tropsch
    b. P-series
    d. Methanol to gasoline (MTG)

DIESEL AND BIODIESEL FUELS

OBJECTIVES

After studying Chapter 7, the reader will be able to:

1. Explain diesel fuel specifications.
2. List the advantages and disadvantages of biodiesel.
3. Discuss API gravity.
4. Explain E-diesel specifications.

KEY TERMS

API gravity 125
ASTM 124
B20 126
Biodiesel 126
Cetane number 124
Cloud point 124
Diesohol 128

E-diesel 128
Petrodiesel 127
PPO 127
SVO 127
UCO 127
ULSD 126
WVO 127

DIESEL FUEL

FEATURES OF DIESEL FUEL   Diesel fuel must meet an entirely different set of standards than gasoline. Diesel fuel contains 12% more heat energy than the same amount of gasoline. The fuel in a diesel engine is not ignited with a spark, but is ignited by the heat generated by high compression. The pressure of compression (400 to 700 PSI or 2,800 to 4,800 kilopascals) generates temperatures of 1200°F to 1600°F (700°C to 900°C), which speeds the preflame reaction to start the ignition of fuel injected into the cylinder.

DIESEL FUEL REQUIREMENTS   All diesel fuel must have the following characteristics:

- **Cleanliness.** It is imperative that the fuel used in a diesel engine be clean and free from water. Unlike the case with gasoline engines, the fuel is the lubricant and coolant for the diesel injector pump and injectors. Good-quality diesel fuel contains additives such as oxidation inhibitors, detergents, dispersants, rust preventatives, and metal deactivators.

- **Low-temperature fluidity.** Diesel fuel must be able to flow freely at all expected ambient temperatures. One specification for diesel fuel is its "pour point," which is the temperature below which the fuel would stop flowing.

- **Cloud point** is another concern with diesel fuel at lower temperatures. Cloud point is the low-temperature point when the waxes present in most diesel fuels tend to form crystals that can clog the fuel filter. Most diesel fuel suppliers distribute fuel with the proper pour point and cloud point for the climate conditions of the area.

CETANE NUMBER   The cetane number for diesel fuel is the opposite of the octane number for gasoline. The **cetane number** is a measure of the ease with which the fuel can be ignited. The cetane rating of the fuel determines, to a great extent, its ability to start the engine at low temperatures and to provide smooth warm-up and even combustion. The cetane rating of diesel fuel should be between 45 and 50. The higher the cetane rating, the more easily the fuel is ignited.

SULFUR CONTENT   The sulfur content of diesel fuel is very important to the life of the engine. Sulfur in the fuel creates sulfuric acid during the combustion process, which can damage engine components and cause piston ring wear. Federal regulations are getting extremely tight on sulfur content to less than 15 parts per million (PPM). High-sulfur fuel contributes to acid rain.

(a)

(b)

FIGURE 7–1 (a) Regular diesel fuel on the left has a clear or greenish tint, whereas fuel for off-road use is tinted red for identification. (b) A fuel pump in a farming area that clearly states the red diesel fuel is for off-road use only.

DIESEL FUEL COLOR   Diesel fuel intended for use on the streets and highways is clear or green in color. Diesel fuel to be used on farms and off-road use is dyed red. ● **SEE FIGURE 7–1.**

GRADES OF DIESEL FUEL   **American Society for Testing Materials (ASTM)** also classifies diesel fuel by volatility (boiling range) into the following grades:

GRADE #1   This grade of diesel fuel has the lowest boiling point and the lowest cloud and pour points, as well as a lower BTU content—less heat per pound of fuel. As a result, grade #1 is suitable for use during low-temperature (winter) operation. Grade #1 produces less heat per

FIGURE 7–2 Testing the API viscosity of a diesel fuel sample using a hydrometer.

API GRAVITY COMPARISON CHART			
Values for API Scale Oil			
API GRAVITY SCALE	SPECIFIC GRAVITY	WEIGHT DENSITY, LB/FT	POUNDS PER GALLON
0			
2			
4			
6			
8			
10	1.0000	62.36	8.337
12	0.9861	61.50	8.221
14	0.9725	60.65	8.108
16	0.9593	59.83	7.998
18	0.9465	59.03	7.891
20	0.9340	58.25	7.787
22	0.9218	57.87	7.736
24	0.9100	56.75	7.587
26	0.8984	56.03	7.490
28	0.8871	55.32	7.396
30	0.8762	54.64	7.305
32	0.8654	53.97	7.215
34	0.8550	53.32	7.128
36	0.8448	52.69	7.043
38	0.8348	51.06	6.960
40	0.8251	50.96	6.879
42	0.8155	50.86	6.799
44	0.8030	50.28	6.722
46	0.7972	49.72	6.646
48	0.7883	49.16	6.572
50	0.7796	48.62	6.499
52	0.7711	48.09	6.429
54	0.7628	47.57	6.359
56	0.7547	47.07	6.292
58	0.7467	46.57	6.225
60	0.7389	46.08	6.160
62	0.7313	45.61	6.097
64	0.7238	45.14	6.034
66	0.7165	44.68	5.973
68	0.7093	44.23	5.913
70	0.7022	43.79	5.854
72	0.6953	43.36	5.797
74	0.6886	42.94	5.741
76	0.6819	42.53	5.685
78	0.6754	41.12	5.631
80	0.6690	41.72	5.577
82	0.6628	41.33	5.526
84	0.6566	40.95	5.474
86	0.6506	40.57	5.424
88	0.6446	40.20	5.374
90	0.6388	39.84	5.326
92	0.6331	39.48	5.278
94	0.6275	39.13	5.231
96	0.6220	38.79	5.186
98	0.6116	38.45	5.141
100	0.6112	38.12	5.096

CHART 7–1

The API gravity scale is based on the specific gravity of the fuel.

pound of fuel compared to grade #2 and may be specified for use in diesel engines involved in frequent changes in load and speed, such as those found in city buses and delivery trucks.

GRADE #2 This grade has a higher boiling point, cloud point, and pour point as compared with grade #1. It is usually specified where constant speed and high loads are encountered, such as in long-haul trucking and automotive diesel applications. Most diesel is Grade #2.

DIESEL FUEL SPECIFIC GRAVITY TESTING The density of diesel fuel should be tested whenever there is a driveability concern. The density or specific gravity of diesel fuel is measured in units of **API gravity.** API gravity is an arbitrary scale expressing the gravity or density of liquid petroleum products devised jointly by the American Petroleum Institute and the National Bureau of Standards. The measuring scale is calibrated in terms of degrees API. Oil with the least specific gravity has the highest API gravity. The formula for determining API gravity is as follows:

Degrees API gravity = (141.5 ÷ specific gravity at 60°F) − 131.5

The normal API gravity for #1 diesel fuel is 39 to 44 (typically 40). The normal API gravity for #2 diesel fuel is 30 to 39 (typically 35). A hydrometer calibrated in API gravity units should be used to test diesel fuel. ● **SEE FIGURE 7–2.**

● **SEE CHART 7–1** for a comparison among specific gravity, weight density, pounds per gallon, and API gravity of diesel fuel.

DIESEL FUEL HEATERS Diesel fuel heaters, either coolant or electric, help prevent power loss and stalling in cold weather. The heater is placed in the fuel line between the tank and the

How Can You Tell If Gasoline Has Been Added to the Diesel Fuel by Mistake?

If gasoline has been accidentally added to diesel fuel and is burned in a diesel engine, the result can be very damaging to the engine. The gasoline can ignite faster than diesel fuel, which would tend to increase the temperature of combustion. This high temperature can harm injectors and glow plugs, as well as pistons, head gaskets, and other major diesel engine components. If contaminated fuel is suspected, first smell the fuel at the filler neck. If the fuel smells like gasoline, then the tank should be drained and refilled with diesel fuel. If the smell test does not indicate a gasoline smell (or any rancid smell), then test a sample for proper API gravity.

NOTE: Diesel fuel designed for on-road use should be green in color. Red diesel fuel (high sulfur) should only be found in off-road or farm equipment.

FIGURE 7–3 An electrical resistance heater coil in the air inlet on a General Motors 6.5-liter V-8 diesel engine used to warm the air entering the engine.

DIESEL FUEL (CONTINUED)

primary filter. Some coolant heaters are thermostatically controlled, which allows fuel to bypass the heater once it has reached operating temperature. ● **SEE FIGURE 7–3.**

ULTRA-LOW-SULFUR DIESEL FUEL Diesel fuel is used in diesel engines and is usually readily available throughout the United States, Canada, and Europe, where many more cars are equipped with diesel engines. Diesel engines manufactured to 2007 or newer standards must use ultra-low-sulfur diesel fuel containing less than 15 parts per million (PPM) of sulfur compared to the older, low-sulfur specification of 500 PPM. The purpose of the lower sulfur amount in diesel fuel is to reduce emissions of sulfur oxides (SO_x) and particulate matter (PM) from heavy-duty highway engines and vehicles that use diesel fuel. The emission controls used on 2007 and newer diesel engines require the use of **ultra-low-sulfur diesel (ULSD)** for reliable operation.

Ultra-low-sulfur diesel (ULSD) will eventually replace the current highway diesel fuel, low-sulfur diesel, which can have as much as 500 PPM of sulfur. ULSD is required for use in all model year 2007 and newer vehicles equipped with advanced emission control systems. ULSD looks lighter in color and has less smell than other diesel fuel.

BIODIESEL

DEFINITION OF BIODIESEL **Biodiesel** is a domestically produced, renewable fuel that can be manufactured from vegetable oils, animal fats, or recycled restaurant greases. Biodiesel is safe, biodegradable, and reduces serious air pollutants such as particulate matter (PM), carbon monoxide, and hydrocarbons. Biodiesel is defined as mono-alkyl esters of long-chain fatty acids derived from vegetable oils or animal fats which conform to ASTM D6751 specifications for use in diesel engines. Biodiesel refers to the pure fuel before blending with diesel fuel. ● **SEE FIGURE 7–4.**

BIODIESEL BLENDS Biodiesel blends are denoted as "BXX" with "XX" representing the percentage of biodiesel contained in the blend (i.e., **B20** is 20% biodiesel, 80% petroleum diesel). Blends of 20% biodiesel with 80% petroleum diesel (B20) can generally be used in unmodified diesel engines; however, users should consult their OEM and engine warranty statement. Biodiesel can also be used in its pure form (B100), but it may require certain engine modifications to avoid maintenance and performance problems and may not be suitable for wintertime use. Most diesel engine or vehicle manufacturers of diesel vehicles allow the use of B5 (5% biodiesel). For example, Cummins, used in Dodge trucks, allows the use of B20 only if the optional extra fuel filter has been installed. Users should consult their engine warranty statement for more information on fuel blends of greater than 20% biodiesel.

FIGURE 7–4 A pump decal indicating that the biodiesel fuel is ultra-low-sulfur diesel (ULSD) and must be used in 2007 and newer diesel vehicles.

In general, B20 costs 30 to 40 cents more per gallon than conventional diesel. Although biodiesel costs more than regular diesel fuel, often called **petrodiesel,** fleet managers can make the switch to alternative fuels without purchasing new vehicles, acquiring new spare parts inventories, rebuilding refueling stations, or hiring new service technicians.

FEATURES OF BIODIESEL Biodiesel has the following characteristics:

1. Purchasing biodiesel in bulk quantities decreases the cost of fuel.
2. Biodiesel maintains similar horsepower, torque, and fuel economy.
3. Biodiesel has a higher cetane number than conventional diesel, which increases the engine's performance.
4. It is nontoxic, which makes it safe to handle, transport, and store. Maintenance requirements for B20 vehicles and petrodiesel vehicles are the same.
5. Biodiesel acts as a lubricant and this can add to the life of the fuel system components.

NOTE: For additional information on biodiesel and the locations where it can be purchased, visit www.bio diesel.org.

 FREQUENTLY ASKED QUESTION

I Thought Biodiesel Was Vegetable Oil?

Biodiesel is vegetable oil with the glycerin component removed by means of reacting the vegetable oil with a catalyst. The resulting hydrocarbon esters are 16 to 18 carbon atoms in length, almost identical to the petroleum diesel fuel atoms. This allows the use of biodiesel fuel in a diesel engine with no modifications needed. Biodiesel-powered vehicles do not *need* a second fuel tank, whereas vegetable-oil-powered vehicles do. There are three main types of fuel used in diesel engines. These are:

- Petroleum diesel, a fossil hydrocarbon with a carbon chain length of about 16 carbon atoms.
- Biodiesel, a hydrocarbon with a carbon chain length of 16 to 18 carbon atoms.
- Vegetable oil is a triglyceride with a glycerin component joining three hydrocarbon chains of 16 to 18 carbon atoms each, called straight vegetable oil **(SVO)**. Other terms used when describing vegetable oil include:
  - Pure plant oil **(PPO)**—a term most often used in Europe to describe SVO
  - Waste vegetable oil **(WVO)**—this oil could include animal or fish oils from cooking
  - Used cooking oil **(UCO)**—a term used when the oil may or may not be pure vegetable oil

Vegetable oil is not liquid enough at common ambient temperatures for use in a diesel engine fuel delivery system designed for the lower-viscosity petroleum diesel fuel. Vegetable oil needs to be heated to obtain a similar viscosity to biodiesel and petroleum diesel. This means that a heat source needs to be provided before the fuel can be used in a diesel engine. This is achieved by starting on petroleum diesel or biodiesel fuel until the engine heat can be used to sufficiently warm a tank containing the vegetable oil. It also requires purging the fuel system of vegetable oil with petroleum diesel or biodiesel fuel prior to stopping the engine to avoid the vegetable oil thickening and solidifying in the fuel system away from the heated tank. The use of vegetable oil in its natural state does, however, eliminate the need to remove the glycerin component. Many vehicle and diesel engine fuel system suppliers permit the use of biodiesel fuel that is certified as meeting testing standards. None permit the use of vegetable oil in its natural state.

E-DIESEL FUEL

DEFINITION OF E-DIESEL

E-diesel, also called **diesohol** outside of the United States, is standard No. 2 diesel fuel that contains up to 15% ethanol. While E-diesel can have up to 15% ethanol by volume, typical blend levels are from 8% to 10%.

CETANE RATING OF E-DIESEL

The higher the cetane number, the shorter the delay between injection and ignition. Normal diesel fuel has a cetane number of about 50. Adding 15% ethanol lowers the cetane number. To increase the cetane number back to that of conventional diesel fuel, a cetane-enhancing additive is added to E-diesel. The additive used to increase the cetane rating of E-diesel is ethylhexylnitrate or ditertbutyl peroxide.

E-diesel has better cold-flow properties than conventional diesel. The heat content of E-diesel is about 6% less than conventional diesel, but the particulate matter (PM) emissions are reduced by as much as 40%, 20% less carbon monoxide, and a 5% reduction in oxides of nitrogen (NO_X).

Currently, E-diesel is considered to be experimental and can be used legally in off-road applications or in mass-transit buses with EPA approval. For additional information, visit www.e-diesel.org.

SUMMARY

1. Diesel fuel produces 12% more heat energy than the same amount of gasoline.
2. Diesel fuel requirements include cleanliness, low-temperature fluidity, and proper cetane rating.
3. Emission control devices used on 2007 and newer engines require the use of ultra-low-sulfur diesel (ULSD) that has less than 15 parts per million (PPM) of sulfur.
4. The density of diesel fuel is measured in a unit called API gravity.
5. The cetane rating of diesel fuel is a measure of the ease with which the fuel can be ignited.
6. Biodiesel is the blend of vegetable-based liquid with regular diesel fuel. Most diesel engine manufacturers allow the use of a 5% blend, called B20 without any changes to the fuel system or engine.
7. E-diesel is a blend of ethanol with diesel fuel up to 15% ethanol by volume.

REVIEW QUESTIONS

1. What is meant by the cloud point?
2. What is ultra-low-sulfur diesel?
3. Biodiesel blends are identified by what designation?

CHAPTER QUIZ

1. What color is diesel fuel dyed if it is for off-road use only?
   a. Red
   b. Green
   c. Blue
   d. Yellow
2. What clogs fuel filters when the temperature is low on a vehicle that uses diesel fuel?
   a. Alcohol
   b. Sulfur
   c. Wax
   d. Cetane
3. The specific gravity of diesel fuel is measured in what units?
   a. Hydrometer units
   b. API gravity
   c. Grade number
   d. Cetane number
4. What rating of diesel fuel indicates how well a diesel engine will start?
   a. Specific gravity rating
   b. Sulfur content
   c. Cloud point
   d. Cetane rating
5. Ultra-low-sulfur diesel fuel has how much sulfur content?
   a. 15 PPM
   b. 50 PPM
   c. 500 PPM
   d. 1,500 PPM
6. E-diesel is diesel fuel with what additive?
   a. Methanol
   b. Sulfur
   c. Ethanol
   d. Vegetable oil
7. Biodiesel is regular diesel fuel with vegetable oil added.
   a. True
   b. False
8. B20 biodiesel has how much regular diesel fuel?
   a. 20%
   b. 40%
   c. 80%
   d. 100%
9. Most diesel fuel is what grade?
   a. Grade #1
   b. Grade #2
   c. Grade #3
   d. Grade #4
10. Most manufacturers of vehicles equipped with diesel engines allow what type of biodiesel?
   a. B100
   b. B80
   c. B20
   d. B5

COOLING SYSTEM OPERATION AND DIAGNOSIS

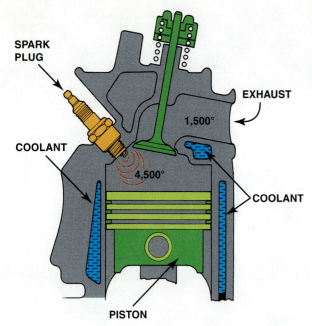

SPARK PLUG

EXHAUST

1,500°

COOLANT

4,500°

COOLANT

PISTON

FIGURE 8–1 Typical combustion and exhaust temperatures.

Satisfactory cooling system operation depends on the design and operating conditions of the system. The design is based on heat output of the engine, radiator size, type of coolant, size of water pump (coolant pump), type of fan, thermostat, and system pressure. Unfortunately, the cooling system is usually neglected until there is a problem. Proper routine maintenance can prevent problems.

COOLING SYSTEM PURPOSE AND FUNCTION

The cooling system must allow the engine to warm up to the required operating temperature as rapidly as possible and then maintain that temperature. It must be able to do this when the outside air temperature is as low as −30°F (−35°C) and as high as 110°F (45°C).

Peak combustion temperatures in the engine cycle run from 4000°F to 6000°F (2200°C to 3300°C). The combustion temperatures will *average* between 1200°F and 1700°F (650°C and 925°C). Continued temperatures as high as this would weaken engine parts, so heat must be removed from the engine. The cooling system keeps the head and cylinder walls at a temperature that is within the range for maximum efficiency. ● **SEE FIGURE 8–1.**

LOW-TEMPERATURE ENGINE PROBLEMS

Engine operating temperatures must be above a minimum temperature for proper engine operation. Gasoline combustion is a rapid oxidation process that releases heat as the hydro-carbon fuel chemically combines with oxygen from the air. *For each gallon of fuel used, moisture equal to a gallon of water is produced*. It is a part of this moisture that condenses and gets into the oil pan, along with unburned fuel and soot, and causes sludge formation. The condensed moisture combines with unburned hydrocarbons and additives to form carbonic acid, sulfuric acid, nitric acid, hydrobromic acid, and hydrochloric acid. These acids are responsible for engine wear by causing corrosion and rust within the engine. Rust occurs rapidly when the coolant temperature is below 130°F (55°C). High cylinder wall wear rates occur whenever the coolant temperature is below 150°F (65°C).

To reduce cold-engine problems and to help start engines in cold climates, most manufacturers offer block heaters as an option. These block heaters are plugged into household current (110 volts AC) and the heating element warms the coolant.

Engine Temperature and Exhaust Emissions

Many areas of the United States and Canada have exhaust emission testing. Hydrocarbon (HC) emissions are simply unburned gasoline. To help reduce HC emissions and be able to pass emission tests, be sure that the engine is at normal operating temperature. Vehicle manufacturers' definition of "normal operating temperature" includes the following:

1. Upper radiator hose is hot and pressurized.
2. Electric cooling fan(s) cycles twice.

Be sure that the engine is operating at normal operating temperature before testing for exhaust emissions. For best results, the vehicle should be driven about *20 miles* (32 kilometers) to be certain that the catalytic converter and engine oil, as well as the coolant, are at normal temperature. This is particularly important in cold weather. Most drivers believe that their vehicle will "warm-up" if allowed to idle until heat starts flowing from the heater. The heat from the heater comes from the coolant. Most manufacturers recommend that idling be limited to a maximum of 5 minutes and that the vehicle should be warmed up by driving slowly after just a minute or two to allow the oil pressure to build.

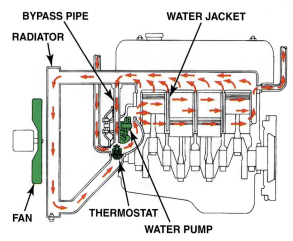

FIGURE 8–2 Coolant flow through a typical engine cooling system.

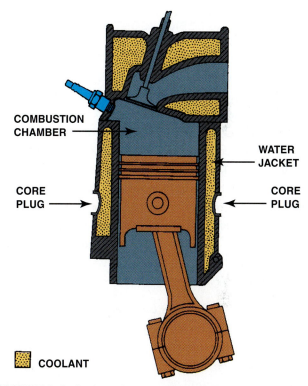

COOLANT

FIGURE 8–3 Coolant circulates through the water jackets in the engine block and cylinder head.

HIGH-TEMPERATURE ENGINE PROBLEMS

Maximum temperature limits are required to protect the engine. High temperatures will oxidize the engine oil. This breaks the oil down, producing hard carbon and varnish. If high temperatures are allowed to continue, the carbon that is produced will plug piston rings. The varnish will cause the hydraulic valve lifter plungers to stick. High temperatures always thin the oil. Metal-to-metal contact within the engine will occur when the oil is too thin. This will cause high friction, loss of power, and rapid wear of the parts. Thinned oil will also get into the combustion chamber by going past the piston rings and through valve guides to cause excessive oil consumption.

High coolant temperatures raise the combustion temperatures to a point that may cause detonation and preignition to occur. These are common forms of abnormal combustion. If they are allowed to continue for any period of time, the engine will be damaged.

COOLING SYSTEM DESIGN

Coolant flows through the engine, where it picks up heat. It then flows to the radiator, where the heat is given up to the outside air. The coolant continually recirculates through the cooling system, as illustrated in ● **FIGURES 8–2 AND 8–3**.

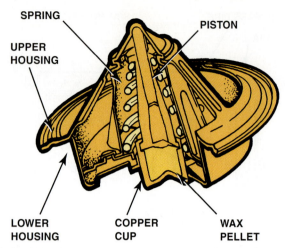

FIGURE 8–4 A cross-section of a typical wax-actuated thermostat showing the position of the wax pellet and spring.

COOLING SYSTEM DESIGN (CONTINUED)

Its temperature rises as much as 15°F (8°C) as it goes through the engine; then it recools as it goes through the radiator. *The coolant flow rate may be as high as 1 gallon (4 liters) per minute for each horsepower the engine produces.*

Hot coolant comes out of the thermostat housing on the top of the engine. The engine coolant outlet is connected to the top of the radiator by the upper hose and clamps. The coolant in the radiator is cooled by air flowing through the radiator. As it cools, it moves from the top to the bottom of the radiator. Cool coolant leaves the lower radiator area through an outlet and lower hose, going into the inlet side of the water pump, where it is recirculated through the engine.

NOTE: Some newer engine designs such as Chrysler's 4.7-L, V-8 and General Motors 4.8-, 5.3-, 5.7-, and 6.0-L V-8s place the thermostat on the inlet side of the water pump. As the cooled coolant hits the thermostat, the thermostat closes until the coolant temperature again causes it to open. Placing the thermostat in the inlet side of the water pump therefore reduces thermal cycling by reducing the rapid temperature changes that could cause stress in the engine, especially if aluminum heads are used with a cast-iron block.

Much of the cooling capacity of the cooling system is based on the functioning of the radiator. Radiators are designed for the maximum rate of heat transfer using minimum space. Cooling airflow through the radiator is aided by a belt- or electric motor-driven cooling fan.

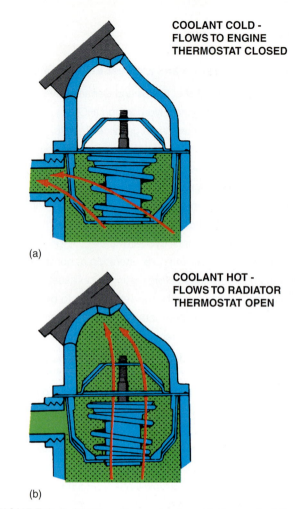

(a)

(b)

FIGURE 8–5 (a) When the engine is cold, the coolant flows through the bypass. (b) When the thermostat opens, the coolant can flow to the radiator.

THERMOSTAT TEMPERATURE CONTROL

There is a normal operating temperature range between low-temperature and high-temperature extremes. The thermostat controls the minimum normal temperature. The **thermostat** is a temperature-controlled valve placed at the engine coolant outlet. An encapsulated, wax-based, plastic-pellet heat sensor is located on the engine side of the thermostatic valve. As the engine warms, heat swells the heat sensor. ● **SEE FIGURE 8–4.**

A mechanical link, connected to the heat sensor, opens the thermostat valve. As the thermostat begins to open, it allows some coolant to flow to the radiator, where it is cooled. The remaining part of the coolant continues to flow through the bypass, thereby bypassing the thermostat and flowing back through the engine. ● **SEE FIGURE 8–5.**

The rated temperature of the thermostat indicates the temperature at which the thermostat starts to open. The

Do Not Take Out the Thermostat!

Some vehicle owners and technicians remove the thermostat in the cooling system to "cure" an overheating problem. In some cases, removing the thermostat can *cause* overheating—not stop overheating. This is true for three reasons:

1. Without a thermostat the coolant can flow more quickly through the radiator. The thermostat adds some restriction to the coolant flow, and therefore keeps the coolant in the radiator longer. The presence of the thermostat thus ensures a greater reduction in the coolant temperature before it returns to the engine.

2. Heat transfer is greater with a greater difference between the coolant temperature and air temperature. Therefore, when coolant flow rate is increased (no thermostat), the temperature difference is reduced.

3. Without the restriction of the thermostat, much of the coolant flow often bypasses the radiator entirely and returns directly to the engine.

If overheating is a problem, removing the thermostat will usually not solve the problem. Remember, the thermostat controls the temperature of the engine coolant by opening at a certain temperature and closing when the temperature falls below the minimum rated temperature of the thermostat. If overheating occurs, two basic problems could be the cause:

1. The engine is producing too much heat for the cooling system to handle. For example, if the engine is running too lean or if the ignition timing is either excessively advanced or excessively retarded, overheating of the engine can result.

2. The cooling system has a malfunction or defect that prevents it from getting rid of its heat.

FIGURE 8–6 A thermostat stuck in the open position caused the engine to operate too cold. The vehicle failed an exhaust emission test because of this defect. If a thermostat is stuck closed, this can cause the engine to overheat.

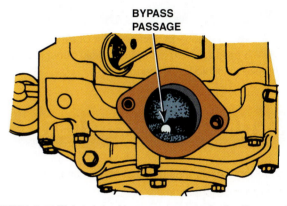

FIGURE 8–7 This Internal bypass passage in the thermostat housing directs cold coolant to the water pump.

If the radiator, water pump, and coolant passages are functioning correctly, the engine should always be operating within the opening and fully open temperature range of the thermostat. ● SEE FIGURE 8–6.

BYPASS A **bypass** around the closed thermostat allows a small part of the coolant to circulate within the engine during warm-up. It is a small passage that leads from the engine side of the thermostat to the inlet side of the water pump. It allows some coolant to bypass the thermostat even when the thermostat is open. The bypass may be cast or drilled into the engine and pump parts. ● SEE FIGURES 8–7 AND 8–8.

The bypass aids in uniform engine warm-up. Its operation eliminates hot spots and prevents the buildup of excessive coolant pressure in the engine when the thermostat is closed.

thermostat is fully open at about 20°F higher than its opening temperature. See the following examples.

Thermostat Temperature Rating	Starts to Open	Fully Open
180°F	180°F	200°F
195°F	195°F	215°F

FIGURE 8–8 A cutaway of a small block Chevrolet V-8 showing the passage from the cylinder head through the front of the intake manifold to the thermostat.

FIGURE 8–9 Setup used to check the opening temperature of a thermostat.

TESTING THE THERMOSTAT

There are three basic methods that can be used to check the operation of the thermostat.

1. **Hot-water method.** If the thermostat is removed from the vehicle and is closed, insert a 0.015-inch (0.4-millimeter) feeler gauge in the opening so that the thermostat will hang on the feeler gauge. The thermostat should then be suspended by the feeler gauge in a bath along with a thermometer. ● **SEE FIGURE 8–9.** The bath should be heated until the thermostat opens enough to release and fall from the feeler gauge. The temperature of the bath when the thermostat falls is the opening temperature of the thermostat. If it is within 5°F (4°C) of the temperature stamped on the thermostat, the thermostat is satisfactory for use. If the temperature difference is greater, the thermostat should be replaced.

2. **Infrared pyrometer method.** An infrared pyrometer can be used to measure the temperature of the coolant near the thermostat. The area on the engine side of the thermostat should be at the highest temperature that exists in the engine. A properly operating cooling system should cause the pyrometer to read as follows:

   a. As the engine warms, the temperature reaches near thermostat-opening temperature.

   b. As the thermostat opens, the temperature drops just as the thermostat opens, sending coolant to the radiator.

   c. As the thermostat cycles, the temperature should range between the opening temperature of the thermostat and 20°F (11°C) above the opening temperature.

   NOTE: If the temperature rises higher than 20°F (11°C) above the opening temperature of the thermostat, inspect the cooling system for a restriction or low coolant flow. A clogged radiator could also cause the excessive temperature rise.

3. **Scan tool method.** A scan tool can be used on many vehicles to read the actual temperature of the coolant as detected by the engine coolant temperature (ECT) sensor. Although the sensor or the wiring to and from the sensor may be defective, at least the scan tool can indicate what the computer "thinks" the engine coolant temperature is.

FIGURE 8–10 Some thermostats are an integral part of the housing. This thermostat and radiator hose housing is serviced as an assembly. Some thermostats simply snap into the engine radiator fill tube underneath the pressure cap.

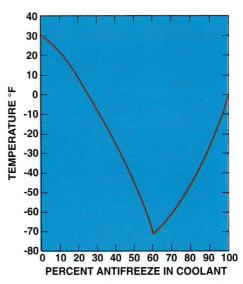

FIGURE 8–11 Graph showing the relationship of the freezing point of the coolant to the percentage of antifreeze used in the coolant.

THERMOSTAT REPLACEMENT

An overheating engine may result from a faulty thermostat. An engine that does not get warm enough always indicates a faulty thermostat.

To replace the thermostat, coolant will have to be drained from the radiator drain petcock to lower the coolant level below the thermostat. It is not necessary to completely drain the system. The upper hose should be removed from the thermostat housing neck; then the housing must be removed to expose the thermostat. ● **SEE FIGURE 8–10**.

The gasket flanges of the engine and thermostat housing should be cleaned, and the gasket surface of the housing must be flat. The thermostat should be placed in the engine with the sensing pellet *toward* the engine. Make sure that the thermostat position is correct, and install the thermostat housing with a new gasket.

CAUTION: Failure to set the thermostat into the recessed groove will cause the housing to become tilted when tightened. If this happens and the housing bolts are tightened, the housing will usually crack, creating a leak.

The upper hose should then be installed and the system refilled. Install the proper size of radiator hose clamp.

ANTIFREEZE/COOLANT

Coolant is a mixture of antifreeze and water. Water is able to absorb more heat per gallon than any other liquid coolant. Under standard conditions, water boils at 212°F (100°C) and freezes at 32°F (0°C). *When water freezes, it increases in volume about 9%.* The expansion of the freezing water can easily crack engine blocks, cylinder heads, and radiators. All manufacturers recommend the use of **ethylene glycol**-based antifreeze mixtures for protection against this problem.

A curve depicting freezing point as compared with the percentage of antifreeze mixture is shown in ● **FIGURE 8–11**.

It should be noted that the freezing point increases as the antifreeze concentration is increased above 60%. The normal mixture is 50% antifreeze and 50% water. Ethylene glycol antifreezes contain anticorrosion additives, rust inhibitors, and water pump lubricants.

At the maximum level of protection, an ethylene glycol concentration of 60% will absorb about 85% as much heat as will water. Ethylene glycol-based antifreeze also has a higher boiling point than water. ● **SEE FIGURE 8–12**.

If the coolant boils, it vaporizes and does not act as a cooling agent because it is not in liquid form and in contact with the cooling surfaces.

All coolants have rust and corrosion inhibitors to help protect the metals in the engine and cooling systems. Most conventional green antifreeze contains inorganic salts such as sodium silicate and phosphates. Organic additive technology (OAT) coolant contains inorganic acid salts (carboxylates)

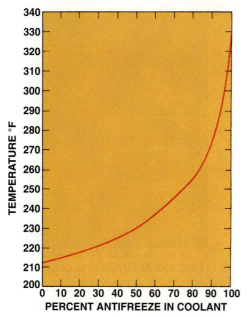

FIGURE 8–12 Graph showing how the boiling point of the coolant increases as the percentage of antifreeze in the coolant increases.

ANTIFREEZE/COOLANT (CONTINUED)

additives that are not abrasive to water pumps. Hybrid organic additive technology (HOAT) coolant contains inorganic acids and some silicate but is phosphate free.

 FREQUENTLY ASKED QUESTION

What Is "Pet Friendly" Coolant?

Similar to ethylene glycol, propylene glycol is a type of coolant that is less harmful to pets and animals because it is not sweet tasting, although it is still harmful if swallowed. This type of coolant should not be mixed with ethylene glycol coolant.

NOTE: Some vehicle manufacturers do not recommend the use of propylene glycol coolant. Check the recommendations in the owner's manual or service manual before using it in a vehicle.

 REAL WORLD FIX

If 50% Is Good, 100% Must Be Better

A vehicle owner said that the cooling system of his vehicle would never freeze or rust. He said that he used 100% antifreeze (ethylene glycol) instead of a 50/50 mixture with water.

However, after the temperature dropped to −20°F (−29°C), the radiator froze and cracked. (Pure antifreeze freezes at about 0°F [−18°C]). After thawing, the radiator had to be repaired. The owner was lucky that the engine block did not also crack.

For best freeze protection with good heat transfer, use a 50/50 mixture of antifreeze and water. A 50/50 mixture of antifreeze and water is the best compromise between temperature protection and the heat transfer that is necessary for cooling system operation. Do not exceed 70% antifreeze (30% water). As the percentage of antifreeze increases, the boiling temperature increases, and freezing protection increases (up to 70% antifreeze), but the heat transfer performance of the mixture decreases.

ANTIFREEZE CAN FREEZE

An antifreeze and water mixture is an example wherein the freezing point differs from the freezing point of either pure antifreeze or pure water.

	Freezing Point
Pure water	32°F (0°C)
Pure antifreeze*	0°F (−18°C)
50/50 mixture	−34°F (−37°C)
70% antifreeze/30% water	−84°F (−64°C)

*Pure antifreeze is usually 95% ethylene glycol, 2% to 3% water, and 2% to 3% additives.

Depending on the exact percentage of water used, antifreeze, as sold in containers, freezes between −8°F and +8°F (−13°C and −22°C). Therefore, it is easiest just to remember that most antifreeze freezes at about 0°F (−18°C).

The boiling point of antifreeze and water is also a factor of mixture concentrations.

	Boiling Point at Sea Level	Boiling Point with 15 PSI Pressure Cap
Pure water	212°F (100°C)	257°F (125°C)
50/50 mixture	218°F (103°C)	265°F (130°C)
70/30 mixture	225°F (107°C)	276°F (136°C)

FIGURE 8–13
Checking the freezing and boiling protection levels of the coolant using a hydrometer.

HYDROMETER TESTING

Coolant can be checked using a coolant hydrometer. The hydrometer measures the density of the coolant. The higher the density, the more concentration of antifreeze in the water. Most coolant hydrometers read the freezing point and boiling point of the coolant. ● **SEE FIGURE 8–13**.

If the engine is overheating and the hydrometer reading is near −50°F (−45.555°C), suspect that pure 100% antifreeze is present. For best results, the coolant should have a freezing point lower than −20°F and a boiling point above 234°F.

RECYCLING COOLANT

Coolant (antifreeze and water) should be recycled. Used coolant may contain heavy metals, such as lead, aluminum, and iron, which are absorbed by the coolant during its use in the engine.

Recycle machines filter out these metals and dirt and reinstall the depleted additives. The recycled coolant, restored to be like new, can be reinstalled into the vehicle.

CAUTION: Most vehicle manufacturers warn that antifreeze coolant should not be reused unless it is recycled and the additives restored.

DISPOSING OF USED COOLANT

Used coolant drained from vehicles can usually be disposed of by combining it with used engine oil. The equipment used for recycling the used engine oil can easily separate the coolant from the waste oil. Check with recycling companies authorized by local or state governments for the exact method recommended for disposal in your area.

RADIATOR DESIGN AND FUNCTION

Two types of radiator cores are in common use in domestic vehicles—the serpentine fin core and the plate fin core. In each of these types the coolant flows through oval-shaped **core tubes**. Heat is transferred through the tube wall and soldered joint to **fins**. The fins are exposed to airflow, which removes heat

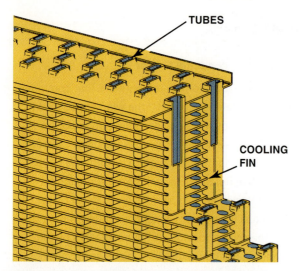

FIGURE 8–14 The tubes and fins of the radiator core.

RADIATOR DESIGN AND FUNCTION (CONTINUED)

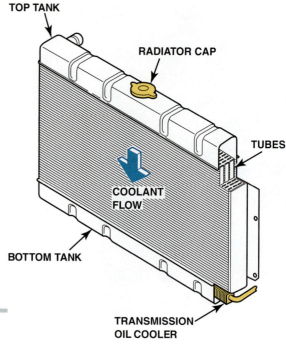

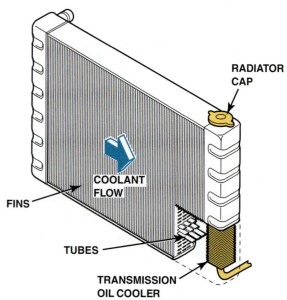

FIGURE 8–15 A radiator may be either a down-flow or a cross-flow type.

from the radiator and carries it away. ● **SEE FIGURES 8–14 THROUGH 8–16**.

Older automobile radiators were made from yellow brass. Since the 1980s, most radiators have been made from aluminum. These materials are corrosion resistant, have good heat-transferring ability, and are easily formed.

Core tubes are made from 0.0045- to 0.012-inch (0.1 to 0.3-millimeter) sheet brass or aluminum, using the thinnest possible materials for each application. The metal is rolled into round tubes and the joints are sealed with a locking seam.

The main limitation of heat transfer in a cooling system is in the transfer from the radiator to the air. Heat transfers from the water to the fins as much as seven times faster than heat transfers from the fins to the air, assuming equal surface exposure. The radiator must be capable of removing an amount of heat energy approximately equal to the heat energy of the power produced by the engine. *Each horsepower is equivalent to 42 BTU (10,800 calories) per minute.* As the engine power is increased, the heat-removing requirement of the cooling system is also increased.

With a given frontal area, radiator capacity may be increased by increasing the core thickness, packing more material into the same volume, or both. The radiator capacity may also be increased by placing a shroud around the fan so that more air will be pulled through the radiator.

NOTE: The lower air dam in the front of the vehicle is used to help direct the air through the radiator. If this air dam is broken or missing, the engine may overheat, especially during highway driving due to the reduced airflow through the radiator.

Radiator headers and tanks that close off the ends of the core were made of sheet brass 0.020 to 0.050 inch (0.5 to 1.25 millimeters) thick and now are made of molded plastic. When a transmission oil cooler is used in the radiator, it is placed in the outlet tank, where the coolant has the lowest temperature. ● **SEE FIGURE 8–17**.

FIGURE 8–16 Cutaway of a typical radiator showing restriction of tubes. Changing antifreeze frequently helps prevent this type of problem.

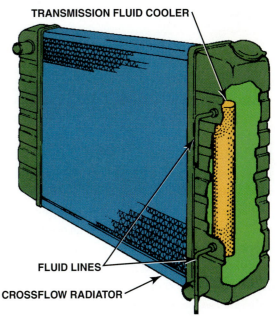

FIGURE 8–17 Many vehicles equipped with an automatic transmission use a transmission fluid cooler installed in one of the radiator tanks.

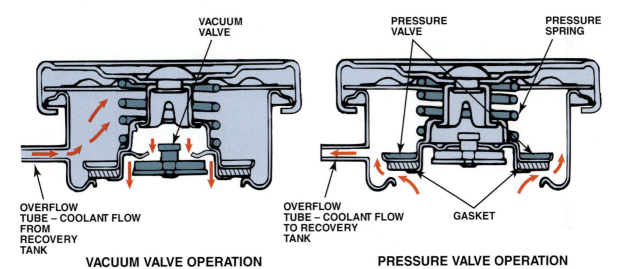

VACUUM VALVE OPERATION PRESSURE VALVE OPERATION

FIGURE 8–18 The pressure valve maintains the system pressure and allows excess pressure to vent. The vacuum valve allows coolant to return to the system from the recovery tank.

PRESSURE CAP

The filler neck is fitted with a pressure cap. The cap has a spring-loaded valve that closes the cooling system vent. This causes cooling pressure to build up to the pressure setting of the cap. At this point, the valve will release the excess pressure to prevent system damage. ● SEE FIGURE 8–18.

Engine cooling systems are pressurized to raise the boiling temperature of the coolant. *The boiling temperature will increase by approximately 3°F (1.6°C) for each pound of increase in pressure.* At standard atmospheric pressure, water will boil at 212°F (100°C). With a 15 PSI (100 kPa) pressure cap, water will boil at 257°F (125°C), which is a maximum operating temperature for an engine.

The high coolant system temperature serves two functions:

1. It allows the engine to run at an efficient temperature, close to 200°F (93°C), with no danger of boiling the coolant.

TECH TIP

Working Better Under Pressure

A problem that sometimes occurs with a high-pressure cooling system involves the water pump. For the pump to function, the inlet side of the pump must have a lower pressure than its outlet side. If inlet pressure is lowered too much, the coolant at the pump inlet can boil, producing vapor. The pump will then spin the coolant vapors and not pump coolant. This condition is called pump **cavitation.** Therefore, a radiator cap could be the cause of an overheating problem. A pump will not pump enough coolant if not kept under the proper pressure for preventing vaporization of the coolant.

PRESSURE CAP (CONTINUED)

2. The higher the coolant temperature, the more heat the cooling system can transfer. The heat transferred by the cooling system is proportional to the temperature difference between the coolant and the outside air. This characteristic has led to the design of small, high-pressure radiators that are capable of handling large quantities of heat. For proper cooling, the system must have the right pressure cap correctly installed.

NOTE: The proper operation of the pressure cap is especially important at high altitudes. The boiling point of water is lowered by about 1°F for every 550-foot increase in altitude. Therefore in Denver, Colorado (altitude 5,280 feet), the boiling point of water is about 202°F, and at the top of Pike's Peak in Colorado (14,110 feet) water boils at 186°F.

SURGE TANK

Some vehicles use a **surge tank**, which is located at the highest level of the cooling system and holds about 1 quart (1 liter) of coolant. A hose attaches to the bottom of the surge tank to the inlet side of the water pump. A smaller bleed hose attaches to the side of the surge tank to the highest point of the radiator. The bleed line allows some coolant circulation through the surge tank, and air in the system will rise below the radiator cap and be forced from the system if the pressure in the system exceeds the rating of the radiator cap. ● SEE FIGURE 8–19.

FIGURE 8–19 Some vehicles use a surge tank, which is located at the highest level of the cooling system, with a radiator cap.

METRIC RADIATOR CAPS

According to the *SAE Handbook*, all radiator caps must indicate their nominal (normal) pressure rating. Most original equipment radiator caps are rated at about 14 to 16 PSI (97 to 110 kPa).

However, many vehicles manufactured in Japan or Europe have the radiator pressure indicated in a unit called a **bar**. One bar is the pressure of the atmosphere at sea level, or about 14.7 PSI. The following conversion can be used when replacing a radiator cap to make certain it matches the pressure rating of the original.

Bar or Atmospheres	Pounds per Square Inch (PSI)
1.1	16
1.0	15
0.9	13
0.8	12
0.7	10
0.6	9
0.5	7

NOTE: Many radiator repair shops use a 7-PSI (0.5-bar) radiator cap on a repaired radiator. A 7-PSI cap can still provide boil protection of 21°F (3°F ×7 PSI = 21°F) above the boiling point of the coolant. For example, if the boiling point of the antifreeze coolant is 223°F, 21°F is added for the pressure cap, and boil over will not occur until about 244°F (223°F + 21°F = 244°F). Even though this lower-pressure radiator cap does provide some protection and will also help protect the radiator repair, the coolant can still boil *before* the "hot" dash warning light comes on and therefore, should not be used.

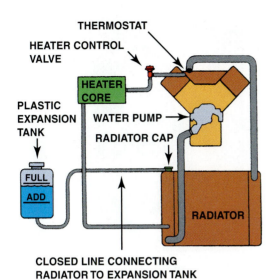

FIGURE 8–20 The level in the coolant recovery system raises and lowers with engine temperature.

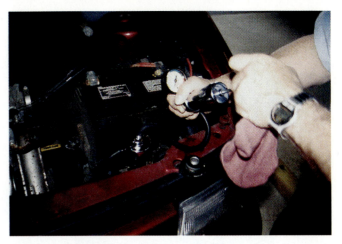

FIGURE 8–21 Pressure testing the cooling system. A typical hand-operated pressure tester applies pressure equal to the radiator cap pressure. The pressure should hold; if it drops, this indicates a leak somewhere in the cooling system. An adapter is used to attach the pump to the cap to determine if the radiator can hold pressure, and release it when pressure rises above its maximum rated pressure setting.

COOLANT RECOVERY SYSTEM

Excess pressure usually forces some coolant from the system through an overflow. Most cooling systems connect the overflow to a plastic reservoir to hold excess coolant while the system is hot. ● SEE FIGURE 8–20.

When the system cools, the pressure in the cooling system is reduced and a partial vacuum forms. This pulls the coolant from the plastic container back into the cooling system, keeping the system full. Because of this action, this system is called a **coolant recovery system**. The filler cap used on a coolant system without a coolant saver is fitted with a vacuum valve. This valve allows air to reenter the system as the system cools so that the radiator parts will not collapse under the partial vacuum.

TESTING THE COOLING SYSTEM

PRESSURE TESTING Pressure testing using a hand-operated pressure tester is a quick and easy cooling system test. The radiator cap is removed (engine cold!) and the tester is attached in the place of the radiator cap. By operating the plunger on the pump, the entire cooling system is pressurized. ● SEE FIGURE 8–21.

CAUTION: Do not pump up the pressure beyond that specified by the vehicle manufacturer. Most systems should not be pressurized beyond 14 PSI (100 kPa). If a greater pressure is used, it may cause the water pump, radiator, heater core, or hoses to fail.

If the cooling system is free from leaks, the pressure should stay and not drop. If the pressure drops, look for evidence of leaks anywhere in the cooling system including:

1. Heater hoses
2. Radiator hoses
3. Radiator
4. Heat core
5. Cylinder head
6. Core plugs in the side of the block or cylinder head

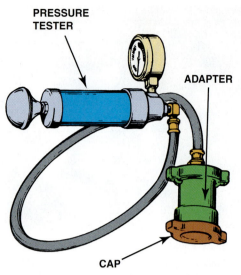

FIGURE 8–22 The pressure cap should be checked for proper operation using a pressure tester as part of the cooling system diagnosis.

FIGURE 8–23 Use dye specifically made for coolant when checking for leaks using a black light.

 TECH TIP

Use Distilled Water in the Cooling System

Two technicians are discussing refilling the radiator after changing antifreeze. One technician says that distilled water is best to use because it does not contain minerals that can coat the passages of the cooling system. The other technician says that any water that is suitable to drink can be used in a cooling system. Both technicians are correct. If water contains minerals, however, it can leave deposits in the cooling system that could prevent proper heat transfer. Because the mineral content of most water is unknown, distilled water, which has no minerals, is better to use. Although the cost of distilled water must be considered, the amount of water required (usually about 2 gallons [8 liters] or less of water) makes the expense minor in comparison with the cost of radiator or cooling system failure.

TESTING THE COOLING SYSTEM (CONTINUED)

Pressure testing should be performed whenever there is a leak or suspected leak. The pressure tester can also be used to test the radiator cap. An adapter is used to connect the pressure tester to the radiator cap. Replace any cap that will not hold pressure. ● SEE FIGURE 8–22.

COOLANT DYE LEAK TESTING One of the best methods to check for a coolant leak is to use a fluorescent dye in the coolant. Use a dye designed for coolant. Operate the vehicle with the dye in the coolant until the engine reaches normal operating temperature. Use a black light to inspect all areas of the cooling system. When there is a leak, it will be easy to spot because the dye in the coolant will be seen as bright green. ● SEE FIGURE 8–23.

FIGURE 8–24 Coolant flow through the impeller and scroll of a coolant pump for a V-type engine.

FIGURE 8–25 A demonstration engine showing the amount of water that can be circulated through the cooling system.

WATER PUMP

OPERATION The water pump (also called a coolant pump) is driven by a belt from the crankshaft or driven by the camshaft. Coolant recirculates from the radiator to the engine and back to the radiator. Low-temperature coolant leaves the radiator by the bottom outlet. It is pumped into the warm engine block, where it picks up some heat. From the block, the warm coolant flows to the hot cylinder head, where it picks up more heat.

NOTE: Some engines use reverse cooling. This means that the coolant flows from the radiator to the cylinder head(s) before flowing to the engine block.

Water pumps are not positive displacement pumps. The water pump is a **centrifugal pump** that can move a large volume of coolant without increasing the pressure of the coolant. The pump pulls coolant in at the center of the **impeller**. Centrifugal force throws the coolant outward so that it is discharged at the impeller tips. This can be seen in ● **FIGURE 8–24**.

As engine speeds increase, more heat is produced by the engine and more cooling capacity is required. The pump impeller speed increases as the engine speed increases to provide extra coolant flow at the very time it is needed.

Coolant leaving the pump impeller is fed through a **scroll**. The scroll is a smoothly curved passage that changes the fluid flow direction with minimum loss in velocity. The scroll is connected to the front of the engine so as to direct the coolant into the engine block. On V-type engines, two outlets are usually used, one for each cylinder bank. Occasionally, diverters are necessary in the water pump scroll to equalize coolant flow

between the cylinder banks of a V-type engine to equalize the cooling.

SERVICE A worn impeller on a water pump can reduce the amount of coolant flow through the engine. ● **SEE FIGURE 8–26**. If the seal of the water pump fails, coolant will leak out of the hole as seen in ● **FIGURE 8–27**. The hole allows coolant to escape without getting trapped and forced into the water pump bearing assembly.

If the bearing is defective, the pump will usually be noisy and will have to be replaced. Before replacing a water pump

? FREQUENTLY ASKED QUESTION

How Much Coolant Can a Water Pump Pump?

A typical water pump can move a maximum of about 7,500 gallons (28,000 liters) of coolant per hour, or recirculate the coolant in the engine over 20 times per minute. This means that a water pump could be used to empty a typical private swimming pool in an hour! The slower the engine speed, the less power is consumed by the water pump. However, even at 35 miles per hour (56 kilometers per hour), the typical water pump still moves about 2,000 gallons (7,500 liters) per hour or 1/2 gallon (2 liters) per second! ● **SEE FIGURE 8–25**.

FIGURE 8–26 This severely corroded water pump could not circulate enough coolant to keep the engine cool. As a result, the engine overheated and blew a head gasket.

BLEED WEEP HOLE

FIGURE 8–27 The bleed weep hole in the water pump allows coolant to leak out of the pump and not be forced into the bearing. If the bearing failed, more serious damage could result.

WATER PUMP (CONTINUED)

that has failed because of a loose or noisy bearing, be sure to do all of the following:

1. Check belt tension
2. Check for bent fan
3. Check fan for balance

If the water pump drive belt is too tight, excessive force may be exerted against the pump bearing. If the cooling fan is bent or out of balance, the resulting vibration can damage the water pump bearing. ● **SEE FIGURE 8–28.**

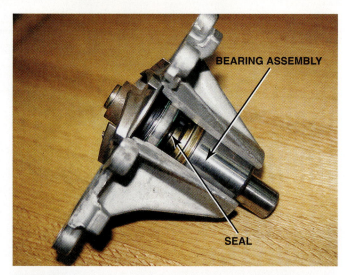

BEARING ASSEMBLY

SEAL

FIGURE 8–28 A cutaway of a typical water pump showing the long bearing assembly and the seal. The weep hole is located between the seal and the bearing. If the seal fails, then coolant flows out of the weep hole to prevent the coolant from damaging the bearing.

COOLING FANS

Air is forced across the radiator core by a cooling fan. On older engines used in rear-wheel-drive vehicles, it is attached to a fan hub that is pressed on the water pump shaft. ● **SEE FIGURE 8–29.**

Many installations with rear-wheel drive and all transverse-engines drive the fan with an electric motor. ● **SEE FIGURE 8–30.**

NOTE: Most electric cooling fans are computer controlled. To save energy, most cooling fans are turned off whenever the vehicle is traveling faster than 35 mph (55 km/h). The ram air from the vehicle's traveling at that speed should be enough to keep the radiator cool. Of course, if the computer senses that the temperature is still too high, the computer will turn on the cooling fan, to "high," if possible, in an attempt to cool the engine to avoid severe engine damage.

The fan is designed to move enough air at the lowest fan speed to cool the engine when it is at its highest coolant temperature. The fan shroud is used to increase the cooling system efficiency. The horsepower required to drive the fan increases at a much faster rate than the increase in fan speed. Higher fan speeds also increase fan noise. Fans with flexible plastic or flexible steel blades have been used. These fans have high blade angles that pull a high volume of air when turning at low speeds. As the fan speed increases, the fan blade angle flattens, reducing the horsepower required to rotate the blade at high speeds. ● **SEE FIGURE 8–31.**

FIGURE 8–29 A typical engine-driven cooling fan.

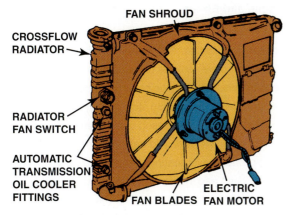

FAN SHROUD

CROSSFLOW RADIATOR

RADIATOR FAN SWITCH

AUTOMATIC TRANSMISSION OIL COOLER FITTINGS

FAN BLADES

ELECTRIC FAN MOTOR

FIGURE 8–30 A typical electric cooling fan assembly showing the radiator and related components.

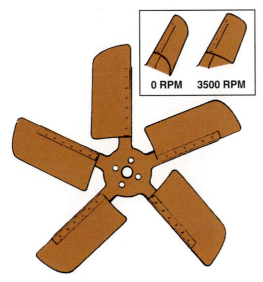

0 RPM   3500 RPM

FIGURE 8–31 Flexible cooling fan blades change shape as the engine speed changes.

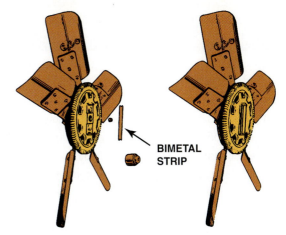

BIMETAL STRIP

FIGURE 8–32 The bimetallic temperature sensor spring controls the amount of silicone that is allowed into the drive unit, which controls the speed of the fan.

THERMOSTATIC FANS

Since the early 1980s, most cooling fans have been computer-controlled electric motor units. On some rear-wheel-drive vehicles, a thermostatic cooling fan is driven by a belt from the crankshaft. It turns faster as the engine turns faster. Generally, the engine is required to produce more power at higher speeds. Therefore, the cooling system will also transfer more heat. Increased fan speed aids in the required cooling. Engine heat also becomes critical at low engine speeds in traffic where the vehicle moves slowly.

The thermal fan is designed so that it uses little power at high engine speeds and minimizes noise. The thermal fan has a **silicone coupling** fan drive mounted between the drive pulley and the fan.

NOTE: Whenever diagnosing an overheating problem, look carefully at the cooling fan. If silicone is leaking, then the fan may not be able to function correctly and should be replaced.

A second type of thermal fan has a **thermostatic spring** added to the silicone coupling fan drive. The thermostatic spring operates a valve that allows the fan to freewheel when the radiator is cold. As the radiator warms to about 150°F (65°C), the air hitting the thermostatic spring will cause the spring to change its shape. The new shape of the spring opens a valve that allows the drive to operate like the silicone coupling drive. When the engine is very cold, the fan may operate at high speeds for a short time until the drive fluid warms slightly. The silicone fluid will then flow into a reservoir to let the fan speed drop to idle. ● **SEE FIGURE 8–32.**

ELECTRIC COOLING FANS

Air is forced across the radiator core by a cooling fan. On older engines used in rear-wheel-drive vehicles, it is attached to a fan hub that is pressed on the water pump shaft. Many installations with rear-wheel drive and all transverse engines drive the fan with an electric motor. ● **SEE FIGURE 8–33**.

A typical engine cooling fan system consists of one cooling fan and two relays or two separate fans. If only one fan is used, the cooling fan has two windings in the motor. One winding is for low speed and the other winding is for high speed. When the cooling fan 1 relay is energized, voltage is sent to the cooling fan low-speed winding. The ECM controls the high-speed fan operation by grounding the cool fan 2 relay control circuit. When the cooling fan 2 relay is energized, voltage is sent to the cooling fan high-speed winding. The cooling fan motor has its own ground circuit.

The ECM commands Low Speed Fans ON under the following conditions:

- Engine coolant temperature (ECT) exceeds approximately 223°F (106°C).
- A/C refrigerant pressure exceeds 190 PSI (1,310 kPa).

After the vehicle is shut off, if the ECT at key-off is greater than 284°F (140°C) and system voltage is more than 12 volts, the fans will stay on for approximately 3 minutes.

The ECM commands High Speed Fans ON under the following conditions:

- ECT reaches 230°F (110°C).
- A/C refrigerant pressure exceeds 240 PSI (1,655 kPa).
- When certain diagnostic trouble codes (DTCs) set.

To prevent a fan from cycling ON and OFF excessively at idle, the fan may not turn OFF until the ignition switch is moved to the OFF position or the vehicle speed exceeds approximately 10 mph.

NOTE: To save energy and to improve fuel economy, most cooling fans are turned off whenever the vehicle is traveling faster than 35 mph (55 km/h). The ram air from the vehicle's traveling at that speed should be enough to keep the radiator cool. Of course, if the computer senses that the temperature is still too high, the computer will turn on the cooling fan, to "high," if possible, in an attempt to cool the engine to avoid severe engine damage. Some engines, such as the General Motors NorthStar engine, can disable four of the eight cylinders from firing to air cool the engine in the event of a severe overheating condition.

FIGURE 8–33 A typical electric cooling fan assembly after being removed from the vehicle.

 **TECH TIP**

Cause and Effect

A common cause of overheating is an inoperative cooling fan. Most front-wheel-drive vehicles and many rear-wheel-drive vehicles use electric motor-driven cooling fans. A fault in the cooling fan circuit often causes overheating during slow city-type driving.

Even slight overheating can soften or destroy rubber vacuum hoses and gaskets. The gaskets most prone to overheating damage are rocker cover (valve cover) and intake manifold gaskets. Gasket and/or vacuum hose failure often results in an air (vacuum) leak that leans the air–fuel mixture. The resulting lean mixture burns hotter in the cylinders and contributes to the overheating problem.

The vehicle computer can often compensate for a minor air leak (vacuum leak), but more severe leaks can lead to driveability problems; especially idle quality problems. If the leak is severe enough, a lean diagnostic trouble code (DTC) may be present. If a lean code is not set, the vehicle's computer may indicate a defective or out-of-range MAP sensor code in diagnostics.

Therefore, a typical severe engine problem can often be traced back to a simple, easily repaired, cooling system-related problem.

COOLANT TEMPERATURE WARNING LIGHT

Most vehicles are equipped with a heat sensor for the engine operating temperature. If the "hot" light comes on during driving (or the temperature gauge goes into the red danger zone), then the coolant temperature is about 250°F to 258°F (120°C to 126°C), which is still *below* the boiling point of the coolant (assuming a properly operating pressure cap and system). If this happens, follow these steps:

STEP 1 Shut off the air conditioning and turn on the heater. The heater will help rid the engine of extra heat. Set the blower speed to high.

STEP 2 If possible, shut the engine off and let it cool. (This may take over an hour.)

STEP 3 Never remove the radiator cap when the engine is hot.

STEP 4 Do *not* continue to drive with the hot light on, or serious damage to your engine could result.

STEP 5 If the engine does not feel or smell hot, it is possible that the problem is a faulty hot light sensor or gauge. Continue to drive, but to be safe, stop occasionally and check for any evidence of overheating or coolant loss.

COMMON CAUSES OF OVERHEATING

Overheating can be caused by defects in the cooling system. Some common causes of overheating include:

1. Low coolant level
2. Plugged, dirty, or blocked radiator
3. Defective fan clutch or electric fan
4. Incorrect ignition timing
5. Low engine oil level
6. Broken fan belt
7. Defective radiator cap
8. Dragging brakes
9. Frozen coolant (in freezing weather)
10. Defective thermostat
11. Defective water pump (the impeller slipping on the shaft internally)

FIGURE 8–34 When an engine overheats, often the coolant overflow container boils.

 REAL WORLD FIX

Highway Overheating

A vehicle owner complained of an overheating vehicle, but the problem occurred only while driving at highway speeds. The vehicle, ● **SEE FIGURE 8–34**, would run in a perfectly normal manner in city-driving situations.

The technician flushed the cooling system and replaced the radiator cap and the water pump, thinking that restricted coolant flow was the cause of the problem. Further testing revealed coolant spray out of one cylinder when the engine was turned over by the starter with the spark plugs removed.

A new head gasket solved the problem. Obviously, the head gasket leak was not great enough to cause any problems until the engine speed and load created enough flow and heat to cause the coolant temperature to soar.

The technician also replaced the oxygen (O_2) sensor, because some coolant contains phosphates and silicates that often contaminate the sensor. The deteriorated oxygen sensor could have contributed to the problem.

COOLING SYSTEM MAINTENANCE

The cooling system is one of the most maintenance-free systems in the engine. Normal maintenance involves an occasional check on the coolant level. It should also include a visual inspection for signs of coolant system leaks and for the condition of the coolant hoses and fan drive belts.

CAUTION: The coolant level should only be checked when the engine is cool. Removing the pressure cap from a hot engine will release the cooling system pressure while the coolant temperature is above its atmospheric boiling temperature. When the cap is removed, the pressure will instantly drop to atmospheric pressure level, causing the coolant to boil immediately. Vapors from the boiling liquid will blow coolant from the system. Coolant will be lost, and someone may be injured or burned by the high-temperature coolant that is blown out of the filler opening.

The coolant-antifreeze mixture is renewed at periodic intervals. Some vehicle manufacturers recommend that coolant system stop-leak pellets be installed whenever the coolant is changed.

CAUTION: General Motors recommends the use of these stop-leak pellets in only certain engines. Using these pellets in some engines could cause a restriction in the cooling system and an overheating condition.

Drive belt condition and proper installation are important for the proper operation of the cooling system.

(a)

(b)

FIGURE 8–35 (a) Chrysler recommends that the bleeder valve be opened whenever refilling the cooling system. (b) Chrysler also recommends that a clear plastic hose (1/4" ID) be attached to the bleeder valve and directed into a suitable container to keep from spilling coolant onto the ground and on the engine and to allow the technician to observe the flow of coolant for any remaining oil bubbles.

FLUSH AND REFILL

Manufacturers recommend that a cooling system be flushed and that the antifreeze be replaced at specified intervals. Draining coolant when the engine is cool eliminates the danger of being injured by hot coolant. The radiator is drained by opening a petcock in the bottom tank, and the coolant in the block is drained into a suitable container by opening plugs located in the lower part of the cooling passage.

Water should be run into the filler opening while the drains remain open. Flushing should be continued until only clear water comes from the system.

The volume of the cooling system must be determined. It is specified in the owner's manual and in the engine service manual. The antifreeze quantity needed for the protection desired is shown on a chart that comes with the antifreeze. Open the bleeder valves and add the correct amount of the specified type of antifreeze followed by enough water to completely fill the system. ● **SEE FIGURE 8–35.** The coolant recovery reservoir should be filled to the "level-cold" mark with the correct antifreeze mixture.

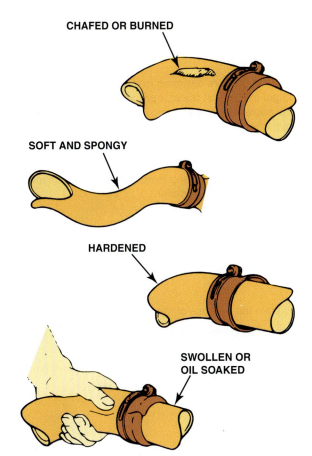

CHAFED OR BURNED

SOFT AND SPONGY

HARDENED

SWOLLEN OR OIL SOAKED

FIGURE 8–36 All cooling system hoses should be checked for wear or damage.

HOSES

Coolant system hoses are critical to engine cooling. As the hoses get old, they become either soft or brittle and sometimes swell in diameter. Their condition depends on their material and on the engine service conditions. If a hose breaks while the engine is running, all coolant will be lost. A hose should be replaced anytime it appears to be abnormal. ● **SEE FIGURE 8–36**.

NOTE: To make hose removal easier and to avoid possible damage to the radiator, use a utility knife and slit the hose lengthwise. Then simply peel the hose off.

Care should be taken to avoid bending the soft metal hose neck on the radiator. The hose neck should be cleaned before a new hose is slipped in place. The clamp is placed on the hose; then the hose is pushed fully over the neck. The hose should be cut so that the clamp is close to the bead on the neck. This is especially important on aluminum hose necks to avoid corrosion. When the hoses are in place and the drain petcock is closed, the cooling system can be refilled with the correct coolant mixture.

CLEANING THE RADIATOR EXTERIOR

Overheating can result from exterior radiator plugging as well as internal plugging. External plugging is caused by dirt and insects. This type of plugging can be seen if you look straight through the radiator while a light is held behind it. It is most likely to occur on off-road vehicles. The plugged exterior of the radiator core can usually be cleaned with water pressure from a hose. The water is aimed at the *engine side* of the radiator. The water should flow freely through the core at all locations. If this does not clean the core, the radiator should be removed for cleaning at a radiator shop.

BURPING THE SYSTEM

In most systems, small air pockets can occur. The engine must be thoroughly warmed to open the thermostat. This allows full coolant flow to remove the air pockets. The heater must also be turned to full heat.

NOTE: The cooling system will not function correctly if air is not released (burped) from the system after a refill. An easy method involves replacing the radiator cap after the refill, but only to the first locked position. Drive the vehicle for several minutes and check the radiator level. Without the radiator cap tightly sealed, no pressure will build in the cooling system. Driving the vehicle helps circulate the coolant enough to force all air pockets up and out of the radiator filler. Top off the radiator after burping and replace the radiator cap to the fully locked position. Failure to burp the cooling system to remove all the air will often result in lack of heat from the heater and may result in engine overheating.

TECH TIP

Quick and Easy Cooling System Problem Diagnosis

If overheating occurs in slow, stop-and-go traffic, the usual cause is low airflow through the radiator. Check for airflow blockages or cooling fan malfunction. If overheating occurs at highway speeds, the cause is usually a radiator or coolant circulation problem. Check for a restricted or clogged radiator.

SUMMARY

1. The purpose and function of the cooling system is to maintain proper engine operating temperature.
2. The thermostat controls engine coolant temperature by opening at its rated opening temperature to allow coolant to flow through the radiator.
3. Most antifreeze coolant is ethylene glycol-based.
4. Used coolant should be recycled whenever possible.
5. Coolant fans are designed to draw air through the radiator to aid in the heat transfer process, drawing the heat from the coolant and transferring it to the outside air through the radiator.
6. The cooling system should be tested for leaks using a hand-operated pressure pump.
7. The freezing and boiling temperature of the coolant can be tested using a hydrometer.

REVIEW QUESTIONS

1. Explain why the normal operating coolant temperature is about 200°F to 220°F (93°C to 104°C).
2. Explain why a 50/50 mixture of antifreeze and water is commonly used as a coolant.
3. Explain the flow of coolant through the engine and radiator.
4. Why is a cooling system pressurized?
5. Describe the ways to test a thermostat.
6. Explain the purpose of the coolant system bypass.
7. Describe how to perform a drain, flush, and refill procedure on a cooling system.
8. Explain the operation of a thermostatic cooling fan.
9. List five common causes of overheating.

CHAPTER QUIZ

1. Permanent antifreeze is mostly _____.
   a. Methanol
   b. Glycerin
   c. Kerosene
   d. Ethylene glycol
2. As the percentage of antifreeze in the coolant increases, _____.
   a. The freeze point decreases (up to a point)
   b. The boiling point decreases
   c. The heat transfer increases
   d. All of the above occurs
3. A stuck open thermostat can cause _____.
   a. Lower fuel economy
   b. Increased exhaust emissions
   c. Failure of a State emission test
   d. All of the above
4. A water pump is a positive displacement-type pump.
   a. True
   b. False
5. The weep hole on a water pump is located where?
   a. Between the impeller and the seal
   b. Between the seal and the bearing
   c. Between the bearing and the engine
   d. Any of the above depending on engine.
6. Technician A says that a bleeder valve is located on many engines to allow air to escape when refilling the cooling system. Technician B says that a hose should be attached to the bleeder valve to allow any escaping coolant to be directed to a suitable container. Which technician is correct?
   a. Technician A only
   b. Technician B only
   c. Both Technicians A and B
   d. Neither Technician A nor B
7. Which statement is *true* about thermostats?
   a. The temperature marked on the thermostat is the temperature at which the thermostat should be fully open.
   b. Thermostats often cause overheating.
   c. The temperature marked on the thermostat is the temperature at which the thermostat should start to open.
   d. Both a and b.
8. Used coolant should be _____.
   a. Reused
   b. Recycled
   c. Disposed of properly
   d. Either b or c

9. An engine fails to reach normal operating temperature. Which is the most likely fault?
   a. Defective thermostat
   b. Low coolant level
   c. Wrong antifreeze coolant
   d. Partially clogged radiator

10. The normal operating temperature (coolant temperature) of an engine equipped with a 195°F thermostat is _____.
   a. 175°F to 195°F
   b. 185°F to 205°F
   c. 195°F to 215°F
   d. 175°F to 215°F

chapter 9
LUBRICATION SYSTEM OPERATION AND DIAGNOSIS

OBJECTIVES

After studying Chapter 9, the reader will be able to:

1. Prepare for Engine Repair (A1) ASE certification test content area "D" (Lubrication and Cooling Systems Diagnosis and Repair).

2. Explain engine oil ratings.

3. Describe how an oil pump and engine lubrication work.

4. Discuss how and when to change the oil and filter.

5. Explain how to inspect an oil pump for wear.

KEY TERMS

boundary lubrication 153
hydrodynamic lubrication 153
longitudinal header 158
oil gallery 158
positive displacement pump 154
pressure regulating valve 155
viscosity 153
windage tray 160

Engine oil is the lifeblood of any engine. The purposes of engine oil include the following:

1. *Lubricating* all moving parts to prevent wear

2. Helping to *cool* the engine

3. Helping to *seal* piston rings

4. *Cleaning*, and holding dirt in suspension in the oil until it can be drained from the engine

5. *Neutralizing* acids that are formed as the result of the combustion process

6. *Reducing* friction

7. *Preventing* rust and corrosion

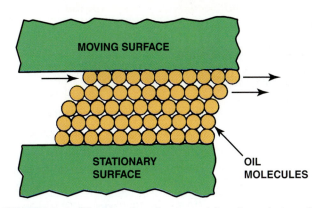

FIGURE 9–1 Oil molecules cling to metal surfaces but easily slide against each other.

LUBRICATION PRINCIPLES

Lubrication between two moving surfaces results from an oil film that separates the surfaces and supports the load. ● **SEE FIGURE 9–1**.

Although oil does not compress, it does leak out around the oil clearance between the shaft and the bearing. In some cases, the oil film is thick enough to keep the surfaces from seizing, but can allow some contact to occur. This condition is called **boundary lubrication**. The specified oil viscosity and oil clearances must be adhered to during service to help prevent boundary lubrication and wear from occurring, which usually happens when the engine is under a heavy load and low speeds. The movement of the shaft helps prevent contact with the bearing. If oil were put on a flat surface and a heavy block were pushed across the surface, the block would slide more easily than if it were pushed across a dry surface. The reason for this is that a wedge-shaped oil film is built up between the moving block and the surface, as illustrated in ● **SEE FIGURE 9–2**. This wedging action is called **hydrodynamic lubrication.** The wedging action depends on the force applied, the speed of difference between objects, and the thickness of the oil. Thickness of oil is called the **viscosity** and is defined as the ability of the oil to resist flow. High-viscosity oil is thick and low-viscosity oil is thin. The prefix *hydro-* refers to liquids, as in hydraulics, and *dynamic* refers to moving materials. Hydrodynamic lubrication occurs when a wedge-shaped film of lubricating oil develops between two surfaces that have relative motion between them. ● **SEE FIGURE 9–3**.

The engine oil pressure system feeds a continuous supply of oil into the lightly loaded part of the bearing oil clearance. Hydrodynamic lubrication takes over as the shaft rotates in the

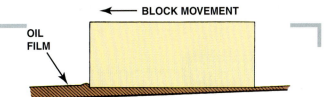

FIGURE 9–2 Wedge-shaped oil film developed below a moving block.

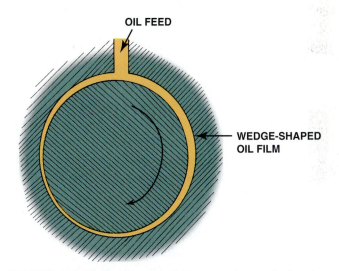

FIGURE 9–3 Wedge-shaped oil film curved around a bearing journal.

bearing to produce a wedge-shaped hydrodynamic oil film that is curved around the bearing. This film supports the bearing and reduces the turning effort to a minimum when oil of the correct viscosity is used.

Most bearing wear occurs during the initial start-up. Wear continues until a hydrodynamic film is established.

ENGINE LUBRICATION SYSTEMS

The primary function of the engine lubrication system is to maintain a positive and continuous oil supply to the bearings. Engine oil pressure must be high enough to get the oil to the bearings with enough force to cause the oil flow that is required for proper cooling. The normal engine oil pressure range is from 10 to 60 PSI (200 to 400 kPa) (10 PSI per 1000 engine RPM). However, hydrodynamic film pressures developed in the high-pressure areas of the engine bearings may be over 1,000 PSI (6,900 kPa). The relatively low engine oil pressures obviously could not support these high bearing loads without hydrodynamic lubrication.

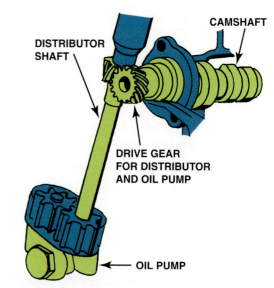

FIGURE 9–4 An oil pump driven by the camshaft.

OIL PUMPS

All production automobile engines have a full-pressure oil system. The oil is drawn from the bottom of the oil pan and is forced into the lubrication system under pressure.

NOTE: The oil pump is the only engine component that uses unfiltered oil.

In most engines that use a distributor, the distributor drive gear meshes with a gear on the camshaft, as shown in ● **FIGURES 9–4 AND 9–5**. The oil pump is driven from the end of the distributor shaft, often with a hexagon-shaped shaft. Some engines have a short shaft gear that meshes with the cam gear to drive both the distributor and oil pump. With these drive methods, the pump turns at one-half engine speed. In other engines, the oil pump is driven by the front of the crankshaft, in a setup similar to that of an automatic transmission pump, so that it turns at the same speed as the crankshaft. Examples of a crankshaft-driven oil pump are shown in ● **FIGURES 9–6 AND 9–7**.

Most automotive engines use one of two types of oil pumps: *gear* or *rotor*. All oil pumps are called **positive displacement pumps**, and each rotation of the pump delivers the same volume of oil; thus, everything that enters must exit. The gear-type oil pump consists of two spur gears in a close-fitting housing—one gear is driven while the other idles. As the gear teeth come out of mesh, they tend to leave a space, which is filled by oil drawn through the pump inlet. When the pump is pumping, oil is carried around the *outside* of each gear in the space between the gear teeth and the housing, as shown in ● **FIGURE 9–8**.

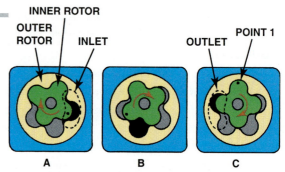

A. OIL IS PICKED UP IN LOBE OF OUTER ROTOR.
B. OIL IS MOVED IN LOBE OF OUTER ROTOR TO OUTLET.
C. OIL IS FORCED OUT OF OUTLET BECAUSE THE INNER AND OUTER ROTORS MESH TOO TIGHTLY AT POINT 1 AND THE OIL CANNOT PASS THROUGH.

FIGURE 9–5 The operation of a rotor-type oil pump.

FIGURE 9–6 A typical oil pump mounted in the front cover of the engine that is driven by the crankshaft.

FIGURE 9–7 Gerotor-type oil pump driven by the crankshaft.

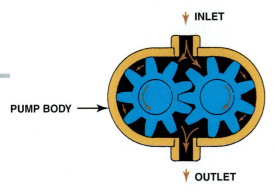

FIGURE 9–8 In a gear-type oil pump, the oil flows through the pump around the outside of each gear. This is an example of a positive displacement pump, where everything entering the pump must leave the pump.

As the teeth mesh in the center, oil is forced from the teeth into an oil passage, thus producing oil pressure. The rotor-type oil pump consists essentially of a special lobe-shape gear meshing with the inside of a lobed rotor. The center lobed section is driven and the outer section idles. As the lobes separate, oil is drawn in just as it is drawn into gear-type pumps. As the pump rotates, it carries oil around and between the lobes. As the lobes mesh, they force the oil out from between them under pressure in the same manner as the gear-type pump. The pump is sized so that it will maintain a pressure of at least 10 PSI (70 kPa) in the oil gallery when the engine is hot and idling. Pressure will increase by about 10 PSI for each 1000 RPM as the engine speed increases, because the engine-driven pump also rotates faster.

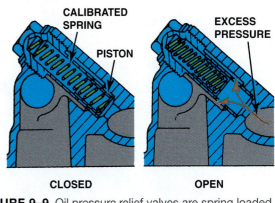

FIGURE 9–9 Oil pressure relief valves are spring loaded. The stronger the spring tension, the higher the oil pressure.

OIL PRESSURE REGULATION

In engines with a full-pressure lubricating system, maximum pressure is limited with a pressure relief valve. The relief valve (sometimes called the **pressure regulating valve**) is located at the outlet of the pump. The relief valve controls maximum pressure by bleeding off oil to the inlet side of the pump. ● **SEE FIGURE 9–9.**

The relief valve spring tension determines the maximum oil pressure. If a pressure relief valve is not used, the engine oil pressure will continue to increase as the engine speed increases. Maximum pressure is usually limited to the lowest pressure that will deliver enough lubricating oil to all engine parts that need to be lubricated. *Three to 6 gallons per minute are required to lubricate the engine.* The oil pump is made so that it is large enough to provide pressure at low engine speeds and small enough so that cavitation will not occur at high speed. Cavitation occurs when the pump tries to pull oil faster than it can flow from the pan to the pickup. When it cannot get enough oil, it will pull air. This puts air pockets or cavities in the oil stream. A pump is cavitating when it is pulling air or vapors.

NOTE: The reason for sheet-metal covers over the pickup screen is to prevent cavitation. Oil is trapped under the cover, which helps prevent the oil pump from drawing in air, especially during sudden stops or during rapid acceleration.

After the oil leaves the pump, it is delivered to the oil filter and then to the moving parts through drilled oil passages. ● **SEE FIGURE 9–10.** It needs no pressure after it reaches the parts that are to be lubricated. The oil film between the parts is developed and maintained by hydrodynamic lubrication. Excessive oil pressure requires more horsepower and provides no better lubrication than the minimum effective pressure.

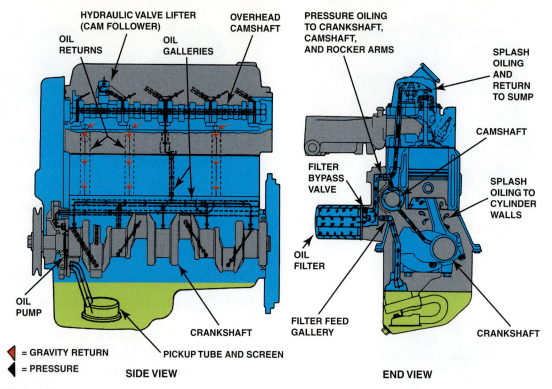

FIGURE 9–10 A typical engine design that uses both pressure and splash lubrication. Oil travels under pressure through the galleries (passages) to reach the top of the engine. Other parts are lubricated as the oil flows back down into the oil pan or is splashed onto parts.

FACTORS AFFECTING OIL PRESSURE

Oil pressure can only be produced when the oil pump has a capacity larger than all the "leaks" in the engine. The leaks are the clearances at end points of the lubrication system. The end points are at the edges of bearings, the rocker arms, the connecting rod spit holes, and so on. These clearances are designed into the engine and are necessary for its proper operation. As the engine parts wear and clearance becomes greater, more oil will leak out. The oil pump *capacity* must be great enough to supply extra oil for these leaks. The capacity of the oil pump results from its size, rotating speed, and physical condition. If the pump is rotating slowly as the engine is idling, oil pump capacity is low. *If the leaks are greater than the pump capacity, engine oil pressure is low.* As the engine speed increases, the pump capacity increases and the pump tries to force more oil out of the leaks. This causes the pressure to rise until it reaches the regulated maximum pressure.

The viscosity of the engine oil affects both the pump capacity and the oil leakage. Thin oil or oil of very low viscosity slips past the edges of the pump and flows freely from the leaks. Hot oil has a low viscosity, and therefore, a hot engine often has low oil pressure. Cold oil is more viscous (thicker) than hot oil. This results in higher pressures, even with the cold engine idling. High oil pressure occurs with a cold engine, because the oil relief valve must open farther to release excess oil than is necessary with a hot engine. This larger opening increases the spring compression force, which in turn increases the oil pressure. Putting higher-viscosity oil in an engine will raise the engine oil pressure to the regulated setting of the relief valve at a lower engine speed.

(a)

(b)

FIGURE 9–11 (a) A visual inspection indicated that this pump cover was worn. (b) An embedded particle of something was found on one of the gears, making this pump worthless except for scrap metal.

OIL PUMP CHECKS

The cover is removed to check the condition of the oil pump. The gears and housing are examined for scoring. If the gears and housing are heavily scored, the entire pump should be replaced. If they are lightly scored, the clearances in the pump should be measured. These clearances include the space between the gears and housing, the space between the teeth of the two gears, and the space between the side of the gear and the pump cover. A feeler gauge is often used to make these measurements. Gauging plastic can be used to measure the space between the side of the gears and the cover. The oil pump should be replaced when excessive clearance or scoring is found. ● **SEE FIGURE 9–11**.

On most engines, the oil pump should be replaced as part of any engine work, especially if the cause for the repair is lack of lubrication.

NOTE: The oil pump is the "garbage pit" of the entire engine. Any and all debris is often forced through the gears and housing of an oil pump. ● SEE FIGURE 9–12.

Always refer to the manufacturer's specifications when checking the oil pump for wear. Typical oil pump clearances include the following:

1. End plate clearance: 0.0015 inch (0.04 millimeter)
2. Side (rotor) clearance: 0.012 inch (0.30 millimeter)
3. Rotor tip clearance: 0.010 inch (0.25 millimeter)
4. Gear end play clearance: 0.004 inch (0.10 millimeter)

All parts should also be inspected closely for wear. Check the relief valve for scoring and check the condition of the spring. When installing the oil pump, coat the sealing surfaces with engine assembly lubricant. This lubricant helps draw oil from the oil pan on initial start-up.

(a)

(b)

FIGURE 9–12 (a) The oil pump is the only part in an engine that gets unfiltered engine oil. The oil is drawn up from the bottom of the oil pan and is pressurized before flowing to the oil filter. (b) If debris gets into an oil pump, the drive or distributor shaft can twist and/or break. When this occurs, the engine will lose all oil pressure.

OIL PASSAGES IN THE BLOCK

From the filter, oil goes through a drilled hole that intersects with a drilled main **oil gallery** or **longitudinal header**. This is a long hole drilled from the front of the block to the back. Inline engines use one oil gallery; V-type engines may use two or three galleries. Passages drilled through the block bulkheads allow the oil to go from the main oil gallery to the main and cam bearings. ● **SEE FIGURE 9–13.** In some engines, oil goes to the cam bearings first, and then to the main bearings.

It is important that the oil holes in the bearings match with the drilled passages in the bearing saddles so that the bearing can be properly lubricated. Over a long period of use, bearings will wear. This wear causes excess clearance. The excess clearance will allow too much oil to leak from the side of the bearing. When this happens, there will be little or no oil left for bearings located farther downstream in the lubricating system. This is a major cause of bearing failure. If a new bearing were installed in place of the oil-starved bearing, it, too, would fail unless the bearing having the excess clearance was also replaced.

VALVE TRAIN LUBRICATION

The valve train components are the last parts to get oil from the oil pump. The oil gallery may intersect or have drilled passages to the valve lifter bores to lubricate the lifters. When hydraulic lifters are used, the oil pressure in the gallery keeps refilling them. On some engines, oil from the lifters goes up the center of a hollow pushrod to lubricate the pushrod ends, the rocker arm pivot, and the valve stem tip. ● **SEE FIGURE 9–14.** In other engines, an oil passage is drilled from either the gallery or a cam bearing to the block deck, where it matches with a gasket hole and a hole drilled in the head to carry the oil to a rocker arm shaft. Some engines use an enlarged bolt hole to carry lubrication oil around the rocker shaft cap screw to the rocker arm shaft. Holes in the bottom of the rocker arm shaft allow lubrication of the rocker arm pivot. Mechanical loads on the valve train hold the rocker arm against the passage in the rocker arm shaft. This prevents excessive oil leakage from the rocker arm shaft. Often, holes are drilled in cast rocker arms to carry oil to the pushrod end and to the valve tip. Rocker arm assemblies need only a surface coating of oil, so the oil flow to the rocker assembly is minimized using restrictions or metered openings.

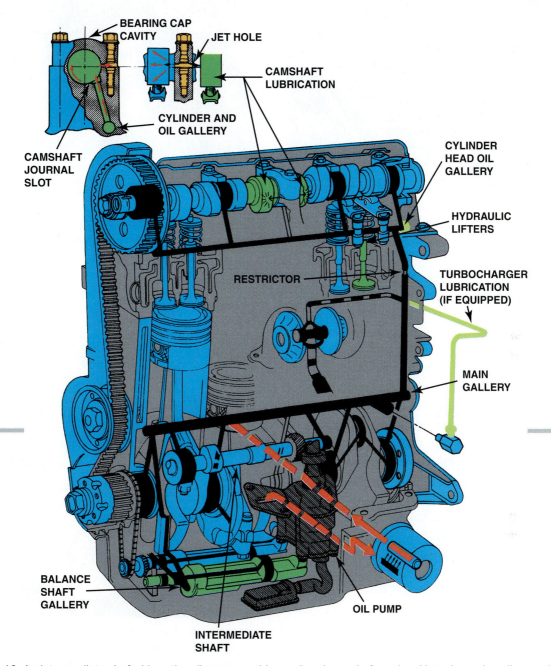

BEARING CAP CAVITY
JET HOLE
CAMSHAFT LUBRICATION
CYLINDER AND OIL GALLERY
CAMSHAFT JOURNAL SLOT
CYLINDER HEAD OIL GALLERY
HYDRAULIC LIFTERS
RESTRICTOR
TURBOCHARGER LUBRICATION (IF EQUIPPED)
MAIN GALLERY
BALANCE SHAFT GALLERY
INTERMEDIATE SHAFT
OIL PUMP

FIGURE 9–13 An intermediate shaft drives the oil pump on this overhead camshaft engine. Note the main gallery and other drilled passages in the block and cylinder head.

The restriction or metering disk is in the lifter when the rocker assembly is lubricated through the pushrod. Cam journal holes that line up with oil passages are often used to meter oil to the rocker shafts.

Oil that seeps from the rocker assemblies is returned to the oil pan through drain holes. These oil drain holes are often placed so that the oil drains on the camshaft or cam drive gears to lubricate them.

Some engines have means of directing a positive oil flow to the cam drive gears or chain. This may be a nozzle or a chamfer on a bearing parting surface that allows oil to spray on the loaded portion of the cam drive mechanism.

FIGURE 9–14 Oil is sent to the rocker arms on this Chevrolet V-8 engine through the hollow pushrods. The oil returns to the oil pan through the oil drainback holes in the cylinder head.

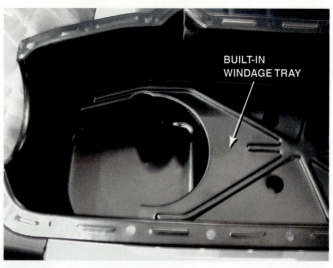

FIGURE 9–15 A typical oil pan with a built-in windage tray used to keep oil from being churned up by the rotating crankshaft.

OIL PANS

As the vehicle accelerates, brakes, or turns rapidly, the oil tends to move around in the pan. Pan baffles and oil pan shapes are often used to keep the oil inlet under the oil at all times. As the crankshaft rotates, it acts like a fan and causes air within the crankcase to rotate with it. This can cause a strong draft on the oil, churning it so that air bubbles enter the oil, which then causes oil foaming. Oil with air will not lubricate like liquid oil, so oil foaming can cause bearings to fail. A baffle or **windage tray** is sometimes installed in engines to eliminate the oil churning problem. This may be an added part, as shown in ● **SEE FIGURE 9–15**, or it may be a part of the oil pan. Windage trays have the good side effect of reducing the amount of air disturbed by the crankshaft, so that less power is drained from the engine at high crankshaft speeds. Oil pans on many engines are a structural part of the engine. ● **SEE FIGURE 9–16**.

OIL COOLERS

Oil temperature must also be controlled on many high-performance or turbocharged engines. ● **SEE FIGURE 9–17** for an example of an engine oil cooler used on a production high-performance engine. A larger-capacity oil pan also helps to control oil temperature. Coolant flows through the oil cooler to help warm the oil when the engine is cold and cool the oil when the engine is hot. Oil temperature should be above 212°F (100°C) to boil off any accumulated moisture, but it should not exceed about 280° to 300°F (138° to 148°C).

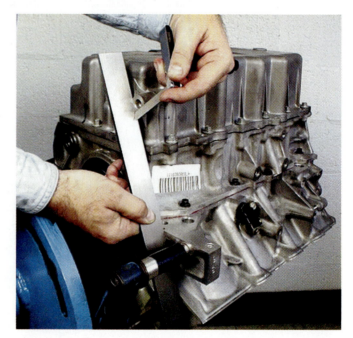

FIGURE 9–16 A straightedge and a feeler gauge are being used to check that the oil pan has been correctly installed on the 5.7-liter Chevrolet V-8 engine. The oil pan is part of the engine itself and must be properly installed to ensure that other parts attached to the engine are not being placed in a bind.

FIGURE 9–17 A typical engine oil cooler. Engine coolant flows through the cooler adjuster that fits between the engine block and the oil filter.

FIGURE 9–19 A typical oil pressure sending unit on a Ford V-8.

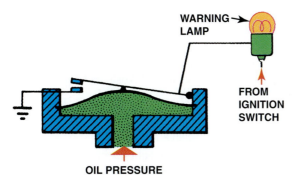

FIGURE 9–18 The oil pressure switch is connected to a warning lamp that alerts the driver of low oil pressure.

OIL PRESSURE WARNING LAMP

All vehicles are equipped with an oil pressure gauge or a warning lamp. The warning lamp comes on whenever the engine oil pressure has dropped to 3 to 7 PSI. Normal oil pressure is considered to be 10 PSI per 1,000 RPM. An electrical switch is used to convert the ground circuit of the oil pressure warning lamp if the oil pressure is below the rating of the sending unit. ● SEE **FIGURES 9–18 AND 9–19**.

● SEE **FIGURES 9–18 AND 9–19**.

? FREQUENTLY ASKED QUESTION

What Is Acceptable Oil Consumption?

There are a number of opinions regarding what is acceptable oil consumption. Most vehicle owners do not want their engine to use *any* oil between oil changes even if they do not change it more often than every 7,500 miles (12,000 kilometers). Engineers have improved machining operations and piston ring designs to help eliminate oil consumption.

Many stationary or industrial engines are not driven on the road; therefore, they do not accumulate miles, yet they still may consume excessive oil.

A general rule for "acceptable" oil consumption is that it should be about 0.002 to 0.004 pounds per horsepower per hour. To figure, use the following:

$$\frac{1.82 \times \text{quarts used}}{\text{Operating hp} \times \text{total hours}} = \text{lb/hp/hr}$$

Therefore, oil consumption is based on the amount of work an engine performs. Although the formula may not be usable for vehicle engines used for daily transportation, it may be usable by the marine or industrial engine builder. Generally, oil consumption that is greater than 1 quart for every 600 miles (1,000 kilometers per liter) is considered to be excessive with a motor vehicle.

SUMMARY

1. Normal engine oil pump pressure ranges from 10 to 60 PSI (200 to 400 kPa) or 10 PSI for every 1000 engine RPM.

2. Hydrodynamic oil pressure around engine bearings is usually over 1,000 PSI (6,900 kPa).

3. The oil pump is driven directly by the crankshaft or by a gear or shaft from the camshaft.

4. The last components to get oil from the oil pump are the valve train parts.

5. Some engines use an oil cooler.

REVIEW QUESTIONS

1. What causes a wedge-shaped film to form in the oil?

2. What is hydrodynamic lubrication?

3. Explain why internal engine leakage affects oil pressure.

4. Describe how the oil flows from the oil pump, through the filter and main engine bearings, to the valve train.

5. What is the purpose of a windage tray?

CHAPTER QUIZ

1. Normal oil pump pressure in an engine is _____.
   a. 3 to 7 PSI
   b. 10 to 60 PSI
   c. 100 to 150 PSI
   d. 180 to 210 PSI

2. The oil pump pressure relief valve is also called _____.
   a. Oil pump valve
   b. Pressure valve
   c. Pressure regulating valve
   d. Pressure dump valve

3. A typical oil pump is what type of pump?
   a. Positive displacement
   b. Centrifugal
   c. Piston-type
   d. Hydraulically driven

4. Engine oil passages in an engine block are called _____.
   a. Oil passages
   b. Oil galleries
   c. Weep holes
   d. Oil holes

5. Technician A says that the oil pump draws unfiltered oil from the bottom of the oil pan. Technician B says that the oil pump is driven from the front of the crankshaft in some engines. Which technician is correct?
   a. Technician A only
   b. Technician B only
   c. Both Technicians A and B
   d. Neither Technician A nor B

6. Technician A says that oil pressure is affected by the amount of main and rod bearing clearance. Technician B says that the oil pressure is lower when the oil gets hot than when it is cold. Which technician is correct?
   a. Technician A only
   b. Technician B only
   c. Both Technicians A and B
   d. Neither Technician A nor B

7. Technician A says that many engines use a windage tray in the oil pan. Technician B says that some engines are equipped with an oil cooler. Which technician is correct?
   a. Technician A only
   b. Technician B only
   c. Both Technicians A and B
   d. Neither Technician A nor B

8. The oil pressure warning light normally comes on to warn the driver if the oil pressure drops below _____.
   a. 50 PSI
   b. 30 PSI
   c. 10 PSI
   d. 3 to 7 PSI

9. A typical oil pump can pump how many gallons per minute?
   a. 3 to 6 gallons
   b. 6 to 10 gallons
   c. 10 to 60 gallons
   d. 50 to 100 gallons

10. In typical engine lubrication systems, what components are the last to receive oil and the first to suffer from a lack of oil or oil pressure?
    a. Main bearings
    b. Rod bearings
    c. Valve train components
    d. Oil filters

chapter 10
INTAKE AND EXHAUST SYSTEMS

OBJECTIVES

After studying Chapter 10, the reader will be able to:

1. Prepare for ASE Engine Performance (A8) certification test content area "C" (Air Induction and Exhaust Systems Diagnosis and Repair).
2. Discuss the purpose and function of intake manifolds.
3. Explain the differences between throttle fuel-injection manifolds and port fuel-injection manifolds.
4. Describe the operation of the exhaust gas recirculation system in the intake manifold.
5. List the materials used in exhaust manifolds and exhaust systems.

KEY TERMS

annealing 170
exhaust gas recirculation (EGR) 169
hangers 173

Helmholtz resonator 166
micron 164
plenum 170

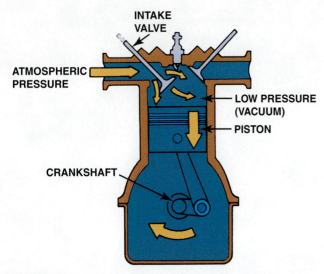

FIGURE 10–1 Downward movement of the piston lowers the air pressure inside the combustion chamber. The pressure differential between the atmosphere and the inside of the engine forces air into the engine.

FIGURE 10–2 Dust and dirt in the air are trapped in the air filter so they do not enter the engine.

AIR INTAKE FILTRATION

Gasoline must be mixed with air to form a combustible mixture. Air movement into an engine occurs due to low pressure (vacuum) being created in the engine. ● **SEE FIGURE 10–1**.

Like gasoline, air contains dirt and other materials which cannot be allowed to reach the engine. Just as fuel filters are used to clean impurities from gasoline, an air cleaner and filter are used to remove contaminants from the air. The three main jobs of the air cleaner and filter are to:

- Clean the air before it is mixed with fuel
- Silence intake noise
- Act as a flame arrester in case of a backfire

The automotive engine uses about 9,000 gallons (34,069 liters) of air for every gallon of gasoline burned at an air–fuel ratio of 14.7 to 1. Without proper filtering of the air before intake, dust and dirt in the air seriously damage engine parts and shorten engine life.

While abrasive particles can cause wear any place inside the engine where two surfaces move against each other, they first attack piston rings and cylinder walls. Contained in the blowby gases, they pass by the piston rings and into the crankcase. From the crankcase, the particles circulate throughout the engine in the oil. Large amounts of abrasive particles in the oil can damage other moving engine parts.

The filter that cleans the intake air is in a two-piece air cleaner housing made either of stamped steel or composite materials. The air cleaner housing is located on top of the throttle-body injection (TBI) unit or is positioned to one side of the engine. ● **SEE FIGURE 10–2**.

FILTER REPLACEMENT Manufacturers recommend cleaning or replacing the air filter element at periodic intervals, usually listed in terms of distance driven or months of service. The distance and time intervals are based on so-called normal driving. More frequent air filter replacement is necessary when the vehicle is driven under dusty, dirty, or other severe conditions.

It is best to replace a filter element before it becomes too dirty to be effective. A dirty air filter passes contaminants that cause engine wear.

AIR FILTER ELEMENTS The paper air filter element is the most common type of filter. It is made of a chemically treated paper stock that contains tiny passages in the fibers. These passages form an indirect path for the airflow to follow. The airflow passes through several fiber surfaces, each of which traps microscopic particles of dust, dirt, and carbon. Most air filters are capable of trapping dirt and other particles larger than 10 to 25 microns in size. One **micron** is equal to 0.000039 in.

NOTE: A person can only see objects that are 40 microns or larger in size. A human hair is about 50 microns in diameter.

FIGURE 10–3 Most air filter housings are located on the side of the engine compartment and use flexible rubber hose to direct the airflow into the throttle body of the engine.

(a)

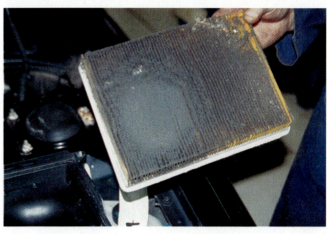

(b)

FIGURE 10–4 (a) Note the discovery as the air filter housing was opened during service on a Pontiac Bonneville. The nuts were obviously deposited by squirrels (or some other animal). (b) Not only was the housing filled with nuts, but also this air filter was extremely dirty, indicating that this vehicle had not been serviced for a long time.

NOTE: Do not attempt to clean a paper element filter by rapping it on a sharp object to dislodge the dirt, or blowing compressed air through the filter. This tends to clog the paper pores and further reduce the airflow capability of the filter.

REMOTELY MOUNTED AIR FILTERS AND DUCTS

Air cleaner and duct design depend on a number of factors such as the size, shape, and location of other engine compartment components, as well as the vehicle body structure.

Port fuel-injection systems generally use a horizontally mounted throttle body. Some systems also have a mass airflow (MAF) sensor between the throttle body and the air cleaner. ● **SEE FIGURE 10–3.** Because placing the air cleaner housing next to the throttle body would cause engine and vehicle design problems, it is more efficient to use this remote air cleaner placement.

Turbocharged engines present a similar problem. The air cleaner connects to the air inlet elbow at the turbocharger. However, the tremendous heat generated by the turbocharger makes it impractical to place the air cleaner housing too close to the turbocharger. For better protection, the MAF sensor is installed between the turbocharger and the air cleaner in some vehicles. Remote air cleaners are connected to the turbocharger air inlet elbow or fuel-injection throttle body by composite ducting, which is usually retained by clamps. The ducting used may be rigid or flexible, but all connections must be airtight.

TECH TIP

Always Check the Air Filter

Always inspect the air filter and the air intake system carefully during routine service. Debris or objects deposited by animals can cause a restriction to the airflow and can reduce engine performance. ● **SEE FIGURE 10–4.**

What Does This Tube Do?

What is the purpose of the odd-shaped tube attached to the inlet duct between the air filter and the throttle body, as seen in ● **FIGURE 10–5**?

The tube shape is designed to dampen out certain resonant frequencies that can occur at certain engine speeds. The length and shape of this tube are designed to absorb shock waves that are created in the air intake system and to provide a reservoir for the air that will then be released into the airstream during cycles of lower pressure. This resonance tube is often called a **Helmholtz resonator**, named for the discoverer of the relationship between shape and value of frequency Herman L. F. von Helmholtz (1821–1894) of the University of Hönizsberg in East Prussia. The overall effect of these resonance tubes is to reduce the noise of the air entering the engine.

FIGURE 10–5 A resonance tube, called a Helmholtz resonator, is used on the intake duct between the air filter and the throttle body to reduce air intake noise during engine acceleration.

ENGINE AIR TEMPERATURE REQUIREMENTS

Some form of thermostatic control has been used on vehicles equipped with a throttle-body fuel injection to control intake air temperature for improved driveability. In a throttle-body fuel injection system, the fuel and air are combined above the throttle plate and must travel through the intake manifold before reaching the cylinders. Air temperature control is needed under these conditions to help keep the gas and air mixture combined.

Heat radiating from the exhaust manifold is retained by the heat stove and sent to the air cleaner inlet to provide heated air to the throttle body.

An air control valve or damper permits the air intake of:

- Heated air from the heat stove
- Cooler air from the snorkel or cold-air duct
- A combination of both

While the air control valve generally is located in the air cleaner snorkel, it may be in the air intake housing or ducting of remote air cleaners. Most fuel-injection systems do not use temperature control.

THROTTLE-BODY INJECTION INTAKE MANIFOLDS

The *intake manifold* is also called the *inlet manifold*. Smooth operation can only occur when each combustion chamber produces the same pressure as every other chamber in the engine. For this to be achieved, each cylinder must receive a charge exactly like the charge going into the other cylinders in quality and quantity. The charges must have the same physical properties and the same air–fuel mixture.

A throttle-body fuel injector forces finely divided droplets of liquid fuel into the incoming air to form a combustible air–fuel mixture. ● **SEE FIGURE 10–6** for an example of a typical throttle-body injection (TBI) unit. These droplets start to evaporate as soon as they leave the throttle-body injector nozzles. *The droplets stay in the charge as long as the charge flows at high velocities.* At maximum horsepower, these velocities may reach 300 feet per second. Separation of the droplets from the charge as it passes through the manifold occurs when the velocity drops below 50 feet per second. Intake charge velocities at idle speeds are often below this value. When separation occurs—at low engine speeds—extra fuel must be supplied to the charge in order to have a combustible mixture reach the combustion chamber.

FIGURE 10–6 A throttle-body injection (TBI) unit used on a GM V-6 engine.

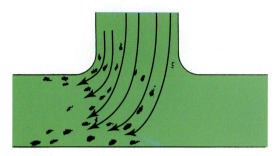

FIGURE 10–7 Heavy fuel droplets separate as they flow around an abrupt bend in an intake manifold.

Manifold sizes represent a compromise. They must have a cross-section large enough to allow charge flow for maximum power. The cross-section must be small enough that the flow velocities of the charge will be high enough to keep the fuel droplets in suspension. This is required so that equal mixtures reach each cylinder. Manifold cross-sectional size is one reason why engines designed especially for racing will not run at low engine speeds. Racing manifolds must be large enough to reach maximum horsepower. This size, however, allows the charge to move slowly, and the fuel will separate from the charge at low engine speeds. Fuel separation leads to poor accelerator response. ● **SEE FIGURE 10–7.** Standard passenger vehicle engines are primarily designed for economy during light-load, partial-throttle operation. Their manifolds, therefore, have a much smaller cross-sectional area than do those of racing engines. This small size will help keep flow velocities of the charge high throughout the normal operating speed range of the engine.

TECH TIP

Check the Intake If an Exhaust Noise

Because many V-type engines equipped with a throttle-body injection and/or EGR valve use a crossover exhaust passage, a leak around this passage will create an exhaust leak and noise. Always check for evidence of an exhaust leak around the intake manifold whenever diagnosing an exhaust sound.

PORT FUEL-INJECTION INTAKE MANIFOLDS

The size and shape of port fuel-injected engine intake manifolds can be optimized because the only thing in the manifold is air. The fuel injection is located in the intake manifold about 3 to 4 inches (70 to 100 mm) from the intake valve. Therefore, the runner length and shape are designed for tuning only. There is no need to keep an air–fuel mixture homogenized throughout its trip from the TBI unit to the intake valve. Typically, long runners build low-RPM torque while shorter runners provide maximum high-RPM power. ● **SEE FIGURES 10–8 AND 10–9.** Some engines with four valve heads utilize a dual or variable intake runner design. At lower engine speeds, long intake runners provide low-speed torque. At higher engine speeds, shorter intake runners are opened by means of a computer-controlled valve to increase high-speed power.

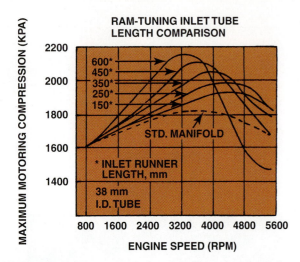

FIGURE 10–8 The graph shows the effect of sonic tuning of the intake manifold runners. The longer runners increase the torque peak and move it to a lower RPM. The 600-mm-long intake runner is about 24 inches long.

FIGURE 10–10 The air flowing into the engine can be directed through long or short runners for best performance and fuel economy.

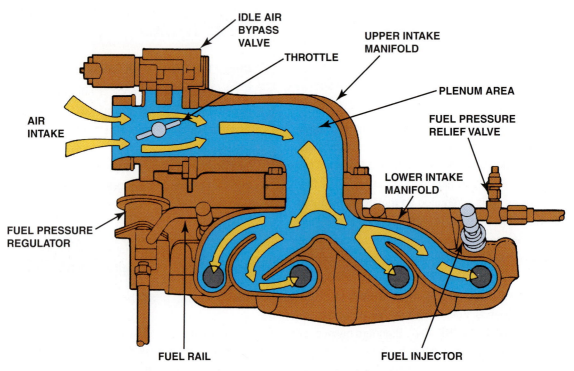

FIGURE 10–9 Airflow through the large diameter upper intake manifold is distributed to smaller diameter individual runners in the lower manifold in this two-piece manifold design.

VARIABLE INTAKES

Many intake manifolds are designed to provide both short runners, best for higher engine speed power, and longer runners, best for lower engine speed torque. The valve(s) that control the flow of air through the passages of the intake manifold are computer controlled. ● SEE FIGURE 10–10.

PLASTIC INTAKE MANIFOLDS

Most thermoplastic intake manifolds are molded from fiberglass-reinforced nylon. The plastic manifolds can be cast or injection molded. Some manifolds are molded in two parts and bonded together. Plastic intake manifolds are lighter than aluminum manifolds and can better insulate engine heat from the fuel injectors.

Plastic intake manifolds have smoother interior surfaces than do other types of manifolds, resulting in greater airflow. ● **SEE FIGURE 10–11**.

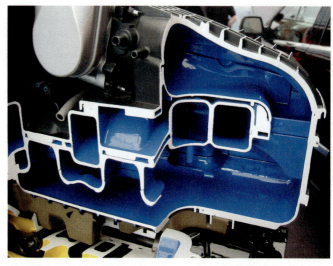

FIGURE 10–11 Many plastic intake manifolds are constructed using many parts glued together to form complex passages for airflow into the engine.

EXHAUST GAS RECIRCULATION PASSAGES

To reduce the emission of oxides of nitrogen (NO_x), engines have been equipped with **exhaust gas recirculation (EGR)** valves. From 1973 until recently, they were used on almost all vehicles. Because of the efficiency of computer-controlled fuel injection, some newer engines do not require an EGR system to meet emission standards. Some engines use intake and exhaust valve overlap as a means of trapping some exhaust in the cylinder as an alternative to using an EGR valve.

The EGR valve opens at speeds above idle on a warm engine. When open, the valve allows a small portion of the exhaust gas (5% to 10%) to enter the intake manifold. Here, the exhaust gas mixes with and takes the place of some of the intake charge. This leaves less room for the intake charge to enter the combustion chamber. The recirculated exhaust gas is inert and does *not* enter into the combustion process. The result is a lower peak combustion temperature. As the combustion temperature is lowered, the production of oxides of nitrogen is also reduced.

The EGR system has some means of interconnecting the exhaust and intake manifolds. The interconnecting passage is controlled by the EGR valve. On V-type engines, the intake manifold crossover is used as a source of exhaust gas for the EGR system. A cast passage connects the exhaust crossover to the EGR valve. On inline-type engines, an external tube is generally used to carry exhaust gas to the EGR valve.

EGR VALVE

EXHAUST GAS TUBE

FIGURE 10–12 The exhaust gas recirculation system is more efficient at controlling NO_x emissions if the exhaust gases are cooled. A long metal tube between the exhaust manifold and the intake manifold allows the exhaust gases to cool before entering the engine.

The exhaust gases are more effective in reducing oxides of nitrogen (NO_x) emissions if the exhaust is cooled before being drawn into the cylinders. This tube is often designed to be long so that the exhaust gas is cooled before it enters the EGR valve. ● **FIGURE 10–12** shows a typical long EGR tube.

UPPER AND LOWER INTAKE MANIFOLDS

Many intake manifolds are constructed in two parts.

- A lower section attaches to the cylinder heads and includes passages from the intake ports.

- An upper manifold, also called the **plenum**, connects to the lower unit and includes the long passages needed to help provide the ram effect that helps the engine deliver maximum torque at low engine speeds. The throttle body attaches to the upper intake.

The use of a two-part intake manifold allows for easier manufacturing as well as assembly, but can create additional locations for leaks. If the lower intake manifold gasket leaks, not only could a vacuum leak occur affecting the operation of the engine, but a coolant leak or an oil leak can also occur. A leak at the gasket(s) of the upper intake manifold usually results in a vacuum (air) leak only.

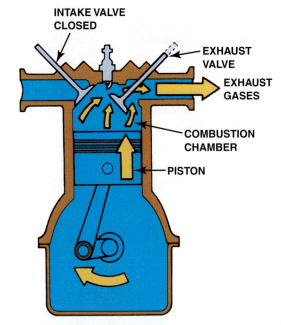

FIGURE 10–13 The exhaust gases are pushed out of the cylinder by the piston on the exhaust stroke.

EXHAUST MANIFOLD DESIGN

The exhaust manifold is designed to collect high-temperature spent gases from the head exhaust ports. ● **SEE FIGURE 10–13.** The hot gases are sent to an exhaust pipe, then to a catalytic converter, to the muffler, to a resonator, and on to the tailpipe, where they are vented to the atmosphere. This must be done with the least-possible amount of restriction or back pressure while keeping the exhaust noise at a minimum.

Exhaust gas temperature will vary according to the power produced by the engine. The manifold must be designed to operate at both engine idle and continuous full power. Under full-power conditions, the exhaust manifold will become red-hot, causing a great deal of expansion.

NOTE: The temperature of an exhaust manifold can exceed 1500°F (815°C).

At idle, the exhaust manifold is just warm, causing little expansion. After casting, the manifold may be annealed. **Annealing** is a heat-treating process that takes out the brittle hardening of the casting to reduce the chance of cracking from the temperature changes. During vehicle operation, manifold temperatures usually reach the high-temperature extremes. Most exhaust manifolds are made from cast iron to withstand extreme and rapid temperature changes. The manifold is bolted to the head in a way that will allow expansion and contraction. In some cases, hollow-headed bolts are used to maintain a gastight seal while still allowing normal expansion and contraction.

The exhaust manifold is designed to allow the free flow of exhaust gas. Some manifolds use internal cast-rib deflectors or dividers to guide the exhaust gases toward the outlet as smoothly as possible.

Some exhaust manifolds are designed to go above the spark plug, whereas others are designed to go below. The spark plug and carefully routed ignition wires are usually shielded from the exhaust heat with sheet-metal deflectors. Many exhaust manifolds have heat shields as seen in ● **FIGURE 10–14.**

Exhaust systems are especially designed for the engine-chassis combination. The exhaust system length, pipe size, and silencer are designed, where possible, to make use of the tuning effect of the gas column resonating within the exhaust system. Tuning occurs when the exhaust pulses from the cylinders are emptied into the manifold between the pulses of other cylinders. ● **SEE FIGURE 10–15.**

FIGURE 10–14 This exhaust manifold has a heat shield to help retain the heat and help reduce exhaust emissions.

FIGURE 10–16 A crack in an exhaust manifold is often not this visible. A crack in the exhaust manifold upstream of the oxygen sensor can fool the sensor and affect engine operation.

FIGURE 10–15 Many exhaust manifolds are constructed of pressed steel and are free flowing to improve engine performance.

EXHAUST MANIFOLD GASKETS

Exhaust heat will expand the manifold more than it will expand the head. It causes the exhaust manifold to slide on the sealing surface of the head. The heat also causes thermal stress. When the manifold is removed from the engine for service, the stress is relieved and this may cause the manifold to warp slightly. Exhaust manifold gaskets are included in gasket sets to seal slightly warped exhaust manifolds. These gaskets *should* be used, even if the engine did not originally use exhaust manifold

? FREQUENTLY ASKED QUESTION

How Can a Cracked Exhaust Manifold Affect Engine Performance?

A crack in an exhaust manifold will not only allow exhaust gases to escape and cause noise but the crack can also allow air to enter the exhaust manifold. ● **SEE FIGURE 10–16.**

Exhaust flows from the cylinders as individual puffs or pressure pulses. Behind each of these pressure pulses, a low pressure (below atmospheric pressure) is created. Outside air at atmospheric pressure is then drawn into the exhaust manifold through the crack. This outside air contains 21% oxygen and is measured by the oxygen sensor (O2S). The air passing the O2S signals the engine computer that the engine is operating too lean (excess oxygen) and the computer, not knowing that the lean indicator is false, adds additional fuel to the engine. The result is that the engine will be operating richer (more fuel than normal) and spark plugs could become fouled causing poor engine operation.

gaskets. When a perforated core exhaust manifold gasket has facing on one side only, put the facing side against the head and put the manifold against the perforated metal core. The manifold can slide on the metal of the gasket just as it slid on the sealing surface of the head.

FIGURE 10–17 Typical exhaust manifold gaskets. Note how they are laminated to allow the exhaust manifold to expand and contract due to heating and cooling.

EXHAUST MANIFOLD SPREADER TOOL

FIGURE 10–18 An exhaust manifold spreader tool is a tool that is absolutely necessary to use when reinstalling exhaust manifolds. When they are removed from the engine, they tend to warp slightly even though the engine is allowed to cool before being removed. The spreader tool allows the technician to line up the bolt holes without doing any harm to the manifold.

EXHAUST MANIFOLD GASKETS (CONTINUED)

Gaskets are used on new engines with tubing- or header-type exhaust manifolds. The gaskets often include heat shields to keep exhaust heat from the spark plugs and spark plug cables. They may have several layers of steel for high-temperature sealing. The layers are spot-welded together. Some are embossed where special sealing is needed. ● SEE FIGURE 10–17.

Many new engines do not use gaskets with cast exhaust manifolds. The flat surface of the new cast-iron exhaust manifold fits tightly against the flat surface of the new head.

TECH TIP

The Correct Tools Save Time

When cast-iron exhaust manifolds are removed, the stresses built up in the manifolds often cause the manifolds to twist or bend. This distortion even occurs when the exhaust manifolds have been allowed to cool before removal. Attempting to reinstall distorted exhaust manifolds is often a time-consuming and frustrating exercise.

However, special spreading jacks can be used to force the manifold back into position so that the fasteners can be lined up with the cylinder head. ● SEE FIGURE 10–18.

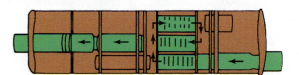

FIGURE 10–19 Exhaust gases expand and cool as they travel through the passages in the muffler.

MUFFLERS

When the exhaust valve opens, it rapidly releases high-pressure gas. This sends a strong air pressure wave through the atmosphere, which produces a sound we call an explosion. It is the same sound produced when the high-pressure gases from burned gunpowder are released from a gun. In an engine, the pulses are released one after another. The explosions come so fast that they blend together in a steady roar.

Sound is air vibration. When the vibrations are large, the sound is loud. The muffler catches the large bursts of high-pressure exhaust gas from the cylinder, smoothing out the pressure pulses and allowing them to be released at an even and constant rate. It does this through the use of perforated tubes within the muffler chamber. The smooth-flowing gases are released to the tailpipe. In this way, the muffler silences engine exhaust noise. Sometimes resonators are used in the exhaust system and the catalytic converter also acts as a muffler. They provide additional expansion space at critical points in the exhaust system to smooth out the exhaust gas flow. ● SEE FIGURE 10–19.

FIGURE 10–20 A hole in the muffler allows condensed water to escape.

![wrench icon] **FREQUENTLY ASKED QUESTION**

Why Is There a Hole in My Muffler?

Many mufflers are equipped with a small hole in the lower rear part to drain accumulated water. About 1 gallon of water is produced in the form of steam for each gallon of gasoline burned. The water vapor often condenses on the cooler surfaces of the exhaust system unless the vehicle has been driven long enough to fully warm the muffler above the boiling point of water (212°F [100°C]). ● **SEE FIGURE 10–20**.

FIGURE 10–21 A high-performance aftermarket air filter often can increase airflow into the engine for more power.

![wrench icon] **TECH TIP**

More Airflow = More Power

One of the most popular high-performance modifications is to replace the factory exhaust system with a low-restriction design and to replace the original air filter and air filter housing with a low-restriction unit as shown in ● **FIGURE 10–21**.

The installation of an aftermarket air filter not only increases power, but also increases air induction noise, which many drivers prefer. The aftermarket filter housing, however, may not be able to effectively prevent water from being drawn into the engine if the vehicle is traveling through deep water.

Almost every modification that increases performance has a negative effect on some other part of the vehicle, or else the manufacturer would include the change at the factory.

Most mufflers have a larger inlet diameter than outlet diameter. As the exhaust enters the muffler, it expands and cools. The cooler exhaust is more dense and occupies less volume. The diameter of the outlet of the muffler and the diameter of the tailpipe can be reduced with no decrease in efficiency.

The tailpipe carries the exhaust gases from the muffler to the air, away from the vehicle. In most cases, the tailpipe exit is at the rear of the vehicle, below the rear bumper. In some cases, the exhaust is released at the side of the vehicle, just ahead of or just behind the rear wheel.

The muffler and tailpipe are supported with brackets called **hangers**. The hangers are made of rubberized fabric with metal ends that hold the muffler and tailpipe in position so that they do not touch any metal part. This helps to isolate the exhaust noise from the rest of the vehicle.

SUMMARY

1. All air entering an engine must be filtered.

2. Engines that use throttle-body injection units are equipped with intake manifolds that keep the airflow speed through the manifold at 50 to 300 feet per second.

3. Most intake manifolds have an EGR valve that regulates the amount of recirculated exhaust that enters the engine to reduce NO_x emissions.

4. Exhaust manifolds can be made from cast iron or stainless steel.

5. The exhaust system also contains a catalytic converter, exhaust pipes, and muffler. The entire exhaust system is supported by rubber hangers that isolate the noise and vibration of the exhaust from the rest of the vehicle.

REVIEW QUESTIONS

1. Why is it necessary to have intake charge velocities of about 50 feet per second?

2. Why can fuel-injected engines use larger (and longer) intake manifolds and still operate at low engine speed?

3. What is a tuned runner in an intake manifold?

4. How does a muffler quiet exhaust noise?

CHAPTER QUIZ

1. Intake charge velocity has to be _____ to prevent fuel droplet separation.
   a. 25 feet per second
   b. 50 feet per second
   c. 100 feet per second
   d. 300 feet per second

2. The intake manifold of a port fuel-injected engine _____.
   a. Uses a dual heat riser
   b. Contains a leaner air–fuel mixture than does the intake manifold of a TBI system
   c. Contains only fuel (gasoline)
   d. Contains only air

3. Why are the EGR gases cooled before entering the engine on some engines?
   a. Cool exhaust gas is more effective at controlling NO_x emissions
   b. To help prevent the exhaust from slowing down
   c. To prevent damage to the intake valve
   d. To prevent heating the air–fuel mixture in the cylinder

4. A heated air intake system is usually necessary for proper cold-engine driveability on _____.
   a. Port fuel-injection systems
   b. Throttle-body fuel-injection systems
   c. Both a port-injected and throttle-body-injected engine
   d. Any fuel-injected engine

5. Air filters can remove particles and dirt as small as _____.
   a. 5 to 10 microns
   b. 10 to 25 microns
   c. 30 to 40 microns
   d. 40 to 50 microns

6. Why do many port fuel-injected engines use long intake manifold runners?
   a. To reduce exhaust emissions
   b. To heat the incoming air
   c. To increase high-RPM power
   d. To increase low-RPM torque

7. Exhaust passages are included in some intake manifolds. Technician A says that the exhaust passages are used for exhaust gas recirculation (EGR) systems. Technician B says that the exhaust heat is used to warm the intake charge on some engines equipped with a throttle-body-type fuel-injection system. Which technician is correct?
   a. Technician A only
   b. Technician B only
   c. Both Technicians A and B
   d. Neither Technician A nor B

8. The upper portion of a two-part intake manifold is often called the _____.
   a. Housing
   b. Lower part
   c. Plenum
   d. Vacuum chamber

9. Technician A says that a cracked exhaust manifold can affect engine operation. Technician B says that a leaking lower intake manifold gasket could cause a vacuum leak. Which technician is correct?
   a. Technician A only
   b. Technician B only
   c. Both Technicians A and B
   d. Neither Technician A nor B

10. Technician A says that some intake manifolds are plastic. Technician B says that some intake manifolds are constructed in two parts or sections: upper and lower. Which technician is correct?
   a. Technician A only
   b. Technician B only
   c. Both Technicians A and B
   d. Neither Technician A nor B

chapter 11

VARIABLE VALVE TIMING SYSTEMS

OBJECTIVES

After studying Chapter 11, the reader will be able to:

1. List the reasons for variable valve timing.
2. Describe how the valve timing is changed.
3. Discuss the various types of variable valve timing.
4. Explain how to diagnose variable valve timing faults.

KEY TERMS

Active fuel management (AFM) 184
Cylinder cut off system 184
Displacement on demand (DOD) 184
EVCP 178
Ground side switching 183
MDS 184
Oil control valve (OCV) 176
Power side switching 183
PWM 181
Spline phaser 178
Vane phaser 178
Variable displacement system 184
VTEC 182
VVT 177

FIGURE 11–1 Camshaft rotation during advance and retard.

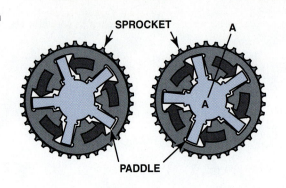

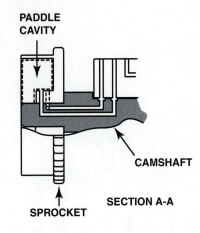

CAMSHAFT POSITION CHART

DRIVING CONDITION	CHANGE IN CAMSHAFT POSITION	OBJECTIVE	RESULT
Idle	No change	Minimize valve overlap	Stabilize idle speed
Light engine load	Retard valve timing	Decrease valve overlap	Stable engine output
Medium engine load	Advance valve timing	Increase valve overlap	Better fuel economy with lower emissions
Low to medium RPM with heavy load	Advance valve timing	Advance intake valve closing	Improve low to midrange torque
High RPM with heavy load	Retard valve timing	Retard intake valve closing	Improve engine output

CHART 11–1

An overview of how variable valve timing is able to improve engine performance and reduce exhaust emissions.

PRINCIPLES OF VARIABLE VALVE TIMING

PURPOSE OF VARIABLE VALVE TIMING Conventional camshafts are permanently synchronized to the crankshaft so that they operate the valves at a specific point in each combustion cycle. In an engine, the intake valve opens slightly before the piston reaches the top of the cylinder and closes about 60 degrees after the piston reaches the bottom of the stroke on every cycle, regardless of the engine speed or load.

Variable-cam timing allows the valves to be operated at different points in the combustion cycle, to improve performance.

There are three basic types of variable valve timing used on vehicles:

1. Exhaust camshaft variable action only on overhead camshaft engines, such as the inline 4.2 liter engine used in Chevrolet Trailblazers.

2. Intake and exhaust camshaft variable action on both camshafts used in many General Motors engines.

3. Overhead valve, cam-in-block engines use variable valve timing by changing the relationship of the camshaft to the crankshaft. See ● **SEE CHART 11–1**.

PARTS AND OPERATION The camshaft position actuator **oil control valve (OCV)** directs oil from the oil feed in the head to the appropriate camshaft position actuator oil passages. There is one OCV for each camshaft position actuator. The OCV is sealed and mounted to the front cover. The ported end of the OCV is inserted into the cylinder head with a sliding fit. A filter screen protects each OCV oil port from any contamination in the oil supply.

The camshaft position actuator is mounted to the front end of the camshaft and the timing notch in the nose of the camshaft aligns with the dowel pin in the camshaft position actuator to ensure proper cam timing and camshaft position actuator oil hole alignment. ● **SEE FIGURE 11–1**.

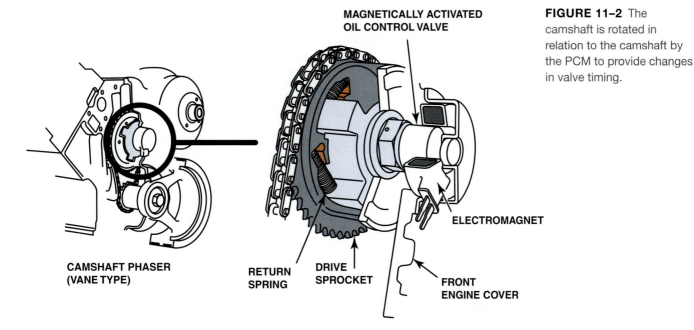

MAGNETICALLY ACTIVATED
OIL CONTROL VALVE

FIGURE 11–2 The camshaft is rotated in relation to the camshaft by the PCM to provide changes in valve timing.

ELECTROMAGNET

CAMSHAFT PHASER
(VANE TYPE)

RETURN
SPRING

DRIVE
SPROCKET

FRONT
ENGINE COVER

? **FREQUENTLY ASKED QUESTION**

What Are The Various Names Used for Variable Valve Timing Systems?

- **BMW**-VANOS (Variable Nockenwellen Steuerung)
- **Ford**-VVT (Variable Valve Timing)
- **GM**-DCVCP–(Double Continuous Variable Cam Phasing) if used for both intake and exhaust camshafts
- **Honda**-VTEC - Variable valve Timing and lift Electronic Control
- **Hyundai**-MPI CVVT (Multiport Injection Continuously Variable Valve Timing)
- **Mazda**-S-VT (Sequential Valve Timing)
- **Mitsubishi**-MIVECC (Mitsubishi Innovative Valve timing Electronic Control system)
- **Nissan**-N-VCTT (Nissan Variable Control Timing)
- **Nissan**-VVL (Variable Valve Lift)
- **Porsche**-variocam–(Variable camshaft timing)
- **Suzuki**-VVT (Variable Valve Timing)
- **Subaru**-AVCS (Active Valve Control System)
- **Toyota**-VVT-i (Variable Valve Timing-intelligent)
- **Toyota**-VVTL-I (Variable Valve Timing and Lift-intelligent)
- **Volkswagen**-VVT (Variable Valve Timing)
- **Volvo**-VVT (Variable Valve Timing)

OHV VARIABLE TIMING

The GM 3900 V-6 engine is an example of an overhead-valve (OHV) cam-in-block engine that uses variable valve timing (VVT) and active fuel management (displacement on demand—DOD). Engine size was increased from 3.5 liters to 3.9 liters because the larger displacement was needed to obtain good performance in the three cylinder mode.

The variable valve timing system uses electronically controlled, hydraulic gear-driven cam phaser that can alter the relationship of the camshaft from 15 degrees retard to 25 degrees advance (40 degrees overall) relative to the crankshaft. By using **variable valve timing (VVT)**, engineers were able to eliminate the EGR valve and still be able to meet the standards for oxides of nitrogen (NO_X). The VVT also works in conjunction with an active manifold that gives the engine a broader torque curve.

A valve in the intake manifold creates a longer path for intake air at low speeds, improving combustion efficiency and torque output. At higher speed the valve opens creating a shorter air path for maximum power production.
● **SEE FIGURE 11–2**.

Varying the exhaust and/or the intake camshaft position allows for reduced exhaust emissions and improved performance. ● **SEE CHART 11–2**.

By varying the exhaust cam phasing, vehicle manufacturers are able to meet newer NO_X reduction standards and eliminate the exhaust gas recirculation (EGR) valve. By using exhaust cam phasing, the PCM can close the exhaust valves sooner than usual, thereby trapping some exhaust gases in the combustion chamber. General Motors uses one or two actuators that allow

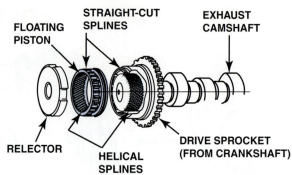

FIGURE 11–3 Spline cam phaser assembly.

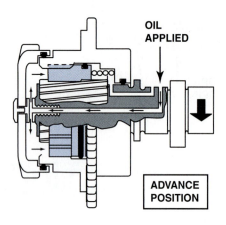

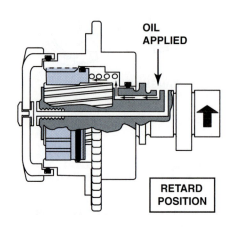

OHV VARIABLE TIMING (CONTINUED)

INTAKE AND EXHAUST CAMSHAFT PHASING CHART

CAMSHAFT PHASING CHANGED	IMPROVES
Exhaust cam phasing	Reduces NO_X exhaust emissions
Exhaust cam phasing	Increases fuel economy (reduced pumping losses)
Intake cam phasing	Increases low-speed torque
Intake cam phasing	Increases high-speed power

CHART 11–2

By varying the intake camshaft timing, engine performance is improved. By varying the exhaust camshaft timing, the exhaust emissions and fuel consumption are reduced.

the camshaft piston to change by up to 50 degrees in relation to the crankshaft position.

There are two types of cam phasing devices used on General Motors engines:

- **Spline phaser**—used on overhead camshaft (OHC) engines

- **Vane phaser**—used on overhead camshaft (OHC) and overhead valve (OHV) cam-in-block engines

SPLINE PHASER SYSTEM   The spline phaser system is also called the **exhaust valve cam phaser (EVCP)** and consists of the following components:

- Engine control module (ECM)

- Four-way pulse-width-modulated (PWM) control valve

- Cam phaser assembly

- Camshaft position (CMP) sensor

  ● **SEE FIGURE 11–3**.

SPLINE PHASER SYSTEM OPERATION   On the 4200 inline six-cylinder engine used in the Chevrolet Trailblazer, the pulse-width-modulated (PWM) control valve is located on the front passenger side of the cylinder head. Oil pressure is regulated by the control valve and then directed to the ports in the cylinder head leading to the camshaft and cam phaser position. The cam phaser is located on the exhaust cams and is part of the exhaust cam sprocket. When the ECM commands an increase in oil pressure, the piston is moved inside the cam phaser and rides along the helical splines, which compresses the coil spring. This movement causes the cam phaser gear and the camshaft to move in an opposite direction, thereby retarding the cam timing. ● **SEE FIGURE 11–4**.

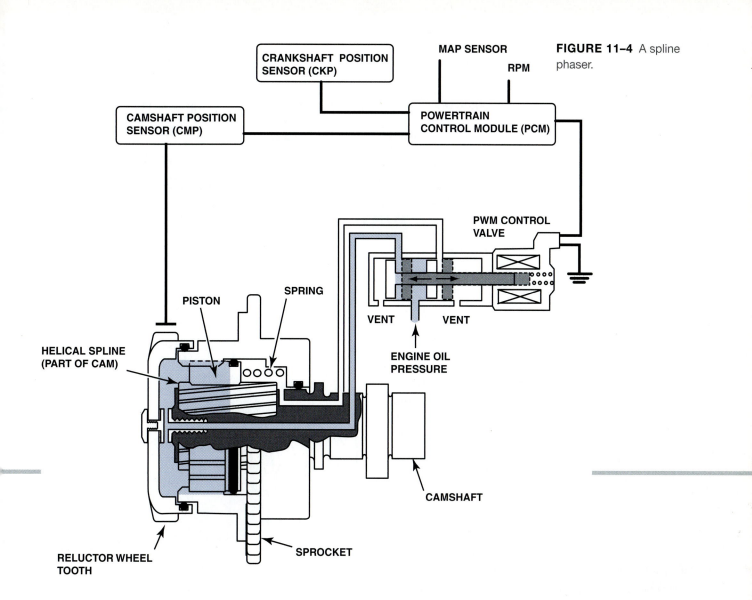

CRANKSHAFT POSITION
SENSOR (CKP)

MAP SENSOR

RPM

FIGURE 11–4 A spline phaser.

CAMSHAFT POSITION
SENSOR (CMP)

POWERTRAIN
CONTROL MODULE (PCM)

PWM CONTROL
VALVE

PISTON

SPRING

VENT

VENT

ENGINE OIL
PRESSURE

HELICAL SPLINE
(PART OF CAM)

CAMSHAFT

RELUCTOR WHEEL
TOOTH

SPROCKET

TECH TIP

**Check the Screen on the Control Valve
If There Are Problems**

If a NO_x emission failure at a state inspection occurs or a diagnostic trouble code is set related to the cam timing, remove the control valve and check for a clogged oil screen. A lack of regular oil changes can cause the screen to become clogged, thereby preventing proper operation. A rough idle is a common complaint because the spring may not be able to return the camshaft to the idle position after a long highway trip. ● **SEE FIGURE 11–5.**

SCREENS

FIGURE 11–5 The screen(s) protect the solenoid valve from dirt and debris that can cause the valve to stick. This fault can set a P0017 diagnostic trouble code (crankshaft position-camshaft position correlation error.)

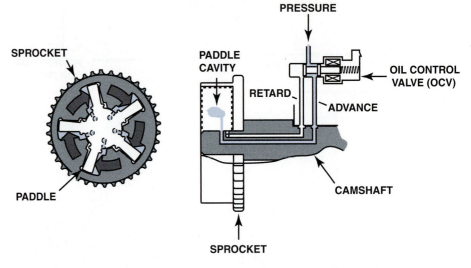

FIGURE 11-6 A vane phaser is used to move the camshaft using changes of oil pressure from the oil control valve.

SPROCKET

PADDLE

ENGINE OIL PRESSURE

PADDLE CAVITY

RETARD

ADVANCE

OIL CONTROL VALVE (OCV)

CAMSHAFT

SPROCKET

OHV VARIABLE TIMING (CONTINUED)

NOTE: A unique cam-within-a-cam is used on the 2008+ Viper V-10 OHV engine. This design allows the exhaust lobes to be moved by up to 36 degrees to improve idle quality and reduction of exhaust emissions.

VANE PHASER SYSTEM ON AN OVERHEAD CAMSHAFT ENGINE
The vane phaser system used on overhead camshaft (OHC) engines uses a camshaft piston (CMP) sensor on each camshaft. Each camshaft has its own actuator and its own oil control valve (OCV). Instead of using a piston along a helical spline, the vane phaser uses a rotor with four vanes, which is connected to the end of the camshaft. The rotor is located inside the stator, which is bolted to the cam sprocket. The stator and rotor are not connected. Oil pressure is controlled on both sides of the vanes of the rotor, which creates a hydraulic link between the two parts. The oil control valve varies the balance of pressure on either side of the vanes and thereby controls the position of the camshaft. A return spring is used under the reluctor of the phaser to help return it to the home or zero degrees position. ● **SEE FIGURE 11-6.**

MAGNETICALLY CONTROLLED VANE PHASER
A magnetically controlled vane phaser is controlled by the ECM by using a 12-volt pulse-width-modulated (PWM) signal to an electromagnet, which operates the oil control valve (OCV). A magnetically controlled vane phaser is used on many General Motors engines that use overhead camshafts on both the intake and exhaust. The OCV directs pressurized engine oil to either advance or retard chambers of the camshaft actuator to change the camshaft position in relation to the crankshaft position. ● **SEE FIGURE 11-7.**

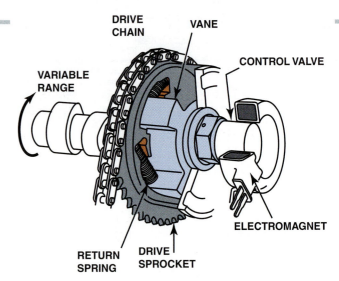

DRIVE CHAIN

VANE

CONTROL VALVE

VARIABLE RANGE

ELECTROMAGNET

RETURN SPRING

DRIVE SPROCKET

FIGURE 11-7 A magnetically controlled vane phaser.

The following occurs when the pulse width is changed:

- **0% pulse width**—The oil is directed to the advance chamber of the exhaust camshaft actuator and the retard chamber of the intake camshaft activator.

- **50% pulse width**—The PCM is holding the cam in the calculated position based on engine RPM and load. At 50% pulse width, the oil flow through the phaser drops to zero. ● **SEE FIGURE 11-8.**

- **100% pulse width**—The oil is directed to the retard chamber of the exhaust camshaft actuator and the advance chamber of the intake camshaft actuator.

The cam phasing is continuously variable with a range from 40 degrees for the intake camshaft and 50 degrees for the

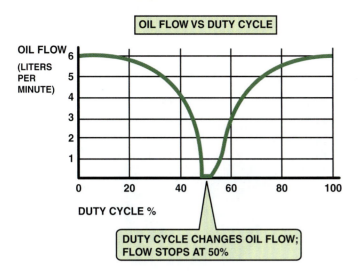

OIL FLOW VS DUTY CYCLE

OIL FLOW (LITERS PER MINUTE)

DUTY CYCLE %

DUTY CYCLE CHANGES OIL FLOW; FLOW STOPS AT 50%

FIGURE 11–8 When the PCM commands 50% duty cycle, the oil flow through the phaser drops to zero.

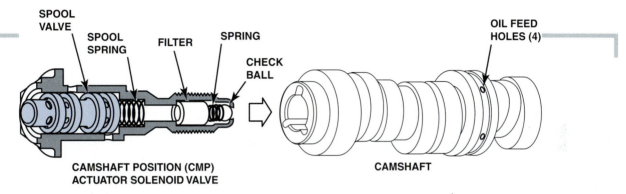

SPOOL VALVE

SPOOL SPRING

FILTER

SPRING

CHECK BALL

OIL FEED HOLES (4)

CAMSHAFT POSITION (CMP) ACTUATOR SOLENOID VALVE

CAMSHAFT

FIGURE 11–9 A camshaft position actuator used in a cam-in-block engine.

exhaust camshaft. The PCM uses the following sensors to determine the best position of the camshaft for maximum power and lowest possible exhaust emissions:

- Engine speed (RPM)
- MAP sensor
- Crankshaft position (CKP) sensor
- Camshaft position (CMP) sensor
- Barometric pressure (BARO) sensor

CAM-IN-BLOCK ENGINE CAM PHASER
Overhead valve engines that use a cam-in-block design use a magnetically controlled cam phaser to vary the camshaft in relation to the crankshaft. This type of phaser is not capable of changing the duration of valve opening or valve lift.

Inside the camshaft actuator is a rotor with vanes that are attached to the camshaft. Oil pressure is supplied to the vanes, which causes the camshaft to rotate in relation to the crankshaft.

The camshaft actuator solenoid valve directs the flow of oil to either the advance or retard side vanes of the actuator. ● SEE **FIGURE 11–9**.

The ECM sends a **pulse-width-modulated (PWM)** signal to the camshaft actuator magnet. The movement of the pintle is used to direct oil flow to the actuator. The higher the duty cycle is, the greater the movement in the valve position and change in camshaft timing.

? FREQUENTLY ASKED QUESTION

What Happens When the Engine Stops?

When the engine stops, the oil pressure drops to zero and a spring-loaded locking pin is used to keep the camshaft locked to prevent noise at engine start. When the engine starts, oil pressure releases the locking pin.

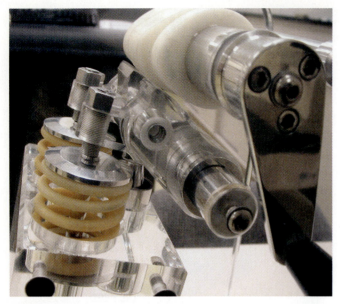

FIGURE 11–10 A plastic mock-up of a Honda VTEC system that uses two different camshaft profiles; one for low-speed engine operation and the other for high speed.

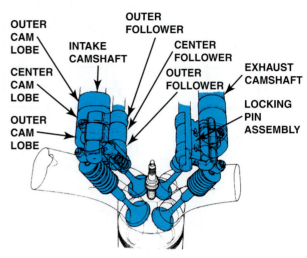

FIGURE 11–11 Engine oil pressure is used to switch cam lobes on a VTEC system.

VARIABLE VALVE TIMING AND LIFT

Many engines use variable valve timing in an effort to improve high-speed performance without the disadvantages of a high-performance camshaft at idle and low speeds. There are two basic systems including:

- Variable camshafts such as the system used by Honda/Acura called **Variable Valve Timing and Lift Electronic Control** or **VTEC**. This system uses two different camshafts for low and high RPM. When the engine is operating at idle and speeds below about 4000 RPM, the valves are opened by camshafts that are optimized by maximum torque and fuel economy. When engine speed reaches a predetermined speed, depending on the exact make and model, the computer turns on a solenoid, which opens a spool valve. When the spool valve opens, engine oil pressure pushes against pins that lock the three intake rocker arms together. With the rocker arms lashed, the valves must follow the profile of the high RPM cam lobe in the center. This process of switching from the low-speed camshaft profile to the high-speed profile takes about 100 milliseconds (0.1 sec). ● SEE **FIGURES 11–10 AND 11–11**.

- Variable camshaft timing is used on many engines including General Motors 4-, 5-, and 6-cylinder engines, as well as engines from BMW, Chrysler, and Nissan. On a system that controls the intake camshaft only, the camshaft timing is advanced at low engine speed, closing the intake valves earlier to improve low RPM torque. At high engine speeds, the camshaft is retarded by using engine oil pressure against a helical gear to rotate the camshaft. When the camshaft is retarded, the intake valve closing is delayed, improving cylinder filling at higher engine speeds. ● SEE FIGURE 11–12. Variable cam timing can be used to control exhaust cam timing only. Engines that use this system, such as the 4.2 liter GM inline 6-cylinder engines, can eliminate the exhaust gas recirculation (EGR) valve because the computer can close the exhaust valve sooner than normal, trapping some exhaust gases in the combustion chamber and therefore eliminating the need for an EGR valve. Some engines use variable camshaft timing on both intake and exhaust cylinder cams.

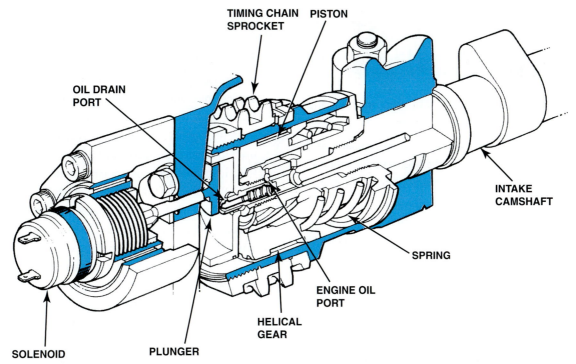

FIGURE 11–12 A typical variable cam timing control valve. The solenoid is controlled by the engine computer and directs engine oil pressure to move a helical gear, which rotates the camshaft relative to the timing chain sprocket.

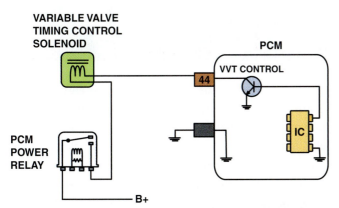

FIGURE 11–13 The schematic of a variable valve timing control circuit, showing that battery power (+) is being applied to the variable valve timing (VVT) solenoid and pulsed to ground by the PCM.

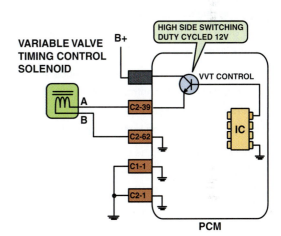

FIGURE 11–14 A variable valve timing solenoid being controlled by applying voltage from the PCM.

COMPUTER CONTROL OF VARIABLE VALVE TIMING

Variable valve timing is controlled by the Powertrain Control Module (PCM) and can be one of two different circuits:

- **Ground side switching** is the most commonly used.
  - ● **SEE FIGURE 11–13**. The variable valve timing (VVT) solenoid usually has 3 to 6 ohms of resistance and therefore requires 2 to 4 amperes of current to operate.

- **Power side switching** is commonly found on General Motors vehicles and the solenoid has 8 to 12 ohms of resistance requiring 1.0 to 1.5 amperes of current to operate. ● **SEE FIGURE 11–14** for an example of a circuit showing high-side switching of the variable valve timing solenoid.

DIAGNOSIS OF VARIABLE VALVE TIMING SYSTEMS

The diagnostic procedure as specified by most vehicle manufacturers usually includes the following steps:

STEP 1 Verify the customer concern. This will usually be a check engine light (MIL) as the engine performance effects would be minor under most operating conditions.

STEP 2 Check for stored diagnostic trouble codes (DTCs). Typical variable valve timing-related DTCs include:
P0011—Intake cam position is over advanced bank 1
P0021—Intake cam position is over advanced bank 2
P0012—Intake cam position is over retarded bank 1
P0022—Intake cam position is over retarded bank 2

STEP 3 Use a scan tool and check for duty cycle on the cam phase solenoid while operating the vehicle at a steady road speed. The commanded pulse width should be 50%. If the pulse width is not 50%, then the PCM is trying to move the phaser to its commanded position and the phaser has not reacted properly. A PWM signal of higher or lower than 50% usually indicates a stuck phaser assembly.

STEP 4 Check the solenoid for proper resistance. If a scan tool with bidirectional control is available, connect an ammeter and measure the current as the solenoid is being commanded on by the scan tool.

STEP 5 Check for proper engine oil pressure. Low oil pressure or restricted flow to the cam phaser can be the cause of many diagnostic trouble codes.

STEP 6 Determine the root cause of the problem and clear all DTCs.

STEP 7 Road test the vehicle to verify the fault has been corrected.

 REAL WORLD FIX

The Case of the Wrong Oil

A 2007 Dodge Durango was in the shop for routine service, including a tire rotation and an oil change. Shortly after, the customer returned and stated that the "check engine" light was on. A scan tool was used to retrieve any diagnostic trouble codes. A P0521, "oil pressure not reaching specified value at 1250 RPM" was set. A check of service information showed that this code could be set if the incorrect viscosity engine oil was used. The shop had used SAE 10W-30 but the 5.7 liter Hemi V-8 with multiple displacement system (MDS) required SAE 5W-20 oil. The correct oil was installed and the DTC cleared. A thorough test drive confirmed that the fault had been corrected and the shop learned that the proper viscosity oil is important to use in all vehicles.

VARIABLE DISPLACEMENT SYSTEMS

PURPOSE AND FUNCTION Some engines are designed to be operated on four of eight or three of six cylinders during low-load conditions to improve fuel economy. The powertrain computer monitors engine speed, coolant temperature, throttle position, and load. It also determines when to deactivate cylinders.

Systems that can deactivate cylinders are called:

- **Cylinder cutoff system**
- **Variable displacement system**
- **Displacement on Demand (DOD)** (now called **Active Fuel Management**) for General Motors
- **Multiple Displacement System (MDS)** for Chrysler

PARTS AND OPERATION The key to this process is the use of two-stage hydraulic valve lifters. In normal operation, the inner and outer lifter sleeves are held together by a pin and operate as an assembly. When the computer determines that the cylinder can be deactivated, oil pressure is delivered to a passage, which depresses the pin and allows the outer portion of the lifter to follow the contour of the cam while the inner portion remains stationary, keeping the valve closed. The electronic operation is achieved through the use of lifter oil manifold containing solenoids to control the oil flow, which is used to activate or deactivate the cylinders. ● **SEE FIGURES 11–15 AND 11–16.**

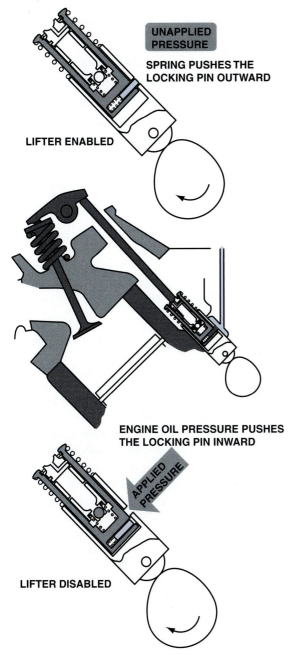

UNAPPLIED PRESSURE

SPRING PUSHES THE LOCKING PIN OUTWARD

LIFTER ENABLED

ENGINE OIL PRESSURE PUSHES THE LOCKING PIN INWARD

APPLIED PRESSURE

LIFTER DISABLED

FIGURE 11–15 Oil pressure applied to the locking pin causes the inside of the lifter to freely move inside the outer shell of the lifter, thereby keeping the valve closed.

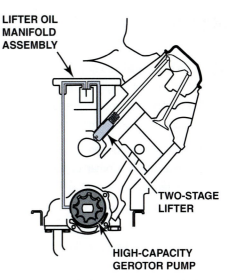

LIFTER OIL MANIFOLD ASSEMBLY

TWO-STAGE LIFTER

HIGH-CAPACITY GEROTOR PUMP

FIGURE 11–16 Active fuel management includes many different components and changes to the oiling system, which makes routine oil changes even more important on engines equipped with this system.

FIGURE 11–17 The driver information display on a Chevrolet Impala with a 5.3 liter V-8 equipped with active fuel management. The transition between 4-cylinder mode and 8-cylinder mode is so smooth that most drivers are not aware that the switch is occurring.

CYLINDER DEACTIVATION SYSTEM DIAGNOSIS

A cylinder deactivation system, also called cylinder cutoff system or variable displacement system, often displays when the system is active on the driver information display. ● **SEE FIGURE 11–17**.

The diagnosis of the variable displacement system usually starts as a result of a check engine light (malfunction indicator lamp or MIL). The diagnostic procedure specified by the vehicle manufacturer usually includes the following steps:

STEP 1 Verify the customer concern. With a cylinder deactivation system, the customer concern could be lower than expected fuel economy.

STEP 2 Check for any stored diagnostic trouble codes (DTCs). A fault code set for an emission-related fault could cause the PCM to disable cylinder deactivation.

STEP 3 Perform a thorough visual inspection, including checking the oil level and condition.

STEP 4 Check scan tool data for related parameters to see if any of the sensors are out of the normal range.

STEP 5 Determine the root cause and perform the repair as specified in service information.

STEP 6 Test drive the vehicle to verify proper operation.

SUMMARY

1. Variable valve timing is used to improve engine performance and reduce exhaust emissions.

2. Intake cam phasing is used to improve low-speed torque and high-speed power.

3. Exhaust cam phasing is used to reduce exhaust emissions and increase fuel economy by reducing pumping losses.

4. Variable valve timing or overhead valve, cam-in-block engines are used to reduce NO_X emissions.

5. Variable valve timing faults are often the result of extended oil change intervals, which can clog the screen on the cam phaser. As a result of the clogged screen, oil cannot flow to and adjust the valve timing, thereby setting valve timing-related diagnostic trouble codes (DTCs).

6. Oil flow to the phasers is controlled by the Powertrain Control Module (PCM). If a 50% duty cycle is shown on a scan tool, this means that the phaser has reached the commanded position.

7. If the duty cycle is other than 50% while operating the vehicle under steady conditions, this means that there is a fault in the system because the cam phaser is not able to reach the commanded position.

8. Variable valve timing and lift electronic control (VTEC) is used on most Honda/Acura vehicles to improve performance.

9. Control of the variable valve timing (VVT) solenoid can be either ground side switching or power side switching.

10. Common variable valve timing diagnostic trouble codes include P0011, P0021, P0012, and P0022.

11. Cylinder deactivation systems improve fuel economy by disabling half of the cylinders during certain driving conditions, such as steady speed cruising.

REVIEW QUESTIONS

1. What is the advantage of varying the intake camshaft timing?

2. What is the advantage of varying the exhaust camshaft timing?

3. Why must the engine oil be changed regularly on an engine equipped with variable valve timing?

4. What sensors does the PCM monitor to determine the best position for the camshaft(s)?

5. What diagnostic trouble codes are associated with the variable valve timing (VVT) system?

1. Variable valve timing can be found on which type of engines?
   a. Cam-in-block
   b. SOHC
   c. DOHC
   d. All of the above

2. To reduce oxides of nitrogen (NO_X) exhaust emissions, which camshaft is varied?
   a. Exhaust camshaft only
   b. Intake camshaft only
   c. Both the intake and exhaust camshaft
   d. The exhaust camshaft is advanced and the intake camshaft is advanced.

3. To increase engine performance, which camshaft is varied?
   a. Exhaust camshaft only
   b. Intake camshaft only
   c. Both the intake and exhaust camshaft
   d. The exhaust camshaft is advanced and the intake camshaft is advanced.

4. What is the commanded pulse width of the camshaft phaser that results in the desired position?
   a. 0%
   b. 25%
   c. 50%
   d. 100%

5. What sensors are used by the PCM to determine the best position of the camshafts for maximum power and lowest possible exhaust emissions?
   a. Engine speed (RPM)
   b. Crankshaft position (CKP) sensor
   c. Camshaft position (CMP) sensor
   d. All of the above

6. How is the camshaft actuator controlled?
   a. On only when conditions are right
   b. Pulse-width-modulated (PWM) signal
   c. Spring-loaded to the correct position based on engine speed
   d. Vacuum-controlled valve

7. If the engine oil is not changed regularly, what is the most likely fault that can occur to an engine equipped with variable valve timing (VVT)?
   a. Low oil pressure diagnostic trouble code (DTC)
   b. A no-start condition because the camshaft cannot rotate
   c. The filter screens on the actuator control valve become clogged
   d. Any of the above

8. How quickly can the rocker arms be switched from the low-speed camshaft profile to the high-speed camshaft profile on a Honda equipped with a VTEC system?
   a. 50 milliseconds
   b. 100 milliseconds
   c. 250 milliseconds
   d. 500 milliseconds

9. Which diagnostic trouble code (DTC) may be set if there is a problem with the intake cam position?
   a. P0300
   b. P042
   c. P0011 or P0021
   d. P0012 or P0022

10. If the incorrect grade of engine oil is used in an engine equipped with a variable displacement engine, what diagnostic trouble code (DTC) could be set?
    a. P0521
    b. P0300
    c. P0420
    d. P0011

TURBOCHARGING AND SUPERCHARGING

OBJECTIVES

After studying Chapter 12, the reader will be able to:

1. Prepare for ASE Engine Performance (A8) certification test content area "C" (Fuel, Air Induction, and Exhaust Systems Diagnosis and Repair).

2. Explain the difference between a turbocharger and a supercharger.

3. Describe how the boost levels are controlled.

4. Discuss maintenance procedures for turbochargers and superchargers.

FIGURE 12–1 A supercharger on a Ford V-8.

FIGURE 12–2 A turbocharger on a Toyota engine.

AIRFLOW REQUIREMENTS

Naturally aspirated engines with throttle bodies rely on atmospheric pressure to push an air–fuel mixture into the combustion chamber vacuum created by the downstroke of a piston. The mixture is then compressed before ignition to increase the force of the burning, expanding gases. The greater the mixture compression, the greater the power resulting from combustion.

All gasoline automobile engines share certain air–fuel requirements. For example, a four-stroke engine can take in only so much air, and how much fuel it consumes depends on how much air it takes in. Engineers calculate engine airflow requirements using these three factors:

- Engine displacement
- Engine revolutions per minute (RPM)
- Volumetric efficiency

VOLUMETRIC EFFICIENCY **Volumetric efficiency** is a comparison of the actual volume of air–fuel mixture drawn into an engine to the theoretical maximum volume that could be drawn in. Volumetric efficiency is expressed as a percentage, and changes with engine speed. For example, an engine might have 75% volumetric efficiency at 1000 RPM. The same engine might be rated at 85% at 2000 RPM and 60% at 3000 RPM.

If the engine takes in the airflow volume slowly, a cylinder might fill to capacity. It takes a definite amount of time for the airflow to pass through all the curves of the intake manifold and valve port. Therefore, volumetric efficiency decreases as engine speed increases. At high speed, it may drop to as low as 50%.

The average street engine never reaches 100% volumetric efficiency. With a street engine, the volumetric efficiency is about 75% at maximum speed, or 80% at the torque peak. A high-performance street engine is about 85% efficient, or a bit more efficient at peak torque. A race engine usually has 95% or better volumetric efficiency. These figures apply only to naturally aspirated engines, however, and turbocharged and supercharged engines easily achieve more than 100% volumetric efficiency. Many vehicles are equipped with a supercharger or a turbocharger to increase power. ● **SEE FIGURES 12–1 AND 12–2.**

ENGINE COMPRESSION Higher compression increases the thermal efficiency of the engine because it raises compression temperatures, resulting in hotter, more complete combustion. However, a higher compression can cause an increase in NO_x emissions and would require the use of high-octane gasoline with effective antiknock additives.

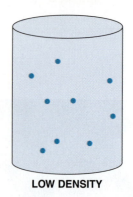
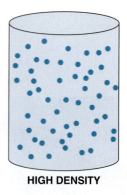

FIGURE 12–3 The more air and fuel that can be packed in a cylinder, the greater the density of the air–fuel charge.

LOW DENSITY   **HIGH DENSITY**

SUPERCHARGING PRINCIPLES

The amount of force an air–fuel charge produces when it is ignited is largely a function of the charge density. Density is the mass of a substance in a given amount of space. ● **SEE FIGURE 12–3**.

The greater the density of an air–fuel charge forced into a cylinder, the greater the force it produces when ignited, and the greater the engine power.

An engine that uses atmospheric pressure for intake is called a **naturally (normally) aspirated** engine. A better way to increase air density in the cylinder is to use a pump.

When air is pumped into the cylinder, the combustion chamber receives an increase of air pressure known as **boost** and is measured in pounds per square inch (PSI), atmospheres (ATM), or **bar**. While boost pressure increases air density, friction heats air in motion and causes an increase in temperature. This increase in temperature works in the opposite direction, decreasing air density. Because of these and other variables, an increase in pressure does not always result in greater air density.

Another way to achieve an increase in mixture compression is called **supercharging.** This method uses a pump to pack a denser air–fuel charge into the cylinders. Since the density of the air–fuel charge is greater, so is its weight—and power is directly related to the weight of an air–fuel charge consumed within a given time period. The result is similar to that of a high-compression ratio, but the effect can be controlled during idle and deceleration to avoid high emissions.

Air is drawn into a naturally aspirated engine by atmospheric pressure forcing it into the low-pressure area of the intake manifold. The low pressure or vacuum in the manifold results from the reciprocating motion of the pistons. When a piston moves downward during its intake stroke, it creates an empty space, or vacuum, in the cylinder. Although atmospheric pressure pushes air to fill up as much of this empty space as possible, it has a difficult path to travel. The air must pass through the air filter, the throttle body, the manifold, and the intake port before entering the cylinder. Bends and restrictions in this pathway limit the amount of air reaching the cylinder before the intake valve closes; therefore, the volumetric efficiency is less than 100%.

Pumping air into the intake system under pressure forces it through the bends and restrictions at a greater speed than it would travel under normal atmospheric pressure, allowing more air to enter the intake port before it closes. By increasing the airflow into the intake, more fuel can be mixed with the air while still maintaining the same air–fuel ratio. The denser the air–fuel charge entering the engine during its intake stroke, the greater the potential energy released during combustion. In addition to the increased power resulting from combustion, there are several other advantages of supercharging an engine including:

- It increases the air–fuel charge density to provide high-compression pressure when power is required, but allows the engine to run on lower pressures when additional power is not required.

- The pumped air pushes the remaining exhaust from the combustion chamber during intake and exhaust valve overlap.

- The forced airflow and removal of hot exhaust gases lowers the temperature of the cylinder head, pistons, and valves, and helps extend the life of the engine.

A supercharger pressurizes air to greater than atmospheric pressure. The pressurization above atmospheric pressure, or boost, can be measured in the same way as atmospheric pressure. Atmospheric pressure drops as altitude increases, but boost pressure remains the same. If a supercharger develops

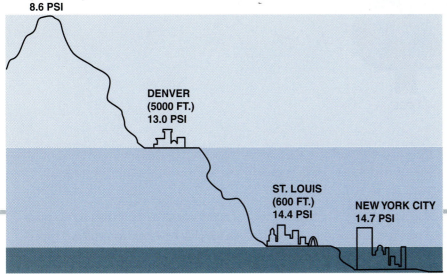

FIGURE 12–4 Atmospheric pressure decreases with increases in altitude.

PIKES PEAK
(14,000 FT.)
8.6 PSI

DENVER
(5000 FT.)
13.0 PSI

ST. LOUIS
(600 FT.)
14.4 PSI

NEW YORK CITY
14.7 PSI

FINAL COMPRESSION RATIO CHART AT VARIOUS BOOST LEVELS

BLOWER BOOST (PSI)

Comp Ratio	2	4	6	8	10	12	14	16	18	20
6.5	7.4	8.3	9.2	10	10.9	11.8	12.7	13.6	14.5	15.3
7	8	8.9	9.9	10.8	11.8	12.7	13.6	14.5	15.3	16.2
7.5	8.5	9.5	10.6	11.6	12.6	13.6	14.6	15.7	16.7	17.8
8	9.1	10.2	11.3	12.4	13.4	14.5	15.6	16.7	17.8	18.9
8.5	9.7	10.8	12	13.1	14.3	15.4	16.6	17.8	18.9	19.8
9	10.2	11.4	12.7	13.9	15.1	16.3	17.6	18.8	20	21.2
9.5	10.8	12.1	13.4	14.7	16	17.3	18.5	19.8	21.1	22.4
10	11.4	12.7	14.1	15.4	16.8	18.2	19.5	20.9	22.2	23.6

CHART 12–1

Equivalent compression ratios for listed boost levels.

12 PSI (83 kPa) boost at sea level, it will develop the same amount at a 5,000-foot altitude because boost pressure is measured inside the intake manifold. ● **SEE FIGURE 12–4.**

BOOST AND COMPRESSION RATIOS Boost increases the amount of air drawn into the cylinder during the intake stroke. This extra air causes the effective compression ratio to be greater than the mechanical compression ratio designed into the engine. The higher the boost pressure, the greater the compression ratio. ● **SEE CHART 12–1** for an example of how much the effective compression ratio is increased compared to the boost pressure.

FIGURE 12–5 A roots-type supercharger uses two lobes to force the air around the outside of the housing and forces it into the intake manifold.

LOBE

SUPERCHARGERS

A supercharger is an engine-driven air pump that supplies more than the normal amount of air into the intake manifold and boosts engine torque and power. A supercharger provides an instantaneous increase in power without the delay or lag often associated with turbochargers. However, a supercharger, because it is driven by the engine, does require horsepower to operate and is not as efficient as a turbocharger.

In basic concept, a supercharger is nothing more than an air pump mechanically driven by the engine itself. Gears, shafts, chains, or belts from the crankshaft can be used to turn the pump. This means that the air pump or supercharger pumps air in direct relation to engine speed.

There are two general types of superchargers:

- **Roots-type supercharger.** Named for Philander and Francis Roots, two brothers from Connersville, Indiana, who patented the design in 1860 as a type of water pump to be used in mines. Later it was used to move air and is used today on two-stroke cycle Detroit diesel engines and other supercharged engines. The **roots-type supercharger** is called a **positive displacement** design because all of the air that enters is forced through the unit. Examples of a roots-type supercharger include the GMC 6-71 (used originally on GMC diesel engines that had six cylinders each with 71 cu. in.) and Eaton used on supercharged 3800 V-6 General Motors engines. ● **SEE FIGURE 12–5.**

- **Centrifugal supercharger.** A centrifugal supercharger is similar to a turbocharger but is mechanically driven by the engine instead of being powered by the hot exhaust gases. A centrifugal supercharger is not a positive

displacement pump and all of the air that enters is not forced through the unit. Air enters a centrifugal supercharger housing in the center and exits at the outer edges of the compressor wheels at a much higher speed due to centrifugal force. The speed of the blades has to be higher than engine speed so a smaller pulley is used on the supercharger and the crankshaft overdrives the impeller through an internal gear box achieving about seven times the speed of the engine. Examples of centrifugal superchargers include Vortech and Paxton.

SUPERCHARGER BOOST CONTROL Many factory-installed superchargers are equipped with a **bypass valve** that allows intake air to flow directly into the intake manifold bypassing the supercharger. The computer controls the bypass valve actuator. ● **SEE FIGURE 12–6.**

The airflow is directed around the supercharger whenever any of the following conditions occur:

- The boost pressure, as measured by the MAP sensor, indicates that the intake manifold pressure is reaching the predetermined boost level.

- During deceleration.

- Whenever reverse gear is selected.

SUPERCHARGER SERVICE Superchargers are usually lubricated with synthetic engine oil inside the unit. This oil level should be checked and replaced as specified by the vehicle or supercharger manufacturer. The drive belt should also be inspected and replaced as necessary.

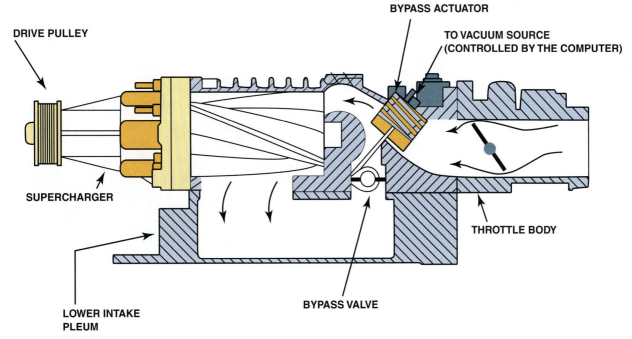

FIGURE 12–6 The bypass actuator opens the bypass valve to control boost pressure.

TURBOCHARGERS

The major disadvantage of a supercharger is its reliance on engine power to drive the unit. In some installations, as much as 20% of the engine's power is used by a mechanical supercharger. However, by connecting a centrifugal supercharger to a turbine drive wheel and installing it in the exhaust path, the lost engine horsepower is regained to perform other work and the combustion heat energy lost in the engine exhaust (as much as 40% to 50%) can be harnessed to do useful work. This is the concept of a **turbocharger.**

The turbocharger's main advantage over a mechanically driven supercharger is that the turbocharger does not drain power from the engine. In a naturally aspirated engine, about half of the heat energy contained in the fuel goes out the exhaust system. ● **SEE FIGURE 12–7.** Another 25% is lost through radiator cooling. Only about 25% is actually converted to mechanical power. A mechanically driven pump uses some of this mechanical output, but a turbocharger gets its energy from the exhaust gases, converting more of the fuel's heat energy into mechanical energy.

A turbocharger turbine looks much like a typical centrifugal pump used for supercharging. ● **SEE FIGURE 12–8.** Hot exhaust gases flow from the combustion chamber to the turbine wheel. The gases are heated and expanded as they leave the engine. It is not the speed of force of the exhaust gases that forces the turbine wheel to turn, as is commonly thought, but the expansion of hot gases against the turbine wheel's blades.

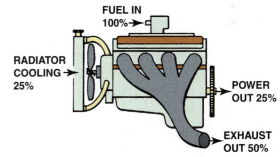

FIGURE 12–7 A turbocharger uses some of the heat energy that would normally be wasted.

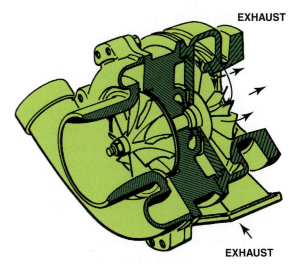

FIGURE 12–8 A turbine wheel is turned by the expanding exhaust gases.

FIGURE 12–9 The exhaust drives the turbine wheel on the left, which is connected to the impeller wheel on the right through a shaft. The bushings that support the shaft are lubricated with engine oil under pressure.

TURBOCHARGER DESIGN AND OPERATION

A turbocharger consists of two chambers connected by a center housing. The two chambers contain a turbine wheel and a compressor wheel connected by a shaft which passes through the center housing.

To take full advantage of the exhaust heat which provides the rotating force, a turbocharger must be positioned as close as possible to the exhaust manifold. This allows the hot exhaust to pass directly into the unit with a minimum of heat loss. As exhaust gas enters the turbocharger, it rotates the turbine blades. The turbine wheel and compressor wheel are on the same shaft so that they turn at the same speed. Rotation of the compressor wheel draws air in through a central inlet and centrifugal force pumps it through an outlet at the edge of the housing. A pair of bearings in the center housing support the turbine and compressor wheel shaft, and are lubricated by engine oil. ● **SEE FIGURE 12–9.**

Both the turbine and compressor wheels must operate with extremely close clearances to minimize possible leakage around their blades. Any leakage around the turbine blades causes a dissipation of the heat energy required for compressor rotation. Leakage around the compressor blades prevents the turbocharger from developing its full boost pressure.

When the engine is started and runs at low speed, both exhaust heat and pressure are low and the turbine runs at a low speed (approximately 1000 RPM). Because the compressor does not turn fast enough to develop boost pressure, air simply passes through it and the engine works like any naturally aspirated engine. As the engine runs faster or load increases, both exhaust heat and flow increases, causing the turbine and compressor wheels to rotate faster. Since there is no brake and very little rotating resistance on the turbocharger shaft, the turbine and compressor wheels accelerate as the exhaust heat energy increases. When an engine is running at full power, the typical turbocharger rotates at speeds between 100,000 and 150,000 RPM.

Engine deceleration from full power to idle requires only a second or two because of its internal friction, pumping resistance, and drivetrain load. The turbocharger, however, has no such load on its shaft, and is already turning many times faster than the engine at top speed. As a result, it can take as much as a minute or more after the engine has returned to idle speed before the turbocharger also has returned to idle. If the engine is decelerated to idle and then shut off immediately, engine lubrication stops flowing to the center housing bearings while the turbocharger is still spinning at thousands of RPM. The oil in the center housing is then subjected to extreme heat and can gradually "coke" or oxidize. The coked oil can clog passages and will reduce the life of the turbocharger.

The high rotating speeds and extremely close clearances of the turbine and compressor wheels in their housings require equally critical bearing clearances. The bearings must keep radial clearances of 0.003 to 0.006 inch (0.08 to 0.15 mm). Axial clearance (end play) must be maintained at 0.001 to 0.003 inch (0.025 to 0.08 mm). If properly maintained, the turbocharger also is a trouble-free device. However, to prevent problems, the following conditions must be met:

- The turbocharger bearings must be constantly lubricated with clean engine oil—turbocharged engines should have regular oil changes at half the time or mileage intervals specified for nonturbocharged engines.

- Dirt particles and other contamination must be kept out of the intake and exhaust housings.

FIGURE 12–10 The unit on top of this Subaru that looks like a radiator is the intercooler, which cools the air after it has been compressed by the turbocharger.

- Whenever a basic engine bearing (crankshaft or camshaft) has been damaged, the turbocharger must be flushed with clean engine oil after the bearing has been replaced.
- If the turbocharger is damaged, the engine oil must be drained and flushed and the oil filter replaced as part of the repair procedure.

Late-model turbochargers all have liquid-cooled center bearings to prevent heat damage. In a liquid-cooled turbocharger, engine coolant is circulated through passages cast in the center housing to draw off the excess heat. This allows the bearings to run cooler and minimize the probability of oil coking when the engine is shut down.

TURBOCHARGER SIZE AND RESPONSE TIME
A time lag occurs between an increase in engine speed and the increase in the speed of the turbocharger. This delay between acceleration and turbo boost is called **turbo lag.** Like any material, moving exhaust gas has inertia. Inertia also is present in the turbine and compressor wheels, as well as the intake airflow. Unlike a supercharger, the turbocharger cannot supply an adequate amount of boost at low speed.

Turbocharger response time is directly related to the size of the turbine and compressor wheels. Small wheels accelerate rapidly; large wheels accelerate slowly. While small wheels would seem to have an advantage over larger ones, they may not have enough airflow capacity for an engine. To minimize turbo lag, the intake and exhaust breathing capacities of an engine must be matched to the exhaust and intake airflow capabilities of the turbocharger.

BOOST CONTROL

Both supercharged and turbocharged systems are designed to provide a pressure greater than atmospheric pressure in the intake manifold. This increased pressure forces additional amounts of air into the combustion chamber over what would normally be forced in by atmospheric pressure. This increased charge increases engine power. The amount of "boost" (or pressure in the intake manifold) is measured in pounds per square inch (PSI), in inches of mercury (in. Hg), in bar, or in atmospheres. The following values will vary due to altitude and weather conditions (barometric pressure).

    1 atmosphere = 14.7 PSI
    1 atmosphere = 29.50 in. Hg
    1 atmosphere = 1.0 bar
    1 bar = 14.7 PSI

The higher the level of boost (pressure), the greater the horsepower potential. However, other factors must be considered when increasing boost pressure:

1. As boost pressure increases, the temperature of the air also increases.

2. As the temperature of the air increases, combustion temperatures also increase, which increases the possibility of detonation.

3. Power can be increased by cooling the compressed air after it leaves the turbocharger. *The power can be increased about 1% per 10°F by which the air is cooled.* A typical cooling device is called an **intercooler** and is similar to a radiator, wherein outside air can pass through, cooling the pressurized heated air. ● **SEE FIGURE 12–10.**

    Some intercoolers use engine coolant to cool the hot compressed air that flows from the turbocharger to the intake.

4. As boost pressure increases, combustion temperature and pressures increase, which, if not limited, can do severe engine damage. The maximum exhaust gas temperature must be 1550°F (840°C). Higher temperatures decrease the durability of the turbocharger *and* the engine.

WASTEGATE
A turbocharger uses exhaust gases to increase boost, which causes the engine to make more exhaust gases, which in turn increases the boost from the turbocharger. To prevent overboost and severe engine damage, most turbocharger systems use a wastegate. A **wastegate** is a valve similar to a door that can open and close. The wastegate is a bypass valve at the exhaust inlet to the turbine. It allows all of

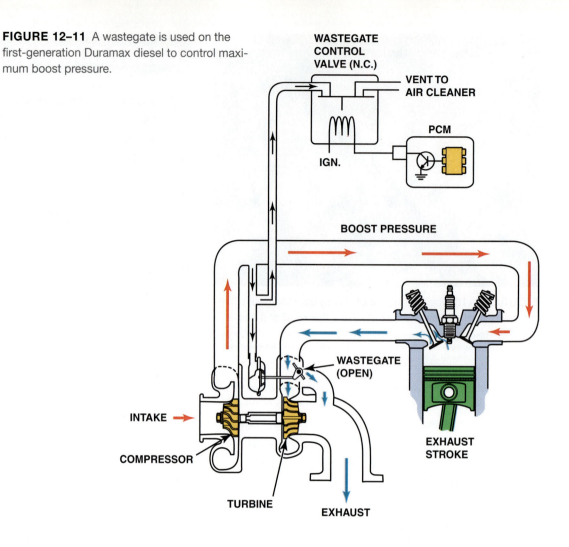

FIGURE 12–11 A wastegate is used on the first-generation Duramax diesel to control maximum boost pressure.

the exhaust into the turbine, or it can route part of the exhaust past the turbine to the exhaust system. If the valve is closed, all of the exhaust travels to the turbocharger. When a predetermined amount of boost pressure develops in the intake manifold, the wastegate valve is opened. As the valve opens, most of the exhaust flows directly out the exhaust system, bypassing the turbocharger. With less exhaust flowing across the vanes of the turbocharger, the turbocharger decreases in speed and boost pressure is reduced. When the boost pressure drops, the wastegate valve closes to direct the exhaust over the turbocharger vanes and again allow the boost pressure to rise. Wastegate operation is a continuous process to control boost pressure.

The wastegate is the pressure control valve of a turbocharger system. The wastegate is usually controlled by the onboard computer through a boost control solenoid. ● **SEE FIGURE 12–11.**

TECH TIP

Boost Is the Result of Restriction

The boost pressure of a turbocharger (or supercharger) is commonly measured in pounds per square inch. If a cylinder head is restricted because of small valves and ports, the turbocharger will quickly provide boost. Boost results when the air being forced into the cylinder heads cannot flow into the cylinders fast enough and "piles up" in the intake manifold, increasing boost pressure. If an engine had large valves and ports, the turbocharger could provide a much greater *amount* of air into the engine at the same boost pressure as an identical engine with smaller valves and ports. Therefore, by increasing the size of the valves, a turbocharged or supercharged engine will be capable of producing much greater power.

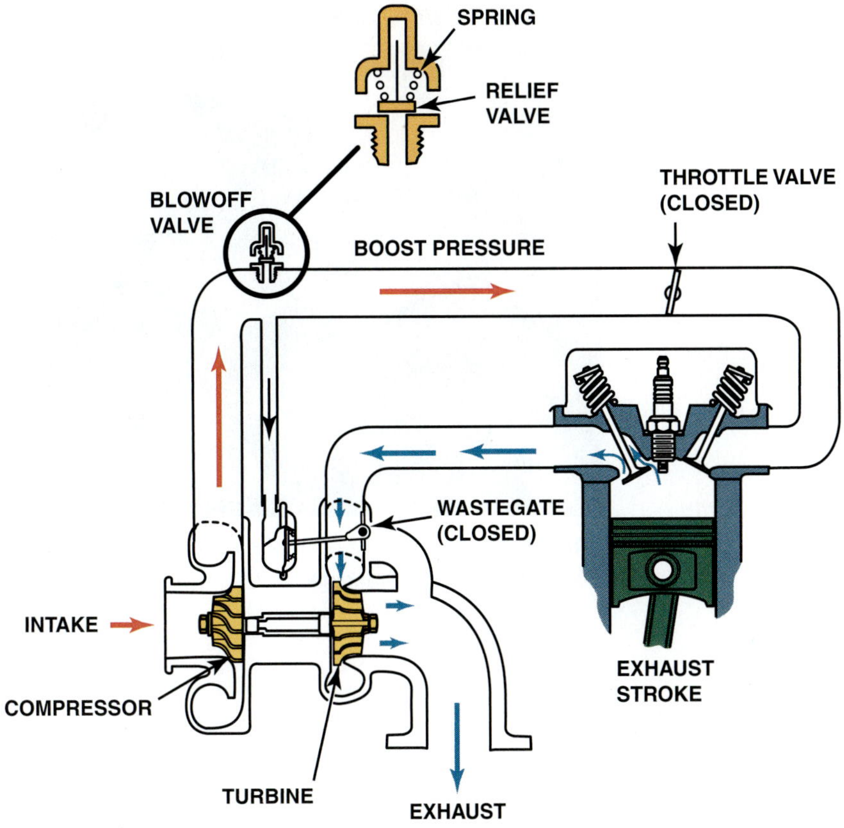

FIGURE 12–12 A blow-off valve is used in some turbocharged systems to relieve boost pressure during deceleration.

RELIEF VALVES A wastegate controls the exhaust side of the turbocharger. A relief valve controls the intake side. A **relief valve** vents pressurized air from the connecting pipe between the outlet of the turbocharger and the throttle whenever the throttle is closed during boost, such as during shifts. If the pressure is not released, the turbocharger turbine wheel will slow down, creating a lag when the throttle is opened again after a shift has been completed. There are two basic types of relief valves including:

- **Compressor bypass valve or CBV** This type of relief valve routes the pressurized air to the inlet side of the turbocharger for reuse and is quiet during operation.

- **Blow-off valve or BOV** This is also called a **dump valve** or **vent valve** and features an adjustable spring design that keeps the valve closed until a sudden release of the throttle. The resulting pressure increase opens the valve and vents the pressurized air directly into the atmosphere. This type of relief valve is noisy in operation and creates a whooshing sound when the valve opens.
- **SEE FIGURE 12–12**.

If One Is Good, Two Are Better

A turbocharger uses the exhaust from the engine to spin a turbine, which is connected to an impeller inside a turbocharger. This impeller then forces air into the engine under pressure higher than is normally achieved without a turbocharger. The more air that can be forced into an engine, the greater the power potential. A V-type engine has two exhaust manifolds and so two small turbochargers can be used to help force greater quantities of air into an engine, as shown in ● **FIGURE 12–13**.

FIGURE 12–13 A dual turbocharger system installed on a small block Chevrolet V-8 engine.

TURBOCHARGER FAILURES

When turbochargers fail to function correctly, a drop in power is noticed. To restore proper operation, the turbocharger must be rebuilt, repaired, or replaced. It is not possible to simply remove the turbocharger, seal any openings, and still maintain decent driveability. Bearing failure is a common cause of turbocharger failure, and replacement bearings are usually only available to rebuilders. Another common turbocharger problem is excessive and continuous oil consumption resulting in blue exhaust smoke. Turbochargers use small rings similar to piston rings on the shaft to prevent exhaust (combustion gases) from entering the central bearing. Because there are no seals to keep oil in, excessive oil consumption is usually caused by:

1. A plugged positive crankcase ventilation (PCV) system resulting in excessive crankcase pressures forcing oil into the air inlet. This failure is not related to the turbocharger, but the turbocharger is often blamed.

2. A clogged air filter, which causes a low-pressure area in the inlet, which can draw oil past the turbo shaft rings and into the intake manifold.

3. A clogged oil return (drain) line from the turbocharger to the oil pan (sump), which can cause the engine oil pressure to force oil past the turbocharger's shaft rings and into the intake *and* exhaust manifolds. Obviously, oil being forced into both the intake and exhaust would create lots of smoke.

SUMMARY

1. Volumetric efficiency is a comparison of the actual volume of air–fuel mixture drawn into the engine to the theoretical maximum volume that can be drawn into the cylinder.

2. A supercharger operates from the engine by a drive belt and, while it does consume some engine power, it forces a greater amount of air into the cylinders for even more power.

3. A turbocharger uses the normally wasted heat energy of the exhaust to turn an impeller at high speed. The impeller is linked to a turbine wheel on the same shaft and is used to force air into the engine.

4. There are two types of superchargers: roots-type and centrifugal.

5. A bypass valve is used to control the boost pressure on most factory-installed superchargers.

6. An intercooler is used on many turbocharged and some supercharged engines to reduce the temperature of air entering the engine for increased power.

7. A wastegate is used on most turbocharger systems to limit and control boost pressures, as well as a relief valve, to keep the speed of the turbine wheel from slowing down during engine deceleration.

1. What are the reasons why supercharging increases engine power?

2. How does the bypass valve work on a supercharged engine?

3. What are the advantages and disadvantages of supercharging?

4. What are the advantages and disadvantages of turbocharging?

5. What turbocharger control valves are needed for proper engine operation?

CHAPTER QUIZ

1. Boost pressure is generally measured in _____.
   a. in. Hg
   b. PSI
   c. in. H_2O
   d. in. lb

2. Two types of superchargers include _____.
   a. Rotary and reciprocating
   b. Roots-type and centrifugal
   c. Double and single acting
   d. Turbine and piston

3. Which valve is used on a factory supercharger to limit boost?
   a. A bypass valve
   b. A wastegate
   c. A blow-off valve
   d. An air valve

4. How are most superchargers lubricated?
   a. By engine oil under pressure through lines from the engine
   b. By an internal oil reservoir
   c. By greased bearings
   d. No lubrication is needed because the incoming air cools the supercharger

5. How are most turbochargers lubricated?
   a. By engine oil under pressure through lines from the engine
   b. By an internal oil reservoir
   c. By greased bearings
   d. No lubrication is needed because the incoming air cools the supercharger

6. Two technicians are discussing the term "turbo lag." Technician A says that it refers to the delay between when the exhaust leaves the cylinder and when it contacts the turbine blades of the turbocharger. Technician B says that it refers to the delay in boost pressure that occurs when the throttle is first opened. Which technician is correct?
   a. Technician A only
   b. Technician B only
   c. Both Technicians A and B
   d. Neither Technician A nor B

7. What is the purpose of an intercooler?
   a. To reduce the temperature of the air entering the engine
   b. To cool the turbocharger
   c. To cool the engine oil on a turbocharged engine
   d. To cool the exhaust before it enters the turbocharger

8. Which type of relief valve used on a turbocharged engine is noisy?
   a. A bypass valve
   b. A BOV
   c. A dump valve
   d. Both b and c

9. Technician A says that a stuck-open wastegate can cause the engine to burn oil. Technician B says that a clogged PCV system can cause the engine to burn oil. Which technician is correct?
   a. Technician A only
   b. Technician B only
   c. Both Technicians A and B
   d. Neither Technician A nor B

10. What service operation is *most* important on engines equipped with a turbocharger?
    a. Replacing the air filter regularly
    b. Replacing the fuel filter regularly
    c. Regular oil changes
    d. Regular exhaust system maintenance

OBJECTIVES

After studying Chapter 13, the reader will be able to:

1. Prepare for ASE Engine Performance (A8) certification test content area "A" (General Engine Diagnosis).
2. List the visual checks to determine engine condition.
3. Discuss engine noise and its relation to engine condition.
4. Describe how to perform a dry and a wet compression test.
5. Explain how to perform a cylinder leakage test.
6. Discuss how to measure the amount of timing chain slack.
7. Describe how an oil sample analysis can be used to determine engine condition.

KEY TERMS

back pressure 214
compression test 208
cranking vacuum test 212
cylinder leakage test 210
dynamic compression test 210
idle vacuum test 212
inches of mercury (in. Hg) 212
paper test 207
power balance test 211
restricted exhaust 214
running compression test 210
vacuum test 212
wet compression test 209

If there is an engine operation problem, then the cause could be any one of many items, including the engine itself. The condition of the engine should be tested anytime the operation of the engine is not satisfactory.

TYPICAL ENGINE-RELATED COMPLAINTS

Many driveability problems are *not* caused by engine mechanical problems. A thorough inspection and testing of the ignition and fuel systems should be performed before testing for mechanical engine problems.

Typical engine mechanical-related complaints include the following:

- Excessive oil consumption
- Engine misfiring
- Loss of power
- Smoke from the engine or exhaust
- Engine noise

ENGINE SMOKE DIAGNOSIS

The color of engine exhaust smoke can indicate what engine problem might exist.

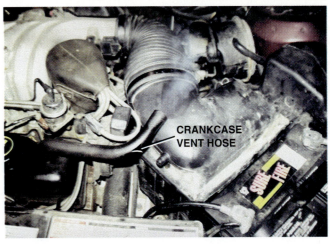

FIGURE 13–1 Blowby gases coming out of the crankcase vent hose. Excessive amounts of combustion gases flow past the piston rings and into the crankcase.

FIGURE 13–2 White steam is usually an indication of a blown (defective) cylinder head gasket that allows engine coolant to flow into the combustion chamber where it is turned to steam.

Typical Exhaust Smoke Color	Possible Causes
Blue	Blue exhaust indicates that the engine is burning oil. Oil is getting into the combustion chamber either past the piston rings or past the valve stem seals. Blue smoke only after start-up is usually due to defective valve stem seals. ● SEE FIGURE 13–1.
Black	Black exhaust smoke is due to excessive fuel being burned in the combustion chamber. Typical causes include a defective or misadjusted throttle body, leaking fuel injector, or excessive fuel-pump pressure.
White (steam)	White smoke or steam from the exhaust is normal during cold weather and represents condensed steam. Every engine creates about 1 gallon of water for each gallon of gasoline burned. If the steam from the exhaust is excessive, then water (coolant) is getting into the combustion chamber. Typical causes include a defective cylinder head gasket, a cracked cylinder head, or in severe cases a cracked block. ● SEE FIGURE 13–2.

Note: White smoke can also be created when automatic transmission fluid (ATF) is burned. A common source of ATF getting into the engine is through a defective vacuum modulator valve on the automatic transmission.

THE DRIVER IS YOUR BEST RESOURCE

The driver of the vehicle knows a lot about the vehicle and how it is driven. *Before* diagnosis is started, always ask the following questions:

- When did the problem first occur?
- Under what conditions does it occur?
  1. Cold or hot?
  2. Acceleration, cruise, or deceleration?
  3. How far was it driven?

After the nature and scope of the problem are determined, the complaint should be verified before further diagnostic tests are performed.

TECH TIP

Your Nose Knows

Whenever diagnosing any vehicle try to use all senses including the smell. Some smells and their cause include:

- **Gasoline:** If the exhaust smells like gasoline or un-burned fuel, then a fault with the ignition system is a likely cause. Unburned fuel due to lean air–fuel mixture causing a lean misfire is also possible.
- **Sweet smell:** A coolant leak often gives off a sweet smell especially if the leaking coolant flows onto the hot exhaust.
- **Exhaust smell:** Check for an exhaust leak including a possible cracked exhaust manifold which can be difficult to find because it often does not make noise.

VISUAL CHECKS

The first and most important "test" that can be performed is a careful visual inspection.

OIL LEVEL AND CONDITION

The first area for visual inspection is oil level and condition.

1. Oil level—oil should be to the proper level
2. Oil condition
   a. Using a match or lighter, try to light the oil on the dipstick; if the oil flames up, gasoline is present in the engine oil.
   b. Drip some of the engine oil from the dipstick onto the hot exhaust manifold. If the oil bubbles or boils, there is coolant (water) in the oil.
   c. Check for grittiness by rubbing the oil between your fingers.

COOLANT LEVEL AND CONDITION

Most mechanical engine problems are caused by overheating. The proper operation of the cooling system is critical to the life of any engine.

NOTE: Check the coolant level in the radiator only if the radiator is cool. If the radiator is hot and the radiator cap is removed, the drop in pressure above the coolant will cause the coolant to boil immediately and can cause severe burns when the coolant explosively expands upward and outward from the radiator opening.

1. The coolant level in the coolant recovery container should be within the limits indicated on the overflow bottle. If this level is too low or the coolant recovery container is empty, then check the level of coolant in the radiator (only when cool) and also check the operation of the pressure cap.

2. The coolant should be checked with a hydrometer for boiling and freezing temperature. This test indicates if the concentration of the antifreeze is sufficient for proper protection.

3. Pressure test the cooling system and look for leakage. Coolant leakage can often be seen around hoses or cooling system components because it will often cause:
   a. A grayish white stain
   b. A rusty color stain
   c. Dye stains from antifreeze (greenish or yellowish depending on the type of coolant)

4. Check for cool areas of the radiator indicating clogged sections.

5. Check operation and condition of the fan clutch, fan, and coolant pump drive belt.

OIL LEAKS

Oil leaks can lead to severe engine damage if the resulting low oil level is not corrected. Besides causing an oily mess where the vehicle is parked, the oil leak can cause

FIGURE 13–3 What looks like an oil pan gasket leak can be a rocker cover gasket leak. Always look up and look for the highest place you see oil leaking; that should be repaired first.

FIGURE 13–4 The transmission and flexplate (flywheel) were removed to check the exact location of this oil leak. The rear main seal and/or the oil pan gasket could be the cause of this leak.

TECH TIP

What's Leaking?

The color of the leaks observed under a vehicle can help the technician determine and correct the cause. Some leaks, such as condensate (water) from the air-conditioning system, are normal, whereas a brake fluid leak is very dangerous. The following are colors of common leaks:

Sooty Black	Engine Oil
Yellow, green, blue, or orange	Antifreeze (coolant)
Red	Automatic transmission fluid
Murky brown	Brake or power steering fluid or very neglected antifreeze (coolant)
Clear	Air-conditioning condensate (water) (normal)

blue smoke to occur under the hood as leaking oil drips on the exhaust system. *Finding* the location of the oil leak can often be difficult. ● **SEE FIGURES 13–3 AND 13–4**. To help find the source of oil leaks follow these steps:

STEP 1 Clean the engine or area around the suspected oil leak. Use a high-powered hot-water spray to wash the engine. While the engine is running, spray the entire engine and the engine compartment. Avoid letting the water come into direct contact with the air inlet and ignition distributor or ignition coil(s).

NOTE: If the engine starts to run rough or stalls when the engine gets wet, then the secondary ignition wires (spark plug wires) or distributor cap may be defective or have weak insulation. Be certain to wipe all wires and the distributor cap dry with a soft, dry cloth if the engine stalls.

An alternative method is to spray a degreaser on the engine, then start and run the engine until warm. Engine heat helps the degreaser penetrate the grease and dirt. Use a water hose to rinse off the engine and engine compartment.

STEP 2 If the oil leak is not visible or oil seems to be coming from "everywhere," use a white talcum powder. The leaking oil will show as a dark area on the white powder. See the Tech Tip, "The Foot Powder Spray Trick."

STEP 3 Fluorescent dye can be added to the engine oil. Add about 1/2 oz (15 cc) of dye per 5 quarts of engine oil. Start the engine and allow it to run about 10 minutes to thoroughly mix the dye throughout the engine. A black

FIGURE 13–5 Using a black light to spot leaks after adding dye to the oil.

FIGURE 13–6 An accessory belt tensioner. Most tensioners have a mark that indicates normal operating location. If the belt has stretched, this indicator mark will be outside of the normal range. Anything wrong with the belt or tensioner can cause noise.

VISUAL CHECKS (CONTINUED)

light can then be shown around every suspected oil leak location. The black light will easily show all oil leak locations because the dye will show as a bright yellow/green area. ● **SEE FIGURE 13–5**.

NOTE: Fluorescent dye works best with clean oil.

TECH TIP

The Foot Powder Spray Trick

The source of an oil or other fluid leak is often difficult to determine. A quick and easy method that works is the following. First, clean the entire area. This can best be done by using a commercially available degreaser to spray the entire area. Let it soak to loosen all accumulated oil and greasy dirt. Clean off the degreaser with a water hose. Let the area dry. Start the engine, and using spray foot powder or other aerosol powder product, spray the entire area. The leak will turn the white powder dark. The exact location of any leak can be quickly located.

NOTE: Most oil leaks appear at the bottom of the engine due to gravity. Look for the highest, most forward location for the source of the leak.

ENGINE NOISE DIAGNOSIS

An engine knocking noise is often difficult to diagnose. Several items that can cause a deep engine knock include:

- **Valves clicking.** This can happen because of lack of oil to the lifters. This noise is most noticeable at idle when the oil pressure is the lowest.

- **Torque converter.** The attaching bolts or nuts may be loose on the flex plate. This noise is most noticeable at idle or when there is no load on the engine.

- **Cracked flex plate.** The noise of a cracked flex plate is often mistaken for a rod- or main-bearing noise.

- **Loose or defective drive belts or tensioners.** If an accessory drive belt is loose or defective, the flopping noise often sounds similar to a bearing knock. ● **SEE FIGURE 13–6**.

- **Piston pin knock.** This knocking noise is usually not affected by load on the cylinder. If the clearance is too great, a double knock noise is heard when the engine idles. If all cylinders are grounded out one at a time and the noise does not change, a defective piston pin could be the cause.

- **Piston slap.** A piston slap is usually caused by an undersized or improperly shaped piston or oversized cylinder bore. A piston slap is most noticeable when the engine is cold and tends to decrease or stop making noise as the piston expands during engine operation.

Typical Noises	Possible Causes
Clicking noise— like the clicking of a ballpoint pen	1. Loose spark plug 2. Loose accessory mount (for air-conditioning compressor, alternator, power steering pump, etc.) 3. Loose rocker arm 4. Worn rocker arm pedestal 5. Fuel pump (broken mechanical fuel pump return spring) 6. Worn camshaft 7. Exhaust leak. ● SEE FIGURE 13–7.
Clacking noise— like tapping on metal	1. Worn piston pin 2. Broken piston 3. Excessive valve clearance 4. Timing chain hitting cover
Knock— like knocking on a door	1. Rod bearing(s) 2. Main bearing(s) 3. Thrust bearing(s) 4. Loose torque converter 5. Cracked flex plate (drive plate)
Rattle—like a baby rattle	1. Manifold heat control valve 2. Broken harmonic balancer 3. Loose accessory mounts 4. Loose accessory drive belt or tensioner
Clatter—like rolling marbles	1. Rod bearings 2. Piston pin 3. Loose timing chain
Whine—like an electric motor running	1. Alternator bearing 2. Drive belt 3. Power steering 4. Belt noise (accessory or timing)
Clunk—like a door closing	1. Engine mount 2. Drive axle shaft U-joint or constant velocity (CV) joint

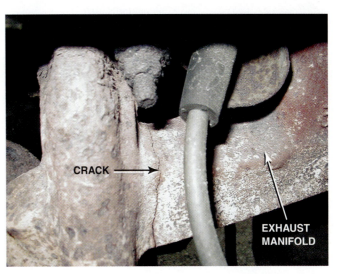

FIGURE 13–7 A cracked exhaust manifold on a Ford V-8.

Regardless of the type of loud knocking noise, after the external causes of the knocking noise have been eliminated, the engine should be disassembled and carefully inspected to determine the exact cause.

TECH TIP

Engine Noise and Cost

A light ticking noise often heard at one-half engine speed and associated with valve train noise is a less serious problem than many deep-sounding knocking noises. Generally, the deeper the sound of the engine noise, the more the owner will have to pay for repairs. A light "tick tick tick," though often not cheap, is usually far less expensive than a deep "knock knock knock" from the engine.

- **Timing chain noise.** An excessively loose timing chain can cause a severe knocking noise when the chain hits the timing chain cover. This noise can often sound like a rod-bearing knock.

- **Rod-bearing noise.** The noise from a defective rod bearing is usually load sensitive and changes in intensity as the load on the engine increases and decreases. A rod-bearing failure can often be detected by grounding out the spark plugs one cylinder at a time. If the knocking noise decreases or is eliminated when a particular cylinder is grounded (disabled), then the grounded cylinder is the one from which the noise is originating.

- **Main-bearing knock.** A main-bearing knock often cannot be isolated to a particular cylinder. The sound can vary in intensity and may disappear at times depending on engine load.

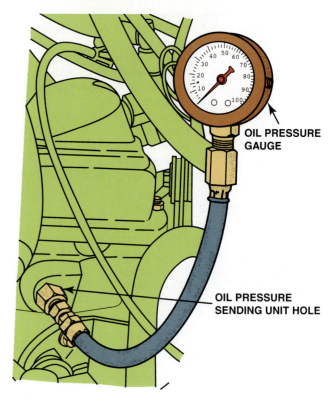

FIGURE 13–8 To measure engine oil pressure, remove the oil pressure sending (sender) unit usually located near the oil filter. Screw the pressure gauge into the oil pressure sending unit hole.

OIL PRESSURE GAUGE

OIL PRESSURE SENDING UNIT HOLE

OIL PRESSURE TESTING

Proper oil pressure is very important for the operation of any engine. *Low oil pressure can cause engine wear, and engine wear can cause low oil pressure.*

If main thrust or rod bearings are worn, oil pressure is reduced because of leakage of the oil around the bearings. Oil pressure testing is usually performed with the following steps:

STEP 1   Operate the engine until normal operating temperature is achieved.

STEP 2   With the engine off, remove the oil pressure sending unit or sender, usually located near the oil filter. Thread an oil pressure gauge into the threaded hole. ● **SEE FIGURE 13–8**.

NOTE: An oil pressure gauge can be made from another gauge, such as an old air-conditioning gauge and a flexible brake hose. The threads are often the same as those used for the oil pressure sending unit.

STEP 3   Start the engine and observe the gauge. Record the oil pressure at idle and at 2500 RPM. Most vehicle manufacturers recommend a minimum oil pressure of 10 PSI per 1000 RPM. Therefore, at 2500 RPM, the oil pressure should be at least 25 PSI. Always compare your test results with the manufacturer's recommended oil pressure.

Besides engine bearing wear, other possible causes for low oil pressure include:

■ Low oil level

■ Diluted oil

■ Stuck oil pressure relief valve

OIL PRESSURE WARNING LAMP

The red oil pressure warning lamp in the dash usually lights when the oil pressure is less than 4 to 7 PSI, depending on vehicle and engine. The oil light should not be on during driving. If the oil warning lamp is on, stop the engine immediately. Always confirm oil pressure with a reliable mechanical gauge before performing engine repairs. The sending unit or circuit may be defective.

 TECH TIP

Use the KISS Test Method

Engine testing is done to find the cause of an engine problem. All the simple things should be tested first. Just remember KISS—"keep it simple, stupid." A loose alternator belt or loose bolts on a torque converter can sound just like a lifter or rod bearing. A loose spark plug can make the engine perform as if it had a burned valve. Some simple items that can cause serious problems include the following:

Oil Burning
- Low oil level
- Clogged PCV valve or system, causing blowby and oil to be blown into the air cleaner
- Clogged drainback passages in the cylinder head
- Dirty oil that has not been changed for a long time (Change the oil and drive for about 1,000 miles (1,600 kilometers) and change the oil and filter again.)

Noises
- Carbon on top of the piston(s) can sound like a bad rod bearing (often called a carbon knock)
- Loose torque-to-flex plate bolts (or nuts), causing a loud knocking noise

NOTE: Often this problem will cause noise only at idle; the noise tends to disappear during driving or when the engine is under load.

- A loose and/or defective drive belt, which may cause a rod- or main-bearing knocking noise (A loose or broken mount for the generator [alternator], power steering pump, or air-conditioning compressor can also cause a knocking noise.)

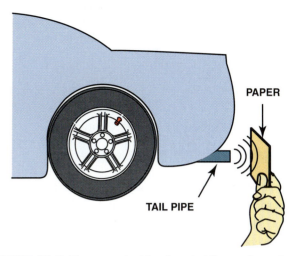

FIGURE 13–9 The paper test involves holding a piece of paper near the tailpipe of an idling engine. A good engine should produce even, outward puffs of exhaust. If the paper is sucked in toward the tailpipe, a burned valve is a possibility.

 **TECH TIP**

The Paper Test

A soundly running engine should produce even and steady exhaust at the tailpipe. You can test this with the **paper test.** Hold a piece of paper or a 3″ × 5″ index card (even a dollar bill works) within 1 inch (25 millimeters) of the tailpipe with the engine running at idle. ● **SEE FIGURE 13–9.**

The paper should blow out evenly without "puffing." If the paper is drawn *toward* the tailpipe at times, the exhaust valves in one or more cylinders could be burned. Other reasons why the paper might be sucked toward the tailpipe include the following:

1. The engine could be misfiring because of a lean condition that could occur normally when the engine is cold.
2. Pulsing of the paper toward the tailpipe could also be caused by a hole in the exhaust system. If exhaust escapes through a hole in the exhaust system, air could be drawn in during the intervals between the exhaust puffs from the tailpipe to the hole in the exhaust, causing the paper to be drawn toward the tailpipe.
3. Ignition fault causing misfire.

FIGURE 13–10 A two-piece compression gauge set. The threaded hose is screwed into the spark plug hole after removing the spark plug. The gauge part is then snapped onto the end of the hose.

COMPRESSION TEST

An engine **compression test** is one of the fundamental engine diagnostic tests that can be performed. For smooth engine operation, all cylinders must have equal compression. An engine can lose compression by leakage of air through one or more of only three routes:

- Intake or exhaust valve
- Piston rings (or piston, if there is a hole)
- Cylinder head gasket

For best results, the engine should be warmed to normal operating temperature before testing. An accurate compression test should be performed as follows:

STEP 1 Remove all spark plugs. This allows the engine to be cranked to an even speed. Be sure to label all spark plug wires.

CAUTION: Disable the ignition system by disconnecting the primary leads from the ignition coil or module or by grounding the coil wire after removing it from the center of the distributor cap. Also disable the fuel-injection system to prevent the squirting of fuel into the cylinder.

STEP 2 Block open the throttle. This permits the maximum amount of air to be drawn into the engine. This step also ensures consistent compression test results.

STEP 3 Thread a compression gauge into one spark plug hole and crank the engine. ● **SEE FIGURE 13–10.**

Continue cranking the engine through *four* compression strokes. Each compression stroke makes a puffing sound.

NOTE: Note the reading on the compression gauge after the first puff. This reading should be at least one-half the final reading. For example, if the final, highest reading is 150 PSI, then the reading after the first puff should be higher than 75 PSI. A low first-puff reading indicates possible weak piston rings. Release the pressure on the gauge and repeat for the other cylinders.

STEP 4 Record the highest readings and compare the results. Most vehicle manufacturers specify the minimum compression reading and the maximum allowable variation among cylinders. Most manufacturers specify a maximum difference of 20% between the highest reading and the lowest reading. For example:

If the high reading is	**150 PSI**
Subtract 20%	**−30 PSI**
Lowest allowable compression is	**120 PSI**

NOTE: To make the math quick and easy, think of 10% of 150, which is 15 (move the decimal point to the left one place). Now double it: 15 × 2 = 30. This represents 20%.

NOTE: During cranking, the oil pump cannot maintain normal oil pressure. Extended engine cranking, such as that which occurs during a compression test, can cause hydraulic lifters to collapse. When the engine starts, loud valve clicking noises may be heard. This should be considered normal after performing a compression test, and the noise should stop after the vehicle has been driven a short distance.

The Hose Trick

Installing spark plugs can be made easier by using a rubber hose on the end of the spark plug. The hose can be a vacuum hose, fuel line, or even an old spark plug wire end. ● **SEE FIGURE 13–11.**

The hose makes it easy to start the threads of the spark plug into the cylinder head. After starting the threads, continue to thread the spark plug for several turns. Using the hose eliminates the chance of cross-threading the plug. This is especially important when installing spark plugs in aluminum cylinder heads.

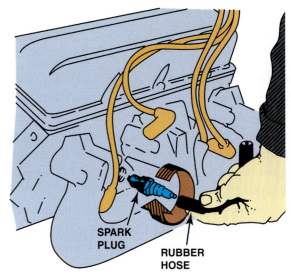

SPARK PLUG

RUBBER HOSE

FIGURE 13–11 Use a vacuum or fuel line hose over the spark plug to install it without danger of cross-threading the cylinder head.

WET COMPRESSION TEST

If the compression test reading indicates low compression on one or more cylinders, add three squirts of oil to the cylinder and retest. This is called a **wet compression test**, when oil is used to help seal around the piston rings.

CAUTION: Do not use more oil than three squirts from a hand-operated oil squirt can. Too much oil can cause a hydrostatic lock, which can damage or break pistons or connecting rods or even crack a cylinder head.

Perform the compression test again and observe the results. If the first-puff readings greatly improve and the readings are much higher than without the oil, the cause of the low compression is worn or defective piston rings. If the compression readings increase only slightly (or not at all), then the cause of the low compression is usually defective valves. ● **SEE FIGURE 13–12.**

NOTE: **During both the dry and wet compression tests, be sure that the battery and starting system are capable of cranking the engine at normal cranking speed.**

FIGURE 13–12 Badly burned exhaust valve. A compression test could have detected a problem, and a cylinder leakage test (leak-down test) could have been used to determine the exact problem.

RUNNING (DYNAMIC) COMPRESSION TEST

A compression test is commonly used to help determine engine condition and is usually performed with the engine cranking.

What is the RPM of a cranking engine? An engine idles at about 600 to 900 RPM, and the starter motor obviously cannot crank the engine as fast as the engine idles. Most manufacturers' specifications require the engine to crank at 80 to 250 cranking RPM. Therefore, a check of the engine's compression at cranking speed determines the condition of an engine that does not run at such low speeds.

But what should be the compression of a running engine? Some would think that the compression would be substantially higher, because the valve overlap of the cam is more effective at higher engine speeds, which would tend to increase the compression.

A **running compression test**, also called a **dynamic compression test**, is a compression test done with the engine running rather than during engine cranking as is done in a regular compression test.

Actually, the compression pressure of a running engine is much *lower* than cranking compression pressure. This results from the volumetric efficiency. The engine is revolving faster, and therefore, there is less *time* for air to enter the combustion chamber. With less air to compress, the compression pressure is lower. Typically, the higher the engine RPM, the lower the running compression. For most engines, the value ranges are as follows:

- Compression during cranking: 125 to 160 PSI
- Compression at idle: 60 to 90 PSI
- Compression at 2000 RPM: 30 to 60 PSI

As with cranking compression, the running compression of all cylinders should be equal. Therefore, a problem is not likely to be detected by single compression values, but by *variations* in running compression values among the cylinders. Broken valve springs, worn valve guides, bent pushrods, and worn cam lobes are some items that would be indicated by a low running compression test reading on one or more cylinders.

PERFORMING A RUNNING COMPRESSION TEST
To perform a running compression test, remove just one spark plug at a time. With one spark plug removed from the engine, use a jumper wire to *ground* the spark plug wire to a good engine ground. This prevents possible ignition coil damage. Start the engine, push the pressure release on the gauge, and read the compression. Increase the engine speed to about 2000 RPM and push the pressure release on the gauge again. Read the gauge. Stop the engine, reattach the spark plug wire, and repeat the test for each of the remaining cylinders. Just like the cranking compression test, the running compression test can inform a technician of the *relative* compression of all the cylinders.

FIGURE 13–13 A typical handheld cylinder leakage tester.

CYLINDER LEAKAGE TEST

One of the best tests that can be used to determine engine condition is the **cylinder leakage test**. This test involves injecting air under pressure into the cylinders one at a time. The amount and location of any escaping air helps the technician determine the condition of the engine. The air is injected into the cylinder through a cylinder leakage gauge into the spark plug hole.
● **SEE FIGURE 13–13**. To perform the cylinder leakage test, take the following steps:

STEP 1   For best results, the engine should be at normal operating temperature (upper radiator hose hot and pressurized).

STEP 2   The cylinder being tested must be at top dead center (TDC) of the compression stroke. ● **SEE FIGURE 13–14**.

NOTE: The greatest amount of wear occurs at the top of the cylinder because of the heat generated near the top of the cylinders. The piston ring flex also adds to the wear at the top of the cylinder.

STEP 3   Calibrate the cylinder leakage unit as per manufacturer's instructions.

STEP 4   Inject air into the cylinders one at a time, rotating the engine as necessitated by firing order to test each cylinder at TDC on the compression stroke.

FIGURE 13–14 A whistle stop used to find top dead center. Remove the spark plug and install the whistle stop, then rotate the engine by hand. When the whistle stops making a sound, the piston is at the top.

STEP 5 Evaluate the results:

Less than 10% leakage: good

Less than 20% leakage: acceptable

Less than 30% leakage: poor

More than 30% leakage: definite problem

NOTE: If leakage seems unacceptably high, repeat the test, being certain that it is being performed correctly and that the cylinder being tested is at TDC on the compression stroke.

STEP 6 Check the source of air leakage.

a. If air is heard escaping from the oil filler cap, the *piston rings* are worn or broken.

b. If air is observed bubbling out of the radiator, there is a possible blown *head gasket* or cracked *cylinder head*.

c. If air is heard coming from the throttle body or air inlet on fuel injection-equipped engines, there is a defective *intake valve(s)*.

d. If air is heard coming from the tailpipe, there is a defective *exhaust valve(s)*.

CYLINDER POWER BALANCE TEST

Most large engine analyzers and scan tools have a cylinder power balance feature. The purpose of a cylinder **power balance test** is to determine if all cylinders are contributing power equally. It determines this by shorting out one cylinder at a time. If the engine speed (RPM) does not drop as much for one cylinder as for other cylinders of the same engine, then the shorted cylinder must be weaker than the other cylinders. For example:

Cylinder Number	RPM Drop When Ignition Is Shorted
1	75
2	70
3	15
4	65
5	75
6	70

Cylinder #3 is the weak cylinder.

NOTE: Most automotive test equipment uses automatic means for testing cylinder balance. Be certain to correctly identify the offending cylinder. Cylinder #3 as identified by the equipment may be the third cylinder in the firing order instead of the actual cylinder #3.

POWER BALANCE TEST PROCEDURE

When point-type ignition was used on all vehicles, the common method for determining which, if any, cylinder was weak was to remove a spark plug wire from one spark plug at a time while watching a tachometer and a vacuum gauge. This method is not recommended on any vehicle with any type of electronic ignition. If any of the spark plug wires are removed from a spark plug with the engine running, the ignition coil tries to supply increasing levels of voltage attempting to jump the increasing gap as the plug wires are removed. This high voltage could easily track the ignition coil, damage the ignition module, or both.

The acceptable method of canceling cylinders, which will work on all types of ignition systems, including distributorless, is to *ground* the secondary current for each cylinder. ● **SEE FIGURE 13–15.** The cylinder with the least RPM drop is the cylinder not producing its share of power.

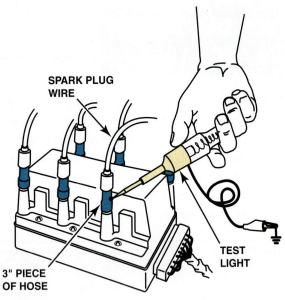

SPARK PLUG
WIRE

3" PIECE
OF HOSE

TEST
LIGHT

FIGURE 13–15 Using a vacuum hose and a test light to ground one cylinder at a time on a distributorless ignition system. This works on all types of ignition systems and provides a method for grounding out one cylinder at a time without fear of damaging any component.

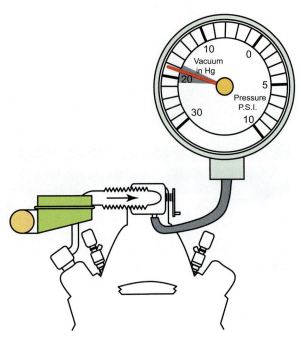

FIGURE 13–16 An engine in good mechanical condition should produce 17 to 21 in. Hg of vacuum at idle at sea level.

VACUUM TESTS

Vacuum is pressure below atmospheric pressure and is measured in **inches** (or millimeters) **of mercury (Hg).** An engine in good mechanical condition will run with high manifold vacuum. Manifold vacuum is developed by the pistons as they move down on the intake stroke to draw the charge from the throttle body and intake manifold. Air to refill the manifold comes past the throttle plate into the manifold. Vacuum will increase anytime the engine turns faster or has better cylinder sealing while the throttle plate remains in a fixed position. Manifold vacuum will decrease when the engine turns more slowly or when the cylinders no longer do an efficient job of pumping. **Vacuum tests** include testing the engine for **cranking vacuum, idle vacuum**, and vacuum at 2500 RPM.

CRANKING VACUUM TEST
Measuring the amount of manifold vacuum during cranking is a quick and easy test to determine if the piston rings and valves are properly sealing. (For accurate results, the engine should be warm and the throttle closed.) To perform the cranking vacuum test, take the following steps:

STEP 1 Disable the ignition or fuel injection.

STEP 2 Connect the vacuum gauge to a manifold vacuum source.

STEP 3 Crank the engine while observing the vacuum gauge.

Cranking vacuum should be higher than 2.5 inches of mercury. (Normal cranking vacuum is 3 to 6 inches Hg.) If it is lower than 2.5 inches Hg, then the following could be the cause:

- Too slow a cranking speed
- Worn piston rings
- Leaking valves
- Excessive amounts of air bypassing the throttle plate (This could give a false low vacuum reading. Common sources include a throttle plate partially open or a high-performance camshaft with excessive overlap.)

IDLE VACUUM TEST
An engine in proper condition should idle with a steady vacuum between 17 and 21 inches Hg.
● **SEE FIGURE 13–16.**

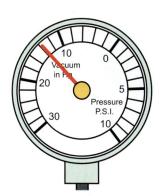

FIGURE 13–17 A steady but low reading could indicate retarded valve or ignition timing.

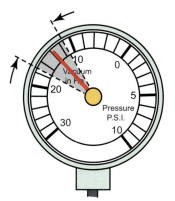

FIGURE 13–18 A gauge reading with the needle fluctuating 3 to 9 in. Hg below normal often indicates a vacuum leak in the intake system.

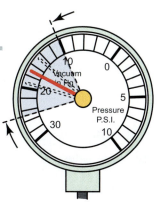

FIGURE 13–19 A leaking head gasket can cause the needle to vibrate as it moves through a range from below to above normal.

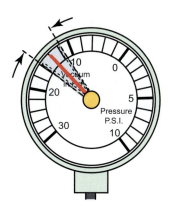

FIGURE 13–20 An oscillating needle 1 or 2 in. Hg below normal could indicate an incorrect air–fuel mixture (either too rich or too lean).

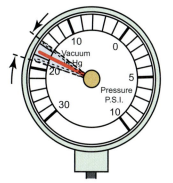

FIGURE 13–21 A rapidly vibrating needle at idle that becomes steady as engine speed is increased indicates worn valve guides.

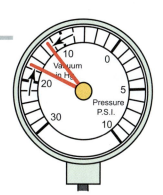

FIGURE 13–22 If the needle drops 1 or 2 in. Hg from the normal reading, one of the engine valves is burned or not seating properly.

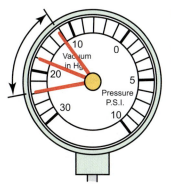

FIGURE 13–23 Weak valve springs will produce a normal reading at idle, but as engine speed increases, the needle will fluctuate rapidly between 12 and 24 in. Hg.

NOTE: Engine vacuum readings vary with altitude. A reduction of 1 inch Hg per 1,000 feet (300 meters) of altitude should be subtracted from the expected values if testing a vehicle above 1,000 feet (300 meters).

LOW AND STEADY VACUUM

If the vacuum is lower than normal, yet the gauge reading is steady, the most common causes include:

- Retarded ignition timing
- Retarded cam timing (check timing chain for excessive slack or timing belt for proper installation)

● **SEE FIGURE 13–17.**

FLUCTUATING VACUUM

If the needle drops, then returns to a normal reading, then drops again, and again returns, this indicates a sticking valve. A common cause of sticking valves is lack of lubrication of the valve stems. ● **SEE FIGURES 13–18 THROUGH 13–26.** If the vacuum gauge fluctuates above and below a center point, burned valves or weak valve springs may be indicated. If the fluctuation is slow and steady, unequal fuel mixture could be the cause.

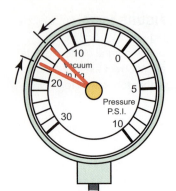

FIGURE 13–24 A steady needle reading that drops 2 or 3 in. Hg when the engine speed is increased slightly above idle indicates that the ignition timing is retarded.

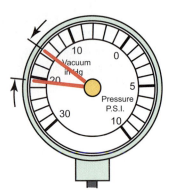

FIGURE 13–25 A steady needle reading that rises 2 or 3 in. Hg when the engine speed is increased slightly above idle indicates that the ignition timing is advanced.

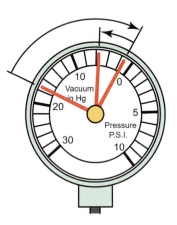

FIGURE 13–26 A needle that drops to near zero when the engine is accelerated rapidly and then rises slightly to a reading below normal indicates an exhaust restriction.

VACUUM TESTS (CONTINUED)

NOTE: A common trick that some technicians use is to squirt some automatic transmission fluid (ATF) down the throttle body or into the air inlet of a warm engine. Often the idle quality improves and normal vacuum gauge readings are restored. The use of ATF does create excessive exhaust smoke for a short time, but it should not harm oxygen sensors or catalytic converters.

EXHAUST RESTRICTION TEST

If the exhaust system is restricted, the engine will be low on power, yet smooth. Common causes of **restricted exhaust** include the following:

- **Clogged catalytic converter.** Always check the ignition and fuel-injection systems for faults that could cause excessive amounts of unburned fuel to be exhausted. Excessive unburned fuel can overheat the catalytic converter and cause the beads or structure of the converter to fuse together, creating the restriction. A defective fuel delivery system could also cause excessive unburned fuel to be dumped into the converter.

- **Clogged or restricted muffler.** This can cause low power. Often a defective catalytic converter will shed particles that can clog a muffler. Broken internal baffles can also restrict exhaust flow.

- **Damaged or defective piping.** This can reduce the power of any engine. Some exhaust pipe is constructed with double walls, and the inside pipe can collapse and form a restriction that is not visible on the outside of the exhaust pipe.

TESTING BACK PRESSURE WITH A VACUUM GAUGE

A vacuum gauge can be used to measure manifold vacuum at a high idle (2000 to 2500 RPM). If the exhaust system is restricted, pressure increases in the exhaust system. This pressure is called **back pressure.** Manifold vacuum will drop gradually if the engine is kept at a constant speed if the exhaust is restricted.

The reason the vacuum will drop is that all exhaust leaving the engine at the higher engine speed cannot get through the restriction. After a short time (within 1 minute), the exhaust tends to "pile up" above the restriction and eventually remains in the cylinder of the engine at the end of the exhaust stroke. Therefore, at the beginning of the intake stroke, when the piston traveling downward should be lowering the pressure (raising the vacuum) in the intake manifold, the extra exhaust in the cylinder *lowers* the normal vacuum. If the exhaust restriction is severe enough, the vehicle can become undriveable because cylinder filling cannot occur except at idle.

FIGURE 13–27 A technician-made adapter used to test exhaust system back pressure.

FIGURE 13–28 A tester that uses a blue liquid to check for exhaust gases in the exhaust, which would indicate a head gasket leak problem.

TESTING BACK PRESSURE WITH A PRESSURE GAUGE

Exhaust system back pressure can be measured directly by installing a pressure gauge into an exhaust opening. This can be accomplished in one of the following ways:

- **With an oxygen sensor.** Use a back pressure gauge and adapter or remove the inside of an old, discarded oxygen sensor and thread in an adapter to convert to a vacuum or pressure gauge.

  NOTE: An adapter can be easily made by inserting a metal tube or pipe. A short section of brake line works great. The pipe can be brazed to the oxygen sensor housing or it can be glued in with epoxy. An 18-millimeter compression gauge adapter can also be adapted to fit into the oxygen sensor opening. ● SEE FIGURE 13–27.

- **With the exhaust gas recirculation (EGR) valve.** Remove the EGR valve and fabricate a plate to connect to a pressure gauge.

- **With the air-injection reaction (AIR) check valve.** Remove the check valve from the exhaust tubes leading down to the exhaust manifold. Use a rubber cone with a tube inside to seal against the exhaust tube. Connect the tube to a pressure gauge.

At idle, the maximum back pressure should be less than 1.5 PSI (10 kPa), and it should be less than 2.5 PSI (15 kPa) at 2500 RPM.

DIAGNOSING HEAD GASKET FAILURE

Several items can be used to help diagnose a head gasket failure:

- **Exhaust gas analyzer.** With the radiator cap removed, place the probe from the exhaust analyzer above the radiator filler neck. If the HC reading increases, the exhaust (unburned hydrocarbons) is getting into the coolant from the combustion chamber.

- **Chemical test.** A chemical tester using blue liquid is also available. The liquid turns yellow if combustion gases are present in the coolant. ● SEE FIGURE 13–28.

- **Bubbles in the coolant.** Remove the coolant pump belt to prevent pump operation. Remove the radiator cap and start the engine. If bubbles appear in the coolant before it begins to boil, a defective head gasket or cracked cylinder head is indicated.

- **Excessive exhaust steam.** If excessive water or steam is observed coming from the tailpipe, this means that coolant is getting into the combustion chamber from a defective head gasket or a cracked head. If there is leakage between cylinders, the engine usually misfires and a power balancer test and/or compression test can be used to confirm the problem.

If any of the preceding indicators of head gasket failure occur, remove the cylinder head(s) and check all of the following:

1. Head gasket

2. Sealing surfaces—for warpage

3. Castings—for cracks

NOTE: A leaking thermal vacuum valve can cause symptoms similar to those of a defective head gasket. Most thermal vacuum valves thread into a coolant passage, and they often leak only after they get hot.

DASH WARNING LIGHTS

Most vehicles are equipped with several dash warning lights often called "telltale" or "idiot" lights. These lights are often the only warning a driver receives that there may be engine problems. A summary of typical dash warning lights and their meanings follows.

OIL (ENGINE) LIGHT   The red oil light indicates that the engine oil pressure is too low (usually lights when oil pressure is 4 to 7 PSI [20 to 50 kPa]). Normal oil pressure should be 10 to 60 PSI (70 to 400 kPa) or 10 PSI per 1000 engine RPM.

When this light comes on, the driver should shut off the engine immediately and check the oil level and condition for possible dilution with gasoline caused by a fuel system fault. If the oil level is okay, then there is a possible serious engine problem or a possible defective oil pressure sending (sender) unit. The automotive technician should always check the oil pressure using a reliable mechanical oil pressure gauge if low oil pressure is suspected.

NOTE: Some automobile manufacturers combine the dash warning lights for oil pressure and coolant temperature into one light, usually labeled "engine." Therefore, when the engine light comes on, the technician should check for possible coolant temperature and/or oil pressure problems.

COOLANT TEMPERATURE LIGHT   Most vehicles are equipped with a coolant temperature gauge or dash warning light. The warning light may be labeled "coolant," "hot," or "temperature." If the coolant temperature warning light comes on during driving, this usually indicates that the coolant temperature is above a safe level, or above about 250°F (120°C). Normal coolant temperature should be about 200° to 220°F (90° to 105°C).

If the coolant temperature light comes on during driving, the following steps should be followed to prevent possible engine damage:

1. Turn off the air conditioning and turn on the heater. The heater will help get rid of some of the heat in the cooling system.

2. Raise the engine speed in neutral or park to increase the circulation of coolant through the radiator.

3. If possible, turn the engine off and allow it to cool (this may take over an hour).

4. Do not continue driving with the coolant temperature light on (or the gauge reading in the red warning section or above 260°F) or serious engine damage may result.

NOTE: If the engine does not feel or smell hot, it is possible that the problem is a faulty coolant temperature sensor or gauge.

TECH TIP

Misfire Diagnosis

If a misfire goes away with propane added to the air inlet, suspect a lean injector.

COMPRESSION TEST

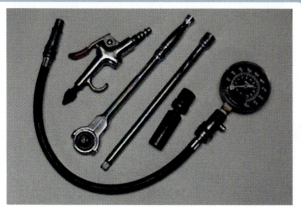

1 The tools and equipment needed to perform a compression test include a compression gauge, an air nozzle, and the socket ratchets and extensions that may be necessary to remove the spark plugs from the engine.

2 To prevent ignition and fuel-injection operation while the engine is being cranked, remove both the fuel-injection fuse and the ignition fuse. If the fuses cannot be removed, disconnect the wiring connectors for the injectors and the ignition system.

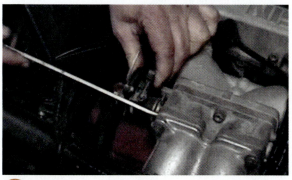

3 Block open the throttle (and choke, if the engine is equipped with a carburetor). Here a screwdriver is being used to wedge the throttle linkage open. Keeping the throttle open ensures that enough air will be drawn into the engine so that the compression test results will be accurate.

4 Before removing the spark plugs, use an air nozzle to blow away any dirt that may be around the spark plug. This step helps prevent debris from getting into the engine when the spark plugs are removed.

5 Remove all of the spark plugs. Be sure to mark the spark plug wires so that they can be reinstalled onto the correct spark plugs after the compression test has been performed.

6 Select the proper adapter for the compression gauge. The threads on the adapter should match those on the spark plug.

CONTINUED ▶

7 If necessary, connect a battery charger to the battery before starting the compression test. It is important that consistent cranking speed be available for each cylinder being tested.

8 Make a note of the reading on the gauge after the first "puff," which indicates the first compression stroke that occurred on that cylinder as the engine was being rotated. If the first puff reading is low and the reading gradually increases with each puff, weak or worn piston rings may be indicated.

9 After the engine has been cranked for four "puffs," stop cranking the engine and observe the compression gauge.

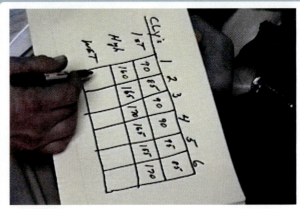

10 Record the first puff and this final reading for each cylinder. The final readings should all be within 20% of each other.

11 If a cylinder(s) is lower than most of the others, use an oil can and squirt two squirts of engine oil into the cylinder and repeat the compression test. This is called performing a wet compression test.

12 If the gauge reading is now much higher than the first test results, then the cause of the low compression is due to worn or defective piston rings. The oil in the cylinder temporarily seals the rings which causes the higher reading.

1. The first step in diagnosing engine condition is to perform a thorough visual inspection, including a check of oil and coolant levels and condition.

2. Oil leaks can be found by using a white powder or a fluorescent dye and a black light.

3. Many engine-related problems make a characteristic noise.

4. Oil analysis by an engineering laboratory can reveal engine problems by measuring the amount of dissolved metals in the oil.

5. A compression test can be used to test the condition of valves and piston rings.

6. A cylinder leakage test fills the cylinder with compressed air, and the gauge indicates the percentage of leakage.

7. A cylinder balance test indicates whether all cylinders are working okay.

8. Testing engine vacuum is another procedure that can help the service technician determine engine condition.

REVIEW QUESTIONS

1. Describe the visual checks that should be performed on an engine if a mechanical malfunction is suspected.

2. List three simple items that could cause excessive oil consumption.

3. List three simple items that could cause engine noises.

4. Describe how to perform a compression test and how to determine what is wrong with an engine based on a compression test result.

5. Describe the cylinder leakage test.

6. Describe how a vacuum gauge would indicate if the valves were sticking in their guides.

7. Describe the test procedure for determining if the exhaust system is restricted (clogged) using a vacuum gauge.

CHAPTER QUIZ

1. Technician A says that the paper test could detect a burned valve. Technician B says that a grayish white stain on the engine could be a coolant leak. Which technician is correct?
   a. Technician A only
   b. Technician B only
   c. Both Technicians A and B
   d. Neither Technician A nor B

2. Two technicians are discussing oil leaks. Technician A says that an oil leak can be found using a fluorescent dye in the oil with a black light to check for leaks. Technician B says that a white spray powder can be used to locate oil leaks. Which technician is correct?
   a. Technician A only
   b. Technician B only
   c. Both Technicians A and B
   d. Neither Technician A nor B

3. Which of the following is the *least likely* to cause an engine noise?
   a. Carbon on the pistons
   b. Cracked exhaust manifold
   c. Loose accessory drive belt
   d. Vacuum leak

4. A good engine should produce how much compression during a running (dynamic) compression test at idle?
   a. 150–200 PSI
   b. 100–150 PSI
   c. 60–90 PSI
   d. 30–60 PSI

5. A smoothly operating engine depends on _____.
   a. High compression on most cylinders
   b. Equal compression between cylinders
   c. Cylinder compression levels above 100 PSI (700 kPa) and within 70 PSI (500 kPa) of each other
   d. Compression levels below 100 PSI (700 kPa) on most cylinders

6. A good reading for a cylinder leakage test would be _____.
   a. Within 20% between cylinders
   b. All cylinders below 20% leakage
   c. All cylinders above 20% leakage
   d. All cylinders above 70% leakage and within 7% of each other

7. Technician A says that during a power balance test, the cylinder that causes the biggest RPM drop is the weak cylinder. Technician B says that if one spark plug wire is grounded out and the engine speed does not drop, a weak or dead cylinder is indicated. Which technician is correct?
   a. Technician A only
   b. Technician B only
   c. Both Technicians A and B
   d. Neither Technician A nor B

8. *Cranking* vacuum should be _____.
   a. 2.5 inches Hg or higher
   b. Over 25 inches Hg
   c. 17 to 21 inches Hg
   d. 6 to 16 inches Hg

9. Technician A says that a leaking head gasket can be tested for using a chemical tester. Technician B says that leaking head gasket can be found using an exhaust gas analyzer.
   a. Technician A only
   b. Technician B only
   c. Both Technicians A and B
   d. Neither Technician A nor B

10. The low oil pressure warning light usually comes on _____.
   a. Whenever an oil change is required
   b. Whenever oil pressure drops dangerously low (4 to 7 PSI)
   c. Whenever the oil filter bypass valve opens
   d. Whenever the oil filter antidrainback valve opens

IN-VEHICLE ENGINE SERVICE

OBJECTIVES

After studying Chapter 14, the reader will be able to:

1. Prepare for ASE certification test content area "A" (General Engine Diagnosis)

2. Diagnose and replace the thermostat.

3. Diagnose and replace the water pump.

4. Diagnose and replace an intake manifold gasket

5. Determine and verify correct cam timing

6. Replace a timing a belt

7. Describe how to adjust valves

8. Explain hybrid engine precautions

KEY TERMS

EREV 226
Fretting 223
HEV 226

Idle stop 226
Skewed 222

FIGURE 14–1 A stuck-open thermostat. This caused the vehicle to set a diagnostic trouble code P0128 (coolant temperature below thermostat regulating temperature).

THERMOSTAT REPLACEMENT

FAILURE PATTERNS All thermostat valves move during operation to maintain the desired coolant temperature. Thermostats can fail in the following ways:

- **Stuck Open**—If a thermostat fails open or partially open, the operating temperature of the engine will be less than normal. ● **SEE FIGURE 14–1.**

- **Stuck Closed**—If the thermostat fails closed or almost closed, the engine will likely overheat.

- **Stuck Partially Open**—This will cause the engine to warm up slowly if at all. This condition can cause the powertrain control module (PCM) to set a P0128 diagnostic trouble code (DTC) which means that the engine coolant temperature does not reach the specified temperature.

- **Skewed**—A **skewed** thermostat works, but not within the correct temperature range. Therefore, the engine could overheat or operate cooler than normal or even do both.

REPLACEMENT PROCEDURE Before replacing the thermostat, double-check that the cooling system problem is not due to another fault, such as being low on coolant or an inoperative cooling fan. Check service information for the specified procedure to follow to replace the thermostat. Most recommended procedures include the following steps:

STEP 1 Allow the engine to cool for several hours so the engine and the coolant should be at room temperature.

STEP 2 Drain the coolant into a suitable container. Most vehicle manufacturers recommend that new coolant be used and the old coolant disposed of properly or recycled.

STEP 3 Remove any necessary components to get access to the thermostat.

STEP 4 Remove the thermostat housing and thermostat.

STEP 5 Replace the thermostat housing gasket and thermostat. Torque all fasteners to specifications.

STEP 6 Refill the cooling system with the specified coolant and bleed any trapped air from the system.

STEP 7 Pressurize the cooling system to verify that there are no leaks around the thermostat housing.

STEP 8 Run the engine until it reaches normal operating temperature and check for leaks.

STEP 9 Verify that the engine is reaching correct operating temperature.

FIGURE 14–2 Use caution if using a steel scraper to remove a gasket from aluminum parts. It is best to use a wood or plastic scraper.

FIGURE 14–3 An intake manifold gasket that failed and allowed coolant to be drawn into the cylinder(s).

WATER PUMP REPLACEMENT

NEED FOR REPLACEMENT A water pump will require replacement if any of the following conditions are present:

- Leaking coolant from the weep hole
- Bearing noisy or loose
- Lack of proper coolant flow caused by worn or slipping impeller blades

REPLACEMENT GUIDELINES After diagnosis has been confirmed that the water pump requires replacement, check service information for the exact procedure to follow. The steps usually include the following:

STEP 1 Allow the engine to cool to room temperature.

STEP 2 Drain the coolant and dispose of properly or recycle.

STEP 3 Remove engine components to gain access to the water pump as specified in service information.

STEP 4 Remove the water pump assembly.

STEP 5 Clean the gasket surfaces and install the new water pump using a new gasket or seal as needed. ● **SEE FIGURE 14–2.** Torque all fasteners to factory specifications.

STEP 6 Install removed engine components.

STEP 7 Fill the cooling system with the specified coolant.

STEP 8 Run the engine, check for leaks, and verify proper operation.

INTAKE MANIFOLD GASKET INSPECTION

CAUSES OF FAILURE Many V-type engines leak oil, coolant, or experience an air (vacuum) leak caused by a leaking intake manifold gasket. This failure can be contributed to one or more of the following:

1. Expansion/contraction rate difference between the cast-iron head and the aluminum intake manifold can cause the intake manifold gasket to be damaged by the relative motion of the head and intake manifold. This type of failure is called **fretting.**

2. Plastic (Nylon 6.6) gasket deterioration caused by the coolant. ● **SEE FIGURE 14–3.**

DIAGNOSIS OF LEAKING INTAKE MANIFOLD GASKET
Because intake manifold gaskets are used to seal oil, air, and coolant in most causes, determining that the intake manifold gasket is the root cause can be a challenge. To diagnose a possible leaking intake manifold gasket, perform the following tests:

Visual inspection—Check for evidence of oil or coolant between the intake manifold and the cylinder heads.

Coolant level—Check the coolant level and determine if the level has been dropping. A leaking intake manifold gasket can cause coolant to leak and then evaporate, leaving no evidence of the leak.

Air (vacuum) leak—If there is a stored diagnostic trouble code (DTC) for a lean exhaust (P0171, P0172, or P0174), a leaking intake manifold gasket could be the cause. Use propane to check if the engine changes when dispensed around the intake manifold gasket. If the engine changes in speed or sound, then this test verifies that an air leak is present.

FIGURE 14–4 The lower intake manifold, attaches to the cylinder heads.

FIGURE 14–5 The upper intake manifold, often called a plenum, attaches to the lower intake manifold.

INTAKE MANIFOLD GASKET REPLACEMENT

When replacing the intake manifold gasket, always check service information for the exact procedure to follow. The steps usually include the following:

STEP 1 Be sure the engine has been off for about an hour and then drain the coolant into a suitable container.

STEP 2 Remove covers and other specified parts needed to get access to the retaining bolts.

STEP 3 To help ensure that the manifold does not warp when removed, loosen all fasteners in the reverse order of the tightening sequence. This means that the bolts should be loosened starting at the ends and working toward the center.

STEP 4 Remove the upper intake manifold, if equipped, and inspect for faults. ● **SEE FIGURES 14–4 AND 14–5.**

STEP 5 Remove the lower intake manifold (plenum), using the same bolt removal procedure of starting at the ends and working toward the center.

STEP 6 Thoroughly clean the area and replace the intake manifold if needed. Check that the correct replacement manifold is being used, and even the current part could look different from the original. ● **SEE FIGURE 14–6.**

STEP 7 Install the intake manifold using new gaskets as specified. Some designs use gaskets that are reusable. Replace as needed.

STEP 8 Torque all fasteners to factory specifications and in the proper sequences. The tightening sequences usually start at the center and work outward to the ends.

FIGURE 14–6 Many aftermarket replacement intake manifolds have a different appearance from the original manifold.

CAUTION: Double-check the torque specifications and be sure to use the correct values. Many intake manifolds use fasteners that are torqued to values expressed in pound-inches and not pound-feet.

STEP 9 Reinstall all parts needed to allow the engine to start and run, including refilling the coolant if needed.

STEP 10 Start the engine and check for leaks and proper engine operation.

STEP 11 Reset or relearn the idle if specified, using a scan tool.

STEP 12 Install all of the remaining parts and perform a test drive to verify proper operation and no leaks.

STEP 13 Check and replace the air filter if needed.

STEP 14 Change the engine oil if the intake manifold leak could have caused coolant to leak into the engine, which would contaminate the oil.

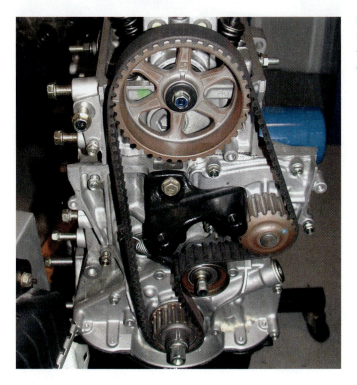

FIGURE 14–7 A single overhead camshaft engine with a timing belt that also rotates the water pump.

TIMING BELT REPLACEMENT

NEED FOR REPLACEMENT Timing belts have a limited service and a specified replacement interval ranging from 60,000 miles (97,000 km) to about 100,000 miles (161,000 km). Timing belts are required to be replaced if any of the following conditions occur:

- Meets or exceeds the vehicle manufacturer's recommended timing belt replacement interval.
- The timing belt has been contaminated with coolant or engine oil.
- The timing belt has failed (missing belt teeth or broken).

TIMING BELT REPLACEMENT GUIDELINES Before replacing the timing belt, check service information for the recommended procedure to follow. Most timing belt replacement procedures include the following steps:

STEP 1 Allow the engine to cool before starting to remove components to help eliminate the possibility of personal injury or warpage of the parts.

STEP 2 Remove all necessary components to gain access to the timing belt and timing marks.

STEP 3 If the timing belt is not broken, rotate the engine until the camshaft and crankshaft timing marks are aligned according to the specified marks. ● **SEE FIGURE 14–7.**

STEP 4 Loosen or remove the tensioner as needed to remove the timing belt.

STEP 5 Replace the timing belt and any other recommended items. Components that some vehicle manufacturers recommend replacing in addition to the timing belt include:

- Tensioner assembly
- Water pump
- Camshaft oil seal(s)
- Front crankshaft seal

STEP 6 Check (verify) that the camshaft timing is correct by rotating the engine several revolutions.

STEP 7 Install enough components to allow the engine to start to verify proper operation. Check for any leaks, especially if seals have been replaced.

STEP 8 Complete the reassembly of the engine and perform a test drive before returning the vehicle to the customer.

FIGURE 14–8 A Toyota/Lexus hybrid electric vehicle has a ready light. If the ready light is on, the engine can start at anytime without warning.

FIGURE 14–9 Always use the viscosity of oil as specified on the oil fill cap.

HYBRID ENGINE PRECAUTIONS

HYBRID VEHICLE ENGINE OPERATION Gasoline engines used in **hybrid electric vehicles (HEVs)** and in **extended range electric vehicles (EREVs)** can be a hazard to be around under some conditions. These vehicles are designed to stop the gasoline engines unless needed. This feature is called **idle stop**. This means that the engine is not running, but could start at any time if the computer detects the need to charge the hybrid batteries or other issue that requires the gasoline engine to start and run.

PRECAUTIONS Always check service information for the exact procedures to follow when working around or under the hood of a hybrid electric vehicle. These precautions could include:

- Before working under the hood or around the engine, be sure that the ignition is off and the key is out of the ignition.
- Check that the "Ready" light is off. ● SEE FIGURE 14–8.

- Do not touch any circuits that have orange electrical wires or conduit. The orange color indicates dangerous high-voltage wires, which could cause serious injury or death if touched.
- Always use high-voltage linesman's gloves whenever depowering the high-voltage system.

HYBRID ENGINE SERVICE The gasoline engine in most hybrid electric vehicles specifies low viscosity engine oil as a way to achieve maximum fuel economy. ● SEE FIGURE 14–9. The viscosity required is often:

- SAE 0W-20
- SAE 5W-20

Many shops do not keep this viscosity in stock so preparations need to be made to get and use the specified engine oil.

In addition to engine oil, some hybrid electric vehicles such as the Honda Insight (1999–2004) require special spark plugs. Check service information for the specified service procedures and parts needed if a hybrid electric vehicle is being serviced.

1 Before starting the process of adjusting the valves, look up the specifications and exact procedures. The technician is checking this information from a computer CD-ROM-based information system.

2 The tools necessary to adjust the valves on an engine with adjustable rocker arms include basic hand tools, feeler gauge, and a torque wrench.

3 An overall view of the four-cylinder engine that is due for a scheduled valve adjustment according to the vehicle manufacturer's recommendations.

4 Start the valve adjustment procedure by first disconnecting and labeling, if necessary, all vacuum lines that need to be removed to gain access to the valve cover.

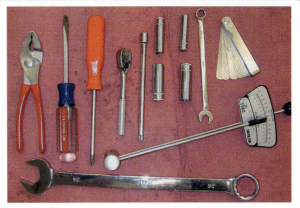

5 The air intake tube is being removed from the throttle body.

6 With all vacuum lines and the intake tube removed, the valve cover can be removed after removing all retaining bolts.

CONTINUED ▶

7 Notice how clean the engine appears. This is a testament of proper maintenance and regular oil changes by the owner.

8 To help locate how far the engine is being rotated, the technician is removing the distributor cap to be able to observe the position of the rotor.

9 The engine is rotated until the timing marks on the front of the crankshaft line up with zero degrees—top dead center (TDC)—with both valves closed on #1 cylinder.

10 With the rocker arms contacting the base circle of the cam, insert a feeler gauge of the specified thickness between the camshaft and the rocker arm. There should be a slight drag on the feeler gauge.

11 If the valve clearance (lash) is not correct, loosen the retaining nut and turn the valve adjusting screw with a screwdriver to achieve the proper clearance.

12 After adjusting the valves that are closed, rotate the engine one full rotation until the engine timing marks again align.

13 The engine is rotated until the timing marks again align indicating that the companion cylinder will now be in position for valve clearance measurement.

14 On some engines, it is necessary to watch the direction the rotor is pointing to help determine how far to rotate the engine. Always follow the vehicle manufacturer's recommended procedure.

15 The technician is using a feeler gauge that is one-thousandth of an inch thinner and another one thousandth of an inch thicker than the specified clearance as a double-check that the clearance is correct.

16 Adjusting a valve takes both hands—one to hold the wrench to loosen and tighten the lock nut and one to turn the adjusting screw. Always doublecheck the clearance after an adjustment is made.

17 After all valves have been properly measured and adjusted as necessary, start the reassembly process by replacing all gaskets and seals as specified by the vehicle manufacturer.

18 Reinstall the valve cover being careful to not pinch a wire or vacuum hose between the cover and the cylinder head.

CONTINUED ▶

19 Use a torque wrench and torque the valve cover retaining bolts to factory specifications.

20 Reinstall the distributor cap.

21 Reinstall the spark plug wires and all brackets that were removed to gain access to the valve cover.

22 Reconnect all vacuum and air hoses and tubes. Replace any vacuum hoses that are brittle or swollen with new ones.

23 Be sure that the clips are properly installed. Start the engine and check for proper operation.

24 Double-check for any oil or vacuum leaks after starting the engine.

SUMMARY

1. Thermostats can fail in the following ways:
   - Stuck open
   - Stuck closed
   - Stuck partially open
   - Skewed

2. A water pump should be replaced if any of the following conditions are present:
   - Leaking from the weep hole
   - Noisy bearing
   - Loose bearing
   - Lack of normal circulation due to worn impeller blades

3. A leaking intake manifold gasket can cause coolant to get into the oil or oil into the coolant, as well as other faults, such as a poor running engine.

4. When a timing belt is replaced, most vehicle manufacturers also recommend that the following items be replaced:
   - Tensioner assembly
   - Water pump
   - Camshaft seal(s)
   - Front crankshaft seal

5. When working on a Toyota/Lexus hybrid electric vehicle (HEV), be sure that the key is off and out of the ignition and the READY light is off.

REVIEW QUESTIONS

1. How can a thermostat fail?

2. How can a water pump fail requiring replacement?

3. What will happen to the engine if the intake manifold gasket fails?

4. Why must timing belts be replaced?

5. Why is it important that the READY light be out on the dash before working under the hood of a hybrid electric vehicle?

CHAPTER QUIZ

1. A thermostat can fail in which way?
   - a. Stuck open
   - b. Stuck closed
   - c. Stuck partially open
   - d. Any of the above

2. A skewed thermostat means it is _____.
   - a. Working, but not at the correct temperature
   - b. Not working
   - c. Missing the thermo wax in the heat sensor
   - d. Contaminated with coolant

3. Coolant drained from the cooling system when replacing a thermostat or water pump should be _____.
   - a. Reused
   - b. Disposed of properly or recycled
   - c. Filtered and reinstalled after the repair
   - d. Poured down a toilet

4. A water pump can fail to provide the proper amount of flow of coolant through the cooling system if what has happened?
   - a. The coolant is leaking from the weep hole
   - b. The bearing is noisy
   - c. The impeller blades are worn or slipping on the shaft
   - d. A bearing failure has caused the shaft to become loose

5. Intake manifold gaskets on a V-type engine can fail due to what factor?
   - a. Fretting
   - b. Coolant damage
   - c. Relative movement between the intake manifold and the cylinder head
   - d. All of the above

6. A defective thermostat can cause the Powertrain Control Module to set what diagnostic trouble code (DTC)?
   - a. P0171
   - b. P0172
   - c. P0128
   - d. P0300

7. A replacement plastic intake manifold may have a different design or appearance from the original factory-installed part.
   - a. True
   - b. False

8. The torque specifications for many plastic intake manifolds are in what unit?
   - a. Pound-inches
   - b. Pound-feet
   - c. Ft-lbs per minute
   - d. Lb-ft per second

9. When replacing a timing belt, many experts and vehicle manufacturers recommend that what other part(s) should be replaced?
   - a. Tensioner assembly
   - b. Water pump
   - c. Camshaft oil seal(s)
   - d. All of the above

10. Hybrid electric vehicles usually require special engine oil of what viscosity?
    - a. SAE 5W-30
    - b. SAE 10W-30
    - c. SAE 0W-20
    - d. SAE 5W-40

After studying Chapter 15, the reader will be able to:

1. Prepare for ASE Engine Performance (A8) certification test content area "F" (Engine Electrical Systems Diagnosis and Repair).

2. Discuss methods that can be used to check the condition of a battery.

3. Describe how to perform a battery drain test and how to isolate the cause.

4. Explain how to test the condition of the starter.

5. List the steps necessary to perform a voltage-drop test.

6. Explain how to test the generator.

AC ripple voltage 253

Ampere-hour 233

Battery 233

Battery electrical drain test 240

Battery voltage correction 234

CA 233

Capacity test 237

CCA 233

Charging circuit 233

Conductance testing 238

Cranking circuit 233

DE 251

ELD 256

Generator (alternator) 233

IOD 240

Load test 237

LRC 256

MCA 233

Neutral safety switch 244

Open-circuit battery voltage test 235

Parasitic load 240

Reserve capacity 233

Ripple current 254

SRE 251

State of charge 239

Surface charge 235

Voltage-drop test 247

FIGURE 15–1 This battery shows a large "1000" on the front panel but this is the CA rating and not the more important CCA rating. Always compare batteries with the same rating.

Just as in the old saying "If Mother isn't happy—no one is happy," the battery, the starter, and the charging system have to function correctly for the engine performance to be satisfactory.

PURPOSE AND FUNCTION OF A BATTERY

The primary purpose of an automotive **battery** is to provide a source of electrical power for starting and for electrical demands that exceed generator output. The battery also acts as a voltage stabilizer for the entire electrical system. The battery is a voltage stabilizer because it acts as a reservoir where large amounts of current (amperes) can be removed quickly during starting and replaced gradually by the **generator (alternator)** during charging. The battery *must* be in good (serviceable) condition before the charging system and the cranking system can be tested. For example, if a battery is discharged, the **cranking circuit** (starter motor) could test as being defective because the battery voltage might drop below specifications. The **charging circuit** could also test as being defective because of a weak or discharged battery. It is important to test the vehicle battery before further testing of the cranking or charging system.

BATTERY RATINGS

Batteries are rated according to the amount of current they can produce under specific conditions.

COLD-CRANKING AMPERES   Every automotive battery must be able to supply electrical power to crank the engine in cold weather and still provide voltage high enough to operate the ignition system for starting. The cold-cranking power of a battery is the number of amperes that can be supplied at 0°F (−18°C) for 30 seconds while the battery still maintains a voltage of 1.2 volts per cell or higher. This means that the battery voltage would be 7.2 volts for a 12-volt battery and 3.6 volts for a 6-volt battery. The cold-cranking performance rating is called **cold-cranking amperes (CCA)**. Try to purchase a battery that offers the highest CCA for the money. ● **SEE FIGURE 15–1**.

CRANKING AMPERES   Cranking amperes (CA) are not the same as CCA, but are often advertised and labeled on batteries. The designation CA refers to the number of amperes that can be supplied by the battery at 32°F (0°C). This rating results in a higher number than the more stringent rating of CCA.

MARINE CRANKING AMPERES   Marine cranking amperes (MCA) rating is similar to the cranking amperes (CA) rating and is tested at 32°F (0°C).

AMPERE-HOUR RATING   The **Ampere-Hour (Ah)** is how many amperes can be discharged from the battery before dropping at 10.5 volts over a 20-hour period. A battery that is able to supply 3.75 amperes for 20 hours has a rating of 75 ampere-hours (3.75 × 20 = 75).

RESERVE CAPACITY   The **reserve capacity** rating for batteries is *the number of minutes* for which the battery can produce 25 amperes and still have a battery voltage of 1.75 volts per cell (10.5 volts for a 12-volt battery). This rating is actually a measurement of the time for which a vehicle can be driven in the event of a charging system failure.

FREQUENTLY ASKED QUESTION

How Can a Defective Battery Affect Engine Performance?

A weak or discharged battery should be replaced as soon as possible. A weak battery causes a constant load on the generator that can cause the stator windings to overheat and fail. Low battery voltage also affects the electronic fuel-injection system. The computer senses low battery voltage and increases the fuel injector on-time to help compensate for the lower voltage to the fuel pump and fuel injectors. This increase in injector pulse time is added to the calculated pulse time and is sometimes called the **battery voltage correction factor.** Reduced fuel economy could therefore be the result of a weak or defective battery.

 FREQUENTLY ASKED QUESTION

Should Batteries Be Kept Off of Concrete Floors?

All batteries should be stored in a cool, dry place when not in use. Many technicians have been warned not to store or place a battery on concrete. According to battery experts, it is the temperature difference between the top and the bottom of the battery that causes a difference in the voltage potential between the top (warmer section) and the bottom (colder section). It is this difference in temperature that causes self-discharge to occur.

In fact, submarines cycle seawater around their batteries to keep all sections of the battery at the same temperature to help prevent self-discharge.

Therefore, always store or place batteries up off the floor and in a location where the entire battery can be kept at the same temperature, avoiding extreme heat and freezing temperatures. Concrete cannot drain the battery directly, because the case of the battery is a very good electrical insulator.

BATTERY SERVICE SAFETY CONSIDERATIONS

Batteries contain acid and release explosive gases (hydrogen and oxygen) during normal charging and discharging cycles. To help prevent physical injury or damage to the vehicle, always adhere to the following safety procedures:

1. Whenever working on any electrical component on a vehicle, disconnect the negative battery cable from the battery. When the negative cable is disconnected, all electrical circuits in the vehicle will be open, which will prevent accidental electrical contact between an electrical component and ground. Any electrical spark has the potential to cause explosion and personal injury.

2. Wear eye protection whenever working around any battery.

3. Wear protective clothing to avoid skin contact with battery acid.

4. Always adhere to all safety precautions as stated in the service procedures for the equipment used for battery service and testing.

5. Never smoke or use an open flame around any battery.

 FREQUENTLY ASKED QUESTION

What Can Cause a Battery to Explode?
Batteries discharge hydrogen gas and oxygen when being charged. If there happens to be a flame or spark, the hydrogen will burn. The oxygen can also help contribute to an explosion of a small pocket of hydrogen.

BATTERY VISUAL INSPECTION

The battery and battery cables should be included in the list of items checked during a thorough visual inspection. Check the battery cables for corrosion and tightness. ● **SEE FIGURE 15–2.**

NOTE: On side-post batteries, grasp the battery cable near the battery and attempt to move the cable in a clockwise direction in an attempt to tighten the battery connection.

If possible, remove the covers and observe the level of the electrolyte. ● **SEE FIGURE 15–3.**

FIGURE 15–2 Corrosion on a battery cable could be an indication that the battery is either being overcharged or is sulfated, creating a lot of gassing of the electrolyte.

FIGURE 15–3 A visual inspection on this battery showed that the electrolyte level was below the plates in all cells.

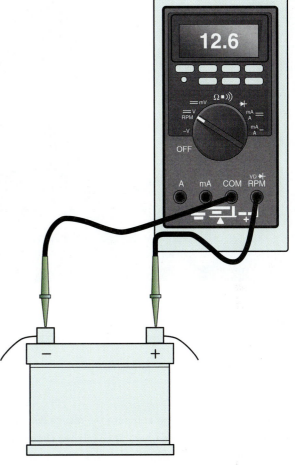

FIGURE 15–4 Using a DMM to measure the open-circuit voltage of a battery.

BATTERY VOLTAGE TEST

Testing the battery voltage with a voltmeter is a simple method for determining the state of charge of any battery. ● **SEE FIGURE 15–4.** The voltage of a battery does not necessarily indicate whether the battery can perform satisfactorily, but it does indicate to the technician more about the battery's condition than a simple visual inspection. A battery that *looks* good may not be good. This test is commonly called an **open-circuit battery voltage test** because it is conducted with an open circuit—with no current flowing and no load applied to the battery.

1. Connect a voltmeter to the positive (+) and negative (−) terminals of the battery. Set the voltmeter to read DC volts.

2. If the battery has just been charged or the vehicle has recently been driven, it is necessary to remove the surface charge from the battery before testing. A **surface charge** is a charge of higher-than-normal voltage that is only on the surface of the battery plates. The surface charge is quickly removed whenever the battery is loaded and therefore does not accurately represent the true state of charge of the battery.

3. To remove the surface charge, turn the headlights on high beam (brights) for 1 minute, then turn the headlights off and wait 2 minutes.

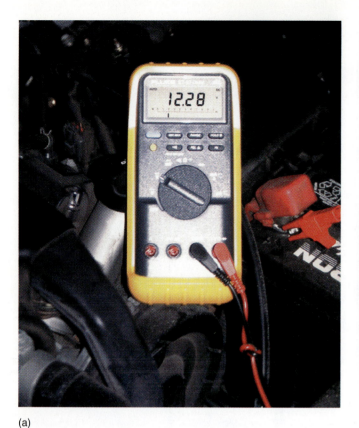
(a)

(b)

FIGURE 15–5 (a) Voltmeter showing the battery voltage after the headlights were on (engine off) for 1 minute. (b) Headlights were turned off and the battery voltage quickly recovered to indicate 12.6 volts.

BATTERY VOLTAGE TEST (CONTINUED)

4. Read the voltmeter and compare the results with the following state-of-charge chart. The voltages shown are for a battery at or near room temperature (70° to 80°F or 21° to 27°C).

NOTE: Watch the voltmeter when the headlights are turned on. A new good battery will indicate a gradual drop in voltage, whereas a weak battery will indicate a more rapid drop in voltage. Soon the voltage will stop dropping and will stabilize. A good new battery will likely stabilize above 12 volts. A weak older battery may drop below 11 volts. After turning off the headlights, the faster the recovery, generally, the better the battery. ● **SEE FIGURE 15–5.**

Battery voltage (V)	State of charge
12.6 or higher	100% charged
12.4	75% charged
12.2	50% charged
12.0	25% charged
11.9 or lower	Discharged

 **TECH TIP**

Use a Scan Tool to Check the Battery, Starter, and Generator!

General Motors and Chrysler vehicles as well as selected others that can display data to a scan tool can be easily checked for proper operating voltage. Most scan tools can display battery or system voltage and engine speed in RPM (revolutions per minute). Connect a scan tool to the data link connector (DLC) and perform the following while watching the scan tool display (● **SEE FIGURE 15–6**).

Many scan tools are also capable of recording or graphing engine data while cranking including:

- RPM during cranking should be 80 to 250 RPMs.
- Battery voltage during cranking should be above 9.6 volts.

  NOTE: Usually readings for a good battery and starter would be 10.5 to 11.5 volts.

- Battery voltage after engine starts should be 13.5 to 15.0 volts.

FIGURE 15–6 Using a scan tool to check battery voltage.

FIGURE 15–7 A Bear Automotive starting and charging tester. This tester automatically loads the battery for 15 seconds to remove the surface charge, waits 30 seconds to allow the battery to recover, and then loads the battery again. The LCD indicates the status of the battery.

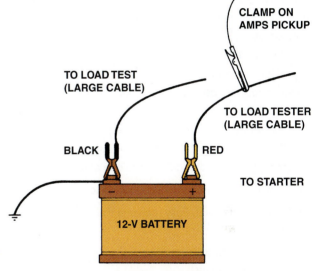

FIGURE 15–8 This shows a typical battery load tester hookup.

BATTERY LOAD TESTING

One method to determine the condition of any battery is the **load test**, also known as a **capacity test**. Most automotive starting and charging testers use a carbon pile to create an electrical load on the battery. The amount of the load is determined by the original capacity of the battery being tested. The capacity is measured in cold-cranking amperes (CCA), which is the number of amperes that a battery can supply at 0°F (−18°C) for 30 seconds. An older type of battery rating is called the ampere-hour rating. The proper electrical load to be used to test a battery is one-half of the CCA rating or three times the ampere-hour rating, with a minimum of a 150-ampere load. Apply the load for a full 15 seconds and observe the voltmeter at the end of the 15-second period while the battery is still under load. A good battery should indicate above 9.6 V.

NOTE: This test is sometimes called the *1-minute test*, because many battery manufacturers recommend performing the load test twice, using the first load period (15 seconds) to remove the surface charge on the battery, then waiting for 30 seconds to allow time for the battery to recover, and then loading the battery again for 15 seconds. Total time required is 60 seconds (15 + 30 + 15 = 60 seconds or 1 minute). This method provides a true indication of the condition of the battery. ● SEE FIGURES 15–7 AND 15–8.

If the battery fails the load test, recharge the battery and retest. If the battery fails the load test again, replace the battery.

FIGURE 15–9 An electronic battery tester.

CONDUCTANCE TESTING

General Motors Corporation, Chrysler Corporation, Ford, and other vehicle manufacturers specify that a **conductance tester** be used to test batteries in vehicles still under factory warranty. The tester uses its internal electronic circuitry to determine the state of charge and capacity of the battery by measuring the voltage and conductance of the plates. ● **SEE FIGURE 15–9**.

Connect the unit to the positive and negative terminals of the battery, and after entering the CCA rating (if known), push the arrow keys. The tester determines one of the following:

- **Good battery.** The battery can return to service.
- **Charge and retest.** Fully recharge the battery and return it to service.
- **Replace the battery.** The battery is not serviceable and should be replaced.
- **Bad cell—replace.** The battery is not serviceable and should be replaced.

CAUTION: Test results can be incorrectly reported on the display if proper, clean connections to the battery are not made. Also be sure that all accessories and the ignition switch are in the off position.

JUMP STARTING

To safely jump start a vehicle without doing any harm, use the following procedure:

1. Be certain the ignition switch is off on both vehicles.
2. Connect good-quality copper jumper cables as indicated in the guide in ● **FIGURE 15–10**.
3. Start the vehicle with the good battery and allow it to run for 5 to 10 minutes. This allows the generator of the good vehicle to charge the battery on the disabled vehicle.
4. Start the disabled vehicle and, after the engine is operating smoothly, disconnect the jumper cables in the reverse order of step 2.

NOTE: To help prevent accidental touching of the jumper cables, simply separate them into two cables and attach using wire (cable) ties or tape so that the clamps are offset from each other, making it impossible for them to touch.

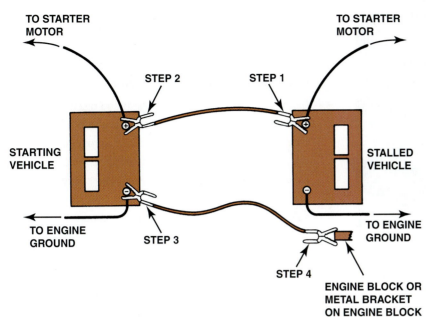

FIGURE 15–10 Jumper cable usage guide.

TO STARTER MOTOR

TO STARTER MOTOR

STEP 2

STEP 1

STARTING VEHICLE

STALLED VEHICLE

TO ENGINE GROUND

STEP 3

TO ENGINE GROUND

STEP 4

ENGINE BLOCK OR METAL BRACKET ON ENGINE BLOCK

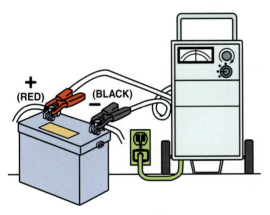

+ (RED)   − (BLACK)

FIGURE 15–11 To use a battery charger, make sure the charger is connected to the battery before plugging in the charger.

OPEN CIRCUIT VOLTAGE, V	STATE OF CHARGE, %	CHARGING TIME (MIN) TO FULL CHARGE AT 80°F (27°C)*					
		at 60 A	at 50 A	at 40 A	at 30 A	at 20 A	at 10 A
12.6	100	Full Charge					
12.4	75	15	20	27	35	48	90
12.2	50	35	45	55	75	95	180
12.0	25	50	65	85	115	145	280
11.8	0	65	85	110	150	195	370

CHART 15–1

A chart that can be used to estimate the charging time based on battery voltage and charging rate.
* If colder, allow additional time.

BATTERY CHARGING

If the **state of charge** of a battery is low, it must be recharged. It is best to slow-charge any battery to prevent possible overheating damage to the battery. Remember, it may take 8 hours or more to charge a fully discharged battery. The initial charge rate should be about 35 amperes for 30 minutes to help start the charging process. Fast-charging a battery increases the temperature of the battery and can cause warping of the plates inside the battery. Fast-charging also increases the amount of gassing (release of hydrogen and oxygen), which can create a health and fire hazard. The battery temperature should not exceed 125°F (hot to the touch). Most batteries should be charged at a rate equal to 1% of the battery's CCA rating.
● **SEE FIGURE 15–11**.

Fast charge: 15 amperes maximum

Slow charge: 5 amperes maximum

● **SEE CHART 15–1** for battery charging times at various battery voltages and charging rates.

FIGURE 15–12 This battery cable was found corroded underneath. The corrosion had eaten through the insulation yet was not noticeable without careful inspection. This cable should be replaced.

BATTERY SERVICE

Before returning the vehicle to the customer, check and service the following items as necessary.

1. Neutralize and clean any corrosion from the battery terminals.

2. Carefully inspect the battery cables by visual inspection.
   ● **SEE FIGURE 15–12**.

3. Check the tightness and cleanliness of all ground connections.

BATTERY ELECTRICAL DRAIN TEST

The **battery electrical drain test** determines if some component or circuit in a vehicle or truck is causing a drain on the battery when everything is off. This test is also called the **ignition off-draw (IOD)** or **parasitic load** test. This test should be performed whenever one of the following conditions exists:

1. Whenever a battery is being charged or replaced (a battery drain could have been the cause for charging or replacing the battery)

2. Whenever the battery is suspected of being drained

Normal battery drain on a vehicle equipped with electronic radio, climate control, computerized fuel injection, and so forth, is usually about 20 to 30 milliamperes (0.02 to 0.03 A). Most vehicle manufacturers recommend repairing the cause of any drain that exceeds 50 mA (0.05 A).

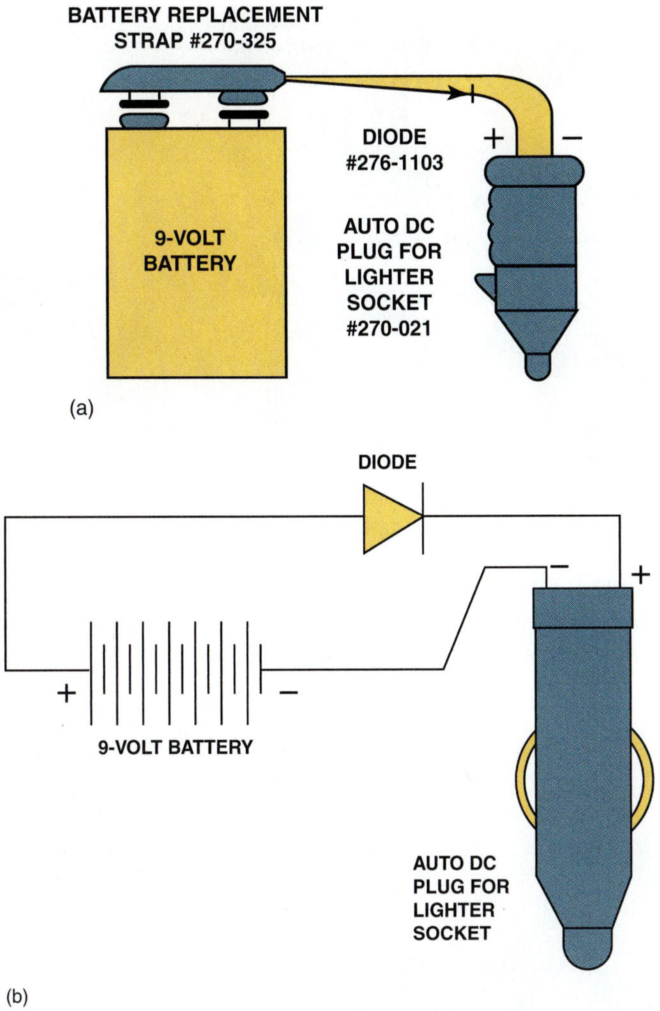

BATTERY REPLACEMENT STRAP #270-325

9-VOLT BATTERY

DIODE #276-1103

AUTO DC PLUG FOR LIGHTER SOCKET #270-021

(a)

DIODE

9-VOLT BATTERY

AUTO DC PLUG FOR LIGHTER SOCKET

(b)

FIGURE 15–13 (a) Memory saver. The part numbers represent components from Radio Shack®. (b) A schematic drawing of the same memory saver.

Use a MIN/MAX Feature to Check for Battery Electrical Drain

Most digital multimeters that feature a "data hold," MIN/MAX, or recording feature can be used when the meter is set up to read DC amperes. This is especially helpful if the battery drain is not found during routine tests in the shop. The cause or source of this drain may only occur when the vehicle cools down at night or after it sits for several hours. Connect the ammeter in series with the disconnected negative battery cable and set the meter to record. Refer to the meter instruction booklet if necessary to be assured of a proper setup. The next morning, check the meter for the maximum, minimum, and average readings. For example,

MAX = 0.89 A (over specifications of 0.05 A)
MIN = 0.02 A (typical normal reading)
Average = 0.76 A

Because the average is close to the maximum, the battery electrical drain was taking place during most of the duration of the test.

NOTE: Some manufacturers relate maximum allowable parasitic load to the size of the battery. The higher the battery capacity, the greater the allowable load. The maximum allowable drain on a battery can be calculated by dividing the reserve capacity of the battery in minutes by 4 to get the maximum allowable drain in milliamps. For example, if a battery had a reserve capacity of 100 minutes, it would have a maximum allowable parasitic load of 25 mA (100 ÷ 4 = 25 mA).

NOTE: Many electronic components do draw a slight amount of current from the battery all the time with the ignition off. These components include:

1. Digital clocks
2. Electronically tuned radios for station memory and clock circuits (if the vehicle is so equipped)
3. The engine control computer (if the vehicle is so equipped), through slight diode leakage
4. The generator, through slight diode leakage

These components may cause a voltmeter to read full battery voltage if it is connected between the negative battery terminal and the removed end of the negative battery cable. Using a voltmeter to measure battery drain is *not* recommended by most vehicle manufacturers. The high internal resistance of the voltmeter results in an irrelevant reading that does not tell the technician if there is a problem.

BATTERY ELECTRICAL DRAIN TESTING USING AN AMMETER

The ammeter method is the most accurate way to test for a possible battery drain. Connect an ammeter in series between the battery terminal (post) and the disconnected cable. (Normal battery drain is 0.020 to 0.030 A and any drain greater than 0.050 A should be found and corrected.) Many digital multimeters have an ammeter scale that can be used to safely and accurately test for an abnormal parasitic drain.

CAUTION: Some vehicle manufacturers recommend that a test light be used before connecting an ammeter when checking for a battery drain. If the drain is large enough to light a test light, the ammeter may be damaged. Be certain to use an ammeter that is rated to read the anticipated amperage.

FIGURE 15–14 This mini clamp-on DMM is being used to measure the amount of battery electrical drain that is present. In this case, a reading of 20 mA (displayed on the meter as 00.02 A) is within the normal range of 20 to 30 mA. Be sure to clamp around all of the positive battery cables or all of the negative battery cables, whichever is easiest to clamp.

PROCEDURE FOR BATTERY ELECTRICAL DRAIN TEST

The fastest and easiest method to measure battery electrical drain is to connect an inductive DC ammeter that is capable of measuring low current (10 mA). ● **SEE FIGURE 15–14** for an example of a clamp-on digital multimeter being used to measure battery drain.

Following is the procedure for performing the battery electrical drain test using a test light:

1. Make certain that all lights, accessories, and the ignition are off.

2. Check all vehicle doors to be certain that the interior courtesy (dome) lights are off.

3. Disconnect the *negative* (−) battery cable and install a parasitic load tool as shown in ● **FIGURE 15–15**.

4. Start the engine and drive the vehicle about 10 minutes, being sure to turn on all the lights and accessories, including the radio.

5. Turn the engine and all accessories off, including the underhood light.

6. Connect an ammeter across the parasitic load tool switch and wait 10 minutes or longer for all computers to go to sleep and circuits to shut down.

FIGURE 15–15 After connecting the shutoff tool, start the engine and operate all accessories. Stop the engine and turn off everything. Connect the ammeter across the shutoff switch in parallel. Wait 20 minutes. This time allows all electronic circuits to "time out" or shut down. Open the switch—all current now will flow through the ammeter. A reading greater than specified, usually greater than 50 mA (0.05 A), indicates a problem that should be corrected.

7. Open the switch on the load tool and read the battery electrical drain on the meter display.

   Results: Normal = 10 to 30 mA (0.02 to 0.03 A)

   Maximum allowable = 50 mA (0.05 A) (Industry standards—some vehicle manufacturers' specifications can vary)

   Be sure to reset the clock and anti-theft radio, if equipped.
   ● **SEE FIGURE 15–16**.

FIGURE 15–16 The battery was replaced in this Acura and the radio displayed "code" when the replacement battery was installed. Thankfully, the owner had the five-digit code required to unlock the radio.

WHAT TO DO IF A BATTERY DRAIN STILL EXISTS AFTER ALL THE FUSES ARE DISCONNECTED

If all the fuses have been disconnected and the drain still exists, the source of the drain has to be between the battery and the fuse box. The most common sources of drain under the hood include the following:

1. **The generator (alternator).** Disconnect the generator wires and retest. If the draw is now within acceptable limits, the problem is a defective diode(s) in the generator.

2. **The starter solenoid (relay) or wiring near its components.** These are also a common source of battery drain, due to high current flows and heat, which can damage the wire or insulation.

FINDING THE SOURCE OF THE DRAIN

If there is a drain, check and temporarily disconnect the following components:

1. Cell phone or MP3 player still connected to the vehicle

2. Glove compartment light

3. Trunk light

If after disconnecting these components the battery drain can still light the test light or draw more than 50 mA (0.05 A), disconnect one fuse at a time from the fuse box until the test light goes out or the ammeter reading drops. If the drain drops to normal after one fuse is disconnected, the source of the drain is located in that particular circuit, as labeled on the fuse box. As fuses are pulled, they should not be reinstalled until the end of the test. Reinstalling a fuse can reset a module and foul up the test. Start at the fuses farthest from the battery and work toward the battery until the faulty circuit is found. Note that many vehicles have multiple fuse boxes. Continue to disconnect the *power-side* wire connectors from each component included in that particular circuit until the ammeter reads a normal amount of draw. The source of the battery drain can then be traced to an individual component or part of one circuit. If none of the fuses causes the drain to stop, disconnect the generator (alternator) output lead. A shorted diode in the generator could be the cause.

CRANKING CIRCUIT

The cranking circuit includes those mechanical and electrical components required to crank the engine for starting. The cranking force in the early 1900s was the driver's arm. Modern cranking circuits include the following:

1. **Starter motor.** The starter is normally a 0.5 to 2.6 horsepower (0.4 to 2.0 kilowatts) electric motor that can develop nearly 8 horsepower (6 kilowatts) for a very short time when first cranking a cold engine.

2. **Battery.** The battery must be of the correct capacity and be at least 75% charged to provide the necessary current and voltage for correct operation of the starter.

3. **Starter solenoid or relay.** The high current required by the starter must be able to be turned on and off. A large switch would be required if the current were controlled by the driver directly. Instead, a small current switch (ignition switch) operates a solenoid or relay that controls the high starter current.

4. **Starter drive.** The starter drive uses a small gear that contacts the engine flywheel gear and transmits starter motor power to rotate the engine.

5. **Ignition switch.** The ignition switch and safety control switches control the starter motor operation. ● **SEE FIGURES 15–17 AND 15–18.**

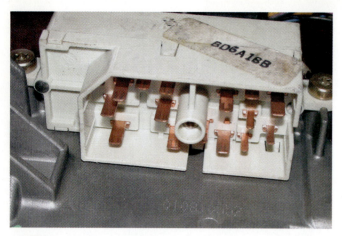

FIGURE 15–17 A typical ignition switch showing all of the electrical terminals after the connector has been removed.

FIGURE 15–18 Some column-mounted ignition switches act directly on the contact points, whereas others use a link from the lock cylinder to the ignition switch.

CRANKING CIRCUIT (CONTINUED)

The engine is cranked by an electric motor that is controlled by a key-operated ignition switch or the PCM on vehicles equipped with electronic starting. The ignition switch will not operate the starter unless the automatic transmission is in neutral or park. This is to prevent an accident that might result from the vehicle moving forward or backward when the engine is started. Many automobile manufacturers use a **neutral safety switch** that opens the circuit between the ignition switch and the starter to prevent starter motor operation unless the gear selector is in neutral or park. The safety switch can either be attached to the steering column inside the vehicle near the floor or on the side of the transmission/transaxle. According to vehicle manufacturing engineers, starters can be expected to start an engine 25,000 times during normal life of the vehicle. ● SEE FIGURE 15–19.

FIGURE 15–19 A typical solenoid-operated starter.

DIAGNOSING STARTER PROBLEMS USING VISUAL INSPECTION

For proper operation, all starters require that the vehicle battery be at least 75% charged and that both power-side and ground-side battery cables be free from excessive voltage drops. The following should be carefully checked as part of a thorough visual inspection:

- Carefully check the battery cables for tightness both at the battery and at the starter, and block connections. ● SEE FIGURE 15–20.
- Check to see if the heat shield (if equipped) is in place.

FIGURE 15–20 Carefully inspect all battery terminals for corrosion.

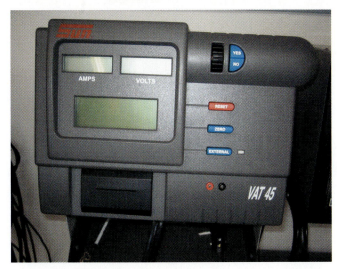

FIGURE 15–21 When connecting a starter tester such as a Sun VAT 45 to the vehicle, make certain that the inductive probe is placed over all of the cables or wires from the battery.

FIGURE 15–22 Always check the battery, using a conductance or load tester. A battery showing a green charge indicator does not mean that the battery is good.

- Check for any nonstock add-on accessories or equipment that may drain the battery such as a sound system, extra lighting, and so on.
- Crank the engine. Feel the battery cables and connections. If any cables or connections are hot to the touch, then an excessive voltage drop is present or the starter is drawing too much current. The engine itself could be binding. Repair or replace the components or connections as needed.

CHECK BATTERY Before performing a starter amperage test, be certain that the battery is sufficiently charged (75% or more) and capable of supplying adequate starting current.

STARTER AMPERAGE TEST A starter amperage test should be performed whenever the starter fails to operate normally (is slow in cranking) or as part of a routine electrical system inspection. Some service manuals specify normal starter amperage for starter motors being tested on the vehicle; however, most service manuals only give the specifications for bench-testing a starter without a load applied. These specifications are helpful in making certain that a repaired starter meets exact specifications, but they do not apply to starter testing on the vehicle. If exact specifications are not available, the following can be used as general maximum specifications for testing a starter on the vehicle. Any ampere reading lower than these are acceptable:

- 4-cylinder engines = 150 to 185 amperes
- 6-cylinder engines = 160 to 200 amperes
- 8-cylinder engines = 185 to 250 amperes

Excessive current draw may indicate one or more of the following:

1. Low battery voltage (discharged or defective battery) (● **SEE FIGURE 15–21.**)
2. Binding of starter armature as a result of worn bushings
3. Oil too thick (viscosity too high) for weather conditions
4. Shorted or grounded starter windings or cables
5. Tight or seized engine

   ● **SEE FIGURE 15–22.**

The Case of the No Crank

A 4-cylinder engine would not crank. Previously the customer said that once in a while, the starter seemed to lock up when the vehicle sat overnight but would then finally crank. The problem only occurred in the morning and the engine would crank and start normally the rest of the day.

The vehicle finally would not start and was towed to the shop. The service technician checked the current draw of the starter and it read higher than the scale on the ammeter. The technician then attempted to rotate the engine by hand and found that the engine would not rotate. Based on this history of not cranking normally in the morning, the technician removed the spark plugs and attempted to crank the engine. This time the engine cranked and coolant was seen shooting from cylinders number two and three. Apparently coolant leaked into the cylinders, due to a fault with the head gasket, causing the engine to hydro-lock or not rotate due to liquid being trapped on top of the piston. Replacing the bad gasket solved the cranking problems in the morning.

TESTING A STARTER USING A SCAN TOOL

A scan tool can be used on most vehicles to check the cranking system. Follow these steps:

1. Connect the scan tool according to the manufacturer's instructions.

2. Select battery voltage and engine RPM on the scan tool.

3. Select "snapshot" and start recording or graphing if the scan tool is capable.

4. Crank the engine. Stop the scan tool recording.

5. Retrieve the scan data and record cranking RPM and battery voltage during cranking. Cranking RPM should be between 80 and 250 RPM. Battery voltage during cranking should be higher than 9.6 volts.

Watch the Dome Light

When diagnosing any starter-related problem, open the door of the vehicle and observe the brightness of the dome or interior light(s). The brightness of any electrical lamp is proportional to the voltage.

Normal operation of the starter results in a slight dimming of the dome light.

- *If the light remains bright*, the problem is usually an open circuit in the control circuit.

- *If the light goes out or almost goes out*, the problem is usually a shorted or grounded armature or field coils inside the starter.

A poor electrical connection that opens under load could also be the cause.

Don't Hit That Starter!

In the past, it was common to see service technicians hitting a starter in their effort to diagnose a no-crank condition. Often the shock of the blow to the starter aligned or moved the brushes, armature, and bushings. Many times, the starter functioned after being hit—even if only for a short time.

However, most of today's starters use permanent-magnet fields, and the magnets can be easily broken if hit. A magnet that is broken becomes two weaker magnets. Some early permanent-magnet (PM) starters used magnets that were glued or bonded to the field housing. If struck with a heavy tool, the magnets could be broken, with parts of the magnet falling onto the armature and into the bearing pockets, making the starter impossible to repair or rebuild.

Is Voltage Drop the Same as Resistance?

Many technicians have asked the question: Why measure voltage drop when the resistance can be easily measured using an ohmmeter? Think of a battery cable with all the strands of the cable broken, except for one. If an ohmmeter is used to measure the resistance of the cable, the reading would be very low, probably less than 1 ohm. However, the cable is not capable of conducting the amount of current necessary to crank the engine. In less severe cases, several strands can be broken and affect the operation of the starter motor. Although the resistance of the battery cable will not indicate any increased resistance, the restriction to current flow will cause heat and a drop in the voltage available at the starter. Because resistance is not effective until current flows, measuring the voltage drop (differences in voltage between two points) is the most accurate method of determining the true resistance in a circuit.

How much is too much? According to Bosch Corporation, all electrical circuits should have a maximum of 3% loss of the voltage of the circuit to resistance. Therefore, in a 12-volt circuit, the maximum loss of voltage in cables and connections should be 0.36 volt ($12 \times 0.03 = 0.36$ volt). The remaining 97% of the circuit voltage (11.64 volt) is available to operate the electrical device (load). Just remember:

- **Low voltage drop = low resistance**
- **High voltage drop = high resistance**

VOLTAGE-DROP TESTING

PURPOSE OF VOLTAGE DROP TESTING
Voltage drop is the drop in voltage that occurs when current is flowing through a resistance. For example, a voltage drop is the difference between voltage at the source and voltage at the electrical device to which it is flowing. The higher the voltage drop, the greater the resistance in the circuit. Even though voltage-drop testing can be performed on any electrical circuit, the most common areas of testing include the cranking circuit and the charging circuit wiring and connections.

RESULTS OF EXCESSIVE VOLTAGE DROP
A high voltage drop (high resistance) in the cranking circuit wiring can cause slow engine cranking with less-than-normal starter amperage drain as a result of the excessive circuit resistance. If the voltage drop is high enough, such as could be caused by dirty battery terminals, the starter may not operate. A typical symptom of low battery voltage or high resistance in the cranking circuit is a "clicking" of the starter solenoid.

PERFORMING A VOLTAGE DROP TEST
Voltage-drop testing of the wire involves connecting any voltmeter (on the low scale) to the suspected high-resistance cable ends and cranking the engine. ● **SEE FIGURES 15–23, 15–24, AND 15–25.**

NOTE: Before a difference in voltage (voltage drop) can be measured between the ends of a battery cable, current must be flowing through the cable. *Resistance is not effective unless current is flowing.* If the engine is not being cranked, current is not flowing through the battery cables and the voltage drop cannot be measured.

Crank the engine with a voltmeter connected to the battery and record the reading. Crank the engine with the voltmeter connected across the starter and record the reading. If the difference in the two readings exceeds 0.5 volt, perform the following steps to determine the exact location of the voltage drop.

1. Connect the positive voltmeter test lead to the most positive end of the cable being tested. The most positive end of a cable is the end closest to the positive terminal of the battery.

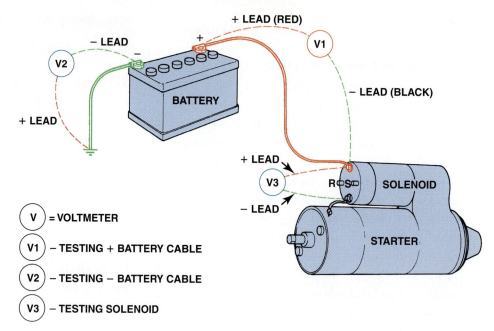

FIGURE 15–23 Voltmeter hookups for voltage-drop testing of a GM-type cranking circuit.

+ LEAD (RED)

V1

− LEAD

V2

− LEAD (BLACK)

BATTERY

+ LEAD

+ LEAD

V3

− LEAD

R S SOLENOID

STARTER

V = VOLTMETER

V1 − TESTING + BATTERY CABLE

V2 − TESTING − BATTERY CABLE

V3 − TESTING SOLENOID

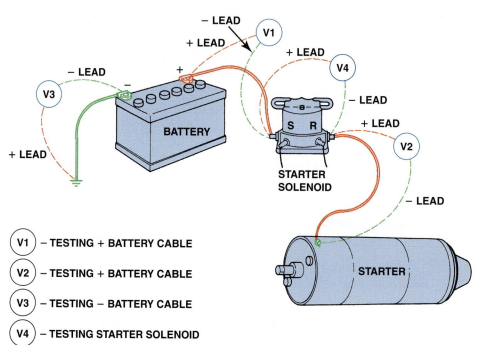

FIGURE 15–24 Voltmeter hookups for voltage-drop testing of a Ford-type cranking circuit.

− LEAD

V1

+ LEAD

+ LEAD

V4

− LEAD

− LEAD

V3

+ LEAD

S R

+ LEAD

BATTERY

V2

+ LEAD

STARTER SOLENOID

− LEAD

STARTER

V1 − TESTING + BATTERY CABLE

V2 − TESTING + BATTERY CABLE

V3 − TESTING − BATTERY CABLE

V4 − TESTING STARTER SOLENOID

FIGURE 15–25 Using the voltmeter leads from a starting and charging test unit to measure the voltage drop between the battery terminal (red lead) and the cable end (black lead). The engine must be cranked to cause current to flow through this connection.

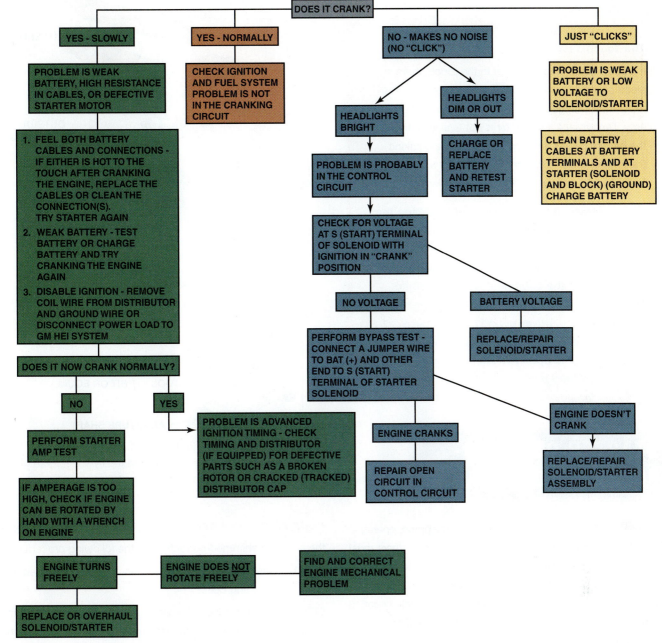

FIGURE 15–26 Starter diagnosis chart.

VOLTAGE-DROP TESTING (CONTINUED)

2. Connect the negative voltmeter test lead to the other end of the cable being tested. With no current flowing through the cable, the voltmeter should read zero because there is the same voltage at both ends of the cable.

3. Crank the engine. The voltmeter should read less than 0.2 volt.

4. Evaluate the results. If the voltmeter reads zero, the cable being tested has no resistance and is good. If the voltmeter reads higher than 0.2 volt, the cable has excessive resistance and should be replaced. However, before replacing the cable, make certain that the connections at both ends of the cable being tested are clean and tight.

● **SEE FIGURE 15–26.**

The Touch Test

If a cable or connection is hot to the touch, there is electrical resistance in the cable or connection. The resistance changes electrical energy into heat energy. Therefore, if a voltmeter is not available, touch the battery cables and connections while cranking the engine. If any cable or connection is warm or hot to the touch, it should be cleaned or replaced.

NOTE: Some experts recommend replacing the entire battery cable if the cable ends become corroded or otherwise unusable. Many "temporary" cable ends do not provide adequate contact areas for the cable and allow the end of the cable strands to be exposed to battery acid corrosion. Also, never pound or hammer a battery cable onto a battery post. Always use a spreader tool to open the clamp wide enough to fit the battery posts.

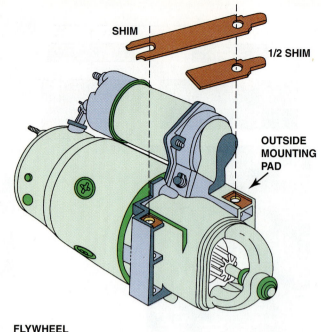

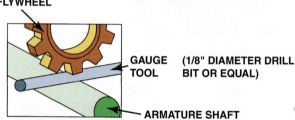

FIGURE 15–27 A shim (or half shim) may be needed to provide the proper clearance between the flywheel teeth of the engine and the pinion teeth of the starter.

STARTER DRIVE-TO-FLYWHEEL CLEARANCE

NEED FOR PROPER CLEARANCE For the proper operation of the starter and absence of abnormal starter noise, there must be a slight clearance between the starter pinion and the engine flywheel ring gear. Many General Motors starters use shims (thin metal strips) between the flywheel and the engine block mounting pad to provide the proper clearance. ● **SEE FIGURE 15–27.**

NOTE: Some manufacturers use shims under the starter drive end housings during production. Other manufacturers *grind* the mounting pads at the factory for proper starter pinion gear clearance. If *any* GM starter is replaced, the starter pinion *must* be checked and corrected as necessary to prevent starter damage and excessive noise.

If the clearance is too great, the starter will produce a high-pitched whine *during* cranking. If the *clearance is too small*, the starter will produce a high-pitched whine *after* the engine starts, just as the ignition key is released.

NOTE: The major cause of broken drive-end housings on starters is too small a clearance. If the clearance cannot be measured, it is better to put a shim between the engine block and the starter than to leave one out and chance breaking a drive-end housing.

CHECKING FOR PROPER CLEARANCE To be sure that the starter is shimmed correctly, use the following procedure:

STEP 1 Place the starter in position and finger-tighten the mounting bolts.

STEP 2 Use a 1/8-inch-diameter drill bit (or gauge tool) and insert between the armature shaft of the starter and a tooth of the engine flywheel.

STEP 3 If the gauge tool cannot be inserted, use a full-length shim across both mounting holes, which moves the starter away from the flywheel.

STEP 4 Remove a shim or shims if the gauge tool is loose between the shaft and the tooth of the engine flywheel.

STEP 5 If no shims have been used and the fit of the gauge tool is too loose, add a half shim to the outside pad only. This moves the starter closer to the teeth of the engine flywheel.

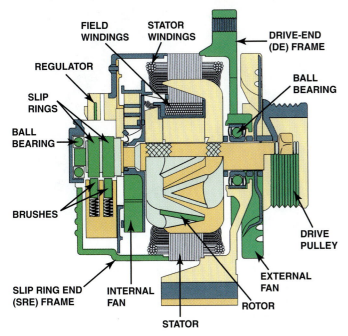

FIGURE 15–28 Cutaway view of a typical AC generator (alternator).

GENERATOR CONSTRUCTION

A generator is constructed of a two-piece cast-aluminum housing. Aluminum is used because of its lightweight, nonmagnetic properties and heat transfer properties which are needed to help keep the generator cool. A front ball bearing is pressed into the front housing (called the **drive-end [DE] housing**) to provide the support and friction reduction necessary for the belt-driven rotor assembly. The rear housing (called the **slip ring end [SRE]**) usually contains a roller-bearing support for the rotor and mounting for the brushes, diodes, and internal voltage regulator (if the generator is so equipped). ● **SEE FIGURE 15–28.**

CHECKING CHARGING SYSTEM VOLTAGE

The charge indicator light on the dash should be on with the ignition on, engine off (KOEO), but should be off when the engine is running (KOER). If the charge light remains on with the engine running, check the charging system voltage. To measure charging system voltage, connect the test leads of a digital multimeter to the positive (+) and negative (−) terminals of the battery. Set the multimeter to read DC volts.

How Many Horsepower Does a Generator Require to Operate?

Many technicians are asked how much power certain accessories require. A 100 A generator requires about 2 horsepower (hp) from the engine. One horsepower is equal to 746 watts (W). Watts are calculated by multiplying amperes times volts.

$$\text{Power in W} = 100 \text{ A} \times 14.5 \text{ V}$$
$$= 1450 \text{ W}$$
$$1 \text{ hp} = 746 \text{ W}$$

Therefore, 1450 W is about 2 hp.

Allowing about 20% for mechanical and electrical losses adds another 0.4 hp. Therefore, when anyone asks how much power it takes to produce 100 A from a generator, the answer is about 2.4 hp.

The Dead Rat Smell Test

When checking for the root cause of a generator failure, the wise technician should sniff (smell) the generator! If the generator smells like a dead rat (rancid), the stator windings have been overheated by trying to charge a discharged or defective battery. If the battery voltage is continuously low, the voltage regulator will continue supplying full-field current to the generator. The voltage regulator is designed to cycle on and off to maintain a narrow charging system voltage range.

If the battery voltage is continually below the cutoff point of the voltage regulator, the generator is continually producing current in the stator windings. This constant charging can often overheat the stator and burn the insulating varnish covering the stator windings. If the generator fails the sniff test, the technician should replace the generator *and* replace or recharge and test the battery.

FIGURE 15–29 The digital multimeter should be set to read DC volts and the red lead connected to the battery positive (+) terminal and the black meter lead connected to the negative (−) battery terminal.

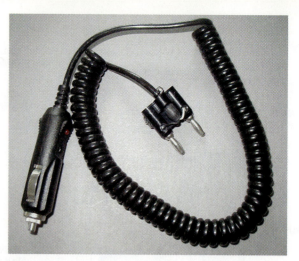

FIGURE 15–30 A simple and easy-to-use tester can be made from a lighter plug and double banana plug that fits the "COM" and "V" terminals of most digital meters. By plugging the lighter plug into the lighter, the charging circuit voltage can be easily measured.

TESTING A GENERATOR USING A VOLTMETER

CHARGING SYSTEM VOLTAGE SPECIFICATIONS Most generators are designed to supply between 13.5 and 15.0 volts at 2000 engine RPM. Be sure to check the vehicle manufacturer's specifications. For example, most General Motors Corporation vehicles specify a charging voltage of 14.7 volts ± 0.5 (or between 14.2 and 15.2 volts) at 2000 RPM and no load.

CHARGING SYSTEM VOLTAGE TEST PROCEDURE Charging system voltage tests should be performed on a vehicle with a battery at least 75% charged. If the battery is discharged (or defective), the charging voltage may be below specifications. To measure charging system voltage, follow these steps:

1. Connect the voltmeter as shown in ● **FIGURE 15–29**.
2. Set the meter to read DC volts.
3. Start the engine and raise to a fast idle (about 2000 RPM).
4. Read the voltmeter and compare with specifications. If lower than specifications, charge the battery and test for excessive charging circuit voltage drop and for a possible open in the sensing wire before replacing the generator.

NOTE: If the voltmeter reading rises, then becomes lower as the engine speed is increased, the generator drive (accessory drive) belt is loose or slipping.

TESTING A GENERATOR USING A SCAN TOOL

A scan tool can be used on most General Motors and Chrysler Corporation vehicles and others that have datastream information. Follow these steps:

1. Connect the scan tool according to the manufacturers' instructions.
2. Select battery voltage and engine RPM on the scan tool.
3. Start the engine and operate at 2000 RPM.
4. Observe the battery voltage. This voltage should be between 13.5 and 15.0 volts (or within manufacturers' specifications).

NOTE: The scan tool voltage should be within 0.5 volt of the charging voltage as tested at the battery. If the scan tool indicates a voltage lower than actual battery voltage by more than 0.5 volt, check all power and ground connections at the computer for corrosion or defects.

The Hand Cleaner Trick

Lower-than-normal generator output could be the result of a loose or slipping drive belt. All belts (V and serpentine multigroove) use an interference angle between the angle of the V's of the belt and the angle of the V's on the pulley. A belt wears this interference angle off the edges of the V of the belt. As a result, the belt may start to slip and make a squealing sound even if tensioned properly.

A common trick used to determine if the noise is belt related is to use grit-type hand cleaner or scouring powder. With the engine off, sprinkle some powder onto the pulley side of the belt. Start the engine. The excess powder will fly into the air, so get away from under the hood when the engine starts. If the belts are now quieter, you know that it was the glazed belt that made the noise.

NOTE: Often, the noise sounds exactly like a noisy bearing. Therefore, before you start removing and replacing parts, try the hand cleaner trick.

The grit from the hand cleaner will often remove the glaze from the belt and the noise will not return. If the belt is worn or loose, however, the noise will return and the belt should be replaced. A fast, alternative method to check for belt noise is to spray water from a squirt bottle at the belt with the engine running. If the noise stops, the belt is the cause of the noise. The water quickly evaporates and therefore, unlike the gritty hand cleaner, water simply finds the problem—it does not provide a short-term fix.

MEASURING THE AC RIPPLE FROM THE ALTERNATOR TELLS A LOT ABOUT ITS CONDITION. IF THE AC RIPPLE IS ABOVE 500 MILLIVOLTS, OR .5 VOLTS, LOOK FOR A PROBLEM IN THE DIODES OR STATOR. IF THE RIPPLE IS BELOW 500 MILLIVOLTS, CHECK THE ALTERNATOR OUTPUT TO DETERMINE ITS CONDITION.

FIGURE 15–31 AC ripple at the output terminal of the battery is more accurate than testing at the battery due to the resistance of the wiring between the generator and the battery. The reading shown on the meter is only 78 mV (0.078V), far below what the reading would be if a diode were defective.

AC RIPPLE VOLTAGE CHECK

A good generator should produce only a small amount of AC voltage. It is the purpose of the diodes in the generator to rectify AC voltage into DC voltage. **AC ripple voltage** is the AC part of the DC charging voltage produced by the generator (alternator). If the AC ripple voltage is higher than 0.5 volt this can cause engine performance problems because the AC voltage can interfere with sensor signals. The procedure to check for AC voltage includes the following steps:

1. Set the digital meter to read AC volts.
2. Start the engine and operate it at 2000 RPM (fast idle).
3. Connect the voltmeter leads to the positive and negative battery terminals.
4. Turn on the headlights to provide an electrical load on the generator.

NOTE: A higher, more accurate reading can be obtained by touching the meter lead to the output terminal of the generator as shown in ● FIGURE 15–31.

FIGURE 15–32 A mini clamp-on digital multimeter can be used to measure generator output and unwanted AC current by switching the meter to read DC amperes.

AC RIPPLE VOLTAGE CHECK (CONTINUED)

The results should be interpreted as follows: If the diodes are good, the voltmeter should read *less* than 0.4 volt AC. If the reading is *over* 0.5 volt AC, the rectifier diodes or stator are defective indicating that the generator (alternator) should be replaced.

NOTE: This test will *not* test for a defective diode trio, which is used in some generators to power the field circuit internally and to turn off the dash charge light.

AC CURRENT CHECK

The amount of AC current (also called **ripple current**) in amperes flowing from the generator to the battery can be measured using a clamp-on digital multimeter set to read AC amperes. Attach the clamp of the meter around the generator output wire or all of the positive or negative battery cables if the output wire is not accessible. Start the engine and turn on all lights and accessories to load the generator and read the meter display. The maximum allowable AC current (amperes) from the generator is less than 10% of the rated output of the generator. Because most newer generators produce about 100 amperes DC, the maximum allowable AC amperes would be 10 amperes. If the reading is above 10 A (or 10%), this indicates that the rectifier diodes or a fault with the stator windings is present. ● **SEE FIGURE 15–32.**

CHARGING SYSTEM VOLTAGE-DROP TESTING

PURPOSE OF CHARGING SYSTEM VOLTAGE DROP TESTING
For the proper operation of any charging system, there must be good electrical connections between the battery positive terminal and the generator output terminal. The generator must also be properly grounded to the engine block.

Many vehicle manufacturers run the lead from the output terminal of the generator to other connectors or junction blocks that are electrically connected to the positive terminal of the battery. If there is high resistance (a high voltage drop) in these connections or in the wiring itself, the battery will not be properly charged.

CHARGING SYSTEM VOLTAGE DROP TESTING PROCEDURE
When there is a suspected charging system problem (with or without a charge indicator light on), simply follow these steps to measure the voltage drop of the insulated (power-side) charging circuit:

1. Start the engine and run it at a fast idle (about 2000 engine RPM).

2. Turn on the headlights to ensure an electrical load on the charging system.

3. Using any voltmeter, connect the positive test lead (usually red) to the output terminal of the generator. Attach the negative test lead (usually black) to the positive post of the battery.

The results should be interpreted as follows:

1. If there is less than a 0.4-volt reading, then all wiring and connections are satisfactory.

2. If the voltmeter reads higher than 0.4 volt, there is excessive resistance (voltage drop) between the generator output terminal and the positive terminal of the battery.

3. If the voltmeter reads battery voltage (or close to battery voltage), there is an open circuit between the battery and the generator output terminal (look for a positive open fusible link).

To determine whether the generator is correctly grounded, maintain the engine speed at 2000 RPM with the headlights on. Connect the positive voltmeter lead to the case of the generator and the negative voltmeter lead to the negative terminal of the battery. The voltmeter should read less than 0.2 volt if the generator is properly grounded. If the reading is over 0.2 volt, connect one end of an auxiliary ground wire to the case of the generator and the other end to a good engine ground. ● **SEE FIGURE 15–33.**

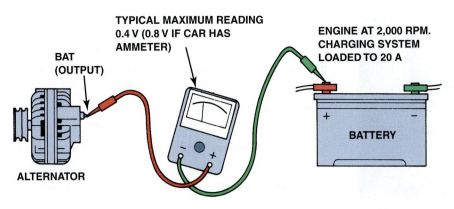

FIGURE 15–33 Voltmeter hookup to test the voltage drop of the charging circuit.

TYPICAL MAXIMUM READING 0.4 V (0.8 V IF CAR HAS AMMETER)

BAT (OUTPUT)

ENGINE AT 2,000 RPM. CHARGING SYSTEM LOADED TO 20 A

BATTERY

ALTERNATOR

VOLTAGE DROP – INSULATED CHARGING CIRCUIT

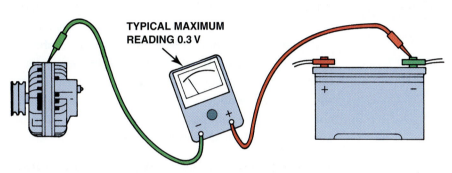

TYPICAL MAXIMUM READING 0.3 V

VOLTAGE DROP – GROUND CHARGING CIRCUIT

TECH TIP

"2 to 4"

Most voltage-drop specifications range between 0.2 and 0.4 volt. Generally, if the voltage loss (voltage drop) in a circuit exceeds 0.5 volt (1/2 volt), the wiring in that circuit should be repaired or replaced. During automotive testing, it is sometimes difficult to remember the exact specification for each test; therefore, the technician can simply remember "2 to 4" and that any voltage drop over that may indicate a problem.

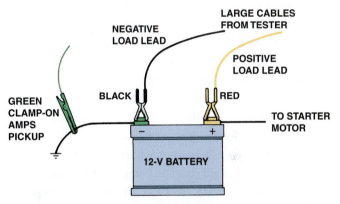

LARGE CABLES FROM TESTER

NEGATIVE LOAD LEAD

POSITIVE LOAD LEAD

GREEN CLAMP-ON AMPS PICKUP

BLACK

RED

TO STARTER MOTOR

12-V BATTERY

TEST LEAD CONNECTIONS FOR TESTING THE STARTING SYSTEM, CHARGING SYSTEM, VOLTAGE REGULATOR, AND DIODE STATOR.

FIGURE 15–34 Typical hookup of a starting and charging tester.

GENERATOR OUTPUT TEST

A charging circuit may be able to produce correct charging circuit voltage, but not be able to produce adequate amperage output. If in doubt about charging system output, first check the condition of the generator drive belt. With the engine off, attempt to rotate the fan of the generator by hand. Replace tensioner or tighten drive belt if the generator fan can be rotated by hand. ● **SEE FIGURE 15–34** for typical test equipment hookup.

The testing procedure for generator output is as follows:

1. Connect the starting and charging test leads according to the manufacturers' instructions.

2. Turn the ignition switch on (engine off) and observe the ammeter. This is the ignition circuit current, and it should be about 2 to 8 amperes.

OUTPUT RATING

FIGURE 15–35 The output on this generator is printed on a label.

 REAL WORLD FIX

The 2-Minute Generator Repair

A Chevrolet pickup truck was brought to a dealer for routine service. The owner stated that the battery required a jump start after a weekend of sitting. Almost immediately, the technician who was assigned to service the truck found a slightly loose generator belt during a visual inspection. The belt felt tight (less than 1/2 inch of deflection), yet the generator cooling fan blade could be turned by hand. After retensioning the generator drive belt, the technician tested the battery and charging system voltage using a small handheld digital multimeter. The battery voltage was 12.4 volts (about 75% charged), but the charging voltage was also 12.4 volts at 2000 RPM. Because normal charging voltage should be 13.5 to 15.0 volts, it was obvious that the charging system was not operating correctly.

The technician checked the dash and found that the "charge" light was not on even though the rear bearing was not magnetized, indicating that the voltage regulator was not working. Before removing the generator for service, the technician checked the wiring connection on the generator. When the two-lead regulator connector was removed, the connector was discovered to be rusty. After the contacts were cleaned, the charging system was restored to normal operation. The technician had learned that the simple things should always be checked first before tearing into a big (or expensive) repair.

3. Start the engine and operate it at 2000 RPM (fast idle). Turn the load increase control slowly to obtain the highest reading on the ammeter scale while maintaining a battery voltage of at least 13 volts. Note the ampere reading.

4. Total the amperes from steps 2 and 3. Results should be within 10% (or 15 amperes) of the rated output. Rated output may be stamped on the generator as shown in ● **FIGURE 15–35**.

NOTE: Almost all vehicle manufacturers are now using some load response control (LRC) also called electronic load detector (ELD), in the control of the voltage output (voltage regulators) of the generator. This means that the regulator does not react immediately to a load change, but rather slowly increases the load on the generator to avoid engine idle problems. This gradual increase of voltage may require as long as 15 seconds. This delay has convinced some technicians that a problem exists in the generator/regulator or computer control of the generator.

NOTE: When applying a load to the battery with a carbon pile tester during a generator output test, do not permit the battery voltage to drop below 13 volts. Most generators will produce their maximum output (in amperes) above 13 volts.

TESTING A GENERATOR USING A SCOPE

Defective diodes and open or shorted stators can be detected on an ignition scope. Connect the scope leads as usual, *except* for the coil negative connection, which attaches to the generator output ("BAT") terminal. With the pattern selection set to "raster" (stacked), start the engine and run to approximately 1000 RPM (slightly higher-than-normal idle speed). The scope should show an even ripple pattern reflecting the slight alternating up-and-down level of the generator output voltage.

If the generator is controlled by an electronic voltage regulator, the rapid on-and-off cycling of the field current can create vertical spikes evenly throughout the pattern. These spikes are normal. If the ripple pattern is jagged or uneven, a defective diode (open or shorted) or a defective stator is indicated. ● **SEE FIGURES 15–36 THROUGH 15–38**. If the generator scope pattern does not show even ripples, the generator should be replaced.

FIGURE 15–36 Normal generator scope pattern. This AC ripple is on top of a DC voltage line. The ripple should be less than 0.50 V high.

FIGURE 15–37 Generator pattern indicating a shorted diode.

FIGURE 15–38 Generator pattern indicating an open diode.

The Start/Stall/Start/Stall Problem

A Chevrolet 4-cylinder engine would stall every time it was started. The engine cranked normally and the engine started quickly. It would just stall once it had run for about 1 second. After hours of troubleshooting, it was discovered that if the "gages" fuse was removed, the engine would start and run normally. Because the generator was powered by the "gages" fuse, the charging voltage was checked and found to be over 16 volts just before the engine stalled. Replacing the generator fixed the problem. The computer shut down to prevent damage when the voltage exceeded 16 volts.

NOTE: A shorted throttle-body injector on a similar vehicle had the same characteristic problem. In this case, the lower resistance caused an increase in current flow (amperes) through the injector and through the computer switching transistor. To protect the transistor, the computer limited current to the injector after the engine started and the charging voltage increased to above 14 volts. As long as the generator was disconnected, the current flow through the injector was okay and the engine ran when the generator was disconnected.

SUMMARY

1. Batteries can be tested with a voltmeter to determine the state of charge. A battery load test loads the battery to one-half of its CCA rating. A good battery should be able to maintain above 9.6 volts for the entire 15-second test period.

2. A battery drain test should be performed if the battery runs down.

3. Proper operation of the starter motor depends on the battery being at least 75% charged and the battery cables being of the correct size (gauge) and having no more than a 0.2-volt drop.

4. Voltage-drop testing includes cranking the engine, measuring the drop in voltage from the battery to the starter, and measuring the drop in voltage from the negative terminal of the battery to the engine block.

5. The cranking circuit should be tested for proper amperage draw.

6. An open in the control circuit can prevent starter motor operation.

7. Charging system testing requires that the battery be at least 75% charged to be assured of accurate test results. The charge indicator light should be on with the ignition switch on, but should go out whenever the engine is running. Normal charging voltage (at 2000 engine RPM) is 13.5 to 15.0 volts.

8. To check for excessive resistance in the wiring between the generator and the battery, perform a voltage-drop test.

1. Describe the results of a voltmeter battery state-of-charge test.

2. List the steps for performing a battery load test.

3. Explain how to perform a battery drain test.

4. Explain how to perform a voltage-drop test of the cranking circuit.

5. Describe how to test the voltage drop of the charging circuit.

6. Discuss how to measure the maximum amperage output of a generator.

CHAPTER QUIZ

1. A battery high-rate discharge (load capacity) test is being performed on a 12-volt battery. Technician A says that a good battery should have a voltage reading of higher than 9.6 volts while under load at the end of the 15-second test. Technician B says that the battery should be discharged (loaded to 2 times its CCA rating). Which technician is correct?
   a. Technician A only
   b. Technician B only
   c. Both Technicians A and B
   d. Neither Technician A nor B

2. Normal battery drain (parasitic drain) with a vehicle with many computer and electronic circuits is _____.
   a. 20 to 30 milliamperes
   b. 2 to 3 amperes
   c. 150 to 300 milliamperes
   d. None of the above

3. When jump starting, _____.
   a. The last connection should be the positive post of the dead battery
   b. The last connection should be the engine block of the dead vehicle
   c. The generator must be disconnected on both vehicles
   d. Both a and c

4. Technician A says that a discharged battery (lower-than-normal battery voltage) can cause solenoid clicking. Technician B says that a discharged battery or dirty (corroded) battery cables can cause solenoid clicking. Which technician is correct?
   a. Technician A only
   b. Technician B only
   c. Both Technicians A and B
   d. Neither Technician A nor B

5. Slow cranking can be caused by all of the following *except* _____.
   a. A low or discharged battery
   b. Corroded or dirty battery cables
   c. Engine mechanical problems
   d. An open neutral safety switch

6. High resistance means _____.
   a. High voltage drop
   b. Low voltage drop
   c. Causes higher than normal current to flow
   d. Normally found in good battery cables

7. An acceptable charging circuit voltage on a 12-volt system is _____.
   a. 13.5 to 15.0 volts
   b. 12.6 to 15.6 volts
   c. 12.0 to 14.0 volts
   d. 14.9 to 16.1 volts

8. Technician A says that a voltage-drop test of the charging circuit should only be performed when current is flowing through the circuit. Technician B says to connect the leads of a voltmeter to the positive and negative terminals of the battery to measure the voltage drop of the charging system. Which technician is correct?
   a. Technician A only
   b. Technician B only
   c. Both Technicians A and B
   d. Neither Technician A nor B

9. Testing the electrical system through the lighter plug using a digital meter can test _____.
   a. Charging system current
   b. Charging system voltage
   c. Cranking system current
   d. All of the above

10. The maximum acceptable AC ripple voltage is _____.
    a. 0.010 V (10 mV)
    b. 0.050 V (50 mV)
    c. 0.100 V (100 mV)
    d. 0.400 V (400 mV)

IGNITION SYSTEM COMPONENTS AND OPERATION

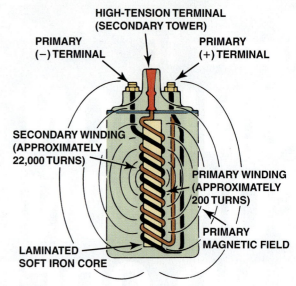

FIGURE 16–1 Internal construction of an oil-cooled ignition coil. Notice that the primary winding is electrically connected to the secondary winding. The polarity (positive or negative) of a coil is determined by the direction in which the coil is wound.

The ignition system includes those parts and wiring required to generate and distribute a high voltage to the spark plugs. A fault anywhere in the primary (low-voltage) ignition circuit can cause a no-start condition. A fault anywhere in the secondary (high-voltage) ignition circuit can cause engine misfire, hesitation, stalling, or excessive exhaust emissions.

IGNITION SYSTEM OPERATION

The ignition system includes components and wiring necessary to create and distribute a high voltage (up to 40,000 volts or more). All ignition systems apply voltage close to battery voltage (12 volts) to the positive side of the ignition coil and pulse the negative side to ground. When the coil negative lead is grounded, the primary (low-voltage) circuit of the coil is complete and a magnetic field is created around the coil windings. When the circuit is opened, the magnetic field collapses and induces a high-voltage spark in the secondary winding of the ignition coil. Early ignition systems used a mechanically opened set of contact points to make and break the electrical connection to ground. Electronic ignition uses a sensor, such as a pickup coil and reluctor (trigger wheel), or trigger to signal an electronic module that makes and breaks the primary connection of the ignition coil.

NOTE: Distributor ignition (DI) is the term specified by the Society of Automotive Engineers (SAE) for an ignition system that uses a distributor. Electronic ignition (EI) is the term specified by the SAE for an ignition system that does not use a distributor.

IGNITION COILS

PURPOSE AND FUNCTION The heart of any ignition system is the **ignition coil.** The coil creates a high-voltage spark by electromagnetic induction. Many ignition coils contain two separate but electrically connected windings of copper wire. Other coils are true transformers in which the primary and secondary windings are not electrically connected. ● **SEE FIGURE 16–1.**

COIL CONSTRUCTION The center of an ignition coil contains a core of laminated soft iron (thin strips of soft iron). This core increases the magnetic strength of the coil. Surrounding the laminated core are approximately 20,000 turns of fine wire (approximately 42 gauge). These windings are called the **secondary** coil windings. Surrounding the secondary windings are approximately 150 turns of heavy wire (approximately 21 gauge). These windings are called the **primary** coil windings. The secondary winding has about 100 times the number of turns of the primary winding, referred to as the **turns ratio** (approximately 100:1). In many coils, these windings are surrounded with a thin metal shield and insulating paper and placed into a metal container. The metal container and shield help retain the magnetic field produced in the coil windings. The primary and secondary windings produce heat because of the electrical resistance in the turns of wire. Many coils contain oil to help cool the ignition coil. Other coil designs, such as those used on GM's **high**

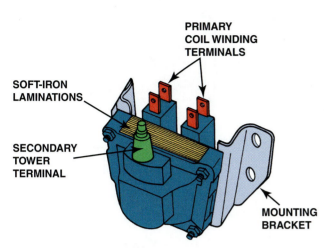

FIGURE 16–2 Typical air-cooled epoxy-filled E coil.

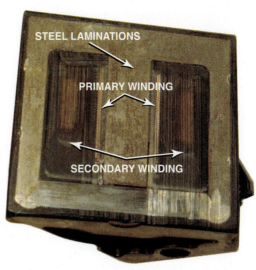

FIGURE 16–3 Cutaway of a General Motors Type II distributorless ignition coil. Note that the primary windings are inside of the secondary windings.

energy ignition (HEI) systems, use an air-cooled, epoxy-sealed **E coil.** The E coil is so named because the laminated, soft-iron core is E-shaped, with the coil wire turns wrapped around the center "finger" of the E and the primary winding wrapped inside the secondary winding. ● **SEE FIGURES 16–2 AND 16–3.**

The primary windings of the coil extend through the case of the coil and are labeled as positive and negative. The positive terminal of the coil attaches to the ignition switch, which supplies current from the positive battery terminal. The negative terminal is attached to an **ignition control module (ICM** or **igniter),** which opens and closes the primary ignition circuit by opening or closing the ground return path of the circuit. When the ignition switch is on, voltage should be available at *both* the positive terminal and the negative terminal of the coil if the primary windings of the coil have continuity. The labeling of positive (+) and negative (−) of the coil indicates that the positive terminal is *more* positive (closer to the positive terminal of the battery) than the negative terminal of the coil. This condition is called the coil **polarity.** The polarity of the coil must be correct to ensure that electrons will flow from the hot center electrode of the spark plug on DI systems. *The polarity of an ignition coil is determined by the direction of rotation of the coil windings.* The correct polarity is then indicated on the primary terminals of the coil. If the coil primary leads are reversed, the voltage required to fire the spark plugs is increased

by 40%. The coil output voltage is directly proportional to the ratio of primary to secondary turns of wire used in the coil.

SELF-INDUCTION   When current starts to flow into a coil, an opposing current is created in the windings of the coil. This opposing current generation is caused by **self-induction** and is called **inductive reactance.** Inductive reactance is similar to resistance because it opposes any changes (increase or decrease) in current flow in a coil. Therefore, when an ignition coil is first energized, there is a slight delay of approximately 0.01 second before the ignition coil reaches its maximum magnetic field strength. The point at which a coil's maximum magnetic field strength is reached is called **saturation.**

MUTUAL INDUCTION   In an ignition coil there are two windings, a primary and a secondary winding. When a *change* occurs in the magnetic field of one coil winding, a change also occurs in the other coil winding. Therefore, if the current is stopped from flowing (circuit is opened), the collapsing magnetic field cuts across the turns of the secondary winding and creates a high voltage in the secondary winding. This generation of an electric current in both coil windings is called **mutual induction.** The collapsing magnetic field also creates a voltage of up to 250 volts in the primary winding.

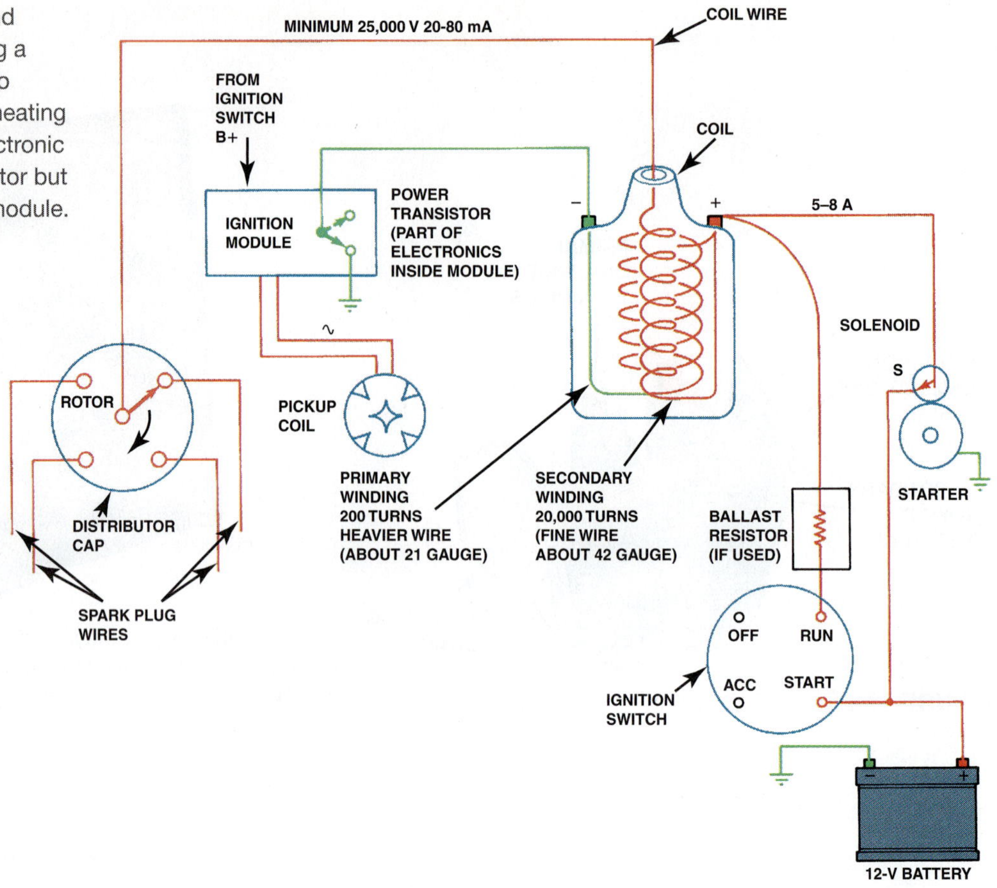

FIGURE 16–4 Typical primary and secondary electronic ignition using a ballast resistor and a distributor. To protect the ignition coil from overheating at lower engine speeds, many electronic ignitions do not use a ballast resistor but use electronic circuits within the module.

Labels in figure:
MINIMUM 25,000 V 20-80 mA
COIL WIRE
FROM IGNITION SWITCH B+
POWER TRANSISTOR (PART OF ELECTRONICS INSIDE MODULE)
COIL
5–8 A
IGNITION MODULE
SOLENOID
S
PICKUP COIL
STARTER
ROTOR
PRIMARY WINDING 200 TURNS HEAVIER WIRE (ABOUT 21 GAUGE)
SECONDARY WINDING 20,000 TURNS (FINE WIRE ABOUT 42 GAUGE)
BALLAST RESISTOR (IF USED)
DISTRIBUTOR CAP
SPARK PLUG WIRES
OFF RUN ACC START
IGNITION SWITCH
12-V BATTERY

IGNITION COILS (CONTINUED)

HOW IGNITION COILS CREATE 40,000 VOLTS

All ignition systems use electromagnetic induction to produce a high-voltage spark from the ignition coil. Electromagnetic induction means that a current can be created in a conductor (coil winding) by a moving magnetic field. The magnetic field in an ignition coil is produced by current flowing through the primary windings of the coil. The current for the primary winding is supplied through the ignition switch to the positive terminal of the ignition coil. The negative terminal is connected to the ground return through an electronic ignition module (igniter).

If the primary circuit is completed, current (approximately 2 to 6 A) can flow through the primary coil windings. This flow creates a strong magnetic field inside the coil. When the primary coil winding ground return path connection is opened, the magnetic field collapses and induces a voltage of from 250 to 400 volts in the primary winding of the coil and a high-voltage (20,000 to 40,000 volts) low-amperage (20 to 80 mA) current in the secondary coil windings. This high-voltage pulse flows through the coil wire (if the vehicle is so equipped), distributor cap, rotor, and spark plug wires to the spark plugs. For each spark that occurs, the coil must be charged with a magnetic field and then discharged. The ignition components that regulate the current in the coil primary winding by turning it on and off are known collectively as the **primary ignition circuit.** The components necessary to create and distribute the high voltage produced in the secondary windings of the coil are called the **secondary ignition circuit.** ● SEE FIGURE 16–4. These circuits include the following components.

PRIMARY IGNITION CIRCUIT

1. Battery
2. Ignition switch
3. Primary windings of coil
4. Pickup coil (crank sensor)
5. Ignition module (igniter)

SECONDARY IGNITION CIRCUIT

1. Secondary windings of coil
2. Distributor cap and rotor (if the vehicle is so equipped)
3. Spark plug wires
4. Spark plugs

FREQUENTLY ASKED QUESTION

What Is a "Married" and "Divorced" Coil Design?

An ignition coil contains two windings, a primary winding and a secondary winding, and these windings can be either connected together at one end or kept separated.

- **Married.** A **married coil** design is also called a tapped transformer design. ● **SEE FIGURE 16–5**. The primary winding is electrically connected to the secondary winding. This method is commonly used in older distributor-type ignition system coils, as well as many coil-on-plug designs. The inductive kick, also called flyback voltage, created when the primary field collapses is used by the PCM to monitor secondary ignition performance.
- **Divorced.** A **divorced coil** design is also called a **true transformer** design and is used by most waste-spark ignition coils to keep both the primary and secondary winding separated.

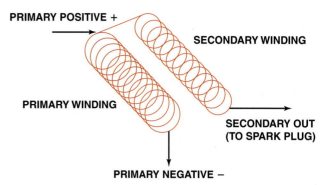

FIGURE 16–5 A tapped- (married) type ignition coil where the primary winding is tapped (connected) to the secondary winding.

IGNITION SWITCHING AND TRIGGERING

For any ignition system to function, the primary current must be turned on to charge the coil and off to allow the coil to discharge, creating a high-voltage spark. This turning on and off of the primary circuit is called **switching.** The unit that does the switching is an electronic switch, such as a power transistor. This power transistor can be located in any of the following locations:

- In the ignition control module (ICM)
- In the PCM (computer)

NOTE: On some coil-on-plug systems, the ICM is part of the ignition coil itself and is serviced as an assembly.

The device that signals the switching of the coil on and off or just on in most instances, is called the **trigger.** A trigger is typically a pickup coil in some distributor-type ignitions and a crankshaft position sensor (CKP) on electronic (waste-spark and coil-on-plug) and many distributor-type ignitions. There are three types of devices used for triggering, including the magnetic sensor, Hall-effect switch, and optical sensor.

PRIMARY CIRCUIT OPERATION

To get a spark out of an ignition coil, the primary coil circuit must be turned on and off. This primary circuit current is controlled by a **transistor** (electronic switch) inside the ignition module or (igniter) that in turn is controlled by one of several devices, including:

- **Pickup coil (pulse generator)**—A simple and common ignition electronic switching device is the magnetic pulse generator system. Most manufacturers use the rotation of the distributor shaft to time the voltage pulses. The **magnetic pulse generator** is installed in the distributor housing. The pulse generator consists of a trigger wheel (reluctor) and a pickup coil. The pickup coil consists of an iron core wrapped with fine wire, in a coil at one end and attached to a permanent magnet at the other end. The center of the coil is called the pole piece. The pickup coil signal triggers the transistor inside the module and is also used by the computer for piston position information and engine speed (RPM). ● **SEE FIGURES 16–6 AND 16–7.**

- **Hall-effect switch**—A **Hall-effect switch** also uses a stationary sensor and rotating trigger wheel (shutter). ● **SEE FIGURE 16–8.** Unlike the magnetic pulse generator, the Hall-effect switch requires a small input voltage to generate an output or signal voltage. Hall effect is the ability to generate a voltage signal in semiconductor material (gallium arsenate crystal) by passing current through it in one direction and applying a magnetic field to it at a right angle to its surface. If the input current is

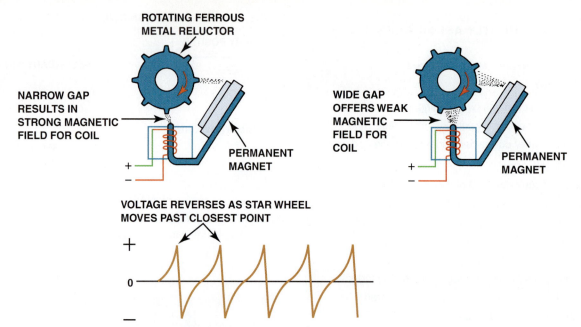

FIGURE 16–6 Operation of a typical pulse generator (pickup coil). At the bottom is a line drawing of a typical scope pattern of the output voltage of a pickup coil. The module receives this voltage from the pickup coil and opens the ground circuit to the ignition coil when the voltage starts down from its peak (just as the reluctor teeth start moving away from the pickup coil).

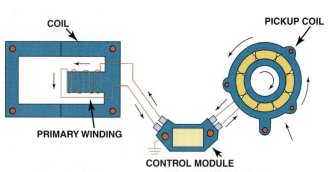

FIGURE 16–7 The varying voltage signal from the pickup coil triggers the ignition module. The ignition module grounds and ungrounds the primary winding of the ignition coil, creating a high-voltage spark.

FIGURE 16–8 Hall-effect switches use metallic shutters to shunt magnetic lines of force away from a silicon chip and related circuits. All Hall-effect switches produce a square wave output for every accurate triggering.

PRIMARY CIRCUIT OPERATION (CONTINUED)

held steady and the magnetic field fluctuates, an output voltage is produced that changes in proportion to field strength. Most Hall-effect switches in distributors have a Hall element or device, a permanent magnet, and a rotating ring of metal blades (shutters) similar to a trigger wheel (another method uses a stationary sensor with a rotating magnet). Some blades are designed to hang down, typically found in Bosch and Chrysler systems; others may be on a separate ring on the distributor shaft, typically found in GM and Ford Hall-effect distributors. When the shutter blade enters the gap between the

magnet and the Hall element, it creates a magnetic shunt that changes the field strength through the Hall element. This analog signal is sent to a **Schmitt trigger** inside the sensor itself, which converts the analog signal into a digital signal. A digital (on or off) voltage signal is created at a varying frequency to the ignition module or onboard computer. ● **SEE FIGURES 16–9 AND 16–10.**

■ **Magnetic crankshaft position sensor—A magnetic sensor** uses the changing strength of the magnetic field surrounding a coil of wire to signal the module and computer. This signal is used by the electronics in the

FIGURE 16–9 Shutter blade of a rotor as it passes between the sensing silicon chip and the permanent magnet.

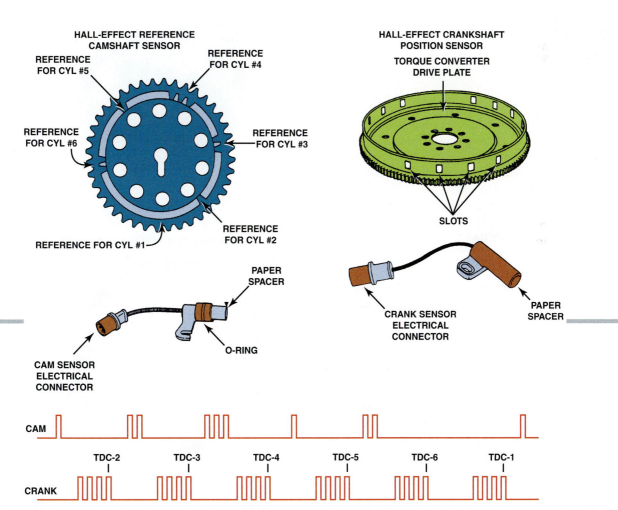

FIGURE 16–10 Some Hall-effect sensors look like magnetic sensors. This Hall-effect camshaft reference sensor and crankshaft position sensor have an electronic circuit built in that creates a 0- to 5-volt signal as shown at the bottom. These Hall-effect sensors have three wires: a power supply (8 volts) from the computer (controller); a signal (0 to 5 volts); and a signal ground.

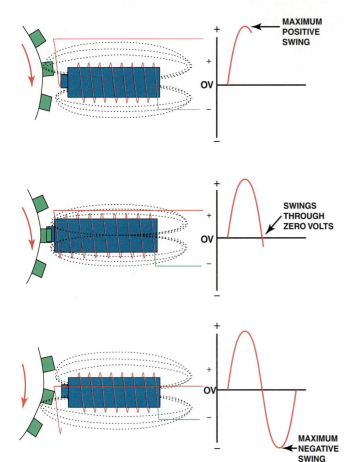

FIGURE 16–11 A magnetic sensor uses a permanent magnet surrounded by a coil of wire. The notches of the crankshaft (or camshaft) create a variable magnetic field strength around the coil. When a metallic section is close to the sensor, the magnetic field is stronger because metal is a better conductor of magnetic lines of force than air.

PRIMARY CIRCUIT OPERATION (CONTINUED)

module and computer as to piston position and engine speed (RPM). ● SEE FIGURES 16–11 AND 16–12.

- **Optical sensors**—These use light from a LED and a phototransistor to signal the computer. An interrupter disc between the LED and the phototransistor has slits that allow the light from the LED to trigger the phototransistor on the other side of the disc. Most **optical sensors** (usually located inside the distributor) use two rows of slits to provide individual cylinder recognition (low-resolution) and precise distributor angle recognition (high-resolution) signals. ● SEE FIGURE 16–13.

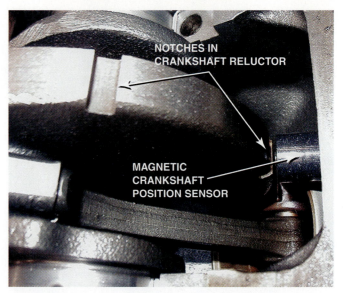

FIGURE 16–12 A typical magnetic crankshaft position sensor.

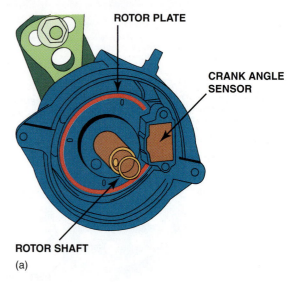

(a)

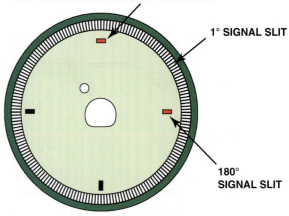

(b)

FIGURE 16–13 (a) Typical optical distributor. (b) Cylinder I slit signals the computer the piston position for cylinder I. The I-degree slits provide accurate engine speed information to the computer.

(a)

(b)

FIGURE 16–14 (a) An optical distributor on a Nissan 3.0 L V-6 shown with the light shield removed. (b) A light shield being installed before the rotor is attached.

TECH TIP

Optical Distributors Do Not Like Light

Optical distributors use the light emitted from LEDs to trigger phototransistors. Most optical distributors use a shield between the distributor rotor and the optical interrupter ring. Sparks jump the gap from the rotor tip to the distributor cap inserts. This shield blocks the light from the electrical arc from interfering with the detection of the light from the LEDs.

If this shield is not replaced during service, the light signals are reduced and the engine may not operate correctly. ● **SEE FIGURE 16–14.** This can be difficult to detect because nothing looks wrong during a visual inspection. Remember that all optical distributors must be shielded between the rotor and the interrupter ring.

TECH TIP

The Tachometer Trick

When diagnosing a no-start or intermittent misfire condition, check the operation of the tachometer. If the tachometer does not indicate engine speed (no-start condition) or drops toward zero (engine misfire), then the problem is due to a defect in the *primary* ignition circuit. The tachometer gets its signal from the pulsing of the primary winding of the ignition coil. The following components in the primary circuit could cause the tachometer to not work when the engine is cranking.

- Pickup coil
- Crankshaft position sensor
- Ignition module (igniter)
- Coil primary wiring

If the vehicle is not equipped with a tachometer, connect a handheld tachometer to the negative terminal of the coil. Remember the following:

- No tachometer reading means the problem is in the primary ignition circuit.
- Tachometer reading okay means the problem is in the secondary ignition circuit or is a fuel-related problem.

DISTRIBUTOR IGNITION

GENERAL MOTORS HEI ELECTRONIC IGNITION As mentioned, high energy ignition (HEI) has been the standard equipment DI system on General Motors vehicles. Some models use an ignition coil inside the distributor cap and some use an externally mounted ignition coil. The operation of both styles is similar. The large-diameter distributor cap provides additional space between the spark plug connections to help prevent crossfire. ● **SEE FIGURE 16–15.** Most HEI distributors also use 8-mm-diameter spark plug wires that use female connections to the distributor cap towers. HEI coils must be replaced (if defective) with the exact replacement style. HEI coils differ and can be identified by the colors of the primary leads. The primary coil leads can be either white and red or yellow and red. The correct color of lead coil must be used for replacement. The colors of the leads indicate the direction in which the coil is wound, and therefore its polarity. ● **SEE FIGURES 16–16 AND 16–17.**

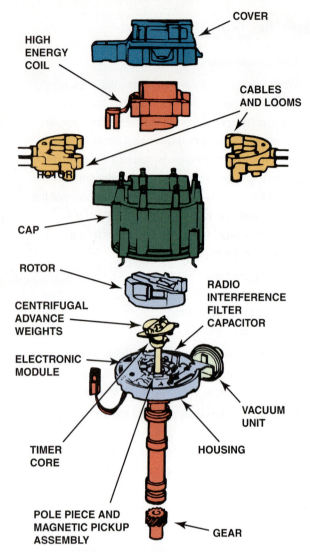

FIGURE 16–15 An HEI distributor.

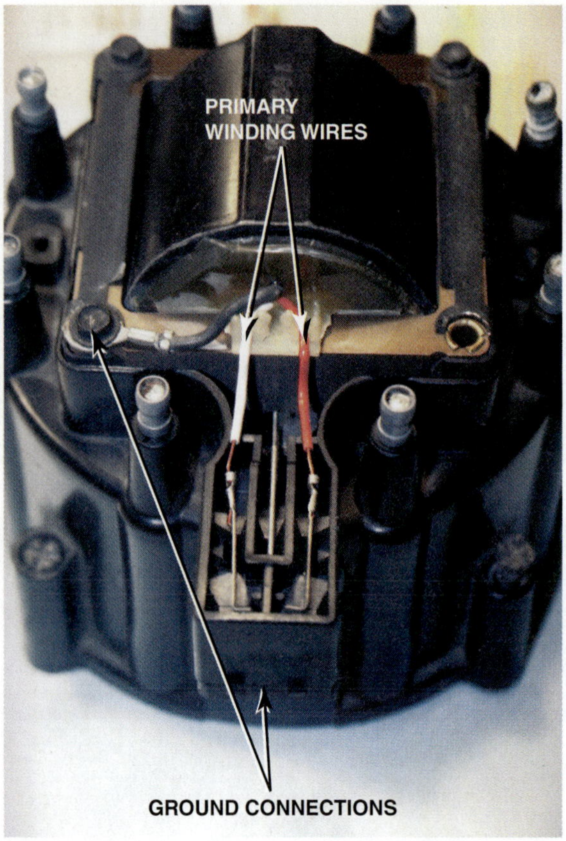

Labels in figure: COVER, HIGH ENERGY COIL, CABLES AND LOOMS, ROTOR, CAP, ROTOR, CENTRIFUGAL ADVANCE WEIGHTS, RADIO INTERFERENCE FILTER CAPACITOR, ELECTRONIC MODULE, VACUUM UNIT, TIMER CORE, HOUSING, POLE PIECE AND MAGNETIC PICKUP ASSEMBLY, GEAR

FIGURE 16–16 A typical General Motors HEI coil installed in the distributor cap. When the coil or distributor cap is replaced, check that the ground clip is transferred from the old distributor cap to the new. Without proper grounding, coil damage is likely. There are two designs of HEI coils. One uses red and white wire as shown, and the other design, which has reversed polarity, uses red and yellow wire for the coil primary.

Labels in figure: PRIMARY WINDING WIRES, GROUND CONNECTIONS

DISTRIBUTOR IGNITION (CONTINUED)

FORD ELECTRONIC IGNITION   Ford electronic ignition systems all function similarly, even though over the years the system has been called by various names.

The EEC IV system uses the thick-film-integration (TFI) ignition system. This system uses a smaller control module attached to the distributor and uses an air-cooled epoxy E coil.
● **SEE FIGURE 16–18**. Thick-film integration means that all electronics are manufactured on small layers built up to form a thick film. Construction includes using pastes of different electrical resistances that are deposited on a thin, flat ceramic material by a process similar to silk-screen printing. These resistors are connected by tracks of palladium silver paste. Then the chips that form the capacitors, diodes, and integrated circuits are soldered directly to the palladium silver tracks. The thick-film manufacturing process is highly automated.

FIGURE 16–17 This distributor ignition system uses a remotely mounted ignition coil.

Labels in figure: PICKUP COIL, IGNITION MODULE

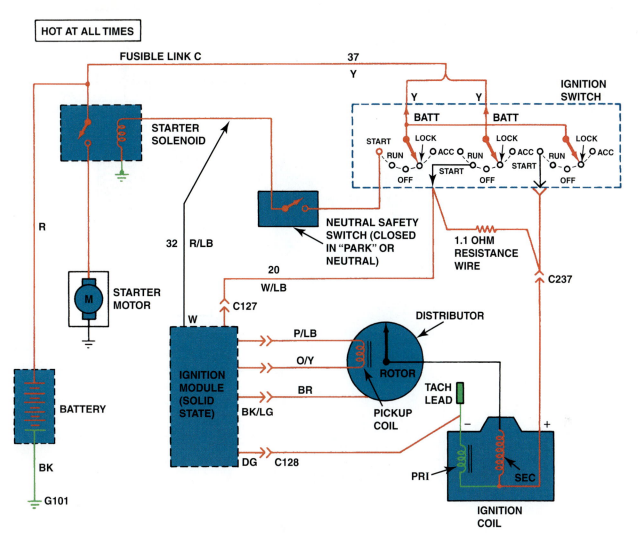

FIGURE 16–18 Wiring diagram of a typical Ford electronic ignition.

OPERATION OF FORD DISTRIBUTOR IGNITION Ford DI systems function in basically the same way regardless of year and name. Under the distributor cap and rotor is a magnetic pickup assembly. This assembly produces a small alternating electrical pulse (approximately 1.5 volts) when the distributor armature rotates past the pickup assembly (stator). This low-voltage pulse is sent to the ignition module. The ignition module then switches (through transistors) off the primary ignition coil current. When the ignition coil primary current is stopped quickly, a high-voltage "spike" discharges from the coil secondary winding. The coil current is controlled in the module circuits by decreasing dwell (coil-charging time), depending on various factors determined by operating conditions. ● **SEE FIGURE 16–19.**

CHRYSLER DISTRIBUTOR IGNITION Chrysler was the first domestic manufacturer to produce electronic ignition as standard equipment. The Chrysler system consists of a pulse generator unit in the distributor (pickup coil and reluctor). Chrysler's name for their electronic ignition is **electronic ignition system (EIS),** and the control unit (module) is called the **electronic control unit (ECU).**

The pickup coil in the distributor (pulse generator) generates the signal to open and close the primary coil circuit. ● **SEE FIGURE 16–20.**

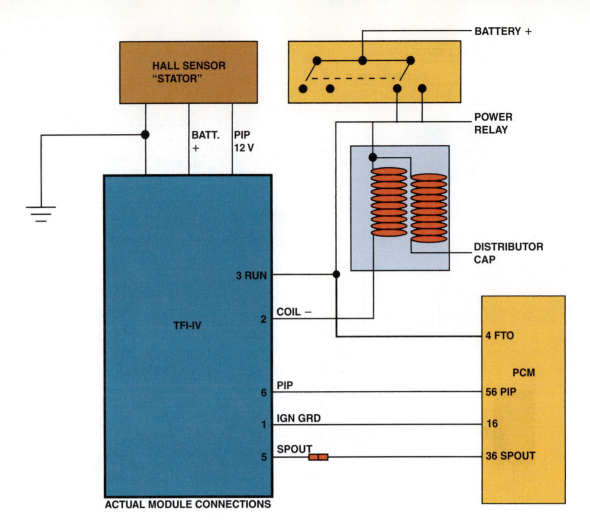

FIGURE 16–19
Schematic of a Ford TFI-IV ignition system. The SPOUT connector is unplugged when ignition timing is being set.

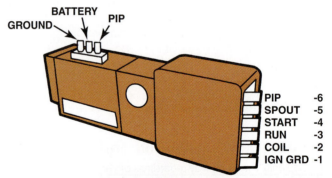

FIGURE 16–20 A Chrysler electronic ignition distributor. This unit is equipped with a vacuum advance mechanism that advances the ignition timing under light engine load conditions.

WASTE-SPARK IGNITION SYSTEMS

Waste-spark ignition is another name for distributorless ignition system (DIS) or **electronic ignition (EI).** Waste-spark ignition was introduced in the mid-1980s and uses the onboard computer to fire the ignition coils. These systems were first used on some Saabs and General Motors engines. A four-cylinder engine uses two ignition coils and a six-cylinder engine uses three ignition coils. Each coil is a true transformer in which the primary winding and secondary winding are not electrically connected. Each end of the secondary winding is connected to a cylinder exactly opposite the other in the firing order, which is called a **companion (paired) cylinder.** ● **SEE FIGURE 16–21.** This means that *both* spark plugs fire at the same time (within nanoseconds of each other). When one cylinder (for example, 6) is on the compression stroke, the other cylinder (3) is on the exhaust stroke. This spark that occurs on the exhaust stroke is called the waste spark, because it does no useful work and is only used as a ground path for the secondary winding of the ignition coil. The voltage required to jump the spark plug gap on cylinder 3 (the exhaust stroke) is only 2 to 3 kV and provides the *ground circuit* for the secondary coil circuit. The remaining coil energy is used by the cylinder on the compression stroke. One spark plug of each pair always fires straight polarity and the other cylinder always fires reverse polarity. Spark plug life is not greatly affected by the reverse polarity. If there is only one defective spark plug wire or spark plug, two cylinders may be affected.

The coil polarity is determined by the direction the coil is wound (left-hand rule for conventional current flow) and cannot be changed. ● **SEE FIGURE 16–22.** Each spark plug for a particular cylinder always will be fired either with straight or reversed polarity, depending on its location in the engine and how the coils are wired. However, the compression and waste-spark condition flip-flops. When one cylinder is on compression, such as cylinder number 1, then the paired cylinder (number 4) is on the exhaust stroke. During the next rotation of the crankshaft, cylinder number 4 is on the compression stroke and cylinder number 1 is on the exhaust stroke.

Cylinder 1 Always fires straight polarity, one time, requiring 10 to 12 kV and one time, requiring 3 to 4 kV.

Cylinder 4 Always fires reverse polarity, one time, requiring 10 to 12 kV and one time, requiring 3 to 4 kV.

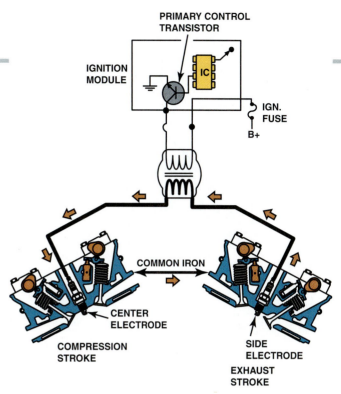

FIGURE 16–21 A waste-spark system fires one cylinder while its piston is on the compression stroke and into paired or companion cylinders while it is on the exhaust stroke. In a typical engine, it requires only about 2 to 3 kV to fire the cylinder on the exhaust strokes. The remaining coil energy is available to fire the spark plug under compression (typically about 8 to 12 kV).

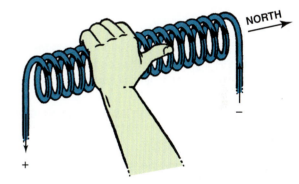

FIGURE 16–22 The left-hand rule states that if a coil is grasped with the left hand, the fingers will point in the direction of current flow and the thumb will point toward the north pole.

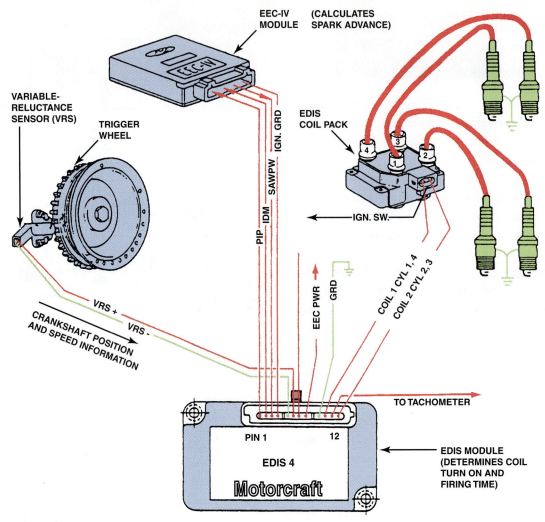

FIGURE 16–23 Typical Ford EDIS 4-cylinder ignition system. The crankshaft sensor, called a variable-reluctance sensor (VRS), sends crankshaft position and speed information to the EDIS module. A modified signal is sent to the computer as a profile ignition pickup (PIP) signal. The PIP is used by the computer to calculate ignition timing, and the computer sends a signal back to the EDIS module as to when to fire the spark plug. This return signal is called the spark angle word (SAW) signal.

WASTE-SPARK IGNITION SYSTEMS (CONTINUED)

NOTE: With a distributor-type ignition system, the coil has two air gaps to fire: one between the rotor tip and the distributor insert (not under compression forces) and the other in the gap at the firing tip of the spark plug (under compression forces). A DIS also fires two gaps: one under compression (compression stroke plug) and one not under compression (exhaust stroke plug).

Waste-spark ignitions require a sensor (usually a crankshaft sensor) to trigger the coils at the correct time. ● **SEE FIGURE 16–23**. The crankshaft sensor cannot be moved to adjust ignition timing. Ignition timing is not adjustable. The slight adjustment of the crankshaft sensor is designed to position the sensor exactly in the middle of the rotating metal disc for maximum clearance. Some engines do not use a camshaft position sensor, but rather double Hall-effect crankshaft sensors and again, ignition timing is not adjustable.

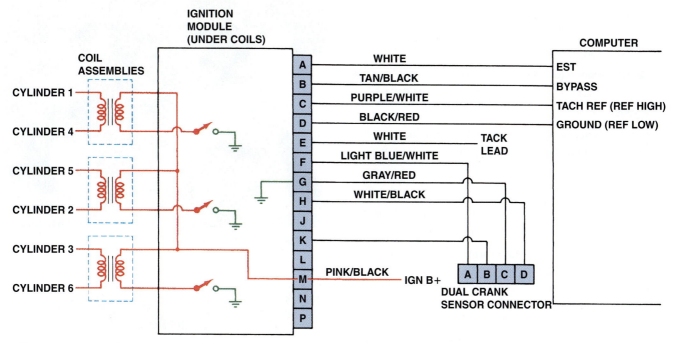

FIGURE 16–24 Typical wiring diagram of a V-6 distributorless (direct fire) ignition system.

TECH TIP

Odds Fire Straight

Waste-spark ignition systems fire two spark plugs at the same time. Most vehicle manufacturers use a waste-spark system that fires the odd-numbered cylinders (1, 3, and 5) by straight polarity (current flow from the top of the spark plug through the gap and to the ground electrode). The even-numbered cylinders (2, 4, and 6) are fired reverse polarity, meaning that the spark jumps from the side electrode to the center electrode. Some vehicle manufacturers equip their vehicles with platinum plugs with the expansive platinum alloy only on one electrode as follows:

- On odd-numbered cylinders (1, 3, 5), the platinum is on the center electrode.
- On even-numbered cylinders (2, 4, 6), the platinum is on the ground electrode.

Replacement spark plugs use platinum on both electrodes (double platinum) and can, therefore, be placed in any cylinder location.

IGNITION CONTROL CIRCUITS

Ignition control (IC) is the OBD-II terminology for the output signal from the PCM to the ignition system that controls engine timing. Previously, each manufacturer used a different term to describe this signal. For instance, Ford referred to this signal as **spark output (SPOUT)** and General Motors referred to this signal as **electronic spark timing (EST)**. This signal is now referred to as the ignition control (IC) signal. The ignition control signal is usually a digital output that is sent to the ignition system as a timing signal. If the ignition system is equipped with an ignition module, then this signal is used by the ignition module to vary the timing as engine speed and load changes. If the PCM directly controls the coils, such as most coil-on-plug ignition systems, then this IC signal directly controls the coil primary and there is a separate IC signal for each ignition coil. The IC signal controls the time that the coil fires; it either advances or retards the timing. On many systems, this signal controls the duration of the primary current flow in the coil, which is referred to as the **dwell.**

BYPASS IGNITION CONTROL A bypass-type ignition control means that the engine starts using the ignition module for timing control and then switches to the PCM for timing control after the engine starts. A **bypass ignition** is commonly used on General Motors engines equipped with distributor ignition (DI), as well as those equipped with waste-spark ignition. ● **SEE FIGURE 16–24**.

The bypass circuit includes four wires:

- **Tach reference (purple/white).** This wire comes from the ignition control (IC) module and is used by the PCM as engine speed information.

- **Ground (black/white).** This ground wire is used to ensure that both the PCM and the ignition control module share the same ground.

- **Bypass (tan/black).** This wire is used to conduct a 5-volt DC signal from the PCM to the ignition control module to switch the timing control from the module to the PCM.

- **EST (ignition control) (white wire).** This is the ignition timing control signal from the PCM to the ignition control module.

NOTE: It is this bypass wire that is disconnected before the ignition timing can be set on many General Motors engines equipped with a distributor ignition.

DIAGNOSING A BYPASS IGNITION SYSTEM One advantage of a bypass-type ignition is that the engine will run without the computer because the module can do the coil switching and can, through electronic circuits inside the module, provide for some spark advance as the engine speed increases. This is a safety feature that helps protect the catalytic converter if the ignition control from the PCM is lost. Therefore, if there is a problem, use a digital meter and check for the presence of 5 volts on the tan bypass wire. If there is not 5 volts present with the engine running, then the PCM or the wiring is at fault.

UP-INTEGRATED IGNITION CONTROL Most coil-on-plug and many waste-spark-type ignition systems use the PCM for ignition timing control. This type of ignition control is called **up-integrated** because all timing functions are interpreted in the PCM, rather than being split between the ignition control module and the PCM. The ignition module, if even used, contains the power transistor for coil switching. The signal as to when the coil fires, is determined and controlled from the PCM.

Unlike a bypass ignition control circuit, it is not possible to separate the PCM from the ignition coil control to help isolate a fault.

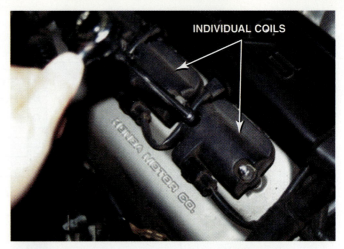

FIGURE 16–25 A coil-on-plug ignition system.

COMPRESSION-SENSING IGNITION

Some waste-spark ignition systems, such as those used on Saturns, use the voltage required to fire the cylinders to determine cylinder position. It requires a higher voltage to fire a spark plug under compression than it does when the spark plug is being fired on the exhaust stroke. The electronics in the coil and the PCM can detect which of the two cylinders that are fired at the same time requires the higher voltage, which indicates the cylinder on the compression stroke. For example, a typical four-cylinder engine equipped with a waste-spark ignition system will fire both cylinders 1 and 4. If cylinder number 4 requires a higher voltage to fire, as determined by the electronics connected to the coil, then the PCM assumes that cylinder number 4 is on the compression stroke. Engines equipped with **compression-sensing ignition** systems, such as Saturns, do not require the use of a camshaft position sensor to determine cylinder number.

COIL-ON-PLUG IGNITION

Coil-on-plug (COP) ignition uses one ignition coil for each spark plug. This system is also called **coil-by-plug, coil-near-plug,** or **coil-over-plug** ignition. ● **SEE FIGURES 16–25 AND 16–26.** The coil-on-plug system eliminates the spark plug wires which are often sources of **electromagnetic interference (EMI)** that can cause problems to some computer signals. The vehicle computer controls the timing of the spark. Ignition timing also can be changed (retarded or advanced) on a cylinder-by-cylinder basis for maximum performance and to respond to knock sensor signals. ● **SEE FIGURE 16–27.**

There are two basic types of coil-on-plug ignition including:

- **Two-wire**—This design uses the vehicle computer to control the firing of the ignition coil. The two wires include

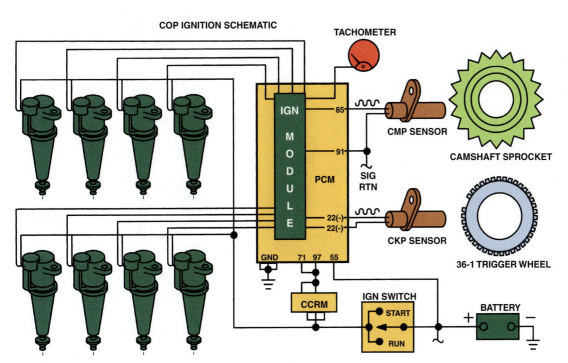

COP IGNITION SCHEMATIC

TACHOMETER

IGN MODULE

PCM

85 — CMP SENSOR

91

SIG RTN

22(-)
22(-) — CKP SENSOR

GND 71 97 55

CAMSHAFT SPROCKET

36-1 TRIGGER WHEEL

CCRM

IGN SWITCH
START
RUN

BATTERY
+ —

FIGURE 16–26 A typical coil-on-plug (COP) ignition system on a V-8 with a separate coil for each cylinder.

FIGURE 16–27 Individual coils with modules shown on the General Motors 4.2-L inline 6-cyliner light-truck engine. Note the aluminum cooling fins (heat sink) on top of each assembly.

＋ SAFETY TIP

Never Disconnect a Spark Plug Wire When the Engine Is Running!

Ignition systems produce a high-voltage pulse necessary to ignite a lean air–fuel mixture. If you disconnect a spark plug wire when the engine is running, this high-voltage spark could cause personal injury or damage to the ignition coil and/or ignition module.

ignition voltage feed and the pulse ground wire, which is controlled by the computer. All ignition timing and dwell control are handled by the computer.

- **Three-wire**—This design includes an ignition module at each coil. The three wires include:
  - Ignition voltage
  - Ground
  - Pulse from the computer to the built-in module

General Motors vehicles use a variety of coil-on-plug-type ignition systems. Many V-8 engines use a coil-near-plug system with individual coils and modules for each individual cylinder

that are placed on the valve covers. Short secondary ignition spark plug wires are used to connect the output terminal of the ignition coil to the spark plug.

Most newer Chrysler engines use coil-over-plug-type ignition systems. Each coil is controlled by the PCM, which can vary the ignition timing separately for each cylinder based on signals the PCM receives from the knock sensor(s). For example, if the knock sensor detects that a spark knock has occurred after firing cylinder 3, then the PCM will continue to monitor cylinder 3 and retard timing on just this one cylinder if necessary to prevent engine-damaging detonation.

ION-SENSING IGNITION

In an **ion-sensing ignition** system, the spark plug itself becomes a sensor. The ignition control (IC) module applies a voltage of about 100 to 400 volts DC across the spark plug gap after the ignition event to sense the plasma inside the cylinder. ● **SEE FIGURE 16–28**. The coil discharge voltage (10 to 15 kV) is electrically isolated from the ion-sensing circuit. The combustion flame is ionized and will conduct some electricity, which can be accurately measured at the spark plug gap. The purpose of this circuit includes:

- Misfire detection (required by OBD-II regulations)
- Knock detection (eliminates the need for a knock sensor)
- Ignition timing control (to achieve the best spark timing for maximum power with lowest exhaust emissions)
- Exhaust gas recirculation (EGR) control
- Air–fuel ratio control on an individual cylinder basis

Ion-sensing ignition systems still function the same as conventional coil-on-plug designs, but the engine does not need to be equipped with a camshaft position sensor for misfire detection, or a knock sensor because both of these faults are achieved using the electronics inside the ignition control circuits.

IGNITION TIMING

THE NEED FOR SPARK ADVANCE Ignition timing refers to when the spark plug fires in relation to piston position. The time when the spark occurs depends on engine speed, and therefore, must be advanced (spark plugs fire some) as the engine rotates faster. The ignition in the cylinder takes a certain amount of time, usually 30 ms (30/1000 of a second). This burning time is relatively constant throughout the entire engine speed range. For maximum efficiency from the expanding gases inside the combustion chamber, the burning of the air–fuel mixture should end by about 10° after top dead center (ATDC). If the burning of the mixture is still occurring after that point, the expanding gases do not exert much force on the piston because it is moving away from the gases (the gases are "chasing" the piston).

Therefore, to achieve the goal of having the air–fuel mixture be completely burned by the time the piston reaches 10° after top dead center, the spark must be advanced (occur sooner) as the

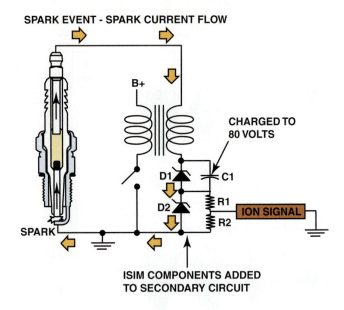

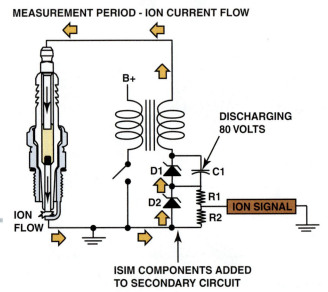

FIGURE 16–28 A DC voltage is applied across the spark plug gap after the plug fires and the circuit can determine if the correct air–fuel ratio was present in the cylinder and if knock occurred.

engine speed increases. This timing advance is determined and controlled by the PCM on most vehicles. ● **SEE FIGURE 16–29**.

INITIAL TIMING If the engine is equipped with a distributor, it may be possible to adjust the base or the **initial timing.** The initial timing is usually set to fire the spark plug between zero degrees (top dead center or TDC) or slightly before TDC (BTDC). Ignition timing does change as the timing chain or gear wears and readjustment is often necessary on high-mileage engines. ● **SEE FIGURE 16–30**. Waste-spark and coil-on-plug ignitions cannot be adjusted.

FIGURE 16–29 Ignition timing marks are found on the harmonic balancers that are equipped with distributor ignition.

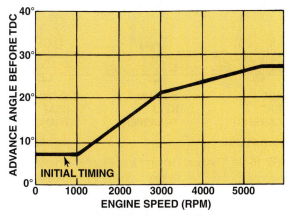

FIGURE 16–30 The initial timing is where the spark plug fires at idle speed. The computer then advances the timing based on engine speed and other factors.

Knock sensors are used to detect abnormal combustion, often called **ping, spark knock,** or **detonation.** Whenever abnormal combustion occurs, a rapid pressure increase occurs in the cylinder, creating a vibration in the engine block. It is this vibration that is detected by the knock sensor. The signal from the knock sensor is used by the PCM to retard the ignition timing until the knock is eliminated, thereby reducing the damaging effects of the abnormal combustion on pistons and other engine parts.

Inside the knock sensor is a piezoelectric element that generates a voltage when pressure or a vibration is applied to the unit. The knock sensor is tuned to the engine knock frequency, which is a range from 5 kHz to 10 kHz, depending on the engine design. The voltage signal from the **knock sensor (KS)** is sent to the PCM. The PCM retards the ignition timing until the knocking stops.

DIAGNOSING THE KNOCK SENSOR If a knock sensor diagnostic trouble code (DTC) is present, follow the specified testing procedure in the service information. A scan tool can be used to check the operation of the knock sensor, using the following procedure.

STEP 1 Start the engine and connect a scan tool to monitor ignition timing and/or knock sensor activity.

STEP 2 Create a simulated engine knocking sound by tapping on the engine block or cylinder head with a soft-faced mallet.

STEP 3 Observe the scan tool display. The vibration from the tapping should have been interpreted by the knock sensor as a knock, resulting in a knock sensor signal and a reduction in the spark advance.

A knock sensor also can be tested using a digital storage oscilloscope. ● **SEE FIGURE 16–31.**

NOTE: Some engine computers are programmed to ignore knock sensor signals when the engine is at idle speed to avoid having the noise from a loose accessory drive belt, or other accessory, interpreted as engine knock. Always follow the vehicle manufacturer's recommended testing procedure.

REPLACING A KNOCK SENSOR If replacing a knock sensor, be sure to purchase the exact replacement needed, because they often look the same, but the frequency range can vary according to engine design, as well as where it is located on the engine. Always tighten the knock sensor using a torque wrench and tighten to the specified torque to avoid causing damage to the piezoelectric element inside the sensor.

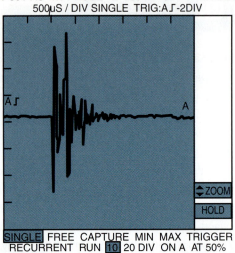

A 50V AC 1:1 PROBE B 200mV OFF 1:1 PROBE
500µS / DIV SINGLE TRIG:A ⌐ -2DIV

SINGLE FREE CAPTURE MIN MAX TRIGGER
RECURRENT RUN 10 20 DIV ON A AT 50%

FIGURE 16–31 A typical waveform from a knock sensor during a spark knock event. This signal is sent to the computer which in turn retards the ignition timing. This timing retard is accomplished by an output command from the computer to either a spark advance control unit or directly to the ignition module.

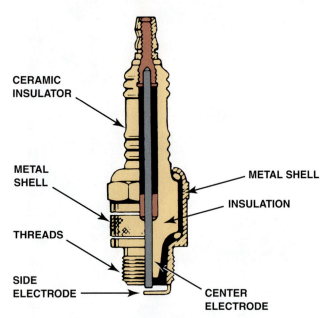

FIGURE 16–32 Parts of a typical spark plug.

SPARK PLUGS

Spark plugs are manufactured from ceramic insulators inside a steel shell. The threads of the shell are rolled and a seat is formed to create a gastight seal with the cylinder head. ● **SEE FIGURE 16–32.** The physical difference in spark plugs includes:

- **Reach.** This is the length of the threaded part of the plug.

- **Heat range.** The heat range of the spark plug refers to how rapidly the heat created at the tip is transferred to the cylinder head. A plug with a long ceramic insulator path will run hotter at the tip than a spark plug that has a shorter path because the heat must travel farther. ● **SEE FIGURE 16–33.**

- **Type of seat.** Some spark plugs use a gasket and others rely on a tapered seat to seal.

RESISTOR SPARK PLUGS
Most spark plugs include a resistor in the center electrode, which helps to reduce electromagnetic noise or radiation from the ignition system. The closer the resistor is to the actual spark or arc, the more effective it becomes. The value of the resistor is usually between 2,500 ohms and 7,500 ohms.

PLATINUM SPARK PLUGS
Platinum spark plugs have a small amount of the precious metal platinum welded onto the end of the center electrode, as well as on the ground or side electrode. Platinum is a grayish-white metal that does not react

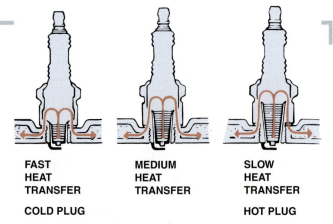

FIGURE 16–33 The heat range of a spark plug is determined by the distance the heat has to flow from the tip to the cylinder head.

with oxygen and therefore, will not erode away as can occur with conventional nickel alloy spark plug electrodes. Platinum is also used as a catalyst in catalytic converters where it is able to start a chemical reaction without itself being consumed.

IRIDIUM SPARK PLUGS
Iridium is a white precious metal and is the most corrosion-resistant metal known. Most **iridium spark plugs** use a small amount of iridium welded onto the tip of a small center electrode 0.0015 to 0.002 inch (0.4 to 0.6 mm) in diameter. The small diameter reduces the voltage required to jump the gap between the center and the side electrode, thereby reducing possible misfires. The ground or side electrode is usually tipped with platinum to help reduce electrode gap wear.

SUMMARY

1. All inductive ignition systems supply battery voltage to the positive side of the ignition coil and pulse the negative side of the coil on and off to ground to create a high-voltage spark.

2. If an ignition system uses a distributor, it is a distributor ignition (DI) system.

3. If an ignition system does not use a distributor, it is called an electronic ignition (EI) system.

4. A waste-spark ignition system fires two spark plugs at the same time.

5. A coil-on-plug ignition system uses an ignition coil for each spark plug.

REVIEW QUESTIONS

1. How can 12 volts from a battery be changed to 40,000 volts for ignition?

2. How does a magnetic sensor work?

3. How does a Hall-effect sensor work?

4. How does a waste-spark ignition system work?

CHAPTER QUIZ

1. The primary (low-voltage) ignition system must be working correctly before any spark occurs from a coil. Which component is *not* in the primary ignition circuit?
   a. Spark plug wiring
   b. Ignition module (igniter)
   c. Pickup coil (pulse generator)
   d. Ignition switch

2. The ignition module has direct control over the firing of the coil(s) of an EI system. Which component(s) triggers (controls) the module?
   a. Pickup coil
   b. Computer
   c. Crankshaft sensor
   d. All of the above

3. A reluctor is a _____.
   a. Type of sensor used in the secondary circuit.
   b. Notched ring or pointed wheel
   c. Type of optical sensor
   d. Type of Hall effect sensor

4. HEI, and EIS are examples of _____.
   a. Waste-spark systems
   b. Coil-on-plug ignition systems
   c. Distributor ignition systems
   d. Pickup coil types

5. Coil polarity is determined by the _____.
   a. Direction of rotation of the coil windings
   b. Turns ratio
   c. Direction of laminations
   d. Saturation direction

6. Because of _____, an ignition coil cannot be fully charged (reach magnetic saturation) until after a delay of about 10 ms.
   a. Voltage drop across the ignition switch and related wiring
   b. Resistance in the coil windings
   c. Inductive reactance
   d. Saturation

7. The pulse generator _____.
   a. Fires the spark plug directly
   b. Signals the electronic control unit (module)
   c. Signals the computer that fires the spark plug directly
   d. Is used as a tachometer reference signal by the computer and has no other function

8. Two technicians are discussing distributor ignition. Technician A says that the pickup coil or optical sensor in the distributor is used to pulse the ignition module (igniter). Technician B says that some distributor ignition systems have the ignition coil inside the distributor cap. Which technician is correct?
   a. Technician A only
   b. Technician B only
   c. Both Technicians A and B
   d. Neither Technician A nor B

9. A waste-spark-type ignition system _____.
   a. Fires two spark plugs at the same time
   b. Fires one spark plug with reverse polarity
   c. Fires one spark plug with straight polarity
   d. All of the above

10. An ion-sensing ignition system allows the ignition system itself to be able to _____.
    a. Detect misfire
    b. Detect spark knock
    c. Detect rich or lean air-fuel mixture
    d. All of the above

chapter 17

IGNITION SYSTEM DIAGNOSIS AND SERVICE

OBJECTIVES

After studying Chapter 17, the reader will be able to:

1. Prepare for ASE Engine Performance (A8) certification test content area "B" (Ignition System Diagnosis and Repair).
2. Describe the procedure used to check for spark.
3. Discuss what to inspect and look for during a visual inspection of the ignition system.
4. List the steps necessary to check and/or adjust ignition timing on engines equipped with a distributor.
5. Describe how to test the ignition system using an oscilloscope.

KEY TERMS

Automatic shutdown (ASD) relay 282
Base timing 295
Burn kV 301
Display 300
Distributor cap 289
Dwell section 300
Firing line 298
Firing order 288
Intermediate oscillations 299
Millisecond (ms) sweep 301

Raster 300
Remove and replace (R & R) 291
Rotor gap 303
Spark line 299
Spark tester 281
Superimposed 300
Track coil 286
Transistor-off point 300
Transistor-on point 300

FIGURE 17–1 A spark tester looks like a regular spark plug with an alligator clip attached to the shell. This tester has a specified gap that requires at least 25,000 volts (25 kV) to fire.

FIGURE 17–2 A close-up showing the recessed center electrode on a spark tester. It is recessed 3/8 in. into the shell and the spark must then jump another 3/8 in. to the shell for a total gap of 3/4 in.

CHECKING FOR SPARK

In the event of a no-start condition, the first step should be to check for secondary voltage out of the ignition coil or to the spark plugs. If the engine is equipped with a separate ignition coil, remove the coil wire from the center of the distributor cap, install a **spark tester,** and crank the engine. See the Tech Tip "Always Use a Spark Tester." A good coil and ignition system should produce a blue spark at the spark tester. ● **SEE FIGURES 17–1 AND 17–2.**

If the ignition system being tested does not have a separate ignition coil, disconnect any spark plug wire from a spark plug and, while cranking the engine, test for spark available at the spark plug wire, again using a spark tester.

NOTE: An intermittent spark should be considered a no-spark condition.

Typical causes of a no-spark (intermittent spark) condition include the following:

1. Weak ignition coil
2. Low or no voltage to the primary (positive) side of the coil
3. High resistance or open coil wire, or spark plug wire
4. Negative side of the coil not being pulsed by the ignition module, also called an ignition control module (ICM)
5. Defective pickup coil
6. Defective module

TECH TIP

Always Use a Spark Tester

A spark tester looks like a spark plug except it has a recessed center electrode and no side electrode. The tester commonly has an alligator clip attached to the shell so that it can be clamped on a good ground connection on the engine. A good ignition system should be able to cause a spark to jump this wide gap at atmospheric pressure. Without a spark tester, a technician might assume that the ignition system is okay, because it can spark across a normal, grounded spark plug. The voltage required to fire a standard spark plug when it is out of the engine and not under pressure is about 3,000 volts or less. An electronic ignition spark tester requires a minimum of 25,000 volts to jump the 3/4-in. gap. Therefore, never assume that the ignition system is okay because it fires a spark plug—always use a spark tester. *Remember that an intermittent spark across a spark tester should be interpreted as a no-spark condition.*

ELECTRONIC IGNITION TROUBLESHOOTING PROCEDURE

When troubleshooting any electronic ignition system for no spark, follow these steps to help pinpoint the exact cause of the problem:

STEP 1   Turn the ignition on (engine off) and, using either a voltmeter or a test light, test for battery voltage available at the positive terminal of the ignition coil. If the voltage is not available, check for an open circuit at the ignition switch or wiring. Also check the condition of the ignition fuse (if used).

> **NOTE: Many Chrysler group products use an automatic shutdown (ASD) relay to power the ignition coil. The ASD relay will not supply voltage to the coil unless the engine is cranking and the computer senses a crankshaft sensor signal. This little known fact has fooled many technicians.**

STEP 2   Connect the voltmeter or test light to the negative side of the coil and crank the engine. The voltmeter should fluctuate or the test light should blink, indicating that the primary coil current is being turned on and off. If there is no pulsing of the negative side of the coil, then the problem is a defective pickup, electronic control module, or wiring.

IGNITION COIL TESTING USING AN OHMMETER

If an ignition coil is suspected of being defective, a simple ohmmeter check can be performed to test the resistance of the primary and secondary winding inside the coil. For accurate resistance measurements, the wiring to the coil should be removed before testing. To test the primary coil winding resistance, take the following steps (● **FIGURE 17–3**):

STEP 1   Set the meter to read low ohms.

STEP 2   Measure the resistance between the positive terminal and the negative terminal of the ignition coil. Most coils will give a reading between 1 and 3 ohms; however, some coils should indicate less than 1 ohm. Check the manufacturer's specifications for the exact resistance values.

To test the secondary coil winding resistance, follow these steps:

STEP 1   Set the meter to read kilohms (kΩ).

STEP 2   Measure the resistance between either primary terminal and the secondary coil tower. The normal resistance of most coils ranges between 6,000 and 30,000 ohms. Check the manufacturer's specifications for the exact resistance values.

> **NOTE: Many ignition coils use a screw that is inside the secondary tower of the ignition coil. If this screw is loose, an intermittent engine misfire could occur. The secondary coil would also indicate high resistance if this screw was loose.**

1. INSERT TEST LEADS IN THE INPUT TERMINALS SHOWN.
2. TURN THE ROTARY SWITCH TO Ω.
3. TOUCH THE PROBES AS SHOWN TO MEASURE RESISTANCE IN PRIMARY WINDINGS.
4. OBSERVE DISPLAY. RESISTANCE SHOULD BE LESS THAN A FEW OHMS.
5. TOUCH PROBES AS SHOWN TO MEASURE RESISTANCE IN SECONDARY WINDINGS.
6. OBSERVE DISPLAY. RESISTANCE SHOULD TYPICALLY BE IN THE 10 KΩ RANGE.

PICKUP COIL TESTING

The pickup coil, located under the distributor cap on many electronic ignition engines, can cause a no-spark condition if defective. The pickup coil must generate an AC voltage pulse to the ignition module so that the module can pulse the ignition coil.

A pickup coil contains a coil of wire, and the resistance of this coil should be within the range specified by the manufacturer. ● SEE FIGURE 17–4. Some common specifications include the following:

Manufacturer	Pickup Coil Resistance (Ohms)
General Motors	500 to 1,500 (white and green leads)
Ford	400 to 1,000 (orange and purple leads)
Chrysler Brand	150 to 900 (orange and black leads)

Also check that the pickup coil windings are insulated from ground by checking for continuity using an ohmmeter. With one ohmmeter lead attached to ground, touch the other lead of the ohmmeter to the pickup coil terminal. The ohmmeter should read OL (over limit) with the ohmmeter set on the high scale. If the pickup coil resistance is not within the specified range, or if it has continuity to ground, replace the pickup coil assembly.

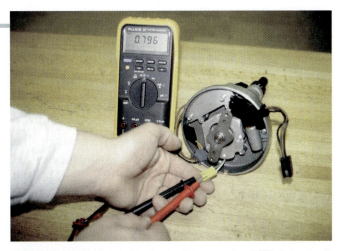

FIGURE 17–4 Measuring the resistance of an HEI pickup coil using a digital multimeter set to the ohms position. The reading on the face of the meter is 0.796 kΩ or 796 ohms in the middle of the 500- to 1,500-ohm specifications.

The pickup coil also can be tested for proper voltage output. During cranking, most pickup coils should produce a minimum of 0.25 volt AC. This can be tested with the distributor out of the vehicle by rotating the distributor drive gear by hand.

FIGURE 17–5 An AC voltage is produced by a magnetic sensor. Most sensors should produce at least 0.1 volt AC while the engine is cranking and can exceed 100 volts with the engine running if the pickup wheel has many teeth. If the pickup wheel has only a few teeth, you may need to switch the meter to read DC volts and watch the display for a jump in voltage as the teeth pass the magnetic sensor.

PERMANENT MAGNET AC GENERATORS DEVELOP THEIR OWN AC VOLTAGE SIGNAL AS THEY OPERATE. A DIGITAL METER CAN MEASURE THE AC SIGNAL FROM THESE SENSORS, TO CONFIRM THEY'RE WORKING PROPERLY.

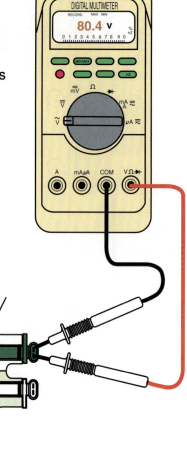

TESTING MAGNETIC SENSORS

First of all, magnetic sensors must be tested to see if they will stick to iron or steel, indicating that the magnetic strength of the sensors is okay. If the permanent magnet inside the sensor has cracked, the result is two weak magnets.

If the sensor is removed from the engine, hold a metal (steel) object against the end of the sensor. It should exert a strong magnetic pull on the steel object. If not, replace the sensor. Second, the sensor can be tested using a digital meter set to read AC volts. ● **SEE FIGURE 17–5.**

TESTING HALL-EFFECT SENSORS

As with any other sensor, the output of the Hall-effect sensor should be tested first. Using a digital voltmeter, check for the presence of changing voltage (pulsed on and off or digital DC) when the engine is being cranked. The best test is to use an oscilloscope and observe the waveform. ● **SEE FIGURE 17–6.**

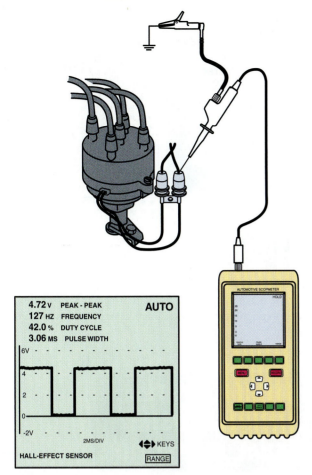

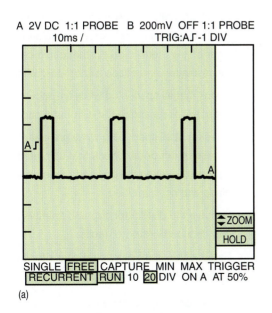

FIGURE 17–6 (a) The connection required to test a Hall-effect sensor. (b) A typical waveform from a Hall-effect sensor.

TESTING OPTICAL SENSORS

Optical sensors will not operate if dirty or covered in oil. Perform a thorough visual inspection and look for an oil leak that could cause dirty oil to get on the LED or phototransistor. Also be sure that the light shield is securely fastened and that the seal is lightproof. An optical sensor also can be checked using an oscilloscope. ● **SEE FIGURE 17–7.** Because of the speed of the engine and the number of slits in the optical sensor disk, a scope is one of the only tools that can capture useful information. For example, a Nissan has 360 slits and if it is running at 2000 RPM, a signal is generated 720,000 times per minute or 12,000 times per second.

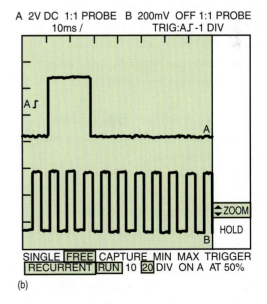

FIGURE 17–7 (a) The low-resolution signal has the same number of pulses as the engine has cylinders. (b) A dual-trace pattern showing both the low-resolution signal and the high-resolution signals that usually represent 1 degree of rotation.

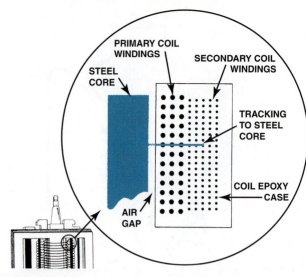

FIGURE 17–8 A track inside an ignition coil is not a short, but rather it is a low-resistance path or hole that has been burned through from the secondary wiring to the steel core.

TECH TIP

Bad Wire? Replace the Coil!

When performing engine testing (such as a compression test), always ground the coil wire. Never allow the coil to discharge without a path to ground for the spark. High-energy electronic ignition systems can produce 40,000 volts or more of electrical pressure. If the spark cannot spark to ground, the coil energy can (and usually does) arc inside the coil itself, creating a low-resistance path to the primary windings or the steel laminations of the coil. ● **SEE FIGURE 17–8.** This low-resistance path is called a **track** and could cause an engine misfire under load even though all of the remaining component parts of the ignition system are functioning correctly. Often these tracks do not show up on any coil test, including most scopes. Because the track is a lower-resistance path to ground than normal, it requires that the ignition system be put under a load for it to be detected, and even then, the problem (engine misfire) may be intermittent.

　　Therefore, when disabling an ignition system, perform one of the following procedures to prevent possible ignition coil damage:

1. Remove the power source wire from the ignition system to prevent any ignition operation.
2. On distributor-equipped engines, remove the secondary coil wire from the center of the distributor cap and connect a jumper wire between the disconnected coil wire and a good engine ground. This ensures that the secondary coil energy will be safely grounded and prevents high-voltage coil damage.

IGNITION SYSTEM DIAGNOSIS USING VISUAL INSPECTION

One of the first steps in the diagnosis process is to perform a thorough visual inspection of the ignition system, including the following items:

- Check all spark plug wires for proper routing. All plug wires should be in the factory wiring separator and be clear of any metallic object that could cause damage to the insulation and cause a short-to-ground fault.

- Check that all spark plug wires are securely attached to the spark plugs and to the distributor cap or ignition coil(s).

- Check that all spark plug wires are clean and free from excessive dirt or oil. Check that all protective covers normally covering the coil and/or distributor cap are in place and not damaged.

- Remove the distributor cap and carefully check the cap and distributor rotor for faults.

- Remove the spark plugs and check for excessive wear or other visible faults. Replace if needed.

NOTE: According to research conducted by General Motors, about one-fifth (20%) of all faults are detected during a *thorough visual inspection*!

FIGURE 17–9 A GM type 2 distributorless ignition system (DIS) can be checked by unplugging *both* spark plug wires from one ignition coil and starting the engine. The spark should be able to jump the 1-in. (25-mm) distance between the terminals of the coil. No damage to the coil (or module) results because a spark occurs and does not find ground elsewhere.

FIGURE 17–10 Using a vacuum hose and a grounded test light to ground one cylinder at a time on a DIS. This works on all types of ignition systems and provides a method for grounding out one cylinder at a time without fear of damaging any component.

TESTING FOR POOR PERFORMANCE

Many diagnostic equipment manufacturers offer methods for testing distributorless ignition systems on an oscilloscope. If using this type of equipment, follow the manufacturer's recommended procedures and interpretation of the specific test results.

A simple method of testing distributorless (waste-spark systems) ignition with the engine off involves removing the spark plug wires (or connectors) from the spark plugs (or coils or distributor cap) and installing short lengths (2 inches) of rubber vacuum hose in series.

NOTE: For best results, use rubber hose that is electrically conductive. Measure the vacuum hose with an ohmmeter. Suitable vacuum hose should give a reading of less than 10,000 ohms (10 kΩ) for a length of about 2 inches. ● **SEE FIGURES 17–9 AND 17–10.**

STEP 1 Start the engine and ground out each cylinder one at a time by touching the tip of a grounded test light to the rubber vacuum hose. Even though the computer will increase idle speed and fuel delivery to compensate for the grounded spark plug wire, a technician should watch for a change in the operation of the engine. If no change is observed or heard, the cylinder being grounded is obviously weak or defective. Check the spark plug wire or connector with an ohmmeter to be certain of continuity.

STEP 2 Check all cylinders by grounding them out one at a time. If one weak cylinder is found (very little RPM drop), check the other cylinder using the same ignition coil (except on engines that use an individual coil for each cylinder). If both cylinders are affected, the problem could be an open spark plug wire, defective spark plug, or defective ignition coil.

STEP 3 To help eliminate other possible problems and determine exactly what is wrong, switch the suspected ignition coil to another position (if possible).

- If the problem now affects the other cylinders, the ignition coil is defective and must be replaced.
- If the problem does not "change positions" with changing the position of the ignition coil, the control module affecting the suspected coil or either cylinder's spark plug or spark plug wire could be defective.

TESTING FOR A NO-START CONDITION

A no-start condition (with normal engine cranking speed) can be the result of either no spark or no fuel delivery.

Computerized engine control systems use the ignition primary pulses as a signal to inject fuel—a port or throttle-body injection (TBI) style of fuel—injection system. If there is no pulse, then there is no squirt of fuel. To determine exactly what is wrong, follow these steps:

STEP 1 Test the output signal from the crankshaft sensor. Most computerized engines with distributorless ignitions use a crankshaft position sensor. These sensors are either the Hall-effect type or the magnetic type. The sensors must be able to produce either a sine or a digital signal. A meter set on AC volts should read a voltage across the sensor leads when the engine is being cranked. If there is no AC voltage output, replace the sensor.

STEP 2 If the sensor tests okay in step 1, check for a changing AC voltage signal at the ignition module.

> **NOTE: Step 2 checks the wiring between the crankshaft position sensor and the ignition control module.**

STEP 3 If the ignition control module is receiving a changing signal from the crankshaft position sensor, it must be capable of switching the power to the ignition coils on and off. Remove a coil or coil package, and with the ignition switched to on (run), check for voltage at the positive terminal of the coil(s).

> **NOTE: Several manufacturers program the current to the coils to be turned off within several seconds of the ignition being switched to on if no pulse is received by the computer. This circuit design helps prevent ignition coil damage in the event of a failure in the control circuit or driver error, by keeping the ignition switch on (run) without operating the starter (start position). Some Chrysler engines do not supply power to the positive (+) side of the coil until a crank pulse is received by the computer which then energizes the coil(s) and injectors through the automatic shutdown (ASD) relay.**

STEP 4 If the module is not pulsing the negative side of the coil or not supplying battery voltage to the positive side of the coil, replace the ignition control module.

> **NOTE: Before replacing the ignition control module, be certain that it is properly grounded (where applicable) and that the module is receiving ignition power from the ignition circuit.**

> **CAUTION: Most distributorless (waste-spark) ignition systems can produce 40,000 volts or more, with energy levels high enough to cause personal injury. Do not open the circuit of an electronic ignition secondary wire, because damage to the system (or to you) can occur.**

FIRING ORDER

Firing order means the order that the spark is distributed to the correct spark plug at the right time. The firing order of an engine is determined by crankshaft and camshaft design. The firing order is determined by the location of the spark plug wires in the distributor cap of an engine equipped with a distributor. The firing order is often cast into the intake manifold for easy reference, as shown in ● **FIGURE 17–11.** Service information also shows the firing order and the direction of the distributor rotor rotation, as well as the location of the spark plug wires on the distributor cap.

> **CAUTION: Ford V-8s use two different firing orders depending on whether the engine is high output (HO) or standard. Using the incorrect firing order can cause the engine to backfire and could cause engine damage or personal injury. General Motors V-6s use different firing orders and different locations for cylinder 1 between the 60-degree V-6 and the 90-degree V-6. Using the incorrect firing order or cylinder number location chart could result in poor engine operation or a no-start condition.**

Firing order is also important for waste-spark-type distributorless (direct-fire) ignition systems. The spark plug wire can often be installed on the wrong coil pack that can create a no-start condition or poor engine operation.

FIGURE 17–11 The firing order is cast or stamped on the intake manifold on most engines that have a distributor ignition.

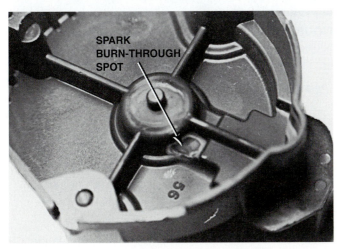

FIGURE 17–12 Note where the high-voltage spark jumped through the plastic rotor to arc into the distributor shaft. Always check for a defective spark plug(s) when a defective distributor cap or rotor is discovered. If a spark cannot jump to a spark plug, it tries to find a ground path wherever it can.

FIGURE 17–13 Carbon track in a distributor cap. These faults are sometimes difficult to spot and can cause intermittent engine misfire. The usual cause of a tracked distributor cap (or coil, if it is distributorless ignition) is a defective (open) spark plug wire.

FIGURE 17–14 Corroded terminals on a waste-spark coil can cause misfire diagnostic trouble codes to be set.

SECONDARY IGNITION INSPECTION

DISTRIBUTOR CAP AND ROTOR   Inspect a **distributor cap** for a worn or cracked center carbon insert, excessive side insert wear or corrosion, cracks, or carbon tracks, and check the towers for burning or corrosion by removing spark plug wires from the distributor cap one at a time. Remember, a defective distributor cap affects starting and engine performance, especially in high-moisture conditions. If a carbon track is detected, it is most likely the result of a high-resistance or open spark plug wire. Replacement of a distributor cap because of a carbon track without checking and replacing the defective spark plug wire(s) often will result in the new distributor cap failing in a short time. It is recommended that the distributor cap and rotor be inspected every year and replaced if defective. The rotor should be replaced every time the spark plugs are replaced, because all ignition current flows through the rotor. Generally, distributor caps should only need replacement after every three or four years of normal service. ● **SEE FIGURES 17–12 AND 17–13.** Check ignition coils of waste-spark and coil-on-plug systems for signs of carbon tracks (black lines) or corrosion. ● **SEE FIGURE 17–14.**

SPARK PLUG WIRE INSPECTION   Spark plug wires should be visually inspected for cuts or defective insulation and checked for resistance with an ohmmeter. Good spark plug wires should measure less than 10,000 ohms per foot of length. ● **SEE FIGURES 17–15 AND 17–16.** Faulty spark plug wire insulation can cause hard starting or no starting in damp weather conditions.

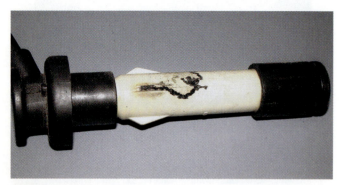

FIGURE 17–15 This spark plug boot on an overhead camshaft engine has been arcing to the valve cover causing a misfire to occur.

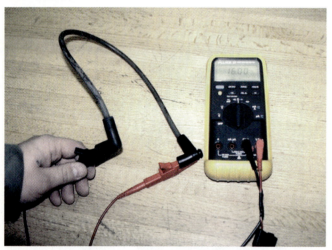

FIGURE 17–16 Measuring the resistance of a spark plug wire with a multimeter set to the ohms position. The reading of 16.03 kΩ (16.030 ohms) is okay because the wire is about 2 feet long. Maximum allowable resistance for a spark plug wire this long would be 20 kΩ (20,000 ohms). High resistance spark plug wires can cause an engine misfire especially during acceleration.

TECH TIP

Spark Plug Wire Pliers Are a Good Investment

Spark plug wires are often difficult to remove. Using a good-quality spark plug wire plier, such as shown in ● **FIGURE 17–17**, saves time and reduces the chance of harming the wire during removal.

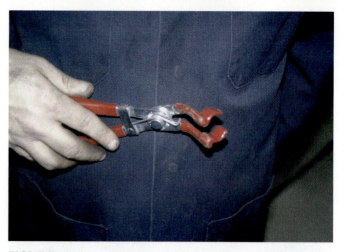

FIGURE 17–17 Spark plug wire boot pliers is a handy addition to any tool box.

TECH TIP

Route the Wires Right!

High voltage is present through spark plug wires when the engine is running. Surrounding the spark plugs is a magnetic field that can affect other circuits or components of the vehicle. For example, if a spark plug wire is routed too closely to the signal wire from a mass airflow (MAF) sensor, the induced signal from the ignition wire could create a false MAF signal to the computer. The computer, not able to detect that the signal was false, would act on the MAF signal and command the appropriate amount of fuel based on the false MAF signal.

To prevent any problems associated with high-voltage spark plug wires, be sure to route them as manufactured using all the factory holding brackets and wiring combs. ● **SEE FIGURE 17–18**. If the factory method is unknown, most factory service information shows the correct routing.

SPARK PLUG SERVICE

THE NEED FOR SERVICE Spark plugs should be inspected when an engine performance problem occurs and should be replaced at specified intervals to ensure proper ignition system performance. Most spark plugs have a service life of over 20,000 miles (32,000 kilometers). Platinum-tipped original equipment spark plugs have a typical service life of 60,000 to 100,000 miles (100,000 to 160,000 kilometers). Used spark plugs should *not* be cleaned and reused unless absolutely necessary.

FIGURE 17–18 Always take the time to install spark plug wires back into the original holding brackets (wiring combs).

FIGURE 17–19 When removing spark plugs, it is wise to arrange them so that they can be compared and any problem can be identified with a particular cylinder.

FIGURE 17–20 A spark plug thread chaser is a low-cost tool that hopefully will not be used often, but is necessary to use to clean the threads before new spark plugs are installed.

FIGURE 17–21 Since 1991, General Motors engines have been equipped with slightly (1/8 in. or 3 mm) longer spark plugs. This requires that a longer spark plug socket should be used to prevent the possibility of cracking a spark plug during installation. The longer socket is shown next to a normal 5/8-in. spark plug socket.

The labor required to **remove and replace (R & R)** spark plugs is the same whether the spark plugs are replaced or cleaned. Although cleaning spark plugs often restores proper engine operation, the service life of cleaned spark plugs is definitely shorter than that of new spark plugs. *Platinum-tipped spark plugs should not be regapped!* Using a gapping tool can break the platinum after it has been used in an engine.

Be certain that the engine is cool before removing spark plugs, especially on engines with aluminum cylinder heads. To help prevent dirt from getting into the cylinder of an engine while removing a spark plug, use compressed air or a brush to remove dirt from around the spark plug before removal. ● SEE **FIGURES 17–19 THROUGH 17–21.**

SPARK PLUG INSPECTION Spark plugs are the windows to the inside of the combustion chamber. A thorough visual inspection of the spark plugs often can lead to the root cause of an engine performance problem. Two indications on

FIGURE 17–22 A normally worn spark plug that has a tapered platinum-tipped center electrode.

FIGURE 17–23 Spark plug removed from an engine after a 500-mile race. Note the clipped side (ground) electrode. The electrode design and narrow (0.025 in.) gap are used to ensure that a spark occurs during extremely high engine speed operation. The color and condition of the spark plug indicate that near-perfect combustion has been occurring.

SPARK PLUG SERVICE (CONTINUED)

spark plugs and their possible root causes in engine performance include the following:

1. **Carbon fouling.** If the spark plug(s) has *dry black carbon* (soot), the usual causes include:
   - Excessive idling
   - Slow-speed driving under light loads that keeps the spark plug temperatures too low to burn off the deposits
   - Overrich air–fuel mixture
   - Weak ignition system output
2. **Oil fouling.** If the spark plug has *wet, oily* deposits with little electrode wear, oil may be getting into the combustion chamber from the following:
   - Worn or broken piston rings
   - Defective or missing valve stem seals

NOTE: If the deposits are heavier on the side of the plug facing the intake valve, the cause is usually due to excessive valve stem clearance or defective intake valve stem seals.

When removing spark plugs, place them in order so that they can be inspected to check for engine problems that might affect one or more cylinders. All spark plugs should be in the same condition, and the color of the center insulator should be light tan or gray. If all the spark plugs are black or dark, the engine should be checked for conditions that could cause an overly rich air–fuel mixture or possible oil burning. If only one or a few spark plugs are black, check those cylinders for proper firing (possible defective spark plug wire) or an engine condition affecting only those particular cylinders. ● **SEE FIGURES 17–22 THROUGH 17–25**.

If all spark plugs are white, check for possible overadvanced ignition timing or a vacuum leak causing a lean air–fuel mixture. If only one or a few spark plugs are white, check for a vacuum leak affecting the fuel mixture only to those particular cylinders.

NOTE: The engine computer "senses" rich or lean air–fuel ratios by means of input from the oxygen sensor. If one cylinder is lean, the computer may make all other cylinders richer to compensate.

FIGURE 17–24 Typical worn spark plug. Notice the rounded center electrode. The deposits indicate a possible oil usage problem.

FIGURE 17–25 New spark plug that was fouled by a too-rich air–fuel mixture. The engine from which this spark plug came had a defective (stuck partially open) injector on this one cylinder only.

Inspect all spark plugs for wear by first checking the condition of the center electrode. As a spark plug wears, the center electrode becomes rounded. If the center electrode is rounded, higher ignition system voltage is required to fire the spark plug. When installing spark plugs, always use the correct tightening torque to ensure proper heat transfer from the spark plug shell to the cylinder head. See the following table.

Spark Plug	Torque with Torque Wrench (lb-ft)		Torque without Torque Wrench (turns)	
	Cast-iron Head	Aluminum Head	Cast-iron Head	Aluminum Head
Gasket				
14 mm	26–30	18–22	1/4	1/4
18 mm	32–38	28–34	1/4	1/4
Tapered seat				
14 mm	7–15	7–15	1/16 (snug)	1/16 (snug)
18 mm	15–20	15–20	1/16 (snug)	1/16 (snug)

NOTE: General Motors does not recommend the use of antiseize compound on the threads of spark plugs being installed in an aluminum cylinder head, because the spark plug will be overtightened. This excessive tightening torque places the threaded portion of the spark plug too far into the combustion chamber where carbon can accumulate and result in the spark plugs being difficult to remove. If antiseize compound is used on spark plug threads, reduce the tightening torque by 40%. Always follow the vehicle manufacturer's recommendations.

 **TECH TIP**

Two-Finger Trick

To help prevent overtightening a spark plug when a torque wrench is not available, simply use two fingers on the ratchet handle. Even the strongest service technician cannot overtighten a spark plug by using two fingers.

Use Original Equipment Manufacturer's Spark Plugs

A technician at an independent service center replaced the spark plugs in a Pontiac with new Champion brand spark plugs of the correct size, reach, and heat range. When the customer returned to pay the bill, he inquired as to the brand name of the replacement parts used for the tune-up. When told that Champion spark plugs were used, he stopped signing his name on the check he was writing. He said that he owned 1,000 shares of General Motors stock and he owned two General Motors vehicles and he expected to have General Motors parts used in his General Motors vehicles. The service manager had the technician replace the spark plugs with AC brand spark plugs because this brand was used in the engine when the vehicle was new. Even though most spark plug manufacturers produce spark plugs that are correct for use, many customers prefer that original equipment manufacturer (OEM) spark plugs be used in their engines.

FIGURE 17–26 A water spray bottle is an excellent diagnostic tool to help find an intermittent engine misfire caused by a break in a secondary ignition circuit component.

QUICK AND EASY SECONDARY IGNITION TESTS

Engine running problems often are caused by defective or out-of-adjustment ignition components. Many ignition problems involve the high-voltage secondary ignition circuit. Following are some quick and easy secondary ignition tests.

TEST 1 If there is a crack in a distributor cap, coil, or spark plug, or if there is a defective spark plug wire, a spark may be visible at night. Because the highest voltage is required during partial throttle acceleration, the technician's assistant should accelerate the engine slightly with the gear selector in drive or second gear (if manual transmission) and the brake firmly applied. If any spark is visible or a "snapping" sound is heard, the location should be closely inspected and the defective parts replaced. A blue glow or "corona" around the shell of the spark plug is normal and not an indication of a defective spark plug.

TEST 2 For intermittent problems, use a spray bottle to apply a water mist to the spark plugs, distributor cap, and spark plug wires. ● **SEE FIGURE 17–26**. With the engine running, the water may cause an arc through any weak insulating materials and cause the engine to misfire or stall.

NOTE: Adding a little salt or liquid soap to the water makes the water more conductive and also makes it easier to find those hard-to-diagnose intermittent ignition faults.

TEST 3 To determine if the rough engine operation is due to secondary ignition problems, connect a 12-volt test light to the negative side (sometimes labeled "tach") of the coil. Connect the other lead of the test light to the positive lead of the coil. With the engine running, the test light should be dim and steady in brightness. If there is high resistance in the secondary circuit (such as that caused by a defective spark plug wire), the test light will pulse brightly at times. If the test light varies noticeably, this indicates that the secondary voltage cannot find ground easily and is feeding back through the primary windings of the coil. This feedback causes the test light to become brighter.

FIGURE 17–27 Typical timing marks. The numbers of the degrees are on the stationary plate and the notch is on the harmonic balancer.

IGNITION TIMING

Ignition timing should be checked and adjusted according to the manufacturer's specifications and procedures on some vehicles equipped with distributor-type ignition systems. Generally, for testing, engines must be at idle with computer engine controls put into **base timing**, the timing of the spark before the computer advances the timing. To be assured of the proper ignition timing, follow exactly the timing procedure indicated on the underhood emission (VECI) decal. ● **SEE FIGURE 17–27** for a typical ignition timing plate and mark.

If the ignition timing is too far *advanced*, for example, if it is set at 12 degrees before top dead center (BTDC) instead of 8 degrees BTDC, the following symptoms may occur:

1. Engine ping or spark knock may be heard, especially while driving up a hill or during acceleration.
2. Cranking (starting) may be slow and jerky, especially when the engine is warm.
3. The engine may overheat.

If the ignition timing is too far *retarded*, for example, if it is set at 4 degrees BTDC instead of 8 degrees BTDC, the following symptoms may occur:

1. The engine may lack power and performance.
2. The engine may require a long period of starter cranking before starting.
3. Poor fuel economy may result.
4. The engine may overheat.

PRETIMING CHECKS Before the ignition timing is checked or adjusted, the following items should be checked to ensure accurate timing results:

1. The engine should be at normal operating temperature (the upper radiator hose should be hot and pressurized).
2. The engine should be at the correct timing RPM (check the specifications).
3. The vacuum hoses should be removed, and the hose from the vacuum advance unit on the distributor (if the vehicle is so equipped) should be plugged unless otherwise specified.
4. If the engine is computer equipped, check the timing procedure specified by the manufacturer. This may include disconnecting a "set timing" connector wire, grounding a diagnostic terminal, disconnecting a four-wire connector, or similar procedure.

NOTE: General Motors specifies many different timing procedures depending on the engine, type of fuel system, and type of ignition system. Always consult the emission decal under the hood or service information for the exact procedure to follow.

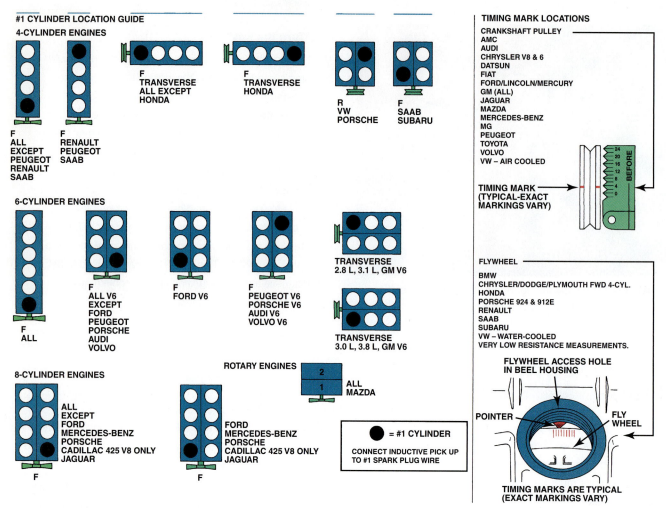

FIGURE 17-28 Cylinder 1 and timing mark location guide.

IGNITION TIMING (CONTINUED)

TIMING LIGHT CONNECTIONS For checking or adjusting ignition timing, make the timing light connections as follows:

1. Connect the timing light battery leads to the vehicle battery: the red to the positive terminal and the black to the negative terminal.

2. Connect the timing light high-tension lead to spark plug cable 1.

DETERMINING CYLINDER 1 The following will help in determining cylinder 1.

1. **Four- or six-cylinder engines.** On all inline four- and six-cylinder engines, cylinder 1 is the *most forward* cylinder.

2. **V-6 or V-8 engines.** Most V-type engines use the left front (driver's side) cylinder as cylinder 1, except for Ford engines and some Cadillacs, which use the right front (passenger's side) cylinder.

3. **Sideways (transverse) engines.** Most front-wheel-drive vehicles with engines installed sideways use the cylinder to the far right (passenger's side) as cylinder 1 (plug wire closest to the drive belt[s]).

Follow this rule of thumb: If cylinder 1 is unknown for a given type of engine, it is the *most forward* cylinder as viewed from above (except in Pontiac V-8 engines). ● **SEE FIGURE 17-28** for typical cylinder 1 locations.

NOTE: Some engines are not timed off of cylinder 1. For example, Jaguar inline six-cylinder engines before 1988 used cylinder 6, but the cylinders were numbered from the firewall (bulkhead) forward. Therefore, cylinder 6 was the most forward cylinder. Always check for the specifications and procedures for the vehicle being tested.

(a)

(b)

FIGURE 17–29 (a) Typical SPOUT connector as used on many Ford engines equipped with distributor ignition (DI). (b) The connector must be opened (disconnected) to check and/or adjust the ignition timing. On DIS/EDIS systems, the connector is called SPOUT/SAW (spark output/spark angle word).

NOTE: If cylinder 1 is difficult to reach, such as up against the bulkhead (firewall) or close to an exhaust manifold, simply use the opposite cylinder in the firing order (paired cylinder). The timing light will not detect the difference and will indicate the correct position of the timing mark in relation to the pointer or degree mark.

CHECKING OR ADJUSTING IGNITION TIMING Use the following steps for checking or adjusting ignition timing:

1. Start the engine and adjust the speed to that specified for ignition timing.

2. With the timing light aimed at the stationary timing pointer, observe the position of the timing mark on the vibration damper with the light flashing. Refer to the manufacturer's specifications on underhood decal for the correct setting.
   ● **SEE FIGURE 17–29.**

NOTE: If the timing mark appears ahead of the pointer in relation to the direction of crankshaft rotation, the timing is advanced. If the timing mark appears behind the pointer in relation to the direction of crankshaft rotation, the timing is retarded.

3. To adjust timing, loosen the distributor locking bolt or nut and turn the distributor housing until the timing mark is in correct alignment. Turn the distributor housing in the direction of rotor rotation to retard the timing and against rotor rotation to advance the timing.

4. After adjusting the timing to specifications, carefully tighten the distributor locking bolt. Sometimes it is necessary to readjust the timing after the initial setting because the distributor may rotate slightly when the hold-down bolt is tightened.

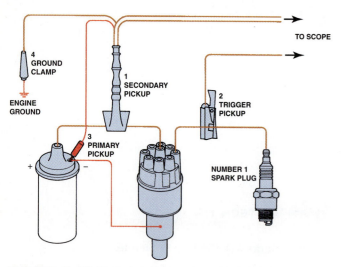

FIGURE 17–30 Typical engine analyzer hookup that includes a scope display. (1) Coil wire on top of the distributor cap if integral type of coil; (2) number 1 spark plug connection; (3) negative side of the ignition coil; (4) ground (negative) connection of the battery.

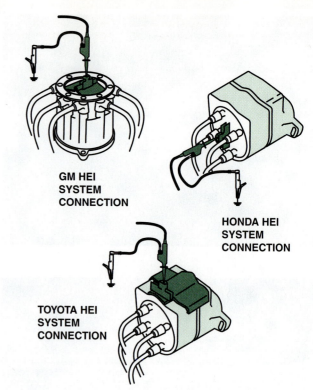

FIGURE 17–31 Clip-on adapters are used with an ignition system that uses an integral ignition coil.

SCOPE-TESTING THE IGNITION SYSTEM

Any automotive scope with the correct probes or adapters will show an ignition system pattern. All ignition systems must charge and discharge an ignition coil. With the engine off, most scopes will display a horizontal line. With the engine running, this horizontal (zero) line is changed to a pattern that will have sections both above and below the zero line. Sections of this pattern that are above the zero line indicate that the ignition coil is discharging. Sections of the scope pattern below the zero line indicate charging of the ignition coil. The height of the scope pattern indicates voltage. The length (from left to right) of the scope pattern indicates time. ● **SEE FIGURES 17–30 AND 17–31** for typical scope hookups.

FIRING LINE The leftmost vertical (upward) line is called the **firing line**. The height of the firing line should be between 5,000 and 15,000 volts (5 and 15 kV) with not more than a 3 kV difference between the highest and the lowest cylinder's firing line. ● **SEE FIGURES 17–32 AND 17–33.**

The height of the firing line indicates the *voltage* required to fire the spark plug. It requires a high voltage to make the air

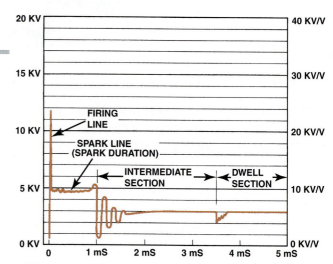

FIGURE 17–32 Typical secondary ignition oscilloscope pattern.

inside the cylinder electrically conductive (to ionize the air). A higher than normal height (or height higher than that of other cylinders) can be caused by one or more of the following:

1. Spark plug gapped too wide
2. Lean fuel mixture
3. Defective spark plug wire

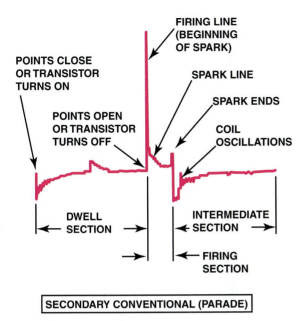

SECONDARY CONVENTIONAL (SINGLE)

FIRING LINE (BEGINNING OF SPARK)

POINTS CLOSE OR TRANSISTOR TURNS ON

SPARK LINE

SPARK ENDS

POINTS OPEN OR TRANSISTOR TURNS OFF

COIL OSCILLATIONS

DWELL SECTION

INTERMEDIATE SECTION

FIRING SECTION

SECONDARY CONVENTIONAL (PARADE)

FIRING LINES SHOULD BE EQUAL. A SHORT LINE INDICATES LOW RESISTANCE IN THE WIRE. A HIGH LINE INDICATES HIGH RESISTANCE IN THE WIRE.

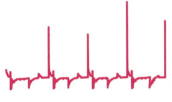

AVAILABLE VOLTAGE SHOULD BE ABOUT 10KV ON A CONVENTIONAL IGNITION SYSTEM AND EVEN GREATER WITH AN ELECTRONIC SYSTEM

SPARK LINES CAN BE VIEWED SIDE-BY-SIDE FOR EASE OF COMPARISON

CYLINDERS ARE DISPLAYED IN FIRING ORDER

FIGURE 17–33 A single cylinder is shown at the top and a four-cylinder engine at the bottom.

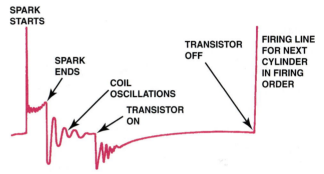

SPARK STARTS

SPARK ENDS

COIL OSCILLATIONS

TRANSISTOR ON

TRANSISTOR OFF

FIRING LINE FOR NEXT CYLINDER IN FIRING ORDER

FIGURE 17–34 Drawing shows what is occurring electrically at each part of the scope pattern.

If the firing lines are higher than normal for *all* cylinders, then possible causes include one or more of the following:

1. Worn distributor cap and/or rotor (if the vehicle is so equipped)
2. Excessive wearing of all spark plugs
3. Defective coil wire (the high voltage could still jump across the open section of the wire to fire the spark plugs)

SPARK LINE   The **spark line** is a short horizontal line immediately after the firing line. The height of the spark line represents the voltage required to maintain the spark across the spark plug after the spark has started. The height of the spark line should be one-fourth of the height of the firing line (between 1.5 and

2.5 kV). The length (from left to right) of the line represents the length of time for which the spark lasts (duration or burn time). The spark duration should be between 0.8 and 2.2 milliseconds (usually between 1.0 and 2.0 ms). The spark stops at the end (right side) of the spark line, as shown in ● **FIGURE 17–34**.

INTERMEDIATE OSCILLATIONS   After the spark has stopped, some energy remains in the coil. This remaining energy dissipates in the coil windings and the entire secondary circuit. The **intermediate oscillations** are also called the "ringing" of the coil as it is pulsed.

The secondary pattern amplifies any voltage variation occurring in the primary circuit because of the turns ratio between the primary and secondary windings of the ignition coil. A correctly operating ignition system should display five or more "bumps" (oscillations) (three or more for a GM HEI system).

TRANSISTOR-ON POINT   After the intermediate oscillations, the coil is empty (not charged), as indicated by the scope pattern being on the zero line for a short period. When the transistor turns on an electronic system, the coil is being charged.

Note that the charging of the coil occurs slowly (coil-charging oscillations) because of the inductive reactance of the coil.

DWELL SECTION　　Dwell is the amount of time that the current is charging the coil from the **transistor-on point** to the **transistor-off point**. At the end of the **dwell section** is the beginning of the next firing line. This point is called "transistor off" and indicates that the primary current of the coil is stopped, resulting in a high-voltage spark out of the coil.

PATTERN SELECTION　　Ignition oscilloscopes use three positions to view certain sections of the basic pattern more closely. These three positions are as follows:

1. **Superimposed.** This **superimposed** position is used to look at differences in patterns between cylinders in all areas except the firing line. There are no firing lines illustrated in superimposed positions. ● **SEE FIGURE 17–35.**

2. **Raster (stacked).** Cylinder 1 is at the bottom on most scopes. Use the **raster** (stacked) position to look at the spark line length and transistor-on point. The raster pattern shows all areas of the scope pattern except the firing lines. ● **SEE FIGURE 17–36.**

3. **Display (parade).** Display (parade) is the only position in which firing lines are visible. The firing line section for cylinder 1 is on the far right side of the screen, with the remaining portions of the pattern on the left side. This selection is used to compare the height of firing lines among all cylinders. ● **SEE FIGURE 17–37.**

READING THE SCOPE ON DISPLAY (PARADE)　　Start the engine and operate at approximately 1000 RPM to ensure a smooth and accurate scope pattern. Firing lines are visible only on the display (parade) position. The firing lines should all be 5 to 15 kV in height and be within 3 kV of each other. If one or more cylinders have high firing lines, this could indicate a defective (open) spark plug wire, a spark plug gapped too far, or a lean fuel mixture affecting only those cylinders.

A lean mixture (not enough fuel) requires a higher voltage to ignite because there are fewer droplets of fuel in the cylinder for the spark to use as "stepping stones" for the voltage to jump across. Therefore, a lean mixture is less conductive than a rich mixture.

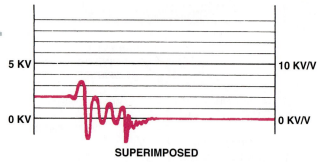

FIGURE 17–35 Typical secondary ignition pattern. Note the lack of firing lines on superimposed pattern.

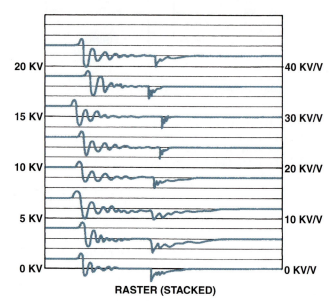

FIGURE 17–36 Raster is the best scope position to view the spark lines of all the cylinders to check for differences. Most scopes display the cylinder 1 at the bottom. The other cylinders are positioned by firing order above cylinder 1.

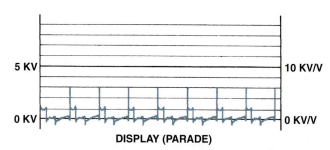

FIGURE 17–37 Display is the only position to view the firing lines of all cylinders. Cylinder 1 is displayed on the left (except for its firing line, which is shown on the right). The cylinders are displayed from left to right by firing order.

A Technician's Toughie

A vehicle ran poorly, yet its scope patterns were "perfect." Remembering that the scope indicates only that a spark has occurred (not necessarily inside the engine), the technician grounded one spark plug wire at a time using a vacuum hose and a test light. Every time a plug wire was grounded, the engine ran worse, until the last cylinder was checked. When the last spark plug wire was grounded, the engine ran the same. The technician checked the spark plug wire with an ohmmeter; it tested within specifications (less than 10,000 ohms per foot of length). The technician also removed and inspected the spark plug. The spark plug looked normal. The spark plug was reinstalled and the engine tested again. The test had the same results as before—the engine seemed to be running on seven cylinders, yet the scope pattern was perfect.

The technician then replaced the spark plug for the affected cylinder. The engine ran correctly. Very close examination of the spark plug showed a thin crack between the wire terminal and the shell of the plug. Why didn't the cracked plug show on the scope? The scope simply indicated that a spark had occurred. The scope cannot distinguish between a spark inside the engine and a spark outside the engine. In this case, the voltage required to travel through the spark plug crack to ground was about the same voltage required to jump the spark plug electrodes inside the engine. The spark that occurred across the cracked spark plug, however, may have been visible at night with the engine running.

READING THE SPARK LINES

Spark lines can easily be seen on either superimposed or raster (stacked) position. On the raster position, each individual spark line can be viewed.

The spark lines should be level and one-fourth as high as the firing lines (1.5 to 2.5 kV, but usually less than 2 kV). The spark line voltage is called the **burn kV.** The *length* of the spark line is the critical factor for determining proper operation of the engine because it represents the spark duration or burn time. There is only a limited amount of energy in an ignition coil. If most of the energy is used to ionize the air gaps of the rotor and the spark plug, there may not be enough energy remaining to create a spark duration long enough to completely burn the air–fuel mixture. Many scopes are equipped with a **millisecond (ms) sweep**. This means that the scope will sweep only that portion of the pattern that can be shown during a 5- or 25-ms setting. Following are guidelines for spark line length:

- 0.8 ms—too short
- 1.5 ms—average
- 2.2 ms—too long

If the spark line is too short, possible causes include the following:

1. Spark plug(s) gap is too wide
2. Rotor tip to distributor cap insert distance gap is too wide (worn cap or rotor)
3. High-resistance spark plug wire
4. Air–fuel mixture too lean (vacuum leak, broken valve spring, etc.)

If the spark line is too long, possible causes include the following:

1. Fouled spark plug(s)
2. Spark plug(s) gap is too narrow
3. Shorted spark plug or spark plug wire

Many scopes do not have a millisecond scale. Some scopes are labeled in degrees and/or percentage (%) of dwell. The following chart can be used to determine acceptable spark line length.

Normal Spark Line Length (at 700 to 1200 RPM)

Number of Cylinders	Milliseconds	Percentage (%) of Dwell Scale	Degrees (°)
4	1.0–2.0	3–6	3–5
6	1.0–2.0	4–9	2–5
8	1.0–2.0	6–13	3–6

SPARK LINE SLOPE

Downward-sloping spark lines indicate that the voltage required to maintain the spark duration is decreasing during the firing of the spark plug. This downward slope usually indicates that the spark energy is finding ground through spark plug deposits (the plug is fouled) or other ignition problems. ● **SEE FIGURE 17–38**.

An upward-sloping spark line usually indicates a mechanical engine problem. A defective piston ring or valve would tend to seal better in the increasing pressures of combustion. As the spark plug fires, the effective increase in pressures increases the

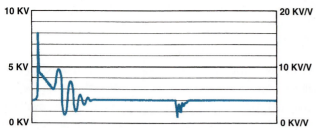

FIGURE 17–38 A downward-sloping spark line usually indicates high secondary ignition system resistance or an excessively rich air–fuel mixture.

SCOPE-TESTING
THE IGNITION SYSTEM (CONTINUED)

voltage required to maintain the spark, and the height of the spark line rises during the duration of the spark. ● **SEE FIGURE 17–39**.

An upward-sloping spark line can also indicate a lean air–fuel mixture. Typical causes include:

1. Clogged injector(s)
2. Vacuum leak
3. Sticking intake valve

● **SEE FIGURE 17–40** for an example showing the relationship between the firing line and the spark line.

READING THE INTERMEDIATE SECTION   The intermediate section should have three or more oscillations (bumps) for a correctly operating ignition system. Because approximately 250 volts are in the primary ignition circuit when the spark stops flowing across the spark plugs, this voltage is reduced by about 75 volts per oscillation. Additional resistances in the primary circuit would decrease the number of oscillations. If there are fewer than three oscillations, possible problems include the following:

1. Shorted ignition coil
2. Loose or high-resistance primary connections on the ignition coil or primary ignition wiring

ELECTRONIC IGNITION AND THE DWELL SECTION
Electronic ignitions also use a dwell period to charge the coil. Dwell is not adjustable with electronic ignition, but it does change with increasing RPM with many electronic ignition systems. This change in dwell with RPM should be considered normal.

Many EI systems also produce a "hump" in the dwell section, which reflects a current-limiting circuit in the control module. These current-limiting humps may have slightly different shapes depending on the exact module used. For example, the humps produced by various GM HEI modules differ slightly.

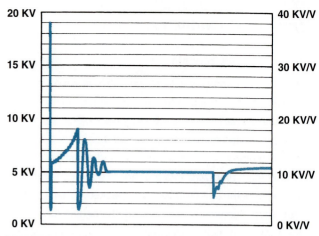

FIGURE 17–39 An upward-sloping spark line usually indicates a mechanical engine problem or a lean air–fuel mixture.

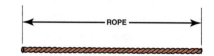

LENGTH OF ROPE REPRESENTS AMOUNT OF ENERGY STORED IN IGNITION COIL

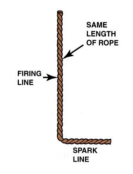

SAME LENGTH OF ROPE

FIRING LINE

SPARK LINE

SAME LENGTH OF ROPE (ENERGY). IF HIGH VOLTAGE IS REQUIRED TO IONIZE SPARK PLUG CAP, LESS ENERGY IS AVAILABLE FOR SPARK DURATION. (A LEAN CYLINDER IS AN EXAMPLE OF WHERE HIGHER VOLTAGE IS REQUIRED TO FIRE WITH A SHORTER-THAN-NORMAL DURATION.)

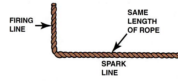

FIRING LINE

SAME LENGTH OF ROPE

SPARK LINE

IF LOW VOLTAGE IS REQUIRED TO FIRE THE SPARK PLUG (LOW FIRING LINE), MORE OF THE COIL'S ENERGY IS AVAILABLE TO PROVIDE A LONG-DURATION SPARK LINE. (A FOULED SPARK PLUG IS AN EXAMPLE OF LOW VOLTAGE TO FIRE, WITH A LONGER-THEN-NORMAL DURATION.)

FIGURE 17–40 The relationship between the height of the firing line and length of the spark line can be illustrated using a rope. Because energy cannot be destroyed, the stored energy in an ignition coil must dissipate totally, regardless of engine operating conditions.

DWELL VARIATION (ELECTRONIC IGNITION)   A worn distributor gear, worn camshaft gear, or other distributor problem may cause engine performance problems, because the signal created in the distributor will be affected by the inaccurate distributor operation. However, many electronic ignitions vary the dwell electronically in the module to maintain acceptable current flow levels through the ignition coil and module without the use of a ballast resistor.

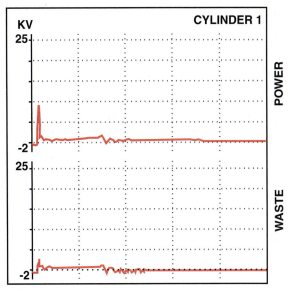

FIGURE 17–41 A dual-trace scope pattern showing both the power and the waste spark from the same coil (cylinders 1 and 6). Note that the firing line is higher on the cylinder that is under compression (power); otherwise, both patterns are almost identical.

COIL POLARITY   With the scope connected and the engine running, observe the scope pattern in the superimposed mode. If the pattern is upside down, the primary wires on the coil may be reversed, causing the coil polarity to be reversed.

ACCELERATION CHECK   With the scope selector set on the display (parade) position, rapidly accelerate the engine (gear selector in park or neutral with the parking brake on). The results should be interpreted as follows:

1. All firing lines should rise evenly (not to exceed 75% of maximum coil output) for properly operating spark plugs.

2. If the firing lines on one or more cylinders fail to rise, this indicates fouled spark plugs.

ROTOR GAP VOLTAGE   The **rotor gap** voltage test measures the voltage required to jump the gap (0.030 to 0.050 in. or 0.8 to 1.3 mm) between the rotor and the inserts (segments) of the distributor cap. Select the display (parade) scope pattern and remove a spark plug wire using a jumper wire to provide a good ground connection. Start the engine and observe the height of the firing line for the cylinder being tested. Because the spark plug wire is connected directly to ground, the firing line height on the scope will indicate the voltage required to jump the air gap between the rotor and the distributor cap insert. The normal rotor gap voltage is 3 to 7 kV, and the voltage should not exceed 8 kV. If the rotor gap voltage indicated is near or above 8 kV, inspect and replace the distributor cap and/or rotor as required.

SCOPE-TESTING A WASTE-SPARK IGNITION SYSTEM

A handheld digital storage oscilloscope can be used to check the pattern of each individual cylinder. Some larger scopes can be connected to all spark plug wires and therefore are able to display both power and waste-spark waveforms. ● **SEE FIGURE 17–41.** Because the waste spark does not require as high a voltage level as the cylinder on the power stroke, the waste form will be normally lower.

SCOPE-TESTING A COIL-ON-PLUG IGNITION SYSTEM

On a coil-on-plug (COP) type of ignition system, each individual coil can be shown on a scope and using the proper cables and adapters, the waveform for all of the cylinders can be viewed at the same time. Always follow the scope equipment manufacturer's instructions. Many Ford coil-on-plug systems

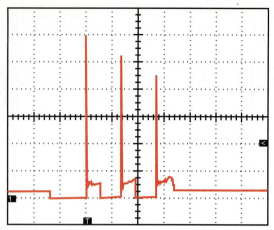

FIGURE 17–42 A secondary waveform of a Ford 4.6 liter V-8, showing three sparks occurring at idle speed.

SCOPE-TESTING A COIL-ON-PLUG IGNITION SYSTEM (CONTINUED)

use a triple-strike secondary spark event. The spark plugs are fired three times when the engine is at idle speed to improve idle quality and to reduce exhaust emissions. Above certain engine speeds, the ignition system switches to a single-fire event. ● **SEE FIGURE 17–42**.

SUMMARY

1. A thorough visual inspection should be performed on all ignition components when diagnosing an engine performance problem.

2. Platinum spark plugs should not be regapped after use in an engine.

3. A secondary ignition scope pattern includes a firing line, spark line, intermediate oscillations, and transistor-on and transistor-off points.

4. The slope of the spark line can indicate incorrect air–fuel ratio or other engine problems.

REVIEW QUESTIONS

1. Why should a spark tester be used to check for spark rather than a standard spark plug?

2. How do you test a pickup coil for resistance and AC voltage output?

3. What harm can occur if the engine is cranked or run with an open (defective) spark plug wire?

4. What are the sections of a secondary ignition scope pattern?

5. What can the slope of the spark line indicate about the engine?

1. Technician A says that the firing line shows the voltage that is required to fire the spark plug. Technician B says that spark line shows the duration of the spark inside the cylinder. Which technician is correct?
   a. Technician A only
   b. Technician B only
   c. Both Technicians A and B
   d. Neither Technician A nor B

2. Technician A says that a defective spark plug wire or boot can cause an engine misfire. Technician B says that a tracked ignition coil can cause an engine misfire. Which technician is correct?
   a. Technician A only
   b. Technician B only
   c. Both Technicians A and B
   d. Neither Technician A nor B

3. The _____ sends a pulse signal to an electronic ignition module.
   a. Ballast resistor
   b. Pickup coil
   c. Ignition coil
   d. Condenser

4. Typical primary coil resistance specifications usually range from _____ ohms.
   a. 100 to 450
   b. 500 to 1,500
   c. Less than 1 to 3
   d. 6,000 to 30,000

5. Typical secondary coil resistance specifications usually range from _____ ohms.
   a. 100 to 450
   b. 500 to 1,500
   c. 1 to 3
   d. 6,000 to 30,000

6. Technician A says that an engine will not start and run if the ignition coil is tracked. Technician B says the engine will not start if the crankshaft position sensor fails. Which technician is correct?
   a. Technician A only
   b. Technician B only
   c. Both Technicians A and B
   d. Neither Technician A nor B

7. Technician A says that a distributor rotor can burn through and cause an engine misfire during acceleration. Technician B says that a defective spark plug wire can cause an engine misfire during acceleration. Which technician is correct?
   a. Technician A only
   b. Technician B only
   c. Both Technicians A and B
   d. Neither Technician A nor B

8. The secondary ignition circuit can be tested using _____.
   a. An ohmmeter
   b. Visual inspection
   c. An ammeter
   d. Both a and b

9. Two technicians are discussing a no-start (no-spark) condition. Technician A says that an open pickup coil could be the cause. Technician B says that a defective ignition control module (ICM) could be the cause. Which technician is correct?
   a. Technician A only
   b. Technician B only
   c. Both Technicians A and B
   d. Neither Technician A nor B

10. Which sensor produces a square wave signal?
    a. Magnetic sensor
    b. Hall-effect sensor
    c. Optical sensor
    d. Both b and c

COMPUTER AND NETWORK FUNDAMENTALS

COMPUTER CONTROL

Modern automotive control systems consist of a network of electronic sensors, actuators, and computer modules designed to regulate the power train and vehicle support systems. The **Powertrain Control Module (PCM)** is the heart of this system. It coordinates engine and transmission operation, processes data, maintains communications, and makes the control decisions needed to keep the vehicle operating.

Automotive computers use voltage to send and receive information. Voltage is electrical pressure and does not flow through circuits, but voltage can be used as a signal. A computer converts input information or data into voltage signal combinations that represent number combinations. The number combinations can represent a variety of information—temperature, speed, or even words and letters. A computer processes the input voltage signals it receives by computing what they represent, and then delivering the data in computed or processed form.

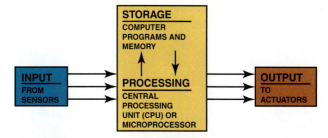

FIGURE 18–1 All computer systems perform four basic functions: input, processing, storage, and output.

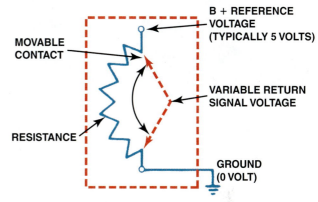

FIGURE 18–2 A potentiometer uses a movable contact to vary resistance and send an analog voltage to the PCM.

THE FOUR BASIC COMPUTER FUNCTIONS

The operation of every computer can be divided into four basic functions. ● **SEE FIGURE 18–1**.

- Input
- Processing
- Storage
- Output

These basic functions are not unique to computers; they can be found in many noncomputer systems. However, we need to know how the computer handles these functions.

INPUT First, the computer receives a voltage signal (input) from an input device. The device can be as simple as a button or a switch on an instrument panel, or a sensor on an automotive engine. ● **SEE FIGURE 18–2** for a typical type of automotive sensor.

Vehicles use various mechanical, electrical, and magnetic sensors to measure factors such as vehicle speed, engine RPM, air pressure, oxygen content of exhaust gas, airflow, and engine coolant temperature. Each sensor transmits its information in the form of voltage signals. The computer receives these voltage signals, but before it can use them, the signals must undergo a process called **input conditioning**. This process includes amplifying voltage signals that are too small for the computer

circuitry to handle. Input conditioners generally are located inside the computer, but a few sensors have their own input-conditioning circuitry.

PROCESSING Input voltage signals received by a computer are processed through a series of electronic logic circuits maintained in its programmed instructions. These logic circuits change the input voltage signals, or data, into output voltage signals or commands.

STORAGE The program instructions for a computer are stored in electronic memory. Some programs may require that certain input data be stored for later reference or future processing. In others, output commands may be delayed or stored before they are transmitted to devices elsewhere in the system.

Computers have two types of memory: permanent and temporary. Permanent memory is called **read-only memory (ROM)** because the computer can only read the contents; it cannot change the data stored in it. This data is retained even when power to the computer is shut off. Part of the ROM is built into the computer, and the rest is located in an IC chip called a **programmable read-only memory (PROM)** or calibration assembly. ● **SEE FIGURE 18–3**. Many chips are erasable, meaning that the program can be changed. These chips are called erasable programmable

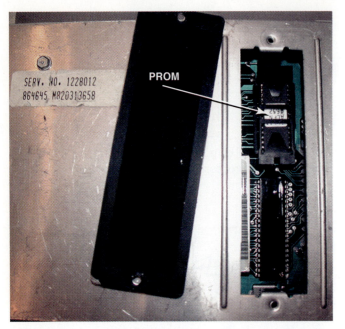

FIGURE 18–3 A replaceable PROM used in an older General Motors computer. Notice that the sealed access panel has been removed to gain access.

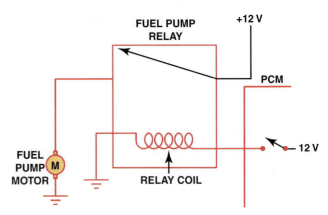

FIGURE 18–4 A typical output driver. In this case, the PCM applies voltage to the fuel pump relay coil to energize the fuel pump.

THE FOUR BASIC COMPUTER FUNCTIONS (CONTINUED)

read-only memory or EPROM. Since the early 1990s most programmable memory has been electronically erasable, meaning that the program in the chip can be reprogrammed by using a scan tool and the proper software. This computer reprogramming is usually called *reflashing*. These chips are electrically erasable programmable read-only memory, abbreviated **EEPROM** or **E²PROM**. All vehicles equipped with onboard diagnosis second generation, called OBD II, are equipped with EEPROMs.

Temporary memory is called **random-access memory (RAM)** because the microprocessor can write or store new data into it as directed by the computer program, as well as read the data already in it. Automotive computers use two types of RAM memory: **volatile** and **nonvolatile**. Volatile RAM memory is lost whenever the ignition is turned off. However, a type of volatile RAM called **keep-alive memory (KAM)** can be wired directly to battery power. This prevents its data from being erased when the ignition is turned off. Both RAM and KAM have the disadvantage of losing their memory when disconnected from their power source. One example of RAM and KAM is the loss of station settings in a programmable radio when the battery is disconnected. Since all the settings are stored in RAM, they have to be reset when the battery is reconnected. System trouble codes are commonly stored in RAM and can be erased by disconnecting the battery.

Nonvolatile RAM memory can retain its information even when the battery is disconnected. One use for this type of RAM is the storage of odometer information in an electronic speedometer.

The memory chip retains the mileage accumulated by the vehicle. When speedometer replacement is necessary, the odometer chip is removed and installed in the new speedometer unit. KAM is used primarily in conjunction with adaptive strategies.

OUTPUT After the computer has processed the input signals, it sends voltage signals or commands to other devices in the system, such as system actuators. An **actuator** is an electrical or mechanical device that converts electrical energy into heat, light, or motion, such as adjusting engine idle speed, altering suspension height, or regulating fuel metering.

Computers also can communicate with, and control, each other through their output and input functions. This means that the output signal from one computer system can be the input signal for another computer system through a network.

Most outputs work electrically in one of three ways:

- Switched
- Pulse width modulated
- Digital

A switched output is an output that is either on or off. In many circuits, the PCM uses a relay to switch a device on or off. This is because the relay is a low-current device that can switch a higher-current device. Most computer circuits cannot handle a lot of current. By using a relay circuit as shown in ● **FIGURE 18–4**, the PCM provides the output control to the relay, which in turn

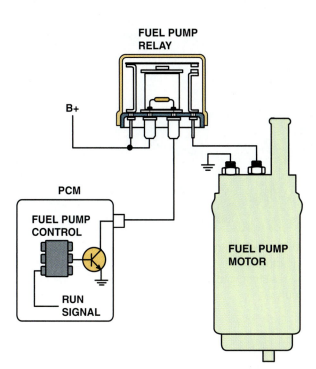

FIGURE 18–5 A typical low-side driver (LSD) which uses a control module to control the ground side of the relay coil.

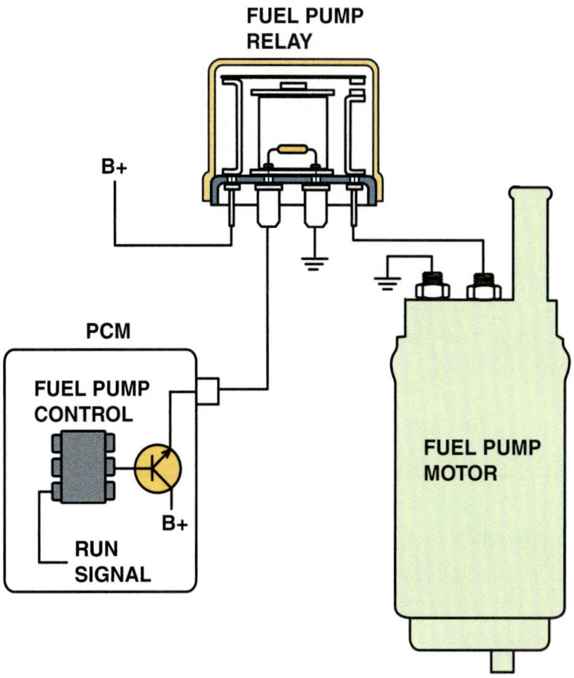

FIGURE 18–6 A typical module-controlled high-side driver (HSD) where the module itself supplies the electrical power to the device. The logic circuit inside the module can detect circuit faults including continuity of the circuit and if there is a short-to-ground in the circuit being controlled.

provides the output control to the device. The relay coil, which the PCM controls, typically draws less than 0.5 amps. The device that the relay controls may draw 30 amps or more. These switches are actually transistors, often called **output drivers**.

LOW-SIDE DRIVERS

Low-side drivers, often abbreviated **LSD**, are transistors that complete the ground path in the circuit. Ignition voltage is supplied to the relay as well as battery voltage. The computer output is connected to the ground side of the relay coil. The computer energizes the fuel pump relay by turning the transistor on and completing the ground path for the relay coil. A relatively low current flows through the relay coil and transistor that is inside the computer. This causes the relay to switch and provides the fuel pump with battery voltage. The majority of switched outputs have typically been low-side drivers. ● **SEE FIGURE 18–5**. Low-side drivers can often perform a diagnostic circuit check by monitoring the voltage from the relay to check that the control circuit for the relay is complete. A low-side driver, however, cannot detect a short-to-ground.

HIGH-SIDE DRIVERS

High-side drivers, often abbreviated **HSD**, control the power side of the circuit. In these applications when the transistor is switched on, voltage is applied to the device. A ground has been provided to the device so when

the high-side driver switches the device will be energized. In some applications, high-side drivers are used instead of low-side drivers to provide better circuit protection. General Motors vehicles have used a high-side driver to control the fuel pump relay instead of a low-side driver. In the event of an accident, should the circuit to the fuel pump relay become grounded, a high-side driver would cause a short circuit, which would cause the fuel pump relay to de-energize. High-side drivers inside modules can detect electrical faults such as a lack of continuity when the circuit is not energized. ● **SEE FIGURE 18–6**.

PULSE WIDTH MODULATION

Pulse width modulation (PWM) is a method of controlling an output using a digital signal. Instead of just turning devices on or off, the computer can control output devices more precisely by using pulse width modulation. For example, a vacuum solenoid could be a pulse-width modulated device. If the vacuum solenoid is controlled by a switched driver, switching either on or off would mean that either full vacuum would flow through the solenoid or no vacuum would flow through the solenoid. However, to control the amount of vacuum that flows through the solenoid, pulse width modulation could be used. A PWM signal is a digital signal, usually 0 volts and 12 volts, that is cycling at a fixed frequency. Varying the length of time that the signal is on, provides a signal

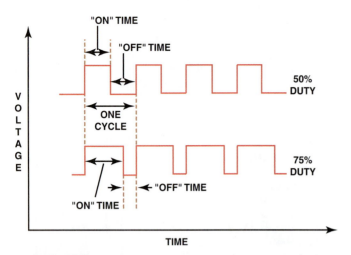

FIGURE 18–7 Both the top and bottom pattern have the same frequency. However, the amount of on-time varies. Duty cycle is the percentage of the time during a cycle that the signal is turned on.

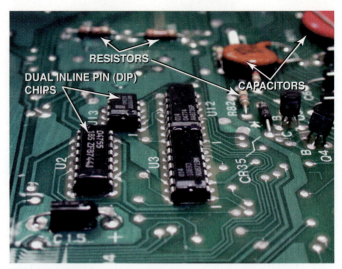

FIGURE 18–8 Many electronic components are used to construct a typical vehicle computer. Notice the quantity of chips, resistors, and capacitors used in this General Motors computer.

THE FOUR BASIC COMPUTER FUNCTIONS (CONTINUED)

that can vary the on and off time of an output. The ratio of on-time relative to the period of the cycle is referred to as **duty cycle**. ● SEE FIGURE 18–7. Depending on the frequency of the signal, which is usually fixed, this signal would turn the device on and off a fixed number of times per second. When, for example, the voltage is high (12 volts) 90% of the time and low (0 volts) the other 10% of the time, the signal has a 90% duty cycle. In other words, if this signal were applied to the vacuum solenoid, the solenoid would be on 90% of the time. This would allow more vacuum to flow through the solenoid. The computer has the ability to vary this on and off time or pulse width modulation at any rate between 0 and 100%.

A good example of pulse width modulation is the cooling fan speed control. The speed of the cooling fan is controlled by varying the amount of on-time that the battery voltage is applied to the cooling fan motor.

100% duty cycle—the fan runs at full speed

75% duty cycle—the fan runs at 3/4 speed

50% duty cycle—the fan runs at 1/2 speed

25% duty cycle—the fan runs at 1/4 speed

The use of PWM, therefore, results in very precise control of an output device to achieve the amount of cooling needed and conserve electrical energy compared to simply timing the cooling fan on high when needed. PWM may be used to control vacuum through a solenoid, the amount of purge of the evaporative purge solenoid, the speed of a fuel pump motor, control of a linear motor, or even the intensity of a lightbulb.

DIGITAL COMPUTERS

In a **digital** computer, the voltage signal or processing function is a simple high/low, yes/no, on/off signal. The digital signal voltage is limited to two voltage levels: high voltage and low voltage. Since there is no stepped range of voltage or current in between, a digital binary signal is a "square wave."

The signal is called "digital" because the on and off signals are processed by the computer as the digits or numbers 0 and 1. The number system containing only these two digits is called the **binary** system. Any number or letter from any number system or language alphabet can be translated into a combination of binary 0s and 1s for the digital computer.

A digital computer changes the analog input signals (voltage) to digital bits (*bi*nary dig*its*) of information through an **analog-to-digital (AD) converter** circuit. The binary digital number is used by the computer in its calculations or logic networks. Output signals usually are digital signals that turn system actuators on and off.

The digital computer can process thousands of digital signals per second because its circuits are able to switch voltage signals on and off in billionths of a second. ● SEE FIGURE 18–8.

PARTS OF A COMPUTER The software consists of the programs and logic functions stored in the computer's circuitry. The hardware is the mechanical and electronic parts of a computer.

CENTRAL PROCESSING UNIT (CPU). The microprocessor is the **central processing unit (CPU)** of a computer. Since it performs

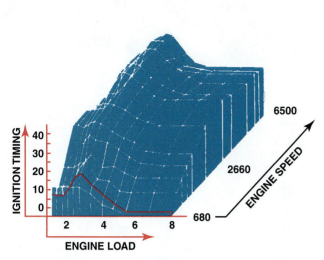

FIGURE 18–9 Typical ignition timing map developed from testing and used by the vehicle computer to provide the optimum ignition timing for all engine speeds and load combinations.

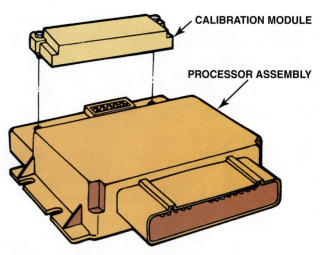

FIGURE 18–10 The calibration module on many Ford computers contains a system PROM.

FIGURE 18–11 The clock generator produces a series of pulses that are used by the microprocessor and other components to stay in step with each other at a steady rate.

the essential mathematical operations and logic decisions that make up its processing function, the CPU can be considered to be the brain of a computer. Some computers use more than one microprocessor, called a coprocessor.

COMPUTER MEMORY. Other IC devices store the computer operating program, system sensor input data, and system actuator output data, information that is necessary for CPU operation.

COMPUTER PROGRAMS By operating a vehicle on a dynamometer and manually adjusting the variable factors such as speed, load, and spark timing, it is possible to determine the optimum output settings for the best driveability, economy, and emission control. This is called **engine mapping**. ● **SEE FIGURE 18–9**.

Engine mapping creates a three-dimensional performance graph that applies to a given vehicle and power train combination. Each combination is mapped in this manner to produce a PROM. This allows an automaker to use one basic computer for all models; a unique PROM individualizes the computer for a particular model. Also, if a driveability problem can be resolved by a change in the program, the manufacturers can release a revised PROM to supersede the earlier part.

Many older vehicle computers used a single PROM that plugged into the computer. ● **SEE FIGURE 18–10**. Some Ford computers used a larger "calibration module" that contained the system PROM.

NOTE: If the onboard computer needs to be replaced, the PROM or calibration module must be removed from the defective unit and installed in the replacement computer. Since the mid-1990s, computers must be programmed or *flashed* before being put into service.

CLOCK RATES AND TIMING The microprocessor receives sensor input voltage signals, processes them by using information from other memory units, and then sends voltage signals to the appropriate actuators. The microprocessor communicates by transmitting long strings of 0s and 1s in a language called binary code. But the microprocessor must have some way of knowing when one signal ends and another begins. That is the job of a crystal oscillator called a **clock generator**. ● **SEE FIGURE 18–11**. The computer's crystal oscillator

FIGURE 18–12 This Powertrain Control Module (PCM) is located under the hood on this Chevrolet pickup truck.

DIGITAL COMPUTERS (CONTINUED)

FIGURE 18–13 This PCM on a Chrysler vehicle can only be seen by hoisting the vehicle because it is located next to the radiator, and in the airflow to help keep it cool.

generates a steady stream of one-bit-long voltage pulses. Both the microprocessor and the memories monitor the clock pulses while they are communicating. Because they know how long each voltage pulse should be, they can distinguish between a 01 and a 0011. To complete the process, the input and output circuits also watch the clock pulses.

COMPUTER SPEEDS Not all computers operate at the same speed; some are faster than others. The speed at which a computer operates is specified by the cycle time, or clock speed, required to perform certain measurements. Cycle time or clock speed is measured in megahertz (4.7 MHz, 8.0 MHz, 15 MHz, 18 MHz, etc.).

BAUD RATE The computer transmits bits of a serial data stream at precise intervals. The computer's processing speed is called the baud rate, or bits per second. Just as mph helps in estimating the length of time required to travel a certain distance, the baud rate is useful in estimating how long a given computer will need to transmit a specified amount of data to another computer. Storage of a single character requires eight bits per byte, plus an additional two bits to indicate stop and start. This means that transmission of one character requires 10 bits. Dividing the baud rate by 10 tells us the maximum number of words per second that can be transmitted. For example, if the computer has a baud rate of 600, approximately 60 words can be received or sent per minute.

Automotive computers have evolved from a baud rate of 160 used in the early 1980s to a baud rate as high as 500,000 for

some networks. The speed of data transmission is an important factor both in system operation and in system troubleshooting.

CONTROL MODULE LOCATIONS The onboard automotive computer has many names. It may be called an **electronic control unit (ECU)**, **electronic control module (ECM)**, **electronic control assembly (ECA)**, or a **controller**, depending on the manufacturer and the computer application. The Society of Automotive Engineers (SAE) bulletin, J-1930, standardizes the name as a powertrain control module (PCM). The computer hardware is all mounted on one or more circuit boards and installed in a metal case to help shield it from electromagnetic interference (EMI). The wiring harnesses that link the computer to sensors and actuators connect to multipin connectors or edge connectors on the circuit boards.

Onboard computers range from single-function units that control a single operation to multifunction units that manage all of the separate (but linked) electronic systems in the vehicle. They vary in size from a small module to a notebook-sized box. Most other engine computers are installed in the passenger compartment either under the instrument panel or in a side kick panel where they can be shielded from physical damage caused by temperature extremes, dirt, and vibration, or interference by the high currents and voltages of various underhood systems. ● **SEE FIGURES 18–12 AND 18–13.**

COMPUTER INPUT SENSORS

The vehicle computer uses the signals (voltage levels) from the following engine sensors:

- **Engine speed (RPM or revolutions per minute) sensor.** This signal comes from the primary signal in the ignition module.

- **MAP (manifold absolute pressure) sensor.** This sensor detects engine load. The computer uses this information for fuel delivery and for onboard diagnosis of other sensors and systems such as the exhaust gas recirculation (EGR) system.

- **MAF (mass airflow) sensor.** This sensor measures the mass (weight and density) of the air entering the engine. The computer uses this information to determine the amount of fuel needed by the engine.

- **ECT (engine coolant temperature) sensor.** This sensor measures the temperature of the engine coolant needed by the computer to determine the amount of fuel and spark advance. This is a major sensor, especially when the engine is cold and when the engine is first started.

- **O2S (oxygen sensor).** This sensor measures the oxygen in the exhaust stream. These sensors are used for fuel control and to check other sensors and systems.

- **TP (throttle position) sensor.** This sensor measures the throttle opening and is used by the computer to control fuel delivery as well as spark advance and the shift points of the automotive transmission/transaxle.

- **VS (vehicle speed) sensor.** This sensor measures the vehicle speed using a sensor located at the output of the transmission/transaxle or by monitoring sensors at the wheel speed sensors.

- **Knock sensor.** The voltage signal from the knock sensor **(KS)** is sent to the PCM. The PCM retards the ignition timing until the knocking stops.

COMPUTER OUTPUTS

A vehicle computer can do just two things.

- Turn a device on.

- Turn a device off.

The computer can turn devices such as fuel injectors on and off very rapidly or keep them on for a certain amount of time. Typical output devices include the following.

- **Fuel injectors.** The computer can vary the amount of time the injectors are held open, thereby controlling the amount of fuel supplied to the engine.

- **Ignition timing.** The computer can trigger the signal to the ignition module to fire the spark plugs based on information from the sensors. The spark is advanced when the engine is cold and/or when the engine is operating under light load conditions.

- **Transmission shifting.** The computer provides a ground to the shift solenoids and torque converter clutch solenoid. The operation of the automatic transmission/transaxle is optimized based on vehicle sensor information.

- **Idle speed control.** The computer can pulse the idle speed control (ISC) or idle air control (IAC) device to maintain engine idle speed and to provide an increased idle speed when needed, such as when the air-conditioning system is operating.

- **Evaporative emission control solenoids.** The computer can control the flow of gasoline fumes from the charcoal canister to the engine and seal off the system to perform a fuel system leak detection test as part of the OBD II onboard diagnosis.

MODULE COMMUNICATION AND NETWORKS

Since the 1990s, vehicles use modules to control most of the electrical component operation. A typical vehicle will have 10 or more modules and they communicate with each other over data lines or hard wiring, depending on the application.

SERIAL DATA   **Serial data** is data that is transmitted by a series of rapidly changing voltage signals pulsed from low to high or from high to low. Most modules are connected together in a network because of the following advantages:

- A decreased number of wires is needed, thereby saving weight, cost, as well as helping with installation at the factory, and decreased complexity, making servicing easier.

- Common sensor data can be shared with those modules that may need the information, such as vehicle speed, outside air temperature, and engine coolant temperature.

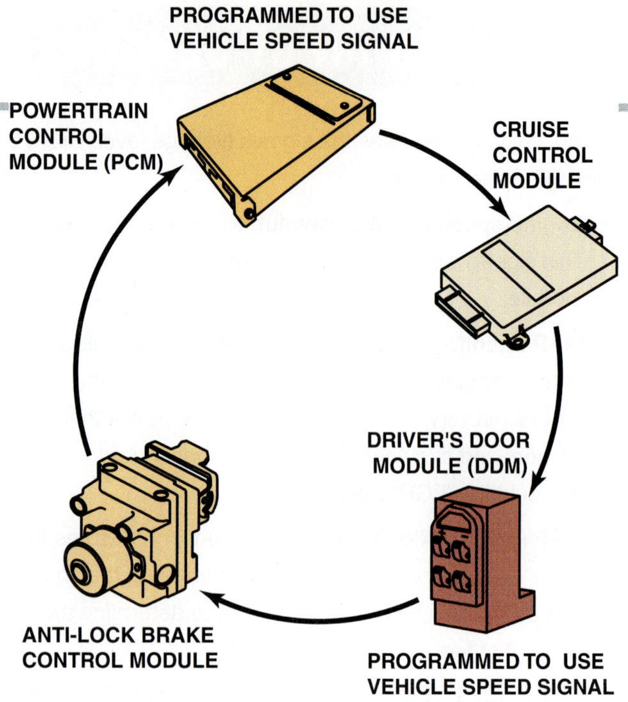

MULTIPLEXING   **Multiplexing** is the process of sending multiple signals of information at the same time over a signal wire and then separating the signals at the receiving end. This system of intercommunication of computers or processors is referred to as a **network**. ● **SEE FIGURE 18–14**. By connecting the computers together on a communications network, they can easily share information back and forth. This multiplexing has a number of advantages, including:

- The elimination of redundant sensors and dedicated wiring for these multiple sensors.

- The reduction of the number of wires, connectors, and circuits.

- Addition of more features and option content to new vehicles.

- Weight reduction, increasing fuel economy.

- Allows features to be changed with software upgrades instead of component replacement.

The three most common types of networks used on General Motors vehicles include:

1. **Ring link networks.** In a ring-type network, all modules are connected to each other by a serial data line in a line until all are connected in a ring. ● **SEE FIGURE 18–15**.

2. **Star link.** In a star link network, a serial data line attaches to each module and then each is connected to a central point. This central point is called a **splice pack**, abbreviated SP

FIGURE 18–14 A network allows all modules to communicate with other modules.

such as in "SP 306." The splice pack uses a bar to splice all of the serial lines together. Some GM vehicles use two or more splice packs to tie the modules together. When more than one splice pack is used, a serial data line connects one splice pack to the others. In most applications the bus bar used in each splice pack can be removed. When the bus bar is removed a special tool (J 42236) can be installed in place of the removed bus bar. Using this tool, the serial data line for each module can be isolated and tested for a possible problem. Using the special tool at the splice pack makes diagnosing this type of network easier than many others. ● **SEE FIGURE 18–16** for an example of a star link network system.

3. **Ring/Star hybrid.** In a ring/star network, the modules are connected using both types of network configuration. Check service information (SI) for details on how this network is connected on the vehicle being diagnosed and always follow the recommended diagnostic steps.

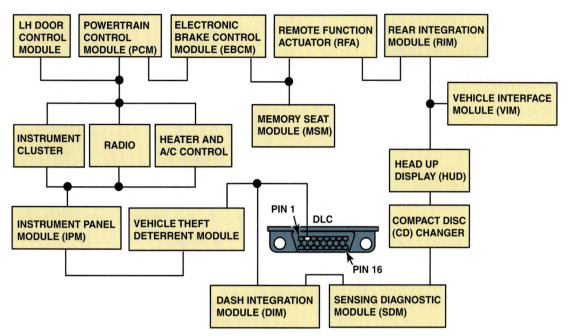

FIGURE 18–15 A ring link network reduces the number of wires it takes to interconnect all of the modules.

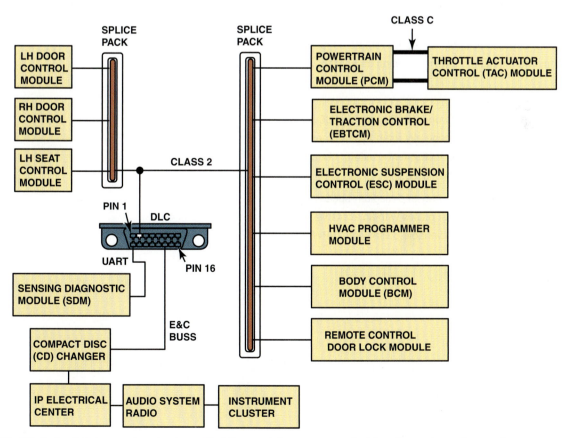

FIGURE 18–16 A star-link-type network where all of the modules are connected together using splice packs.

SAE COMMUNICATION CLASSIFICATIONS

The Society of Automotive Engineers (SAE) standards include three categories of in-vehicle network communications, including the following.

CLASS A   Low-speed networks (less than 10,000 bits per second [10 kbs]) are generally used for trip computers, entertainment, and other convenience features. Most low-speed Class A communication functions are performed using the following:

- UART standard (Universal Asynchronous Receive/Transmit) used by General Motors (8192 bps).
- CCD (Chrysler Collision Detection) used by Chrysler (7812.5 bps).

   NOTE: The "collision" in CCD-type bus communication refers to the program that avoids conflicts of information exchange within the bus, and does not refer to airbags or other accident-related circuits of the vehicle.

- Chrysler SCI (Serial Communications Interface) is used to communicate between the engine controller and a scan tool (62.5 kbps).
- ACP (Audio Control Protocol) is used for remote control of entertainment equipment (twisted pairs) on Ford vehicles.

CLASS B   Medium-speed networks (10,000 to 125,000 bits per second [10 to 125 kbs]) are generally used for information transfer among modules, such as instrument clusters, temperature sensor data, and other general uses.

- General Motors GMLAN; both low- and medium-speed and Class 2, which uses 0-to 7-volt pulses with an available pulse width. Meets SAE 1850 variable pulse width (VPW).

? FREQUENTLY ASKED QUESTION

What Is a Bus?

A bus is a term used to describe a communication network. Therefore, there are *connections to the bus* and *bus communications*, both of which refer to digital messages being transmitted among electronic modules or computers.

- Chrysler Programmable Communication Interface (PCI). Meets SAE standard J-1850 pulse-width modulated (PWM).
- Ford Standard Corporate Protocol (SCP). Meets SAE standard J-1850 pulse-width modulated (PWM).

CLASS C   High-speed networks (125,000 to 1,000,000 bits per second [125,000 to 1,000,000 kbs]) are generally used for real-time powertrain and vehicle dynamic control. Most high-speed bus communication is **controller area network** or **CAN**. ● **SEE FIGURE 18–17**.

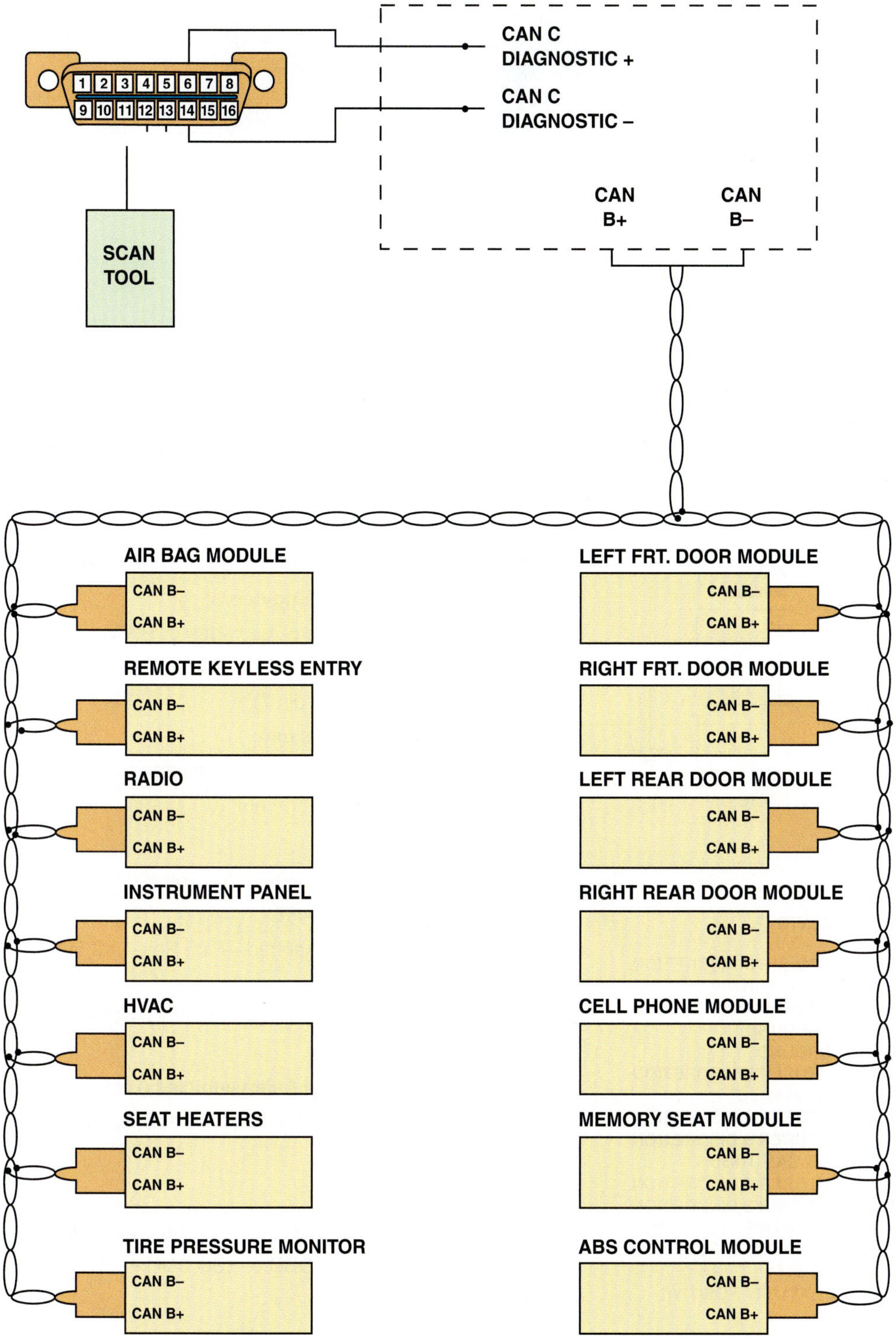

FIGURE 18–17 A typical bus system showing module CAN communications and twisted pairs of wire.

MODULE COMMUNICATION DIAGNOSIS

Most vehicle manufacturers specify that a scan tool be used to diagnose modules and module communications. Always follow the recommended testing procedures, which usually require the use of a factory scan tool.

Some tests of the communication bus (network) and some of the service procedures require the service technician to at-tach a DMM, set to DC volts, to monitor communications. A variable voltage usually indicates that messages are being sent and received.

Most high-speed bus systems use resistors at each end called **terminating resistors**. These resistors are used to help reduce interference into other systems in the vehicle.

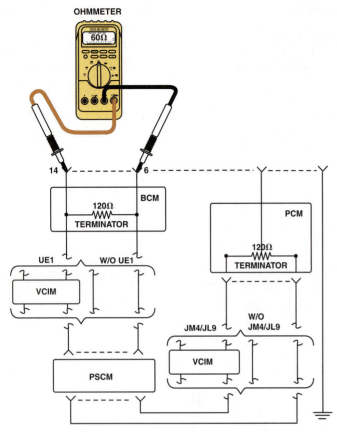

FIGURE 18–18 Checking the terminating resistors using an ohmmeter at the DLC.

OBD-II DLC

PIN NO.	ASSIGNMENTS
1.	MANUFACTURER'S DISCRETION
2.	BUS + LINE, SAE J1850
3.	MANUFACTURER'S DISCRETION
4.	CHASSIS GROUND
5.	SIGNAL GROUND
6.	MANUFACTURER'S DISCRETION
7.	K LINE, ISO 9141
8.	MANUFACTURER'S DISCRETION
9.	MANUFACTURER'S DISCRETION
10.	BUS – LINE, SAE J1850
11.	MANUFACTURER'S DISCRETION
12.	MANUFACTURER'S DISCRETION
13.	MANUFACTURER'S DISCRETION
14.	MANUFACTURER'S DISCRETION
15.	L LINE, ISO 9141
16.	VEHICLE BATTERY POSITIVE (4A MAX)

FIGURE 18–19 Sixteen-pin OBD II DLC with terminals identified. Scan tools use the power pin (16) ground pin (4) for power so that a separate cigarette lighter plug is not necessary on OBD II vehicles.

MODULE COMMUNICATION DIAGNOSIS (CONTINUED)

Usually two 120-ohm resistors are installed at each end and are therefore connected electrically in parallel. Two 120-ohm resistors connected in parallel would measure 60 ohms if being tested using an ohmmeter. ● **SEE FIGURE 18–18.**

OBD II DATA LINK CONNECTOR

All OBD II vehicles use a 16-pin connector that includes:
● **SEE FIGURE 18–19.**

> Pin 4 = chassis ground
>
> Pin 5 = signal ground
>
> Pin 16 = battery power (4A max)

Vehicles may use one of two major standards including:

- **ISO 9141-2 Standard (ISO = International Standards Organization)**

  Pins 7 and 15 (or wire at pin 7 and no pin at 2 or a wire at 7 and at 2 and/or 10)

- **SAE J-1850 Standard (SAE = Society of Automotive Engineers)**

  Two types: **VPW** (variable pulse width) or **PWM** (pulse-width modulated)

  Pins 2 and 10 (no wire at pin 7)

  General Motors vehicles use:

- SAE J-1850 (VPW—Class 2—10.4 kb) standard, which uses pins 2, 4, 5, and 16 and not 10

- **GM Domestic OBD II**

  Pin 1 and 9—CCM (Comprehensive Component Monitor) slow baud rate—8192 UART

  Pins 2 and 10—OEM Enhanced—Fast Rate—40,500 baud rate

  Pins 7 and 15—Generic OBD II—ISO 9141—10,400 baud rate

  Chrysler, European, and Asian vehicles use:

- ISO 9141-2 standard, which uses pins 4, 5, 7, 15, and 16

- **Chrysler OBD II**

  Pins 2 and 10—CCM

  Pins 3 and 14—OEM Enhanced—60,500 baud rate

  Pins 7 and 15—Generic OBD II—ISO 9141—10,400 baud rate

  Ford vehicles use:

- SAE J-1850(PWM) (PWM—41.6 kb) standard, which uses pins 2, 4, 5, 10, and 16

- **Ford Domestic OBD II**

  Pins 2 and 10—CCM

  Pins 6 and 14—OEM Enhanced—Class C—40,500 baud rate

  Pins 7 and 15—Generic OBD II—ISO 9141—10,400 baud rate

SUMMARY

1. The Society of Automotive Engineers (SAE) standard J-1930 specifies that the term Powertrain Control Module (PCM) be used for the computer that controls the engine and transmission in a vehicle.

2. The four basic computer functions include input, processing, storage, and output.

3. Read-only memory (ROM) can be programmable (PROM), erasable (EPROM), or electrically erasable (EEPROM).

4. Computer input sensors include engine speed (RPM), MAP, MAF, ECT, O2S, TP, and VS.

5. A computer can only turn a device on or turn a device off, but it can do the operation very rapidly.

REVIEW QUESTIONS

1. What part of the vehicle computer is considered to be the brain?

2. What is the difference between volatile and nonvolatile RAM?

3. List four input sensors.

4. List four output devices.

CHAPTER QUIZ

1. What unit of electricity is used as a signal for a computer?
   a. Volt
   b. Ohm
   c. Ampere
   d. Watt

2. The four basic computer functions include _____.
   a. Writing, processing, printing, and remembering
   b. Input, processing, storage, and output
   c. Data gathering, processing, output, and evaluation
   d. Sensing, calculating, actuating, and processing

3. All OBD II vehicles use what type of read-only memory?
   a. ROM
   b. PROM
   c. EPROM
   d. EEPROM

4. The "brain" of the computer is the _____.
   a. PROM
   b. RAM
   c. CPU
   d. AD converter

5. Computer processing speed is measured in _____.
   a. Baud rate
   b. Clock speed (Hz)
   c. Voltage
   d. Bytes

6. Which item is a computer input sensor?
   a. RPM
   b. Throttle position angle
   c. Engine coolant temperature
   d. All of the above

7. Which item is a computer output device?
   a. Fuel injector
   b. Transmission shift solenoid
   c. Evaporative emission control solenoid
   d. All of the above

8. The SAE term for the vehicle computer is _____.
   a. PCM
   b. ECM
   c. ECA
   d. Controller

9. What two things can a vehicle computer actually perform (output)?
   a. Store and process information
   b. Turn something on or turn something off
   c. Calculate and vary temperature
   d. Control fuel and timing only

10. Analog signals from sensors are changed to digital signals for processing by the computer through which type of circuit?
    a. Digital
    b. Analog
    c. AD converter
    d. PROM

ONBOARD DIAGNOSIS

After studying Chapter 19, the reader will be able to:

1. Prepare for ASE Electrical/Electronic Systems (A6) certification test content area "A" (General Electrical/Electronic Systems Diagnosis).
2. Explain the purpose and function of onboard diagnosis.
3. List the various duties of the diagnostic executive (task master).
4. List five continuous monitors.
5. List five noncontinuous monitors.

California Air Resources Board (CARB) 321

Component identification (CID) 329

Comprehensive component monitor (CCM) 322

Diagnostic executive 322

Enable criteria 325

Exponentially weighted moving average (EWMA) monitor 324

Federal Test Procedure (FTP) 321

Freeze-frame 322

Functionality 323

Malfunction indicator lamp (MIL) 321

On-board diagnosis (OBD) 321

Parameter identification (PID) 329

Rationality 323

Society of Automotive Engineers (SAE) 326

Test identification (TID) 329

Task manager 322

ON-BOARD DIAGNOSTICS GENERATION-II (OBD-II) SYSTEMS

PURPOSE AND FUNCTION OF OBD II During the 1980s, most manufacturers began equipping their vehicles with full-function control systems capable of alerting the driver of a malfunction and of allowing the technician to retrieve codes that identify circuit faults. These early diagnostic systems were meant to reduce emissions and speed up vehicle repair.

The automotive industry calls these systems **On-Board Diagnostics (OBDs)**. The **California Air Resources Board (CARB)** developed the first regulation requiring manufacturers selling vehicles in that state to install OBD. OBD Generation I (OBD I) applies to all vehicles sold in California beginning with the 1988 model year. It specifies the following requirements:

1. An instrument panel warning lamp able to alert the driver of certain control system failures, now called a **malfunction indicator lamp (MIL)**. ● SEE FIGURE 19–1.

2. The system's ability to record and transmit DTCs for emission-related failures.

3. Electronic system monitoring of the HO2S, EGR valve, and evaporative purge solenoid. Although not U.S. EPA-required, during this time most manufacturers also equipped vehicles sold outside of California with OBD I.

By failing to monitor the catalytic converter, the evaporative system for leaks, and the presence of engine misfire, OBD I did not do enough to lower automotive emissions. This led the CARB and the EPA to develop OBD Generation II (OBD II).

OBD-II OBJECTIVES Generally, the CARB defines an OBD-II-equipped vehicle by its ability to do the following:

1. Detect component degradation or a faulty emission-related system that prevents compliance with federal emission standards.

2. Alert the driver of needed emission-related repair or maintenance.

3. Use standardized DTCs and accept a generic scan tool.

These requirements apply to all 1996 and later model light-duty vehicles. The Clean Air Act of 1990 directed the EPA to develop new regulations for OBD. The primary purpose of OBD II is emission-related, whereas the primary purpose of OBD I (1988) was to detect faults in sensors or sensor circuits. OBD-II regulations require that not only sensors be tested but also all exhaust emission control devices, and that they be verified for proper operation.

All new vehicles must pass the **Federal Test Procedure (FTP)** for exhaust emissions while being tested for 505 seconds on rollers that simulate the urban drive cycle around downtown Los Angeles.

NOTE: IM 240 is simply a shorter 240-second version of the 505-second federal test procedure.

The regulations for OBD-II vehicles state that the vehicle computer must be capable of testing for, and determining, if the exhaust emissions are within 1.5 times the FTP limits. To achieve this goal, the computer must do the following:

1. Test all exhaust emission system components for correct operation.

2. Actively operate the system and measure the results.

3. Continuously monitor all aspects of the engine operation to be certain that the exhaust emissions do not exceed 1.5 times the FTP.

4. Check engine operation for misfire.

5. Turn on the MIL (check engine) if the computer senses a fault in a circuit or system.

6. Record a **freeze-frame,** which is a snapshot of all of the engine data at the time the DTC was set.

7. Flash the MIL if an engine misfire occurs that could damage the catalytic converter.

DIAGNOSTIC EXECUTIVE AND TASK MANAGER

On OBD-II systems, the PCM incorporates a special segment of software. On Ford and GM systems, this software is called the **diagnostic executive.** On Chrysler systems, it is called the **task manager.** This software program is designed to manage the operation of all OBD-II monitors by controlling the sequence of steps necessary to execute the diagnostic tests and monitors.

MONITORS

A monitor is an organized method of testing a specific part of the system. Monitors are simply tests that the computer performs to evaluate components and systems. If a component or system failure is detected while a monitor is running, a DTC will be stored and the MIL illuminated by the second trip. The two types of monitors are continuous and noncontinuous.

CONTINUOUS MONITORS As required conditions are met, continuous monitors begin to run. These continuous monitors will run for the remainder of the vehicle drive cycle. The three continuous monitors are as follows:

- **Comprehensive component monitor (CCM).** This monitor watches the sensors and actuators in the OBD-II system. Sensor values are constantly compared with known-good values stored in the PCM's memory.

  The CCM is an internal program in the PCM designed to monitor a failure in any electronic component or circuit (including emission-related and non-emission-related circuits) that provide input or output signals to the PCM. The PCM considers that an input or output signal is inoperative when a failure exists due to an open circuit, out-of-range value, or if an onboard rationality check fails. If an emission-related fault is detected, the PCM will set a code and activate the MIL (requires two consecutive trips).

  Many PCM sensors and output devices are tested at key-on or immediately after engine start-up. However, some devices, such as the IAC, are only tested by the CCM after the engine meets certain engine conditions. The number of times the CCM must detect a fault before it will activate the MIL depends upon the manufacturer, but most require two consecutive trips to activate the MIL. The components tested by the CCM include:

  Four-wheel-drive low switch

  Brake switch

  Camshaft (CMP) and crankshaft (CKP) sensors

  Clutch switch (manual transmissions/transaxles only)

  Cruise servo switch

  Engine coolant temperature (ECT) sensor

  EVAP purge sensor or switch

  Fuel composition sensor

  Intake air temperature (IAT) sensor

  Knock sensor (KS)

  Manifold absolute pressure (MAP) sensor

Mass airflow (MAF) sensor

Throttle-position (TP) sensor

Transmission temperature sensor

Transmission turbine speed sensor

Vacuum sensor

Vehicle speed (VS) sensor

EVAP canister purge and EVAP purge vent solenoid

Idle air control (IAC) solenoid

Ignition control system

Transmission torque converter clutch solenoid

Transmission shift solenoids

- **Misfire monitor.** This monitor looks at engine misfire. The PCM uses the information received from the crankshaft position sensor (CKP) to calculate the time between the edges of the reluctor, as well as the rotational speed and acceleration. By comparing the acceleration of each firing event, the PCM can determine if a cylinder is not firing correctly.

  Misfire type A. Upon detection of a misfire type A (200 revolutions), which would cause catalyst damage, the MIL will blink once per second during the actual misfire, and a DTC will be stored.

  Misfire type B. Upon detection of a misfire type B (1,000 revolutions), which will exceed 1.5 times the EPA federal test procedure (FTP) standard or cause a vehicle to fail an inspection and maintenance tailpipe emissions test, the MIL will illuminate and a DTC will be stored.

The DTC associated with multiple cylinder misfire for a type A or type B misfire is DTC P0300. The DTCs associated with an individual cylinder misfire for a type A or type B misfire are DTCs P0301, P0302, P0303, P0304, P0305, P0306, P0307, P0308, P0309, and P0310.

- **Fuel trim monitor.** The PCM continuously monitors short- and long-term fuel trim. Constantly updated adaptive fuel tables are stored in long-term memory (KAM), and used by the PCM for compensation due to wear and aging of the fuel system components. The MIL will illuminate when the PCM determines the fuel trim values have reached and stayed at their limits for too long a period of time.

NONCONTINUOUS MONITORS   Noncontinuous monitors run (at most) once per vehicle drive cycle. The noncontinuous monitors are as follows:

O2S monitor

O2S heater monitor

Catalyst monitor

EGR monitor

EVAP monitor

Secondary AIR monitor

Transmission monitor

PCV system monitor

Thermostat monitor

Once a noncontinuous monitor has run to completion, it will not be run again until the conditions are met during the next vehicle drive cycle. Also after a noncontinuous monitor has run to completion, the readiness status on your scan tool will show "complete" or "done" for that monitor. Monitors that have not run to completion will show up on your scanner as "incomplete."

OBD-II MONITOR INFORMATION

COMPREHENSIVE COMPONENT MONITOR   The circuits and components covered by the comprehensive component monitor (CCM) do not include those directly monitored by another monitor.

However, OBD II also requires that inputs from powertrain components to the PCM be tested for **rationality,** and that outputs to powertrain components from the PCM be tested for **functionality.** Both inputs and outputs are to be checked *electrically.* Rationality checks refer to a PCM comparison of input value to values.

Example:

TPS	3 V
MAP	18 in./Hg
RPM	700 RPM
PRNDL	Park

NOTE: Comprehensive component monitors are continuous. Therefore enabling conditions do not apply.

- Monitor runs continuously
- Monitor includes sensors, switches, relays, solenoids, and PCM hardware
- All are checked for opens, shorts-to-ground, and shorts-to-voltage
- Inputs are checked for rationality
- Outputs are checked for functionality
- Most are one-trip DTCs
- Freeze-frame is priority 3
- Three consecutive good trips are used to extinguish the MIL
- Forty warm-up cycles are used to erase DTC and freeze-frame
- Two minutes run time without reoccurrence of the fault constitutes a "good trip"

CONTINUOUS RUNNING MONITORS

- Monitors run continuously, only stop if they fail
- Fuel system: rich/lean
- Misfire: catalyst damaging/FTP (emissions)
- Two-trip faults (except early generation catalyst damaging misfire)
- MIL, DTC, freeze-frame after two consecutive faults
- Freeze-frame is priority 2 on first trip
- Freeze-frame is priority 4 on maturing trip
- Three consecutive good trips in a similar condition window are used to extinguish the MIL
- Forty warm-up cycles are used to erase DTC and freeze-frame (80 to erase one-trip failure if similar conditions cannot be met)

ONCE PER TRIP MONITORS

- Monitor runs once per trip, pass or fail
- O$_2$ response, O$_2$ heaters, EGR, purge flow EVAP leak, secondary air, catalyst
- Two-trip DTCs
- MIL, DTC, freeze-frame after two consecutive faults
- Freeze-frame is priority 1 on first trip
- Freeze-frame is priority 3 on maturing trip

- Three consecutive good trips are used to extinguish the MIL
- Forty warm-up cycles are used to erase DTC and freeze-frame

EXPONENTIALLY WEIGHTED MOVING AVERAGE (EWMA) MONITORS

The **exponentially weighted moving average (EWMA) monitor** is a mathematical method used to determine performance.

- Catalyst monitor
- EGR monitor
- PCM runs six consecutive failed tests; fails in one trip
- Three consecutive failed tests on next trip, then fails
- Freeze-frame is priority 3
- Three consecutive good trips are used to extinguish the MIL
- Forty warm-up cycles are used to erase DTC and freeze-frame

NONCONTINUOUS MONITORS

Noncontinuous monitors run (at most) once per vehicle drive cycle. The noncontinuous monitors are as follows:

O2S monitor

O2S heater monitor

Catalyst monitor

EGR monitor

EVAP monitor

Secondary AIR monitor

Transmission monitor

PCV system monitor

Thermostat monitor

Once a noncontinuous monitor has run to completion, it will not be run again until the conditions are met during the next vehicle drive cycle. Also after a noncontinuous monitor has run to completion, the readiness status on your scan tool will show "complete" or "done" for that monitor. Monitors that have not run to completion will show up on your scanner as "incomplete."

ENABLING CRITERIA

With so many different tests (monitors) to run, the PCM needs an internal director to keep track of when each monitor should run. As mentioned, different manufacturers have different names for this director, such as the diagnostic executive or the task manager. Each monitor has enabling criteria. These criteria are a set of conditions that must be met before the task manager will give the go-ahead for each monitor to run. Most enabling criteria follow simple logic, for example:

- The task manager will not authorize the start of the O2S monitor until the engine has reached operating temperature and the system has entered closed loop.

- The task manager will not authorize the start of the EGR monitor when the engine is at idle, because the EGR is always closed at this time.

Because each monitor is responsible for testing a different part of the system, the enabling criteria can differ greatly from one monitor to the next. The task manager must decide when each monitor should run, and in what order, to avoid confusion.

There may be a conflict if two monitors were to run at the same time. The results of one monitor might also be tainted if a second monitor were to run simultaneously. In such cases, the task manager decides which monitor has a higher priority. Some monitors also depend on the results of other monitors before they can run.

A monitor may be classified as pending if a failed sensor or other system fault is keeping it from running on schedule.

The task manager may suspend a monitor if the conditions are not correct to continue. For example, if the catalyst monitor is running during a road test and the PCM detects a misfire, the catalyst monitor will be suspended for the duration of the misfire.

TRIP   A trip is defined as a key-on condition that contains the necessary conditions for a particular test to be performed followed by a key-off. These conditions are called the **enable criteria.** For example, for the EGR test to be performed, the engine must be at normal operating temperature and decelerating for a minimum amount of time. Some tests are performed when the engine is cold, whereas others require that the vehicle be cruising at a steady highway speed.

WARM-UP CYCLE   Once a MIL is deactivated, the original code will remain in memory until 40 warm-up cycles are completed without the fault reappearing. A warm-up cycle is defined as a trip with an engine temperature increase of at least 40°F and where engine temperature reaches at least 160°F (71°C).

MIL CONDITION: OFF   This condition indicates that the PCM has not detected any faults in an emissions-related component or system, or that the MIL circuit is not working.

MIL CONDITION: ON STEADY   This condition indicates a fault in an emissions-related component or system that could affect the vehicle emission levels.

MIL CONDITION: FLASHING   This condition indicates a misfire or fuel control system fault that could damage the catalytic converter.

NOTE: In a misfire condition with the MIL on steady, if the driver reaches a vehicle speed and load condition with the engine misfiring at a level that could cause catalyst damage, the MIL would start flashing. It would continue to flash until engine speed and load conditions caused the level of misfire to subside. Then the MIL would go back to the on-steady condition. This situation might result in a customer complaint of a MIL with an intermittent flashing condition.

MIL: OFF   The PCM will turn off the MIL if any of the following actions or conditions occur:

- The codes are cleared with a scan tool.
- Power to the PCM is removed at the battery or with the PCM power fuse for an extended period of time (may be up to several hours or longer).
- A vehicle is driven on three consecutive trips with a warm-up cycle and meets all code set conditions without the PCM detecting any faults.

The PCM will set a code if a fault is detected that could cause tailpipe emissions to exceed 1.5 times the FTP standard; however, the PCM will not deactivate the MIL until the vehicle has been driven on three consecutive trips with vehicle conditions similar to actual conditions present when the fault was detected. This is not merely three vehicle start-ups and trips. It means three trips during which certain engine operating conditions are met so that the OBD-II monitor that found the fault can run again and pass the diagnostic test.

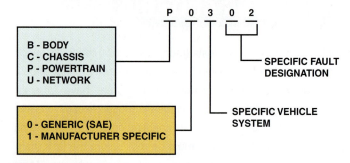

FIGURE 19–2 OBD-II DTC identification format.

EXAMPLE: P0302 = CYLINDER #2 MISFIRE DETECTED

OBD-II DTC NUMBERING DESIGNATION

A scan tool is required to retrieve DTCs from an OBD-II vehicle. Every OBD-II scan tool will be able to read all generic **Society of Automotive Engineers (SAE)** DTCs from any vehicle. ● **SEE FIGURE 19–2** for definitions and explanations of OBD alphanumeric DTCs. The diagnostic trouble codes (DTCs) are grouped into major categories, depending on the location of the fault on the system involved.

> Pxxx codes—powertrain DTCs (engine, transmission-related faults)
>
> Bxxx codes—body DTCs (accessories, interior-related faults)
>
> Cxxx codes—chassis DTCs (suspension and steering-related faults)
>
> Uxxx codes—network DTCs (module communication-related faults)

DTC NUMBERING EXPLANATION
The number in the hundredth position indicates the specific vehicle system or subgroup that failed. This position should be consistent for P0xxx and P1xxx type codes. The following numbers and systems were established by SAE:

- P0100—Air metering and fuel system fault
- P0200—Fuel system (fuel injector only) fault
- P0300—Ignition system or misfire fault
- P0400—Emission control system fault
- P0500—Idle speed control, vehicle speed (VS) sensor fault
- P0600—Computer output circuit (relay, solenoid, etc.) fault
- P0700—Transaxle, transmission faults

NOTE: The tens and ones numbers indicate the part of the system at fault.

TYPES OF DTCs
Not all OBD-II DTCs are of the same importance for exhaust emissions. Each type of DTC has different requirements for it to set, and the computer will only turn on the MIL for emissions-related DTCs.

TYPE A CODES A type A DTC is emission-related and will cause the MIL to be turned on the *first trip* if the computer has detected a problem. Engine misfire or a very rich or lean air–fuel ratio, for example, would cause a type A DTC. These codes alert the driver to an emission problem that may cause damage to the catalytic converter.

TYPE B CODES A type B code will be stored and the MIL will be turned on during the *second consecutive trip*, alerting the driver to the fact that a diagnostic test was performed and failed.

NOTE: Type A and B codes are emission-related codes that will cause the lighting of the malfunction indicator lamp (MIL), usually labeled "check engine" or "service engine soon."

TYPE C AND D CODES. Type C and D codes are for use with non-emission-related diagnostic tests; they will cause the lighting of a "service" lamp (if the vehicle is so equipped). Type C codes are also called type C1 codes and D codes are also called type C0 codes.

DIAGNOSTIC TROUBLE CODE PRIORITY
CARB has also mandated that all diagnostic trouble codes (DTCs) be stored according to individual priority. DTCs with a higher priority overwrite those with a lower priority. The OBD-II System DTC Priority is listed below.

> Priority 0—Non-emission-related codes
>
> Priority 1—One-trip failure of two-trip fault for non-fuel, non-misfire codes
>
> Priority 2—One-trip failure of two-trip fault for fuel or misfire codes
>
> Priority 3—Two-trip failure or matured fault of non-fuel, non-misfire codes
>
> Priority 4—Two-trip failure or matured fault for fuel or misfire codes

Monitor Name	Monitor Type (How Often It Completes)	Number of Faults on Separate Trips to Set a Pending DTC	Number of Separate Consecutive Trips to Light MIL, Store a DTC	Number of Trips with No Faults to Erase a Maturing DTC	Number of Trips with No Fault to Turn the MIL Off	Number of Warm-Up Cycles to Erase DTC after MIL Is Turned Off
CCM	Continuous (when trip conditions allow it)	1	2	1–Trip	3–Trips	40
Catalyst	Once per drive cycle	1	3	1	3–OBD-II drive cycle	40
Misfire Type A	Continuous		1		3–Similar conditions	80
Misfire Type B	Continuous	1	2	1	3–Similar conditions	80
Fuel System	Continuous	1	2	1	3–Similar conditions	80
Oxygen Sensor	Once per trip	1	2	1–Trip	3–Trips	40
EGR	Once per trip	1	2	1–Trip	3–Trips	40
EVAP	Once per trip	1	1	1–Trip	3–Trips	40
AIR	Once per trip	1	2	1–Trip	3–Trips	40

CHART 19–1

PCM Determination of Faults Chart

OBD-II FREEZE-FRAME

To assist the service technician, OBD II requires the computer to take a "snapshot" or freeze-frame of all data at the instant an emission-related DTC is set. A scan tool is required to retrieve this data.

NOTE: Although OBD II requires that just one freeze-frame of data be stored, the instant an emission-related DTC is set, vehicle manufacturers usually provide expanded data about the DTC beyond that required. However, retrieving this enhanced data usually requires the use of the vehicle-specific scan tool.

Freeze-frame items include:

- Calculated load value
- Engine speed (RPM)
- Short-term and long-term fuel trim percent
- Fuel system pressure (on some vehicles)
- Vehicle speed (mph)
- Engine coolant temperature
- Intake manifold pressure
- Closed-open-loop status
- Fault code that triggered the freeze-frame
- If a misfire code is set, identify which cylinder is misfiring

A DTC should not be cleared from the vehicle computer memory unless the fault has been corrected and the technician is so directed by the diagnostic procedure. If the problem that caused the DTC to be set has been corrected, the computer will automatically clear the DTC after 40 consecutive warm-up cycles with no further faults detected (misfire and excessively rich or lean condition codes require 80 warm-up cycles). The codes can also be erased by using a scan tool. **SEE CHART 19–1**.

NOTE: Disconnecting the battery may not erase OBD-II DTCs or freeze-frame data. Most vehicle manufacturers recommend using a scan tool to erase DTCs rather than disconnecting the battery, because the memory for the radio, seats, and learned engine operating parameters is lost if the battery is disconnected.

? FREQUENTLY ASKED QUESTION

What Are Pending Codes?

Pending codes are set when operating conditions are met and the component or circuit is not within the normal range, yet the conditions have not yet been met to set a DTC. For example, a sensor may require two consecutive faults before a DTC is set. If a scan tool displays a pending code or a failure, a driveability concern could also be present. The pending code can help the technician to determine the root cause before the customer complains of a check engine light indication.

ENABLING CONDITIONS OR CRITERIA

These are the exact engine operating conditions required for a diagnostic monitor to run.

Example:

Specific RPM
Specific ECT, MAP, run time, VSS, etc.

PENDING Under some situations the PCM will not run a monitor if the MIL is illuminated and a fault is stored from another monitor. In these situations, the PCM postpones monitors pending a resolution of the original fault. The PCM does not run the test until the problem is remedied.

For example, when the MIL is illuminated for an oxygen sensor fault, the PCM does not run the catalyst monitor until the oxygen sensor fault is remedied. Since the catalyst monitor is based on signals from the oxygen sensor, running the test would produce inaccurate results.

CONFLICT There are also situations when the PCM does not run a monitor if another monitor is in progress. In these situations, the effects of another monitor running could result in an erroneous failure. If this conflict is present, the monitor is not run until the conflicting condition passes. Most likely, the monitor will run later after the conflicting monitor has passed.

For example, if the fuel system monitor is in progress, the PCM does not run the EGR monitor. Since both tests monitor changes in air–fuel ratio and adaptive fuel compensation, the monitors conflict with each other.

SUSPEND Occasionally, the PCM may not allow a two-trip fault to mature. The PCM will suspend the maturing fault if a condition exists that may induce erroneous failure. This prevents illuminating the MIL for the wrong fault and allows more precise diagnosis.

For example, if the PCM is storing a one-trip fault for the oxygen sensor and the EGR monitor, the PCM may still run the EGR monitor but will suspend the results until the oxygen sensor monitor either passes or fails. At that point, the PCM can determine if the EGR system is actually failing or if an oxygen sensor is failing.

PCM TESTS

RATIONALITY TEST While input signals to the PCM are constantly being monitored for electrical opens and shorts, they are also tested for rationality. This means that the input signal is compared against other inputs and information to see if it makes sense under the current conditions.

PCM sensor inputs that are checked for rationality include:

- MAP sensor
- O_2 sensor
- ECT
- Camshaft position sensor (CMP)
- VS sensor
- Crankshaft position sensor (CKP)
- IAT sensor
- TP sensor
- Ambient air temperature sensor
- Power steering switch
- O_2 sensor heater
- Engine controller
- Brake switch
- P/N switch
- Transmission controls

FUNCTIONALITY TEST A functionality test refers to PCM inputs checking the operation of the outputs.

Example:

PCM commands the IAC open; expected change in engine RPM is not seen
IAC 60 counts
RPM 700 RPM

PCM outputs that are checked for functionality include:

- EVAP canister purge solenoid
- EVAP purge vent solenoid
- Cooling fan
- Idle air control solenoid
- Ignition control system
- Transmission torque converter clutch solenoid
- Transmission shift solenoids (A,B,1–2, etc.)

ELECTRICAL TEST Refers to the PCM check of both input and outputs for the following:

- Open
- Shorts
- Ground

Example:

ECT

Shorted high (input to PCM) above capable voltage, i.e., 5-volt sensor with 12-volt input to PCM would indicate a short to voltage or a short high.

Monitor Type	Conditions to Set DTC and Illuminate MIL	Extinguish MIL	Clear DTC Criteria	Applicable DTC
Compre-hensive Monitor	Contin-uous 1-trip monitor	(See note below) Input and output failure—rationally, functionally, electrically	3 con-secutive pass trips	40 warm-up cycles	P0123

NOTE: The number of times the comprehensive component monitor must detect a fault depends on the vehicle manufacturer. On some vehicles, the comprehensive component monitor will activate the MIL as soon as it detects a fault. On other vehicles, the comprehensive component monitor must fail two times in a row.

- Freeze-frame captured on first-trip failure.
- Enabling conditions: Many PCM sensors and output devices are tested at key-on or immediately after engine start-up. However, some devices (ECT, idle speed control) are only tested by the comprehensive component monitor after the engine meets particular engine conditions.
- Pending: No pending condition
- Conflict: No conflict conditions
- Suspend: No suspend conditions

GLOBAL OBD-II

All OBD-II vehicles must be able to display data on a global (also called *generic*) scan tool under nine different modes of operation. These modes include:

Mode One	Current power train data (**parameter identification** display or **PID**)
Mode Two	Freeze-frame data
Mode Three	Diagnostic trouble codes
Mode Four	Clear and reset diagnostic trouble codes (DTCs), freeze-frame data, and readiness status monitors for noncontinuous monitors only
Mode Five	Oxygen sensor monitor test results
Mode Six	Onboard monitoring of test results for non-continuously monitored systems
Mode Seven	Onboard monitoring of test results for con-tinuously monitored systems
Mode Eight	Bidirectional control of onboard systems
Mode Nine	Module identification

The global (generic) data is used by most state emission programs. Global OBD-II displays often use hexadecimal numbers, which use 16 numbers instead of 10. The numbers 0 to 9 (zero counts as a number) make up the first 10 and then capital letters A to F complete the 16 numbers. To help identify the number as being in a hexadecimal format, a dollar sign ($) is used in front of the number or letter. See the conversion chart below:

Decimal Number	Hexadecimal Code
0	$0
1	$1
2	$2
3	$3
4	$4
5	$5
6	$6
7	$7
8	$8
9	$9
10	$A
11	$B
12	$C
13	$D
14	$E
15	$F

Hexadecimal coding is also used to identify tests (**test identification [TID]** and **component identification [CID]**).

FREQUENTLY ASKED QUESTION

How Can You Tell Generic from Factory?

When using a scan tool on an OBD-II-equipped vehicle, if the display asks for make, model, and year, then the factory or enhanced part of the PCM is being accessed. If the generic or global part of the PCM is being scanned, then there is no need to know the vehicle details.

DIAGNOSING PROBLEMS USING MODE SIX

Mode six information can be used to diagnose faults by following three steps:

1. Check the monitor status before starting repairs. This step will show how the system failed.

2. Look at the component or parameter that triggered the fault. This step will help pin down the root cause of the failure.

3. Look to the monitor enable criteria, which will show what it takes to fail or pass the monitor.

SUMMARY

1. If the MIL is on, retrieve the DTC and follow the manufacturer's recommended procedure to find the root cause of the problem.

2. All monitors must have the enable criteria achieved before a test is performed.

3. OBD-II vehicles use common generic DTCs.

4. OBD II includes generic (SAE), as well as vehicle manufacturer-specific DTCs, and data display.

REVIEW QUESTIONS

1. What does the PCM do during a trip to test emission-related components?

2. What is the difference between a type A and type B OBD-II DTC?

3. What is the difference between a trip and a warm-up cycle?

4. What could cause the MIL to flash?

CHAPTER QUIZ

1. A freeze-frame is generated on an OBD-II vehicle _____.
   a. When a type C or D diagnostic trouble code is set
   b. When a type A or B diagnostic trouble code is set
   c. Every other trip
   d. When the PCM detects a problem with the O2S

2. An ignition misfire or fuel mixture problem is an example of what type of DTC?
   a. Type A
   b. Type B
   c. Type C
   d. Type D

3. The comprehensive component monitor checks computer-controlled devices for_____.
   a. opens
   b. rationality
   c. shorts-to-ground
   d. All of the above

4. OBD II has been on all passenger vehicles in the United States since _____.
   a. 1986
   b. 1991
   c. 1996
   d. 2000

5. Which is a continuous monitor?
   a. Fuel system monitor
   b. EGR monitor
   c. Oxygen sensor monitor
   d. Catalyst monitor

6. DTC P0302 is a _____.
   a. Generic DTC
   b. Vehicle manufacturer-specific DTC
   c. Idle speed-related DTC
   d. Transmission/transaxle-related DTC

7. Global (generic) OBD II contains some data in what format?
   a. Plain English
   b. Hexadecimal
   c. Roman numerals
   d. All of the above

8. By looking at the way diagnostic trouble codes are formatted, which DTC could indicate that the gas cap is loose or defective?
   a. P0221   c. P0442
   b. P1301   d. P1603

9. The computer will automatically clear a DTC if there are no additional detected faults after _____.
   a. Forty consecutive warm-up cycles
   b. Eighty warm-up cycles
   c. Two consecutive trips
   d. Four key-on/key-off cycles

10. A pending code is set when a fault is detected on _____.
    a. A one-trip fault item
    b. The first fault of a two-trip failure
    c. The catalytic converter efficiency
    d. Thermostat problem (too long to closed-loop status)

chapter 20

TEMPERATURE SENSORS

OBJECTIVES

After studying Chapter 20, the reader will be able to:

1. Prepare for ASE Engine Performance (A8) certification test content area "E" (Computerized Engine Controls Diagnosis and Repair).

2. Explain the purpose and function of the ECT and IAT temperature sensors.

3. Describe how to test temperature sensors.

4. Discuss how automatic fluid temperature sensor valves can affect transmission operation.

KEY TERMS

Cylinder head temperature (CHT) 342

Engine coolant temperature (ECT) 333

Engine fuel temperature (EFT) 342

Negative temperature coefficient (NTC) 333

Throttle-body temperature (TBT) 340

Transmission fluid temperature (TFT) 341

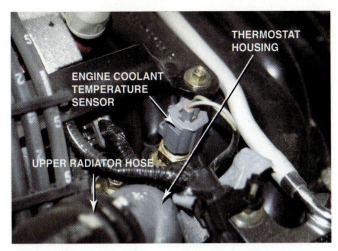

FIGURE 20–1 A typical engine coolant temperature (ECT) sensor. ECT sensors are located near the thermostat housing on most engines.

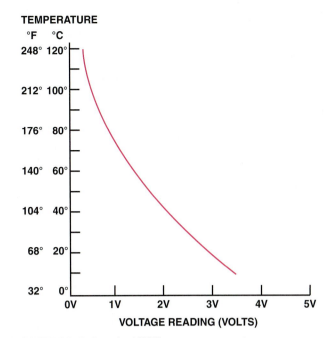

FIGURE 20–2 A typical ECT sensor temperature versus voltage curve.

ENGINE COOLANT TEMPERATURE SENSORS

PURPOSE AND FUNCTION Computer-equipped vehicles use an **engine coolant temperature (ECT)** sensor. When the engine is cold, the fuel mixture must be richer to prevent stalling and engine stumble. When the engine is warm, the fuel mixture can be leaner to provide maximum fuel economy with the lowest possible exhaust emissions. Because the computer controls spark timing and fuel mixture, it will need to know the engine temperature. An engine coolant temperature sensor (ECT) screwed into the engine coolant passage will provide the computer with this information. ● **SEE FIGURE 20–1**. This will be the most important (high-authority) sensor while the engine is cold. The ignition timing can also be tailored to engine (coolant) temperature. A hot engine cannot have the spark timing as far advanced as can a cold engine. The ECT sensor is also used as an important input for the following:

- Idle air control (IAC) position
- Oxygen sensor closed-loop status
- Canister purge on/off times
- Idle speed

ECT SENSOR CONSTRUCTION Engine coolant temperature sensors are constructed of a semiconductor material that decreases in resistance as the temperature of the sensor increases. Coolant sensors have very high resistance when the coolant is cold and low resistance when the coolant is hot. This is referred to as having a **negative temperature coefficient (NTC)**,

which is opposite to the situation with most other electrical components. ● **SEE FIGURE 20–2**. Therefore, if the coolant sensor has a poor connection (high resistance) at the wiring connector, the computer will supply a richer-than-normal fuel mixture based on the resistance of the coolant sensor. Poor fuel economy and a possible-rich code can be caused by a defective sensor or high resistance in the sensor wiring. If the sensor was shorted or defective and had too low a resistance, a leaner-than-normal fuel mixture would be supplied to the engine. A too-lean fuel mixture can cause driveability problems and a possible-lean computer code.

STEPPED ECT CIRCUITS Some vehicle manufacturers use a step-up resistor to effectively broaden the range of the ECT sensor. Chrysler and General Motors vehicles use the same sensor as a non-stepped ECT circuit, but instead apply the sensor voltage through two different resistors.

- When the temperature is cold, usually below 120°F (50°C), the ECT sensor voltage is applied through a high-value resistor inside the PCM.
- When the temperature is warm, usually above 120°F (50°C), the ECT sensor voltage is applied through a much lower resistance value inside the PCM. ● **SEE FIGURE 20–3**.

The purpose of this extra circuit is to give the PCM a more accurate reading of the engine coolant temperature compared to the same sensor with only one circuit. ● **SEE FIGURE 20–4**.

FIGURE 20–3 A typical two-step ECT circuit showing that when the coolant temperature is low, the PCM applies a 5-volt reference voltage to the ECT sensor through a higher resistance compared to when the temperature is higher.

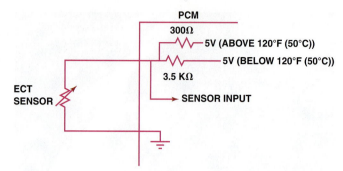

FIGURE 20–4 The transition between steps usually occurs at a temperature that would not interfere with cold engine starts or the cooling fan operation. In this example, the transition occurs when the sensor voltage is about 1 volt and rises to about 3.6 volts.

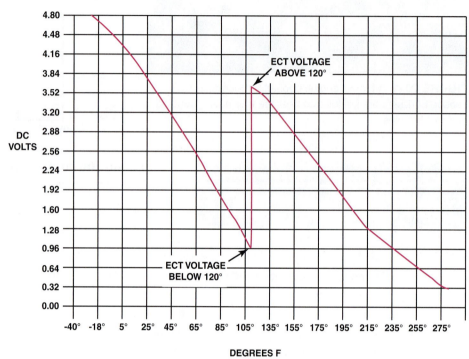

TESTING THE ENGINE COOLANT TEMPERATURE SENSOR

TESTING THE ENGINE COOLANT TEMPERATURE BY VISUAL INSPECTION

The correct functioning of the engine coolant temperature (ECT) sensor depends on the following items that should be checked or inspected:

- **Properly filled cooling system.** Check that the radiator reservoir bottle is full and that the radiator itself is filled to the top.

CAUTION: Be sure that the radiator is cool before removing the radiator cap to avoid being scalded by hot coolant.

The ECT sensor must be submerged in coolant to be able to indicate the proper coolant temperature.

- **Proper pressure maintained by the radiator cap.** If the radiator cap is defective and cannot allow the cooling

system to become pressurized, air pockets could develop. These air pockets could cause the engine to operate at a hotter-than-normal temperature and prevent proper temperature measurement, especially if the air pockets occur around the sensor.

- **Proper antifreeze–water mixture.** Most vehicle manufacturers recommend a 50/50 mixture of antifreeze and water as the best compromise between freezing protection and heat transfer ability.

- **Proper operation of the cooling fan.** If the cooling fan does not operate correctly, the engine may overheat.

TESTING THE ECT USING A MULTIMETER

Both the resistance (in ohms) and the voltage drop across the sensor can be measured and compared with specifications.

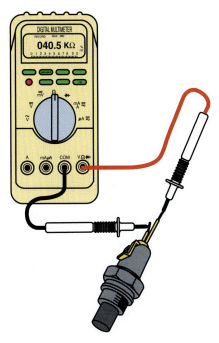

FIGURE 20–5 Measuring the resistance of the ECT sensor. The resistance measurement can then be compared with specifications. *(Courtesy of Fluke Corporation)*

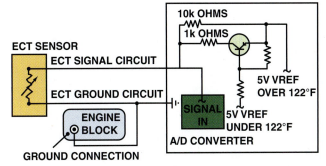

FIGURE 20–6 When the voltage drop reaches approximately 1.20 volts, the PCM turns on a transistor. The transistor connects a 1-kΩ resistor in parallel with the 10-kΩ resistor. Total circuit resistance now drops to around 909 ohms. This function allows the PCM to have full binary control at cold temperatures up to approximately 122°F, and a second full binary control at temperatures greater than 122°F.

● **SEE FIGURE 20–5.** See the following charts showing examples of typical engine coolant temperature sensor specifications. Some vehicles use the PCM to attach another resistor in the ECT circuit to provide a more accurate measure of the engine temperature. ● **SEE FIGURE 20–6.**

If resistance values match the approximate coolant temperature and there is still a coolant sensor trouble code, the problem is generally in the wiring between the sensor and the computer. Always consult the manufacturers' recommended procedures for checking this wiring. If the resistance values do not match, the sensor may need to be replaced.

General Motors ECT Sensor with Pull-up Resistor

°F	°C	Ohms	Voltage Drop Across Sensor
−40	−40	100,000 +	4.95
18	−8	14,628	4.68
32	0	9,420	4.52
50	10	5,670	4.25
68	20	3,520	3.89
86	30	2,238	3.46
104	40	1,459	2.97
122	50	973	2.47
140	60	667	2.00
158	70	467	1.59
176	80	332	1.25
194	90	241	0.97
212	100	177	0.75

General Motors ECT Sensor without Pull-up Resistor

°F	°C	Ohms	Voltage Drop Across Sensor
−40	−40	100,000	5
−22	−30	53,000	4.78
−4	−20	29,000	4.34
14	−10	16,000	3.89
32	0	9,400	3.45
50	10	5,700	3.01
68	20	3,500	2.56
86	30	2,200	1.80
104	40	1,500	1.10
122	50	970	3.25
140	60	670	2.88
158	70	470	2.56
176	80	330	2.24
194	90	240	1.70
212	100	177	1.42
230	110	132	1.15
248	120	100	.87

Ford ECT Sensor

°F	°C	Resistance (Ω)	Voltage (V)
50	10	58,750	3.52
68	20	37,300	3.06
86	30	24,270	2.26
104	40	16,150	2.16
122	50	10,970	1.72
140	60	7,600	1.35
158	70	5,370	1.04
176	80	3,840	0.80
194	90	2,800	0.61
212	100	2,070	0.47
230	110	1,550	0.36
248	120	1,180	0.28

Chrysler ECT Sensor without Pull-up Resistor

°F	°C	Voltage (V)
130	54	3.77
140	60	3.60
150	66	3.40
160	71	3.20
170	77	3.02
180	82	2.80
190	88	2.60
200	93	2.40
210	99	2.20
220	104	2.00
230	110	1.80
240	116	1.62
250	121	1.45

Chrysler ECT Sensor with Pull-up Resistor

°F	°C	Volts
−20	−29	4.70
−10	−23	4.57
0	−18	4.45
10	−12	4.30
20	−7	4.10
30	−1	3.90
40	4	3.60
50	10	3.30
60	16	3.00
70	21	2.75
80	27	2.44
90	32	2.15
100	38	1.83

	Pull-up Resistor Switched by PCM	
110	43	4.20
120	49	4.10
130	54	4.00
140	60	3.60
150	66	3.40
160	71	3.20
170	77	3.02
180	82	2.80
190	88	2.60
200	93	2.40
210	99	2.20
220	104	2.00
230	110	1.80
240	116	1.62
250	121	1.45

Nissan ECT Sensor

°F	°C	Resistance (Ω)
14	−10	7,000–11,400
68	20	2,100–2,900
122	50	680–1,000
176	80	260–390
212	100	180–200

Mercedes ECT

°F	°C	Voltage (DCV)
60	20	3.5
86	30	3.1
104	40	2.7
122	50	2.3
140	60	1.9
158	70	1.5
176	80	1.2
194	90	1.0
212	100	0.8

European Bosch ECT Sensor

°F	°C	Resistance (Ω)
32	0	6,500
50	10	4,000
68	20	3,000
86	30	2,000
104	40	1,500
122	50	900
140	60	650
158	70	500
176	80	375
194	90	295
212	100	230

Honda ECT Sensor (Resistance Chart)

°F	°C	Resistance (Ω)
0	−18	15,000
32	0	5,000
68	20	3,000
104	40	1,000
140	60	500
176	80	400
212	100	250

Honda ECT Sensor (Voltage Chart)

°F	°C	Voltage (V)
0	−18	4.70
10	−12	4.50
20	−7	4.29
30	−1	4.10
40	4	3.86
50	10	3.61
60	16	3.35
70	21	3.08
80	27	2.81
90	32	2.50
100	38	2.26
110	43	2.00
120	49	1.74
130	54	1.52
140	60	1.33
150	66	1.15
160	71	1.00
170	77	0.88
180	82	0.74
190	88	0.64
200	93	0.55
210	99	0.47

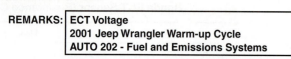

REMARKS:
ECT Voltage
2001 Jeep Wrangler Warm-up Cycle
AUTO 202 - Fuel and Emissions Systems

FORM SAVED TIME: 2/18/04 4:11:55 PM
UPLOAD TIME: 2/18/04 4:09:05 PM
METER ID: FLUKE 189 V2.02 0085510089

SHOW DATA: ALL GRAPH VIEW: ALL

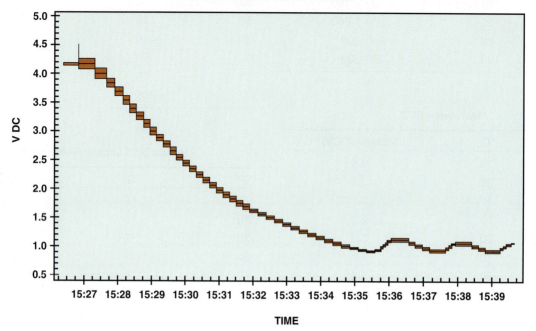

FIGURE 20–7 An ECT sensor being tested using a digital meter set to DC volts. A chart showing the voltage decrease of the ECT sensor as the temperature increases from a cold start. The bumps at the bottom of the waveform represent temperature decreases when the thermostat opens and is controlling coolant temperature.

TESTING THE ENGINE COOLANT TEMPERATURE SENSOR (CONTINUED)

Normal operating temperature varies with vehicle make and model. Some vehicles are equipped with a thermostat with an opening temperature of 180°F (82°C), whereas other vehicles use a thermostat that is 195°F (90°C) or higher. Before replacing the ECT sensor, be sure that the engine is operating at the temperature specified by the manufacturer. Most manufacturers recommend checking the ECT sensor after the cooling fan has cycled twice, indicating a fully warmed engine. To test for voltage at the ECT sensor, select DC volts on a digital meter and carefully back probe the sensor wire and read the voltage. ● SEE FIGURE 20–7.

NOTE: Many manufacturers install another resistor in parallel inside the computer to change the voltage drop across the ECT sensor. This is done to expand the scale of the ECT sensor and to make the sensor more sensitive. Therefore, if measuring *voltage* at the ECT sensor, check with the service manual for the proper voltage at each temperature.

TESTING THE ECT SENSOR USING A SCAN TOOL
Follow the scan tool manufacturer's instructions and connect a scan tool to the data link connector (DLC) of the vehicle. Comparing the temperature of the engine coolant as displayed on a scan tool with the actual temperature of the engine is an excellent method to test an engine coolant temperature sensor.

1. Record the scan tool temperature of the coolant (ECT).

2. Measure the actual temperature of the coolant using an infrared pyrometer or contact-type temperature probe.

NOTE: Often the coolant temperature gauge in the dash of the vehicle can be used to compare with the scan tool temperature. Although not necessarily accurate, it may help to diagnose a faulty sensor, especially if the temperature shown on the scan tool varies greatly from the temperature indicated on the dash gauge.

The maximum difference between the two readings should be 10°F (5°C). If the actual temperature varies by more than 10°F from the temperature indicated on the scan tool, check the ECT sensor wiring and connector for damage or corrosion. If the connector and wiring are okay, check the sensor with a DVOM for resistance and compare to the actual engine temperature chart. If that checks out okay, check the computer.

NOTE: Some manufacturers use two coolant sensors, one for the dash gauge and another one for the computer.

FIGURE 20–8 The IAT sensor on this General Motors 3800 V-6 engine is in the air passage duct between the air cleaner housing and the throttle body.

INTAKE AIR TEMPERATURE SENSOR

PURPOSE AND FUNCTION The intake air temperature (IAT) sensor is a negative temperature coefficient (NTC) thermistor that decreases in resistance as the temperature of the sensor increases. The IAT sensor can be located in one of the following locations:

- In the air cleaner housing
- In the air duct between the air filter and the throttle body, as shown in ● **FIGURE 20–8**
- Built into the mass air flow (MAF) or airflow sensor
- Screwed into the intake manifold where it senses the temperature of the air entering the cylinders

NOTE: An IAT installed in the intake manifold is the most likely to suffer damage due to an engine backfire, which can often destroy the sensor.

The purpose and function of the intake air temperature sensor is to provide the engine computer (PCM) the temperature of the air entering the engine. The IAT sensor information is used for fuel control (adding or subtracting fuel) and spark timing, depending on the temperature of incoming air.

- If the air temperature is cold, the PCM will modify the amount of fuel delivery and add fuel.
- If the air temperature is hot, the PCM will subtract the calculated amount of fuel.
- Spark timing is also changed, depending on the temperature of the air entering the engine. The timing is advanced if the temperature is cold and retarded from the base-programmed timing if the temperature is hot.
- Cold air is more dense, contains more oxygen, and therefore requires a richer mixture to achieve the proper air–fuel mixture. Air at 32°F (0°C) is 14% denser than air at 100°F (38°C).
- Hot air is less dense, contains less oxygen, and therefore requires less fuel to achieve the proper air–fuel mixture.

The IAT sensor is a low-authority sensor and is used by the computer to modify the amount of fuel and ignition timing as determined by the engine coolant temperature sensor.

The IAT sensor is used by the PCM as a backup in the event that the ECT sensor is determined to be inoperative.

Poor Fuel Economy? Black Exhaust Smoke? Look at the IAT

If the intake air temperature sensor is defective, it may be signaling the computer that the intake air temperature is extremely cold when in fact it is warm. In such a case the computer will supply a mixture that is much richer than normal.

If a sensor is physically damaged or electrically open, the computer will often set a diagnostic trouble code (DTC). This DTC is based on the fact that the sensor temperature did not change for a certain amount of time, usually about 8 minutes. If, however, the wiring or the sensor itself has excessive resistance, a DTC will not be set and the result will be lower-than-normal fuel economy, and in serious cases, black exhaust smoke from the tailpipe during acceleration.

INTAKE AIR TEMPERATURE SENSOR (CONTINUED)

NOTE: Some engines use a throttle-body temperature (TBT) sensor to sense the temperature of the air entering the engine, instead of an intake air temperature sensor.

Engine temperature is most accurately determined by looking at the engine coolant temperature (ECT) sensor. In certain conditions, the IAT has an effect on performance and driveability. One such condition is a warm engine being stopped in very cold weather. In this case, when the engine is restarted, the ECT may be near normal operating temperature such as 200°F (93°C) yet the air temperature could be −20°F (−30°C). In this case, the engine requires a richer mixture due to the cold air than the ECT would seem to indicate.

TESTING THE INTAKE AIR TEMPERATURE SENSOR

If the intake air temperature sensor circuit is damaged or faulty, a diagnostic trouble code (DTC) is set and the malfunction indicator lamp (MIL) may or may not turn on depending on the condition and the type and model of the vehicle. To diagnose the IAT sensor follow these steps:

STEP 1 After the vehicle has been allowed to cool for several hours, use a scan tool, observe the IAT, and compare it to the engine coolant temperature (ECT). The two temperatures should be within 5°F of each other.

STEP 2 Perform a thorough visual inspection of the sensor and the wiring. If the IAT is screwed into the intake manifold, remove the sensor and check for damage.

STEP 3 Check the voltage and compare to the following chart.

Intake Air Temperature Sensor Temperature vs. Resistance and Voltage Drop (Approximate)

°F	°C	Ohms	Voltage Drop Across the Sensor
−40	−40	100,000	4.95
+18	−8	15,000	4.68
32	0	9,400	4.52
50	10	5,700	4.25
68	20	3,500	3.89
86	30	2,200	3.46
104	40	1,500	2.97
122	50	1,000	2.47
140	60	700	2.00
158	70	500	1.59
176	80	300	1.25
194	90	250	0.97
212	100	200	0.75

TRANSMISSION FLUID TEMPERATURE SENSOR

The **transmission fluid temperature (TFT),** also called *transmission oil temperature (TOT),* sensor is an important sensor for the proper operation of the automatic transmission. A TFT sensor is a negative temperature coefficient (NTC) thermistor that decreases in resistance as the temperature of the sensor increases.

General Motors
Transaxle Sensor—Temperature to Resistance (approximate)

°F	°C	Resistance Ohms
32	0	7,987–10,859
50	10	4,934–6,407
68	20	3,106–3,923
86	30	1,991–2,483
104	40	1,307–1,611
122	50	878–1,067
140	60	605–728
158	70	425–507
176	80	304–359
194	90	221–259
212	100	163–190

Chrysler
Sensor Resistance (Ohms)—Transmission Temperature Sensor

°F	°C	Resistance Ohms
−40	−40	291,490–381,710
−4	−20	85,850–108,390
14	−10	49,250–61,430
32	0	29,330–35,990
50	10	17,990–21,810
68	20	11,370–13,610
77	25	9,120–10,880
86	30	7,370–8,750
104	40	4,900–5,750
122	50	3,330–3,880
140	60	2,310–2,670
158	70	1,630–1,870
176	80	1,170–1,340
194	90	860–970
212	100	640–720
230	110	480–540
248	120	370–410

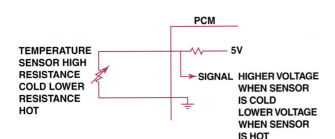

FIGURE 20–9 A typical temperature sensor circuit.

? FREQUENTLY ASKED QUESTION

What Exactly Is an NTC Sensor?

A negative temperature coefficient (NTC) thermistor is a semiconductor whose resistance decreases as the temperature increases. In other words, the sensor becomes more electrically conductive as the temperature increases. Therefore, when a voltage is applied, typically 5 volts, the signal voltage is high when the sensor is cold because the sensor has a high resistance and little current flows through to ground. ● SEE FIGURE 20–9.

However, when the temperature increases, the sensor becomes more electrically conductive and takes more of the 5 volts to ground, resulting in a lower signal voltage as the sensor warms.

Ford
Transmission Fluid Temperature

°F	°C	Resistance Ohms
−40 to −4	−40 to −20	967K–284K
−3 to 31	−19 to −1	284K–100K
32 to 68	0 to 20	100K–37K
69 to 104	21 to 40	37K–16K
105 to 158	41 to 70	16K–5K
159 to 194	71 to 90	5K–2.7K
195 to 230	91 to 110	2.7K–1.5K
231 to 266	111 to 130	1.5K–0.8K
267 to 302	131 to 150	0.8K–0.54K

The transmission fluid temperature signal is used by the Powertrain Control Module (PCM) to perform certain strategies based on the temperature of the automatic transmission fluid. For example:

- If the temperature of the automatic transmission fluid is low (typically below 32°F [0°C]), the shift points may be delayed and overdrive disabled. The torque converter clutch also may not be applied to assist in the heating of the fluid.

- If the temperature of the automatic transmission fluid is high (typically above 260°F [130°C]), the overdrive is disabled and the torque converter clutch is applied to help reduce the temperature of the fluid.

NOTE: Check service information for the exact shift strategy based on high and low transmission fluid temperatures for the vehicle being serviced.

CYLINDER HEAD TEMPERATURE SENSOR

Some vehicles are equipped with **cylinder head temperature (CHT)** sensors.

VW Golf

$$14°F (−10°C) = 11,600 \ \Omega$$

$$68°F (20°C) = 2,900 \ \Omega$$

$$176°F (80°C) = 390 \ \Omega$$

ENGINE FUEL TEMPERATURE (EFT) SENSOR

Some vehicles, such as many Ford vehicles that are equipped with an electronic returnless type of fuel injection, use an **engine fuel temperature (EFT)** sensor to give the PCM information regarding the temperature and, therefore, the density of the fuel.

EXHAUST GAS RECIRCULATION (EGR) TEMPERATURE SENSOR

Some engines, such as Toyota, are equipped with exhaust gas recirculation (EGR) temperature sensors. EGR is a well-established method for reduction of NO_X emissions in internal combustion engines. The exhaust gas contains unburned hydrocarbons, which are recirculated in the combustion process. Recirculation is controlled by valves, which operate as a function of exhaust gas speed, load, and temperature. The gas reaches a temperature of about 850°F (450°C) for which a special heavy-duty glass-encapsulated NTC sensor is available.

The PCM monitors the temperature in the exhaust passage between the EGR valve and the intake manifold. If the temperature increases when the EGR is commanded on, the PCM can determine that the valve or related components are functioning.

ENGINE OIL TEMPERATURE SENSOR

Engine oil temperature sensors are used on many General Motors vehicles and are used as an input to the oil life monitoring system. The computer program inside the PCM calculates engine oil life based on run time, engine RPM, and oil temperature.

TEMPERATURE SENSOR DIAGNOSTIC TROUBLE CODES

The OBD-II diagnostic trouble codes that relate to temperature sensors include both high- and low-voltage codes, as well as intermittent codes.

Diagnostic Trouble Code	Description	Possible Causes
P0112	IAT sensor low voltage	• IAT sensor internally shorted-to-ground • IAT sensor wiring shorted-to-ground • IAT sensor damaged by backfire (usually associated with IAT sensors that are mounted in the intake manifold) • Possible defective PCM
P0113	IAT sensor high voltage	• IAT sensor internally (electrically) open • IAT sensor signal, circuit, or ground circuit open • Possible defective PCM
P0117	ECT sensor low voltage	• ECT sensor internally shorted-to-ground • The ECT sensor circuit wiring shorted-to-ground • Possible defective PCM
P0118	ECT sensor high voltage	• ECT sensor internally (electrically) open • ECT sensor signal, circuit, or ground circuit open • Engine operating in an overheated condition • Possible defective PCM

SUMMARY

1. The ECT sensor is a high-authority sensor at engine start-up and is used for closed-loop control, as well as idle speed.
2. All temperature sensors decrease in resistance as the temperature increases. This is called negative temperature coefficient (NTC).
3. The ECT and IAT sensors can be tested visually, as well as by using a digital multimeter or a scan tool.
4. Some vehicle manufacturers use a stepped ECT circuit inside the PCM to broaden the accuracy of the sensor.
5. Other temperature sensors include transmission fluid temperature (TFT), engine fuel temperature (EFT), exhaust gas recirculation (EGR) temperature, and engine oil temperature.

REVIEW QUESTIONS

1. How does a typical NTC temperature sensor work?
2. What is the difference between a stepped and a non-stepped ECT circuit?
3. What temperature should be displayed on a scan tool if the ECT sensor is unplugged with the key on, engine off?
4. What are the three ways that temperature sensors can be tested?
5. If the transmission fluid temperature (TFT) sensor were to fail open (as if it were unplugged), what would the PCM do to the transmission shifting points?

1. The sensor that most determines fuel delivery when a fuel-injected engine is first started is the _____.
   a. O2S
   b. ECT sensor
   c. Engine MAP sensor
   d. IAT sensor

2. What happens to the voltage measured at the ECT sensor when the thermostat opens?
   a. Increases slightly
   b. Increases about 1 volt
   c. Decreases slightly
   d. Decreases about 1 volt

3. Two technicians are discussing a stepped ECT circuit. Technician A says that the sensor used for a stepped circuit is different than one used in a non-stepped circuit. Technician B says that a stepped ECT circuit uses different internal resistance inside the PCM. Which technician is correct?
   a. Technician A only
   b. Technician B only
   c. Both Technicians A and B
   d. Neither Technician A nor B

4. When testing an ECT sensor on a vehicle, a digital multimeter can be used and the signal wires back probed. What setting should the technician use to test the sensor?
   a. AC volts
   b. DC volts
   c. Ohms
   d. Hz (hertz)

5. When testing the ECT sensor with the connector disconnected, the technician should select what position on the DMM?
   a. AC volts
   b. DC volts
   c. Ohms
   d. Hz (hertz)

6. When checking the ECT sensor with a scan tool, about what temperature should be displayed if the connector is removed from the sensor with the key on, engine off?
   a. 284°F (140°C)
   b. 230°F (110°C)
   c. 120°F (50°C)
   d. −40°F (−40°C)

7. Two technicians are discussing the IAT sensor. Technician A says that the IAT sensor is more important to the operation of the engine (higher authority) than the ECT sensor. Technician B says that the PCM will add fuel if the IAT indicates that the incoming air temperature is cold. Which technician is correct?
   a. Technician A only
   b. Technician B only
   c. Both Technicians A and B
   d. Neither Technician A nor B

8. A typical IAT or ECT sensor reads about 3,000 ohms when tested using a DMM. This resistance represents a temperature of about _____.
   a. −40°F (−40°C)
   b. 70°F (20°C)
   c. 120°F (50°C)
   d. 284°F (140°C)

9. If the transmission fluid temperature (TFT) sensor indicates cold automatic transmission fluid temperature, what would the PCM do to the shifts?
   a. Normal shifts and normal operation of the torque converter clutch
   b. Disable torque converter clutch; normal shift points
   c. Delayed shift points and torque converter clutch disabled
   d. Normal shifts but overdrive will be disabled

10. A P0118 DTC is being discussed. Technician A says that the ECT sensor could be shorted internally. Technician B says that the signal wire could be open. Which technician is correct?
    a. Technician A only
    b. Technician B only
    c. Both Technicians A and B
    d. Neither Technician A nor B

THROTTLE POSITION (TP) SENSORS

OBJECTIVES

After studying Chapter 21, the reader will be able to:

1. Prepare for ASE Engine Performance (A8) certification test content area "E" (Computerized Engine Controls Diagnosis and Repair).
2. Discuss how throttle position sensors work.
3. List the methods that can be used to test TP sensors.
4. Describe the symptoms of a failed TP sensor.
5. List how the operation of the TP sensor affects vehicle operation.
6. Discuss TP sensor rationality tests.

KEY TERMS

Potentiometer 346
Skewed 349

Throttle position (TP) sensor 346

FIGURE 21–1 A typical TP sensor mounted on the throttle plate of this port-injected engine.

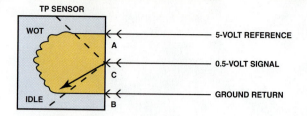

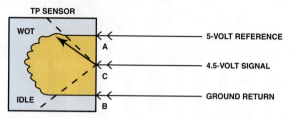

FIGURE 21–2 The signal voltage from a throttle position increases as the throttle is opened because the wiper arm is closer to the 5-volt reference. At idle, the resistance of the sensor winding effectively reduces the signal voltage output to the computer.

THROTTLE POSITION SENSOR CONSTRUCTION

Most computer-equipped engines use a **throttle position (TP) sensor** to signal to the computer the position of the throttle. ● **SEE FIGURE 21–1.** The TP sensor consists of a **potentiometer,** a type of variable resistor.

POTENTIOMETERS A potentiometer is a variable-resistance sensor with three terminals. One end of the resistor receives reference voltage, while the other end is grounded. The third terminal is attached to a movable contact that slides across the resistor to vary its resistance. Depending on whether the contact is near the supply end or the ground end of the resistor, return voltage is high or low. ● **SEE FIGURE 21–2.**

Throttle position (TP) sensors are among the most common potentiometer-type sensors. The computer uses their input to determine the amount of throttle opening and the rate of change.

A typical sensor has three wires:

- A 5-volt reference feed wire from the computer
- Signal return (A ground wire back to the computer)
- A voltage signal wire back to the computer; as the throttle is opened, the voltage to the computer changes

Normal throttle position voltage on most vehicles is about 0.5 volt at idle (closed throttle) and 4.5 volts at wide-open throttle (WOT).

NOTE: The TP sensor voltage at idle is usually about 10% of the TP sensor voltage when the throttle is wide open, but can vary from as low as 0.3 volt to 1.2 volts, depending on the make and model of vehicle.

TP SENSOR COMPUTER INPUT FUNCTIONS

- The computer senses any change in throttle position and changes the fuel mixture and ignition timing. The actual change in fuel mixture and ignition timing is also partly determined by the other sensors, such as the manifold pressure (engine vacuum), engine RPM, the coolant temperature, and oxygen sensor(s). Some throttle position sensors are adjustable and should be set according to the exact engine manufacturer's specifications.

- The throttle position (TP) sensor used on fuel-injected vehicles acts as an "electronic accelerator pump." This means that the computer will pulse additional fuel from the injectors when the throttle is depressed. Because the air can quickly flow into the engine when the throttle is opened, additional fuel must be supplied to prevent the air–fuel mixture from going less, causing the engine to hesitate when the throttle is depressed. If the TP sensor is unplugged or defective, the engine may still operate satisfactorily, but hesitate upon acceleration.

- The PCM supplies the TP sensor with a regulated voltage that ranges from 4.8 to 5.1 volts. This reference voltage is usually referred to as a 5-volt reference or "Vref." The TP output signal is an input to the PCM, and the TP sensor ground also flows through the PCM.

The TP sensor is used by the Powertrain Control Module (PCM) for the following reasons.

CLEAR FLOOD MODE   If the throttle is depressed to the floor during engine cranking, the PCM will either greatly reduce or entirely eliminate any fuel-injector pulses to aid in cleaning a flooded engine. If the throttle is depressed to the floor and the engine is not flooded with excessive fuel, the engine may not start.

TORQUE CONVERTER CLUTCH ENGAGEMENT AND RELEASE   The torque converter clutch will be released if the PCM detects rapid acceleration to help the transmission deliver maximum torque to the drive wheels. The torque converter clutch is also disengaged when the accelerator pedal is released with the vehicle moving to help engine braking.

RATIONALITY TESTING FOR MAP AND MAF SENSORS
As part of the rationality tests for the MAP and/or MAF sensor, the TP sensor signal is compared to the reading from other sensors to determine if they match. For example, if the throttle position sensor is showing wide-open throttle (WOT), the MAP and/or MAF reading should also indicate that this engine is under a heavy load. If not, a diagnostic trouble code could be set for the TP, as well as the MAP and/or MAF sensors.

AUTOMATIC TRANSMISSION SHIFT POINTS   The shift points are delayed if the throttle is opened wide to allow the engine speed to increase, thereby producing more power and aiding in the acceleration of the vehicle. If the throttle is barely open, the shift point occurs at the minimum speed designed for the vehicle.

TARGET IDLE SPEED (IDLE CONTROL STRATEGY)
When the TP sensor voltage is at idle, the PCM then controls idle speed using the idle air control (IAC) and/or spark timing variation to maintain the commanded idle speed. If the TP sensor indicates that the throttle has moved off idle, fuel delivery and spark timing are programmed for acceleration. Therefore, if the throttle linkage is stuck or binding, the idle speed may not be correct.

AIR-CONDITIONING COMPRESSOR OPERATION   The TP sensor is also used as an input sensor for traction control and air-conditioning compressor operation. If the PCM detects

See the Ford throttle position (TP) sensor chart for an example of how sensor voltage changes with throttle angle.

Ford Throttle Position (TP) Sensor Chart

Throttle Angle (Degrees)	Voltage (V)
0	0.50
10	0.97
20	1.44
30	1.90
40	2.37
50	2.84
60	3.31
70	3.78
80	4.24

NOTE: Generally, any reading higher than 80% represents wide-open throttle to the computer.

that the throttle is at or close to wide open, the air-conditioning compressor is disengaged.

BACKS UP OTHER SENSORS   The TP sensor is used as a backup to the MAP sensor and/or MAF in the event the PCM detects that one or both are not functioning correctly. The PCM then calculates fuel needs and spark timing based on the engine speed (RPM) and throttle position.

TESTING THE THROTTLE POSITION SENSOR

A TP sensor can be tested using one or more of the following tools:

- A digital voltmeter with three test leads connected in series between the sensor and the wiring harness connector or back probing using T-pins or other recommended tool that will not cause harm to the connector or wiring.

- A scan tool or a specific tool recommended by the vehicle manufacturer.

- A breakout box that is connected in series between the computer and the wiring harness connector(s). A typical breakout box includes test points at which TP voltages can be measured with a digital voltmeter.

- An oscilloscope.

Use jumper wires, T-pins to back-probe the wires, or a breakout box to gain electrical access to the wiring to the TP sensor. ● **SEE FIGURE 21–3**.

NOTE: The procedure that follows is the usual method used by many manufacturers. Always refer to service information for the exact recommended procedure and specifications for the vehicle being tested.

The procedure for testing the sensor using a digital multimeter is as follows:

1. Turn the ignition switch on (engine off).

2. Set the digital meter to read to DC volts and measure the voltage between the signal wire and ground (reference low) wire. The voltage should be about 0.5 volt.

   NOTE: Consult the service information for exact wire colors or locations.

3. With the engine still not running (but with the ignition still on), slowly increase the throttle opening. The voltage

FIGURE 21–3 A meter lead connected to a T-pin that was gently pushed along the signal wire of the TP sensor until the point of the pin touched the metal terminal inside the plastic connector.

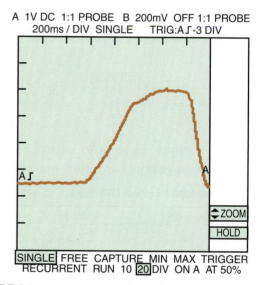

A 1V DC 1:1 PROBE   B 200mV OFF 1:1 PROBE
200ms / DIV SINGLE   TRIG:A↲-3 DIV

SINGLE FREE CAPTURE MIN MAX TRIGGER
RECURRENT RUN 10 20 DIV ON A AT 50%

FIGURE 21–4 A typical waveform of a TP sensor signal as recorded on a DSO when the accelerator pedal was depressed with the ignition switch on (engine off). Clean transitions and the lack of any glitches in this waveform indicate a good sensor. *(Courtesy of Fluke Corporation)*

signal from the TP sensor should also increase. Look for any "dead spots" or open circuit readings as the throttle is increased to the wide-open position. ● **SEE FIGURE 21–4** for an example of how a good TP sensor would look when tested with a digital storage oscilloscope (DSO).

NOTE: Use the accelerator pedal to depress the throttle because this applies the same forces on the TP sensor as the driver does during normal driving. Moving the throttle by hand under the hood may not accurately test the TP sensor.

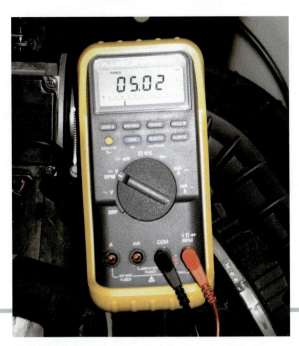

FIGURE 21–5 Checking the 5-volt reference from the computer being applied to the TP sensor with the ignition switch on (engine off).

FIGURE 21–6 Checking the voltage drop between the TP sensor ground and a good engine ground with the ignition on (engine off). A reading of greater than 0.2 volt (200 mV) represents a bad computer ground.

4. With the voltmeter still connected, slowly return the throttle down to the idle position. The voltage from the TP sensor should also decrease evenly on the return to idle.

The TP sensor voltage at idle should be within the acceptable range as specified by the manufacturer. Some TP sensors can be adjusted by loosening their retaining screws and moving the sensor in relation to the throttle opening. This movement changes the output voltage of the sensor.

 TECH TIP

Check Power and Ground Before Condemning a Bad Sensor

Most engine sensors use a 5-volt reference and a ground. If the 5 volts to the sensor is too high (shorted to voltage) or too low (high resistance), then the sensor output will be **skewed** or out of range. Before replacing the sensor that did not read correctly, measure both the 5-volt reference and ground. To measure the ground, simply turn the ignition on (engine off) and touch one test lead of a DMM set to read DC volts to the sensor ground and the other to the negative terminal of the battery. Any reading higher than 0.2 volt (200 mV) represents a poor ground. ● **SEE FIGURES 21–5 AND 21–6.**

All TP sensors should also provide a smooth transition voltage reading from idle to WOT and back to idle. Replace the TP sensor if erratic voltage readings are obtained or if the correct setting at idle cannot be obtained.

TESTING A TP SENSOR USING THE MIN/MAX FUNCTION

Many digital multimeters are capable of recording voltage readings over time and then displaying the minimum, maximum, and average readings. To perform a MIN/MAX test of the TP sensor, manually set the meter to read higher than 4 volts.

STEP 1 Connect the red meter lead to the signal wire and the black meter lead to a good ground on the ground return wire at the TP sensor.

STEP 2 With the ignition on, engine off, slowly depress and release the accelerator pedal from inside the vehicle.

STEP 3 Check the minimum and maximum voltage reading on the meter display. Any 0- or 5-volt reading would indicate a fault or short in the TP sensor.

TESTING THE TP SENSOR USING A SCAN TOOL

A scan tool can be used to check for proper operation of the throttle position sensor using the following steps.

STEP 1 With the key on, engine off, the TP sensor voltage display should be about 0.5 volt, but can vary from as low as 0.3 volt to as high as 1.2 volts.

STEP 2 Check the scan tool display for the percentage of throttle opening. The reading should be zero and gradually increase in percentage as the throttle is depressed.

STEP 3 The idle air control (IAC) counts should increase as the throttle is opened and decrease as the throttle is closed. Start the engine and observe the IAC counts as the throttle is depressed.

STEP 4 Start the engine and observe the TP sensor reading. Use a wedge or thin object to increase the throttle opening slightly. The throttle percentage reading should increase. Shut off and restart the engine. If the percentage of throttle opening returns to 0%, the PCM determines that the increased throttle opening is now the new minimum and resets the idle position of the TP sensor. Remove the wedge and cycle the ignition key. The throttle position sensor should again read zero percentage.

NOTE: Some engine computers are not capable of resetting the throttle position sensor.

TP SENSOR DIAGNOSTIC TROUBLE CODES

The diagnostic trouble codes (DTCs) associated with the throttle position sensor include the following.

Diagnostic Trouble Code	Description	Possible Causes
P0122	TP sensor low voltage	■ TP sensor internally shorted-to-ground ■ TP sensor wiring shorted-to-ground ■ TP sensor or wiring open
P0123	TP sensor high voltage	■ TP sensor internally shorted to 5-volt reference ■ TP sensor ground open ■ TP sensor wiring shorted-to-voltage
P0121	TP sensor signal does not agree with MAP	■ Defective TP sensor ■ Incorrect vehicle-speed (VS) sensor signal ■ MAP sensor out-of-calibration or defective

SUMMARY

1. A throttle position (TP) sensor is a three-wire variable resistor called a potentiometer.
2. The three wires on the TP sensor include a 5-volt reference voltage from the PCM, plus the signal wire to the PCM, and a ground, which also goes to the PCM.
3. The TP sensor is used by the PCM for clear flood mode, torque converter engagement and release, and automotive transmission shift points, as well as for rationality testing for the MAP and MAF sensors.
4. The TP sensor signal voltage should be about 0.5 volt at idle and increase to about 4.5 volts at wide-open throttle (WOT).
5. A TP sensor can be tested using a digital multimeter, a digital storage oscilloscope (DSO), or a scan tool.

REVIEW QUESTIONS

1. What is the purpose of each of the three wires on a typical TP sensor?
2. What all does the PCM do with the TP sensor signal voltage?
3. What is the procedure to follow when checking the 5-volt reference and TP sensor ground?
4. How can a TP sensor be diagnosed using a scan tool?

1. Which sensor is generally considered to be the electronic accelerator pump of a fuel-injected engine?
   - a. O2S
   - b. ECT sensor
   - c. Engine MAP sensor
   - d. TP sensor

2. Typical TP sensor voltage at idle is about _____.
   - a. 2.50 to 2.80 volts
   - b. 0.5 volt or 10% of WOT TP sensor voltage
   - c. 1.5 to 2.8 volts
   - d. 13.5 to 15.0 volts

3. A TP sensor is what type of sensor?
   - a. Rheostat
   - b. Voltage generating
   - c. Potentiometer
   - d. Piezoelectric

4. Most TP sensors have how many wires?
   - a. 1
   - b. 2
   - c. 3
   - d. 4

5. Which sensor does the TP sensor back up if the PCM determines that a failure has occurred?
   - a. Oxygen sensor
   - b. MAF sensor
   - c. MAP sensor
   - d. Either b or c

6. Which wire on a TP sensor should be back-probed to check the voltage signal to the PCM?
   - a. 5-volt reference (Vref)
   - b. Signal
   - c. Ground
   - d. Meter should be connected between the 5-volt reference and the ground

7. After a TP sensor has been tested using the MIN/MAX function on a DMM, a reading of zero volts is displayed. What does this reading indicate?
   - a. The TP sensor is open at one point during the test.
   - b. The TP sensor is shorted.
   - c. The TP sensor signal is shorted to 5-volt reference.
   - d. Both b and c are possible.

8. After a TP sensor has been tested using the MIN/MAX function on a DMM, a reading of 5 volts is displayed. What does this reading indicate?
   - a. The TP sensor is open at one point during the test.
   - b. The TP sensor is shorted.
   - c. The TP sensor signal is shorted to 5-volt reference.
   - d. Both b and c are possible.

9. A technician attaches one lead of a digital voltmeter to the ground terminal of the TP sensor and the other meter lead to the negative terminal of the battery. The ignition is switched to on, engine off and the meter displays 37.3 mV. Technician A says that this is the signal voltage and is a little low. Technician B says that the TP sensor ground circuit has excessive resistance. Which technician is correct?
   - a. Technician A only
   - b. Technician B only
   - c. Both Technicians A and B
   - d. Neither Technician A nor B

10. A P0122 DTC is retrieved using a scan tool. This DTC means _____.
    - a. The TP sensor voltage is low
    - b. The TP sensor could be shorted-to-ground
    - c. The TP sensor signal circuit could be shorted-to-ground
    - d. All of the above are correct.

chapter 22

MAP/BARO SENSORS

OBJECTIVES

After studying Chapter 22, the reader will be able to:

1. Prepare for ASE Engine Performance (A8) certification test content area "E" (Computerized Engine Controls Diagnosis and Repair).

2. Discuss how MAP sensors work.

3. List the methods that can be used to test MAP sensors.

4. Describe the symptoms of a failed MAP sensor.

5. List how the operation of the MAP sensor affects vehicle operation.

6. Discuss MAP sensor rationality tests.

7. Describe how the BARO sensor is used to determine altitude.

KEY TERMS

Barometric manifold absolute pressure (BMAP) sensor 358

Barometric pressure (BARO) sensor 358

Manifold absolute pressure (MAP) sensor 354

Piezoresistivity 354

Pressure differential 353

Speed density 357

Vacuum 353

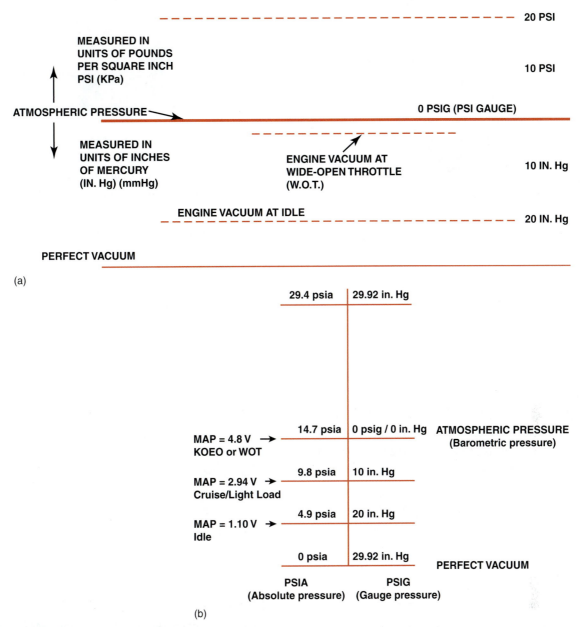

FIGURE 22–1 (a) As an engine is accelerated under a load, the engine vacuum drops. This drop in vacuum is actually an increase in absolute pressure in the intake manifold. A MAP sensor senses all pressures greater than that of a perfect vacuum. (b) The relationship between absolute pressure, vacuum and gauge pressure.

AIR PRESSURE—HIGH AND LOW

Think of an internal combustion engine as a big air pump. As the pistons move up and down in the cylinders, they pump in air and fuel for combustion and pump out exhaust gases. They do this by creating a difference in air pressure. The air outside an engine has weight and exerts pressure, as does the air inside an engine.

As a piston moves down on an intake stroke with the intake valve open, it creates a larger area inside the cylinder for the air to fill. This lowers the air pressure within the engine.

Because the pressure inside the engine is lower than the pressure outside, air flows into the engine to fill the low-pressure area and equalize the pressure.

The low pressure within the engine is called **vacuum.** Vacuum causes the higher-pressure air on the outside to flow into the low-pressure area inside the cylinder. The difference in pressure between the two areas is called a **pressure differential.**
● SEE FIGURE 22–1.

FIGURE 22–2 A plastic MAP sensor used for training purposes showing the electronic circuit board and electrical connections.

PRINCIPLES OF PRESSURE SENSORS

Intake manifold pressure changes with changing throttle positions. At wide-open throttle, manifold pressure is almost the same as atmospheric pressure. On deceleration or at idle, manifold pressure is below atmospheric pressure, thus creating a vacuum. In cases where turbo- or supercharging is used, under part- or full-load condition, intake manifold pressure rises above atmospheric pressure. Also, oxygen content and barometric pressure change with differences in altitude, and the computer must be able to compensate by making changes in the flow of fuel entering the engine. To provide the computer with changing airflow information, a fuel-injection system may use the following:

- Manifold absolute pressure (MAP) sensor
- Manifold absolute pressure (MAP) sensor plus barometric absolute pressure (BARO) sensor
- Barometric and manifold absolute pressure sensors combined (BMAP)

The **manifold absolute pressure (MAP) sensor** may be a ceramic capacitor diaphragm, an aneroid bellows, or a piezoresistive crystal. It has a sealed vacuum reference input on one side; the other side is connected (vented) to the intake manifold. This sensor housing also contains signal conditioning circuitry. ● **SEE FIGURE 22–2.** Pressure changes in the manifold cause the sensor to deflect, varying its analog or digital return signal to the computer. As the air pressure increases, the MAP sensor generates a higher voltage or frequency return signal to the computer.

CONSTRUCTION OF MANIFOLD ABSOLUTE PRESSURE (MAP) SENSORS

The manifold absolute pressure (MAP) sensor is used by the engine computer to sense engine load. The typical MAP sensor consists of a ceramic or silicon wafer sealed on one side with a perfect vacuum and exposed to intake manifold vacuum on the other side. As the engine vacuum changes, the pressure difference on the wafer changes the output voltage or frequency of the MAP sensor.

A manifold absolute pressure (MAP) sensor is used on many engines for the PCM to determine the load on the engine. The relationship among barometer pressure, engine vacuum, and MAP sensor voltage includes:

- Absolute pressure is equal to barometric pressure minus intake manifold vacuum.
- A decrease in manifold vacuum means an increase in manifold pressure.
- The MAP sensor compares manifold vacuum to a perfect vacuum.
- Barometric pressure minus MAP sensor reading equals intake manifold vacuum. Normal engine vacuum is 17–21 in. Hg.
- Supercharged and turbocharged engines require a MAP sensor that is calibrated for pressures above atmospheric, as well as for vacuum.

SILICON-DIAPHRAGM STRAIN GAUGE MAP SENSOR
This is the most commonly used design for a MAP sensor and the output is a DC analog (variable) voltage. One side of a silicon wafer is exposed to engine vacuum and the other side is exposed to a perfect vacuum.

There are four resistors attached to the silicon wafer, which changes in resistance when strain is applied to the wafer. This change in resistance due to strain is called **piezoresistivity.** The resistors are electrically connected to a Wheatstone bridge circuit and then to a differential amplifier, which creates a voltage in proportion to the vacuum applied.

A typical General Motors MAP sensor voltage varies from 0.88 to 1.62 at engine idle.

- 17 in. Hg is equal to about 1.62 volts
- 21 in. Hg is equal to about 0.88 volts

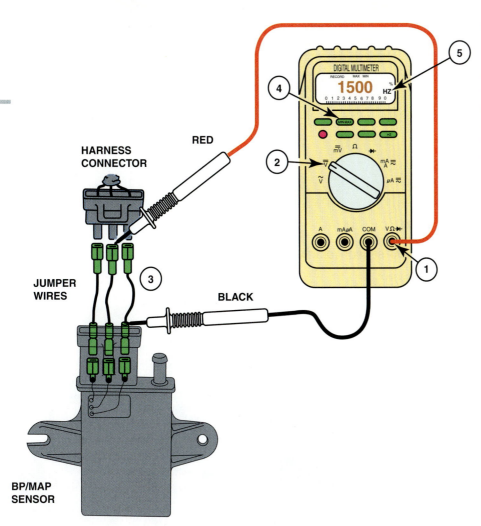

FIGURE 22-3 MAP sensors use three wires: 1. 5-volt reference from the PCM 2. Sensor signal (output signal) 3. Ground. A DMM set to test a MAP sensor. (1) Connect the red meter lead to the V meter terminal and the black meter lead to the COM meter terminal. (2) Select DC volts. (3) Connect the test leads to the sensor signal wire and the ground wire. (4) Select hertz (Hz) if testing a MAP sensor whose output is a varying frequency; otherwise keep it on DC volts. (5) Read the change of voltage (frequency) as the vacuum is applied to the sensor. Compare the vacuum reading and the frequency (or voltage) reading to the specifications. *(Courtesy of Fluke Corporation).*

Therefore, a good reading should be about 1.0 volt from the MAP sensor on a sound engine at idle speed. See the following chart that shows engine load, engine vacuum, and MAP.

Engine Load	Manifold Vacuum	Manifold Absolute Pressure	MAP Sensor Volt Signal
Heavy (WOT)	Low (almost 0 in. Hg)	High (almost atmospheric)	High (4.6–4.8 V)
Light (idle)	High (17–21 in. Hg)	Low (lower than atmospheric)	Low (0.8–1.6 V)

CAPACITOR-CAPSULE MAP SENSOR

A capacitor-capsule is a type of MAP sensor used by Ford which uses two ceramic (alumina) plates with an insulating washer spacer in the center to create a capacitor. Changes in engine vacuum cause the plates to deflect, which changes the capacitance. The electronics in the sensor then generate a varying digital frequency

output signal, which is proportional to the engine vacuum.
● **SEE FIGURE 22–3.** ● **SEE FIGURE 22–4** for a scope waveform of a digital MAP sensor. Also see the Ford MAP sensor chart.

Ford MAP Sensor Chart

MAP Sensor Output (Hz)	Engine Operating Conditions	Intake Manifold Vacuum (in. Hg)
156–159 Hz	Key on, engine off	0 in. Hg
102–109 Hz	Engine at idle (sea level)	17–21 in. Hg
156–159 Hz	Engine at wide-open throttle (WOT)	About 0 in. Hg

CERAMIC DISC MAP SENSOR

The ceramic disc MAP sensor is used by Chrysler and it converts manifold pressure into a capacitance discharge. The discharge controls the amount of voltage delivered by the sensor to the PCM. The output is the same as the previously used strain gauge/Wheatstone bridge design and is interchangeable. ● **SEE FIGURE 22–5.** See the Chrysler MAP sensor chart.

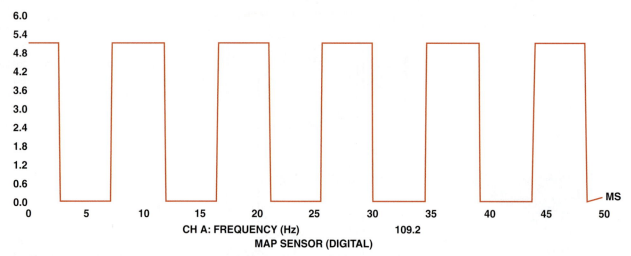

FIGURE 22–4 A waveform of a typical digital MAP sensor.

CONSTRUCTION OF MANIFOLD ABSOLUTE PRESSURE (MAP) SENSORS (CONTINUED)

Chrysler MAP Sensor Chart

Vacuum (in. Hg)	MAP Sensor Signal Voltage (V)
0.5	4.8
1.0	4.6
3.0	4.1
5.0	3.8
7.0	3.5
10.0	2.9
15.0	2.1
20.0	1.2
25.0	0.5

 **TECH TIP**

If It's Green, It's a Signal Wire

Ford-built vehicles usually use a green wire as the signal wire back to the computer from the sensors. It may not be a solid green, but if there is green somewhere on the wire, then it is the signal wire. The other wires are the power and ground wires to the sensor.

FIGURE 22–5 Shown is the electronic circuit inside a ceramic disc MAP sensor used on many Chrysler engines. The black areas are carbon resistors that are applied to the ceramic, and lasers are used to cut lines into these resistors during testing to achieve the proper operating calibration.

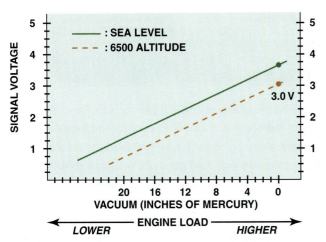

FIGURE 22–6 Altitude affects the MAP sensor voltage.

PCM USES OF THE MAP SENSOR

The PCM uses the MAP sensor to determine the following:

- **The load on the engine.** The MAP sensor is used on a **speed density**-type fuel-injection system to determine the load on the engine, and therefore the amount of fuel needed. On engines equipped with a mass air flow (MAF) sensor, the MAP is used as a backup to the MAF, for diagnosis of other sensors, and systems such as the EGR system.

- **Altitude, fuel, and spark control calculations.** At key on, the MAP sensor determines the altitude (acts as a BARO sensor) and adjusts the fuel delivery and spark timing accordingly.

  - If the altitude is high, generally over 5,000 feet (1,500 meters), the PCM will reduce fuel delivery and advance the ignition timing.

  - The altitude is also reset when the engine is accelerated to wide-open throttle and the MAP sensor is used to reset the altitude reading. ● SEE FIGURE 22–6.

- **EGR system operation.** As part of the OBD-II standards, the exhaust gas recirculation (EGR) system must be checked for proper operation. One method used by many vehicle manufacturers is to command the EGR valve on and then watch the MAP sensor signal. The opening of the EGR pistle should decrease engine vacuum. If the MAP sensor does not react with the specified drop in manifold vacuum (increase in manifold pressure), an EGR flow rate problem diagnostic trouble code is set.

 **TECH TIP**

Use the MAP Sensor as a Vacuum Gauge

A MAP sensor measures the pressure inside the intake manifold compared with absolute zero (perfect vacuum). For example, an idling engine that has 20 inches of mercury (in. Hg) of vacuum has a lower pressure inside the intake manifold than when the engine is under a load and the vacuum is at 10 in. Hg. A decrease in engine vacuum results in an increase in manifold pressure. A normal engine should produce between 17 and 21 in. Hg at idle. Comparing the vacuum reading with the voltage reading output of the MAP sensor indicates that the reading should be between 1.62 and 0.88 volt or 109 to 102 Hz or lower on Ford MAP sensors. Therefore, a digital multimeter (DMM), scan tool, or scope can be used to measure the MAP sensor voltage and be used instead of a vacuum gauge.

NOTE: This chart was developed by testing a MAP sensor at a location about 600 feet above sea level. For best results, a chart based on your altitude should be made by applying a known vacuum, and reading the voltage of a known-good MAP sensor. Vacuum usually drops about 1 inch per 1,000 feet of altitude.

Vacuum (in. Hg)	GM (DC volts)	Ford (Hz)
0	4.80	156–159
1	4.52	
2	4.46	
3	4.26	
4	4.06	
5	3.88	141–143
6	3.66	
7	3.50	
8	3.30	
9	3.10	
10	2.94	127–130
11	2.76	
12	2.54	
13	2.36	
14	2.20	
15	2.00	114–117
16	1.80	
17	1.62	
18	1.42	108–109
19	1.20	
20	1.10	102–104
21	0.88	
22	0.66	

- **Detect deceleration (vacuum increases).** The engine vacuum rises when the accelerator is released, which changes the MAP sensor voltage. When deceleration is detected by the PCM, fuel is either stopped or greatly reduced to improve exhaust emissions.

- **Monitor engine condition.** As an engine wears, the intake manifold vacuum usually decreases. The PCM is programmed to detect the gradual change in vacuum and is able to keep the air–fuel mixture in the correct range. If the PCM were not capable of making adjustments for engine wear, the lower vacuum could be interpreted as increased load on the engine, resulting in too much fuel being injected, thereby reducing fuel economy and increasing exhaust emissions.

- **Load detection for returnless-type fuel injection.** On fuel delivery systems that do not use a return line back to the fuel tank, the engine load calculation for the fuel needed is determined by the signals from the MAP sensor.

- **Altitude and MAP sensor values.** On an engine equipped with a speed-density-type fuel injection, the MAP sensor is the most important sensor needed to determine injection pulse width. Changes in altitude change the air density as well as weather conditions. Barometric pressure and altitude are inversely related:

  - As altitude increases—barometric pressure decreases
  - As altitude decreases—barometric pressure increases

  As the ignition switch is rolled from off to the start position, the PCM reads the MAP sensor value to determine atmospheric and air pressure conditions. This barometric pressure reading is updated every time the engine is started and whenever wide-open throttle is detected. The barometric pressure reading at that time is updated. See the chart that compares altitude to MAP sensor voltage.

Altitude and MAP Sensor Voltage

Altitude	MAP Sensor Voltage (can vary due to atmospheric conditions)
Sea level	4.6 to 4.8 volts
2,500 (760 m)	4.0 volts
5,000 (1,520 m)	3.7 volts
7,500 (2,300 m)	3.35 volts
10,000 (3,050 m)	3.05 volts
12,500 (3,800 m)	2.80 volts
15,000 (4,600 m)	2.45 volts

BAROMETRIC PRESSURE SENSOR

A **barometric pressure (BARO) sensor** is similar in design, but senses more subtle changes in barometric absolute pressure (atmospheric air pressure). It is vented directly to the atmosphere. The **barometric manifold absolute pressure (BMAP) sensor** is actually a combination of a BARO and MAP sensor in the same housing. The BMAP sensor has individual circuits to measure barometric and manifold pressure. This input not only allows the computer to adjust for changes in atmospheric pressure due to weather, but also is the primary sensor used to determine altitude.

NOTE: A MAP sensor and a BARO sensor are usually the same sensor, but the MAP sensor is connected to the manifold and a BARO sensor is open to the atmosphere. The MAP sensor is capable of reading barometric pressure just as the ignition switch is turned to the on position before the engine starts. Therefore, altitude and weather changes are available to the computer. During mountainous driving, it may be an advantage to stop and then restart the engine so that the engine computer can take another barometric pressure reading and recalibrate fuel delivery based on the new altitude. See the Ford/BARO altitude chart for an example of how altitude affects intake manifold pressure. The computer on some vehicles will monitor the throttle position sensor and use the MAP sensor reading at wide-open throttle (WOT) to update the BARO sensor if it has changed during driving.

Ford MAP/BARO Altitude Chart

Altitude (feet)	Volts (V)
0	1.59
1,000	1.56
2,000	1.53
3,000	1.50
4,000	1.47
5,000	1.44
6,000	1.41
7,000	1.39

NOTE: Some older Chrysler brand vehicles were equipped with a combination BARO and IAT sensor. The sensor was mounted on the bulkhead (firewall) and sensed the underhood air temperature.

TESTING THE MAP SENSOR

Most pressure sensors operate on 5 volts from the computer and return a signal (voltage or frequency) based on the pressure (vacuum) applied to the sensor. If a MAP sensor is being tested, make certain that the vacuum hose and hose fittings are sound and making a good, tight connection to a manifold vacuum source on the engine.

Four different types of test instruments can be used to test a pressure sensor:

1. A digital voltmeter with three test leads connected in series between the sensor and the wiring harness connector or back-probe the terminals.

2. A scope connected to the sensor output, power, and ground.

3. A scan tool or a specific tool recommended by the vehicle manufacturer.

4. A breakout box connected in series between the computer and the wiring harness connection(s). A typical breakout box includes test points at which pressure sensor values can be measured with a digital voltmeter set on DC volts (or frequency counter, if a frequency-type MAP sensor is being tested).

NOTE: Always check service information for the exact testing procedures and specifications for the vehicle being tested.

TESTING THE MAP SENSOR USING A DMM OR SCOPE

Use jumper wires, T-pins to back-probe the connector, or a breakout box to gain electrical access to the wiring to the pressure sensor. Most pressure sensors use three wires:

1. A 5-volt wire from the computer

2. A variable-signal wire back to the computer

3. A ground or reference low wire

   The procedure for testing the sensor is as follows:

1. Turn the ignition on (engine off)

2. Measure the voltage (or frequency) of the sensor output

3. Using a hand-operated vacuum pump (or other variable vacuum source), apply vacuum to the sensor

A good pressure sensor should change voltage (or frequency) in relation to the applied vacuum. If the signal does not change or the values are out of range according to the manufacturers' specifications, the sensor must be replaced.

REAL WORLD FIX

The Cavalier Convertible Story

The owner of a Cavalier convertible stated to a service technician that the "check engine" (MIL) was on. The technician found a diagnostic trouble code (DTC) for a MAP sensor. The technician removed the hose at the MAP sensor and discovered that gasoline had accumulated in the sensor and dripped out of the hose as it was being removed. The technician replaced the MAP sensor and test drove the vehicle to confirm the repair. Almost at once the check engine light came on with the same MAP sensor code. After several hours of troubleshooting without success in determining the cause, the technician decided to start over again. Almost at once, the technician discovered that no vacuum was getting to the MAP sensor where a vacuum gauge was connected with a T-fitting in the vacuum line to the MAP sensor. The vacuum port in the base of the throttle body was clogged with carbon. After a thorough cleaning, and clearing the DTC, the Cavalier again performed properly and the check engine light did not come on again. The technician had assumed that if gasoline was able to reach the sensor through the vacuum hose, surely vacuum could reach the sensor. The technician learned to stop assuming when diagnosing a vehicle and concentrate more on testing the simple things first.

TECH TIP

Visual Check of the MAP Sensor

A defective vacuum hose to a MAP sensor can cause a variety of driveability problems including poor fuel economy, hesitation, stalling, and rough idle. A small air leak (vacuum leak) around the hose can cause these symptoms and often set a trouble code in the vehicle computer. When working on a vehicle that uses a MAP sensor, make certain that the vacuum hose travels consistently *downward* on its route from the sensor to the source of manifold vacuum. Inspect the hose, especially if another technician has previously replaced the factory-original hose. It should not be so long that it sags down at any point. Condensed fuel and/or moisture can become trapped in this low spot in the hose and cause all types of driveability problems and MAP sensor codes.

When checking the MAP sensor, if anything comes out of the sensor itself, it should be replaced. This includes water, gasoline, or any other substance.

FIGURE 22–7 A typical hand-operated vacuum pump.

TESTING THE MAP SENSOR USING A SCAN TOOL

A scan tool can be used to test a MAP sensor by monitoring the injector pulse width (in milliseconds) when vacuum is being applied to the MAP sensor using a hand-operated vacuum pump. ● **SEE FIGURE 22–7.**

STEP 1 Apply about 20 in. Hg of vacuum to the MAP sensor and start the engine.

STEP 2 Observe the injector pulse width. On a warm engine, the injector pulse width will normally be 1.5 to 3.5 ms.

STEP 3 Slowly reduce the vacuum to the MAP sensor and observe the pulse width. A lower vacuum to the MAP sensor indicates a heavier load on the engine and the injector pulse width should increase.

NOTE: If 23 in. Hg or more vacuum is applied to the MAP sensor with the engine running, this high vacuum will often stall the engine. The engine stalls because the high vacuum is interpreted by the PCM to indicate that the engine is being decelerated, which shuts off the fuel. During engine deceleration, the PCM shuts off the fuel injectors to reduce exhaust emissions and increase fuel economy.

FUEL-RAIL PRESSURE SENSOR

A fuel-rail pressure (FRP) sensor is used on some vehicles such as Fords that are equipped with electronic returnless fuel injection. This sensor provides fuel pressure information to the PCM for fuel injection pulse width calculations.

MAP/BARO DIAGNOSTIC TROUBLE CODES

The diagnostic trouble codes (DTCs) associated with the MAP and BARO sensors include:

Diagnostic Trouble Code	Description	Possible Causes
P0106	BARO sensor out-of-range at key on	■ MAP sensor fault ■ MAP sensor O-ring damaged or missing
P0107	MAP sensor low voltage	■ MAP sensor fault ■ MAP sensor signal circuit shorted-to-ground ■ MAP sensor 5-volt supply circuit open
P0108	Map sensor high voltage	■ MAP sensor fault ■ MAP sensor O-ring damaged or missing ■ MAP sensor signal circuit shorted-to-voltage

1. Pressure below atmospheric pressure is called vacuum and is measured in inches of mercury.

2. A manifold absolute pressure sensor uses a perfect vacuum (zero absolute pressure) in the sensor to determine the pressure.

3. Three types of MAP sensors include:
   • Silicon-diaphragm strain gauge
   • Capacitor-capsule design
   • Ceramic disc design

4. A heavy engine load results in low intake manifold vacuum and a high MAP sensor signal voltage.

5. A light engine load results in high intake manifold vacuum and a low MAP sensor signal voltage.

6. A MAP sensor is used to detect changes in altitude, as well as check other sensors and engine systems.

7. A MAP sensor can be tested by visual inspection, testing the output using a digital meter or scan tool.

REVIEW QUESTIONS

1. What is the relationship among atmospheric pressure, vacuum, and boost pressure in PSI?

2. What are two types (construction) of MAP sensors?

3. What is the MAP sensor signal voltage or frequency at idle on a typical General Motors, Chrysler, and Ford engine?

4. What are three uses of a MAP sensor by the PCM?

CHAPTER QUIZ

1. As the load on an engine increases, the manifold vacuum decreases and the manifold absolute pressure _____.
   a. Increases
   b. Decreases
   c. Changes with barometric pressure only (altitude or weather)
   d. Remains constant (absolute)

2. A typical MAP sensor compares the vacuum in the intake manifold to _____.
   a. Atmospheric pressure
   b. A perfect vacuum
   c. Barometric pressure
   d. The value of the IAT sensor

3. Which statement is *false*?
   a. Absolute pressure is equal to barometric pressure plus intake manifold vacuum.
   b. A decrease in manifold vacuum means an increase in manifold pressure.
   c. The MAP sensor compares manifold vacuum to a perfect vacuum.
   d. Barometric pressure minus the MAP sensor reading equals intake manifold vacuum.

4. Which design of MAP sensor produces a frequency (digital) output signal?
   a. Silicon-diaphragm strain gauge
   b. Piezoresistivity design
   c. Capacitor-capsule
   d. Ceramic disc

5. The frequency output of a digital MAP sensor is reading 114 Hz. What is the approximate engine vacuum?
   a. Zero
   b. 5 in. Hg
   c. 10 in. Hg
   d. 15 in. Hg

6. Which is *not* a purpose or function of the MAP sensor?
   a. Measures the load on the engine
   b. Measures engine speed
   c. Calculates fuel delivery based on altitude
   d. Helps diagnose the EGR system

7. When measuring the output signal of a MAP sensor on a General Motors vehicle, the digital multimeter should be set to read _____.
   a. DC V
   b. AC V
   c. Hz
   d. DC A

8. Two technicians are discussing testing MAP sensors. Technician A says that the MAP sensor voltage on a General Motors vehicle at idle should be about 1.0 volt. Technician B says that the MAP sensor frequency on a Ford vehicle at idle should be about 105–108 Hz. Which technician is correct?
   a. Technician A only
   b. Technician B only
   c. Both Technicians A and B
   d. Neither Technician A nor B

9. Technician A says that MAP sensors use a 5-volt reference voltage from the PCM. Technician B says that the MAP sensor voltage will be higher at idle at high altitudes compared to when the engine is operating at near sea level. Which technician is correct?
   a. Technician A only
   b. Technician B only
   c. Both Technicians A and B
   d. Neither Technician A nor B

10. A P0107 DTC is being discussed. Technician A says that a defective MAP sensor could be the cause. Technician B says that a MAP sensor signal wire shorted-to-ground could be the cause. Which technician is correct?
    a. Technician A only
    b. Technician B only
    c. Both Technicians A and B
    d. Neither Technician A nor B

MASS AIR FLOW SENSORS

After studying Chapter 23, the reader will be able to:

1. Prepare for ASE Engine Performance (A8) certification test content area "E" (Computerized Engine Controls Diagnosis and Repair).

2. Discuss how MAF sensors work.

3. List the methods that can be used to test MAF sensors.

4. Describe the symptoms of a failed MAF sensor.

5. List how the operation of the MAF sensor affects vehicle operation.

6. Discuss MAF sensor rationality tests.

False air 367

Mass airflow (MAF) sensor 364

Speed density 363

Tap test 367

Vane airflow (VAF) sensor 363

Engines that do not use an airflow meter or sensor rely on calculating the amount of air entering the engine by using the MAP sensor and engine speed as the major factors. The method of calculating the amount of fuel needed by the engine is called **speed density**.

AIRFLOW SENSORS

Older electronic fuel-injection systems that use airflow volume for fuel calculation usually have a movable vane in the intake stream. The vane is part of the **vane airflow (VAF) sensor.** The vane is deflected by intake airflow. ● **SEE FIGURE 23–1.**

The vane airflow sensor used in Bosch L-Jetronic, Ford, and most Japanese electronic port fuel-injection systems is a movable vane connected to a laser-calibrated potentiometer. The vane is mounted on a pivot pin and is deflected by intake airflow proportionate to air velocity. As the vane moves, it also moves the potentiometer. This causes a change in the signal voltage supplied to the computer. ● **SEE FIGURE 23–2.** For example, if the reference voltage is 5 volts, the potentiometer's signal to the computer will vary from a 0 voltage signal (no airflow) to almost a 5-volt signal (maximum airflow). In this way, the potentiometer provides the information the computer needs to vary the injector pulse width proportionate to airflow. There is a special "dampening chamber" built into the VAF to smooth out vane pulsations which would be created by intake manifold air-pressure fluctuations caused by the valve opening and closing. Many vane airflow sensors include a switch to energize the electric fuel pump. This is a safety feature that prevents the operation of the fuel pump if the engine stalls.

FREQUENTLY ASKED QUESTION

What Is the Difference Between an Analog and a Digital MAF Sensor?

Some MAF sensors produce a digital DC voltage signal whose frequency changes with the amount of airflow through the sensor. The frequency range also varies with the make of sensor and can range from 0- to 300-Hz for older General Motors MAF sensors to 1,000- to 9,000-Hz for most newer designs.

Some MAF sensors, such as those used by Ford and others, produce a changing DC voltage, rather than frequency, and range from 0- to 5-volts DC.

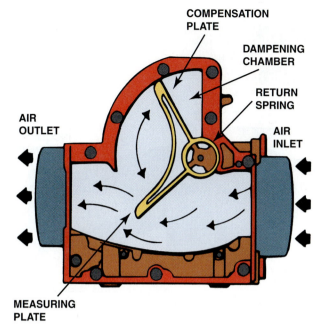

FIGURE 23–1 A vane air flow (VAF) sensor.

FIGURE 23–2 A typical air vane sensor with the cover removed. The movable arm contacts a carbon resistance path as the vane opens. Many air vane sensors also have contacts that close to supply voltage to the electric fuel pump as the air vane starts to open when the engine is being cranked and air is being drawn into the engine.

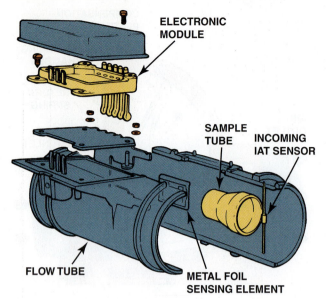

FIGURE 23–3 This five-wire mass air flow sensor consists of a metal foil sensing unit, an intake air temperature (IAT) sensor, and the electronic module.

FIGURE 23–4 The sensing wire in a typical hot wire mass air flow sensor.

MASS AIRFLOW SENSOR TYPES

There are several types of mass airflow sensors.

HOT FILM SENSOR The hot film sensor uses a temperature-sensing resistor (thermistor) to measure the temperature of the incoming air. Through the electronics within the sensor, a conductive film is kept at a temperature 70°C above the temperature of the incoming air. ● **SEE FIGURE 23–3.**

Because the amount and density of the air both tend to contribute to the cooling effect as the air passes through the sensor, this type of sensor can actually produce an output based on the *mass* of the airflow. *Mass equals volume times density.* For example, cold air is denser than warm air so a small amount of cold air may have the same mass as a larger amount of warm air. Therefore, a mass airflow sensor is designed to measure the mass, not the volume, of the air entering the engine.

The output of this type of sensor is usually a frequency based on the amount of air entering the sensor. The more air that enters the sensor, the more the hot film is cooled. The electronics inside the sensor, therefore, increase the current flow through the hot film to maintain the 70°C temperature differential between the air temperature and the temperature of the hot film. This change in current flow is converted to a frequency output that the computer can use as a measurement of airflow. Most of these types of sensors are referred to as **mass airflow (MAF) sensors** because, unlike the air vane sensor, the MAF

sensor takes into account relative humidity, altitude, and temperature of the air. The denser the air, the greater the cooling effect on the hot film sensor and the greater the amount of fuel required for proper combustion.

HOT WIRE SENSOR The hot wire sensor is similar to the hot film type, but uses a hot wire to sense the mass airflow instead of the hot film. Like the hot film sensor, the hot wire sensor uses a temperature-sensing resistor (thermistor) to measure the temperature of the air entering the sensor. ● **SEE FIGURE 23–4.** The electronic circuitry within the sensor keeps the temperature of the wire at 70°C above the temperature of the incoming air.

Both designs operate in essentially the same way. A resistor wire or screen installed in the path of intake airflow is heated to a constant temperature by electric current provided by the computer. Air flowing past the screen or wire cools it. The degree of cooling varies with air velocity, temperature, density, and humidity. These factors combine to indicate the mass of air entering the engine. As the screen or wire cools, more current is required to maintain the specified temperature. As the screen or wire heats up, less current is required. The operating principle can be summarized as follows:

- More intake air volume = cooler sensor, more current.
- Less intake air volume = warmer sensor, less current.

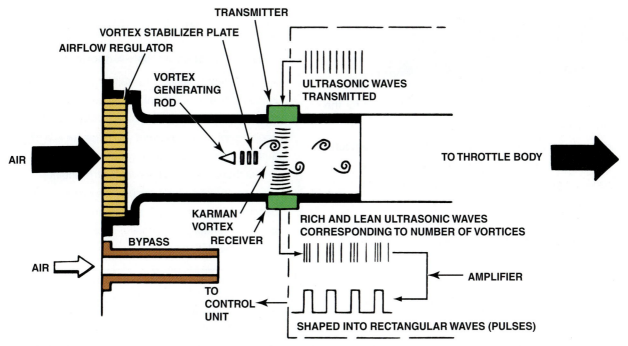

FIGURE 23–5 A Karman Vortex air flow sensor uses a triangle-shaped rod to create vortexes as the air flows through the sensor. The electronics in the sensor itself converts these vortexes to a digital square wave signal.

The computer constantly monitors the change in current and translates it into a voltage signal that is used to determine injector pulse width.

BURN-OFF CIRCUIT. Some MAF sensors use a burn-off circuit to keep the sensing wire clean of dust and dirt. A high current is passed through the sensing wire for a short time, but long enough to cause the wire to glow due to the heat. The burn-off circuit is turned on when the ignition switch is switched off after the engine has been operating long enough to achieve normal operating temperature.

KARMAN VORTEX SENSORS

In 1912, a Hungarian scientist named Theodore Van Karman observed that vortexes were created when air passed over a pointed surface. This type of sensor sends a sound wave through the turbulence created by incoming air passing through the sensor. Air mass is calculated based on the time required for the sound waves to cross the turbulent air passage.

There are two basic designs of Karman Vortex air flow sensors. The two types include:

- **Ultrasonic.** This type of sensor uses ultrasonic waves to detect the vortexes that are produced, and produce a digital (on-and-off) signal where frequency is proportional to the amount of air passing through the sensor. ● **SEE FIGURE 23–5.**

- **Pressure-type.** Chrysler uses a pressure-type Karman Vortex sensor that uses a pressure sensor to detect the vortexes. As the airflow through the sensor increases, so do the number of pressure variations. The electronics in the sensor convert these pressure variations to a square wave (digital DC voltage) signal, whose frequency is in proportion to the airflow through the sensor.

PCM USES FOR AIRFLOW SENSORS

The PCM uses the information from the airflow sensor for the following purposes:

- Airflow sensors are used mostly to determine the amount of fuel needed and base pulse-width numbers. The greater the mass of the incoming air, the longer the injectors are pulsed on.

- Airflow sensors back up the TP sensor in the event of a loss of signal or an inaccurate throttle position sensor signal. If the MAF sensor fails, then the PCM will calculate the fuel delivery needs of the engine based on throttle position and engine speed (RPM).

 REAL WORLD FIX

The Dirty MAF Sensor Story

The owner of a Buick Park Avenue equipped with a 3800 V-6 engine complained that the engine would hesitate during acceleration, showed lack of power, and seemed to surge or miss at times. A visual inspection found everything to be like new, including a new air filter. There were no stored diagnostic trouble codes (DTCs). A look at the scan data showed airflow to be within the recommended 3 to 7 grams per second. A check of the frequency output showed the problem.

Idle frequency = 2.177 kHz (2,177 Hz)

Normal frequency at idle speed should be 2.37 to 2.52 kHz. Cleaning the hot wire of the MAF sensor restored proper operation. The sensor wire was covered with what looked like fine fibers, possibly from the replacement air filter.

NOTE: Older GM MAF sensors operated at a lower frequency of 32 to 150 Hz, with 32 Hz being the average reading at idle and 150 Hz for wide-open throttle.

 FREQUENTLY ASKED QUESTION

What Is Meant By a "High-Authority Sensor"?

A high-authority sensor is a sensor that has a major influence over the amount of fuel being delivered to the engine. For example, at engine start-up, the engine coolant temperature (ECT) sensor is a high-authority sensor and the oxygen sensor (O2S) is a low-authority sensor. However, as the engine reaches operating temperature, the oxygen sensor becomes a high-authority sensor and can greatly affect the amount of fuel being supplied to the engine. See the chart.

High-Authority Sensors	Low-Authority Sensors
ECT (especially when the engine starts and is warming up)	IAT (intake air temperature) sensors modify and back up the ECT
O2S (after the engine reaches closed-loop operation)	TFT (transmission fluid temperature)
MAP	PRNDL (shift position sensor)
MAF	KS (knock sensor)
TP (high authority during acceleration and deceleration)	EFT (engine fuel temperature)

TESTING MASS AIRFLOW SENSORS

VISUAL INSPECTION Start the testing of a MAF sensor by performing a thorough visual inspection. Look at all the hoses that direct and send air, especially between the MAF sensor and the throttle body. Also check the electrical connector for:

- Corrosion
- Terminals that are bent or pushed out of the plastic connector
- Frayed wiring

MAF SENSOR OUTPUT TEST A digital multimeter, set to read DC volts, can be used to check the MAF sensor. See the chart that shows the voltage output compared with the grams per second of airflow through the sensor. Normal airflow is 3 to 7 grams per second.

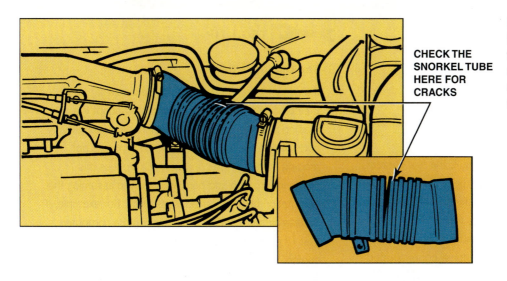

CHECK THE SNORKEL TUBE HERE FOR CRACKS

FIGURE 23–6 Carefully check the hose between the MAF sensor and the throttle plate for cracks or splits that could create extra (false) air into the engine that is not measured by the MAF sensor.

Analog MAF Sensor Grams per Second/Voltage Chart

Grams per Second	Sensor Voltage
0	0.2
2	0.7
4	1.0 (typical idle value)
8	1.5
15	2.0
30	2.5
50	3.0
80	3.5
110	4.0
150	4.5
175	4.8

TAP TEST With the engine running at idle speed, *gently* tap the MAF sensor with the fingers of an open hand. If the engine stumbles or stalls, the MAF sensor is defective. This test is commonly called the **tap test**.

DIGITAL METER TEST OF A MAF SENSOR A digital multimeter can be used to measure the frequency (Hz) output of the sensor and compare the reading with specifications.

The frequency output and engine speed in RPM can also be plotted on a graph to check to see if the frequency and RPM are proportional, resulting in a straight line on the graph.

? FREQUENTLY ASKED QUESTION

What Is False Air?

Airflow sensors and mass airflow (MAF) sensors are designed to measure *all* the air entering the engine. If an air inlet hose was loose or had a hole, extra air could enter the engine without being measured. This extra air is often called **false air.** ● SEE FIGURE 23–6. Because this extra air is unmeasured, the computer does not provide enough fuel delivery and the engine operates too lean, especially at idle. A small hole in the air inlet hose would represent a fairly large percentage of false air at idle, but would represent a very small percentage of extra air at highway speeds.

To diagnose for false air, look at long-term fuel trim numbers at idle and at 3000 RPM.

NOTE: **If the engine runs well in reverse, yet runs terrible in any forward gear, carefully look at the inlet hose for air leaks that would open when the engine torque moves the engine slightly on its mounts.**

MAF SENSOR CONTAMINATION

Dirt, oil, silicon, or even spiderwebs can coat the sensing wire. Because it tends to insulate the sensing wire at low airflow rates, a contaminated sensor often overestimates the amount of air entering the engine at idle, and therefore causes the fuel system to go rich. At higher engine speeds near wide-open throttle (WOT), the contamination can cause the sensor to underestimate the

MAF SENSOR CONTAMINATION (CONTINUED)

amount of air entering the engine. As a result, the fuel system will go lean, causing spark knock and lack of power concerns. To check for contamination, check the fuel trim numbers.

If the fuel trim is negative (removing fuel) at idle, yet is positive (adding fuel) at higher engine speeds, a contaminated MAF sensor is a likely cause. Other tests for a contaminated MAF sensor include:

- At WOT, the grams per second, as read on a scan tool, should exceed 100.

- At WOT, the voltage, as read on a digital voltmeter, should exceed 4 volts for an analog sensor.

- At WOT, the frequency, as read on a meter or scan tool, should exceed 7 kHz for a digital sensor.

If the readings do not exceed these values, then the MAF sensor is contaminated.

MAF-RELATED DIAGNOSTIC TROUBLE CODES

The diagnostic trouble codes (DTCs) associated with the mass airflow and air vane sensors include:

Diagnostic Trouble Code	Description	Possible Causes
P0100	Mass or volume airflow circuit problems	■ Open or short in mass airflow circuit ■ Defective MAF sensor
P0101	Mass airflow circuit range problems	■ Defective MAF sensor (check for false air)
P0102	Mass airflow circuit low output	■ Defective MAF sensor ■ MAF sensor circuit open or shorted-to-ground ■ Open 12-volt supply voltage circuit
P0103	Mass airflow circuit high output	■ Defective MAF sensor ■ MAF sensor circuit shorted-to-voltage

1. A mass airflow sensor actually measures the density and amount of air flowing into the engine, which results in accurate engine control.

2. An air vane sensor measures the volume of the air, and the intake air temperature sensor is used by the PCM to calculate the mass of the air entering the engine.

3. A hot wire MAF sensor uses the electronics in the sensor itself to heat a wire 70°C above the temperature of the air entering the engine.

REVIEW QUESTIONS

1. How does a hot film MAF sensor work?

2. What type of voltage signal is produced by a MAF?

3. What change in the signal will occur if engine speed is increased?

4. How is a MAF sensor tested?

5. What is the purpose of a MAF sensor?

6. What are the types of airflow sensors?

CHAPTER QUIZ

1. A fuel-injection system that does not use a sensor to measure the amount (or mass) of air entering the engine is usually called a(n) _____ type of system.
   a. Air vane-controlled
   b. Speed density
   c. Mass airflow
   d. Hot wire

2. Which type of sensor uses a burn-off circuit?
   a. Hot wire MAF sensor
   b. Hot film MAF sensor
   c. Vane-type airflow sensor
   d. Both a and b

3. Which sensor has a switch that controls the electric fuel pump?
   a. VAF
   b. Hot wire MAF
   c. Hot filter MAF
   d. Karman Vortex sensor

4. Two technicians are discussing Karman Vortex sensors. Technician A says that they contain a burn-off circuit to keep them clean. Technician B says that they contain a movable vane. Which technician is correct?
   a. Technician A only
   b. Technician B only
   c. Both Technicians A and B
   d. Neither Technician A nor B

5. The typical MAF reading on a scan tool with the engine at idle speed and normal operating temperature is _____.
   a. 1 to 3 grams per second
   b. 3 to 7 grams per second
   c. 8 to 12 grams per second
   d. 14 to 24 grams per second

6. Two technicians are diagnosing a poorly running engine. There are no diagnostic trouble codes. When the MAF sensor is unplugged, the engine runs better. Technician A says that this means that the MAF is supplying incorrect airflow information to the PCM. Technician B says that this indicates that the PCM is defective. Which technician is correct?
   a. Technician A only
   b. Technician B only
   c. Both Technicians A and B
   d. Neither Technician A nor B

7. A MAF sensor on a General Motors 3800 V-6 is being tested for contamination. Technician A says that the sensor should show over 100 grams per second on a scan tool display when the accelerator is depressed to WOT on a running engine. Technician B says that the output frequency should exceed 7,000 Hz when the accelerator pedal is depressed to WOT on a running engine. Which technician is correct?
   a. Technician A only
   b. Technician B only
   c. Both Technicians A and B
   d. Neither Technician A nor B

8. Which airflow sensor has a dampening chamber?
   a. A vane airflow
   b. A hot film MAF
   c. A hot wire MAF
   d. A Karman Vortex

9. Air that enters the engine without passing through the airflow sensor is called _____.
   a. Bypass air
   b. Dirty air
   c. False air
   d. Measured air

10. A P0102 DTC is being discussed. Technician A says that a sensor circuit shorted-to-ground can be the cause. Technician B says that an open sensor voltage supply circuit could be the cause. Which technician is correct?
    a. Technician A only
    b. Technician B only
    c. Both Technicians A and B
    d. Neither Technician A nor B

chapter 24
OXYGEN SENSORS

OBJECTIVES

After studying Chapter 24, the reader will be able to:

1. Prepare for ASE Engine Performance (A8) certification test content area "E" (Computerized Engine Controls Diagnosis and Repair).
2. Discuss how O2S sensors work.
3. List the methods that can be used to test O2S sensors.
4. Describe the symptoms of a failed O2S sensor.
5. List how the operation of the O2S sensor affects vehicle operation.

KEY TERMS

Bias voltage 375

Closed-loop operation 374

Cross counts 377

False lean indication 386

False rich indication 386

Open-loop operation 374

Oxygen sensor (O2S) 371

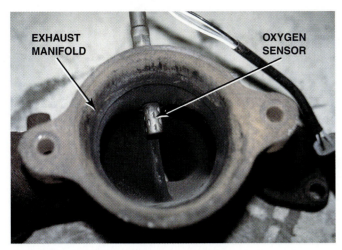

FIGURE 24–1 Many fuel-control oxygen sensors are located in the exhaust manifold near its outlet so that the sensor can detect the presence or absence of oxygen in the exhaust stream for all cylinders that feed into the manifold.

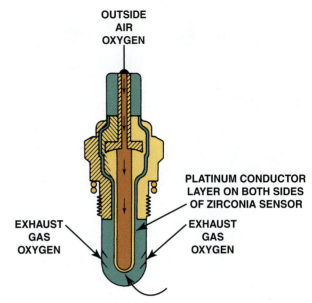

FIGURE 24–2 A cross-sectional view of a typical zirconia oxygen sensor.

OXYGEN SENSORS

PURPOSE AND FUNCTION Automotive computer systems use a sensor in the exhaust system to measure the oxygen content of the exhaust. These sensors are called **oxygen sensors (O2S).** The oxygen sensor is installed in the exhaust manifold or located downstream from the manifold in the exhaust pipe. ● **SEE FIGURE 24–1.** The oxygen sensor is directly in the path of the exhaust gas stream where it monitors oxygen level in both the exhaust stream and the ambient air. In a zirconia oxygen sensor, the tip contains a thimble made of zirconium dioxide (ZrO_2), an electrically conductive material capable of generating a small voltage in the presence of oxygen. The oxygen sensor is used by the PCM to control fuel delivery.

CONSTRUCTION AND OPERATION Exhaust from the engine passes through the end of the sensor where the gases contact the outer side of the thimble. Atmospheric air enters through the other end of the sensor or through the wire of the sensor and contacts the inner side of the thimble. The inner and outer surfaces of the thimble are plated with platinum. The inner surface becomes a negative electrode; the outer surface is a positive electrode. The atmosphere contains a relatively constant 21% of oxygen. Rich exhaust gases contain little oxygen. Exhaust from a lean mixture contains more oxygen.

Negatively charged oxygen ions are drawn to the thimble where they collect on both the inner and outer surfaces. ● **SEE FIGURE 24–2.** Because the percentage of oxygen present in

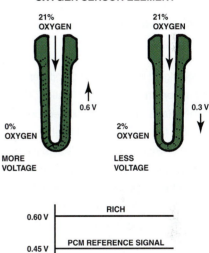

FIGURE 24–3 A difference in oxygen content between the atmosphere and the exhaust gases enables an O2S sensor to generate voltage.

the atmosphere exceeds that in the exhaust gases, the atmosphere side of the thimble draws more negative oxygen ions than the exhaust side. The difference between the two sides creates an electrical potential, or voltage. When the concentration of oxygen on the exhaust side of the thimble is low (risk effort), a high voltage (0.60 to 1.0 volts) is generated between the electrodes. As the oxygen concentration on the exhaust side increases (lean exhaust), the voltage generated drops low (0.00 to 0.3 volts). ● **SEE FIGURE 24–3.**

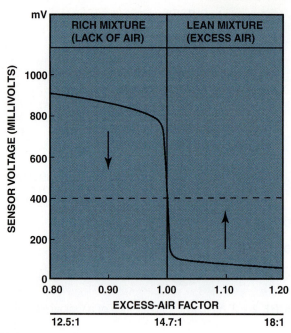

FIGURE 24-4 The oxygen sensor provides a quick response at the stoichiometric air–fuel ratio of 14.7:1.

OXYGEN SENSORS (CONTINUED)

This voltage signal is sent to the computer where it passes through the input conditioner for amplification. The computer interprets a high-voltage signal (low-oxygen content) as a rich air–fuel ratio, and a low-voltage signal (high-oxygen content) as a lean air–fuel ratio. Based on the O2S signal (above or below 0.45 volts), the computer compensates by making the mixture either leaner or richer as required to continually vary close to a 14.7:1 air–fuel ratio to satisfy the needs of the three-way catalytic converter. The O2S is the key sensor of an electronically controlled fuel metering system for emission control.

An O2S does not send a voltage signal until its tip reaches a temperature of about 572°F (300°C). Also, O2 sensors provide their fastest response to mixture changes at about 1472°F (800°C). When the engine starts and the O2S is cold, the computer runs the engine in the open-loop mode, drawing on prerecorded data in the PROM for fuel control on a cold engine, or when O2S output is not within certain limits.

If the exhaust contains very little oxygen (O2S), the computer assumes that the intake charge is rich (too much fuel) and reduces fuel delivery. ● **SEE FIGURE 24-4.** However, when the oxygen level is high, the computer assumes that the intake charge is lean (not enough fuel) and increases fuel delivery.

There are several different designs of oxygen sensors, including:

- **One-wire oxygen sensor.** The one wire of the one-wire oxygen sensor is the O2S signal wire. The ground for the O2S is through the shell and threads of the sensor and through the exhaust manifold.

- **Two-wire oxygen sensor.** The two-wire sensor has a signal wire and a ground wire for the O2S.

- **Three-wire oxygen sensor.** The three-wire sensor design uses an electric resistance heater to help get the O2S up to temperature more quickly and to help keep the sensor at operating temperature even at idle speeds. The three wires include the O2S signal, the power, and ground for the heater.

- **Four-wire oxygen sensor.** The four-wire sensor is a heated O2S (HO2S) that uses an O2S signal wire and signal ground. The other two wires are the power and ground for the heater.

FIGURE 24–5 A typical zirconia oxygen sensor.

ZIRCONIA OXYGEN SENSORS

The most common type of oxygen sensor is made from zirconia (zirconium dioxide). It is usually constructed using powder that is pressed into a thimble shape and coated with porous platinum material that acts as electrodes. All zirconia sensors use 18-mm-diameter threads with a washer. ● **SEE FIGURE 24–5.**

Zirconia oxygen sensors (O2S) are constructed so that oxygen ions flow through the sensor when there is a difference between the oxygen content inside and outside of the sensor. An ion is an electrically charged particle. The greater the differences between the oxygen content between the inside and outside of the sensor the higher the voltage created.

- **Rich mixture.** A rich mixture results in little oxygen in the exhaust stream. Compared to the outside air, this represents a large difference and the sensors create a relatively high voltage of about 1.0 volt (1,000 mV).

- **Lean mixture.** A lean mixture leaves some oxygen in the exhaust stream that did not combine with the fuel. This leftover oxygen reduces the difference between the oxygen content of the exhaust compared to the oxygen content of the outside air. As a result, the sensor voltage is low or almost 0 volt.

- **O2S voltage above 450 mV.** This is produced by the sensor when the oxygen content in the exhaust is low. This is interpreted by the engine computer (PCM) as being a rich exhaust.

- **O2S voltage below 450 mV.** This is produced by the sensor when the oxygen content is high. This is interpreted by the engine computer (PCM) as being a lean exhaust.

TITANIA OXYGEN SENSOR

The titania (titanium dioxide) oxygen sensor does not produce a voltage but rather changes in resistance with the presence of oxygen in the exhaust. All titania oxygen sensors use a four-terminal variable resistance unit with a heating element. A titania sensor samples exhaust air only and uses a reference voltage from the PCM. Titania oxide oxygen sensors use a 14-mm thread and are not interchangeable with zirconia oxygen sensors. One volt is applied to the sensor and the changing resistance of the titania oxygen sensor changes the voltage of the sensor circuit. As with a zirconia oxygen sensor, the voltage signal is above 450 mV when the exhaust is rich, and low (below 450 mV) when the exhaust is lean.

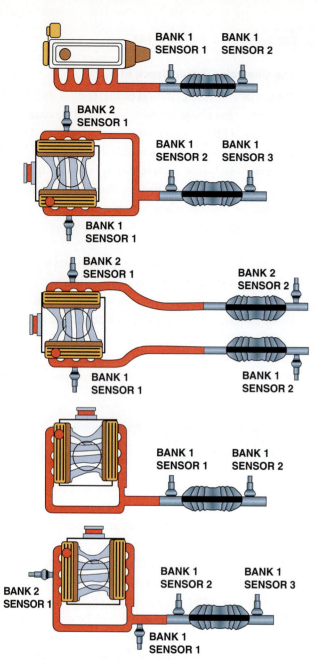

FIGURE 24–6 Number and label designations for oxygen sensors. Bank 1 is the bank where cylinder number 1 is located.

CLOSED LOOP AND OPEN LOOP

The amount of fuel delivered to an engine is determined by the Powertrain Control Module (PCM) based on inputs from the engine coolant temperature (ECT), throttle position (TP) sensor, and others until the oxygen sensor is capable of supplying a usable signal. When the PCM alone (without feedback) is determining the amount of fuel needed, it is called **open-loop operation.** As soon as the oxygen sensor (O2S) is capable of supplying rich and lean signals, adjustments by the computer can be made to fine-tune the correct air–fuel mixture. This checking and adjusting by the computer is called **closed-loop operation.**

PCM USES OF THE OXYGEN SENSOR

FUEL CONTROL The upstream oxygen sensors are among the main sensor(s) used for fuel control while operating in closed loop. Before the oxygen sensors are hot enough to give accurate exhaust oxygen information to the computer, fuel control is determined by other sensors and the anticipated injector pulse width determined by those sensors. After the control system achieves closed-loop status, the oxygen sensor provides feedback with actual exhaust gas oxygen content.

FUEL TRIM Fuel trim is a computer program that is used to compensate for a too rich or a too lean air–fuel exhaust as detected by the oxygen sensor(s). Fuel trim is necessary to keep the air–fuel mixture within limits to allow the catalytic converter to operate efficiently. If the exhaust is too lean or too rich for a long time, the catalytic converter can be damaged. The fuel trim numbers are determined from the signals from the oxygen sensor(s). If the engine has been operating too lean, short-term and long-term fuel time programming inside the PCM can cause an increase in the commanded injector pulse width to bring the air–fuel mixture back into the proper range. Fuel trim can be negative (subtracting fuel) or positive (adding fuel).

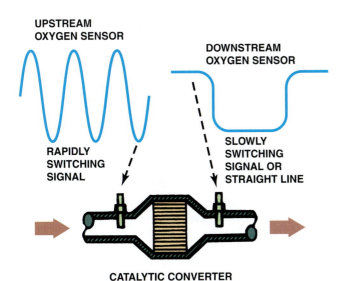

FIGURE 24–7 The OBD-II catalytic converter monitor compares the signals of the upstream and downstream oxygen sensor to determine converter efficiency.

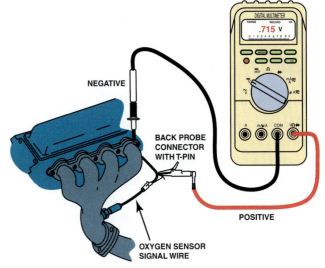

FIGURE 24–8 Testing an oxygen sensor using a DMM set on DC volts. With the engine operating in closed loop, the oxygen voltage should read over 800 mV and lower than 200 mV and be constantly fluctuating.

OXYGEN SENSOR DIAGNOSIS

The oxygen sensors are used for diagnosis of other systems and components. For example, the exhaust gas recirculation (EGR) system is tested by the PCM by commanding the valve to open during the test. Some PCMs determine whether enough exhaust gas flows into the engine by looking at the oxygen sensor response (fuel trim numbers). The upstream and downstream oxygen sensors are also used to determine the efficiency of the catalytic converter. ● SEE FIGURE 24–7.

TESTING AN OXYGEN SENSOR USING A DIGITAL VOLTMETER
The oxygen sensor can be checked for proper operation using a digital high-impedance voltmeter.

1. With the engine off, connect the red lead of the meter to the oxygen sensor signal wire. ● SEE FIGURE 24–8.

2. Start the engine and allow it to reach closed-loop operation.

3. In closed-loop operation, the oxygen sensor voltage should be constantly changing as the fuel mixture is being controlled.

The results should be interpreted as follows:

- If the oxygen sensor fails to respond, and its voltage remains at about 450 millivolts, the sensor may be defective and require replacement. Before replacing the oxygen sensor, check the manufacturers' recommended procedures.

- If the oxygen sensor reads high all the time (above 550 millivolts), the fuel system could be supplying too rich a fuel mixture or the oxygen sensor may be contaminated.

? **FREQUENTLY ASKED QUESTION**

What Happens to the Bias Voltage?

Some vehicle manufacturers such as General Motors Corporation have the computer apply 450 mV (0.450 V) to the O2S signal wire. This voltage is called the **bias voltage** and represents the threshold voltage for the transition from rich to lean.

This bias voltage is displayed on a scan tool when the ignition switch is turned on with the engine off. When the engine is started, the O2S becomes warm enough to produce a usable voltage and bias voltage "disappears" as the O2S responds to a rich and lean mixture. What happened to the bias voltage that the computer applied to the O2S? The voltage from the O2S simply overcame the very weak voltage signal from the computer. This bias voltage is so weak that even a 20-megohm impedance DMM will affect the strength enough to cause the voltage to drop to 426 mV. Other meters with only 10 megohms of impedance will cause the bias voltage to read less than 400 mV.

Therefore, even though the O2S voltage is relatively low powered, it is more than strong enough to override the very weak bias voltage the computer sends to the O2S.

REAL WORLD FIX

The Oxygen Sensor Is Lying to You

A technician was trying to solve a driveability problem with an older V-6 passenger car. The car idled roughly, hesitated, and accelerated poorly. A thorough visual inspection did not indicate any possible problems and there were no diagnostic trouble codes stored.

A check was made on the oxygen sensor activity using a DMM. The voltage stayed above 600 mV most of the time. If a large vacuum hose was removed, the oxygen sensor voltage would temporarily drop to below 450 mV and then return to a reading of over 600 mV. Remember:

- High O2S readings = rich exhaust (low O_2 content in the exhaust)
- Low O2S readings = lean exhaust (high O_2 content in the exhaust)

As part of a thorough visual inspection, the technician removed and inspected the spark plugs. All the spark plugs were white, indicating a lean mixture, not the rich mixture that the oxygen sensor was indicating. The high O2S reading signaled the computer to reduce the amount of fuel, resulting in an excessively lean operation.

After replacing the oxygen sensor, the engine ran great. But what killed the oxygen sensor? The technician finally learned from the owner that the head gasket had been replaced over a year ago. The phosphate and silicate additives in the antifreeze coolant had coated the oxygen sensor. Because the oxygen sensor was coated, the oxygen content of the exhaust could not be detected—the result: a false rich signal from the oxygen sensor.

- If the oxygen sensor voltage remains low (below 350 millivolts), the fuel system could be supplying too lean a fuel mixture. Check for a vacuum leak or partially clogged fuel injector(s). Before replacing the oxygen sensor, check the manufacturer's recommended procedures.

TESTING THE OXYGEN SENSOR USING THE MIN/MAX METHOD

A digital meter set on DC volts can be used to record the minimum and maximum voltage with the engine running. A good oxygen sensor should be able to produce

 REAL WORLD FIX

The Missing Ford Escort

A Ford Escort was being analyzed for poor engine operation. The engine ran perfectly during the following conditions:

1. With the engine cold or operating in open loop
2. With the engine at idle
3. With the engine operating at or near wide-open throttle

After hours of troubleshooting, the cause was found to be a poor ground connection for the oxygen sensor. The engine ran okay during times when the computer ignored the oxygen sensor. Unfortunately, the service technician did not have a definite plan during the diagnostic process and as a result checked and replaced many unnecessary parts. An oxygen sensor test early in the diagnostic procedure would have indicated that the oxygen (O2S) signal was not correct. The poor ground caused the oxygen sensor voltage level to be too high, indicating to the computer that the mixture was too rich. The computer then subtracted fuel, which caused the engine to miss and run rough as the result of the now too lean air–fuel mixture.

 FREQUENTLY ASKED QUESTION

Why Does the Oxygen Sensor Voltage Read 5 Volts on Many Chrysler Vehicles?

Many Chrysler vehicles apply a 5-volt reference to the signal wire of the oxygen sensor. The purpose of this voltage is to allow the computer to detect if the oxygen sensor signal circuit is open or grounded.

- If the voltage on the signal wire is 4.5 volts or more, the computer assumes that the sensor is open.
- If the voltage on the signal wire is zero, the computer assumes that the sensor is shorted-to-ground.

If either condition exists, the computer can set a diagnostic trouble code (DTC).

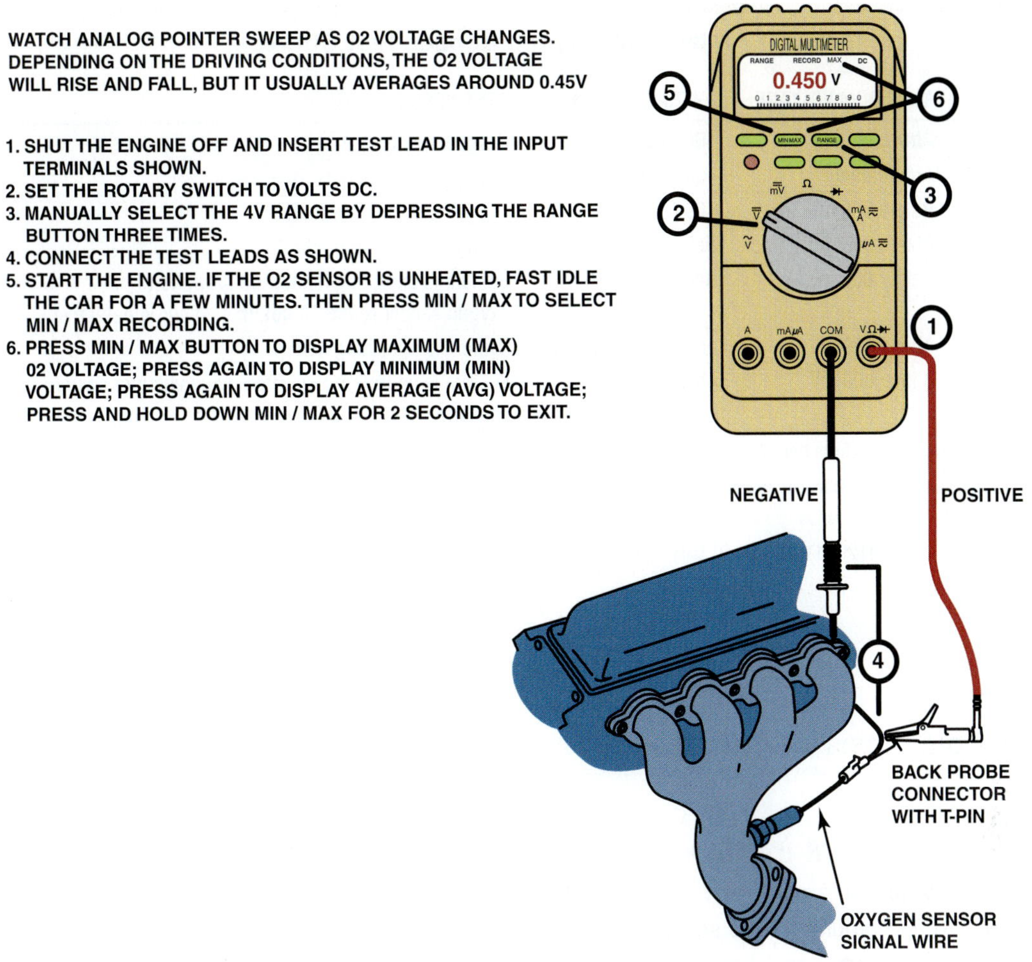

WATCH ANALOG POINTER SWEEP AS O2 VOLTAGE CHANGES.
DEPENDING ON THE DRIVING CONDITIONS, THE O2 VOLTAGE
WILL RISE AND FALL, BUT IT USUALLY AVERAGES AROUND 0.45V

1. SHUT THE ENGINE OFF AND INSERT TEST LEAD IN THE INPUT
   TERMINALS SHOWN.
2. SET THE ROTARY SWITCH TO VOLTS DC.
3. MANUALLY SELECT THE 4V RANGE BY DEPRESSING THE RANGE
   BUTTON THREE TIMES.
4. CONNECT THE TEST LEADS AS SHOWN.
5. START THE ENGINE. IF THE O2 SENSOR IS UNHEATED, FAST IDLE
   THE CAR FOR A FEW MINUTES. THEN PRESS MIN / MAX TO SELECT
   MIN / MAX RECORDING.
6. PRESS MIN / MAX BUTTON TO DISPLAY MAXIMUM (MAX)
   02 VOLTAGE; PRESS AGAIN TO DISPLAY MINIMUM (MIN)
   VOLTAGE; PRESS AGAIN TO DISPLAY AVERAGE (AVG) VOLTAGE;
   PRESS AND HOLD DOWN MIN / MAX FOR 2 SECONDS TO EXIT.

NEGATIVE   POSITIVE

BACK PROBE
CONNECTOR
WITH T-PIN

OXYGEN SENSOR
SIGNAL WIRE

FIGURE 24–9 Using a digital multimeter to test an oxygen sensor using the MIN/MAX record function of the meter.

a value of less than 300 millivolts and a maximum voltage above 800 millivolts. Replace any oxygen sensor that fails to go above 700 millivolts or lower than 300 millivolts. ● **SEE FIGURE 24–9.** See the MIN/MAX oxygen sensor test chart.

TESTING AN OXYGEN SENSOR USING A SCAN TOOL

A good oxygen sensor should be able to sense the oxygen content and change voltage outputs rapidly. How fast an oxygen sensor switches from high (above 450 millivolts) to low (below 350 millivolts) is measured in oxygen sensor **cross counts.** Cross counts are the number of times an oxygen sensor changes voltage from high to low (from low to high voltage is not counted) in 1 second (or 1.25 second, depending on scan tool and computer speed).

NOTE: On a fuel-injected engine at 2000 engine RPM, 8 to 10 cross counts is normal.

Oxygen sensor cross counts can only be determined using a scan tool or other suitable tester that reads computer data. ● **SEE CHART 24–1.**

If the cross counts are low (or zero), the oxygen sensor may be contaminated, or the fuel delivery system is delivering a constant rich or lean air–fuel mixture. To test an engine using a scan tool, follow these steps:

1. Connect the scan tool to the DLC and start the engine.

2. Operate the engine at a fast idle (2500 RPM) for 2 minutes to allow time for the oxygen sensor to warm to operating temperature.

3. Observe the oxygen sensor activity on the scan tool to verify closed-loop operation. Select "snapshot" mode and hold the engine speed steady and start recording.

4. Play back snapshot and place a mark beside each range of oxygen sensor voltage for each frame of the snapshot.

A good oxygen sensor and computer system should result in most snapshot values at both ends (0 to 300 and 600 to 1,000 mV). If most of the readings are in the middle, the oxygen sensor is not working correctly.

MIN/MAX Oxygen Sensor Test Chart

MINIMUM VOLTAGE	MAXIMUM VOLTAGE	AVERAGE VOLTAGE	TEST RESULTS
Below 200 mV	Above 800 mV	400 to 500 mV	Oxygen sensor is okay.
Above 200 mV	Any reading	400 to 500 mV	Oxygen sensor is defective.
Any reading	Below 800 mV	400 to 500 mV	Oxygen sensor is defective.
Below 200 mV	Above 800 mV	Below 400 mV	System is operating lean.*
Below 200 mV	Below 800 mV	Below 400 mV	System is operating lean. (Add propane to the intake air to see if the oxygen sensor reacts. If not, the sensor is defective.)
Below 200 mV	Above 800 mV	Above 500 mV	System is operating rich.
Above 200 mV	Above 800 mV	Above 500 mV	System is operating rich. (Remove a vacuum hose to see if the oxygen sensor reacts. If not, the sensor is defective.)

*Check for an exhaust leak upstream from the O2S or ignition misfire that can cause a false lean indication before further diagnosis.

CHART 24–1

Use this chart to check for proper operation of the oxygen sensors and fuel system after checking them using a multimeter set to read Min/Max.

OXYGEN SENSOR DIAGNOSIS (CONTINUED)

TESTING AN OXYGEN SENSOR USING A SCOPE A scope can also be used to test an oxygen sensor. Connect the scope to the signal wire and ground for the sensor (if it is so equipped). ● **SEE FIGURE 24–10.** With the engine operating in closed loop, the voltage signal of the sensor should be constantly changing. ● **SEE FIGURE 24–11.** Check for rapid switching from rich to lean and lean to rich and change between once every 2 seconds and five times per second (0.5 to 5.0 Hz). ● **SEE FIGURES 24–12, 24–13, AND 24–14.**

NOTE: General Motors warns not to base the diagnosis of an oxygen sensor problem solely on its scope pattern. The varying voltage output of an oxygen sensor can easily be mistaken for a fault in the sensor itself, rather than a fault in the fuel delivery system.

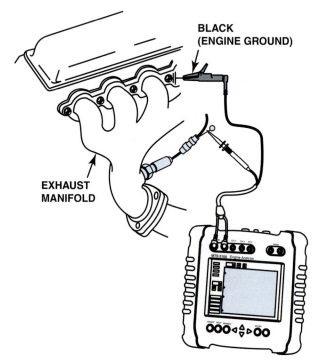

FIGURE 24–10 Connecting a handheld digital storage oscilloscope to an oxygen sensor signal wire. The use of the low-pass filter helps eliminate any low-frequency interference from affecting the scope display.

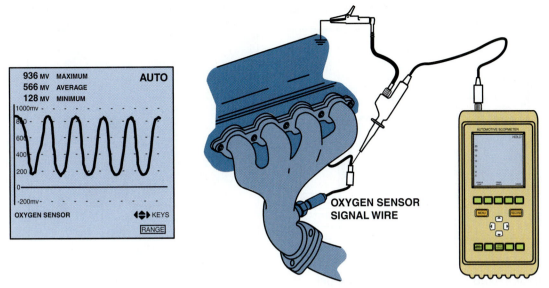

FIGURE 24–11 The waveform of a good oxygen sensor as displayed on a digital storage oscilloscope (DSO). Note that the maximum reading is above 800 mV and the minimum reading is less than 200 mV.

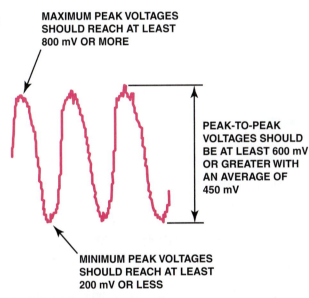

MAXIMUM PEAK VOLTAGES SHOULD REACH AT LEAST 800 mV OR MORE

PEAK-TO-PEAK VOLTAGES SHOULD BE AT LEAST 600 mV OR GREATER WITH AN AVERAGE OF 450 mV

MINIMUM PEAK VOLTAGES SHOULD REACH AT LEAST 200 mV OR LESS

FIGURE 24–12 A typical good oxygen sensor waveform as displayed on a digital storage oscilloscope. Look for transitions that occur between once every two seconds at idle and five times per second at higher engine speeds (0.5 and 5 Hz). *(Courtesy of Fluke Corporation)*

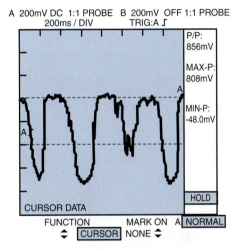

ONCE YOU'VE ACTIVATED "PEAK-TO-PEAK," "MAX-PEAK," AND "MIN-PEAK," FRAME THE WAVEFORM WITH CURSORS - LOOK FOR THE MINIMUM AND MAXIMUM VOLTAGES AND THE DIFFERENCE BETWEEN THEM IN THE RIGHT DISPLAY.

FIGURE 24–13 Using the cursors on the oscilloscope, the high- and low-oxygen sensor values can be displayed on the screen. *(Courtesy of Fluke Corporation)*

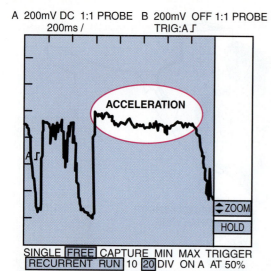

A 200mV DC 1:1 PROBE   B 200mV OFF 1:1 PROBE
    200ms /   TRIG:A ⌐

ACCELERATION

↕ZOOM
HOLD

SINGLE FREE CAPTURE MIN MAX TRIGGER
RECURRENT RUN 10 20 DIV ON A AT 50%

**UNDER HARD ACCELERATION, THE AIR–FUEL
MIXTURE SHOULD BECOME RICH - THE
VOLTAGE SHOULD STAY FAIRLY HIGH**

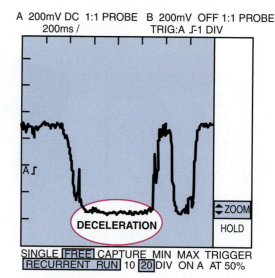

A 200mV DC 1:1 PROBE   B 200mV OFF 1:1 PROBE
    200ms /   TRIG:A ⌐-1 DIV

DECELERATION

↕ZOOM
HOLD

SINGLE FREE CAPTURE MIN MAX TRIGGER
RECURRENT RUN 10 20 DIV ON A AT 50%

**WHILE DECELERATING, MIXTURES BECOME LEAN.
LOOK FOR LOW VOLTAGE LEVELS.**

FIGURE 24–14 When the air–fuel mixture rapidly changes such as during a rapid acceleration, look for a rapid response. The transition from low to high should be less than 100 ms. *(Courtesy of Fluke Corporation)*

🔧 **TECH TIP**

The Key On, Engine Off Oxygen Sensor Test

This test works on General Motors vehicles and may work on others if the PCM applies a bias voltage to the oxygen sensors. Zirconia oxygen sensors become more electrically conductive as they get hot. To perform this test, be sure that the vehicle has not run for several hours.

STEP 1 Connect a scan tool and get the display ready to show oxygen sensor data.

STEP 2 Key the engine on *without* starting the engine. The heater in the oxygen sensor will start heating the sensor.

STEP 3 Observe the voltage of the oxygen sensor. The applied bias voltage of 450 mV should slowly decrease for all oxygen sensors as they become more electrically conductive and other bias voltage is flowing to ground.

STEP 4 A good oxygen sensor should indicate a voltage of less than 100 mV after 3 minutes. Any sensor that displays a higher-than-usual voltage or seems to stay higher longer than the others could be defective or skewed high.

🔧 **TECH TIP**

The Propane Oxygen Sensor Test

Adding propane to the air inlet of a running engine is an excellent way to check if the oxygen sensor is able to react to changes in air–fuel mixture. Follow these steps in performing the propane trick:

1. Connect a digital storage oscilloscope to the oxygen sensor signal wire.

2. Start and operate the engine until up to operating temperature and in closed-loop fuel control.

3. While watching the scope display, add some propane to the air inlet. The scope display should read full rich (over 800 mV), as shown in
  ● **FIGURE 24–15.**

4. Shut off the propane. The waveform should drop to less than 200 mV (0.200 V), as shown in
  ● **FIGURE 24–16.**

5. Quickly add some propane while the oxygen sensor is reading low and watch for a rapid transition to rich. The transition should occur in less than 100 milliseconds (ms).

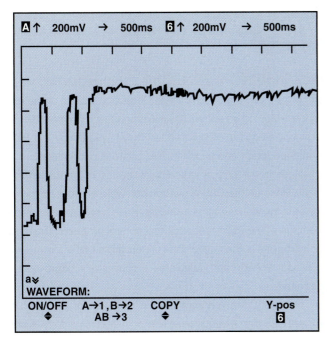

FIGURE 24–15 Adding propane to the air inlet of an engine operating in closed loop with a working oxygen sensor causes the oxygen sensor voltage to read high.

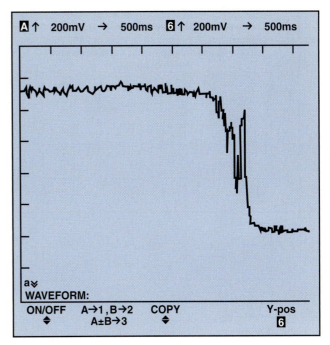

FIGURE 24–16 When the propane is shut off, the oxygen sensor should read below 200 mV.

OXYGEN SENSOR WAVEFORM ANALYSIS

As the O_2 sensor warms up, the sensor voltage begins to rise. When the sensor voltage rises above 450 mV, the PCM determines that the sensor is up to operating temperature, takes control of the fuel mixture, and begins to cycle rich and lean. At this point, the system is considered to be in closed loop.
● **SEE FIGURE 24–17.**

FREQUENCY The frequency of the O_2 sensor is important in determining the condition of the fuel control system. The higher the frequency the better, but the frequency must not exceed 6 Hz. For its OBD-II standards, the government has stated that a frequency greater than 6 Hz represents a misfire.

THROTTLE-BODY FUEL-INJECTION SYSTEMS. Normal TBI system rich/lean switching frequencies are from about 0.5 Hz at idle to about 3 Hz at 2500 RPM. Additionally, due to the TBI design limitations, fuel distribution to individual cylinders may not always be equal (due to unequal intake runner length, etc.). This may be normal unless certain other conditions are present at the same time.

PORT FUEL-INJECTION SYSTEMS. Specification for port fuel-injection systems is 0.5 Hz at idle to 5 Hz at 2500 RPM.

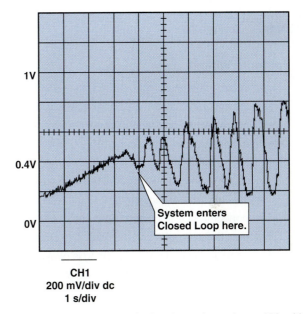

CH1
200 mV/div dc
1 s/div

FIGURE 24–17 When the O2S voltage rises above 450 mV, the PCM starts to control the fuel mixture based on oxygen sensor activity.

● **SEE FIGURE 24–18.** Port fuel-injection systems have more rich/lean O2S voltage transitions (cross counts) for a given amount of time than any other type of system, due to the greatly improved system design compared to TBI units.

Port fuel-injection systems take the least amount of time to react to the fuel adaptive command (for example, changing injector pulse width).

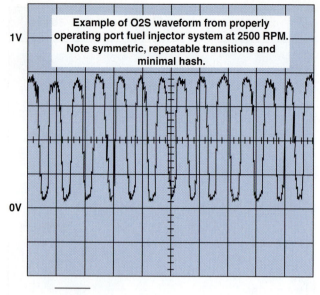

Example of O2S waveform from properly operating port fuel injector system at 2500 RPM. Note symmetric, repeatable transitions and minimal hash.

1V

0V

CH1
200 mV/div dc
1 s/div

FIGURE 24–18 Normal oxygen sensor frequency is from about one to five times per second.

TECH TIP

Sensor or Wiring?

When troubleshooting a diagnostic trouble code, it is sometimes difficult to determine if the sensor itself is defective or its wiring and ground connections are defective. For example, when diagnosing an O2S code, perform the following to check the wiring:

1. Connect a scan tool and observe the O2S voltage with the ignition on (engine off).
2. Disconnect the O2S pigtail to open the circuit between the computer and the O2S. The scan tool should read 450 mV if the wiring is okay and the scan tool is showing the bias voltage.

   NOTE: Some vehicle manufacturers do not apply a bias voltage to the O2S and the reading on the scan tool may indicate zero and be okay.

3. Ground the O2S wire from the computer. The scan tool should read 0 volts if the wiring is okay.

HASH

BACKGROUND INFORMATION Hash on the O2S waveform is defined as a series of high-frequency spikes, or the fuzz (or noise) viewed on some O2S waveforms, or more specifically, oscillation frequencies higher than those created by the PCM normal feedback operation (normal rich/lean oscillations).

Hash is the critical indicator of reduced combustion efficiency. Hash on the O2S waveform can warn of reduced performance in individual engine cylinders. Hash also impedes proper operation of the PCM feedback fuel control program. The feedback program is the active software program that interprets the O_2 sensor voltage and calculates a corrective mixture control command.

Generally, the program for the PCM is not designed to process O2S signal frequencies efficiently that result from events other than normal system operation and fuel control commands. The high-frequency oscillations of the hash can cause the PCM to lose control. This, in turn, has several effects. When the operating strategy of the PCM is adversely affected, the air–fuel ratio drifts out of the catalyst window, which affects converter operating efficiency, exhaust emissions, and engine performance.

Hash on the O2S waveform indicates an exhaust charge imbalance from one cylinder to another, or more specifically, a higher oxygen content sensed from an individual combustion event. Most oxygen sensors, when working properly, can react fast enough to generate voltage deflections corresponding to a single combustion event. The bigger the amplitude of the deflection (hash), the greater the differential in oxygen content sensed from a particular combustion event.

There are vehicles that will have hash on their O2S waveforms and are operating perfectly normal. Small amounts of hash may not be of concern and larger amounts of hash may be all important. A good rule concerning hash is, if engine performance is good, there are no vacuum leaks, and if exhaust HC (hydrocarbon) and oxygen levels are okay while hash is present on the O2S waveform, then the hash is nothing to worry about.

CAUSES OF HASH Hash on the O2S signal can be caused by the following:

1. Misfiring cylinders
   - Ignition misfire
   - Lean misfire
   - Rich misfire
   - Compression-related misfire
   - Vacuum leaks
   - Injector imbalance

2. System design, such as different intake runner length

3. System design amplified by engine and component degradation caused by aging and wear

4. System manufacturing variances, such as intake tract blockage and valve stem mismachining

The spikes and hash on the waveform during a misfire event are created by incomplete combustion, which results in only partial use of the available oxygen in the cylinder. The left-over oxygen goes out the exhaust port and travels past the oxygen sensor. When the oxygen sensor "sees" the oxygen-filled exhaust charge, it quickly generates a low voltage, or spike. A series of these high-frequency spikes make up what we are calling "hash."

CLASSIFICATIONS OF HASH

CLASS 1: AMPLIFIED AND SIGNIFICANT HASH. Amplified hash is the somewhat unimportant hash that is often present between 300 and 600 millivolts on the O2S waveform. This type of hash is usually not important for diagnosis. That is because amplified hash is created largely as a result of the electrochemical properties of the O2S itself and many times not an engine or other unrelated problem. Hash between 300 and 600 mV is not particularly conclusive, so for all practical purposes it is insignificant. ● **SEE FIGURE 24–19**.

Significant hash is defined as the hash that occurs above 600 mV and below 300 mV on the O2S waveform. This is the area of the waveform that the PCM is watching to determine the fuel mixture. Significant hash is important for diagnosis because it is caused by a combustion event. If the waveform exhibits class 1 hash, the combustion event problem is probably occurring in only one of the cylinders. If the event happens in a greater number of the cylinders the waveform will become class 3 or be fixed lean or rich the majority of the time.

CLASS 2: MODERATE HASH. Moderate hash is defined as spikes shooting downward from the top arc of the waveform as the waveform carves its arc through the rich phase. Moderate hash spikes are not greater than 150 mV in amplitude. They may get as large as 200 mV in amplitude as the O2S waveform goes through 450 mV. Moderate hash may or may not be significant to a particular diagnosis. ● **SEE FIGURE 24–20**. For instance, most vehicles will exhibit more hash on the O2S waveform at idle. Additionally, the engine family or type of O2S could be

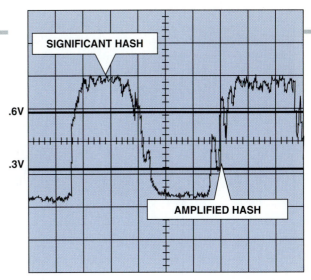

FIGURE 24–19 Significant hash can be caused by faults in one or more cylinders, whereas amplified hash is not as important for diagnosis.

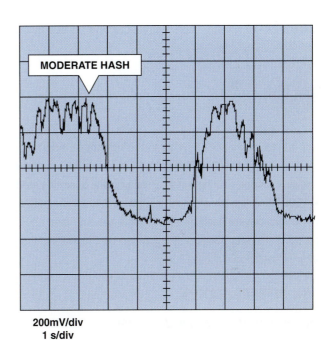

200mV/div
1 s/div

FIGURE 24–20 Moderate hash may or may not be significant for diagnosis.

important factors when considering the significance of moderate hash on the O2S waveform.

CLASS 3: SEVERE HASH. Severe hash is defined as hash whose amplitude is greater than 200 mV. Severe hash may even cover the entire voltage range of the sensor for an extended period of operation. Severe hash on the DSO display appears as spikes that shoot downward, over 200 mV from the top of the operating

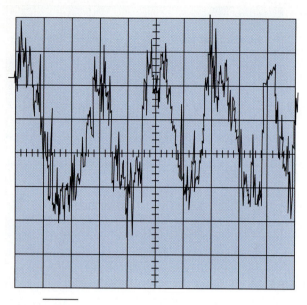

CH1
200 mV/div dc
500 ms/div

FIGURE 24–21 Severe hash is almost always caused by cylinder misfire conditions.

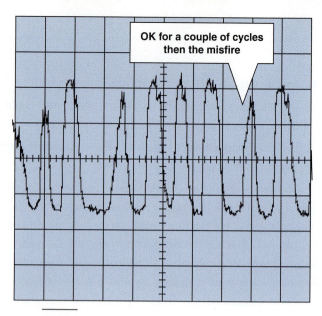

OK for a couple of cycles then the misfire

CH1
200 mV/div dc
500 ms/div

FIGURE 24–22 An ignition- or mixture-related misfire can cause hash on the oxygen sensor waveform.

HASH (CONTINUED)

range of the sensor, or as far as to the bottom of the sensor's operating range. ● SEE FIGURE 24–21. If severe hash is present for several seconds during a steady state engine operating mode, say 2500 RPM, it is almost always significant to the diagnosis of any vehicle. Severe hash of this nature is almost never caused by a normal system design. It is caused by cylinder misfire or mixture imbalance.

HASH INTERPRETATION

TYPES OF MISFIRES THAT CAN CAUSE HASH.

1. Ignition misfire caused by a bad spark plug, spark plug wire, distributor cap, rotor, ignition coil, or ignition primary problem. Usually an engine analyzer is used to eliminate these possibilities or confirm these problems. ● SEE FIGURE 24–22.

2. Rich misfire from an excessively rich fuel delivery to an individual cylinder (various potential root causes). Air–fuel ratio in a given cylinder ventured below approximately 13:1.

3. Lean misfire from an excessively lean fuel delivery to an individual cylinder (various potential root causes). Air–fuel ratio in a given cylinder ventured above approximately 17:1.

4. Compression-related misfire from a mechanical problem that reduces compression to the point that not enough heat

is generated from compressing the air–fuel mixture prior to ignition, preventing combustion. This raises O2S content in the exhaust (for example, a burned valve, broken or worn ring, flat cam lobe, or sticking valve).

5. Vacuum leak misfire unique to one or two individual cylinders. This possibility is eliminated or confirmed by inducing propane around any potential vacuum leak area (intake runners, intake manifold gaskets, vacuum hoses, etc.) while watching the DSO to see when the signal goes rich and the hash changes from ingesting the propane. Vacuum leak misfires are caused when a vacuum leak unique to one cylinder or a few individual cylinders causes the air–fuel ratio in the affected cylinder(s) to venture above approximately 17:1, causing a lean misfire.

6. Injector imbalance misfire (on port fuel-injected engines only); one cylinder has a rich or lean misfire due to an individual injector(s) delivering the wrong quantity of fuel. Injector imbalance misfires are caused when an injector on one cylinder or a few individual cylinders causes the air–fuel ratio in its cylinder(s) to venture above approximately 17:1, causing a lean misfire, or below approximately 13.7:1, causing a rich misfire. ● SEE FIGURE 24–23.

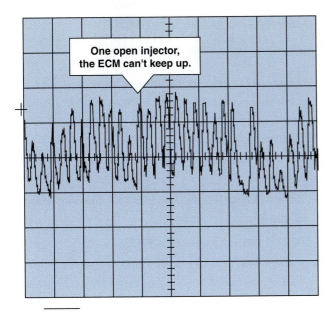

Memory 4
200 mV/div
200 ms/div

FIGURE 24–23 An injector imbalance can cause a lean or a rich misfire.

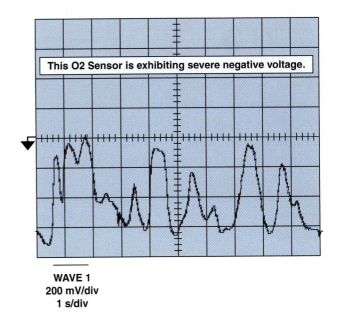

WAVE 1
200 mV/div
1 s/div

FIGURE 24–24 Negative reading oxygen sensor voltage can be caused by several problems.

OTHER RULES CONCERNING HASH ON THE O2S WAVEFORM

If there is significant hash on the O2S signal that is not normal for that type of system, it will usually be accompanied by a repeatable and generally detectable engine miss at idle (for example, a thump, thump, thump every time the cylinder fires). Generally, if the hash is significant, the engine miss will correlate in time with individual spikes seen on the waveform.

Hash that may be difficult to get rid of (and is normal in some cases) will not be accompanied by a significant engine miss that corresponds with the hash. When the individual spikes that make up the hash on the waveform do not correlate in time with an engine miss, less success can usually be found in getting rid of them by performing repairs.

A fair rule of thumb is if you are sure there are no intake vacuum leaks, and the exhaust gas HC (hydrocarbon) and oxygen levels are normal, and the engine does not run or idle rough, the hash is probably acceptable or normal.

NEGATIVE O2S VOLTAGE

When testing O2S waveforms, some O_2 sensors will exhibit some negative voltage. The acceptable amount of negative O2S voltage is -0.75 mV, providing that the maximum voltage peak exceeds 850 mV. ● SEE FIGURE 24–24. Testing has shown that negative voltage signals from an O_2 sensor have usually been caused by the following:

1. Chemical poisoning of sensing element (silicon, oil, etc.).
2. Overheated engines.
3. Mishandling of new O_2 sensors (dropped and banged around, resulting in a cracked insulator).
4. Poor O_2 sensor ground.

TECH TIP

Look for Missing Shield

In rare (very rare) instances, the metal shield on the exhaust side of the O_2 sensor (the shield over the zirconia thimble) may be damaged (or missing) and may create hash on the O2S waveform that could be mistaken for bad injectors or other misfires, vacuum leaks, or compression problems. After you have checked everything, and possibly replaced the injectors, pull the O2S to check for rare situations.

LOW O2S READINGS

An oxygen sensor reading that is low could be due to other things besides a lean air–fuel mixture. Remember, an oxygen sensor senses oxygen, not unburned gas, even though a high reading generally indicates a rich exhaust (lack of oxygen) and a low reading indicates a lean mixture (excess oxygen).

FALSE LEAN If an oxygen sensor reads low as a result of a factor besides a lean mixture, it is often called a **false lean indication.**

False lean indications (low O2S readings) can be attributed to the following:

1. **Ignition misfire.** An ignition misfire due to a defective spark plug wire, fouled spark plug, and so forth, causes no burned air and fuel to be exhausted past the O2S. The O2S "sees" the oxygen (not the unburned gasoline) and the O2S voltage is low.

2. **Exhaust leak in front of the O2S.** An exhaust leak between the engine and the oxygen sensor causes outside oxygen to be drawn into the exhaust and past the O2S. This oxygen is "read" by the O2S and produces a lower-than-normal voltage. The computer interrupts the lower-than-normal voltage signal from the O2S as meaning that the air–fuel mixture is lean. The computer will cause the fuel system to deliver a richer air–fuel mixture.

3. **A spark plug misfire represents a false lean signal to the oxygen sensor.** The computer does not know that the extra oxygen going past the oxygen sensor is not due to a lean air–fuel mixture. The computer commands a richer mixture, which could cause the spark plugs to foul, increasing the rate of misfirings.

HIGH O2S READINGS

An oxygen sensor reading that is high could be due to other things beside a rich air–fuel mixture. When the O2S reads high as a result of other factors besides a rich mixture, it is often called a **false rich indication**.

False rich indication (high O2S readings) can be attributed to the following:

1. Contaminated O2S due to additives in the engine coolant or due to silicon poisoning

2. A stuck-open EGR valve (especially at idle)

3. A spark plug wire too close to the oxygen sensor signal wire, which can induce a higher-than-normal voltage in the signal wire, thereby indicating to the computer a false rich condition

4. A loose oxygen sensor ground connection, which can cause a higher-than-normal voltage and a false rich signal

5. A break or contamination of the wiring and its connectors, which could prevent reference oxygen from reaching the oxygen sensor, resulting in a false rich indication. (All oxygen sensors require an oxygen supply inside the sensor itself for reference to be able to sense exhaust gas oxygen.)

POST-CATALYTIC CONVERTER OXYGEN SENSOR TESTING

The oxygen sensor located behind the catalytic converter is used on OBD-II vehicles to monitor converter efficiency. A changing air–fuel mixture is required for the most efficient operation of the converter. If the converter is working correctly, the oxygen content after the converter should be fairly constant. ● **SEE FIGURE 24–25.**

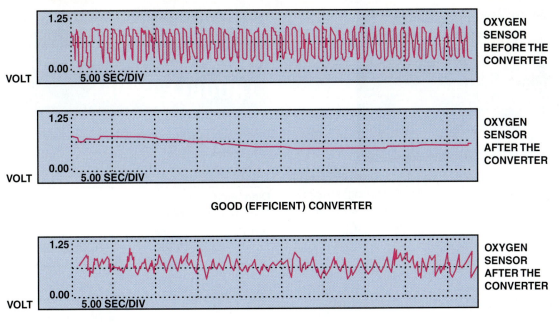

FIGURE 24–25 The post-catalytic converter oxygen sensor should display very little activity if the catalytic converter is efficient.

OXYGEN SENSOR VISUAL INSPECTION

Whenever an oxygen sensor is replaced, the old sensor should be carefully inspected to help determine the cause of the failure. This is an important step because if the cause of the failure is not discovered, it could lead to another sensor failure.

Inspection may reveal the following:

1. **Black sooty deposits** usually indicate a rich air–fuel mixture.

2. **White chalky deposits** are characteristic of silica contamination. Usual causes for this type of sensor failure include silica deposits in the fuel or a technician having used the wrong type of silicone sealant during the servicing of the engine.

3. **White sandy or gritty deposits** are characteristic of antifreeze (ethylene glycol) contamination. A defective cylinder head or intake manifold gasket could be the cause, or a cracked cylinder head or engine block. Antifreeze may also cause the oxygen sensor to become green as a result of the dye used in antifreeze.

4. **Dark brown deposits** are an indication of excessive oil consumption. Possible causes include a defective positive crankcase ventilation (PCV) system or a mechanical engine problem such as defective valve stem seals or piston rings.

CAUTION: Do not spray any silicone spray near the engine where the engine vacuum could draw the fumes into the engine. This can also cause silica damage to the oxygen sensor. Also be sure that the silicone sealer used for gaskets is rated oxygen-sensor safe.

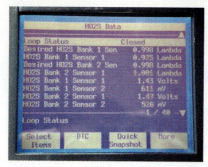

FIGURE 24–26 The target lambda on this vehicle is slightly lower than 1.0 indicating that the PCM is attempting to supply the engine with an air–fuel mixture that is slightly richer than stoichiometric. Multiply the lambda number by 14.7 to find the actual air–fuel ratio.

? FREQUENTLY ASKED QUESTION

What Is Lambda?

An oxygen sensor is also called a lambda sensor because the voltage changes at the air–fuel ratio of 14.7:1, which is the stoichiometric rate for gasoline. If this mixture of gasoline and air is burned, all of the gasoline is burned and uses all of the oxygen in the mixture. This exact ratio represents a lambda of 1.0. If the mixture is richer (more fuel or less air), the number is less than 1.0, such as 0.850. If the mixture is leaner than 14.7:1 (less fuel or more air), the lambda number is higher than 1.0, such as 1.130. Often, the target lambda is displayed on a scan tool.
● **SEE FIGURE 24–26.**

OXYGEN SENSOR-RELATED DIAGNOSTIC TROUBLE CODES

Diagnostic trouble codes (DTCs) associated with the oxygen sensor include:

Diagnostic Trouble Code	Description	Possible Causes
P0131	Upstream HO2S grounded	■ Exhaust leak upstream of HO2S (bank 1) ■ Extremely lean air–fuel mixture ■ HO2S defective or contaminated ■ HO2S signal wire shorted-to-ground
P0132	Upstream HO2S shorted	■ Upstream HO2S (bank 1) shorted ■ Defective HO2S ■ Fuel-contaminated HO2S
P0133	Upstream HO2S slow response	■ Open or short in heater circuit ■ Defective or fuel-contaminated HO2S ■ EGR or fuel-system fault

SUMMARY

1. An oxygen sensor produces a voltage output signal based on the oxygen content of the exhaust stream.

2. If the exhaust has little oxygen, the voltage of the oxygen sensor will be close to 1 volt (1,000 mV) and close to zero if there is high oxygen content in the exhaust.

3. Oxygen sensors can have one, two, three, four, or more wires, depending on the style and design.

4. A wide-band oxygen sensor, also called a lean air–fuel (LAF) or linear air–fuel ratio sensor, can detect air–fuel ratios from as rich as 12:1 to as lean as 18:1.

5. The oxygen sensor signal determines fuel trim, which is used to tailor the air–fuel mixture for the catalytic converter.

6. Conditions can occur that cause the oxygen sensor to be fooled and give a false lean or false rich signal to the PCM.

7. Oxygen sensors can be tested using a digital meter, a scope, or a scan tool.

REVIEW QUESTIONS

1. How does an oxygen sensor detect oxygen levels in the exhaust?

2. What are three basic designs of oxygen sensors and how many wires may be used for each?

3. What is the difference between open-loop and closed-loop engine operation?

4. What are three ways oxygen sensors can be tested?

5. How can the oxygen sensor be fooled and provide the wrong information to the PCM?

CHAPTER QUIZ

1. The sensor that must be warmed and functioning before the engine management computer will go to closed loop is the _____.
   a. O2S
   b. ECT sensor
   c. Engine MAP sensor
   d. BARO sensor

2. The voltage output of a zirconia oxygen sensor when the exhaust stream is lean (excess oxygen) is _____.
   a. Relatively high (close to 1 volt)
   b. About in the middle of the voltage range
   c. Relatively low (close to 0 volt)
   d. Either a or b, depending on atmospheric pressure

3. Where is sensor 1, bank 1 located?
   a. On the same bank where number 1 cylinder is located
   b. In the exhaust manifold
   c. On the bank opposite cylinder number 1
   d. Both a and b

4. A heated zirconia oxygen sensor will have how many wires?
   a. 2
   b. 3
   c. 4
   d. Either b or c

5. A high O2S voltage could be due to _____.
   a. A rich exhaust
   b. A lean exhaust
   c. A defective spark plug wire
   d. Both a and c

6. A low O2S voltage could be due to _____.
   a. A rich exhaust
   b. A lean exhaust
   c. A defective spark plug wire
   d. Both b and c

7. An oxygen sensor is being tested with digital multimeter (DMM), using the MIN/MAX function. The readings are: minimum = 78 mV; maximum = 932 mV; average = 442 mV. Technician A says that the engine is operating correctly. Technician B says that the oxygen sensor is skewed too rich. Which technician is correct?
   a. Technician A only
   b. Technician B only
   c. Both Technicians A and B
   d. Neither Technician A nor B

8. An oxygen sensor is being tested using a digital storage oscilloscope (DSO). A good oxygen sensor should display how many switches per second?
   a. 1 to 5
   b. 5 to 10
   c. 10 to 15
   d. 15 to 20

9. When testing an oxygen sensor using a digital storage oscilloscope (DSO), how quickly should the voltage change when either propane is added to the intake stream or when a vacuum leak is created?
   a. Less than 50 ms
   b. 1 to 3 seconds
   c. 100 to 200 ms
   d. 450 to 550 ms

10. A P0133 DTC is being discussed. Technician A says that a defective heater circuit could be the cause. Technician B says that a contaminated sensor could be the cause. Which technician is correct?
    a. Technician A only
    b. Technician B only
    c. Both Technicians A and B
    d. Neither Technician A nor B

Wide-Band Oxygen Sensors

OBJECTIVES

After studying Chapter 25, the reader will be able to:

1. Prepare for the ASE certification test content Engine Performance (A8) content area "E" (Computerized Engine Controls Diagnosis and Repair)

2. Describe the difference between a two-band and a wide-band oxygen sensor.

3. Explain the difference between a thimble design and a planar design.

4. Discuss the operation of a wide-band oxygen sensor.

5. List the test procedure for testing a dual cell and a single cell wide-band oxygen sensor.

KEY TERMS

Air–fuel ratio sensor 398
Air reference chamber 394
Ambient air electrode 393
Ambient side electrode 393
Cup design 392
Diffusion chamber 394
Dual cell 394
Exhaust side electrode 393
Finger design 392

Lean air–fuel (LAF) sensor 391
Light-off time (LOT) 394
Nernst cell 394
Planar design 394
Pump cell 394
Reference electrode 393
Reference voltage 394
Signal electrode 393
Single cell 398
Thimble design 392

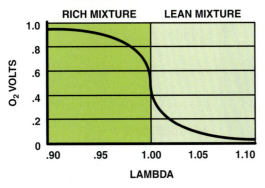

FIGURE 25–1 A conventional zirconia oxygen sensor can only reset to exhaust mixtures that are richer or leaner than 14.7:1 (lambda 1.00).

TERMINOLOGY

Wide-band oxygen sensors have been used since 1992 on some Hondas. Wide-band oxygen sensors are used by most vehicle manufacturers to ensure that the exhaust emissions can meet the current standard. Wide-band oxygen sensors are also called by various names, depending on the vehicle and/or oxygen sensor manufacturer. The terms used include:

- **Wide-band oxygen sensor**
- **Broadband oxygen sensor**
- **Wide-range oxygen sensor**
- **Air–fuel ratio (AFR) sensor**
- **Wide-range air–fuel (WRAF) sensor**
- **Lean air–fuel (LAF) sensor**
- **Air–fuel (AF) sensor**

Wide-band oxygen sensors are also manufactured in dual cell and single cell designs.

NEED FOR WIDE-BAND SENSORS

INTRODUCTION A conventional zirconia oxygen sensor resets to an air–fuel mixture of either richer or leaner than 14.7:1. This means that the sensor cannot be used to detect the exact air–fuel mixture. ● **SEE FIGURE 25–1.**

The need for more stringent exhaust emission standards such as the natural low-emission vehicle (NLEV), plus the ultra low-emission vehicle (ULEV), and the super ultra low-emission vehicle (SULEV) require more accurate fuel control than can be provided by a traditional oxygen sensor.

PURPOSE AND FUNCTION A wide-band oxygen sensor is capable of supplying air–fuel ratio information to the PCM over a much broader range. The use of a wide-band oxygen sensor compared with a conventional zirconia oxygen sensor differs as follows:

1. Able to detect exhaust air–fuel ratio from as rich as 10:1 and as lean as 23:1 in some cases.

2. Cold-start activity within as little as 10 seconds.

? **FREQUENTLY ASKED QUESTION**

How Quickly Can a Wide-Band Oxygen Sensor Achieve Closed Loop?

In a Toyota Highlander hybrid electric vehicle, the gasoline engine start is delayed for a short time when first started. It is capable of being driven immediately using electric power alone and the oxygen sensor heaters are turned on at first start. The gasoline engine often achieves closed loop operation during *cranking* because the oxygen sensors are fully warm and ready to go at the same time the engine is started. Having the gasoline engine achieve closed loop quickly, allows it to meet the stringent SULEV standards.

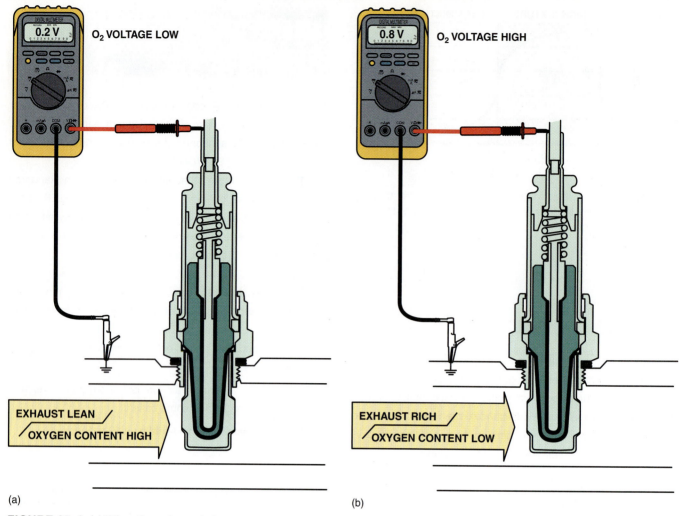

FIGURE 25–2 (a) When the exhaust is lean, the output of a zirconia oxygen sensor is below 450 mV. (b) When the exhaust is rich, the output of a zirconia oxygen sensor is above 450 mV.

CONVENTIONAL O2S REVIEW

NARROW BAND A conventional zirconia oxygen sensor (O2S) is only able to detect if the exhaust is richer or leaner than 14.7:1. A conventional oxygen sensor is therefore referred to as:

- **2-step sensor**—either rich or lean
- **Narrow band sensor**—informs the PCM whether the exhaust is rich or lean only

The voltage value where a zirconia oxygen sensor switches from rich to lean or from lean to rich is 0.450 V (450 mV).

- Above 0.450 V = rich
- Below 0.450 V = lean
  - ● **SEE FIGURE 25–2.**

CONSTRUCTION A typical zirconia oxygen sensor has the sensing element in the shape of a thimble and is often referred to as:

- **Thimble design**
- **Cup design**
- **Finger design**
  - ● **SEE FIGURE 25–3.**

A typical zirconia oxygen sensor has a heater inside the thimble and does not touch the inside of the sensor. The sensor is similar to a battery that has two electrodes and an electrolyte. The electrolyte is solid and is the zirconia (zirconium dioxide).

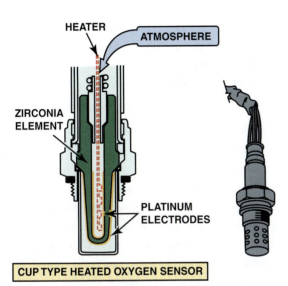

FIGURE 25-3 Most conventional zirconia oxygen sensors and some wide-band oxygen sensors use the cup-type design.

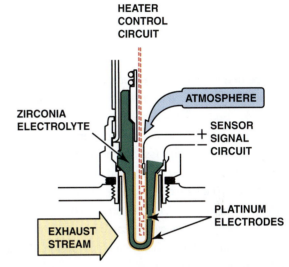

FIGURE 25-4 A typical heated zirconia oxygen sensor, showing the sensor signal circuit that uses the outer (exhaust) electrode as negative and the ambient air side electrode as the positive.

There are also two porous platinum electrodes, which have the following functions:

- **Exhaust side electrode**—This electrode is exposed to the exhaust stream.
- **Ambient side electrode**—This electrode is exposed to outside (ambient) air and is the **signal electrode,** also called the **reference electrode** or **ambient air electrode.**
  - ● **SEE FIGURE 25-4.**

The electrolyte (zirconia) is able to conduct electrons as follows:

- If the exhaust is rich, O_2 from the reference (inner) electrode wants to flow to the exhaust side electrode, which results in the generation of a voltage.

- If the exhaust is lean, O_2 flow is not needed and as a result, there is little if any, electron movement and, therefore, no voltage is being produced.

HEATER CIRCUITS The heater circuit on conventional oxygen sensors requires 0.8 to 2.0 amperes and it keeps the sensor at about 600°F (315°C).

A wide-band oxygen sensor operates at a higher temperature than a conventional HO2S from 1,200°F to 1,400°F (650°C to 760°C). The amount of electrical current needed for a wide-band oxygen sensor is about 8 to 10 amperes.

PLANAR DESIGN In 1998, Bosch introduced a wide-band oxygen sensor that is flat and thin (1.5 mm or 0.006 inch) and not

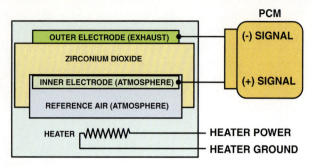

FIGURE 25–5 A planar design zirconia oxygen sensor places all of the elements together, which allows the sensor to reach operating temperature quickly.

CONVENTIONAL 02S REVIEW (CONTINUED)

in the shape of a thimble, as previously constructed. Now several manufacturers produce a similar planar design wide-band oxygen sensor. Because it is thin, it is easier to heat than older styles of oxygen sensors and as a result can achieve closed loop in less than 10 seconds. This fast heating, called **light-off time (LOT),** helps improve fuel economy and reduces cold-start exhaust emissions. The type of construction is not noticed by the technician, nor does it affect the testing procedures.

A conventional oxygen sensor can be constructed using a **planar design** instead of the thimble-type design. A planar design has the following features:

- The elements including the zirconia electrolyte and the two electrodes and heater are stacked together in a flat-type design.

- The planar design allows faster warm-up because the heater is in direct contact with the other elements.

- Planar oxygen sensors are the most commonly used. Some planar designs are used as a conventional narrow-band oxygen sensor.

The sandwich-type design of the planar style of oxygen sensor has the same elements and operates the same, but is stacked in the following way from the exhaust side to the ambient air side:

Exhaust stream

Outer electrode

Zirconia (ZiO$_2$) (electrolyte)

Inner electrode (reference or signal)

Outside (ambient) air

Heater

Another name for a conventional oxygen sensor is a **Nernst cell.** The Nernst cell is named for Walther Nernst, 1864–1941, a German physicist known for his work in electro-chemistry. ● **SEE FIGURE 25–5.**

DUAL CELL PLANAR WIDE-BAND SENSOR OPERATION

In a conventional zirconia oxygen sensor, a bias or **reference voltage** can be applied to the two platinum electrodes, and then oxygen ions can be forced (pumped) from the ambient reference air side to the exhaust side of the sensor. If the polarity is reversed, the oxygen ion can be forced to travel in the opposite direction.

A **dual cell** planar-type wide-band oxygen sensor is made like a conventional planar O2S and is labeled Nernst cell. Above the Nernst cell is another zirconia layer with two electrodes, which is called the **pump cell.** The two cells share a common ground, which is called the reference.

There are two internal chambers:

- The **air reference chamber** is exposed to ambient air.

- The **diffusion chamber** is exposed to the exhaust gases.

Platinum electrodes are on both sides of the zirconia electrolyte elements, which separate the air reference chamber and the exhaust-exposed diffusion chamber.

The basic principle of operation of a typical wide-band oxygen sensor is that it uses a positive or negative voltage signal to keep a balance between two sensors. Oxygen sensors do not measure the quantity of free oxygen in the exhaust. Instead, oxygen sensors produce a voltage that is based on the ion flow between the platinum electrodes of the sensor to maintain a stoichiometric balance.

For example:

- If there is a lean exhaust, there is oxygen in the exhaust and the ion flow from the ambient side to the exhaust side is low.

- If there were rich exhaust, the ion flow is increased to help maintain balance between the ambient air side and the exhaust side of the sensor.

The PCM can apply a small current to the pump cell electrodes, which causes oxygen ions through the zirconia into or out of the diffusion chamber. The PCM pumps O$_2$ ions in and out of the diffusion chamber to bring the voltage back to 0.450, using the pump cell.

The operation of a wide-band oxygen sensor is best described by looking at what occurs when the exhaust is stoichiometric, rich, and lean. ● **SEE FIGURE 25–6.**

STOICHIOMETRIC

- When the exhaust is at stoichiometric (14.7:1 air–fuel ratio), the voltage of the Nernst cell is 450 mV (0.450 V).

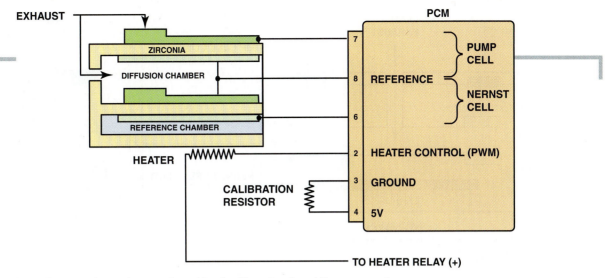

FIGURE 25–6 The reference electrodes are shared by the Nernst cell and the pump cell.

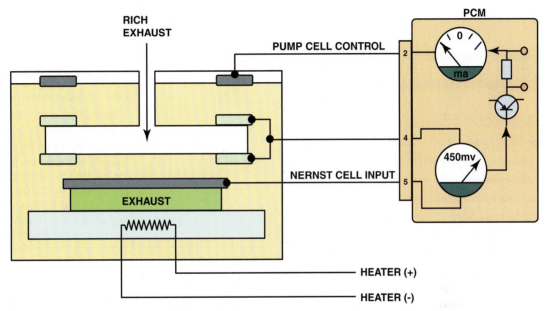

FIGURE 25–7 When the exhaust is rich, the PCM applies a negative current into the pump cell.

- The voltage between the diffusion chamber and the air reference chamber changes from 0.450 V. This voltage will be:
  - Higher if the exhaust is rich
  - Lower if the exhaust is lean

The reference voltage remains constant, usually at 2.5 volts, but can vary depending on the year, make, and model of vehicle and the type of sensor. Typical reference voltages include:

- 2.2
- 2.5
- 2.7
- 3.3
- 3.6

RICH EXHAUST. When the exhaust is rich, the voltage between the common (reference) electrode and the Nernst cell electrode that is exposed to ambient air is lower than 0.450 V. The PCM applies a negative current in milliamperes to the pump cell electrode to bring the circuit back into balance. ● **SEE FIGURE 25–7.**

LEAN EXHAUST. When the exhaust is lean, the voltage between the common (reference) electrode and the Nernst cell electrode is higher than 0.450 V. The PCM applies a positive current in milliamperes to the pump cell to bring the circuit back into balance. ● **SEE FIGURE 25–8.**

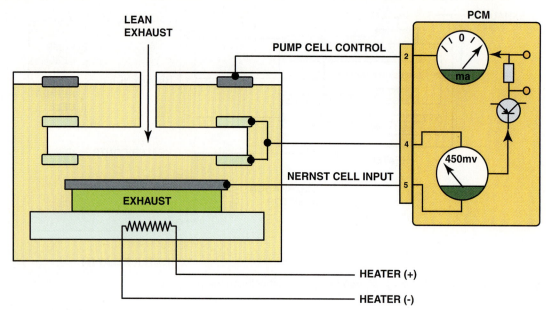

FIGURE 25–8 When the exhaust is lean, the PCM applies a positive current into the pump cell.

DUAL CELL DIAGNOSIS

SCAN TOOL DIAGNOSIS Most service information specifies that a scan tool be used to check the wide-band oxygen sensor. This is because the PCM performs tests of the unit and can identify faults. However, even wide-band oxygen sensors can be fooled if there is an exhaust manifold leak or other fault which could lead to false or inaccurate readings. If the oxygen sensor reading is false, the PCM will command an incorrect amount of fuel. The scan data shown on a generic (global) OBD-II scan tool will often be different than the reading on the factory scan tool. ● **SEE CHART 25–1** for an example of a Toyota wide-band oxygen sensor being tested using a factory scan tool and a generic OBD-II scan tool.

Master Tech Toyota (Factory Scan Tool)	OBD-II Scan Tool	Air–Fuel Ratio
2.50 V	0.50 V	12.5:1
3.00 V	0.60 V	14.0:1
3.30 V	0.66 V	14.7:1
3.50 V	0.70 V	15.5:1
4.00 V	0.80 V	18.5:1

CHART 25–1

A comparison showing what a factory scan tool and a generic OBD-II scan tool might display at various air–fuel ratios.

SCAN TOOL DATA (PID) The following information will be displayed on a scan tool when looking at data for a wide-band oxygen sensor:

HOS21 = _____ mA		If the current is positive, this means that the PCM is pumping current in the diffusion gap due to a rich exhaust.
		If the current is negative, the PCM is pumping current out of the diffusion gap due to a lean exhaust.
Air–fuel ratio =		Usually expressed in lambda. One means that the exhaust is at stoichiometric (14.7:1 air–fuel ratio) and numbers higher than 1 indicate a lean exhaust and numbers lower than 1 indicate a rich exhaust.

DIGITAL MULTIMETER TESTING

When testing a wide-band oxygen sensor for proper operation, perform the following steps:

STEP 1 Check service information and determine the circuit and connector terminal identification.

STEP 2 Measure the calibration resistor. While the value of this resistor can vary widely, depending on the type of sensor, the calibrating resistor should still be checked for opens and shorts.

NOTE: The calibration resistor is usually located within the connector itself.

- If open, the ohmmeter will read OL (infinity ohms).
- If shorted, the ohmmeter will read zero or close to zero.

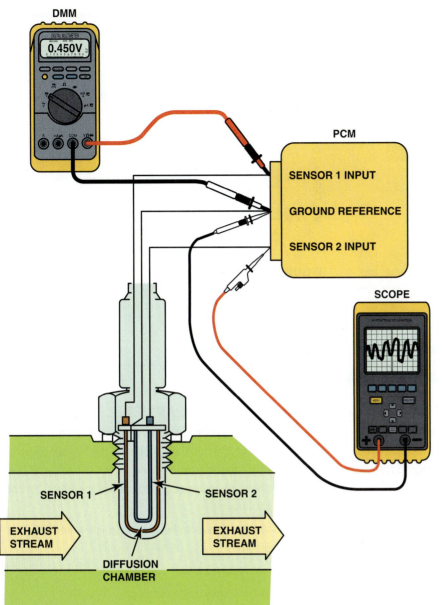

DMM

0.450V

PCM

SENSOR 1 INPUT

GROUND REFERENCE

SENSOR 2 INPUT

SCOPE

SENSOR 1

SENSOR 2

EXHAUST STREAM

EXHAUST STREAM

DIFFUSION CHAMBER

FIGURE 25–9 Testing a dual cell wide-band oxygen sensor can be done using a voltmeter or a scope. The meter reading is attached to the Nernst cell and should read stoichiometric (450 mV) at all times. The scope is showing activity to the pump cell with commands from the PCM to keep the Nernst cell at 14.7:1 air–fuel ratio.

STEP 3 Measure the heater circuit for proper resistance or current flow.

STEP 4 Measure the reference voltage relative to ground. This can vary but is generally 2.4 to 2.6 volts.

STEP 5 Using jumper wires, connect an ammeter and measure the current in the pump cell control wire.

RICH EXHAUST (LAMBDA LESS THAN 1.00)   When the exhaust is rich, the Nernst cell voltage will move higher than 0.45 volts. The PCM will pump oxygen from the exhaust into the diffusion gap by applying a negative voltage to the pump cell.

LEAN EXHAUST (LAMBDA HIGHER THAN 1.00)

When the exhaust is lean, the Nernst cell voltage will move lower than 0.45 volts. The PCM will pump oxygen out of the diffusion gap by applying a positive voltage to the pump cell.

The pump cell is used to pump oxygen into the diffusion gap when the exhaust is rich. The pump cell applies a negative voltage to do this.

- Positive current = lean exhaust
- Negative current = rich exhaust
- **SEE FIGURE 25–9.**

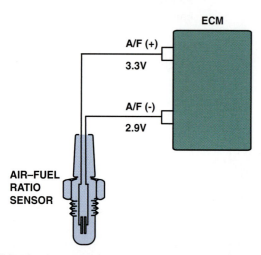

FIGURE 25–10 A single cell wide-band oxygen sensor has four wires with two for the heater and two for the sensor itself. The voltage applied to the sensor is 0.4 volt (3.3 − 2.9 = 0.4) across the two leads of the sensor.

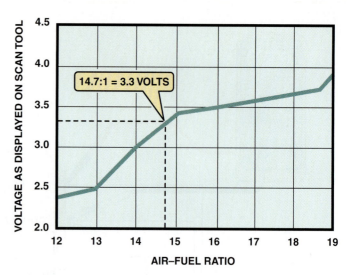

FIGURE 25–11 The scan tool can display various voltage but will often show 3.3 volts because the PCM is controlling the sensor by applying a low current to the sensor to achieve balance.

SINGLE CELL WIDE-BAND OXYGEN SENSORS

CONSTRUCTION   A typical **single cell** wide-band oxygen sensor looks similar to a conventional four-wire zirconia oxygen sensor. The typical single cell wide-band oxygen sensor, usually called an **air–fuel ratio sensor,** has the following construction features:

- Can be made using the cup or planar design
- Oxygen (O_2) is pumped into the diffusion layer similar to the operation of a dual cell wide-band oxygen sensor.
  ● **SEE FIGURE 25–10.**
- Current flow reverses positive and negative
- Consists of two cell wires and two heater wires (power and ground)
- The heater usually requires 6 amperes and the ground side is pulse-width modulated.

TESTING WITH A MILLIAMMETER   The PCM controls the single cell wide-band oxygen sensor by maintaining a voltage difference of 300 mV (0.3 V) between the two sensor leads. The PCM keeps the voltage difference constant under all operating conditions by increasing or decreasing current between the element of the cell.

- Zero (0 mA) represents lambda or stoichiometric air–fuel ratio of 14.7:1
- +10 mA indicates a lean condition
- −10 mA indicates a rich condition

TESTING USING A SCAN TOOL   A scan tool will display a voltage reading but can vary depending on the type and maker of scan tool. ● **SEE FIGURE 25–11.**

WIDE-BAND OXYGEN SENSOR PATTERN FAILURES

Wide-band oxygen sensors have a long life but can fail. Most of the failures will cause a diagnostic trouble code (DTC) to set, usually causing the malfunction indicator (check engine) lamp to light.

However, one type of failure may not set a DTC when the following occurs:

1. Voltage from the heater circuit bleeds into the Nernst cell.
2. This voltage will cause the engine to operate extremely lean and may or may not set a diagnostic trouble code.

3. When testing indicates an extremely lean condition, unplug the connector to the oxygen sensor. If the engine starts to operate correctly with the sensor unplugged, this is confirmation that the wide-band oxygen sensor has failed and requires replacement.

1. Wide-band oxygen sensors are known by many different terms, including:
   - Broadband oxygen sensor
   - Wide-range oxygen sensor
   - Air–fuel ratio (AFR) sensor
   - Wide-range air–fuel (WRAF) sensor
   - Lean air–fuel (LAF) sensor
   - Air–fuel (AF) sensor

2. Wide-band oxygen sensors are manufactured using a cup or planar design and are dual cell or single cell design.

3. A wide-band oxygen sensor is capable of furnishing the PCM with exhaust air–fuel ratios as rich as 10:1 and as lean as 23:1.

4. The use of a wide-band oxygen sensor allows the engine to achieve more stringent exhaust emission standards.

5. A conventional zirconia oxygen sensor can be made in a cup shape or planar design and is sometimes called a narrow band or 2-step sensor.

6. The heater used on a conventional zirconia oxygen sensor uses up to 2 amperes and heats the sensor to about 600°F (315°C). A broadband sensor heater has to heat the sensor to 1,200°F to 1,400°F (650°C to 760°C) and requires up to 8 to 10 amperes.

7. A typical dual cell wide-band oxygen sensor uses the PCM to apply a current to the pump cell to keep the Nernst cell at 14.7:1.
   - When the exhaust is rich, the PCM applies a negative current to the pump cell.
   - When the exhaust is lean, the PCM applies a positive current to the pump cell.

8. Wide-band oxygen sensors can also be made using a single cell design.

9. Wide-band oxygen sensors can be best tested using a scan tool, but dual cell sensors can be checked with a voltmeter or scope. Single cell sensors can be checked using a milliammeter.

REVIEW QUESTIONS

1. What type of construction is used to make wide-band oxygen sensors?

2. Why are wide-band oxygen sensors used instead of conventional zirconia sensors?

3. How is the heater different for a wide-band oxygen sensor compared with a conventional zirconia oxygen sensor?

4. How does a wide-range oxygen sensor work?

5. How can a wide-band oxygen sensor be tested?

CHAPTER QUIZ

1. A wide-band oxygen sensor was first used on a Honda in what model year?
   - **a.** 1992
   - **b.** 1996
   - **c.** 2000
   - **d.** 2006

2. A wide-band oxygen sensor is capable of detecting the air–fuel mixture in the exhaust from _____ (rich) to _____ (lean).
   - **a.** 12:1 to 15:1
   - **b.** 13:1 to 16.7:1
   - **c.** 10:1 to 23:1
   - **d.** 8:1 to 18:1

3. A conventional zirconia oxygen sensor can be made with what designs?
   - **a.** Cup and thimble
   - **b.** Cup and planar
   - **c.** Finger and thimble
   - **d.** Dual cell and single cell

4. A wide-band oxygen sensor can be made using what design?
   - **a.** Cup and thimble
   - **b.** Cup and planar
   - **c.** Finger and thimble
   - **d.** Dual cell and single cell

5. A wide-band oxygen sensor heater could draw how much current (amperes)?
   - **a.** 0.8 to 2.0 A
   - **b.** 2 to 4 A
   - **c.** 6 to 8 A
   - **d.** 8 to 10 A

6. A wide-band oxygen sensor needs to be heated to what operating temperature?
   - **a.** 600°F (315°C)
   - **b.** 800°F (427°C)
   - **c.** 1,400°F (760°C)
   - **d.** 2,000°F (1,093°C)

7. The two internal chambers of a dual cell wide-band oxygen sensor include _____.
   - **a.** Single and dual
   - **b.** Nernst and pump
   - **c.** Air reference and diffusion
   - **d.** Inside and outside

8. When the exhaust is rich, the PCM applies a _____ current into the pump cell.
   - **a.** Positive
   - **b.** Negative

9. When the exhaust is lean, the PCM applies a _____ current into the pump cell.
   - **a.** Positive
   - **b.** Negative

10. A dual cell wide-band oxygen sensor can be tested using a _____.
    - **a.** Scan tool
    - **b.** Voltmeter
    - **c.** Scope
    - **d.** All of the above

FUEL PUMPS, LINES, AND FILTERS

After studying Chapter 26, the reader will be able to:

1. Prepare for ASE Engine Performance (A8) certification test content area "C" (Fuel, Air Induction, and Exhaust Systems Diagnosis and Repair).
2. Describe how to check an electric fuel pump for proper pressure and volume delivery.
3. Explain how to check a fuel-pressure regulator.
4. Describe how to test fuel injectors.
5. Explain how to diagnose electronic fuel-injection problems.

Accumulator 410
Baffle 401
Check valve 403
Delivery system 401
Filter basket 412
Gerotor 407
Hydrokinetic pump 407
Inertia switch 403
Onboard refueling vapor recovery (ORVR) 402
Peripheral pump 407
Residual or rest pressure 407
Roller cell 406
Rotary vane pump 407
Side-channel pump 407
Turbine pump 407
Vacuum lock 403
Vapor lock 404
Volatile organic compound (VOC) 406

FUEL DELIVERY SYSTEM

Creating and maintaining a correct air–fuel mixture requires a properly functioning fuel and air **delivery system**. Fuel delivery (and return) systems use many if not all of the following components to make certain that fuel is available under the right conditions to the fuel-injection system:

- Fuel storage tank, filler neck, and gas cap
- Fuel tank pressure sensor
- Fuel pump
- Fuel filter(s)
- Fuel delivery lines and fuel rail
- Fuel-pressure regulator
- Fuel return line (if equipped with a return-type fuel delivery system)

FUEL TANKS

A vehicle fuel tank is made of corrosion-resistant steel or polyethylene plastic. Some models, such as sport utility vehicles (SUVs) and light trucks, may have an auxiliary fuel tank.

Tank design and capacity are a compromise between available space, filler location, fuel expansion room, and fuel movement. Some later-model tanks deliberately limit tank capacity by extending the filler tube neck into the tank low enough to prevent complete filling, or by providing for expansion room.
● **SEE FIGURE 26–1**. A vertical **baffle** in this same tank limits fuel sloshing as the vehicle moves.

Regardless of size and shape, all fuel tanks incorporate most if not all of the following features:

- Inlet or filler tube through which fuel enters the tank
- Filler cap with pressure holding and relief features
- An outlet to the fuel line leading to the fuel pump or fuel injector
- Fuel pump mounted within the tank
- Tank vent system
- Fuel pickup tube and fuel level sending unit

TANK LOCATION AND MOUNTING   Most vehicles use a horizontally suspended fuel tank, usually mounted below the rear of the floor pan, just ahead of or behind the rear axle. Fuel tanks are located there so that frame rails and body components protect the tank in the event of a crash. To prevent squeaks,

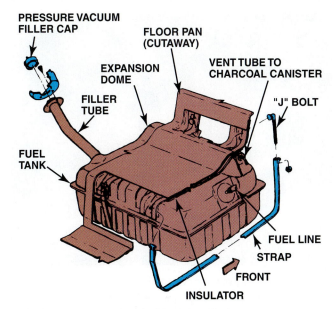

FIGURE 26–1 A typical fuel tank installation.

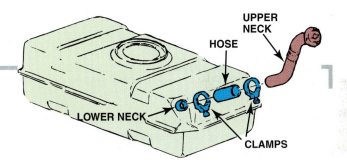

FIGURE 26–2 A three-piece filler tube assembly.

some models have insulated strips cemented on the top or sides of the tank wherever it contacts the underbody.

Fuel inlet location depends on the tank design and filler tube placement. It is located behind a filler cap and is often a hinged door in the outer side of either rear fender panel.

Generally, a pair of metal retaining straps holds a fuel tank in place. Underbody brackets or support panels hold the strap ends using bolts. The free ends are drawn underneath the tank to hold it in place, then bolted to other support brackets or to a frame member on the opposite side of the tank.

FILLER TUBES   Fuel enters the tank through a large tube extending from the tank to an opening on the outside of the vehicle. ● **SEE FIGURE 26–2**.

Effective in 1993, federal regulations require manufacturers to install a device to prevent fuel from being siphoned through the filler neck. Federal authorities recognized methanol as a poison, and methanol used in gasoline is a definite health hazard. Additionally, gasoline is a suspected carcinogen (cancer-causing agent). To prevent siphoning, manufacturers welded a filler-neck check-ball tube in fuel tanks. To drain check-ball-equipped fuel

FIGURE 26–3 A view of a typical filler tube with the fuel tank removed. Notice the ground strap used to help prevent the buildup of static electricity as the fuel flows into the plastic tank. The check ball looks exactly like a ping-pong ball.

FIGURE 26–4 Vehicles equipped with onboard refueling vapor recovery usually have a reduced-size fill tube.

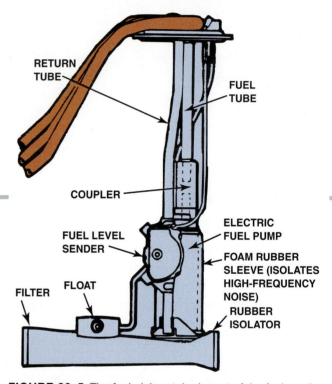

FIGURE 26–5 The fuel pickup tube is part of the fuel sender and pump assembly.

FUEL TANKS (CONTINUED)

tanks, a technician must disconnect the check-ball tube at the tank and attach a siphon directly to the tank. ● SEE FIGURE 26–3.

Onboard refueling vapor recovery (ORVR) systems have been developed to reduce evaporative emissions during refueling. ● SEE FIGURE 26–4. These systems add components to the filler neck and the tank. One ORVR system utilizes a tapered filler neck with a smaller diameter tube and a check valve. When fuel flows down the neck, it opens the normally closed check valve. The vapor passage to the charcoal canister is opened. The decreased size neck and the opened air passage allow fuel and vapor to flow rapidly into the tank and the canister respectively. When the fuel has reached a predetermined level, the check valve closes, and the fuel tank pressure increases. This forces the nozzle to shut off, thereby preventing the tank from being overfilled.

PRESSURE-VACUUM FILLER CAP
Fuel and vapors are sealed in the tank by the safety filler cap. The safety cap must release excess pressure or excess vacuum. Either condition could cause fuel tank damage, fuel spills, and vapor escape. Typically, the cap will release if the pressure is over 1.5 to 2.0 PSI (10 to 14 kPa) or if the vacuum is 0.15 to 0.30 PSI (1 to 2 kPa).

FUEL PICKUP TUBE
The fuel pickup tube is usually a part of the fuel sender assembly or the electric fuel pump assembly. Since dirt and sediment eventually gather on the bottom of a fuel tank, the fuel pickup tube is fitted with a filter sock or strainer to prevent contamination from entering the fuel lines. The woven plastic strainer also acts as a water separator by preventing water from being drawn up with the fuel. The filter sock usually is designed to filter out particles that are larger than 70 to 100 microns, or 30 microns if a gerotor-type fuel pump is used. One micron is 0.000039 in. ● SEE FIGURE 26–5.

NOTE: The human eye cannot see anything smaller than about 40 microns.

The filter is made from woven Saran resin (copolymer of vinylidene chloride and vinyl chloride). The filter blocks any water that may be in the fuel tank, unless it is completely submerged in water. In that case, it will allow water through the filter. This filter should be replaced whenever the fuel pump is replaced.

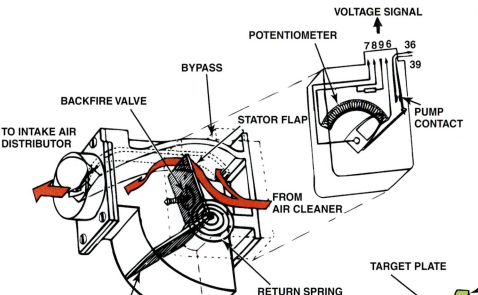

VOLTAGE SIGNAL

POTENTIOMETER

BYPASS

BACKFIRE VALVE

STATOR FLAP

TO INTAKE AIR DISTRIBUTOR

PUMP CONTACT

FROM AIR CLEANER

RETURN SPRING

BALANCE FLAP

BALANCE CHAMBER

7 8 9 6   36

39

FIGURE 26–6 On some vehicles equipped with an airflow sensor, a switch is used to energize the fuel pump. In the event of a collision, the switch opens and the fuel flow stops.

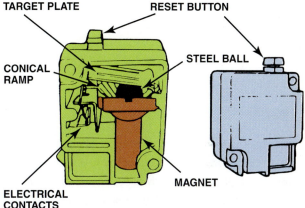

TARGET PLATE

RESET BUTTON

CONICAL RAMP

STEEL BALL

ELECTRICAL CONTACTS

MAGNET

FIGURE 26–7 Ford uses an inertia switch to turn off the electric fuel pump in an accident.

TANK VENTING REQUIREMENTS Fuel tanks must be vented to prevent a **vacuum lock** as fuel is drawn from the tank. As fuel is used and its level drops in the tank, the space above the fuel increases. As the air in the tank expands to fill this greater space, its pressure drops. Without a vent, the air pressure inside the tank would drop below atmospheric pressure, developing a vacuum which prevents the flow of fuel. Under extreme pressure variance, the tank could collapse. Venting the tank allows outside air to enter as the fuel level drops, preventing a vacuum from developing.

An EVAP system vents gasoline vapors from the fuel tank directly to a charcoal-filled vapor storage canister, and uses an unvented filler cap. Many filler caps contain valves that open to relieve pressure or vacuum above specified safety levels. Systems that use completely sealed caps have separate pressure and vacuum relief valves for venting.

Because fuel tanks are not vented directly to the atmosphere, the tank must allow for fuel expansion, contraction, and overflow that can result from changes in temperature or overfilling. One way is to use a dome in the top of the tank. Many General Motors vehicles use a design that includes a vertical slosh baffle which reserves up to 12% of the total tank capacity for fuel expansion.

ROLLOVER LEAKAGE PROTECTION

All vehicles have one or more devices to prevent fuel leaks in case of vehicle rollover or a collision in which fuel may spill.

Variations of the basic one-way **check valve** may be installed in any number of places between the fuel tank and the engine. The valve may be installed in the fuel return line, vapor vent line, or fuel tank filler cap.

In addition to the rollover protection devices, some vehicles use devices to ensure that the fuel pump shuts off when an accident occurs. Some pumps depend upon an oil pressure or an engine speed signal to continue operating; these pumps turn off whenever the engine dies. On some air vane sensors, a microswitch is built into the sensor to switch on the fuel pump as soon as intake airflow causes the vane to lift from its rest position. ● **SEE FIGURE 26–6**.

Ford vehicles use an **inertia switch**. ● **SEE FIGURE 26–7**. The inertia switch is installed in the rear of the vehicle between the electric fuel pump and its power supply. With any sudden impact, such as a jolt from another vehicle in a parking lot, the inertia switch opens and shuts off power to the fuel pump. The switch must be reset manually by pushing a button to restore current to the pump.

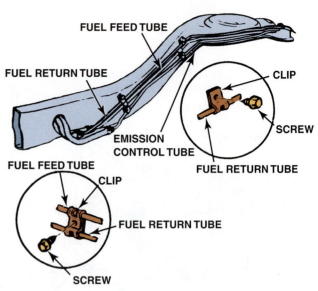

FIGURE 26–8 Fuel lines are routed along the frame or body and secured with clips.

FUEL LINES

Fuel and vapor lines made of steel, nylon tubing, or fuel-resistant rubber hoses connect the parts of the fuel system. Fuel lines supply fuel to the throttle body or fuel rail. They also return excess fuel and vapors to the tank. Depending on their function, fuel and vapor lines may be either rigid or flexible.

Fuel lines must remain as cool as possible. If any part of the line is located near too much heat, the gasoline passing through it vaporizes and **vapor lock** occurs. When this happens, the fuel pump supplies only vapor that passes into the injectors. Without liquid gasoline, the engine stalls and a hot restart problem develops.

The fuel delivery system supplies 10 to 15 PSI (69 to 103 kPa) or up to 35 PSI (241 kPa) to many throttle-body injection units and up to 50 PSI (345 kPa) for multiport fuel-injection systems. Fuel-injection systems retain residual or rest pressure in the lines for a half hour or longer when the engine is turned off to prevent hot engine restart problems. Higher-pressure systems such as these require special fuel lines.

RIGID LINES

All fuel lines fastened to the body, frame, or engine are made of seamless steel tubing. Steel springs may be wound around the tubing at certain points to protect against impact damage.

Only steel tubing, or that recommended by the manufacturer, should be used when replacing rigid fuel lines. *Never substitute copper or aluminum tubing for steel tubing*. These materials do not withstand normal vehicle vibration and could combine with the fuel to cause a chemical reaction.

FLEXIBLE LINES

Most fuel systems use synthetic rubber hose sections where flexibility is needed. Short hose sections often connect steel fuel lines to other system components. The fuel delivery hose inside diameter (ID) is generally larger (3/16 to 3/8 inches or 8 to 10 millimeters) than the fuel return hose ID (1/4 inches or 6 millimeters).

Fuel-injection systems require special-composition reinforced hoses specifically made for these higher-pressure systems. Similarly, vapor vent lines must be made of materials that resist fuel vapors. Replacement vent hoses are usually marked with the designation "EVAP" to indicate their intended use.

FUEL LINE MOUNTING

Fuel supply lines from the tank to a throttle body or fuel rail are routed to follow the frame along the underbody of the vehicle. Vapor and return lines may be routed with the fuel supply line. All rigid lines are fastened to the frame rail or underbody with screws and clamps, or clips. ● **SEE FIGURE 26–8.**

FUEL-INJECTION LINES AND CLAMPS

Hoses used for fuel-injection systems are made of materials with high resistance to oxidation and deterioration. Replacement hoses for injection systems should always be equivalent to original equipment manufacturer (OEM) hoses.

Screw-type clamps are essential on injected engines and should have rolled edges to prevent hose damage.

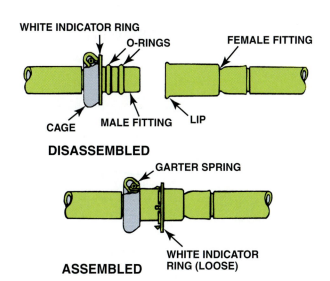

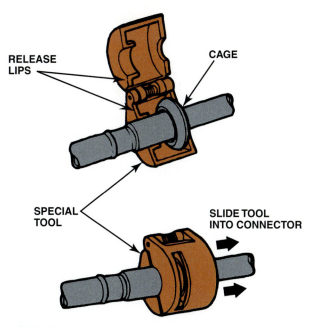

FIGURE 26–9 Some Ford metal line connections use spring-locks and O-rings.

FIGURE 26–10 Ford spring-lock connectors require a special tool for disassembly.

CAUTION: *Do not use spring-type clamps on fuel-injected engines—they cannot withstand the fuel pressures involved.*

FUEL-INJECTION FITTINGS AND NYLON LINES

Because of their operating pressures, fuel-injection systems often use special kinds of fittings to ensure leakproof connections. Some high-pressure fittings on GM vehicles with port fuel-injection systems use O-ring seals instead of the traditional flare connections. When disconnecting such a fitting, inspect the O-ring for damage and replace it if necessary. *Always* tighten O-ring fittings to the specified torque value to prevent damage.

Other manufacturers also use O-ring seals on fuel line connections. In all cases, the O-rings are made of special materials that withstand contact with gasoline and oxygenated fuel blends. Some manufacturers specify that the O-rings be replaced every time the fuel system connection is opened. When replacing one of these O-rings, a new part specifically designed for fuel system service must be used.

Ford also uses spring-lock connectors to join male and female ends of steel tubing. ● **SEE FIGURE 26–9.** The coupling is held together by a garter spring inside a circular cage. The flared end of the female fitting slips behind the spring to lock the coupling together.

General Motors has used nylon fuel lines with quick-connect fittings at the fuel tank and fuel filter since the early 1990s. Like the GM threaded couplings used with steel lines, nylon line couplings use internal O-ring seals. Unlocking the metal connectors requires a special quick-connector separator tool; plastic connectors can be released without the tool. ● **SEE FIGURES 26–10 AND 26–11.**

FUEL LINE LAYOUT

Fuel pressures have tended to become higher to prevent vapor lock, and a major portion of the fuel routed to the fuel-injection system returns to the tank by way of a fuel return line or return-type systems. This allows better control, within limits, of heat absorbed by the gasoline as it is routed through the engine compartment. Throttle-body and multiport injection systems have typically used a pressure regulator to control fuel pressure in the throttle body or fuel rail, and also allow excess fuel not used by the injectors to return to the tank. However, the warmer fuel in the tank may create problems, such as an excessive rise in fuel vapor pressures in the tank.

 ? FREQUENTLY ASKED QUESTION

Just How Much Fuel Is Recirculated?

Approximately 80% of the available fuel-pump volume is released to the fuel tank bypassing the fuel-pressure regulator at idle speed. As an example, a passenger vehicle cruising down the road at 60 mph gets 30 mpg. With a typical return-style fuel system pumping about 30 gallons per hour from the tank, it would therefore burn 2 gallons per hour, and return about 28 gallons per hour to the tank!

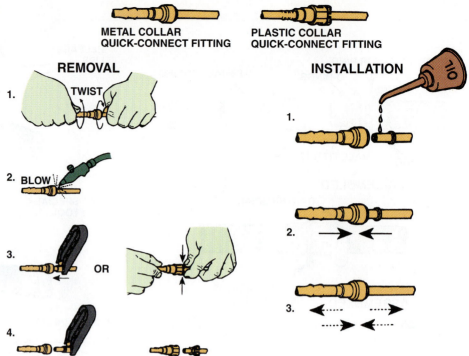

FIGURE 26–11 Typical quick-connect steps.

METAL COLLAR QUICK-CONNECT FITTING

PLASTIC COLLAR QUICK-CONNECT FITTING

REMOVAL

1. TWIST
2. BLOW
3.
OR
4.

INSTALLATION

1.
2.
3.

FUEL LINES (CONTINUED)

With late-model vehicles, there has been some concern about too much heat being sent back to the fuel tank, causing rising in-tank temperatures and increases in fuel vaporization and **volatile organic compound (VOC)** (hydrocarbon) emissions. To combat this problem, manufacturers have placed the pressure regulator back by the tank instead of under the hood on mechanical returnless systems. In this way, returned fuel is not subjected to the heat generated by the engine and the underhood environment. To prevent vapor lock in these systems, pressures have been raised in the fuel rail, and injectors tend to have smaller openings to maintain control of the fuel spray under pressure.

Not only must the fuel be filtered and supplied under adequate pressure, but there must also be a consistent *volume* of fuel to assure smooth engine performance even under the heaviest of loads.

 FREQUENTLY ASKED QUESTION

How Can an Electric Pump Work Inside a Gas Tank and Not Cause a Fire?

Even though fuel fills the entire pump, no burnable mixture exists inside the pump because there is no air and no danger of commutator brush arcing, igniting the fuel.

ELECTRIC FUEL PUMPS

The electric fuel pump is a pusher unit. When the pump is mounted in the tank, the entire fuel supply line to the engine can be pressurized. Because the fuel, when pressurized, has a higher boiling point, it is unlikely that vapor will form to interfere with fuel flow.

Most vehicles use the impeller or turbine pumps. ● **SEE FIGURE 26–12.** All electrical pumps are driven by a small electric motor, but the turbine pump turns at higher speeds and is quieter than the others.

POSITIVE DISPLACEMENT PUMP A positive displacement pump is a design that forces everything that enters the pump to leave the pump.

In the **roller cell** or vane pump, the impeller draws fuel into the pump, and then pushes it out through the fuel line to the injection system. All designs of pumps use a variable-sized chamber to draw in fuel. When the maximum volume has been reached, the supply port closes and the discharge opens. Fuel is then forced out the discharge as this volume decreases. The chambers are formed by rollers or gears in a rotor plate. Since this type of pump uses no valves to move the fuel, the fuel flows steadily through the pump housing. Since fuel flows steadily through the entire pump, including the electrical portion, the pump stays cool. Usually, only when a vehicle runs out of fuel is there a risk of pump damage.

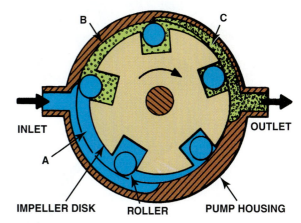

FIGURE 26–13 The pumping action of an impeller or rotary vane pump.

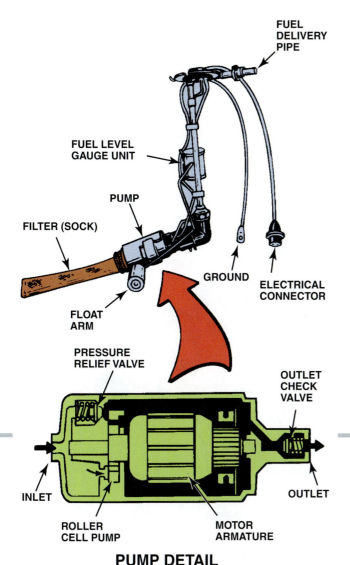

PUMP DETAIL

FIGURE 26–12 A roller cell-type electric fuel pump.

Most electric fuel pumps are equipped with a fuel outlet check valve that closes to maintain fuel pressure when the pump shuts off. **Residual or rest pressure** prevents vapor lock and hot-start problems on these systems.

● **FIGURE 26–13** shows the pumping action of a **rotary vane pump**. The pump consists of a central impeller disk, several rollers or vanes that ride in notches in the impeller, and a pump housing that is offset from the impeller centerline. The impeller is mounted on the end of the motor armature and spins whenever the motor is running. The rollers are free to slide in and out within the notches in the impeller to maintain sealing contact. Unpressurized fuel enters the pump, fills the spaces between the rollers, and is trapped between the impeller, the housing, and two rollers. An internal gear pump, called a **gerotor**, is another type of positive displacement pump that is often used in engine oil pumps. It uses the meshing of internal and external gear teeth to

pressurize the fuel. ● **SEE FIGURE 26–14** for an example of a gerotor-type fuel pump that uses an impeller as the first stage and is used to move the fuel gerotor section where it is pressurized.

HYDROKINETIC FLOW PUMP DESIGN The word *hydro* means liquid and the term *kinetic* refers to motion, so the term **hydrokinetic pump** means that this design of pump rapidly moves the fuel to create pressure. This design of pump is a nonpositive displacement pump design.

A **turbine pump** is the most common because it tends to be less noisy. Sometimes called **turbine**, **peripheral**, and **side-channel**, these units use an impeller that accelerates the fuel particles before actually discharging them into a tract where they generate pressure via pulse exchange. Actual pump volume is controlled by using a different number of impeller blades, and in some cases a higher number of impellers, or different shapes along the side discharge channels. These units are fitted more toward lower operating pressures of less than 60 PSI. ● **SEE FIGURE 26–15** for an example of a two-stage turbine pump. The turbine impeller has a staggered blade design to minimize pump harmonic noise and to separate vapor from the liquid fuel. The end cap assembly contains a pressure relief valve and a radio-frequency interference (RFI) suppression module. The check valve is usually located in the upper fuel pipe connector assembly.

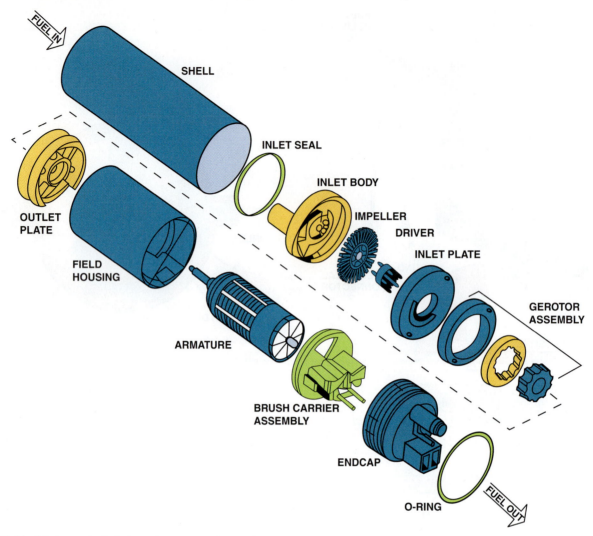

FIGURE 26–14 An exploded view of a gerotor electric fuel pump.

After it passes through the strainer, fuel is drawn into the lower housing inlet port by the impellers. It is pressurized and delivered to the convoluted fuel tube for transfer through a check valve into the fuel feed pipe. A typical electric fuel pump used on a fuel-injection system delivers about 40 to 50 gallons per hour or 0.6 to 0.8 gallons per minute at a pressure of 70 to 90 PSI.

MODULAR FUEL SENDER ASSEMBLY The modular fuel sender consists of a replaceable fuel level sensor, a turbine pump, and a jet pump. The reservoir housing is attached to the cover containing fuel pipes and the electrical connector. Fuel is transferred from the pump to the fuel pipe through a convoluted (flexible) fuel pipe. The convoluted fuel pipe eliminates the need for rubber hoses, nylon pipes, and clamps. The reservoir dampens fuel slosh to maintain a constant fuel level available to the roller vane pump; it also reduces noise.

Some of the flow, however, is returned to the jet pump for recirculation. Excess fuel is returned to the reservoir through one of the three hollow support pipes. The hot fuel quickly mixes with the cooler fuel in the reservoir; this minimizes the possibility of vapor lock. In these modules, the reservoir is filled by the jet pump. Some of the fuel from the pump is sent through the jet pump to lift fuel from the tank into the reservoir.

ELECTRIC PUMP CONTROL CIRCUITS Fuel-pump circuits are controlled by the fuel-pump relay. Fuel-pump relays are activated initially by turning the ignition key to on, which allows the pump to pressurize the fuel system. As a safety precaution, the relay de-energizes after a few seconds until the key is moved to the crank position. On some systems, once an ignition coil signal, or "tach" signal, is received by the engine control computer, indicating the engine is rotating, the relay remains energized even with the key released to the run position.

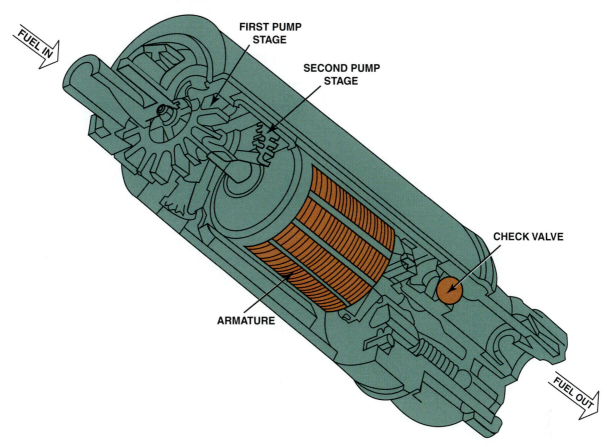

FIGURE 26–15 A cutaway view of a typical two-stage turbine electric fuel pump.

 FREQUENTLY ASKED QUESTION

Why Are Many Fuel-Pump Modules Spring-Loaded?

Fuel modules that contain the fuel pickup sock, fuel pump, and fuel level sensor are often spring-loaded when fitted to a plastic fuel tank. The plastic material shrinks when cold and expands when hot, so having the fuel module spring-loaded ensures that the fuel pickup sock will always be the same distance from the bottom of the tank. ● **SEE FIGURE 26–16**.

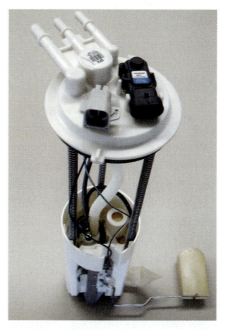

FIGURE 26–16 A typical fuel-pump module assembly, which includes the pickup strainer and fuel pump, as well as the fuel-pressure sensor and fuel level sensing unit.

CHRYSLER. On Chrysler vehicles, the PCM must receive an engine speed (RPM) signal during cranking before it can energize a circuit driver inside the power module to activate an automatic shutdown (ASD) relay to power the fuel pump, ignition coil, and injectors. As a safety precaution, if the RPM signal to the logic module is interrupted, the logic module signals the power module to deactivate the ASD, turning off the pump, coil, and injectors. In some vehicles, the oil pressure switch circuit may be used as a safety circuit to activate the pump in the ignition switch run position.

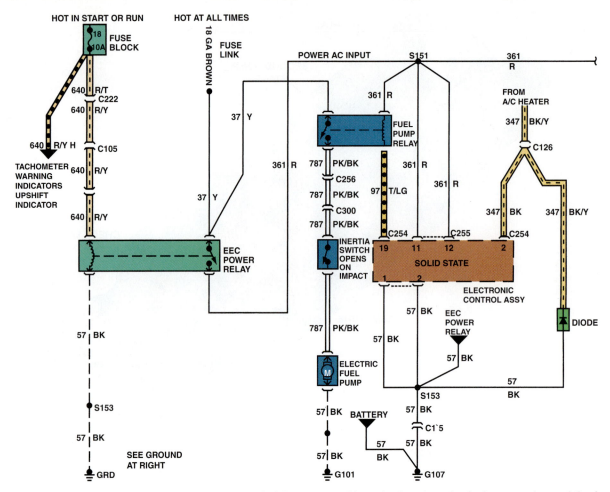

FIGURE 26-17 A schematic showing that an inertia switch is connected in series between the fuel-pump relay and the fuel pump.

ELECTRIC FUEL PUMPS (CONTINUED)

GENERAL MOTORS. General Motors systems energize the pump with the ignition switch to initially pressurize the fuel lines, but then deactivate the pump if an RPM signal is not received within one or two seconds. The pump is reactivated as soon as engine cranking is detected. The oil pressure sending unit serves as a backup to the fuel-pump relay on some vehicles. In case of pump relay failure, the oil pressure switch will operate the fuel pump once oil pressure reaches about 4 PSI (28 kPa).

FORD. Most Ford vehicles with fuel injection have an inertia switch in the trunk between the fuel-pump relay and fuel pump. When the ignition switch is turned to the On position, the electronic engine control (EEC) power relay energizes, providing current to the fuel-pump relay and a timing circuit in the EEC module. If the ignition key is not turned to the Start position within about one second, the timing circuit opens the ground circuit to de-energize the fuel-pump relay and shut down the pump. This circuit is designed to prepressurize the system. Once the key is turned to the start position, power to the pump is sent through the relay and inertia switch.

The inertia switch opens under a specified impact, such as a collision. When the switch opens, current to the pump shuts off because the fuel-pump relay will not energize. The switch must be reset manually by opening the trunk and depressing the reset button before current flow to the pump can be restored.
● **SEE FIGURE 26-17** for a schematic of a typical fuel system that uses an injector switch in the power feed circuit to the electric fuel pump.

PUMP PULSATION DAMPENING
Some manufacturers use an **accumulator** in the system to reduce pressure pulses and noise. Others use a pulsator located at the outlet of the fuel pump to absorb pressure pulsations that are created by the pump. These pulsators are usually used on roller vane pumps and are a source of many internal fuel leaks. ● **SEE FIGURE 26-18**.

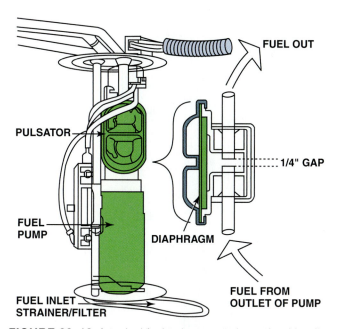

FIGURE 26–18 A typical fuel pulsator used mostly with roller vane-type pumps to help even out the pulsation in pressure that can cause noise.

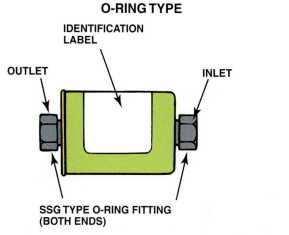

O-RING TYPE

FIGURE 26–19 Inline fuel filters are usually attached to the fuel line with screw clamps or threaded connections. The fuel filter must be installed in the proper direction or a restricted fuel flow can result.

NOTE: Some experts suggest that the pulsator be removed and replaced with a standard section of fuel line to prevent the loss of fuel pressure that results when the connections on the pulsator loosen and leak fuel back into the tank.

VARIABLE SPEED PUMPS   Another way to help reduce noise, current draw, and pump wear is to reduce the speed of the pump when less than maximum output is required. Pump speed and pressure can be regulated by controlling the voltage supplied to the pump with a resistor switched into the circuit, or by letting the engine-control computer pulse-width modulate (PWM) the voltage supply to the pump, through a separate fuel pump driver electronic module. With slower pump speed and pressure, less noise is produced.

FUEL FILTERS

Despite the care generally taken in refining, storing, and delivering gasoline, some impurities get into the automotive fuel system. Fuel filters remove dirt, rust, water, and other contamination from the gasoline before it can reach the fuel injectors. Most fuel filters are designed to filter particles that are 10 to 20 microns or larger in size.

The useful life of many filters is limited, but vehicles that use a returnless-type fuel injection system usually use filters that are part of the fuel pump assembly and do have any specified replacement interval. This means that they, should last the life of the vehicle. If fuel filters are not replaced according to the manufacturer's recommendations, they can become clogged and restrict fuel flow.

In addition to using several different types of fuel filters, a single fuel system may contain two or more filters. The inline filter is located in the line between the fuel pump and the throttle body or fuel rail. ● **SEE FIGURE 26–19.** This filter protects the system from contamination, but does not protect the fuel pump.

The inline filter usually is a metal or plastic container with a pleated paper element sealed inside.

Fuel filters may be mounted on a bracket on the fender panel, a shock tower, or another convenient place in the engine compartment. They may also be installed under the vehicle near the fuel tank. Fuel filters should be replaced according to the vehicle manufacturer's recommendations, which range from every 30,000 miles (48,000 km) to 100,000 miles (160,000 km) or longer. Fuel filters that are part of the fuel-pump module assemblies usually do not have any specified service interval.

 TECH TIP

Be Sure That the Fuel Filter Is Installed Correctly

The fuel filter has flow direction and if it is installed backwards, the vehicle will most likely have a restricted exhaust (low power at higher engine speeds and loads).

All injectors, throttle body or port, are fitted with one or more filter screens or strainers to remove any particles (generally 10 microns or 0.00039 in.) that might have passed through the other filters. These screens, which surround the fuel inlet, are on the side of throttle-body injectors and are inserted in the top of port injectors. ● SEE FIGURE 26–20.

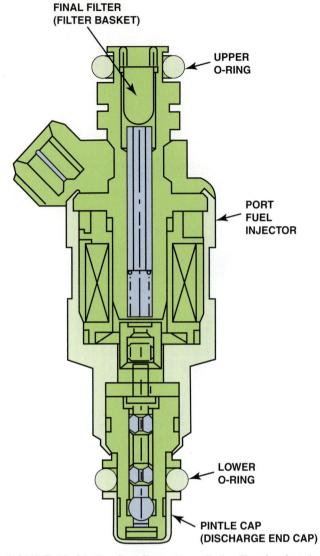

FIGURE 26–20 The final filter, also called a **filter basket,** is the last filter in the fuel system.

FUEL-PUMP TESTING

Fuel-pump testing includes many different tests and procedures. Even though a fuel pump can pass one test, it does not mean that there is not a fuel-pump problem. For example, if the pump motor is rotating slower than normal, it may be able to produce the specified pressure, but not enough volume to meet the needs of the engine while operating under a heavy load.

TESTING FUEL-PUMP PRESSURE Fuel-pump-regulated pressure has become more important than ever with a more exact fuel control. Although an increase in fuel pressure does increase fuel volume to the engine, this is *not* the preferred method to add additional fuel as some units will not open correctly at the increased fuel pressure. On the other side of the discussion, many newer engines will not start when fuel pressure is just a few PSI low. Correct fuel pressure is very important for proper engine operation. Most fuel-injection systems operate at either

 TECH TIP

The Ear Test

No, this is not a test of your hearing, but rather using your ear to check that the electric fuel pump is operating. The electric fuel pump inside the fuel tank is often difficult to hear running, especially in a noisy shop environment. A commonly used trick to better hear the pump is to use a funnel in the fuel filter neck. ● SEE FIGURE 26–21.

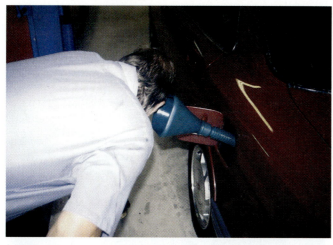

(a)

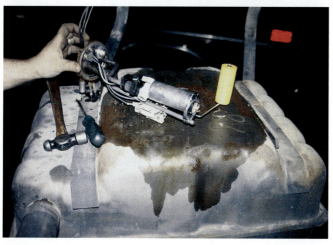

(b)

FIGURE 26–21 (a) A funnel helps in hearing if the electric fuel pump inside the gas tank is working. (b) If the pump is not running, check the wiring and current flow before going through the process of dropping the fuel tank to remove the pump.

FIGURE 26–22 The Schrader valve on this General Motors 3800 V-6 is located next to the fuel-pressure regulator.

a low pressure of about 10 PSI or a high pressure of between 35 and 45 PSI.

Normal Operating Pressure	(PSI)	Maximum Pump Pressure (PSI)
Low-pressure TBI units	9–13	18–20
High-pressure TBI units	25–35	50–70
Port fuel-injection systems	35–45	70–90
Central port fuel injection (GM)	55–64	90–110

In both types of systems, maximum fuel-pump pressure is about double the normal operating pressure to ensure that a continuous flow of cool fuel is being supplied to the injector(s) to help prevent vapor from forming in the fuel system. Although vapor or foaming in a fuel system can greatly affect engine operation, the cooling and lubricating flow of the fuel must be maintained to ensure the durability of injector nozzles.

To measure fuel-pump pressure, locate the Schrader valve and attach a fuel-pressure gauge. ● **SEE FIGURE 26–22.**

TECH TIP

The Rubber Mallet Trick

Often a no-start condition is due to an inoperative electric fuel pump. A common trick is to tap on the bottom of the fuel tank with a rubber mallet in an attempt to jar the pump motor enough to work. Instead of pushing a vehicle into the shop, simply tap on the fuel tank and attempt to start the engine. This is not a repair, but rather a confirmation that the fuel pump does indeed require replacement.

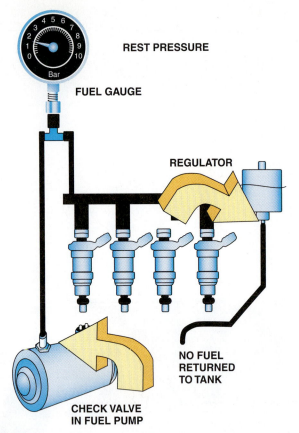

REST PRESSURE

FUEL GAUGE

REGULATOR

NO FUEL
RETURNED
TO TANK

CHECK VALVE
IN FUEL PUMP

FIGURE 26–23 The fuel system should hold pressure if the system is leak free.

FUEL-PUMP TESTING (CONTINUED)

NOTE: Some vehicles, such as those with General Motors TBI fuel-injection systems, require a specific fuel-pressure gauge that connects to the fuel system. Always follow the manufacturers' recommendations and procedures.

REST PRESSURE TEST If the fuel pressure is acceptable, then check the system for leakdown. Observe the pressure gauge after five minutes. ● **SEE FIGURE 26–23**. The pressure should be the same as the initial reading. If not, then the pressure regulator, fuel-pump check valve, or the injectors are leaking.

DYNAMIC PRESSURE TEST To test the pressure dynamically, start the engine. If the pressure is vacuum referenced, then the pressure should change when the throttle is cycled. If it does not, then check the vacuum supply circuit. Remove the vacuum line from the regulator and inspect for any presence of fuel. ● **SEE FIGURE 26–24**. There should never be any fuel present on the vacuum side of the regulator diaphragm. When the engine speed is increased, the pressure reading should remain within the specifications.

FUEL
PRESSURE
REGULATOR

FIGURE 26–24 If the vacuum hose is removed from the fuel-pressure regulator when the engine is running, the fuel pressure should increase. If it does not increase, then the fuel pump is not capable of supplying adequate pressure or the fuel-pressure regulator is defective. If gasoline is visible in the vacuum hose, the regulator is leaking and should be replaced.

> **🔧 TECH TIP**
>
> **The Fuel-Pressure Stethoscope Test**
>
> When the fuel pump is energized and the engine is not running, fuel should be heard flowing back to the fuel tank at the outlet of the fuel-pressure regulator. ● **SEE FIGURE 26–25**. If fuel is heard flowing through the return line, the fuel-pump pressure is higher than the regulator pressure. If no sound of fuel is heard, either the fuel pump or the fuel-pressure regulator is at fault.

Some engines do not use a vacuum-referenced regulator. The running pressure remains constant, which is typical for a mechanical returnless-type fuel system. On these systems, the pressure is higher than on return-type systems to help reduce the formation of fuel vapors in the system.

FIGURE 26–25 Fuel should be heard returning to the fuel tank at the fuel return line if the fuel pump and fuel-pressure regulator are functioning correctly.

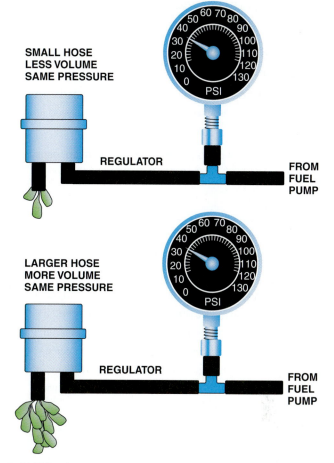

SMALL HOSE
LESS VOLUME
SAME PRESSURE

REGULATOR

FROM FUEL PUMP

LARGER HOSE
MORE VOLUME
SAME PRESSURE

REGULATOR

FROM FUEL PUMP

FIGURE 26–26 A fuel-pressure reading does not confirm that there is enough fuel volume for the engine to operate correctly.

TESTING FUEL-PUMP VOLUME Fuel pressure alone is not enough for proper engine operation. ● **SEE FIGURE 26–26**. Sufficient fuel capacity (flow) should be at least 2 pints (1 liter) every 30 seconds or 1 pint in 15 seconds. Fuel flow specifications are usually expressed in gallons per minute. A typical specification would be 0.5 gallons per minute or more. Volume testing is shown in ● **FIGURE 26–27**.

All fuel must be filtered to prevent dirt and impurities from damaging the fuel system components and/or engine. The first filter is inside the gas tank and is usually not replaceable separately but is attached to the fuel pump (if the pump is electric) and/or fuel gauge sending unit. The replaceable fuel filter is usually located between the fuel tank and the fuel rail or inlet to the fuel-injection system. Most vehicle manufacturers state in service information when to replace the fuel filter. Most newer vehicles, that use returnless-type fuel injection systems, do not have replaceable filters as they are built into the fuel pump module assembly. (Check the vehicle manufacturers' recommendations for exact time and mileage intervals.)

FIGURE 26–27 A fuel system tester connected in series in the fuel system so all of the fuel used flows through the meter which displays the rate-of-flow and the fuel pressure.

If the fuel filter becomes partially clogged, the following are likely to occur:

1. There will be low power at higher engine speeds. The vehicle usually will not go faster than a certain speed (engine acts as if it has a built-in speed governor).

2. The engine will cut out or miss on acceleration, especially when climbing hills or during heavy-load acceleration.

TECH TIP

Quick and Easy Fuel Volume Test

Testing for pump volume involves using a specialized tester or a fuel-pressure gauge equipped with a hose to allow the fuel to be drawn from the system into a container with volume markings to allow for a volume measurement. This test can be hazardous because of expanding gasoline. An alternative test involves connecting a fuel-pressure gauge to the system with the following steps:

STEP 1 Start the engine and observe the fuel-pressure gauge. The reading should be within factory specifications (typically between 35 PSI and 45 PSI).

STEP 2 Remove the hose from the fuel-pressure regulator. The pressure should increase if the system uses a demand-type regulator.

STEP 3 Rapidly accelerate the engine while watching the fuel-pressure gauge. If the fuel volume is okay, the fuel pressure should not drop more than 2 PSI. If the fuel pressure drops more than 2 PSI, replace the fuel filter and retest.

STEP 4 After replacing the fuel filter, accelerate the engine and observe the pressure gauge. If the pressure drops more than 2 PSI, replace the fuel pump.

NOTE: The fuel pump could still be delivering less than the specified volume of fuel, but as long as the volume needed by the engine is met, the pressure will not drop. If, however, the vehicle is pulling a heavy load, the demand for fuel volume may exceed the capacity of the pump.

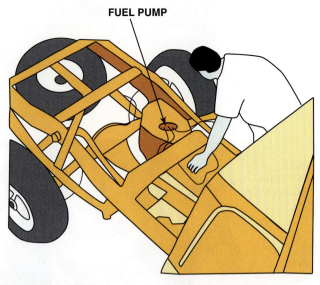

FUEL PUMP

FIGURE 26–28 Removing the bed from a pickup truck makes gaining access to the fuel pump a lot easier.

TECH TIP

Remove the Bed to Save Time?

The electric fuel pump is easier to replace on many General Motors pickup trucks if the bed is removed. Access to the top of the fuel tank, where the access hole is located, for the removal of the fuel tank sender unit and pump is restricted by the bottom of the pickup truck bed. Rather than drop the tank, it is often much easier to use an engine hoist or a couple of other technicians to lift the bed from the frame after removing only a few fasteners. ● **SEE FIGURE 26–28**.

CAUTION: Be sure to clean around the fuel pump opening so that dirt or debris does not enter the tank when the fuel pump is removed.

A weak or defective fuel pump can also be the cause of the symptoms just listed. If an electric fuel pump for a fuel-injected engine becomes weak, additional problems include the following:

1. The engine may be hard to start.

2. There may be a rough idle and stalling.

3. There may be erratic shifting of the automatic transmission as a result of engine missing due to lack of fuel-pump pressure and/or volume.

CAUTION: Be certain to consult the vehicle manufacturers' recommended service and testing procedures before attempting to test or replace any component of a high-pressure electronic fuel-injection system.

FUEL-PUMP CURRENT DRAW TEST

Another test that can and should be performed on a fuel pump is to measure the current draw in amperes. This test is most often performed by connecting a digital multimeter set to read DC amperes and test the current draw. ● **SEE FIGURE 26–29** for the hookup for vehicles equipped with a fuel-pump relay. Compare the reading to factory specifications. See the chart for an example of typical fuel-pump current draw readings.

NOTE: Testing the current draw of an electric fuel pump may not indicate whether the pump is good. A pump that is not rotating may draw normal current.

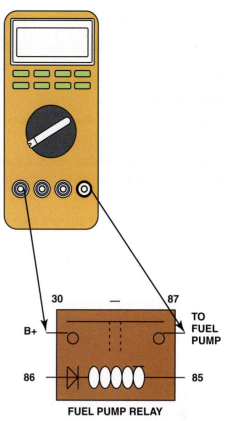

FIGURE 26–29 Hookup for testing fuel-pump current draw on any vehicle equipped with a fuel-pump relay.

Fuel-Pump Current Draw Table

Amperage Reading	Expected Value	Amperage Too High	Amperage Too Low
Throttle-Body Fuel-Injection Engines	2 to 5 amps	• Check the fuel filter. • Check for restrictions in other fuel line areas. • Replace the fuel pump.	• Check for a high-resistance connection. • Check for a high-resistance ground fault. • Replace the fuel pump.
Port Fuel-Injection Engines	4 to 8 amps	• Check the fuel filter. • Check for restrictions in other fuel line areas. • Replace the fuel pump.	• Check for a high-resistance connection. • Check for a high-resistance ground fault. • Replace the fuel pump.
Turbo Engines	6 to 10 amps	• Check the fuel filter. • Check for restrictions in other fuel line areas. • Replace the fuel pump.	• Check for a high-resistance connection. • Check for a high-resistance ground fault. • Replace the fuel pump.
GM CPI Truck Engines	8 to 12 amps	• Check the fuel filter. • Check for restrictions in other fuel line areas. • Replace the fuel pump.	• Check for a high-resistance connection. • Check for a high-resistance ground fault. • Replace the fuel pump.

FUEL-PUMP REPLACEMENT

The following recommendations should be followed whenever replacing an electric fuel pump:

- The fuel-pump strainer (sock) should be replaced with the new pump.

- If the original pump had a defector shield, it should always be used to prevent fuel return bubbles from blocking the inlet to the pump.

- Always check the interior of the fuel tank for evidence of contamination or dirt.

- Double-check that the replacement pump is correct for the application.

- Check that the wiring and electrical connectors are clean and tight.

Fuel Supply-Related Symptom Guide

Problem	Possible Causes
Pressure too high after engine start-up.	1. Defective fuel-pressure regulator 2. Restricted fuel return line 3. Excessive system voltage 4. Restricted return line 5. Wrong fuel pump
Pressure too low after engine start-up.	1. Stuck-open pressure regulator 2. Low voltage 3. Poor ground 4. Plugged fuel filter 5. Faulty inline fuel pump 6. Faulty in-tank fuel pump 7. Partially clogged filter sock 8. Faulty hose coupling 9. Leaking fuel line 10. Wrong fuel pump 11. Leaking pulsator 12. Restricted accumulator 13. Faulty pump check valves 14. Faulty pump installation
Pressure drops off with key on/engine off. **With key off, the pressure does not hold.**	1. Leaky pulsator 2. Leaking fuel-pump coupling hose 3. Faulty fuel pump (check valves) 4. Faulty pressure regulator 5. Leaking fuel injector 6. Leaking cold-start fuel injector 7. Faulty installation 8. Lines leaking

SUMMARY

1. The fuel delivery system includes the following items:
   - Fuel tank
   - Fuel pump
   - Fuel filter(s)
   - Fuel lines
2. A fuel tank is either constructed of steel with a tin plating for corrosion resistance or polyethylene plastic.
3. Fuel tank filler tubes contain an anti-siphoning device.
4. Accident and rollover protection devices include check valves and inertia switches.
5. Most fuel lines are made of nylon plastic.
6. Electric fuel-pump types include: roller cell, gerotor, and turbine.
7. Fuel filters remove particles that are 10 to 20 microns or larger in size and should be replaced regularly.
8. Fuel pumps can be tested by checking:
   - Pressure
   - Volume
   - Specified current draw

REVIEW QUESTIONS

1. What are the two materials used to construct fuel tanks?

2. What are the three most commonly used pump designs?

3. What is the proper way to disconnect and connect plastic fuel line connections?

4. Where are the fuel filters located in the fuel system?

5. What accident and rollover devices are installed in a fuel delivery system?

6. What three methods can be used to test a fuel pump?

1. The first fuel filter in the sock inside the fuel tank normally filters particles larger than _____.
   a. 0.001 to 0.003 in.
   b. 0.010 to 0.030 in.
   c. 10 to 20 microns
   d. 70 to 100 microns

2. If it is tripped, which type of safety device will keep the electric fuel pump from operating?
   a. Rollover valve
   b. Inertia switch
   c. Anti-siphoning valve
   d. Check valve

3. Fuel lines are constructed from _____.
   a. Seamless steel tubing
   b. Nylon plastic
   c. Copper and/or aluminum tubing
   d. Both a and b are used

4. What prevents the fuel pump inside the fuel tank from catching the gasoline on fire?
   a. Electricity is not used to power the pump
   b. No air is around the motor brushes
   c. Gasoline is hard to ignite in a closed space
   d. All of the above

5. A good fuel pump should be able to supply how much fuel per minute?
   a. 1/4 pint
   b. 1/2 pint
   c. 1 pint
   d. 0.6 to 0.8 gallons

6. Technician A says that fuel pump modules are spring-loaded so that they can be compressed to fit into the opening. Technician B says that they are spring-loaded to allow for expansion and contraction of plastic fuel tanks. Which technician is correct?
   a. Technician A only
   b. Technician B only
   c. Both Technicians A and B
   d. Neither Technician A nor B

7. Most fuel filters are designed to remove particles larger than _____.
   a. 10 microns
   b. 20 microns
   c. 70 microns
   d. 100 microns

8. The amperage draw of an electric fuel pump is higher than specified. All of the following are possible causes *except:*
   a. Corroded electrical connections at the pump motor
   b. Clogged fuel filter
   c. Restriction in the fuel line
   d. Defective fuel pump

9. A fuel pump is being replaced for the third time. Technician A says that the gasoline could be contaminated. Technician B says that wiring to the pump could be corroded. Which technician is correct?
   a. Technician A only
   b. Technician B only
   c. Both Technicians A and B
   d. Neither Technician A nor B

10. A fuel filter has been accidentally installed backwards. What is the most likely result?
    a. Nothing will be noticed
    b. Reduced fuel economy
    c. Lower power at higher engine speeds and loads
    d. Fuel system pulsation noises may be heard

FUEL-INJECTION COMPONENTS AND OPERATION

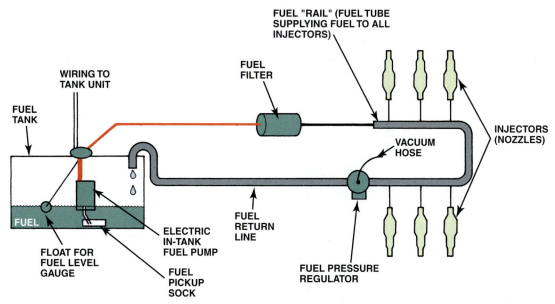

FIGURE 27–1 Typical port fuel-injection system, indicating the location of various components. Notice that the fuel-pressure regulator is located on the fuel return side of the system. The computer does not control fuel pressure. But does control the operation of the electric fuel pump (on most systems) and the pulsing on and off of the injectors.

ELECTRONIC FUEL-INJECTION OPERATION

Electronic fuel-injection systems use the computer to control the operation of fuel injectors and other functions based on information sent to the computer from the various sensors. Most electronic fuel-injection systems share the following:

1. Electric fuel pump (usually located inside the fuel tank)

2. Fuel-pump relay (usually controlled by the computer)

3. Fuel-pressure regulator (mechanically operated spring-loaded rubber diaphragm maintains proper fuel pressure)

4. Fuel-injector nozzle or nozzles

● **SEE FIGURE 27–1.** Most electronic fuel-injection systems use the computer to control these aspects of their operation:

1. **Pulsing the fuel injectors on and off.** The longer the injectors are held open, the greater the amount of fuel injected into the cylinder.

2. **Operating the fuel pump relay circuit.** The computer usually controls the operation of the electric fuel pump located inside (or near) the fuel tank. The computer uses signals from the ignition switch and RPM signals from the ignition module or system to energize the fuel-pump relay circuit.

NOTE: This is a safety feature, because if the engine stalls and the tachometer (engine speed) signal is lost, the computer will shut off (de-energize) the fuel-pump relay and stop the fuel pump.

Computer-controlled fuel-injection systems are normally reliable systems if the proper service procedures are followed. Fuel-injection systems use the gasoline flowing through the injectors to lubricate and cool the injector electrical windings and pintle valves.

NOTE: The fuel does not actually make contact with the electrical windings because the injectors have O-rings at the top and bottom of the winding spool to keep fuel out.

 **TECH TIP**

"Two Must-Do's"

For long service life of the fuel system always do the following:
1. Avoid operating the vehicle on a near-empty tank of fuel. The water or alcohol becomes more concentrated when the fuel level is low. Dirt that settles near the bottom of the fuel tank can be drawn through the fuel system and cause damage to the pump and injector nozzles.
2. Replace the fuel filter at regular service intervals.

FIGURE 27–2 A dual-nozzle TBI unit on a Chevrolet 4.3-L V-6 engine. The fuel is squirted above the throttle plate where the fuel mixes with air before entering the intake manifold.

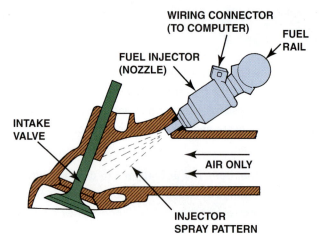

FIGURE 27–3 A typical port fuel-injection system squirts fuel into the low pressure (vacuum) of the intake manifold, about 3 in. (70 to 100 mm) from the intake valve.

ELECTRONIC FUEL-INJECTION OPERATION (CONTINUED)

There are two types of electronic fuel-injection systems:

- **Throttle-body-injection (TBI)** type. A TBI system delivers fuel from a nozzle(s) into the air above the throttle plate. ● **SEE FIGURE 27–2.**

- **Port fuel-injection**-type. A port fuel-injection design uses a nozzle for each cylinder and the fuel is squirted into the intake manifold about 2 to 3 inches (70 to 100 mm) from the intake valve. ● **SEE FIGURE 27–3.**

SPEED-DENSITY FUEL-INJECTION SYSTEMS

Fuel-injection computer systems require a method for measuring the amount of air the engine is breathing in, in order to match the correct fuel delivery. There are two basic methods used:

1. Speed density
2. Mass airflow

The speed-density method does not require an air quantity sensor, but rather calculates the amount of fuel required by the engine. The computer uses information from sensors such as the MAP and TP to calculate the needed amount of fuel.

- **MAP sensor.** The value of the intake (inlet) manifold pressure (vacuum) is a direct indication of engine load.

- **TP sensor.** The position of the throttle plate and its rate of change are used as part of the equation to calculate the proper amount of fuel to inject.

- **Temperature sensors.** Both engine coolant temperature (ECT) and intake air temperature (IAT) are used to calculate the density of the air and the need of the engine for fuel. A cold engine (low-coolant temperature) requires a richer air–fuel mixture than a warm engine.

On speed-density systems, the computer calculates the amount of air in each cylinder by using manifold pressure and engine rpm. The amount of air in each cylinder is the major factor in determining the amount of fuel needed. Other sensors provide information to modify the fuel requirements. The formula used to determine the injector pulse width (PW) in milliseconds (ms) is:

Injector pulse width = MAP/BARO × RPM/maximum rpm

The formula is modified by values from other sensors, including:

- Throttle position (TP)
- Engine coolant temperature (ECT)
- Intake air temperature (IAT)
- Oxygen sensor voltage (O2S)
- Adaptive memory

A fuel injector delivers atomized fuel into the airstream where it is instantly vaporized. All throttle-body (TB) fuel-injection systems and many multipoint (port) injection systems use the speed-density method of fuel calculation.

MASS AIRFLOW FUEL-INJECTION SYSTEMS

The formula used by fuel-injection systems that use a mass airflow (MAF) sensor to calculate the injection base pulse width is:

Injector pulse width = airflow/rpm

The formula is modified by other sensor values such as:

- Throttle position
- Engine coolant temperature
- Barometric pressure
- Adaptive memory

NOTE: Many four-cylinder engines do not use a MAF sensor because, due to the time interval between intake events, some reverse airflow can occur in the intake manifold. The MAF sensor would "read" this flow of air as being additional air entering the engine, giving the PCM incorrect airflow information. Therefore, most four-cylinder engines use the speed-density method of fuel control.

THROTTLE-BODY INJECTION

The computer controls injector pulses in one of two ways:

- Synchronized
- Nonsynchronized

If the system uses a synchronized mode, the injector pulses once for each distributor reference pulse. In some vehicles, when dual injectors are used in a synchronized system, the injectors pulse alternately. In a nonsynchronized system, the injectors are pulsed once during a given period (which varies according to calibration) completely independent of distributor reference pulses.

The injector always opens the same distance, and the fuel pressure is maintained at a controlled value by the pressure regulator. The regulators used on throttle-body injection systems are not connected to a vacuum like many port fuel-injection systems. The strength of the spring inside the regulator determines at what pressure the valve is unseated, sending the fuel back to the tank and lowering the pressure. ● **SEE FIGURE 27–4.** The amount of fuel delivered by the injector depends on the amount of time (on-time) that the nozzle is open. This is the injector pulse width—the on-time in milliseconds that the nozzle is open.

The PCM commands a variety of pulse widths to supply the amount of fuel that an engine needs at any specific moment.

- A long pulse width delivers more fuel.
- A short pulse width delivers less fuel.

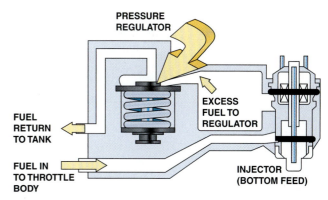

FIGURE 27–4 The tension of the spring in the fuel-pressure regulator determines the operating pressure on a throttle-body fuel-injection unit.

? FREQUENTLY ASKED QUESTION

How Do the Sensors Affect the Pulse Width?

The base pulse width of a fuel-injection system is primarily determined by the value of the MAF or MAP sensor and engine speed (RPM). However, the PCM relies on the input from many other sensors to modify the base pulse width as needed. For example,

- **TP Sensor.** This sensor causes the PCM to command up to 500% (5 times) the base pulse width if the accelerator pedal is depressed rapidly to the floor. It can also reduce the pulse width by about 70% if the throttle is rapidly closed.
- **ECT.** The value of this sensor determines the temperature of the engine coolant, helps determine the base pulse width, and can account for up to 60% of the determining factors.
- **BARO.** The BARO sensor compensates for altitude and adds up to about 10% under high-pressure conditions and subtracts as much as 50% from the base pulse width at high altitudes.
- **IAT.** The intake air temperature is used to modify the base pulse width based on the temperature of the air entering the engine. It is usually capable of adding as much as 20% if very cold air is entering the engine or reduce the pulse width by up to 20% if very hot air is entering the engine.
- **O2S.** This is one of the main modifiers to the base pulse width and can add or subtract up to about 20% to 25% or more, depending on the oxygen sensor activity.

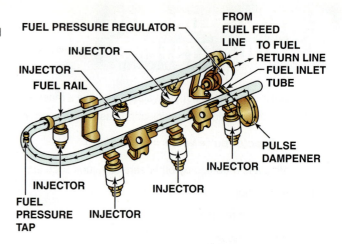

FIGURE 27–5 The injectors receive fuel and are supported by the fuel rail.

FIGURE 27–6 Cross-section of a typical port fuel-injection nozzle assembly. These injectors are serviced as an assembly only; no part replacement or service is possible except for replacement of external O-ring seals.

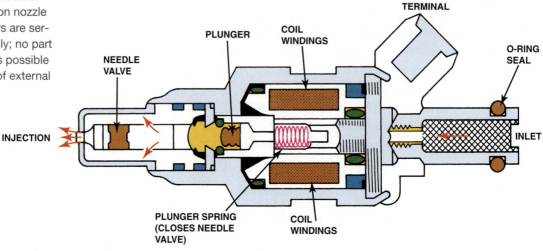

PORT-FUEL INJECTION

The advantages of port fuel-injection design also are related to characteristics of intake manifolds:

- Fuel distribution is equal to all cylinders because each cylinder has its own injector. ● SEE FIGURE 27–5.

- The fuel is injected almost directly into the combustion chamber, so there is no chance for it to condense on the walls of a cold intake manifold.

- Because the manifold does not have to carry fuel to properly position a TBI unit, it can be shaped and sized to tune the intake airflow to achieve specific engine performance characteristics.

An EFI injector is simply a specialized solenoid. ● SEE FIGURE 27–6. It has an armature winding to create a magnetic field, and a needle (pintle), a disc, or a ball valve. A spring holds the needle, disc, or ball closed against the valve seat, and when energized, the armature winding pulls open the valve when it receives a current pulse from the Powertrain Control Module (PCM). When the solenoid is energized, it unseats the valve to inject fuel.

Electronic fuel-injection systems use a solenoid-operated injector to spray atomized fuel in timed pulses into the manifold or near the intake valve. ● SEE FIGURE 27–7. Injectors may be sequenced and fired in one of several ways, but their pulse width is determined and controlled by the engine computer.

Port systems have an injector for each cylinder, but they do not all fire the injectors in the same way. Domestic systems use one of three ways to trigger the injectors:

- Grouped double-fire

- Simultaneous double-fire

- Sequential

GROUPED DOUBLE-FIRE This system divides the injectors into two equalized groups. The groups fire alternately; each group fires once each crankshaft revolution, or twice per four-stroke cycle. The fuel injected remains near the intake valve and enters the engine when the valve opens. This method of pulsing injectors in groups is sometimes called **gang fired.**

FIGURE 27–8 A port fuel-injected engine that is equipped with long, tuned intake manifold runners.

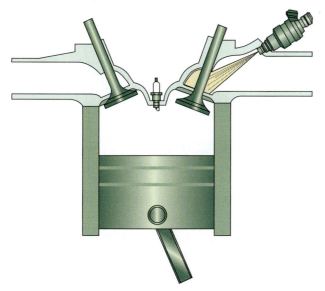

FIGURE 27–7 Port fuel injectors spray atomized fuel into the intake manifold about 3 inches (75 mm) from the intake valve.

? **FREQUENTLY ASKED QUESTION**

How Can It Be Determined If the Injection System Is Sequential?

Look at the color of the wires at the injectors. If a sequentially fired injector is used, then one wire color (the pulse wire) will be a different color for each injector. The other wire is usually the same color because all injectors receive voltage from some source. If a group- or batch-fired injection system is being used, then the wire colors will be the same for the injectors that are group fired. For example, a V-6 group-fired engine will have three injectors with a pink and blue wire (power and pulse) and the other three will have pink and green wires.

SIMULTANEOUS DOUBLE-FIRE   This design fires all of the injectors at the same time once every engine revolution: two pulses per four-stroke cycle. Many port fuel-injection systems on four-cylinder engines use this pattern of injector firing. It is easier for engineers to program this system and it can make relatively quick adjustments in the air–fuel ratio, but it still requires the intake charge to wait in the manifold for varying lengths of time.

SEQUENTIAL   Sequential firing of the injectors according to engine firing order is the most accurate and desirable method of regulating port fuel injection. However, it is also the most complex and expensive to design and manufacture. In this system, the injectors are timed and pulsed individually, much like the spark plugs are sequentially operated in firing order of the engine. This system is often called **sequential fuel injection** or **SFI.** Each cylinder receives one charge every two crankshaft revolutions, just before the intake valve opens. This means that the mixture is never static in the intake manifold and mixture adjustments can be made almost instantaneously between the firing of one injector and the next. A camshaft position sensor (CMP) signal or a special distributor reference pulse informs the PCM when the No. 1 cylinder is on its compression stroke. If the sensor fails or the reference pulse is interrupted, some injection systems shut down, while others revert to pulsing the injectors simultaneously.

The major advantage of using port injection instead of the simpler throttle-body injection is that the intake manifolds on port fuel-injected engines only contain air, not a mixture of air and fuel. This allows the engine design engineer the opportunity to design long, "tuned" intake-manifold runners that help the engine produce increased torque at low engine speeds. ● **SEE FIGURE 27–8.**

NOTE: Some port fuel-injection systems used on engines with four or more valves per cylinder may use two injectors per cylinder. One injector is used all the time, and the second injector is operated by the computer when high engine speed and high-load conditions are detected by the computer. Typically, the second injector injects fuel into the high-speed intake ports of the manifold. This system permits good low-speed power and throttle responses as well as superior high-speed power.

FUEL-PRESSURE REGULATOR

The pressure regulator and fuel pump work together to maintain the required pressure drop at the injector tips. The fuel-pressure regulator typically consists of a spring-loaded, diaphragm-operated valve in a metal housing.

Fuel-pressure regulators on fuel-return-type fuel-injection systems are installed on the return (downstream) side of the injectors at the end of the fuel rail, or are built into or mounted upon the throttle-body housing. Downstream regulation minimizes fuel-pressure pulsations caused by pressure drop across the injectors as the nozzles open. It also ensures positive fuel pressure at the injectors at all times and holds residual pressure in the lines when the engine is off. On mechanical returnless systems, the regulator is located back at the tank with the fuel filter.

In order for excess fuel (about 80% to 90% of the fuel delivered) to return to the tank, fuel pressure must overcome spring pressure on the spring-loaded diaphragm to uncover the return line to the tank. This happens when system pressure exceeds operating requirements. With TBI, the regulator is close to the injector tip, so the regulator senses essentially the same air pressure as the injector.

The pressure regulator used in a port fuel-injection system has an intake manifold vacuum line connection on the regulator vacuum chamber. This allows fuel pressure to be modulated by a combination of spring pressure and manifold vacuum acting on the diaphragm. ● SEE FIGURES 27–9 AND 27–10.

In both TBI and port fuel-injection systems, the regulator shuts off the return line when the fuel pump is not running. This maintains pressure at the injectors for easy restarting after hot soak as well as reducing vapor lock.

NOTE: Some General Motors throttle-body units do not hold pressure and are called nonchecking.

Port fuel-injection systems generally operate with pressures at the injector of about 30 to 55 PSI (207 to 379 kPa), while

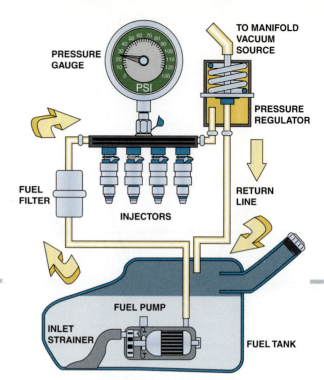

FIGURE 27–9 A typical port fuel-injected system showing a vacuum-controlled fuel-pressure regulator.

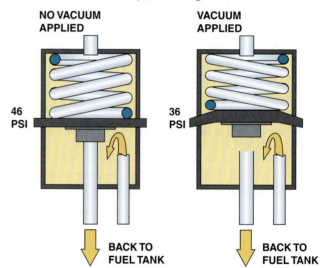

FIGURE 27–10 A typical fuel-pressure regulator that has a spring that exerts 46 pounds of force against the fuel. If 20 inches of vacuum are applied above the spring, the vacuum reduces the force exerted by the spring on the fuel, allowing the fuel to return to the tank at a lower pressure.

TBI systems work with injector pressures of about 10 to 20 PSI (69 to 138 kPa). The difference in system pressures results from the difference in how the systems operate. Since injectors in a TBI system inject the fuel into the airflow at the manifold inlet (above the throttle), there is more time for atomization in the manifold before the air–fuel charge reaches the intake valve. This allows TBI injectors to work at lower pressures than injectors used in a port system.

FIGURE 27–11 A lack of fuel flow could be due to a restricted fuel-pressure regulator. Notice the fine screen filter. If this filter were to become clogged, higher than normal fuel pressure would occur.

 TECH TIP

Don't Forget the Regulator

Some fuel-pressure regulators contain a 10-micron filter. If this filter becomes clogged, a lack of fuel flow would result. ● SEE FIGURE 27–11.

VACUUM-BIASED FUEL-PRESSURE REGULATOR

The primary reason why many port fuel-injected systems use a vacuum-controlled fuel-pressure regulator is to ensure that there is a constant pressure drop across the injectors. In a throttle-body fuel-injection system, the injector squirts into the atmospheric pressure regardless of the load on the engine. In a port fuel-injected engine, however, the pressure inside the intake manifold changes as the load on the engine increases.

Engine Operating Condition	Intake Manifold Vacuum	Fuel Pressure
Idle or cruise	High	Lower
Heavy load	Low	Higher

The computer can best calculate injector pulse width based on all sensors if the pressure drop across the injector is the same under all operating conditions. A vacuum-controlled fuel-pressure regulator allows the equal pressure drop by reducing the force exerted by the regulator spring at high vacuum (low-load condition), yet allowing the full force of the regulator spring to be exerted when the vacuum is low (high-engine-load condition).

ELECTRONIC RETURNLESS FUEL SYSTEM

This system is unique because it does not use a mechanical valve to regulate rail pressure. Fuel pressure at the rail is sensed by a pressure transducer, which sends a low-level signal to a controller. The controller contains logic to calculate a signal to the pump power driver. The power driver contains a high-current transistor that controls the pump speed using pulse width modulation (PWM). This system is called the **electronic returnless fuel system (ERFS)**. ● SEE FIGURE 27–12. This transducer can be differentially referenced to manifold pressure for closed-loop feedback, correcting and maintaining the output of the pump to a desired rail setting. This system is capable of continuously varying rail pressure as a result of engine vacuum, engine fuel demand, and fuel temperature (as sensed by an external temperature transducer, if necessary). A **pressure vent valve (PVV)** is employed at the tank to relieve overpressure due to thermal expansion of fuel. In addition, a supply-side bleed, by means of an in-tank reservoir using a supply-side jet pump, is necessary for proper pump operation.

MECHANICAL RETURNLESS FUEL SYSTEM

The first production returnless systems employed the **mechanical returnless fuel system (MRFS)** approach. This system has a bypass regulator to control rail pressure that is located in close proximity to the fuel tank. Fuel is sent by the in-tank pump to a chassis-mounted inline filter with excess fuel returning to the tank through a short return line. ● SEE FIGURE 27–13. The inline filter may be mounted directly to the tank, thereby eliminating the shortened return line. Supply pressure is regulated on the downstream side of the inline filter to accommodate changing restrictions throughout the filter's service life. This system is limited to constant rail pressure (*CRP) system calibrations, whereas with ERFS, the pressure transducer can be referenced to atmospheric pressure for CRP systems or differentially referenced to intake manifold pressure for constant differential injector pressure (**CIP) systems.

NOTE: *CRP is referenced to atmospheric pressure, has lower operating pressure, and is desirable for calibrations using speed/air density sensing. **CIP is referenced to manifold pressure, varies rail pressure, and is desirable in engines that use mass airflow sensing.

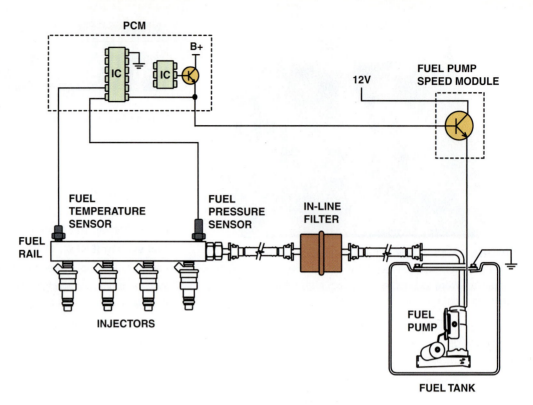

FIGURE 27-12 The fuel-pressure sensor and fuel-temperature sensor are often constructed together in one assembly to help give the PCM the needed data to control the fuel-pump speed.

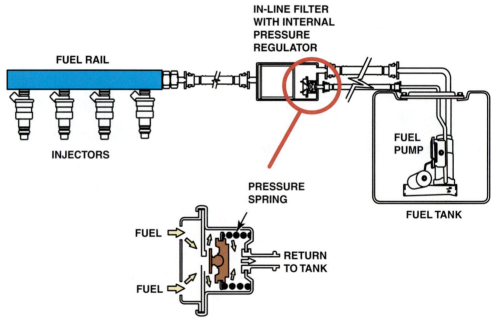

FIGURE 27-13 A mechanical returnless fuel system. The bypass regulator in the fuel tank controls fuel line pressure.

DEMAND DELIVERY SYSTEM (DDS)

Given the experience with both ERFS and MRFS, a need was recognized to develop new returnless technologies that could combine the speed control and constant injector pressure attributes of ERFS together with the cost savings, simplicity, and reliability of MRFS. This new technology also needed to address pulsation dampening/hammering and fuel transient response. Therefore, the **demand delivery system (DDS)** technology was developed.

A different form of demand pressure regulator has been applied to the fuel rail. It mounts at the head or port entry and regulates the pressure downstream at the injectors by admitting the precise quantity of fuel into the rail as consumed by the engine. Having demand regulation at the rail improves pressure response to flow transients and provides rail pulsation dampening. A fuel pump and a low-cost, high-performance bypass regulator are used

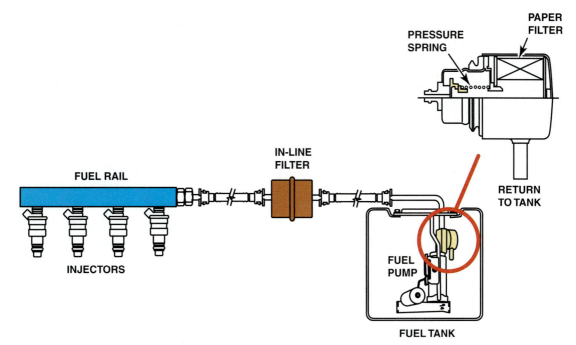

FIGURE 27–14 A demand delivery system uses an intake regulator.

FIGURE 27–15 A rectangular-shaped fuel rail is used to help dampen fuel system pulsations and noise caused by the injectors opening and closing.

? FREQUENTLY ASKED QUESTION

Why Are Some Fuel Rails Rectangular Shaped?

A port fuel-injection system uses a pipe or tubes to deliver fuel from the fuel line to the intended fuel injectors. This pipe or tube is called the **fuel rail.** Some vehicle manufacturers construct the fuel rail in a rectangular cross-section. ● **SEE FIGURE 27–15.** The sides of the fuel rail are able to move in and out slightly, thereby acting as a fuel pulsator evening out the pressure pulses created by the opening and closing of the injectors to reduce underhood noise. A round cross-section fuel rail is not able to deform and, as a result, some manufacturers have had to use a separate dampener.

within the appropriate fuel sender. ● **SEE FIGURE 27–14.** They supply a pressure somewhat higher than the required rail set pressure to accommodate dynamic line and filter pressure losses. Electronic pump speed control is accomplished using a smart regulator as an integral flow sensor. A **pressure control valve (PCV)** may also be used and can readily reconfigure an existing design fuel sender into a returnless sender.

FUEL INJECTORS

EFI systems use solenoid-operated injectors. ● **SEE FIGURE 27–16.** This electromagnetic device contains an armature and a spring-loaded needle valve or ball valve assembly. When the computer energizes the solenoid, voltage is applied to the solenoid coil until the current reaches a specified level. This permits a quick pull-in of the armature during turn-on. The armature is pulled off of its seat against spring force, allowing

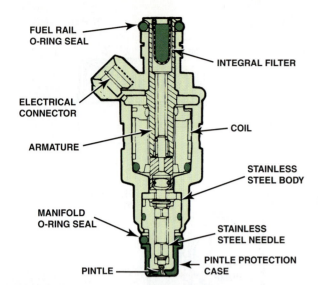

FIGURE 27–16 A multiport fuel injector. Notice that the fuel flows straight through and does not come in contact with the coil windings.

FIGURE 27–17 Each of the eight injectors shown are producing a correct spray pattern for the applications. While all throttle-body injectors spray a conical pattern, most port fuel injections do not.

FUEL INJECTORS (CONTINUED)

fuel to flow through the inlet filter screen to the spray nozzle, where it is sprayed in a pattern that varies with application. ● **SEE FIGURE 27–17.** The injector opens the same amount each time it is energized, so the amount of fuel injected depends on the length of time the injector remains open. By angling the director hole plates, the injector sprays fuel more directly at the intake valves, which further atomizes and vaporizes the fuel before it enters the combustion chamber. PFI injectors typically are a top-feed design in which fuel enters the

top of the injector and passes through its entire length to keep it cool before being injected.

Ford introduced two basic designs of deposit-resistant injectors on some engines. The design, manufactured by Bosch, uses a four-hole director/metering plate similar to that used by the Rochester Multec injectors. The design manufactured by Nippondenso uses an internal upstream orifice in the adjusting tube. It also has a redesigned pintle/seat containing a wider tip opening that tolerates deposit buildup without affecting injector performance.

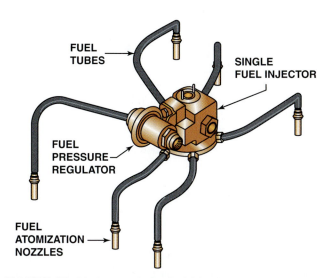

FIGURE 27–18 A central port fuel-injection system.

FIGURE 27–19 A factory replacement unit for a CSFI unit that has individual injectors at the ends that go into the intake manifold instead of poppet valves.

CENTRAL PORT INJECTION

A cross between port fuel injection and throttle-body injection, CPI was introduced in the early 1990s by General Motors. The CPI assembly consists of a single fuel injector, a pressure regulator, and six poppet nozzle assemblies with nozzle tubes. ● **SEE FIGURE 27–18.** The central sequential fuel injection (CSFI) system has six injectors in place of just one used on the CPI unit.

When the injector is energized, its armature lifts off of the six fuel tube seats and pressurized fuel flows through the nozzle tubes to each poppet nozzle. The increased pressure causes each poppet nozzle ball to also lift from its seat, allowing fuel to flow from the nozzle. This hybrid injection system combines the single injector of a TBI system with the equalized fuel distribution of a PFI system. It eliminates the individual fuel rail while allowing more efficient manifold tuning than is otherwise possible with a TBI system. Newer versions use six individual solenoids to fire one for each cylinder. ● **SEE FIGURE 27–19.**

FUEL-INJECTION MODES OF OPERATION

All fuel-injection systems are designed to supply the correct amount of fuel under a wide range of engine operating conditions. These modes of operation include:

Starting (cranking)	Acceleration enrichment
Clear flood	Deceleration enleanment
Idle (run)	Fuel shutoff

STARTING MODE When the ignition is turned to the start (on) position, the engine cranks and the PCM energizes the fuel pump relay. The PCM also pulses the injectors on, basing the pulse width on engine speed and engine coolant temperature. The colder the engine is, the greater the pulse width. Cranking mode air–fuel ratio varies from about 1.5:1 at −40°F (−40°C) to 14.7:1 at 200°F (93°C).

CLEAR FLOOD MODE If the engine becomes flooded with too much fuel, the driver can depress the accelerator pedal to greater than 80% to enter the clear flood mode. When the PCM detects that the engine speed is low (usually below 600 RPM) and the throttle-position (TP) sensor voltage is high (WOT), the injector pulse width is greatly reduced or even shut off entirely, depending on the vehicle.

OPEN-LOOP MODE   Open-loop operation occurs during warm-up before the oxygen sensor can supply accurate information to the PCM. The PCM determines injector pulse width based on values from the MAF, MAP, TP, ECT, and IAT sensors.

CLOSED-LOOP MODE   Closed-loop operation is used to modify the base injector pulse width as determined by feedback from the oxygen sensor to achieve proper fuel control.

ACCELERATION ENRICHMENT MODE   During acceleration, the throttle-position (TP) voltage increases, indicating that a richer air–fuel mixture is required. The PCM then supplies a longer injector pulse width and may even supply extra pulses to supply the needed fuel for acceleration.

DECELERATION ENLEANMENT MODE   When the engine decelerates, a leaner air–fuel mixture is required to help reduce emissions and to prevent deceleration backfire. If the deceleration is rapid, the injector may be shut off entirely for a short time and then pulsed on enough to keep the engine running.

FUEL SHUTOFF MODE   Besides shutting off fuel entirely during periods of rapid deceleration, PCM also shuts off the injector when the ignition is turned off to prevent the engine from continuing to run.

 FREQUENTLY ASKED QUESTION

What Is Battery Voltage Correction?

Battery voltage correction is a program built into the PCM that causes the injector pulse width to increase if there is a drop in electrical system voltage. Lower battery voltage would cause the fuel injectors to open slower than normal and the fuel pump to run slower. Both of these conditions can cause the engine to run leaner than normal if the battery voltage is low. Because a lean air–fuel mixture can cause the engine to overheat, the PCM compensates for the lower voltage by adding a percentage to the injector pulse width. This richer condition will help prevent serious engine damage. The idle speed is also increased to turn the generator (alternator) faster if low battery voltage is detected.

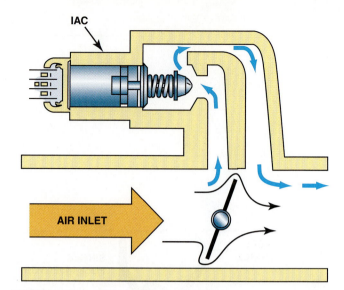

FIGURE 27–20 The small arrows indicate the air bypassing the throttle plate in the closed throttle position. This air is called minimum air. The air flowing through the IAC is the airflow that determines the idle speed.

IDLE CONTROL

Port fuel-injection systems generally use an auxiliary air bypass. ● **SEE FIGURE 27–20.** This air bypass or regulator provides needed additional airflow, and thus more fuel. The engine needs more power when cold to maintain its normal idle speed to overcome the increased friction from cold lubricating oil. It does this by opening an intake air passage to let more air into the engine just as depressing the accelerator pedal would open the throttle valve, allowing more air into the engine. The system is calibrated to maintain engine idle speed at a specified value regardless of engine temperature.

Most PFI systems use an idle air control (IAC) motor to regulate idle bypass air. The IAC is computer-controlled, and is either a solenoid-operated valve or a stepper motor that regulates the airflow around the throttle. The idle air control valve is also called an **electronic air control (EAC)** valve.

When the engine stops, most IAC units will retract outward to get ready for the next engine start. When the engine starts, the engine speed is high to provide for proper operation when the engine is cold. Then, as the engine gets warmer, the computer reduces engine idle speed gradually by reducing the number of counts or steps commanded by the IAC.

When the engine is warm and restarted, the idle speed should momentarily increase, then decrease to normal idle speed. This increase and then decrease in engine speed is often called an engine **flare.** If the engine speed does not flare, then the IAC may not be working (it may be stuck in one position).

STEPPER MOTOR OPERATION

A digital output is used to control stepper motors. Stepper motors are direct-current motors that move in fixed steps or increments from de-energized (no voltage) to fully energized (full voltage). A stepper motor often has as many as 120 steps of motion.

A common use for stepper motors is as an idle air control (IAC) valve, which controls engine idle speeds and prevents stalls due to changes in engine load. When used as an IAC, the stepper motor is usually a reversible DC motor that moves in increments, or steps. The motor moves a shaft back and forth to operate a conical valve. When the conical valve is moved back, more air bypasses the throttle plates and enters the engine, increasing idle speed. As the conical valve moves inward, the idle speed decreases.

When using a stepper motor that is controlled by the PCM, it is very easy for the PCM to keep track of the position of the stepper motor. By counting the number of steps that have been sent to the stepper motor, the PCM can determine the relative position of the stepper motor. While the PCM does not actually receive a feedback signal from the stepper motor, it does know how many steps forward or backward the motor should have moved.

A typical stepper motor uses a permanent magnet and two electromagnets. Each of the two electromagnetic windings is controlled by the computer. The computer pulses the windings and changes the polarity of the windings to cause the armature of the stepper motor to rotate 90 degrees at a time. Each 90-degree pulse is recorded by the computer as a "count" or "step"; therefore, the name given to this type of motor. ● **SEE FIGURE 27–21.**

Idle airflow in a TBI system travels through a passage around the throttle and is controlled by a stepper motor. In some applications, an externally mounted permanent magnet motor called the **idle speed control (ISC) motor** mechanically advances the throttle linkage to advance the throttle opening.

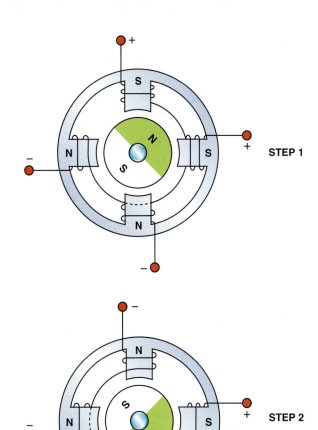

FIGURE 27–21 Most stepper motors use four wires, which are pulsed by the computer to rotate the armature in steps.

? FREQUENTLY ASKED QUESTION

Why Does the Idle Air Control Valve Use Milliamperes?

Some Chrysler vehicles, such as the Dodge minivan, use linear solenoid idle air control valves (LSIAC). The PCM uses regulated current flow through the solenoid to control idle speed and the scan tool display is in milliamperes (mA).

Closed position = 180 to 200 mA

Idle = 300 to 450 mA

Light cruise = 500 to 700 mA

Fully open = 900 to 950 mA

SUMMARY

1. A fuel-injection system includes the electric fuel pump and fuel pump relay, fuel-pressure regulator, and fuel injectors (nozzles).

2. The two types of fuel-injection systems are the throttle-body design and the port fuel-injection design.

3. The two methods of fuel-injection control are the speed-density system, which uses the MAP to measure the load on the engine, and the mass airflow, which uses the MAF sensor to directly measure the amount of air entering the engine.

4. The amount of fuel supplied by fuel injectors is determined by how long they are kept open. This opening time is called the pulse width and is measured in milliseconds.

5. The fuel-pressure regulator is usually located on the fuel return on return-type fuel-injection systems.

6. TBI-type fuel-injection systems do not use a vacuum-controlled fuel-pressure regulator, whereas many port fuel-injection systems use a vacuum-controlled regulator to monitor equal pressure drop across the injectors.

7. Other fuel designs include the electronic returnless, the mechanical returnless, and the demand delivery systems.

REVIEW QUESTIONS

1. What are the two basic types of fuel-injection systems?

2. What is the purpose of the vacuum-controlled (biased) fuel-pressure regulator?

3. How many sensors are used to determine the base pulse width on a speed-density system?

4. How many sensors are used to determine the base pulse width on a mass airflow system?

5. What are the three types of returnless fuel injection systems?

CHAPTER QUIZ

1. Technician A says that the fuel pump relay is usually controlled by the PCM. Technician B says that a TBI injector squirts fuel above the throttle plate. Which technician is correct?
   a. Technician A only
   b. Technician B only
   c. Both Technicians A and B
   d. Neither Technician A nor B

2. Why are some fuel rails rectangular in shape?
   a. Increases fuel pressure
   b. Helps keep air out of the injectors
   c. Reduces noise
   d. Increases the speed of the fuel through the fuel rail

3. Which fuel-injection system uses the MAP sensor as the primary sensor to determine the base pulse width?
   a. Speed density
   b. Mass airflow
   c. Demand delivery
   d. Mechanical returnless

4. Why is a vacuum line attached to a fuel-pressure regulator on many port-fuel-injected engines?
   a. To draw fuel back into the intake manifold through the vacuum hose
   b. To create an equal pressure drop across the injectors
   c. To raise the fuel pressure at idle
   d. To lower the fuel pressure under heavy engine load conditions to help improve fuel economy

5. Which sensor has the greatest influence on injector pulse width besides the MAF sensor?
   a. IAT
   b. BARO
   c. ECT
   d. TP

6. Technician A says that the port fuel-injection injectors operate using 5 volts from the computer. Technician B says that sequential fuel injectors all use a different wire color on the injectors. Which technician is correct?
   a. Technician A only
   b. Technician B only
   c. Both Technicians A and B
   d. Neither Technician A nor B

7. Which type of port fuel-injection system uses a fuel temperature and/or fuel-pressure sensor?
   a. All port-fuel-injected engines
   b. TBI units only
   c. Electronic returnless systems
   d. Demand delivery systems

8. Dampeners are used on some fuel rails to _____.
   a. Increase the fuel pressure in the rail
   b. Reduce (decrease) the fuel pressure in the rail
   c. Reduce noise
   d. Trap dirt and keep it away from the injectors

9. Where is the fuel-pressure regulator located on a vacuum-biased port fuel-injection system?
   a. In the tank
   b. At the inlet of the fuel rail
   c. At the outlet of the fuel rail
   d. Near or on the fuel filter

10. What type of device is used in a typical idle air control?
    a. DC motor
    b. Stepper motor
    c. Pulsator-type actuator
    d. Solenoid

GASOLINE DIRECT-INJECTION SYSTEMS

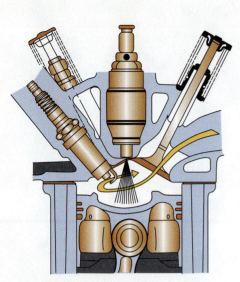

FIGURE 28–1 A gasoline direct-injection system injects fuel under high pressure directly into the combustion chamber.

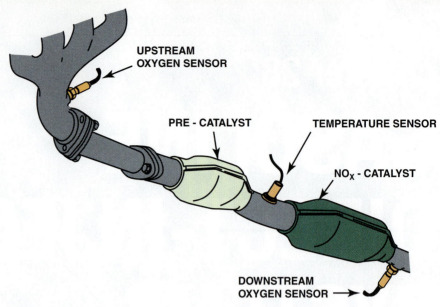

FIGURE 28–2 An engine equipped with a gasoline direct injection (GDI) sometimes requires a NO_X catalyst to meet exhaust emission standards.

DIRECT FUEL INJECTION

Several vehicle manufacturers such as Audi, Mitsubishi, Mercedes, BMW, Toyota/Lexus, Mazda, Ford, and General Motors are using **gasoline direct injection (GDI)** systems, which General Motors refers to as a **Spark Ignition Direct Injection (SIDI)** system. A direct-injection system sprays high-pressure fuel, up to 2,900 PSI, into the combustion chamber as the piston approaches the top of the compression stroke. With the combination of high-pressure swirl injectors and modified combustion chamber, almost instantaneous vaporization occurs. This combined with a higher compression ratio allows a direct-injected engine to operate using a leaner-than-normal air–fuel ratio, which results in improved fuel economy with higher power output and reduced exhaust emissions. ● **SEE FIGURE 28–1.**

ADVANTAGES OF GASOLINE DIRECT INJECTION

The use of direct injection compared with port fuel-injection has many advantages including:

- Improved fuel economy due to reduced pumping losses and heat loss
- Allows a higher compression ratio for higher engine efficiency

- Allows the use of lower-octane gasoline
- The volumetric efficiency is higher
- Less need for extra fuel for acceleration
- Improved cold starting and throttle response
- Allows the use of greater percentage of EGR to reduce exhaust emissions
- Up to 25% improvement in fuel economy
- 12% to 15% reduction in exhaust emissions

DISADVANTAGES OF GASOLINE DIRECT INJECTION

- Higher cost due to high-pressure pump and injectors
- More components compared with port fuel-injection
- Due to the high compression, a NO_X storage catalyst is sometimes required to meet emission standards, especially in Europe. (● **SEE FIGURE 28–2**)
- Uses up to six operating modes depending on engine load and speed, which requires more calculations to be performed by the Powertrain Control Module (PCM).

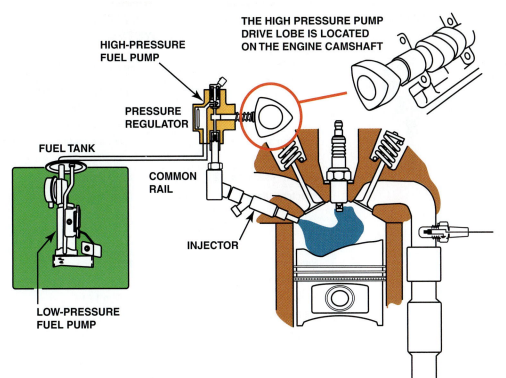

HIGH-PRESSURE FUEL PUMP

THE HIGH PRESSURE PUMP DRIVE LOBE IS LOCATED ON THE ENGINE CAMSHAFT

PRESSURE REGULATOR

FUEL TANK

COMMON RAIL

INJECTOR

LOW-PRESSURE FUEL PUMP

FIGURE 28–3 A typical direct-injection system uses two pumps—one low-pressure electric pump in the fuel tank and the other a high-pressure pump driven by the camshaft. The high pressure fuel system operates at a pressure as low as 500 PSI during light load conditions and as high as 2,900 PSI under heavy loads.

DIRECT-INJECTION FUEL DELIVERY SYSTEM

LOW-PRESSURE SUPPLY PUMP The fuel pump in the fuel tank supplies fuel to the high-pressure fuel pump at a pressure of approximately 60 PSI. The fuel filter is located in the fuel tank and is part of the fuel pump assembly. It is not usually serviceable as a separate component, the engine control module (ECM) controls the output of the high-pressure pump, which has a range between 500 PSI (3,440 kPa) and 2,900 PSI (15,200 kPa) during engine operation. ● **SEE FIGURE 28–3**.

HIGH-PRESSURE PUMP In a General Motors system, the engine control module (ECM) controls the output of the high-pressure pump, which has a range between 500 PSI (3,440 kPa) and 2,900 PSI (15,200 kPa) during engine operation. The high-pressure fuel pump connects to the pump in the fuel tank through the low-pressure fuel line. The pump consists of a single-barrel piston pump, which is driven by the engine camshaft. The pump plunger rides on a three-lobed cam on the camshaft. The high-pressure pump is cooled and lubricated by the fuel itself. ● **SEE FIGURE 28–4**.

FUEL RAIL The fuel rail stores the fuel from the high-pressure pump and stores high pressure fuel for use to each injector. All injectors get the same pressure fuel from the fuel rail.

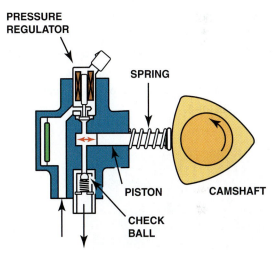

PRESSURE REGULATOR

SPRING

PISTON

CAMSHAFT

CHECK BALL

FIGURE 28–4 A typical camshaft-driven high-pressure pump used to increase fuel pressure to 2,000 PSI or higher.

FUEL PRESSURE REGULATOR An electric pressure-control valve is installed between the pump inlet and outlet valves. The fuel rail pressure sensor connects to the PCM with three wires:

- 5-volt reference
- ground
- signal

The sensor signal provides an analog signal to the PCM that varies in voltage as fuel rail pressure changes. Low pressure results in a low-voltage signal and high pressure results in a high-voltage signal.

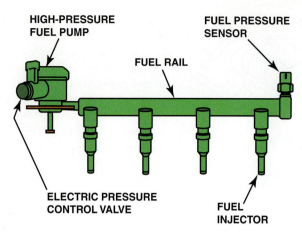

FIGURE 28–5 A gasoline direct-injection (GDI) fuel rail and pump assembly with the electric pressure control valve.

DIRECT-INJECTION FUEL DELIVERY SYSTEM (CONTINUED)

The PCM uses internal drivers to control the power feed and ground for the pressure control valve. When both PCM drivers are deactivated, the inlet valve is held open by spring pressure. This causes the high pressure fuel pump to default to low-pressure mode. The fuel from the high-pressure fuel pump flows through a line to the fuel rail and injectors. The actual operating pressure can vary from as low as 900 PSI (6,200 kPa) at idle to over 2,000 PSI (13,800 kPa) during high speed or heavy load conditions.
● **SEE FIGURE 28–5.**

GASOLINE DIRECT-INJECTION FUEL INJECTORS

Each high-pressure fuel injector assembly is an electrically magnetic injector mounted in the cylinder head. In the GDI system, the PCM controls each fuel injector with 50 to 90 volts (usually 60–70 volts), depending on the system, which is created by a boost capacitor in the PCM. During the high-voltage boost phase, the capacitor is discharged through an injector, allowing for initial injector opening. The injector is then held open with 12 volts. The high-pressure fuel injector has a small slit or six precision-machined holes that generate the desired spray pattern. The injector also has an extended tip to allow for cooling from a water jacket in the cylinder head.
● **SEE CHART 28–1** for an overview of the differences between a port fuel-injection system and a gasoline direct-injection system.

PORT FUEL-INJECTION SYSTEM COMPARED WITH GDI SYSTEM

	PORT FUEL-INJECTION	GASOLINE DIRECT INJECTION
Fuel pressure	35 to 60 PSI	Lift pump—50 to 60 PSI High-pressure pump—500 to 2,900 PSI
Injection pulse width at idle	1.5 to 3.5 ms	About 0.4 ms (400 μs)
Injector resistance	12 to 16 ohms	1 to 3 ohms
Injector voltage	6 V for low-resistance injectors, 12 V for most injectors	50 to 90 V
Number of injections per event	One	1 to 3
Engine compression ratio	8:1 to 11:1	11:1 to 13:1

CHART 28–1

A comparison chart showing the major differences between a port fuel-injection system and a gasoline direct-injection system.

MODES OF OPERATION

The two basic modes of operation include:

1. **Stratified mode.** In this mode of operation, the air–fuel mixture is richer around the spark plug than it is in the rest of the cylinder.

2. **Homogeneous mode.** In this mode of operation, the air–fuel mixture is the same throughout the cylinder.

There are variations of these modes that can be used to fine-tune the air–fuel mixture inside the cylinder. For example, Bosch, a supplier to many vehicle manufacturers, uses six modes of operation including:

■ **Homogeneous mode.** In this mode, the injector is pulsed one time to create an even air–fuel mixture in the cylinder. The injection occurs during the intake stroke. This mode is used during high-speed and/or high-torque conditions.

■ **Homogeneous lean mode.** Similar to the homogeneous mode except that the overall air–fuel mixture is slightly lean for better fuel economy. The injection occurs during the intake stroke. This mode is used under steady, light-load conditions.

■ **Stratified mode.** In this mode of operation, the injection occurs just before the spark occurs resulting in lean combustion, reducing fuel consumption.

■ **Homogeneous stratified mode.** In this mode, there are two injections of fuel:

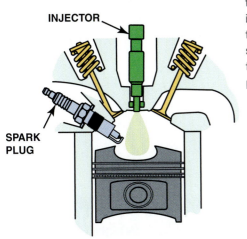

SPRAY - GUIDED COMBUSTION

INJECTOR

SPARK PLUG

FIGURE 28–6
In this design, the fuel injector is at the top of the cylinder and sprays fuel into the cavity of the piston.

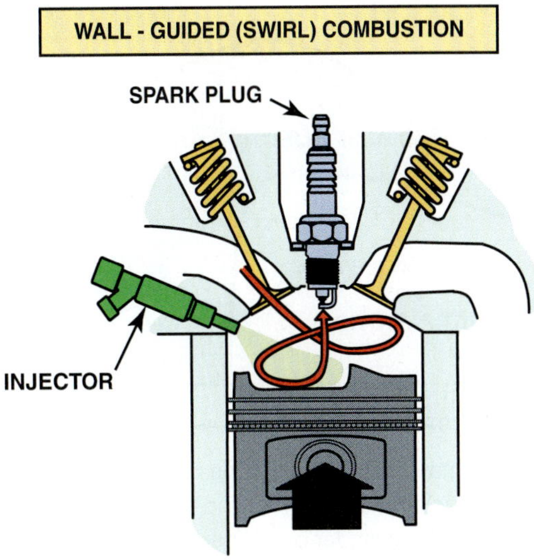

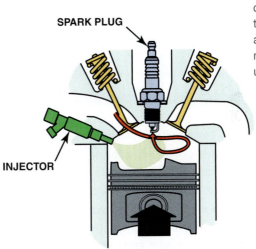

WALL - GUIDED (SWIRL) COMBUSTION

SPARK PLUG

INJECTOR

FIGURE 28–7
The side injector combines with the shape of the piston to create a swirl as the piston moves up on the compression stroke.

WALL - GUIDED (TUMBLE) COMBUSTION

SPARK PLUG

INJECTOR

FIGURE 28–8
The piston creates a tumbling force as the piston moves upward.

- The first injection is during the intake stroke.

- The second injection is during the compression stroke. As a result of these double injections, the rich air–fuel mixture around the spark plug is ignited first. Then, the rich mixture ignites the leaner mixture. The advantages of this mode include lower exhaust emissions than the stratified mode and less fuel consumption than the homogeneous lean mode.

- **Homogeneous knock protection mode.** The purpose of this mode is to reduce the possibility of spark knock from occurring under heavy loads at low engine speeds. There are two injections of fuel:

  - The first injection occurs on the intake stroke.

  - The second injection occurs during the compression stroke with the overall mixture being stoichiometric.
  As a result of this mode, the PCM does not need to retard ignition timing as much to operate knock-free.

- **Stratified catalyst heating mode.** In this mode, there are two injections:

  - The first injection is on the compression stroke just before combustion.

  - The second injection occurs after combustion occurs to heat the exhaust. This mode is used to quickly warm the catalytic converter and to burn the sulfur from the NO_x catalyst.

PISTON TOP DESIGNS

Gasoline direct injection (GDI) systems use a variety of shapes of piston and injector locations depending on make and model of engine. Three of the most commonly used designs include:

- **Spray-guided combustion.** In this design, the injector is placed in the center of the combustion chamber and injects fuel into the dished out portion of the piston. The shape of the piston helps guide and direct the mist of fuel in the combustion chamber. ● **SEE FIGURE 28–6.**

- **Swirl combustion.** This design uses the shape of the piston and the position of the injector at the side of the combustion chamber to create turbulence and swirl of the air–fuel mixture. ● **SEE FIGURE 28–7.**

- **Tumble combustion.** Depending on when the fuel is injected into the combustion chamber, helps determine how the air–fuel is moved or tumbled. ● **SEE FIGURE 28–8.**

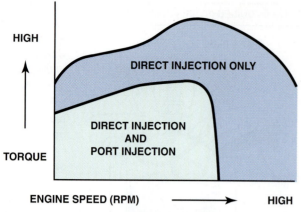

FIGURE 28–9 Notice that there are conditions when the port fuel-injector located in the intake manifold, and the gasoline direct injector, located in the cylinder both operate to provide the proper air–fuel mixture.

LEXUS PORT- AND DIRECT-INJECTION SYSTEMS

OVERVIEW Many Lexus vehicles use gasoline direct injection (GDI) and in some engines, they also use a conventional port fuel-injection system. The Lexus D-4S system combines direct-injection injectors located in the combustion chamber with port fuel-injectors in the intake manifold near the intake valve. The two injection systems work together to supply the fuel needed by the engine. ● **SEE FIGURE 28–9** for how the two systems are used throughout the various stages of engine operation.

COLD-START WARM-UP To help reduce exhaust emissions after a cold start, the fuel system uses a stratified change mode. This results in a richer air–fuel mixture near the spark plug and allows for the spark to be retarded to increase the temperature of the exhaust. As a result of the increased exhaust temperature, the catalytic converter rapidly reaches operating temperature, which reduces exhaust emissions.

ENGINE START SYSTEM

An engine equipped with gasoline direct injection could use the system to start the engine. This is most useful during idle stop mode when the engine is stopped while the vehicle is at a traffic light to save fuel. The steps used in the Mitsubishi start-stop system, called the *smart idle stop system (SISS)*, allow the engine to be started without a starter motor and include the following steps:

STEP 1 The engine is stopped. The normal stopping position of an engine when it stops is 70 degrees before top dead center, plus or minus 20 degrees. This is because the engine stops with one cylinder on the compression stroke and the PCM can determine the cylinder position, using the crankshaft and camshaft position sensors.

STEP 2 When a command is made to start the engine by the PCM, fuel is injected into the cylinder that is on the compression stroke and ignited by the spark plug.

STEP 3 The piston on the compression stroke is forced downward forcing the crankshaft to rotate counterclockwise or in the opposite direction to normal operation.

STEP 4 The rotation of the crankshaft then forces the companion cylinder toward the top of the cylinder.

STEP 5 Fuel is injected and the spark plug is fired, forcing the piston down, causing the crankshaft to rotate in the normal (clockwise) direction. Normal combustion events continue allowing the engine to keep running.

GASOLINE DIRECT-INJECTION SERVICE

NOISE ISSUES Gasoline direct injection (GDI) systems operate at high pressure and the injectors can often be heard with the engine running and the hood open. This noise can be a customer concern because the clicking sound is similar to noisy valves. If a noise issue is the customer concern, check the following:

- Check a similar vehicle to determine if the sound is louder or more noticeable than normal.
- Check that nothing under the hood is touching the fuel rail. If another line or hose is in contact with the fuel rail, the sound of the injectors clicking can be transmitted throughout the engine, making the sound more noticeable.
- Check for any technical service bulletins (TSBs) that may include new clips or sound insulators to help reduce the noise.

CARBON ISSUES Carbon is often an issue in engines equipped with gasoline direct-injection systems. Carbon can affect engine operation by accumulating in two places:

- **On the injector itself.** Because the injector tip is in the combustion chamber, fuel residue can accumulate on the injector, reducing its ability to provide the proper spray pattern and amount of fuel. Some injector designs are more likely to be affected by carbon than others. For example, if the injector uses small holes, these tend to become clogged more than an injector that uses a single slit opening where the fuel being sprayed out tends to blast away any carbon. ● **SEE FIGURE 28–10.**
- **The backside of the intake valve.** This is a common place for fuel residue and carbon to accumulate on engines equipped with gasoline direct injection. The

FIGURE 28–10 There may become a driveability issue because the gasoline direct-injection injector is exposed to combustion carbon and fuel residue.

accumulation of carbon on the intake valve can become so severe that the engine will start and idle, but lack power to accelerate the vehicle. The carbon deposits restrict the airflow into the cylinder enough to decrease engine power.

NOTE: Lexus engines that use both port and gasoline direct-injection injectors do not show intake valve deposits. It is thought that the fuel being sprayed onto the intake valve from the port injector helps keep the intake valve clean.

CARBON CLEANING. Most experts recommend the use of Techron®, a fuel system dispersant, to help keep carbon from accumulating. The use of a dispersant every six months or every 6,000 miles has proven to help prevent injector and intake valve deposits.

If the lack of power is discovered and there are no stored diagnostic trouble codes, a conventional carbon cleaning procedure will likely restore power if the intake valves are coated.

SUMMARY

1. A gasoline direct-injection system uses a fuel injector that delivers a short squirt of fuel directly into the combustion chamber rather than in the intake manifold, near the intake valve on a port fuel-injection system.

2. The advantages of using gasoline direct injection instead of port fuel-injection include:
   - Improved fuel economy
   - Reduced exhaust emissions
   - Greater engine power

3. Some of the disadvantages of gasoline direct-injection systems compared with a port fuel-injection system include:
   - Higher cost
   - The need for NO_x storage catalyst in some applications
   - More components

4. The operating pressure can vary from as low as 500 PSI during some low-demand conditions to as high as 2,900 PSI.

5. The fuel injectors are open for a very short period of time and are pulsed using a 50 to 90 V pulse from a capacitor circuit.

6. GDI systems can operate in many modes, which are separated into the two basic modes:
   - Stratified mode
   - Homogeneous mode

7. GDI can be used to start an engine without the use of a starter motor for idle-stop functions.

8. GDI does create a louder clicking noise from the fuel injectors than port fuel-injection injectors.

9. Carbon deposits on the injector and the backside of the intake valve are a common problem with engines equipped with gasoline direct-injection systems.

REVIEW QUESTIONS

1. What are two advantages of gasoline direct injection compared with port fuel-injection?

2. What are two disadvantages of gasoline direct injection compared with port fuel-injection?

3. How is the fuel delivery system different from a port fuel-injection system?

4. What are the basic modes of operation of a GDI system?

CHAPTER QUIZ

1. Where is the fuel injected in an engine equipped with gasoline direct injection?
   a. Into the intake manifold near the intake valve
   b. Directly into the combustion chamber
   c. Above the intake port
   d. In the exhaust port

2. The fuel pump inside the fuel tank on a vehicle equipped with gasoline direct injection produces about what fuel pressure?
   a. 5 to 10 PSI
   b. 10 to 20 PSI
   c. 20 to 40 PSI
   d. 50 to 60 PSI

3. The high-pressure fuel pumps used in gasoline direct injection (GDI) systems are powered by _____.
   a. Electricity (DC motor)
   b. Electricity (AC motor)
   c. The camshaft
   d. The crankshaft

4. The high-pressure fuel pressure is regulated by using _____.
   a. An electric pressure-control valve
   b. A vacuum-biased regulator
   c. A mechanical regulator at the inlet to the fuel rail
   d. A non-vacuum biased regulator

5. The fuel injectors operate under a fuel pressure of about _____.
   a. 35 to 45 PSI
   b. 90 to 150 PSI
   c. 500 to 2,900 PSI
   d. 2,000 to 5,000 PSI

6. The fuel injectors used on a gasoline direct-injection system are pulsed on using what voltage?
   a. 12 to 14 V
   b. 50 to 90 V
   c. 100 to 110 V
   d. 200 to 220 V

7. Which mode of operation results in a richer air–fuel mixture near the spark plug?
   a. Stoichiometric
   b. Homogeneous
   c. Stratified
   d. Knock protection

8. Some engines that use a gasoline direct-injection system also have port injection.
   a. True
   b. False

9. A gasoline direct-injection system can be used to start an engine without the need for a starter.
   a. True
   b. False

10. A lack of power from an engine equipped with gasoline direct injection could be due to _____.
    a. Noisy injectors
    b. Carbon on the injectors
    c. Carbon on the intake valves
    d. Both b and c

ELECTRONIC THROTTLE CONTROL SYSTEM

After studying Chapter 29, the reader will be able to:

1. Prepare for ASE test content area "E" (Computerized Engine Controls Diagnosis and Repair).

2. Describe the purpose and function of an electronic throttle control (ETC) system.

3. Explain how an electronic throttle control system works.

4. List the parts of a typical electronic throttle control system.

5. Describe how to diagnose faults in an electronic throttle control system.

Accelerator pedal position (APP) sensor 444
Coast-down stall 451
Default position 445
Drive-by-wire 444
Electronic throttle control (ETC) 444
Fail safe position 445
Neutral position 445
Servomotor 445
Throttle position (TP) sensor 444

ELECTRONIC THROTTLE CONTROL (ETC) SYSTEM

ADVANTAGES OF ETC The absence of any mechanical linkage between the throttle pedal and the throttle body requires the use of an electric actuator motor. The electronic throttle system has the following advantages over the conventional cable:

- Eliminates the mechanical throttle cable, thereby reducing the number of moving parts.

- Eliminates the need for cruise control actuators and controllers.

- Helps reduce engine power for traction control (TC and electronic stability control [ESC] systems).

- Used to delay rapid applications of torque to the transmission/transaxle to help improve driveability and to smooth shifts.

- Helps reduce pumping losses by using the electronic throttle to open at highway speeds with greater fuel economy. The electronic throttle control (ETC) opens the throttle to maintain engine and vehicle speed as the Powertrain Control Module (PCM) leans the air–fuel ratio, retards ignition timing, and introduces additional exhaust gas recirculation (EGR) to reducing pumping losses.

- Used to provide smooth engine operation, especially during rapid acceleration.

- Eliminates the need for an idle air control valve.

The electronic throttle can be called **drive-by-wire**, but most vehicle manufacturers use the term **electronic throttle control (ETC)** to describe the system that opens the throttle valve electrically.

PARTS INVOLVED The typical ETC system includes the following components:

1. **Accelerator pedal position (APP)** sensor, also called *accelerator pedal sensor (APS)*

2. The electronic throttle actuator (servomotor), which is part of the electronic throttle body

3. A **throttle position (TP) sensor**

4. An electronic control unit, which is usually the Powertrain Control Module (PCM)
   ● **SEE FIGURE 29–1.**

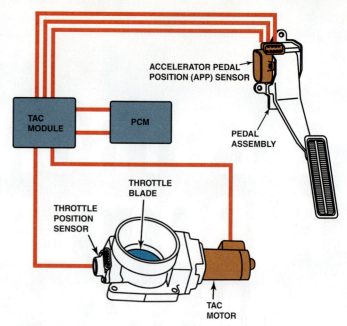

FIGURE 29–1 The throttle pedal is connected to the accelerator pedal position (APP) sensor. The electronic throttle body includes a throttle position sensor to provide throttle angle feedback to the vehicle computer. Some systems use a Throttle Actuator Control (TAC) module to operate the throttle blade (plate).

NORMAL OPERATION OF THE ETC SYSTEM

Driving a vehicle equipped with an electronic throttle control (ETC) system is about the same as driving a vehicle with a conventional mechanical throttle cable and throttle valve. However, the driver may notice some differences, which are to be considered normal. These normal conditions include:

- The engine may not increase above idle speed when depressing the accelerator pedal when the gear selector is in PARK.

- If the engine speed does increase when the accelerator is depressed with the transmission in PARK or NEUTRAL, the engine speed will likely be limited to less than 2000 RPM.

- While accelerating rapidly, there is often a slight delay before the engine responds. ● **SEE FIGURE 29–2.**

- While at cruise speed, the accelerator pedal may or may not cause the engine speed to increase if the accelerator pedal is moved slightly.

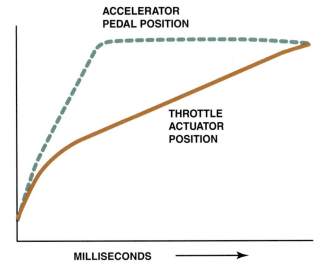

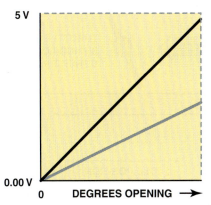

FIGURE 29–2 The opening of the throttle plate can be delayed as long as 30 milliseconds (0.030 sec.) to allow time for the amount of fuel needed to catch up to the opening of the throttle plate.

FIGURE 29–3 A typical accelerator pedal position (APP) sensor, showing two different output voltage signals that are used by the PCM to determine accelerator pedal position. Two (or three in some applications) are used as a double check because this is a safety-related sensor.

ACCELERATOR PEDAL POSITION SENSOR

CABLE-OPERATED SYSTEM Honda Accords until 2008 model year used a cable attached to the accelerator pedal to operate the APP sensor located under the hood. A similar arrangement was used in Dodge RAM trucks in 2003. In both of these applications, the throttle cable was simply moving the APP sensor and not moving the throttle plate. The throttle plate is controlled by the PCM and moved by the electronic throttle control motor.

TWO SENSORS The accelerator pedal position sensor uses two and sometimes three separate sensors, which act together to give accurate accelerator pedal position information to the controller, but also are used to check that the sensor is working properly. They function just like a throttle position sensor, and two are needed for proper system function. One APP sensor output signal increases as the pedal is depressed and the other signal decreases. The controller compares the signals with a look-up table to determine the pedal position. Using two or three signals improves redundancy should one sensor fail, and allows the PCM to quickly detect a malfunction. When three sensors are used, the third signal can either decrease or increase with pedal position, but its voltage range will still be different from the other two. ● **SEE FIGURE 29–3.**

THROTTLE BODY ASSEMBLY

The throttle body assembly contains the following components:

- Throttle plate
- Electric actuator DC motor
- Dual throttle position (TP) sensors
- Gears used to multiply the torque of the DC motor
- Springs used to hold the throttle plate in the default location

THROTTLE PLATE AND SPRING The throttle plate is held slightly open by a concentric clock spring. The spring applies a force that will close the throttle plate if power is lost to the actuator motor. The spring is also used to open the throttle plate slightly from the fully closed position.

ELECTRONIC THROTTLE BODY MOTOR The actuator is a DC electric motor and is often called a **servomotor.** The throttle plate is held in a **default position** by a spring inside the throttle body assembly. This partially open position, also called the **neutral position** or the **fail safe position,** is about 16% to 20% open. This default position varies depending on the vehicle and usually results in an engine speed of 1200 to 1500 RPM.

- The throttle plate is driven closed to achieve speeds lower than the default position, such as idle speed.

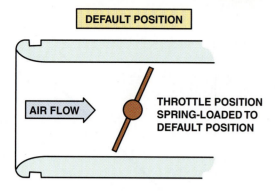

DEFAULT POSITION

AIR FLOW → THROTTLE POSITION SPRING-LOADED TO DEFAULT POSITION

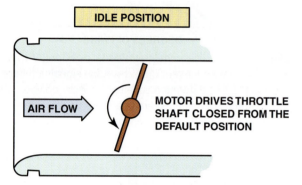

IDLE POSITION

AIR FLOW → MOTOR DRIVES THROTTLE SHAFT CLOSED FROM THE DEFAULT POSITION

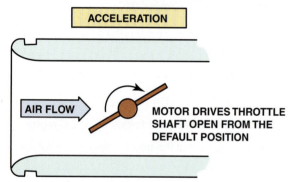

ACCELERATION

AIR FLOW → MOTOR DRIVES THROTTLE SHAFT OPEN FROM THE DEFAULT POSITION

FIGURE 29–4 The default position for the throttle plate is in slightly open position. The servomotor then is used to close it for idle and open it during acceleration.

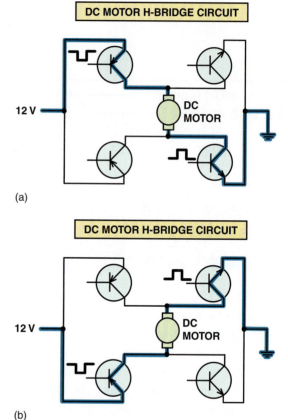

FIGURE 29–5 (a) An H-bridge circuit is used to control the direction of the DC electric motor of the electronic throttle control unit. (b) To reverse the direction of operation, the polarity of the current through the motor is reversed.

THROTTLE BODY ASSEMBLY (CONTINUED)

■ The throttle plate is driven open to achieve speeds higher than the default position, such as during acceleration. ● **SEE FIGURE 29–4.**

The throttle plate motor is driven by a bidirectional pulse-width modulated (PWM) signal from the PCM or electronic throttle control module using an H-bridge circuit. ● **SEE FIGURE 29–5a, b.**

The H-bridge circuit is controlled by the Powertrain Control Module (PCM) by:

■ Reversing the polarity of power and ground brushes to the DC motor

■ Pulse-width modulating (PWM) the current through the motor

The PCM monitors the position of the throttle from the two throttle position (TP) sensors. The PCM then commands the throttle plate to the desired position. ● **SEE FIGURE 29–6.**

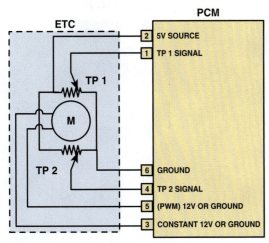

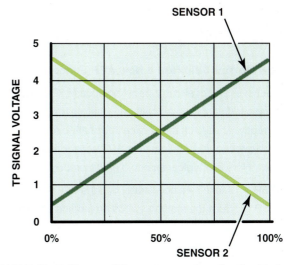

FIGURE 29–6 Schematic of a typical electronic throttle control (ETC) system. Note that terminal #5 is always pulse-width modulated and that terminal #3 is always constant, but both power and ground are switched to change the direction of the motor.

FIGURE 29–7 The two TP sensors used on the throttle body of an electronic throttle body assembly produce opposite voltage signals as the throttle is opened. The total voltage of both combined at any throttle plate position is 5 volts.

? **FREQUENTLY ASKED QUESTION**

What Is the "Spring Test"?

The spring test is a self-test performed by the PCM whenever the engine is started. The PCM operates the throttle to check if it can react to the command and return to the default (home) position. This self-test is used by the PCM to determine that the spring and motor are working correctly and may be noticed by some vehicle owners by the following factors:

- A slight delay in the operation of the starter motor. It is when the ignition is turned to the on position that the PCM performs the test. While it takes just a short time to perform the test, it can be sensed by the driver that there could be a fault in the ignition switch or starter motor circuits.
- A slight "clicking" sound may also be heard coming from under the hood when the ignition is turned on. This is normal and is related to the self-test on the throttle as it opens and closes.

THROTTLE POSITION (TP) SENSOR

Two throttle position (TP) sensors are used in the throttle body assembly to provide throttle position signals to the PCM. Two sensors are used as a fail-safe measure and for diagnosis. There are two types of TP sensors used in electronic throttle control (ETC) systems: potentiometers and Hall-effect.

THREE-WIRE POTENTIOMETER SENSORS These sensors use a 5-volt reference from the PCM and produce an analog (variable) voltage signal that is proportional to the throttle plate position. The two sensors produce opposite signals as the throttle plate opens:

- One sensor starts at low voltage (about 0.5 V) and increases as the throttle plate is opened.
- The second sensor starts at a higher voltage (about 4.5 V) and produces a lower voltage as the throttle plate is opened. ● **SEE FIGURE 29–7.**

HALL-EFFECT TP SENSORS Some vehicle manufacturers, Honda for example, use a non-contact Hall-effect throttle position sensor. Because there is not physical contact, this type of sensor is less likely to fail due to wear.

? **FREQUENTLY ASKED QUESTION**

Why Not Use a Stepper Motor for ETC?

A stepper motor is a type of motor that has multiple windings and is pulsed by a computer to rotate a certain number of degrees when pulsed. The disadvantage is that a stepper motor is too slow to react compared with a conventional DC electric motor and is the reason a stepper motor is not used in electronic throttle control systems.

How Do You Calibrate a New APP Sensor?

Whenever an accelerator pedal position (APP) sensor is replaced, it should be calibrated before it will work correctly. Always check service information for the exact procedure to follow after APP sensor replacement. Here is a typical example of the procedure:

STEP 1 Make sure accelerator pedal is fully released.

STEP 2 Turn the ignition switch on (engine off) and wait at least 2 seconds.

STEP 3 Turn the ignition switch off and wait at least 10 seconds.

STEP 4 Turn the ignition switch on (engine on) and wait at least 2 seconds.

STEP 5 Turn the ignition switch off and wait at least 10 seconds.

(a)

(b)

FIGURE 29–8 (a) A "reduced power" warning light indicates a fault with the electronic throttle control system on some General Motors vehicles. (b) A symbol showing an engine with an arrow pointing down is used on some General Motors vehicles to indicate a fault with the electronic throttle control system.

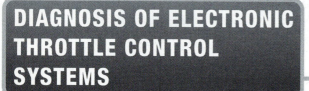

DIAGNOSIS OF ELECTRONIC THROTTLE CONTROL SYSTEMS

FAULT MODE Electronic throttle control (ETC) systems can have faults like any other automatic system. Due to the redundant sensors in accelerator pedal position (APP) sensors and throttle position (TP) sensor, many faults result in a "limp home" situation instead of a total failure. The limp home mode is also called the "fail-safe mode" and indicates the following actions performed by the Powertrain Control Module (PCM).

- Engine speed is limited to the default speed (about 1200 to 1600 RPM).
- There is slow or no response when the accelerator pedal is depressed.
- The cruise control system is disabled.
- A diagnostic trouble code (DTC) is set.
- An ETC warning lamp on the dash will light. The warning lamp may be labeled differently, depending on the vehicle manufacturer. For example:
  - General Motors vehicle—Reduced power lamp
    (● **SEE FIGURE 29–8**)
  - Ford—Wrench symbol (amber or green)
    (● **SEE FIGURE 29–9**)
  - Chrysler—Red lightning bolt symbol
    (● **SEE FIGURE 29–10**)
- The engine will run and can be driven slowly. This limp-in mode operation allows the vehicle to be driven off of the road and to a safe location.

The ETC may enter the limp-in mode if any of the following has occurred:

- Low battery voltage has been detected
- PCM failure

FIGURE 29–9 A wrench symbol warning lamp on a Ford vehicle. The symbol can also be green.

FIGURE 29–10 A symbol used on a Chrysler vehicle indicating a fault with the electronic throttle control.

- One TP and the MAP sensor have failed
- Both TP sensors have failed
- The ETC actuator motor has failed
- The ETC throttle spring has failed

VACUUM LEAKS   The electronic throttle control (ETC) system is able to compensate for many vacuum leaks. A vacuum leak at the intake manifold for example will allow air into the engine that is not measured by the mass airflow sensor. The ETC system will simply move the throttle as needed to achieve the proper idle speed to compensate for the leak.

DIAGNOSTIC PROCEDURE   If a fault occurs in the ETC system, check service information for the specified procedure to follow for the vehicle being checked. Most vehicle service information includes the following steps:

STEP 1   Verify the customer concern.

STEP 2   Use a factory scan tool or an aftermarket scan tool with original equipment capability and check for diagnostic trouble codes (DTCs).

STEP 3   If there are stored diagnostic trouble codes, follow service information instructions for diagnosing the system.

STEP 4   If there are no stored diagnostic trouble codes, check scan tool data for possible fault areas in the system.

SCAN TOOL DATA   Scan data related to the electronic throttle control system can be confusing. Typical data and the meaning include:

- **APP indicated angle.** The scan tool will display a percentage ranging from 0% to 100%. When the throttle is released, the indicated angle should be 0%. When the throttle is depressed to wide open, the reading should indicate 100%.
- **TP desired angle.** The scan tool will display a percentage ranging from 0% to 100%. This represents the desired throttle angle as commanded by the driver of the vehicle.

The High Idle Toyota

The owner of a Toyota Camry complained that the engine would idle at over 1200 RPM compared with a normal 600 to 700 RPM. The vehicle would also not accelerate. Using a scan tool, a check for diagnostic trouble codes showed one code: P2101—"TAC motor circuit low."

Checking service information led to the inspection of the electronic throttle control throttle body assembly. With the ignition key out of the ignition and the inlet air duct off the throttle body, the technician used a screwdriver to see if the throttle plate worked.

Normal operation—The throttle plate should move and then spring back quickly to the default position.

Abnormal operation—If the throttle plate stays where it is moved or does not return to the default position, there is a fault with the throttle body assembly. ● **SEE FIGURE 29–11.**

Solution: The technician replaced the throttle body assembly with an updated version and proper engine operation was restored. The technician disassembled the old throttle body and found it was corroded inside due to moisture entering the unit through the vent hose. ● **SEE FIGURE 29–12.**

FIGURE 29–11 The throttle plate stayed where it was moved, which indicates that there is a problem with the electronic throttle body control assembly.

FIGURE 29–12 A corroded electronic throttle control assembly shown with the cover removed.

DIAGNOSIS OF ELECTRONIC THROTTLE CONTROL SYSTEMS (CONTINUED)

- **TP indicated angle.** The TP indicated angle is the angle of the measured throttle opening and it should agree with the TP desired angle.

- **TP sensors 1 and 2.** The scan tool will display "agree" or "disagree." If the PCM or throttle actuator control (TAC) module receives a voltage signal from one of the TP sensors that is not in the proper relationship to the other TP sensor, the scan tool will display *disagree*.

ETC THROTTLE FOLLOWER TEST

On some vehicles, such as many Chrysler vehicles, the operation of the electronic throttle control can be tested using a factory or factory-level scan tool. To perform this test, use the "throttle follower test" procedure as shown on the scan tool. An assistant is needed to check that the throttle plate is moving as the accelerator pedal is depressed. This test cannot be done normally because the PCM does not normally allow the throttle plate to be moved unless the engine is running.

SERVICING ELECTRONIC THROTTLE SYSTEMS

ETC-RELATED PERFORMANCE ISSUES The only service that an electronic throttle control system may require is a cleaning of the throttle body. Throttle body cleaning is a routine service procedure on port fuel-injected engines and is still needed when the throttle is being opened by an electric motor rather than a throttle cable tied to a mechanical accelerator pedal. The throttle body may need cleaning if one or more of the following symptoms are present:

- Lower than normal idle speed
- Rough idle
- Engine stalls when coming to a stop (called a **coast-down stall**)

If any of the above conditions exists, a throttle body cleaning will often correct these faults.

CAUTION: Some vehicle manufacturers add a nonstick coating to the throttle assembly and warn that cleaning could remove this protective coating. Always follow the vehicle manufacturer's recommended procedures.

THROTTLE BODY CLEANING PROCEDURE Before attempting to clean a throttle body on an engine equipped with an electronic throttle control system, be sure that the ignition key is out of the vehicle and the ready light is off if working on a Toyota/Lexus hybrid electric vehicle to avoid the possibility of personal injury.

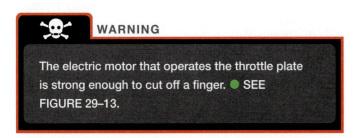

☠ **WARNING**

The electric motor that operates the throttle plate is strong enough to cut off a finger. ● SEE FIGURE 29–13.

To clean the throttle, perform the following steps:

STEP 1 With the ignition off and the key removed from the ignition, remove the air inlet hose from the throttle body.

STEP 2 Spray throttle body cleaner onto a shop cloth.

STEP 3 Open the throttle body and use the shop cloth to remove the varnish and carbon deposits from the throttle body housing and throttle plate.

FIGURE 29–13 Notice the small motor gear on the left drives a larger plastic gear (black), which then drives the small gear in mesh with the section of a gear attached to the throttle plate. This results in a huge torque increase from the small motor and helps explain why it could be dangerous to insert a finger into the throttle body assembly.

CAUTION: Do not spray cleaner into the throttle body assembly. The liquid cleaner could flow into and damage the throttle position (TP) sensors.

STEP 4 Reinstall the inlet hose being sure that there are no air leaks between the hose and the throttle body assembly.

STEP 5 Start the engine and allow the PCM to learn the correct idle. If the idle is not correct, check service information for the specified procedures to follow to perform a throttle relearn.

THROTTLE BODY RELEARN PROCEDURE When installing a new throttle body or Powertrain Control Module (PCM) or sometimes after cleaning the throttle body, the throttle position has to be learned by the PCM. After the following conditions have been met, a typical throttle body relearn procedure for a General Motors vehicle includes:

- Accelerator pedal released
- Battery voltage higher than 8 volts
- Vehicle speed must be zero
- Engine coolant temperature (ECT) higher than 40°F (5°C) and lower than 212°F (100°C)
- Intake air temperature (IAT) higher than 40°F (5°C)
- No throttle diagnostic trouble codes set

If all of the above conditions are met, perform the following steps:

STEP 1 Turn the ignition on (engine off) for 30 seconds.

STEP 2 Turn the ignition off and wait 30 seconds.

Start the engine and the idle learn procedure should cause the engine to idle at the correct speed.

SUMMARY

1. Using an electronic throttle control (ETC) system on an engine has many advantages over a conventional method that uses a mechanical cable between the accelerator pedal and the throttle valve.

2. The major components of an electronic throttle control system include:
   - Accelerator pedal position (APP) sensor
   - Electronic throttle control actuator motor and spring
   - Throttle position (TP) sensor
   - Electronic control unit

3. The throttle position (TP) sensor is actually two sensors that share the 5-volt reference from the PCM and produce opposite signals as a redundant check.

4. Limp-in mode is commanded if there is a major fault in the system, which can allow the vehicle to be driven enough to be pulled off the road to safety.

5. The diagnostic procedure for the ETC system includes verifying the customer concern, using a scan tool to check for diagnostic trouble codes, and checking the value of the TP and APP sensors.

6. Servicing the ETC system includes cleaning the throttle body and throttle plate.

REVIEW QUESTIONS

1. What parts can be deleted if an engine uses an electronic throttle control (ETC) system instead of a conventional accelerator pedal and cable to operate the throttle valve?

2. How can the use of an electronic throttle control (ETC) system improve fuel economy?

3. How is the operation of the throttle different on a system that uses an electronic throttle control system compared with a conventional mechanical system?

4. What component parts are included in an electronic throttle control system?

5. What is the default or limp-in position of the throttle plate?

6. What dash warning light indicates a fault with the ETC system?

CHAPTER QUIZ

1. The use of an electronic throttle control (ETC) system allows the elimination of all *except* _____.
   a. Accelerator pedal
   b. Mechanical throttle cable (most systems)
   c. Cruise control actuator
   d. Idle air control

2. The throttle plate is spring loaded to hold the throttle slightly open how far?
   a. 3% to 5%
   b. 8% to 10%
   c. 16% to 20%
   d. 22% to 28%

3. The throttle plate actuator motor is what type of electric motor?
   a. Stepper motor
   b. DC motor
   c. AC motor
   d. Brushless motor

4. The actuator motor is controlled by the PCM through what type of circuit?
   a. Series
   b. Parallel
   c. H-bridge
   d. Series-parallel

5. When does the PCM perform a self-test of the ETC system?
   a. During cruise speed when the throttle is steady
   b. During deceleration
   c. During acceleration
   d. When the ignition switch is first rotated to the on position before the engine starts

6. The throttle position sensor used in the throttle body assembly of an electronic throttle control (ETC) system is what type?
   a. A single potentiometer
   b. Two potentiometers that read in the opposite direction
   c. A Hall-effect sensor
   d. Either b or c

7. A green wrench symbol is displayed on the dash. What does this mean?
   a. A fault in the ETC in a Ford has been detected
   b. A fault in the ETC in a Honda has been detected
   c. A fault in the ETC in a Chrysler has been detected
   d. A fault in the ETC in a General Motors vehicle has been detected

8. A technician is checking the operation of the electronic throttle control system by depressing the accelerator pedal with the ignition in the on (run) position (engine off). What is the most likely result if the system is functioning correctly?
   a. The throttle goes to wide open when the accelerator pedal is depressed all the way
   b. No throttle movement
   c. The throttle will open partially but not all of the way
   d. The throttle will perform a self-test by closing and then opening to the default position

9. With the ignition off and the key out of the ignition, what should happen if a technician uses a screwdriver and pushes on the throttle plate in an attempt to open the valve?
   a. Nothing. The throttle should be kept from moving by the motor, which is not energized with the key off.
   b. The throttle should move and stay where it is moved and not go back unless moved back.
   c. The throttle should move, and then spring back to the home position when released.
   d. The throttle should move closed, but not open further than the default position.

10. The throttle body may be cleaned (if recommended by the vehicle manufacturer) if what conditions are occurring?
    a. Coast-down stall
    b. Rough idle
    c. Lower-than-normal idle speed
    d. Any of the above

FUEL-INJECTION SYSTEM DIAGNOSIS AND SERVICE

After studying Chapter 30, the reader will be able to:

1. Prepare for ASE Engine Performance (A8) certification test content area "C" (Fuel, Air Induction, and Exhaust Systems Diagnosis and Repair).

2. Describe how to check an electric fuel pump for proper pressure and volume delivery.

3. Explain how to check a fuel-pressure regulator.

4. Describe how to test fuel injectors.

5. Explain how to diagnose electronic fuel-injection problems.

6. Describe how to service the fuel-injection system.

KEY TERMS

Graphing multimeter (GMM) 456	Peak-and-hold injector 465
IAC counts 457	Pressure transducer 456
Idle air control (IAC) 466	Saturation 464
Noid light 459	

PORT FUEL-INJECTION PRESSURE REGULATOR DIAGNOSIS

Most port-fuel-injected engines use a vacuum hose connected to the fuel-pressure regulator. At idle, the pressure inside the intake manifold is low (high vacuum). Manifold vacuum is applied above the diaphragm inside the fuel-pressure regulator. This reduces the pressure exerted on the diaphragm and results in a lower, about 10 PSI (69 kPa), fuel pressure applied to the injectors. To test a vacuum-controlled fuel-pressure regulator, follow these steps:

1. Connect a fuel-pressure gauge to monitor the fuel pressure.

2. Locate the fuel-pressure regulator and disconnect the vacuum hose from the regulator.

   NOTE: If gasoline drips out of the vacuum hose when removed from the fuel-pressure regulator, the regulator is defective and will require replacement.

3. With the engine running at idle speed, reconnect the vacuum hose to the fuel-pressure regulator while watching the fuel-pressure gauge. The fuel pressure should drop (about 10 PSI or 69 kPa) when the hose is reattached to the regulator.

4. Using a hand-operated vacuum pump, apply vacuum (20 in. Hg) to the regulator. The regulator should hold vacuum. If the vacuum drops, replace the fuel-pressure regulator. ● **SEE FIGURE 30–1.**

NOTE: Some vehicles do not use a vacuum-regulated fuel-pressure regulator. Many of these vehicles use a regulator located inside the fuel tank that supplies a constant fuel pressure to the fuel injectors.

FUEL PRESSURE REGULATOR

FIGURE 30–1 If the vacuum hose is removed from the fuel-pressure regulator when the engine is running, the fuel pressure should increase. If it does not increase, then the fuel pump is not capable of supplying adequate pressure or the fuel-pressure regulator is defective. If gasoline is visible in the vacuum hose, the regulator is leaking and should be replaced.

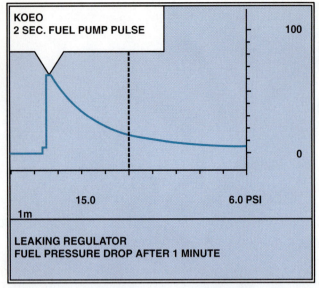

KOEO
2 SEC. FUEL PUMP PULSE

100

15.0   6.0 PSI

1m

LEAKING REGULATOR
FUEL PRESSURE DROP AFTER 1 MINUTE

(a)

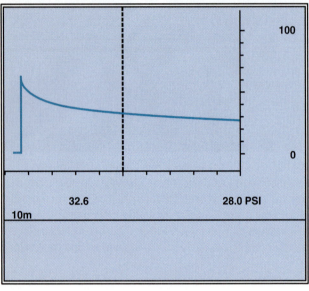

100

0

32.6   28.0 PSI

10m

(b)

FIGURE 30–2 (a) A fuel-pressure graph after key on, engine off (KOEO) on a TBI system. (b) Pressure drop after 10 minutes on a normal port fuel-injection system.

 TECH TIP

Pressure Transducer Fuel Pressure Test

Using a **pressure transducer** and a **graphing multimeter (GMM)** or digital storage oscilloscope (DSO) allows the service technician to view the fuel pressure over time. ● **SEE FIGURE 30–2(a).** Note that the fuel pressure dropped from 15 PSI down to 6 PSI on a TBI-Equipped vehicle after just one minute. A normal pressure holding capability is shown in ● **FIGURE 30–2(b)** when the pressure dropped only about 10% after 10 minutes on a port-fuel injection system.

FIGURE 30–3 A clogged PCV system caused the engine oil fumes to be drawn into the air cleaner assembly. This is what the technician discovered during a visual inspection.

DIAGNOSING ELECTRONIC FUEL-INJECTION PROBLEMS USING VISUAL INSPECTION

All fuel-injection systems require the proper amount of clean fuel delivered to the system at the proper pressure and the correct amount of filtered air. The following items should be carefully inspected before proceeding to more detailed tests.

- Check the air filter and replace as needed.
- Check the air induction system for obstructions.
- Check the conditions of all vacuum hoses. Replace any hose that is split, soft (mushy), or brittle.
- Check the positive crankcase ventilation (PCV) valve for proper operation or replacement as needed. ● **SEE FIGURE 30–3.**

NOTE: The use of an incorrect PCV valve can cause a rough idle or stalling.

- Check all fuel-injection electrical connections for corrosion or damage.
- Check for gasoline at the vacuum port of the fuel-pressure regulator if the vehicle is so equipped. Gasoline in the vacuum hose at the fuel-pressure regulator indicates that the regulator is defective and requires replacement.

FIGURE 30–4 All fuel injectors should make the same sound with the engine running at idle speed. A lack of sound indicates a possible electrically open injector or a break in the wiring. A defective computer could also be the cause of a lack of clicking (pulsing) of the injectors.

FUEL PRESSURE REGULATOR

FUEL RETURN LINE TO TANK

FIGURE 30–5 Fuel should be heard returning to the fuel tank at the fuel return line if the fuel-pump and fuel-pressure regulator are functioning correctly.

 TECH TIP

Stethoscope Fuel-Injection Test

A commonly used test for injector operation is to listen to the injector using a stethoscope with the engine operating at idle speed. ● **SEE FIGURE 30–4.** All injectors should produce the same clicking sound. If any injector makes a clunking or rattling sound, it should be tested further or replaced. With the engine still running, place the end of the stethoscope probe to the return line from the fuel-pressure regulator. ● **SEE FIGURE 30–5.** Fuel should be heard flowing back to the fuel tank if the fuel-pump pressure is higher than the fuel-regulator pressure. If no sound of fuel is heard, then either the fuel pump or the fuel-pressure regulator is at fault.

 TECH TIP

Quick and Easy Leaking Injector Test

Leaking injectors may be found by disabling the ignition, unhooking all injectors, and checking exhaust for hydrocarbons (HC) using a gas analyzer while cranking the engine (maximum HC = 300 PPM).

SCAN TOOL VACUUM LEAK DIAGNOSIS

If a vacuum (air) leak occurs on an engine equipped with a speed-density-type of fuel injection, the extra air would cause the following to occur:

- The idle speed increases due to the extra air just as if the throttle pedal was depressed.

- The MAP sensor reacts to the increased air from the vacuum leak as an additional load on the engine.

- The computer increases the injector pulse width slightly longer due to the signal from the MAP sensor.

- The air–fuel mixture remains unchanged.

- The idle air control (IAC) counts will decrease, thereby attempting to reduce the engine speed to the target idle speed stored in the computer memory. ● **SEE FIGURE 30–6.**

Therefore, one of the best indicators of a vacuum leak on a speed-density fuel-injection system is to look at the IAC counts or percentage. Normal **IAC counts** or percentage is usually 15 to 25. A reading of less than 5 indicates a vacuum leak.

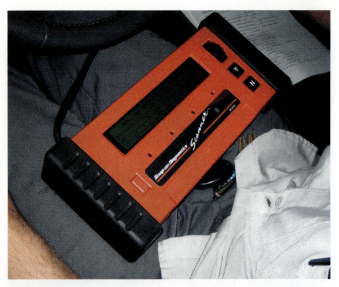

FIGURE 30–6 Using a scan tool to check for IAC counts or percentage as part of a diagnostic routine.

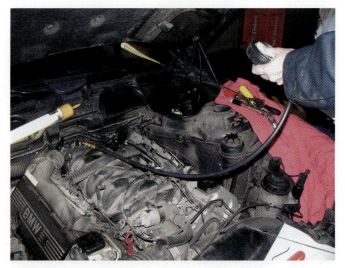

FIGURE 30–7 Checking the fuel pressure using a fuel-pressure gauge connected to the Schrader valve.

SCAN TOOL VACUUM LEAK DIAGNOSIS (CONTINUED)

If a vacuum leak occurs on an engine equipped with a mass airflow-type fuel-injection system, the extra air causes the following to occur:

- The engine will operate leaner-than-normal because the extra air has not been measured by the MAF sensor.

- The idle speed will likely be lower due to the leaner-than-normal air–fuel mixture.

- The idle air control (IAC) counts or percentage will often increase in an attempt to return the engine speed to the target speed stored in the computer.

 **TECH TIP**

No Spark, No Squirt

Most electronic fuel-injection computer systems use the ignition primary (pickup coil or crank sensor) pulse as the trigger for when to inject (squirt) fuel from the injectors (nozzles). If this signal were not present, no fuel would be injected. Because this pulse is also necessary to trigger the module to create a spark from the coil, it can be said that "no spark" could also mean "no squirt." Therefore, if the cause of a no-start condition is observed to be a lack of fuel injection, do not start testing or replacing fuel-system components until the ignition system is checked for proper operation.

PORT FUEL-INJECTION SYSTEM DIAGNOSIS

To determine if a port fuel-injection system—including the fuel pump, injectors, and fuel-pressure regulator—is operating correctly, take the following steps.

1. Attach a fuel-pressure gauge to the Schrader valve on the fuel rail. ● **SEE FIGURE 30–7.**

2. Turn the ignition key on or start the engine to build up the fuel-pump pressure (to about 35 to 45 PSI).

3. Wait 20 minutes and observe the fuel pressure retained in the fuel rail and note the PSI reading. The fuel pressure should not drop more than 20 PSI (140 kPa) in 20 minutes. If the drop is less than 20 PSI in 20 minutes, everything is okay; if the drop is *greater,* then there is a possible problem with:
   - The check valve in the fuel pump
   - Leaking injectors, lines, or fittings
   - A defective (leaking) fuel-pressure regulator

To determine which unit is defective, perform the following:

- Reenergize the electric fuel pump.

- Clamp the fuel *supply* line, and wait 10 minutes (see Caution box). If the pressure drop does not occur, replace the fuel pump. If the pressure drop still occurs, continue with the next step.

FIGURE 30–8 Shutoff valves must be used on vehicles equipped with plastic fuel lines to isolate the cause of a pressure drop in the fuel system.

(a)

(b)

FIGURE 30–9 (a) Noid lights are usually purchased as an assortment so that one is available for any type or size of injector wiring connector. (b) The connector is unplugged from the injector and a noid light is plugged into the injector connector. The noid light should flash when the engine is being cranked if the power circuit and the pulsing to ground by the computer are functioning okay.

- Repeat the pressure buildup of the electric pump and clamp the fuel return line. If the pressure drop time is now okay, replace the fuel-pressure regulator.

- If the pressure drop still occurs, one or more of the injectors is leaking. Remove the injectors with the fuel rail and hold over paper. Replace those injectors that drip one or more drops after 10 minutes with pressurized fuel.

CAUTION: Do not clamp plastic fuel lines. Connect shutoff valves to the fuel system to shut off supply and return lines. ● SEE FIGURE 30–8.

TESTING FOR AN INJECTOR PULSE

One of the first checks that should be performed when diagnosing a no-start condition is whether the fuel injectors are being pulsed by the computer. Checking for proper pulsing of the injector is also important in diagnosing a weak or dead cylinder.

A **noid light** is designed to electrically replace the injector in the circuit and to flash if the injector circuit is working correctly. ● **SEE FIGURE 30–9.** To use a noid light, disconnect the electrical connector at the fuel injector and plug the noid light into the injector harness connections. Crank or start the engine. The noid light should flash regularly.

NOTE: The term *noid* is simply an abbreviation of the word sole*noid*. Injectors use a movable iron core and are therefore solenoids. Therefore, a noid light is a replacement for the solenoid (injector).

Possible noid light problems and causes include the following:

1. **The light is off and does not flash.** The problem is an open in either the power side or ground side (or both) of the injector circuit.

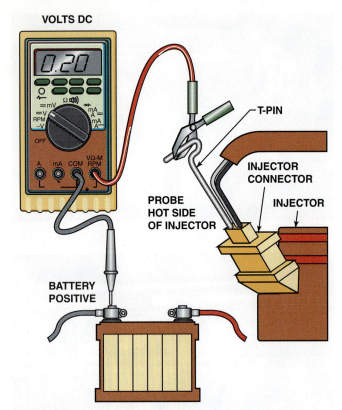

VOLTS DC

T-PIN

INJECTOR CONNECTOR

INJECTOR

PROBE
HOT SIDE
OF INJECTOR

BATTERY
POSITIVE

FIGURE 30–10 Use a DMM set to read DC volts to check the voltage drop of the positive circuit to the fuel injector. A reading of 0.5 volt or less is generally considered to be acceptable.

TESTING FOR AN INJECTOR PULSE (CONTINUED)

2. **The noid light flashes dimly.** A dim noid light indicates excessive resistance or low voltage available to the injector. Both the power and ground side must be checked.

3. **The noid light is on and does not flash.** If the noid light is on, then both a power and a ground are present. Because the light does not flash (blink) when the engine is being cranked or started, then a short-to-ground fault exists either in the computer itself or in the wiring between the injector and the computer.

CAUTION: A noid lamp must be used with caution. The computer may show a good noid light operation and have low supply voltage. ● **SEE FIGURE 30–10.**

CHECKING FUEL-INJECTOR RESISTANCE

Each port fuel injector must deliver an equal amount of fuel or the engine will idle roughly or perform poorly.

The electrical balance test involves measuring the injector coil-winding resistance. For best engine operation, all injectors should have the same electrical resistance. To measure the resistance, carefully release the locking feature of the connector and remove the connector from the injector.

Injector Resistance Table

Manufacturer	Injector Application	Resistance Values
General Motors		
	Quad 4	1.95–2.15 Ω
	CPI Vortec 4.3L	1.48–1.52 Ω
	MFI Bosch Style Injector (1985–1989) 2.8L	15.95–16.35 Ω
	MFI Black Multec Injector 2.8L, 3.1L, 3.3L, 3.4L	11.8–12.6 Ω
	MFI 3800	14.3–14.7 Ω
	MFI 3.8L, 5.0L, 5.7L	15.8–16.6 Ω
	MFI 5.7 LT5-ZR1	11.8–12.6 Ω
	TBI 220 Series 2.8L, 3.1L, 4.3L, 5.0L, 5.7L, 7.4L	1.16–1.36 Ω
	TBI 295 Series 4.3L, 6.0L, 7.0L	1.42–1.62 Ω
	TBI 700 Series 2.0L, 2.2L, 2.5L	1.42–1.62 Ω
Chrysler Brand		
	MFI Early Years through 1992 (majority of)	2.4 Ω
	MFI Later Years after 1992 (majority of)	14.5 Ω
	TBI Low-Pressure Systems (majority of)	1.3 Ω
	TBI High-Pressure Systems (majority of)	0.7 Ω
Ford		
	MFI (majority of)	15.0–18.0 Ω
	TBI Low-Pressure 1.9L (1987–1990)	1.0–2.0 Ω
	TBI Low-Pressure 2.3L (1985–1987)	1.0–2.0 Ω
	TBI Low-Pressure 2.5L (1986–1990)	1.0–2.0 Ω
	TBI High-Pressure 3.8L (1984–1987)	1.5–2.5 Ω
	TBI High-Pressure 5.0L (1981–1985)	1.5–3.5 Ω

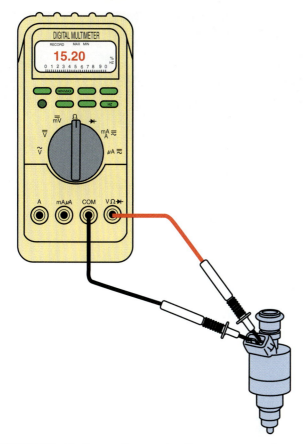

FIGURE 30–11 Connections and settings necessary to measure fuel-injector resistance.

NOTE: Some engines require specific procedures to gain access to the injectors. Always follow the manufacturers' recommended procedures.

With an ohmmeter, measure the resistance across the injector terminals. Be sure to use the low-ohms feature of the digital ohmmeter to read in tenths (0.1) of an ohm. ● **SEE FIGURES 30–11 AND 30–12.** Check service information for the resistance specification of the injectors. Measure the resistance of all of the injectors. Replace any injector that does not fall within the resistance range of the specification. The resistance of the injectors should be measured twice—once when the engine (and injectors) are cold and once after the engine has reached normal operating temperature. If any injector measures close to specification, make certain that the terminals of the injector are electrically sound, and perform other tests to confirm an injector problem before replacement.

FIGURE 30–12 To measure fuel-injector resistance, a technician constructed a short wiring harness with a double banana plug that fits into the V and COM terminals of the meter and an injector connector at the other end. This setup makes checking resistance of fuel injectors quick and easy.

MEASURING RESISTANCE OF GROUPED INJECTORS

Many vehicles are equipped with a port fuel-injection system that "fires" two or more injectors at a time. For example, a V-6 may group all three injectors on one bank to pulse on at the same time. Then the other three injectors will be pulsed on. This sequence alternates. To measure the resistance of these injectors, it is often easiest to measure each group of three that is wired in parallel. The resistance of three injectors wired in parallel is one-third of the resistance of each individual injector. For example,

Injector resistance = 12 ohms (Ω)

Three injectors in parallel = 4 ohms (Ω)

A V-6 has two groups of three injectors. Therefore, both groups should measure the same resistance. If both groups measure 4 ohms, then it is likely that all six injectors are okay. However, if one group measures only 2.9 ohms and the other group measures 4 ohms, then it is likely that one or more fuel injectors are defective (shorted). This means that the technician now has reasonable cause to remove the intake manifold to get access to each injector for further testing. ● **SEE FIGURE 30–13.**

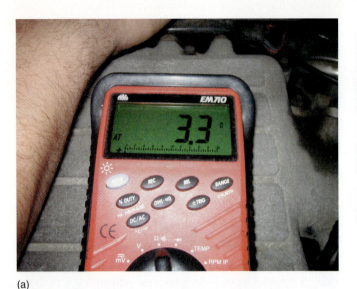
(a)

(b)

FIGURE 30–13 (a) The meter is connected to read one group of three 12-ohm injectors. The result should be 4 ohms and this reading is a little low indicating that at least one injector is shorted (low resistance). (b) This meter is connected to the other group of three injectors and indicates that most, if not all three, injectors are shorted. The technician replaced all six injectors and the engine ran great.

FIGURE 30–14 If an injector has the specified resistance, this does not mean that it is okay. This injector had the specified resistance yet it did not deliver the correct amount of fuel because it was clogged.

TECH TIP

Equal Resistance Test

All fuel injectors should measure the specified resistance. However the specification often indicates the temperature of the injectors be at room temperature and of course will vary according to the temperature. Rather than waiting for all of the injectors to achieve room temperature, measure the resistance and check that they are all within 0.4 ohm of each other. To determine the difference, record the resistance of each injector and then subtract the lowest resistance reading from the highest resistance reading to get the difference. If more than 0.4 ohm then further testing will be needed to verify defective injector(s).

MEASURING RESISTANCE OF INDIVIDUAL INJECTORS

While there are many ways to check injectors, the first test is to measure the resistance of the coil inside and compare it to factory specifications. ● **SEE FIGURE 30–14.** If the injectors are not accessible, check service information for the location of the electrical connector for the injectors. Unplug the connector and measure the resistance of each injector at the injector side of the connector. Use service information to determine the wire colors for the power side and the pulse side of each injector.

PRESSURE-DROP BALANCE TEST

The pressure balance test involves using an electrical timing device to pulse the fuel injectors on for a given amount of time, usually 500 ms or 0.5 second, and observing the drop in pressure that accompanies the pulse. If the *fuel flow* through each injector is equal, the drop in pressure in the system will be equal. Most manufacturers recommend that the pressures be within about 1.5 PSI (10 kPa) of each other for satisfactory engine performance. This test method not only tests the electrical functioning of the injector (for definite time and current pulse), but also tests for mechanical defects that could affect fuel flow amounts.

The purpose of running this injector balance test is to determine which injector is restricted, inoperative, or delivering fuel differently than the other injectors. Replacing a complete set of injectors can be expensive. The basic tools needed are:

- Accurate pressure gauge with pressure relief
- Injector pulser with time control
- Necessary injector connection adapters
- Safe receptacle for catching and disposing of any fuel released

STEP 1 Attach the pressure gauge to the fuel delivery rail on the supply side. Make sure the connections are safe and leakproof.

STEP 2 Attach the injector pulser to the first injector to be tested.

STEP 3 Turn the ignition key to the on position to prime the fuel rail. Note the static fuel-pressure reading. ● **SEE FIGURE 30–15.**

STEP 4 Activate the pulser for the timed firing pulses.

STEP 5 Note and record the new static rail pressure after the injector has been pulsed.

STEP 6 Reenergize the fuel pump and repeat this procedure for all of the engine injectors.

STEP 7 Compare the two pressure readings and compute the pressure drop for each injector. Compare the pressure drops of the injectors to each other. Any variation in pressure drops will indicate an uneven fuel delivery rate between the injectors.

For example:

Injector	1	2	3	4	5	6
Initial pressure	40	40	40	40	40	40
Second pressure	30	30	35	30	20	30
Pressure drop	10	10	5	10	20	10
Possible problem	OK	OK	Restriction	OK	Leak	OK

FIGURE 30–16 An injector tester being used to check the voltage drop through the injector while the tester is sending current through the injectors. This test is used to check the coil inside the injector. This same tester can be used to check for equal pressure drop of each injector by pulsing the injector on for 500 ms.

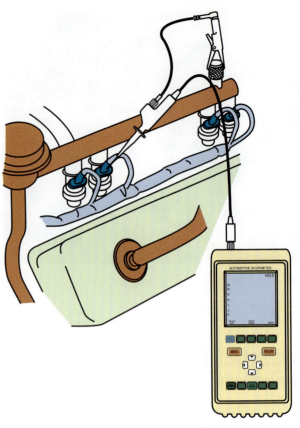

FIGURE 30–17 A digital storage oscilloscope can be easily connected to an injector by carefully back probing the electrical connector.

INJECTOR VOLTAGE-DROP TESTS

Another test of injectors involves pulsing the injector and measuring the voltage drop across the windings as current is flowing. A typical voltage-drop tester is shown in ● **FIGURE 30–16.** The tester, which is recommended for use by General Motors Corporation, pulses the injector while a digital multimeter is connected to the unit, which will display the voltage drop as the current flows through the winding.

CAUTION: Do not test an injector using a pulse-type tester more than one time without starting the engine to help avoid a hydrostatic lock caused by the flow of fuel into the cylinder during the pulse test.

Record the highest voltage drop observed on the meter display during the test. Repeat the voltage-drop test for all of the injectors. The voltage drop across each injector should be within 0.1 volt of each other. If an injector has a higher-than-normal voltage drop, the injector windings have higher-than-normal resistance.

SCOPE-TESTING FUEL INJECTORS

A scope (analog or digital storage) can be connected into each injector circuit. There are three types of injector drive circuits and each type of circuit has its own characteristic pattern. ● **SEE FIGURE 30–17** for an example of how to connect a scope to read a fuel-injector waveform.

SATURATED SWITCH TYPE In a saturated switch-type injector-driven circuit, voltage (usually a full 12 volts) is applied to the injector. The ground for the injector is provided by the vehicle computer. When the ground connection is completed, current flows through the injector windings. Due to the resistance and inductive reactance of the coil itself, it requires a fraction of a second (about 3 milliseconds or 0.003 seconds) for the coil to reach **saturation** or maximum current flow. Most saturated switch-type fuel injectors have 12 to 16 ohms of resistance. This resistance, as well as the computer switching circuit, control and limit the current flow through the injector. A voltage spike

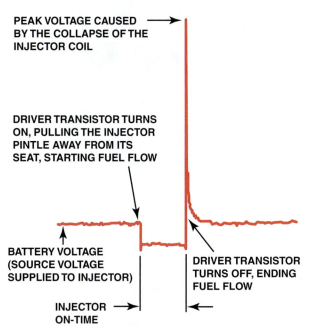

FIGURE 30–18 The injector on-time is called the pulse width. *(Courtesy of Fluke Corporation)*

In figure 30-18:
- PEAK VOLTAGE CAUSED BY THE COLLAPSE OF THE INJECTOR COIL
- DRIVER TRANSISTOR TURNS ON, PULLING THE INJECTOR PINTLE AWAY FROM ITS SEAT, STARTING FUEL FLOW
- BATTERY VOLTAGE (SOURCE VOLTAGE SUPPLIED TO INJECTOR)
- DRIVER TRANSISTOR TURNS OFF, ENDING FUEL FLOW
- INJECTOR ON-TIME

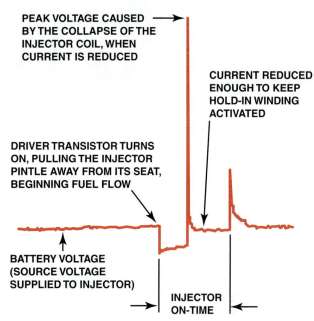

FIGURE 30–19 A typical peak-and-hold fuel-injector waveform. Most fuel injectors that measure less than 6 ohms will usually display a similar waveform.

In figure 30-19:
- PEAK VOLTAGE CAUSED BY THE COLLAPSE OF THE INJECTOR COIL, WHEN CURRENT IS REDUCED
- CURRENT REDUCED ENOUGH TO KEEP HOLD-IN WINDING ACTIVATED
- DRIVER TRANSISTOR TURNS ON, PULLING THE INJECTOR PINTLE AWAY FROM ITS SEAT, BEGINNING FUEL FLOW
- BATTERY VOLTAGE (SOURCE VOLTAGE SUPPLIED TO INJECTOR)
- INJECTOR ON-TIME

occurs when the computer shuts off (opens the injector ground-side circuit) the injectors. ● SEE FIGURE 30–18.

PEAK-AND-HOLD TYPE

A **peak-and-hold** type is typically used for TBI and some port low-resistance injectors. Full battery voltage is applied to the injector and the ground side is controlled through the computer. The computer provides a high initial current flow (about 4 amperes) to flow through the injector windings to open the injector core. Then the computer reduces the current to a lower level (about 1 ampere). The hold current is enough to keep the injector open, yet conserves energy and reduces the heat buildup that would occur if the full current flow remains on as long as the injector is commanded on. Typical peak-and-hold-type injector resistance ranges from 2 to 4 ohms.

The scope pattern of a typical peak-and-hold-type injector shows the initial closing of the ground circuit, then a voltage spike as the current flow is reduced. Another voltage spike occurs when the lower level current is turned off (opened) by the computer. ● SEE FIGURE 30–19.

PULSE-WIDTH MODULATED TYPE

A pulse-width modulated type of injector drive circuit uses lower-resistance coil injectors. Battery voltage is available at the positive terminal of the injector and the computer provides a variable-duration connection to ground on the negative side of the injector. The computer can vary the time intervals that the injector is grounded for very precise fuel control.

Each time the injector circuit is turned off (ground circuit opened), a small voltage spike occurs. It is normal to see multiple voltage spikes on a scope connected to a pulse-width modulated type of fuel injector.

FIGURE 30–20 A set of six reconditioned injectors. The sixth injector is barely visible at the far right.

IDLE AIR SPEED CONTROL DIAGNOSIS

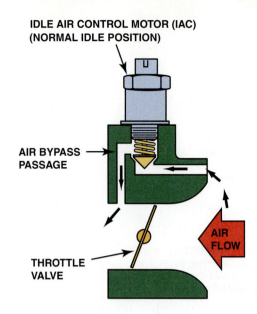

FIGURE 30–21 An IAC controls idle speed by controlling the amount of air that passes around the throttle plate. More airflow results in a higher idle speed.

FIGURE 30–22 A typical IAC.

On an engine equipped with fuel injection (TBI or port injection), the idle speed is controlled by increasing or decreasing the amount of air bypassing the throttle plate. Again, an electronic stepper motor or pulse-width modulated solenoid is used to maintain the correct idle speed. This control is often called the **idle air control (IAC)**. ● **SEE FIGURES 30–21 THROUGH 30–23.**

When the engine stops, most IAC units will retract outward to get ready for the next engine start. When the engine starts, the engine speed is high to provide for proper operation when the engine is cold. Then, as the engine gets warmer, the computer reduces engine idle speed gradually by reducing the number of counts or steps commanded by the IAC.

When the engine is warm and restarted, the idle speed should momentarily increase, then decrease to normal idle speed. This increase and then decrease in engine speed is often called an engine-flare. If the engine speed does not flare, then the IAC may not be working (it may be stuck in one position).

FIGURE 30–23 Some IAC units are purchased with the housing as shown. Carbon buildup in these passages can cause a rough or unstable idling or stalling.

 REAL WORLD FIX

There Is No Substitute for a Thorough Visual Inspection

An intermittent "check engine" light and a random-misfire diagnostic trouble code (DTC) P0300 was being diagnosed. A scan tool did not provide any help because all systems seemed to be functioning normally. Finally, the technician removed the engine cover and discovered a mouse nest. ● **SEE FIGURE 30–24.**

FUEL-INJECTION SERVICE

After many years of fuel-injection service, some service technicians still misunderstand the process of proper fuel-system handling. Much has been said over the years with regard to when and how to perform injector cleaning. Some manufacturers have suggested methods of cleaning while others have issued bulletins to prohibit any cleaning at all.

All engines using fuel injection do require some type of fuel-system maintenance. Normal wear and tear with today's underhood temperatures and changes in gasoline quality contribute to the buildup of olefin wax, dirt, water, and many other additives. Unique to each engine is an air-control design that also may contribute different levels of carbon deposits, such as oil control.

Fuel-injection system service should include the following operations:

1. **Check fuel-pump operating pressure and volume.** The missing link here is volume. Most working technicians assume that if the pressure is correct, the volume is also

(a)

(b)

FIGURE 30–24 (a) Nothing looks unusual when the hood is first opened. (b) When the cover is removed from the top of the engine, a mouse or some other animal nest is visible. The animal had already eaten through a couple of injector wires. At least the cause of the intermittent misfire was discovered.

okay. Hook up a fuel-pressure tester to the fuel rail inlet to quickly test the fuel pressure with the engine running. At the same time, test the volume of the pump by sending fuel into the holding tank. (One ounce per second is the usual specification.) ● **SEE FIGURE 30–25.** A two-line system tester is the recommended procedure to use and is attached to the fuel inlet and the return on the fuel rail. The vehicle onboard system is looped and returns fuel to the tank.

2. **Test the fuel-pressure regulator for operation and leakage.** At this time, the fuel-pressure regulator would be tested for operational pressure and proper regulation, including leakage. (This works well as the operator has total control

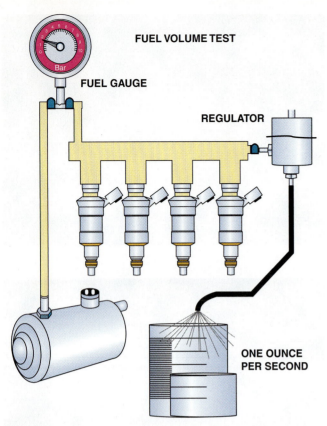

FUEL VOLUME TEST

FUEL GAUGE

REGULATOR

ONE OUNCE
PER SECOND

FIGURE 30–25 Checking fuel-pump volume using a hose from the outlet of the fuel-pressure regulator into a calibrated container.

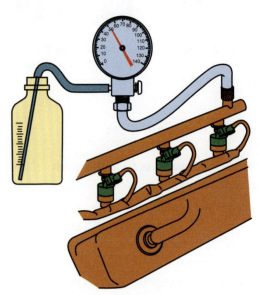

FIGURE 30–26 Testing fuel-pump volume using a fuel-pressure gauge with a bleed hose inserted into a suitable container. The engine is running during this test.

FUEL-INJECTION SERVICE (CONTINUED)

of rail pressure with a unit control valve.) Below are some points to ponder:

- Good pressure does not mean proper volume. For example, a clogged filter may test okay on pressure but the restriction may not allow proper volume under load. ● **SEE FIGURE 30–26.**
- It is a good idea to use the vehicle's own gasoline to service the system versus a can of shop gasoline that has been sitting around for some time.
- Pressure regulators do fail and a lot more do not properly shut off fuel, causing higher-than-normal pump wear and shorter service life.

3. **Flush the entire fuel rail and upper fuel-injector screens including the fuel-pressure regulator.** Raise the input pressure to a point above regulator setting to allow a constant flow of fuel through the inlet pressure side of the system, through the fuel rail, and out the open fuel-pressure regulator. In most cases the applied pressure is 75 to 90 PSI (517 to 620 kPa), but will be maintained by the presence of a regulator. At this point, cleaning chemical is added to the

fuel at a 5:1 mixture and allowed to flow through the system for 15 to 30 minutes. ● **SEE FIGURE 30–27.** Results are best on a hot engine with the fuel supply looped and the engine not running. Below are some points to ponder:

- This flush is the fix most vehicles need first. The difference is that the deposits are removed to a remote tank and filter versus attempting to soften the deposits and blow them through the upper screens.
- Most injectors use a 10-micron final filter screen. A 25% restriction in the upper screen would increase the injector on-time approximately 25%.
- **Clean the fuel injectors.** Start the engine and adjust the output pressure closer to regulator pressure or lower than in the previous steps. Lower pressure will cause the pulse width to open up somewhat longer and allow the injectors to be cleaned. Slow speed (idle) position will take a longer time frame and operating temperature will be reached. Clean injectors are the objective, but the chemical should also decarbon the engine valves, pistons, and oxygen sensor.

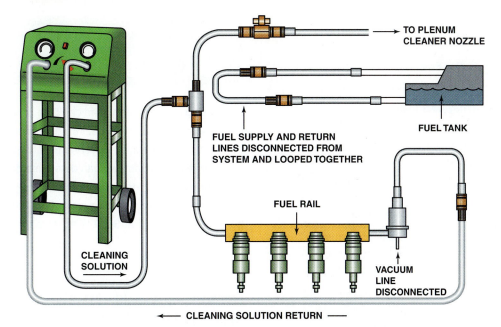

FIGURE 30–27 A typical two-line cleaning machine hookup, showing an extension hose that can be used to squirt a cleaning solution into the throttle body while the engine is running on the cleaning solution and gasoline mixture.

TECH TIP

Check the Injectors at the "Bends and the Ends"

Injectors that are most likely to become restricted due to clogging of the filter basket screen are the injectors at the ends of the rail especially on returnless systems where dirt can accumulate. Also the injectors that are located at the bends of the fuel rail are also subject to possible clogging due to the dirt being deposited where the fuel makes a turn in the rail.

FIGURE 30–28 To thoroughly clean a throttle body, it is sometimes best to remove it from the vehicle.

4. **Decarbon the engine assembly.** On most vehicles, the injector spray will help the decarboning process. On others, you may need to enhance the operation with external addition of a mixture through the PCV hose, throttle plates, or idle air controls.

5. **Clean the throttle plate and idle air control passages.** Doing this service alone on most late-model engines will show a manifold vacuum increase of up to 2 in. Hg. Stop the engine and clean the areas as needed, then use a handheld fuel injector connected in parallel with the pressure hose, along with a pulser to allow cleaning of the throttle plates with the same chemical as injectors are running on. ● **SEE FIGURE 30–28.** This works well as air is drawn into IAC passages on a running engine and will clean the passages without IAC removal.

6. **Relearn the onboard computer.** Some vehicles may have been running in such a poor state of operation that the onboard computer may need to be relearned. Consult service information for the suggested relearn procedures for each particular vehicle.

This service usually takes approximately one hour for the vehicle to run out of fuel and the entire service to be performed. The good thing is that the technician may do other services while this is being performed. Some technicians may install a set of plugs or change the fuel filter while the engine is flushing. This service should restore the fuel system to original operations.

All of the previously listed steps may be performed using a *two-line* fuel-injector service unit such as: Carbon Clean, Auto Care, Injector Test, DeCarbon, or Motor-Vac.

Be Sure to Clean the Fuel Rail

Whenever you service the fuel injectors, or if you suspect that there may be a fuel-injector problem, remove the entire fuel rail assembly and check the passages for contamination. Always thoroughly clean the rail when replacing fuel injectors.

Fuel-Injection Symptom Chart

Symptom	Possible Causes
Hard cold starts	• Low fuel pressure • Leaking fuel injectors • Contaminated fuel • Low-volatility fuel • Dirty throttle plate
Garage stalls	• Low fuel pressure • Insufficient fuel volume • Restricted fuel injector • Contaminated fuel • Low-volatility fuel
Poor cold performance	• Low fuel pressure • Insufficient fuel volume • Contaminated fuel • Low-volatility fuel
Tip-in hesitation (hesitation just as the accelerator pedal is depressed)	• Low fuel pressure • Insufficient fuel volume • Intake valve deposits • Contaminated fuel • Low-volatility fuel

FUEL-SYSTEM SCAN TOOL DIAGNOSTICS

Diagnosing a faulty fuel system can be a difficult task. However, it can be made easier by utilizing the information available via the serial data stream. By observing the long-term fuel trim and the short-term fuel trim, we can determine how the fuel system is performing. Short-term fuel trim and long-term fuel trim can help us to zero in on specific areas of trouble. Readings should be taken at idle and at 3000 RPM. Use the following chart as a guide.

Condition	Long-Term Fuel Trim at Idle	Long-Term Fuel Trim at 3000 RPM
System normal	0% ± 10%	0% ± 10%
Vacuum leak	HIGH	OK
Fuel flow problem	OK	HIGH
Low fuel pressure	HIGH	HIGH
High fuel pressure	*OK or LOW	*OK or LOW

*High fuel pressure will affect trim at idle, at 3000 RPM, or both.

FUEL-PUMP RELAY CIRCUIT DIAGNOSIS

1 The tools needed to diagnose a circuit containing a relay include a digital multimeter (DMM), a fused jumper wire, and an assortment of wiring terminals.

2 Start the diagnosis by locating the relay center. It is under the hood on this General Motors vehicle, so access is easy. Not all vehicles are this easy.

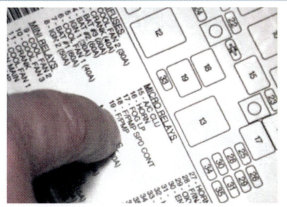

3 The chart under the cover for the relay center indicates the location of the relay that controls the electric fuel pump.

4 Locate the fuel-pump relay and remove by using a puller if necessary. Try to avoid rocking or twisting the relay to prevent causing damage to the relay terminals or the relay itself.

5 Terminals 85 and 86 represent the coil inside the relay. Terminal 30 is the power terminal, 87a is the normally closed contact, and 87 is the normally open contact.

6 The terminals are also labeled on most relays.

CONTINUED ▶

FUEL-PUMP RELAY CIRCUIT DIAGNOSIS (CONTINUED)

7 To help make good electrical contact with the terminals without doing any harm, select the proper-size terminal from the terminal assortment.

8 Insert the terminals into the relay socket in 30 and 87.

9 To check for voltage at terminal 30, use a test light or a voltmeter. Start by connecting the alligator clip of the test light to the positive (+) terminal of the battery.

10 Touch the test light to the negative (−) terminal of the battery or a good engine ground to check the test light.

11 Use the test light to check for voltage at terminal 30 of the relay. The ignition may have to be in the on (run) position.

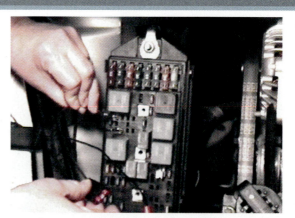

12 To check to see if the electric fuel pump can be operated from the relay contacts, use a fused jumper wire and touch the relay contacts that correspond to terminals 30 and 87 of the relay.

13 Connect the leads of the meter to contacts 30 and 87 of the relay socket. The reading of 4.7 amperes is okay because the specification is 4 to 8 amperes.

14 Set the meter to read ohms (Ω) and measure the resistance of the relay coil. The usual reading for most relays is between 60 and 100 ohms.

15 Measure between terminal 30 and 87a. Terminal 87a is the normally closed contact, and there should be little, if any, resistance between these two terminals, as shown.

16 To test the normally open contacts, connect one meter lead to terminal 30 and the other lead to terminal 87. The ohmmeter should show an open circuit by displaying OL.

17 Connect a fused jumper wire to supply 12 volts to terminal 86 and a ground to terminal 85 of the relay. If the relay clicks, then the relay coil is able to move the armature (movable arm) of the relay.

18 After testing, be sure to reinstall the relay and the relay cover.

FUEL INJECTOR CLEANING

1 Start the fuel injector cleaning process by bringing the vehicle's engine up to operating temperature. Shut off the engine, remove the cap from the fuel rail test port, and install the appropriate adapter.

2 The vehicle's fuel pump is disabled by removing its relay or fuse. In some cases, it may be necessary to disconnect the fuel pump at the tank if the relay or fuse powers more than just the pump.

3 Turn the outlet valve of the canister to the OFF or CLOSED position.

4 Remove the fuel injector cleaning canister's top and regulator assembly. Note that there is an O-ring seal located here that must be in place for the canister's top to seal properly.

5 Pour the injection system cleaning fluid into the open canister. Rubber gloves are highly recommended for this step as the fluid is toxic.

6 Replace the canister's top (making sure it is tight) and connect its hose to the fuel rail adapter. Be sure that the hose is routed away from exhaust manifolds and other hazards.

7 Hang the canister from the vehicle's hood and adjust the air pressure regulator to full OPEN position (CCW).

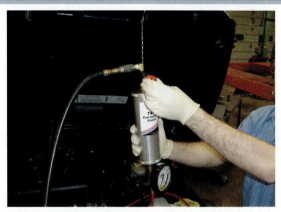

8 Connect shop air to the canister and adjust the air pressure regulator to the desired setting. Canister pressure can be read directly from the gauge.

9 Canister pressure should be adjusted to 5 PSI below system fuel pressure. An alternative for return-type systems is to block the fuel return line to the tank.

10 Open the outlet valve on the canister.

11 Start the vehicle's engine and let run at 1000–1500 RPM. The engine is now running on fuel injector cleaning fluid provided by the canister.

12 Continue the process until the canister is empty and the engine stalls. Remove the cleaning equipment, enable the vehicle's fuel pump, and run the engine to check for leaks.

1. A typical throttle-body fuel injector uses a computer-controlled injector solenoid to spray fuel into the throttle-body unit above the throttle plates.

2. A typical port fuel-injection system uses an individual fuel injector for each cylinder and squirts fuel directly into the intake manifold about 3 inches (80 millimeters) from the intake valve.

3. A typical fuel-injection system fuel pressure should not drop more than 20 PSI in 20 minutes.

4. A noid light can be used to check for the presence of an injector pulse.

5. Injectors can be tested for resistance and should be within 0.3 to 0.4 ohms of each other.

6. Different designs of injectors have a different scope waveform depending on how the computer pulses the injector on and off.

7. An idle air control unit controls idle speed and can be tested for proper operation using a scan tool or scope.

REVIEW QUESTIONS

1. List the ways fuel injectors can be tested.

2. List the steps necessary to test a fuel-pressure regulator.

3. Describe why it may be necessary to clean the throttle plate of a port fuel-injected engine.

CHAPTER QUIZ

1. Most port fuel-injected engines operate on how much fuel pressure?
   a. 3 to 5 PSI (21 to 35 kPa)
   b. 9 to 13 PSI (62 to 90 kPa)
   c. 35 to 45 PSI (240 to 310 kPa)
   d. 55 to 65 PSI (380 to 450 kPa)

2. Fuel injectors can be tested using _____.
   a. An ohmmeter
   b. A stethoscope
   c. A scope
   d. All of the above

3. Throttle-body fuel-injection systems use what type of injector driver?
   a. Peak and hold
   b. Saturated switch
   c. Pulse-width modulated
   d. Pulsed

4. Port fuel-injection systems generally use what type of injector driver?
   a. Peak and hold
   b. Saturated switch
   c. Pulse-width modulated
   d. Pulsed

5. The vacuum hose from the fuel-pressure regulator was removed from the regulator and gasoline dripped out of the hose. Technician A says that is normal and that everything is okay. Technician B says that one or more of the injectors may be defective, causing the fuel to get into the hose. Which technician is correct?
   a. Technician A only
   b. Technician B only
   c. Both Technicians A and B
   d. Neither Technician A nor B

6. The fuel pressure drops rapidly when the engine is turned off. Technician A says that one or more injectors could be leaking. Technician B says that a defective check valve in the fuel pump could be the cause. Which technician is correct?
   a. Technician A only
   b. Technician B only
   c. Both Technicians A and B
   d. Neither Technician A nor B

7. In a typical port fuel-injection system, which injectors are most subject to becoming restricted?
   a. Any of them equally
   b. The injectors at the end of the rail on a returnless system
   c. The injectors at the bends in the rail
   d. Either b or c

8. What component pulses the fuel injector on most vehicles?
   a. Electronic control unit (computer)
   b. Ignition module
   c. Crankshaft sensor
   d. Both b and c

9. Fuel-injection service is being discussed. Technician A says that the throttle plate(s) should be cleaned. Technician B says that the fuel rail should be cleaned. Which technician is correct?
   a. Technician A only
   b. Technician B only
   c. Both Technicians A and B
   d. Neither Technician A nor B

10. If the throttle plate needs to be cleaned, what symptoms will be present regarding the operation of the engine?
    a. Stalls
    b. Rough idle
    c. Hesitation on acceleration
    d. All of the above

After studying Chapter 31, the reader will be able to:

1. Prepare for ASE A8 certification test content area "D" (Emissions Control Systems Diagnosis and Repair) and ASE L1 certification test content area "F" (I/M Failure Diagnosis).

2. Discuss emission standards.

3. Identify the reasons why excessive amounts of HC, CO, and NO_X exhaust emissions are created.

4. Describe how to baseline a vehicle after an exhaust emission failure.

5. List acceptable levels of HC, CO, CO_2, and O_2 with and without a catalytic converter.

6. List four possible causes for high readings for HC, CO, and NO_X.

Acceleration simulation mode (ASM) 481

ASM 25/25 test 482

ASM 50/15 test 481

Federal Test Procedure (FTP) 480

I/M 240 test 482

Lean indicator 485

Non-methane hydrocarbon (NMHC) 484

Ozone 487

Rich indicator 485

Sealed Housing for Evaporative Determination (SHED) test 480

Smog 487

State Implementation Plan (SIP) 480

EMISSION STANDARDS IN THE UNITED STATES

In the United States, emissions standards are managed by the Environmental Protection Agency (EPA) as well as some U.S. state governments. Some of the strictest standards in the world are formulated in California by the California Air Resources Board (CARB).

TIER 1 AND TIER 2

Federal emission standards are set by the clean air act amendments (CAAA) of 1990 grouped by tier. All vehicles sold in the United States must meet Tier 1 standards that went into effect in 1994 and are the least stringent. Additional Tier 2 standards have been optional since 2001, and are currently being phased-in to be fully adopted by 2009. The current Tier 1 standards are different between automobiles and light trucks (SUVs, pickup trucks, and minivans), but Tier 2 standards will be the same for both types.

There are several ratings that can be given to vehicles, and a certain percentage of a manufacturer's vehicles must meet different levels in order for the company to sell its products in affected regions. Beyond Tier 1, and in order by stringency, are the following levels:

- **TLEV Transitional Low-Emission Vehicle.** More stringent for HC than Tier 1.

- **LEV:** (also known as: **LEV I**) **Low-Emission Vehicle,** an intermediate California standard about twice as stringent as Tier 1 for HC and NO_X.

- **ULEV** (also known as **ULEV I**): **Ultra-Low-Emission Vehicle.** A stronger California standard emphasizing very low HC emissions.

- **ULEV II: Ultra-Low-Emission Vehicle.** A cleaner-than-average vehicle certified under the Phase II LEV standard. Hydrocarbon and carbon monoxide emissions levels are nearly 50% lower than those of a LEV II-certified vehicle.
  ● **SEE FIGURE 31–1.**

- **SULEV: Super-Ultra-Low-Emission Vehicle.** A California standard even tighter than ULEV, including much lower HC and NO_X emissions; roughly equivalent to Tier 2 Bin 2 vehicles.

- **ZEV: Zero-Emission Vehicle.** A California standard prohibiting any tailpipe emissions. The ZEV category is largely restricted to electric vehicles and hydrogen-fueled vehicles. In these cases, any emissions that are created are produced at another site, such as a power plant or hydrogen reforming center, unless such sites run on renewable energy.

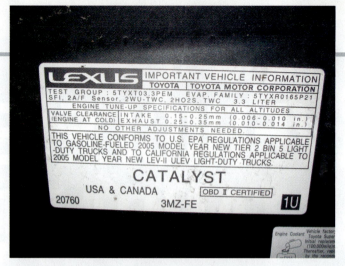

FIGURE 31–1 The underhood decal showing that this Lexus RX-330 meets both national (Tier 2; BIN 5) and California LEV-II (ULEV) regulation standards.

NOTE: A battery-powered electric vehicle charged from the power grid will still be up to 10 times cleaner than even the cleanest gasoline vehicles over their respective lifetimes.

- **PZEV: Partial Zero-Emission Vehicle.** Compliant with the SULEV standard; additionally has near-zero evaporative emissions and a 15-year/150,000-mile warranty on its emission control equipment.

Tier 2 standards are even more stringent. Tier 2 variations are appended with "II," such as LEV II or SULEV II. Other categories have also been created:

- **ILEV: Inherently Low-Emission Vehicle**

- **AT-PZEV: Advanced Technology Partial Zero-Emission Vehicle.** If a vehicle meets the PZEV standards and is using high-technology features, such as an electric motor or high-pressure gaseous fuel tanks for compressed natural gas, it qualifies as an AT-PZEV. Hybrid electric vehicles such as the Toyota Prius can qualify, as can internal combustion engine vehicles that run on natural gas (CNG), such as the Honda Civic GX. These vehicles are classified as "partial" ZEV because they receive partial credit for the number of ZEV vehicles that automakers would otherwise be required to sell in California.

- **NLEV: National Low-Emission Vehicle.** All vehicles nationwide must meet this standard, which started in 2001.

FEDERAL EPA BIN NUMBER

The higher the tier number, the newer the regulation; the lower the bin number, the cleaner the vehicle. The Toyota Prius is a very clean Bin 3, while the Hummer H2 is a dirty Bin 11. ● **SEE CHARTS 31–1, 31–2, AND 31–3.**

CERTIFICATION LEVEL	NMOG (G/MI)	CO (G/MI)	NO$_X$ (G/MI)
Bin 1	0.0	0.0	0.0
Bin 2	0.010	2.1	0.02
Bin 3	0.055	2.1	0.03
Bin 4	0.070	2.1	0.04
Bin 5	0.090	4.2	0.07
Bin 6	0.090	4.2	0.10
Bin 7	0.090	4.2	0.15
Bin 8a	0.125	4.2	0.20
Bin 8b	0.156	4.2	0.20
Bin 9a	0.090	4.2	0.30
Bin 9b	0.130	4.2	0.30
Bin 9c	0.180	4.2	0.30
Bin 10a	0.156	4.2	0.60
Bin 10b	0.230	6.4	0.60
Bin 10c	0.230	6.4	0.60
Bin 11	0.230	7.3	0.90

CHART 31–1

EPA Tier 2—120,000-Mile Tailpipe Emission Limits. After January 2007, the highest allowable Bin is 7.
Source: Data compiled from the Environmental Protection Agency EPA).
Note: The bin number is determined by the type and weight of the vehicle.

U.S. EPA VEHICLE INFORMATION PROGRAM (THE HIGHER THE SCORE, THE LOWER THE EMISSIONS)	
SELECTED EMISSIONS STANDARDS	SCORE
Bin 1 and ZEV	10
PZEV	9.5
Bin 2	9
Bin 3	8
Bin 4	7
Bin 5 and LEV II cars	6
Bin 6	5
Bin 7	4
Bin 8	3
Bin 9a and LEV I cars	2
Bin 9b	2
Bin 10a	1
Bin 10b and Tier 1 cars	1
Bin 11	0

CHART 31–2

Air Pollution Score
Source: Courtesy of the Environmental Protection Agency (EPA).

MINIMUM FUEL ECONOMY (MPG) COMBINED CITY-HIGHWAY LABEL VALUE					
SCORE	GASOLINE	DIESEL	E-85	LPG	CNG*
10	44	50	31	28	33
9	36	41	26	23	27
8	30	35	22	20	23
7	26	30	19	17	20
6	23	27	17	15	18
5	21	24	15	14	16
4	19	22	14	12	14
3	17	20	12	11	13
2	16	18	—	—	12
1	15	17	11	10	11
0	14	16	10	9	10

CHART 31–3

Greenhouse Gas Score
Source: Courtesy of the Environmental Protection Agency (EPA).
*CNG assumes a gallon equivalent of 121.5 cubic feet.

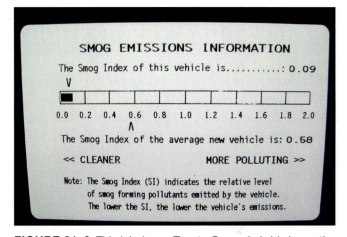

FIGURE 31–2 This label on a Toyota Camry hybrid shows the relative smog-producing emissions, but this does not include carbon dioxide (CO_2), which may increase global warming.

SMOG EMISSION INFORMATION New vehicles are equipped with a sticker that shows the relative level of smog-causing emissions created by the vehicle compared to others on the market. Smog-causing emissions include unburned hydrocarbons (HC) and oxides of nitrogen (NO$_X$). ● **SEE FIGURE 31–2.**

CALIFORNIA STANDARDS The pre-2004 California Air Resources Board (CARB) standards as a whole were known as LEV I. Within that, there were four possible ratings: Tier 1, TLEV, LEV, and ULEV. The newest CARB rating system (since January 1, 2004) is known as LEV II. Within that rating system there are three primary ratings: LEV, ULEV, and SULEV. States other than California are given the option to use the federal EPA standards, or they can adopt California's standards.

EUROPEAN STANDARDS

Europe has its own set of standards that vehicles must meet, which includes the following tiers:

- Euro I (1992–1995)
- Euro II (1995–1999)
- Euro III (1999–2005)
- Euro IV (2005–2008)
- Euro V (2008+)

Vehicle emission standards and technological advancements have successfully reduced pollution from cars and trucks by about 90% since the 1970s. Unfortunately, there currently are more vehicles on the road and they are being driven more miles each year, partially offsetting the environmental benefits of individual vehicle emissions reductions.

FIGURE 31–3 Photo of a sign taken at an emissions test facility.

EXHAUST ANALYSIS TESTING

The Clean Air Act Amendments require enhanced I/M programs in areas of the country that have the worst air quality and the Northeast Ozone Transport region. The states must submit to the EPA a **State Implementation Plan (SIP)** for their programs. Each enhanced I/M program is required to include as a minimum the following items:

- Computerized emission analyzers
- Visual inspection of emission control items
- Minimum waiver limit (to be increased based on the inflation index)
- Remote on-road testing of one-half of 1% of the vehicle population
- Registration denial for vehicles not passing an I/M test
- Denial of waiver for vehicles that are under warranty or that have been tampered with
- Annual inspections
- OBD-II systems check for 1996 and newer vehicles

FEDERAL TEST PROCEDURE (FTP) The **Federal Test Procedure (FTP)** is the test used to certify all new vehicles before they can be sold. Once a vehicle meets these standards, it is certified by the EPA for sale in the United States. The FTP test procedure is a loaded-mode test lasting for a total duration of 505 seconds and is designed to simulate an urban driving trip. A cold start-up representing a morning start and a hot start after a soak period is part of the test. In addition to this drive cycle, a vehicle must undergo evaporative testing. Evaporative emissions are determined using the **Sealed Housing for Evaporative Determination (SHED)** test, which measures the evaporative emissions from the vehicle after a heat-up period representing a vehicle sitting in the sun. In addition, the vehicle is driven and then tested during the hot soak period.

NOTE: A SHED is constructed entirely of stainless steel. The walls, floors, and ceiling, plus the door, are all constructed of stainless steel because it does not absorb hydrocarbons, which could offset test results.

The FTP is a much more stringent test of vehicle emissions than is any test type that uses equipment that measures percentages of exhaust gases. The federal emission standards for each model year vehicle are the same for that model regardless of what size engine the vehicle is equipped with. This is why larger V-8 engines often are equipped with more emission control devices than smaller four- and six-cylinder engines.

I/M TEST PROGRAMS There are a variety of I/M testing programs that have been implemented by the various states. These programs may be centralized testing programs or decentralized testing programs. Each state is free to develop a testing program suitable to their needs as long as they can demonstrate to the EPA that their plan will achieve the attainment levels set by the EPA. This approach has led to a variety of different testing programs. ● SEE FIGURE 31–3.

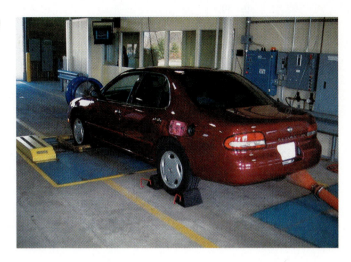

FIGURE 31–4 A vehicle being tested during an enhanced emission test.

VISUAL TAMPERING CHECKS Visual tampering checks may be part of an I/M testing program and usually include checking for the following items:

- Catalytic converter
- Fuel tank inlet restrictor
- Exhaust gas recirculation (EGR)
- Evaporative emission system
- Air-injection reaction system (AIR)
- Positive crankcase ventilation (PCV)

If any of these systems are missing, not connected, or tampered with, the vehicle will fail the emissions test and will have to be repaired/replaced by the vehicle owner before the vehicle can pass the emission test. Any cost associated with repairing or replacing these components may not be used toward the waiver amount required for the vehicle to receive a waiver.

ONE-SPEED AND TWO-SPEED IDLE TEST The one-speed and two-speed idle test measures the exhaust emissions from the tailpipe of the vehicle at idle and/or at 2500 RPM. This uses stand-alone exhaust gas sampling equipment that measures the emissions in percentages. Each state chooses the standards that the vehicle has to meet in order to pass the test. The advantage to using this type of testing is that the equipment is relatively cheap and allows states to have decentralized testing programs because many facilities can afford the necessary equipment required to perform this test.

LOADED MODE TEST The loaded mode test uses a dynamometer that places a "single weight" load on the vehicle. The load applied to the vehicle varies with the speed of the vehicle. Typically, a four-cylinder vehicle speed would be 24 mph, a six-cylinder vehicle speed would be 30 mph, and an eight-cylinder vehicle speed would be 34 mph. Conventional stand-alone sampling equipment is used to measure HC and CO emissions. This type of test is classified as a Basic I/M test by the EPA. ● **SEE FIGURE 31–4.**

ACCELERATION SIMULATION MODE (ASM) The **ASM-type** of test uses a dynamometer that applies a heavy load on the vehicle at a steady-state speed. The load applied to the vehicle is based on the acceleration rate on the second simulated hill of the FTP. This acceleration rate is 3.3 mph/sec/sec (read as 3.3 mph per second per second, which is the unit of acceleration). There are different ASM tests used by different states.

The **ASM 50/15** test places a load of 50% on the vehicle at a steady 15 mph. This load represents 50% of the horsepower required to simulate the FTP acceleration rate of 3.3 mph/sec. This type of test produces relatively high levels of NO_X emissions; therefore, it is useful in detecting vehicles that are emitting excessive NO_X.

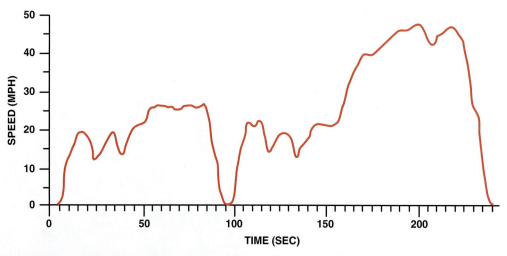

FIGURE 31–5 Trace showing the Inspection/Maintenance 240 test. The test duplicates an urban test loop around Los Angeles, California. The first "hump" in the curve represents the vehicle being accelerated to about 20 mph, then driving up a small hill to about 30 mph and coming to a stop. At about 94 seconds, the vehicle stops and again accelerates while climbing a hill and speeding up to about 50 mph during this second phase of the test.

EXHAUST ANALYSIS TESTING (CONTINUED)

The **ASM 25/25** test places a 25% load on the vehicle while it is driven at a steady 25 mph. This represents 25% of the load required to simulate the FTP acceleration rate of 3.3 mph/sec. Because this applies a smaller load on the vehicle at a higher speed, it will produce a higher level of HC and CO emissions than the ASM 50/15. NO_x emissions will tend to be lower with this type of test.

I/M 240 TEST

The **I/M 240** test is the EPA's enhanced test. It is actually a portion of the 505-second FTP test used by the manufacturers to certify their new vehicles. The "240" stands for 240 seconds of drive time on a dynamometer. This is a loaded-mode transient test that uses constant volume sampling equipment to measure the exhaust emissions in mass just as is done during the FTP. The I/M 240 test simulates the first two hills of the FTP drive cycle. ● **FIGURE 31–5** shows the I/M 240 drive trace.

OBD-II TESTING

In 1999, the EPA requested that states adopt OBD-II systems testing for 1996 and newer vehicles. The OBD-II system is designed to illuminate the MIL light and store trouble codes any time a malfunction exists that would cause the vehicle emissions to exceed 1 1/2 times the FTP limits. If the OBD-II system is working correctly, the system should be able to detect a vehicle failure that would cause emissions to increase to an unacceptable level. The EPA has determined that the OBD-II system should detect emission failures of a vehicle even before that vehicle would fail an emissions test of the type that most states are employing. Furthermore, the EPA has determined that, as the population of OBD-II-equipped vehicles increases and the population of older non-OBD-II-equipped vehicles decreases, tailpipe testing will no longer be necessary.

The OBD-II testing program consists of a computer that can scan the vehicle OBD-II system using the DLC connector. The technician first performs a visual check of the vehicle MIL light to determine if it is working correctly. Next, the computer is connected to the vehicle's DLC connector. The computer will scan the vehicle OBD-II system and determine if there are any codes stored that are commanding the MIL light on. In addition, it will scan the status of the readiness monitors and determine if they have all run and passed. If the readiness monitors have all run and passed, it indicates that the OBD-II system has tested all the components of the emission control system. An OBD-II vehicle would fail this OBD-II test if:

- The MIL light does not come on with the key on, engine off
- The MIL is commanded on
- A number (varies by state) of the readiness monitors have not been run

If none of these conditions are present, the vehicle will pass the emissions test.

FIGURE 31–6 A partial stream sampling exhaust probe being used to measure exhaust gases in parts per million (PPM) or percent (%).

REMOTE SENSING The EPA requires that, in high-enhanced areas, states perform on-the-road testing of vehicle emissions. The state must sample 0.5% of the vehicle population base in high-enhanced areas. This may be accomplished by using a remote sensing device. This type of sensing may be done through equipment that projects an infrared light through the exhaust stream of a passing vehicle. The reflected beam can then be analyzed to determine the pollutant levels coming from the vehicle. If a vehicle fails this type of test, the vehicle owner will receive notification in the mail that he or she must take the vehicle to a test facility to have the emissions tested.

RANDOM ROADSIDE TESTING Some states may implement random roadside testing that would usually involve visual checks of the emission control devices to detect tampering. Obviously, this method is not very popular as it can lead to traffic tie-ups and delays on the part of commuters.

Exhaust analysis is an excellent tool to use for the diagnosis of engine performance concerns. In areas of the country that require exhaust testing to be able to get license plates, exhaust analysis must be able to:

- Establish a baseline for failure diagnosis and service.
- Identify areas of engine performance that are and are not functioning correctly.
- Determine that the service and repair of the vehicle have been accomplished and are complete.

EXHAUST ANALYSIS AND COMBUSTION EFFICIENCY

A popular method of engine analysis, as well as emission testing, involves the use of five-gas exhaust analysis equipment. ● **SEE FIGURE 31–6.** The five gases analyzed and their significance include:

HYDROCARBONS Hydrocarbons (HC) are unburned gasoline and are measured in parts per million (ppm). A correctly operating engine should burn (oxidize) almost all the gasoline; therefore, very little unburned gasoline should be present in the exhaust. Acceptable levels of HC are 50 PPM or less. High levels of HC could be due to excessive oil consumption caused by weak piston rings or worn valve guides. The most common cause of excessive HC emissions is a fault in the ignition system. Items that should be checked include:

- Spark plugs
- Spark plug wires
- Distributor cap and rotor (if the vehicle is so equipped)
- Ignition timing (if possible)
- Ignition coil

CARBON MONOXIDE Carbon monoxide (CO) is unstable and will easily combine with any oxygen to form stable carbon dioxide (CO_2). The fact that CO combines with oxygen is the reason that CO is a poisonous gas (in the lungs, it combines

What Does NMHC Mean?

NMHC means **non-methane hydrocarbon** and it is the standard by which exhaust emission testing for hydrocarbons is evaluated. Methane is natural gas and can come from animals, animal waste, and other natural sources. By not measuring methane gas, all background sources are eliminated, giving better results as to the true amount of unburned hydrocarbons that are present in the exhaust stream.

with oxygen to form CO_2 and deprives the brain of oxygen). CO levels of a properly operating engine should be less than 0.5%. High levels of CO can be caused by clogged or restricted crankcase ventilation devices such as the PCV valve, hose(s), and tubes. Other items that might cause excessive CO include:

- Clogged air filter
- Incorrect idle speed
- Too-high fuel-pump pressure
- Any other items that can cause a rich condition

CARBON DIOXIDE (CO_2)
Carbon dioxide (CO_2) is the result of oxygen in the engine combining with the carbon of the gasoline. An acceptable level of CO_2 is between 12% and 15%. A high reading indicates an efficiently operating engine. If the CO_2 level is low, the mixture may be either too rich or too lean.

OXYGEN
The next gas is oxygen (O_2). There is about 21% oxygen in the atmosphere, and most of this oxygen should be "used up" during the combustion process to oxidize all the hydrogen and carbon (hydrocarbons) in the gasoline. Levels of O_2 should be very low (about 0.5%). High levels of O_2, especially at idle, could be due to an exhaust system leak.

NOTE: Adding 10% alcohol to gasoline provides additional oxygen to the fuel and will result in lower levels of CO and higher levels of O_2 in the exhaust.

OXIDES OF NITROGEN (NO_X)
An oxide of nitrogen (NO) is a colorless, tasteless, and odorless gas when it leaves the engine, but as soon as it reaches the atmosphere and mixes with more oxygen, nitrogen oxides (NO_2) are formed. NO_2 is reddish-brown and has an acid and pungent smell. NO and NO_2 are

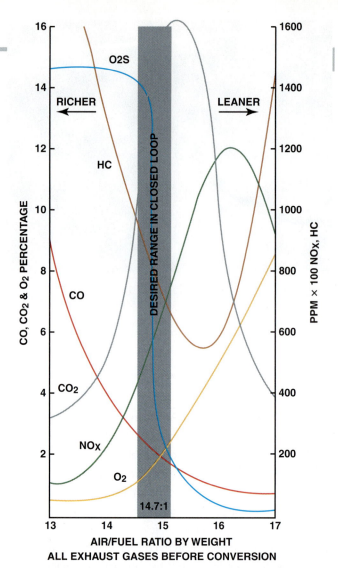

FIGURE 31–7 Exhaust emissions are very complex. When the air–fuel mixture becomes richer, some exhaust emissions are reduced, while others increase.

grouped together and referred to as NO_X, where x represents any number of oxygen atoms. NO_X, the symbol used to represent all oxides of nitrogen, is the fifth gas commonly tested using a five-gas analyzer. The exhaust gas recirculation (EGR) system is the major controlling device limiting the formation of NO_X.

Acceptable exhaust emissions include:

	Without Catalytic Converter	With Catalytic Converter
HC	300 PPM or less	30 to 50 PPM or less
CO	3% or less	0.3% to 0.5% or less
O_2	0% to 2%	0% to 2%
CO_2	12% to 15% or higher	12% to 15% or higher
NO_X	Less than 100 PPM at idle and less than 1,000 PPM at WOT	Less than 100 PPM at idle and less than 1,000 PPM at WOT

● **SEE FIGURE 31–7.**

How Can My Worn-Out, Old, High-Mileage Vehicle Pass an Exhaust Emission Test?

Age and mileage of a vehicle are generally not factors when it comes to passing an exhaust emission test. Regular maintenance is the most important factor for passing an enhanced Inspection and Maintenance (I/M) exhaust analysis test. Failure of the vehicle owner to replace broken accessory drive belts, leaking air pump tubes, defective spark plug wires, or a cracked exhaust manifold can lead to failure of other components such as the catalytic converter. Tests have shown that if the vehicle is properly cared for, even an engine that has 300,000 miles (483,000 km) can pass an exhaust emission test.

HC TOO HIGH

High hydrocarbon exhaust emissions are usually caused by an engine misfire. What burns the fuel in an engine? The ignition system ignites a spark at the spark plug to ignite the *proper* mixture inside the combustion chamber. If a spark plug does not ignite the mixture, the resulting unburned fuel is pushed out of the cylinder on the exhaust stroke by the piston through the exhaust valves and into the exhaust system. Therefore, if any of the following ignition components or adjustments are not correct, excessive HC emission is likely.

1. Defective or worn spark plugs
2. Defective or loose spark plug wires
3. Defective distributor cap and/or rotor
4. Incorrect ignition timing (either too far advanced or too far retarded)
5. A lean air–fuel mixture can also cause a misfire. This condition is referred to as a lean misfire. A lean air-fuel mixture can be caused by low fuel pump pressure, a clogged fuel filter or a restricted fuel injector.

NOTE: To make discussion easier in future reference to these items, this list of ignition components and checks will be referred to simply as "spark stuff."

CO TOO HIGH

Excessive carbon monoxide is an indication of too rich an air–fuel mixture. CO is the **rich indicator**. The higher the CO reading, the richer the air–fuel mixture. High concentrations of CO indicate that not enough oxygen was available for the amount of fuel. Common causes of high CO include:

- Too-high fuel-pump pressure
- Defective fuel-pressure regulator
- Clogged air filter or PCV valve

NOTE: One technician remembers "CO" as meaning "clogged oxygen" and always looks for restricted airflow into the engine whenever high CO levels are detected.

- Defective injectors

TECH TIP

CO Equals O_2

If the exhaust is rich, CO emissions will be higher than normal. If the exhaust is lean, O_2 emissions will be higher than normal. Therefore, if the CO reading is the same as the O_2 reading, then the engine is operating correctly. For example, if both CO and O_2 are 0.5% and the engine develops a vacuum leak, the O_2 will rise. If a fuel-pressure regulator were to malfunction, the resulting richer air–fuel mixture would increase CO emissions. Therefore, if both the rich indicator (CO) and the lean indicator (O_2) are equal, the engine is operating correctly.

MEASURING OXYGEN (O_2) AND CARBON DIOXIDE (CO_2)

Two gas exhaust analyzers (HC and CO) work well, but both HC and CO are consumed (converted) inside the catalytic converter. The amount of leftover oxygen coming out of the tailpipe is an indication of leanness. The higher the O_2 level, the leaner the exhaust. Oxygen therefore is the **lean indicator.** Acceptable levels of O_2 are 0% to 2%.

NOTE: A hole in the exhaust system can draw outside air (oxygen) into the exhaust system. Therefore, to be assured of an accurate reading, carefully check the exhaust system for leaks. Using a smoke machine is an easy method to locate leaks in the exhaust system.

Carbon dioxide (CO_2) is a measure of efficiency. The higher the level of CO_2 in the exhaust stream, the more efficiently the engine is operating. Levels of 12% to 17% are considered to be acceptable. Because CO_2 levels peak at an air–fuel mixture of 14.7:1, a lower level of CO_2 indicates either a too-rich or a too-lean condition. The CO_2 measurement by itself does not indicate which condition is present. For example:

CO_2 = 8% (This means efficiency is low and the air–fuel mixture is not correct.)

Look at O_2 and CO levels.

A high O_2 indicates lean and a high CO indicates rich.

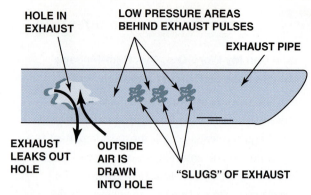

FIGURE 31–8 A hole in the exhaust system can cause outside air (containing oxygen) to be drawn into the exhaust system. This extra oxygen can be confusing to a service technician because the extra O_2 in the exhaust stream could be misinterpreted as a too-lean air–fuel mixture.

TECH TIP

How to Find a Leak in the Exhaust System

A hole in the exhaust system can dilute the exhaust gases with additional oxygen (O_2). ● SEE FIGURE 31–8.

This additional O_2 in the exhaust can lead the service technician to believe that the air–fuel mixture is too lean. To help identify an exhaust leak, perform an exhaust analysis at idle and at 2500 RPM (fast idle) and compare with the following:

- If the O_2 is high at idle and at 2500 RPM, the mixture is lean at both idle and at 2500 RPM.
- If the O_2 is low at idle and high at 2500 RPM, this usually means that the vehicle is equipped with a working AIR pump.
- If the O_2 is high at idle, but okay at 2500 RPM, a hole in the exhaust or a small vacuum leak that is "covered up" at higher speed is indicated.

TECH TIP

Your Nose Knows

Using the nose, a technician can often identify a major problem without having to connect the vehicle to an exhaust analyzer. For example,

- The strong smell of exhaust is due to excessive unburned hydrocarbon (HC) emissions. Look for an ignition system fault that could prevent the proper burning of the fuel. A vacuum leak could also cause a lean misfire and cause excessive HC exhaust emissions.
- If your eyes start to burn or water, suspect excessive oxides of nitrogen (NO_X) emissions. The oxides of nitrogen combine with the moisture in the eyes to form a mild solution of nitric acid. The acid formation causes the eyes to burn and water. Excessive NO_X exhaust emissions can be caused by:
  - A vacuum leak causing higher-than-normal combustion chamber temperature
  - Overadvanced ignition timing causing higher-than-normal combustion chamber temperature
  - Lack of proper amount of exhaust gas recirculation (EGR) (This is usually noticed above idle on most vehicles.)
- Dizzy feeling or headache. This is commonly caused by excessive carbon monoxide (CO) exhaust emissions. Get into fresh air as soon as possible. A probable cause of high levels of CO is an excessively rich air–fuel mixture.

PHOTOCHEMICAL SMOG FORMATION

Oxides of nitrogen are formed by high temperature—over 2500°F (1370°C)—and/or pressures inside the combustion chamber. Oxides of nitrogen contribute to the formation of photochemical **smog** when sunlight reacts chemically with NO_X and unburned hydrocarbons (HC). Smog is a term derived by combining the words *smoke* and *fog*. Ground-level ozone is a constituent of smog. **Ozone** is an enriched oxygen molecule with three atoms of oxygen (O_3) instead of the normal two atoms of oxygen (O_2).

Ozone in the upper atmosphere is beneficial because it blocks out harmful ultraviolet rays that contribute to skin cancer. However, at ground level, this ozone (smog) is an irritant to the respiratory system.

TESTING FOR OXIDES OF NITROGEN

Because the formation of NO_X occurs mostly under load, the most efficient method to test for NO_X is to use a portable exhaust analyzer that can be carried in the vehicle while the vehicle is being driven under a variety of conditions.

SPECIFICATIONS FOR NO_X From experience, a maximum reading of 1,000 parts per million (PPM) of NO_X under loaded driving conditions will generally mean that the vehicle will pass an enhanced I/M roller test. A reading of over 100 PPM at idle should be considered excessive.

TECH TIP

Check for Dog Food?

A commonly experienced problem in many parts of the country involves squirrels or other animals placing dog food into the air intake ducts of vehicles. Dog food is often found packed tight in the ducts against the air filter. An air intake restriction occurs and drives the fuel mixture richer than normal and reduces engine power and vehicle performance as well as creating high CO exhaust emissions.

REAL WORLD FIX

The Case of the Retarded Exhaust Camshaft

A Toyota equipped with a double overhead camshaft (DOHC) inline six-cylinder engine failed the state-mandated enhanced exhaust emission test for NO_X. The engine ran perfectly without spark knocking (ping), which is usually a major reason for excessive NO_X emissions. The technician checked the following:

- The ignition timing, which was found to be set to specifications (if too far advanced, can cause excessive NO_X)
- The cylinders, which were decarbonized using top engine cleaner
- The EGR valve, which was inspected and the EGR passages cleaned

After all the items were completed, the vehicle was returned to the inspection station where the vehicle again failed for excessive NO_X emissions (better, but still over the maximum allowable limit).

After additional hours of troubleshooting, the technician decided to go back to basics and start over again. A check of the vehicle history with the owner indicated that the only previous work performed on the engine was a replacement timing belt over a year before. The technician discovered that the exhaust cam timing was retarded two teeth, resulting in late closing of the exhaust valve. The proper exhaust valve timing resulted in a slight amount of exhaust being retained in the cylinder. This extra exhaust was added to the amount supplied by the EGR valve and helped reduce NO_X emissions. After repositioning the timing belt, the vehicle passed the emissions test well within the limits.

Exhaust Gas Summary Chart

Gas	Cause and Correction
High HC	Engine misfire or incomplete burning of fuel caused by: 1. Ignition system fault 2. Lean misfire 3. Too low an engine temperature (thermostat)
High CO	Rich condition caused by: 1. Leaking fuel injectors or fuel-pressure regulator 2. Clogged air filter or PCV system 3. Excessive fuel pressure
High HC and CO	Excessively rich condition caused by: 1. All items included under high CO 2. Fouled spark plugs causing a misfire to occur 3. Possible nonoperating catalytic converter
High NO$_X$	Excessive combustion chamber temperature: 1. Nonoperating EGR valve 2. Clogged EGR passages 3. Engine operating temperature too high due to cooling system restriction, worn water pump impeller, or other faults in the cooling system 4. Lean air–fuel mixture 5. High compression caused by excessive carbon buildup in the cylinders

REAL WORLD FIX

O2S Shows Rich, but Pulse Width Is Low

A service technician was attempting to solve a drive-ability problem. The computer did not indicate any diagnostic trouble codes (DTCs). A check of the oxygen sensor voltage indicated a higher-than-normal reading almost all the time. The pulse width to the port injectors was lower than normal. The lower-than-normal pulse width indicates that the computer is attempting to reduce fuel flow into the engine by decreasing the amount of on-time for all the injectors.

What could cause a rich mixture if the injectors were being commanded to deliver a lean mixture? Finally the technician shut off the engine and took a careful look at the entire fuel-injection system. Although the vacuum hose was removed from the fuel-pressure regulator, fuel was found dripping from the vacuum hose. The problem was a defective fuel-pressure regulator that allowed an uncontrolled amount of fuel to be drawn by the intake manifold vacuum into the cylinders. While the computer tried to reduce fuel by reducing the pulse width signal to the injectors, the extra fuel being drawn directly from the fuel rail caused the engine to operate with too rich an air–fuel mixture.

SUMMARY

1. Excessive hydrocarbon (HC) exhaust emissions are created by a lack of proper combustion such as a fault in the ignition system, too lean an air–fuel mixture, or too-cold engine operation.

2. Excessive carbon monoxide (CO) exhaust emissions are usually created by a rich air–fuel mixture.

3. Excessive oxides of nitrogen (NO$_X$) exhaust emissions are usually created by excessive heat or pressure in the combustion chamber or a lack of the proper amount of exhaust gas recirculation (EGR).

4. Carbon dioxide (CO$_2$) levels indicate efficiency. The higher the CO$_2$, the more efficient the engine operation.

5. Oxygen (O$_2$) indicates leanness. The higher the O$_2$, the leaner the air–fuel mixture.

6. A vehicle should be driven about 20 miles, especially during cold weather, to allow the engine to be fully warm before an enhanced emissions test.

REVIEW QUESTIONS

1. List the five exhaust gases and their maximum allowable readings for a fuel-injected vehicle equipped with a catalytic converter.

2. List two causes of a rich exhaust.

3. List two causes of a lean exhaust.

4. List those items that should be checked if a vehicle fails an exhaust test for excessive NO$_X$ emissions.

1. Technician A says that high HC emission levels are often caused by a fault in the ignition system. Technician B says that high CO_2 emissions are usually caused by a richer-than-normal air–fuel mixture. Which technician is correct?
   a. Technician A only
   b. Technician B only
   c. Both Technicians A and B
   d. Neither Technician A nor B

2. HC and CO are high and CO_2 and O_2 are low. This could be caused by a _____.
   a. Rich mixture
   b. Lean mixture
   c. Defective ignition component
   d. Clogged EGR passage

3. Which gas is generally considered to be the rich indicator? (The higher the level of this gas, the richer the air–fuel mixture.)
   a. HC   c. CO_2
   b. CO   d. O_2

4. Which gas is generally considered to be the lean indicator? (The higher the level of this gas, the leaner the air–fuel mixture.)
   a. HC   c. CO_2
   b. CO   d. O_2

5. Which exhaust gas indicates efficiency? (The higher the level of this gas, the more efficient the engine operates.)
   a. HC   c. CO_2
   b. CO   d. O_2

6. All of the gases are measured in percentages *except* _____.
   a. HC   c. CO_2
   b. CO   d. O_2

7. After the following exhaust emissions were measured, how was the engine operating?
   HC = 766 PPM CO_2 = 8.2%   CO = 4.6% O_2 = 0.1%
   a. Too rich
   b. Too lean

8. Technician A says that carbon inside the engine can cause excessive NO_X to form. Technician B says that excessive NO_X could be caused by a cooling system fault causing the engine to operate too hot. Which technician is correct?
   a. Technician A only
   b. Technician B only
   c. Both Technicians A and B
   d. Neither Technician A nor B

9. A clogged EGR passage could cause excessive _____ exhaust emissions.
   a. HC   c. NO_X
   b. CO   d. CO_2

10. An ignition fault could cause excessive _____ exhaust emissions.
   a. HC   c. NO_X
   b. CO   d. CO_2

chapter 32

EMISSION CONTROL DEVICES OPERATION AND DIAGNOSIS

FIGURE 32–1 Notice the reddish-brown haze caused by nitrogen oxides that is often over many major cities.

SMOG

The common term used to describe air pollution is *smog*, a word that combines the two words *smoke* and *fog*. Smog is formed in the atmosphere when sunlight combines with unburned fuel (hydrocarbon, or HC) and oxides of nitrogen (NO_X) produced during the combustion process inside the cylinders of an engine. Smog is ground-level ozone (O_3), a strong irritant to the lungs and eyes.

NOTE: Although upper-atmospheric ozone is desirable because it blocks out harmful ultraviolet rays from the sun, ground-level ozone is considered to be unhealthy smog.

- **HC (unburned hydrocarbons).** Excessive HC emissions (unburned fuel) are controlled by the evaporative system (charcoal canister), the positive crankcase ventilation (PCV) system, the air-pump system, and the catalytic converter.

- **CO (carbon monoxide).** Excessive CO emissions are controlled by the PCV system, the air-pump system, and the catalytic converter.

- **NO_X (oxides of nitrogen).** Excessive NO_X emissions are controlled by the exhaust gas recirculation (EGR) system and the catalytic converter. An oxide of nitrogen (NO) is a colorless, tasteless, and odorless gas when it leaves the engine, but as soon as it reaches the atmosphere and mixes with more oxygen, nitrogen oxides (NO_2) are formed, which appear as reddish-brown. ● SEE FIGURE 32–1.

EXHAUST GAS RECIRCULATION SYSTEMS

Exhaust gas recirculation (EGR) is an emission control that lowers the amount of **nitrogen oxides (NO_X)** formed during combustion. In the presence of sunlight, NO_X reacts with hydrocarbons in the atmosphere to form ozone (O_3) or photochemical smog, an air pollutant.

NO_X FORMATION   Nitrogen N_2 and oxygen O_2 molecules are separated into individual atoms of nitrogen and oxygen during the combustion process. These then bond to form NO_X (NO, NO_2). When combustion flame-front temperatures exceed 2500°F (1370°C), NO_X formation increases dramatically.

CONTROLLING NO_X   To handle the NO_X generated above 2500°F (1370°C), the most efficient methods to meet NO_X emissions without significantly affecting engine performance, fuel economy, and other exhaust emissions is to use exhaust gas recirculation. The EGR system routes small quantities, usually between 6% and 10%, of exhaust gas into the intake manifold. Here, the exhaust gas mixes with and takes the place of some of the intake charge. This leaves less room for the intake charge to enter the combustion chamber. The recirculated exhaust gas is **inert** (chemically inactive) and does not enter into the combustion process. The result is a lower peak combustion temperature. As the combustion temperature is lowered, the production of oxides of nitrogen is also reduced.

The EGR system has some means of interconnecting the exhaust and intake manifolds. ● **SEE FIGURES 32–2 AND 32–3.** The interconnecting passage is controlled by the EGR valve. On V-type engines, the intake manifold crossover is used as a source of exhaust gas for the EGR system. A cast passage connects the exhaust crossover to the EGR valve. The gas is sent from the EGR valve to openings in the manifold. On inline-type engines, an external tube is generally used to carry exhaust gas to the EGR valve. This tube is often designed to be long so that the exhaust gas is cooled before it enters the EGR valve.

NOTE: The amount of EGR is subtracted from the mass airflow calculations. While the EGR gases do occupy space, they do not affect the air–fuel mixture.

EGR SYSTEM OPERATION   Since small amounts of exhaust are all that is needed to lower peak combustion temperatures, the orifice that the exhaust passes through is small. Because combustion temperatures are low, EGR is usually *not*

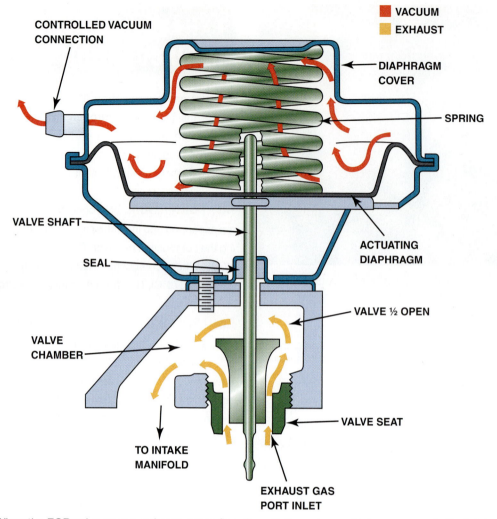

CONTROLLED VACUUM CONNECTION

VACUUM
EXHAUST

DIAPHRAGM COVER

SPRING

VALVE SHAFT

ACTUATING DIAPHRAGM

SEAL

VALVE ½ OPEN

VALVE CHAMBER

VALVE SEAT

TO INTAKE MANIFOLD

EXHAUST GAS PORT INLET

FIGURE 32–2 When the EGR valve opens, exhaust gases flow through the valve and into passages in the intake manifold.

FIGURE 32–3 A vacuum-operated EGR valve. The vacuum to the EGR valve is computer controlled by the EGR valve control solenoid.

required during the following conditions because the combustion temperatures are low.

- Idle speed
- When the engine is cold
- At wide-open throttle (WOT)

The level of NO_X emission changes according to engine speed, temperature, and load. EGR is not used at wide-open throttle (WOT) because it would reduce engine performance and the engine does not operate under these conditions for a long period of time.

In addition to lowering NO_X levels, the EGR system also helps control detonation. Detonation, or ping, occurs when high pressure and heat cause the air–fuel mixture to ignite. This uncontrolled combustion can severely damage the engine.

Using the EGR system allows for greater ignition timing advance and for the advance to occur sooner without detonation problems, which increases power and efficiency.

POSITIVE AND NEGATIVE BACKPRESSURE EGR VALVES

Some EGR valves used on older engines are designed with a small valve inside that bleeds off any applied vacuum and prevents the valve from opening. These types of EGR valves require a positive backpressure in the exhaust system. This is called a **positive backpressure** EGR valve. At low engine speeds and light engine loads, the EGR system is not needed, and the backpressure in it is also low. Without sufficient backpressure, the EGR valve does not open even though vacuum may be present at the EGR valve.

On each exhaust stroke, the engine emits an exhaust "pulse." Each pulse represents a positive pressure. Behind each pulse is a small area of low pressure. Some EGR valves react to this low pressure area by closing a small internal valve, which allows the EGR valve to be opened by vacuum. This type of EGR valve is called a **negative backpressure** EGR valve. The following conditions must occur:

1. Vacuum must be applied to the EGR valve itself. This is usually ported vacuum on some TBI fuel-injected systems. The vacuum source is often manifold vacuum and is controlled by the computer through a solenoid valve.

2. Exhaust backpressure must be present to close an internal valve inside the EGR to allow the vacuum to move the diaphragm.

NOTE: The installation of a low-restriction exhaust system could prevent the proper operation of the backpressure-controlled EGR valve.

FIGURE 32–4 An EGR valve position sensor on top of an EGR valve.

COMPUTER-CONTROLLED EGR SYSTEMS

Many computer-controlled EGR systems have one or more solenoids controlling the EGR vacuum. The computer controls a solenoid to shut off vacuum to the EGR valve at cold engine temperatures, idle speed, and wide-open throttle operation. If two solenoids are used, one acts as an off/on control of supply vacuum, while the second solenoid vents vacuum when EGR flow is not desired or needs to be reduced. The second solenoid is used to control a vacuum air bleed, allowing atmospheric pressure in to modulate EGR flow according to vehicle operating conditions.

TECH TIP

Find the Root Cause

Excessive backpressure, such as that caused by a partially clogged exhaust system, could cause the plastic sensors on the EGR valve to melt. Always check for a restricted exhaust whenever replacing a failed EGR valve sensor.

The top of the valve contains a vacuum regulator and EGR pintle-position sensor in one assembly sealed inside a nonremovable plastic cover. The pintle-position sensor provides a voltage output to the PCM, which increases as the duty cycle increases, allowing the PCM to monitor valve operation. ● **SEE FIGURE 32–4.**

FIGURE 32–5 A General Motors linear EGR Valve.

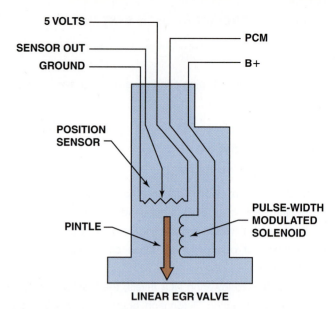

FIGURE 32–6 The EGR valve pintle is pulse-width modulated and a three-wire potentiometer provides pintle-position information back to the PCM.

EXHAUST GAS RECIRCULATION SYSTEMS (CONTINUED)

EGR VALVE POSITION SENSORS
Late-model, computer-controlled EGR systems use a sensor to indicate EGR operation. On-board diagnostics generation-II (OBD-II) EGR system monitors require an EGR sensor to do their job. A linear potentiometer on the top of the EGR valve stem indicates valve position for the computer. This is called an **EGR valve position (EVP)** sensor. Some later-model Ford EGR systems, however, use a feedback signal provided by an EGR exhaust backpressure sensor which converts the exhaust backpressure to a voltage signal. This sensor is called a **pressure feedback EGR (PFE)** sensor.

DIGITAL EGR VALVES
GM introduced a **digital EGR** valve design on some engines. Unlike vacuum-operated EGR valves, the digital EGR valve consists of three solenoids controlled by the PCM. Each solenoid controls a different size orifice in the base—small, medium, and large. The PCM controls each solenoid ground individually. It can produce any of seven different flow rates, using the solenoids to open the three valves in different combinations. The digital EGR valve offers precise control, and using a swivel pintle design helps prevent carbon deposit problems.

LINEAR EGR
Most General Motors and many other vehicles use a **linear EGR** that contains a pulse-width modulated solenoid to precisely regulate exhaust gas flow and a feedback potentiometer that signals the computer regarding the actual position of the valve. ● **SEE FIGURES 32–5 AND 32–6.**

OBD-II EGR MONITORING STRATEGIES

In 1996, the U.S. EPA began requiring OBD-II systems in all passenger cars and most light-duty trucks. These systems include emissions system monitors that alert the driver and the technician if an emissions system is malfunctioning. To be certain the EGR system is operating, the PCM runs a functional test of the system, when specific operating conditions exist. The OBD-II system tests by opening and closing the EGR valve. The PCM monitors an EGR function sensor for a change in signal voltage. If the EGR system fails, a diagnostic trouble code (DTC) is set. If the system fails two consecutive times, the malfunction indicator light (MIL) is lit.

Chrysler monitors the difference in the exhaust oxygen sensor's voltage activity as the EGR valve opens and closes. Oxygen in the exhaust decreases when the EGR valve is open and increases when the EGR valve is closed. The PCM sets a DTC if the sensor signal does not change.

Most Fords use an EGR monitor test sensor called a **Delta Pressure Feedback EGR (DPFE)** sensor. This sensor measures the pressure differential between two sides of a metered orifice positioned just below the EGR valve's exhaust side. Pressure between the orifice and the EGR valve decreases when the EGR opens because it becomes exposed to the lower pressure in the intake. The DPFE sensor recognizes this pressure drop, compares it to the relatively higher pressure on the exhaust side of the orifice, and signals the value of the pressure difference to the

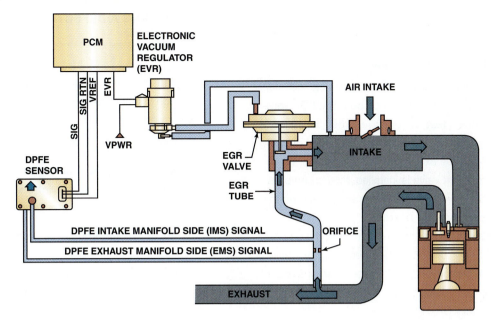

FIGURE 32–7 A DPFE sensor and related components.

DPFE EGR Sensor Chart

Pressure			Voltage
PSI	**In. Hg**	**kPa**	**Volts**
4.34	8.83	29.81	4.56
3.25	6.62	22.36	3.54
2.17	4.41	14.90	2.51
1.08	2.21	7.46	1.48
0	0	0	0.45

PCM. ● **SEE FIGURE 32–7.** When the EGR valve is closed, the exhaust-gas pressure on both sides of the orifice is equal.

The OBD-II EGR monitor for this second system runs when programmed operating conditions (enable criteria) have been met. The monitor evaluates the pressure differential while the PCM commands the EGR valve to open. Like other systems, the monitor compares the measured value with the look-up table value. If the pressure differential falls outside the acceptable value, a DTC sets.

Many vehicle manufacturers use the manifold absolute pressure (MAP) sensor as the EGR monitor on some applications. After meeting the enable criteria (operating condition requirements), the EGR monitor is run. The PCM monitors the MAP sensor while it commands the EGR valve to open. The MAP sensor signal should change in response to the sudden change in manifold pressure or the fuel trim changes created by a change in the oxygen sensor voltage. If the signal value falls outside the acceptable value in the look-up table, a DTC sets. ● **SEE FIGURE 32–8.** If the EGR fails on two consecutive trips the PCM lights the MIL.

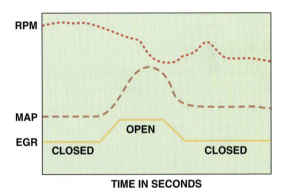

FIGURE 32–8 An OBD-II active test. The PCM opens the EGR valve and then monitors the MAP sensor and/or engine speed (RPM) to verify that it meets acceptable values.

DIAGNOSING A DEFECTIVE EGR SYSTEM

If the EGR valve is not opening or the flow of the exhaust gas is restricted, then the following symptoms are likely:

- Ping (spark knock or detonation) during acceleration or during cruise (steady-speed driving)
- Excessive oxides of nitrogen (NO_X) exhaust emissions

  If the EGR valve is stuck open or partially open, then the following symptoms are likely:

- Rough idle or frequent stalling
- Poor performance/low power, especially at low engine speed

TECH TIP

Watch Out for Carbon Balls!

Exhaust gas recirculation (EGR) valves can get stuck partially open by a chunk of carbon. The EGR valve or solenoid will test as defective. When the valve (or solenoid) is removed, small chunks or balls of carbon often fall into the exhaust manifold passage. When the replacement valve is installed, the carbon balls can be drawn into the new valve again, causing the engine to idle roughly or stall.

To help prevent this problem, start the engine with the EGR valve or solenoid removed. Any balls or chunks of carbon will be blown out of the passage by the exhaust. Stop the engine and install the replacement EGR valve or solenoid.

REAL WORLD FIX

The Blazer Story

The owner of a Chevrolet Blazer equipped with a 4.3-L, V-6 engine complained that the engine would stumble and hesitate at times. Everything seemed to be functioning correctly, except that the service technician discovered a weak vacuum going to the EGR valve at idle. This vehicle was equipped with an EGR valve-control solenoid, called an **electronic vacuum regulator valve** or **EVRV** by General Motors Corporation. The computer pulses the solenoid to control the vacuum that regulates the operation of the EGR valve. The technician checked service information for details on how the system worked. The technician discovered that vacuum should be present at the EGR valve only when the gear selector indicates a drive gear (drive, low, reverse). Because the technician discovered the vacuum at the solenoid to be leaking, the solenoid was obviously defective and required replacement. After replacement of the solenoid (EVRV), the hesitation problem was solved.

NOTE: The technician also discovered in the service manual that blower-type exhaust hoses should not be connected to the tailpipe on any vehicle while performing an inspection of the EGR system. The vacuum created by the system could cause false EGR valve operation to occur.

The first step in almost any diagnosis is to perform a thorough visual inspection. To check for proper operation of a vacuum-operated EGR valve, follow these steps:

1. Check the vacuum diaphragm to see if it can hold vacuum.

   NOTE: Because many EGR valves require exhaust backpressure to function correctly, the engine should be running at a fast idle.

2. Apply vacuum from a hand-operated vacuum pump and check for proper operation. The valve itself should move when vacuum is applied, and the engine operation should be affected. The EGR valve should be able to hold the vacuum that was applied. If the vacuum drops off, then the valve is likely to be defective. If the EGR valve is able to hold vacuum, but the engine is not affected when the valve is opened, then the exhaust passage(s) must be checked for restriction. See the Tech Tip "The Snake Trick." If the EGR valve will not hold vacuum, the valve itself is likely to be defective and require replacement.

3. Connect a vacuum gauge to an intake manifold vacuum source and monitor the engine vacuum at idle (should be 17 to 21 in. Hg at sea level). Raise the speed of the engine to 2500 RPM and note the vacuum reading (should be 17 to 21 in. Hg or higher). Activate the EGR valve using a scan tool or vacuum pump, if vacuum controlled, and observe the vacuum gauge. The results are as follows:
   - The vacuum should drop 6 to 8 in. Hg.
   - If the vacuum drops less than 6 to 8 in. Hg, the valve or the EGR passages are clogged.

EGR-Related OBD-II Diagnostic Trouble Codes

Diagnostic Trouble Code	Description	Possible Causes
P0400	Exhaust gas recirculation flow problems	• EGR valve • EGR valve hose or electrical connection • Defective PCM
P0401	Exhaust gas recirculation flow insufficient	• EGR valve • Clogged EGR ports or passages
P0402	Exhaust gas recirculation flow excessive	• Stuck-open EGR valve • Vacuum hose(s) misrouted • Electrical wiring shorted

FIGURE 32–10 A PCV valve shown in a cutaway valve cover showing the baffles that prevent liquid oil from being drawn into the intake manifold.

FIGURE 32–9 Removing the EGR passage plugs from the intake manifold on a Honda.

CRANKCASE VENTILATION

The problem of crankcase ventilation has existed since the beginning of the automobile, because no piston ring, new or old, can provide a perfect seal between the piston and the cylinder wall. When an engine is running, the pressure of combustion forces the piston downward. This same pressure also forces gases and unburned fuel from the combustion chamber, past the piston rings, and into the crankcase. This process of gases leaking past the rings is called **blowby,** and the gases form crankcase vapors.

These combustion by-products, particularly unburned hydrocarbons caused by blowby, must be ventilated from the crankcase. However, the crankcase cannot be vented directly to the atmosphere, because the hydrocarbon vapors add to air pollution. **Positive crankcase ventilation (PCV)** systems were developed to ventilate the crankcase and recirculate the vapors to the engine's induction system so they can be burned in the cylinders. All systems use a PCV valve, calibrated orifice or separator, an air inlet filter, and connecting hoses. ● **SEE FIGURE 32–10.** An oil/vapor or oil/water separator is used in some systems instead of a valve or orifice, particularly with turbocharged and fuel-injected engines. The oil/vapor separator lets oil condense and drain back into the crankcase. The oil/water separator accumulates moisture and prevents it from freezing during cold engine starts.

The air for the PCV system is drawn after the air cleaner filter, which acts as a PCV filter.

NOTE: Some older designs drew from the dirty side of the air cleaner, where a separate crankcase ventilation filter was used.

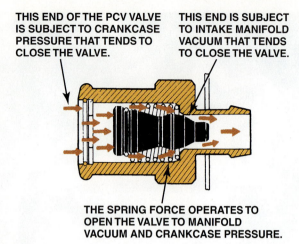

THIS END OF THE PCV VALVE IS SUBJECT TO CRANKCASE PRESSURE THAT TENDS TO CLOSE THE VALVE.

THIS END IS SUBJECT TO INTAKE MANIFOLD VACUUM THAT TENDS TO CLOSE THE VALVE.

THE SPRING FORCE OPERATES TO OPEN THE VALVE TO MANIFOLD VACUUM AND CRANKCASE PRESSURE.

FIGURE 32–11 Spring force, crankcase pressure, and intake manifold vacuum work together to regulate the flow rate through the PCV valve.

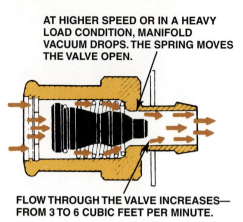

AT HIGHER SPEED OR IN A HEAVY LOAD CONDITION, MANIFOLD VACUUM DROPS. THE SPRING MOVES THE VALVE OPEN.

FLOW THROUGH THE VALVE INCREASES— FROM 3 TO 6 CUBIC FEET PER MINUTE.

FIGURE 32–13 Air flows through the PCV valve during acceleration and when the engine is under a heavy load.

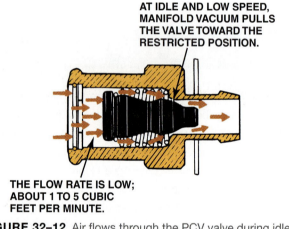

AT IDLE AND LOW SPEED, MANIFOLD VACUUM PULLS THE VALVE TOWARD THE RESTRICTED POSITION.

THE FLOW RATE IS LOW; ABOUT 1 TO 5 CUBIC FEET PER MINUTE.

FIGURE 32–12 Air flows through the PCV valve during idle, cruising, and light-load conditions.

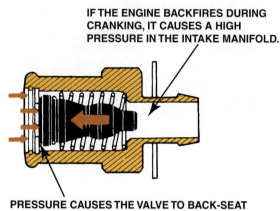

IF THE ENGINE BACKFIRES DURING CRANKING, IT CAUSES A HIGH PRESSURE IN THE INTAKE MANIFOLD.

PRESSURE CAUSES THE VALVE TO BACK-SEAT AND SEAL OFF THE INLET. THIS KEEPS THE BACKFIRE OUT OF THE CRANKCASE.

FIGURE 32–14 PCV valve operation in the event of a backfire.

PCV VALVES

The PCV valve in most systems is a one-way valve containing a spring-operated plunger that controls valve flow rate. ● SEE **FIGURE 32–11.** Flow rate is established for each engine and a valve for a different engine should not be substituted. The flow rate is determined by the size of the plunger and the holes inside the valve. PCV valves usually are located in the valve cover or intake manifold.

The PCV valve regulates airflow through the crankcase under all driving conditions and speeds. When manifold vacuum is high (at idle, cruising, and light-load operation), the PCV valve restricts the airflow to maintain a balanced air–fuel ratio. ● SEE **FIGURE 32–12.** It also prevents high intake manifold vacuum from pulling oil out of the crankcase and into the intake manifold. Under high speed or heavy loads, the valve opens and allows maximum air flow. ● SEE **FIGURE 32–13.** If the engine backfires, the valve will close instantly to prevent a crankcase explosion. ● SEE **FIGURE 32–14.**

ORIFICE-CONTROLLED SYSTEMS

The closed PCV system used on some four-cylinder engines contains a calibrated orifice instead of a PCV valve. The orifice may be located in the valve cover or intake manifold, or in a hose connected between the valve cover, air cleaner, and intake manifold.

While most orifice flow control systems work the same as a PCV valve system, they may not use fresh air scavenging of the crankcase. Crankcase vapors are drawn into the intake manifold in calibrated amounts depending on manifold pressure and the orifice size. If vapor availability is low, as during idle, air is drawn in with the vapors. During off-idle operation, excess vapors are sent to the air cleaner.

At idle, PCV flow is controlled by a 0.050-inch (1.3-mm) orifice. As the engine moves off-idle, ported vacuum pulls a spring-loaded valve off of its seat, allowing PCV flow to pass through a 0.090-inch (2.3-mm) orifice.

SEPARATOR SYSTEMS Turbocharged and many fuel-injected engines use an oil/vapor or oil/water separator and a calibrated orifice instead of a PCV valve. In the most common applications, the air intake throttle body acts as the source for crankcase ventilation vacuum and a calibrated orifice acts as the metering device.

PCV SYSTEM DIAGNOSIS

When intake air flows freely, the PCV system functions properly, as long as the PCV valve or orifice is not clogged. Modern engine design includes the air and vapor flow as a calibrated part of the air–fuel mixture. In fact, some engines receive as much as 30% of their idle air through the PCV system. For this reason, a flow problem in the PCV system results in driveability problems.

A blocked or plugged PCV system is a major cause of high oil consumption, and contributes to many oil leaks. Before expensive engine repairs are attempted, check the condition of the PCV system.

PCV SYSTEM PERFORMANCE CHECK A properly operating positive crankcase ventilation system should be able to draw vapors from the crankcase and into the intake manifold. If the pipes, hoses, and PCV valve itself are not restricted, vacuum is applied to the crankcase. A slight vacuum is created in the crankcase (usually less than 1 in. Hg if measured at the dipstick) and is also applied to other areas of the engine. Oil drainback holes provide a path for oil to drain back into the oil pan. These holes also allow crankcase vacuum to be applied under the rocker covers and in the valley area of most V-type engines. There are several methods that can be used to test a PCV system.

THE RATTLE TEST The rattle test is performed by simply removing the PCV valve and shaking it in your hand.

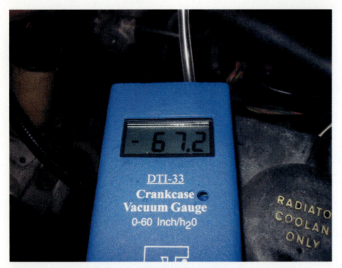

FIGURE 32–15 Using a gauge that measures vacuum in units of inches of water to test the vacuum at the dipstick tube, checking that the PCV system is capable of drawing a vacuum on the crankcase (28 inches of water equals 1 PSI or about 2 in. Hg of vacuum).

PCV SYSTEM DIAGNOSIS (CONTINUED)

- If the PCV valve does *not* rattle, it is definitely defective and must be replaced.
- If the PCV valve *does* rattle, it does not necessarily mean that the PCV valve is good. All PCV valves contain springs that can become weaker with age and heating and cooling cycles. Replace any PCV valve with the *exact* replacement according to vehicle manufacturers' recommended intervals (usually every 3 years or 36,000 miles, or 60,000 km).

THE 3 × 5 CARD TEST   Remove the oil-fill cap (where oil is added to the engine) and start the engine.

NOTE: Use care on some overhead camshaft engines. With the engine running, oil may be sprayed from the open oil-fill opening.

Hold a 3 × 5 card over the opening (a dollar bill or any other piece of paper can be used for this test).

- If the PCV system, including the valve and hoses, is functioning correctly, the card should be held down on the oil-fill opening by the slight vacuum inside the crankcase.
- If the card will not stay, carefully inspect the PCV valve, hose(s), and manifold vacuum port for carbon buildup (restriction). Clean or replace as necessary.

NOTE: On some four-cylinder engines, the 3 × 5 card may vibrate on the oil-fill opening when the engine is running at idle speed. This is normal because of the time intervals between intake strokes on a four-cylinder engine.

THE SNAP-BACK TEST   The proper operation of the PCV valve can be checked by placing a finger over the inlet hole in the valve when the engine is running and removing the finger rapidly. Repeat several times. The valve should "snap back." If the valve does not snap back, replace the valve.

CRANKCASE VACUUM TEST   Sometimes the PCV system can be checked by testing for a weak vacuum at the oil dipstick tube using an inches-of-water manometer or gauge as follows:

STEP 1   Remove the oil-filler cap and cover the opening.

STEP 2   Remove the oil-level indicator (dipstick).

STEP 3   Connect a water manometer or gauge to the dipstick tube.

STEP 4   Start the engine and observe the gauge at idle and at 2500 RPM. ● **SEE FIGURE 32–15.**

The gauge should show some vacuum, especially at 2500 RPM. If not, carefully inspect the PCV system for blockages or other faults.

FIGURE 32–16 Most PCV valves used on newer vehicles are secured with fasteners, which makes it more difficult to disconnect and thereby less likely to increase emissions.

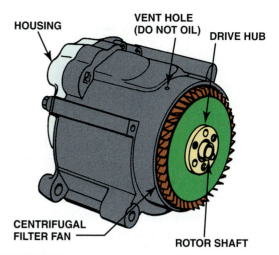

HOUSING · VENT HOLE (DO NOT OIL) · DRIVE HUB · CENTRIFUGAL FILTER FAN · ROTOR SHAFT

FIGURE 32–17 A typical belt-driven AIR pump. Air enters through the revolving fins behind the drive pulley. The fins act as an air filter because dirt is heavier than air and therefore the dirt is deflected off of the fins at the same time air is being drawn into the pump.

PCV MONITOR

Starting with 2004 and newer vehicles, all vehicles must be checked for proper operation of the PCV system. The PCV monitor will fail if the PCM detects an opening between the crankcase and the PCV valve or between the PCV valve and the intake manifold. ● **SEE FIGURE 32–16.**

PCV-Related Diagnostic Trouble Code

Diagnostic Trouble Code	Description	Possible Causes
P1480	PCV solenoid circuit fault	• Defective PCV solenoid • Loose or corroded electrical connection • Loose defective vacuum hoses/connections

SECONDARY AIR INJECTION SYSTEM

An air pump provides the air necessary for the oxidizing process inside the catalytic converter. The system of adding air to the exhaust is commonly called **secondary air injection (SAI).**

NOTE: This system is commonly called AIR, meaning air injection reaction. Therefore, an AIR pump does pump air.

The AIR pump, sometimes referred to as a **smog pump** *or* **thermactor pump,** is mounted at the front of the engine and driven by a belt from the crankshaft pulley. It pulls fresh air in through an external filter and pumps the air under slight pressure to each exhaust port through connecting hoses or a manifold.

- A belt-driven pump with inlet air filter (older models).
  ● **SEE FIGURE 32–17.**
- An electronic air pump (newer models)
- One or more air distribution manifolds and nozzles
- One or more exhaust check valves
- Connecting hoses for air distribution
- Air management valves and solenoids on all newer applications

With the introduction of NO_x reduction converters (also called dual-bed, three-way converters, or TWC), the output of the AIR pump is sent to the center of the converter where the extra air can help oxidize HC and CO into H_2O and CO_2.

The computer controls the airflow from the pump by switching on and off various solenoid valves. When the engine is cold, the air pump output is directed to the exhaust manifold to help provide enough oxygen to convert HC (unburned gasoline) and CO (carbon monoxide) to H_2O (water) and CO_2 (carbon dioxide). When the engine becomes warm and is operating in closed loop, the computer operates the air valves so as to direct the air pump output to the catalytic converter. When the vacuum rapidly increases above the normal idle level, as during rapid deceleration, the computer diverts the air pump output to the air cleaner assembly to silence the air. Diverting the air to the air cleaner prevents exhaust backfire during deceleration.

AIR DISTRIBUTION MANIFOLDS AND NOZZLES

The air-injection system sends air from the pump to a nozzle installed near each exhaust port in the cylinder head. This provides equal air injection for the exhaust from each cylinder and makes it available at a point in the system where exhaust gases are the hottest.

Air is delivered to the exhaust system in one of two ways:

- An external air manifold, or manifolds, distributes the air through injection tubes with stainless steel nozzles. The nozzles are threaded into the cylinder heads or exhaust manifolds close to each exhaust valve. This method is used primarily with smaller engines.

- An internal air manifold distributes the air to the exhaust ports near each exhaust valve through passages cast in the cylinder head or the exhaust manifold. This method is used mainly with larger engines.

EXHAUST CHECK VALVES
All air-injection systems use one or more one-way check valves to protect the air pump and other components from reverse exhaust flow. A **check valve** contains a spring-type metallic disc or reed that closes the air line under exhaust backpressure. Check valves are located between the air manifold and the diverter valve. If exhaust pressure exceeds injection pressure, or if the air pump fails, the check valve spring closes the valve to prevent reverse exhaust flow.

All air pump systems use one-way check valves to allow air to flow into the exhaust manifold and to prevent the hot exhaust from flowing into the valves on the air pump itself. ● **SEE FIGURE 32–18.**

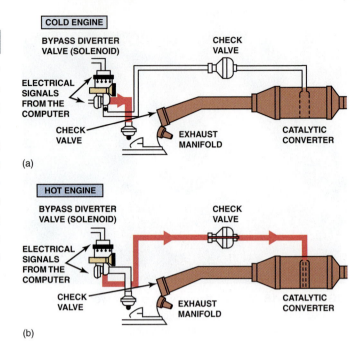

FIGURE 32–18 (a) When the engine is cold and before the oxygen sensor is hot enough to achieve closed-loop, the airflow from the air pump is directed to the exhaust manifold(s) through the one-way check valves which keep the exhaust gases from entering the switching solenoids and the pump itself. (b) When the engine achieves closed-loop, the air is directed to the catalytic converter.

NOTE: These check valves commonly fail, resulting in excessive exhaust emissions (CO especially). When the check valve fails, hot exhaust can travel up to and destroy the switching valve(s) and air pump itself.

BELT-DRIVEN AIR PUMPS
The belt-driven air pump uses a centrifugal filter just behind the drive pulley. As the pump rotates, underhood air is drawn into the pump and slightly compressed. The air is then directed to:

- The exhaust manifold when the engine is cold to help oxidize CO and HC into carbon dioxide (CO_2) and water vapor (H_2O)

- The catalytic converter on many models to help provide the extra oxygen needed for the efficient conversion of CO and HC into CO_2 and H_2O.

- The air cleaner during deceleration or wide-open throttle (WOT) engine operation.

ELECTRIC MOTOR-DRIVEN AIR PUMPS
This style of pump is generally used only during cold engine operation and is computer controlled. The air injection reaction (AIR) system helps reduce hydrocarbon (HC) and carbon monoxide (CO). It also helps to warm up the three-way catalytic converters

FIGURE 32–19 A typical electric motor-driven AIR pump. This unit is on a Chevrolet Corvette and only works when the engine is cold.

quickly on engine start-up so conversion of exhaust gases may occur sooner.

The AIR pump and solenoid is controlled by the PCM. The PCM turns on the AIR pump by providing the ground to complete the circuit which energizes the AIR pump solenoid relay. When air to the exhaust ports is desired, the PCM energizes the relay in order to turn on the solenoid and the AIR pump. ● **SEE FIGURE 32–19.**

The PCM turns on the AIR pump during start-up any time the engine coolant temperature is above 32°F (0°C). A typical electric AIR pump operates for a maximum of 240 seconds, or until the system enters closed-loop operation. The AIR system is disabled under the following conditions:

- The PCM recognizes a problem and sets a diagnostic trouble code.
- The AIR pump has been on for 240 seconds.
- The engine speed is more than 2825 RPM.
- The manifold absolute pressure (MAP) is less than 6 in. Hg (20 kPa).
- Increased temperature detected in three-way catalytic converter during warm-up.
- The short- and long-term fuel trim are not in their normal ranges.
- Power enrichment is detected.

If no air (oxygen) enters the exhaust stream at the exhaust ports, the HC and CO emission levels will be higher than normal.

Air flowing to the exhaust ports at all times could increase temperature of the three-way catalytic converter (TWC).

The diagnostic trouble codes P0410 and/or P0418 set if there is a malfunction in the following components:

- The AIR pump
- The AIR solenoid
- The AIR pump solenoid relay
- Leaking hoses or pipes
- Leaking check valves
- The circuits going to the AIR pump and the AIR pump solenoid relay

The AIR pump is an electric-type pump that requires no periodic maintenance. To check the operation of the AIR pump, the engine should be at normal operating temperature in neutral at idle. Using a scan tool, enable the AIR pump system and watch the heated oxygen sensor (HO2S) voltages for both bank 1 and bank 2 HO2S. The HO2S voltages for both sensors should remain under 350 mV because air is being directed to the exhaust ports. If the HO2S voltages remain low during this test, the AIR pump, solenoid, and shut-off valve are operating satisfactorily. If the HO2S voltage does not remain low when the AIR pump is enabled, inspect for the following:

- Voltage at the AIR pump when energized
- A seized AIR pump
- The hoses, vacuum lines, pipes, and all connections for leaks and proper routing
- Airflow going to the exhaust ports

- AIR pump for proper mounting
- Hoses and pipes for deterioration or holes

If a leak is suspected on the pressure side of the system, or if a hose or pipe has been disconnected on the pressure side, the connections should be checked for leaks with a soapy water solution. With the AIR pump running, bubbles form if a leak exists.

The check valves should be inspected whenever the hose is disconnected or whenever check valve failure is suspected. An AIR pump that had become inoperative and had shown indications of having exhaust gases in the outlet port would indicate check valve failure.

SECONDARY AIR INJECTION SYSTEM DIAGNOSIS

The air pump system should be inspected if an exhaust emissions test failure occurs. In severe cases, the exhaust will enter the air cleaner assembly, resulting in a horribly running engine because the extra exhaust displaces the oxygen needed for proper combustion. With the engine running, check for normal operation:

Engine Operation	Normal Operation of a Typical Secondary Air Injection (SAI) System
Cold engine (open-loop operation)	Air is diverted to the exhaust manifold(s) or cylinder head
Warm engine (closed-loop operation)	Air is diverted to the catalytic converter
Deceleration	Air is diverted to the air cleaner assembly
Wide-open throttle	Air is diverted to the air cleaner assembly

VISUAL INSPECTION Carefully inspect all air injection reaction (AIR) system hoses and pipes. Any pipes that have holes and leak air or exhaust require replacement. The check valve(s) should be checked when a pump has become inoperative. Exhaust gases could have gotten past the check valve and damaged the pump. Check the drive belt on an engine-driven pump for wear and proper tension.

FOUR-GAS EXHAUST ANALYSIS An AIR system can be easily tested using an exhaust gas analyzer. Follow these steps:

1. Start the engine and allow it to run until normal operating temperature is achieved.

2. Connect the analyzer probe to the tailpipe and observe the exhaust readings for hydrocarbons (HC) and carbon monoxide (CO).

3. Using the appropriate pinch-off pliers, shut off the airflow from the AIR system. Observe the HC and CO readings. If the AIR system is working correctly, the HC and CO should increase when the AIR system is shut off.

4. Record the O_2 reading with the AIR system still inoperative. Unclamp the pliers and watch the O_2 readings. If the system is functioning correctly, the O_2 level should increase by 1% to 4%.

Air-Related Diagnostic Trouble Code

Diagnostic Trouble Code	Description	Possible Causes
P0411	SAI system problem	• Defective AIR solenoid • Loose or corroded electrical connections • Loose, missing, or defective rubber hose(s)

FIGURE 32–20 Most catalytic converters are located as close to the exhaust manifold as possible as seen in this display of a Chevrolet Corvette.

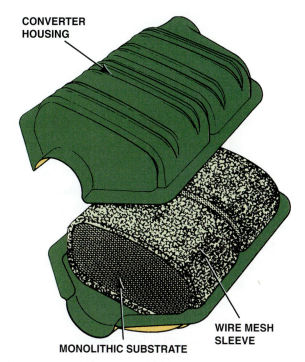

FIGURE 32–21 A typical catalytic converter with a monolithic substrate.

CATALYTIC CONVERTERS

A **catalytic converter** is an after-treatment device used to reduce exhaust emissions outside of the engine. This device is installed in the exhaust system between the exhaust manifold and the muffler, and usually is positioned beneath the passenger compartment. The location of the converter is important, since as much of the exhaust heat as possible must be retained for effective operation. The nearer it is to the engine, the better. ● **SEE FIGURE 32–20.**

CERAMIC MONOLITH CATALYTIC CONVERTER

Most catalytic converters are constructed of a ceramic material in a honeycomb shape with square openings for the exhaust gases. There are approximately 400 openings per square inch (62 per sq cm) and the wall thickness is about 0.006 in. (1.5 mm). The substrate is then coated with a porous aluminum material called the **washcoat,** which makes the surface rough. The catalytic materials are then applied on top of the washcoat. The substrate is contained within a round or oval shell made by welding together two stamped pieces of aluminum or stainless steel. ● **SEE FIGURE 32–21.**

The ceramic substrate in monolithic converters is not restrictive, but the converter breaks more easily when subject to shock or severe jolts and is more expensive to manufacture. Monolithic converters can be serviced only as a unit.

An exhaust pipe is connected to the manifold or header to carry gases through a catalytic converter and then to the muffler or silencer. V-type engines usually route the exhaust into one catalytic converter.

CATALYTIC CONVERTER OPERATION The converter contains small amounts of **rhodium, palladium,** and **platinum.** These elements act as catalysts. A **catalyst** is an element that starts a chemical reaction without becoming a part of, or being consumed in, the process. In a **three-way catalytic converter (TWC)** all three exhaust emissions (NO_X, HC, and CO) are converted to carbon dioxide (CO_2) and water (H_2O). As the exhaust gas passes through the catalyst, oxides of nitrogen (NO_x) are chemically reduced (that is, nitrogen and oxygen are separated)

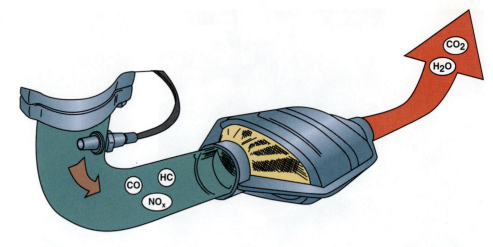

FIGURE 32–22 The three-way catalytic converter first separates the NO_x into nitrogen and oxygen and then converts the HC and CO into harmless water (H_2O) and carbon dioxide (CO_2).

CERAMIC MONOLITH CATALYTIC CONVERTER (CONTINUED)

in the first section of the catalytic converter. In the second section of the catalytic converter, most of the hydrocarbons and carbon monoxide remaining in the exhaust gas are oxidized to form harmless carbon dioxide (CO_2) and water vapor (H_2O). ● SEE FIGURE 32–22.

Since the early 1990s, many converters also contain **cerium,** an element that can store oxygen. The purpose of the cerium is to provide oxygen to the oxidation bed of the converter when the exhaust is rich and lacks enough oxygen for proper oxidation. When the exhaust is lean, the cerium absorbs the extra oxygen. The converter must have a varying rich-to-lean exhaust for proper operation:

- A rich exhaust is required for reduction—stripping the oxygen (O_2) from the nitrogen in NO_x

- A lean exhaust is required to provide the oxygen necessary to oxidize HC and CO (combining oxygen with HC and CO to form H_2O and CO_2)

If the catalytic converter is not functioning correctly, check to see that the air–fuel mixture being supplied to the engine is correct and that the ignition system is free of defects.

CONVERTER LIGHT-OFF The catalytic converter does not work when cold and it must be heated to its **light-off** temperature of close to 500°F (260°C) before it starts working at 50% effectiveness. When fully effective, the converter reaches a temperature range of 900° to 1600°F (482° to 871°C). In spite

of the intense heat, however, catalytic reactions do not generate a flame associated with a simple burning reaction. Because of the extreme heat (almost as hot as combustion chamber temperatures), a converter remains hot long after the engine is shut off. Most vehicles use a series of heat shields to protect the passenger compartment and other parts of the chassis from excessive heat. Vehicles have been known to start fires because of the hot converter causing tall grass or dry leaves beneath the just-parked vehicle to ignite, especially if the engine is idling.

CONVERTER USAGE A catalytic converter must be located as close as possible to the exhaust manifold to work effectively. The farther back the converter is positioned in the exhaust system, the more gases cool before they reach the converter. Since positioning in the exhaust system affects the oxidation process, cars that use only an oxidation converter generally locate it underneath the front of the passenger compartment.

Some vehicles have used a small, quick-heating oxidation converter called a **preconverter, pup,** or **mini-converter** that connects directly to the exhaust manifold outlet. These have a small catalyst surface area close to the engine that heats up rapidly to start the oxidation process more quickly during cold engine warm-up. For this reason, they were often called **light-off converters,** or **LOC.** The oxidation reaction started in the LOC is completed by the larger main converter under the passenger compartment.

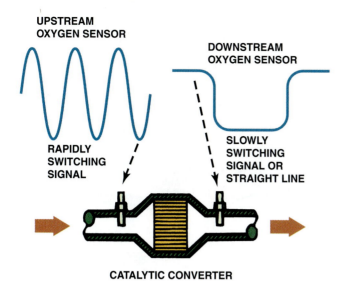

UPSTREAM OXYGEN SENSOR

DOWNSTREAM OXYGEN SENSOR

RAPIDLY SWITCHING SIGNAL

SLOWLY SWITCHING SIGNAL OR STRAIGHT LINE

CATALYTIC CONVERTER

FIGURE 32–23 The OBD-II catalytic converter monitor compares the signals of the upstream and downstream O2Ss to determine converter efficiency.

OBD-II CATALYTIC CONVERTER PERFORMANCE

With OBD-II-equipped vehicles, catalytic converter performance is monitored by **heated oxygen sensors (HO2Ss),** both before and after the converter. The converters used on these vehicles have what is known as **OSC** or **oxygen storage capacity.** OSC is due mostly to the cerium coating in the catalyst rather than the precious metals used. When the TWC is operating as it should, the postconverter HO2S is far less active than the preconverter sensor. The converter stores, then releases the oxygen during normal reduction and oxidation of the exhaust gases, smoothing out the variations in O_2 being released.

Where a cycling sensor voltage output is expected before the converter, because of the converter action, the postconverter HO2S should read a steady signal without much fluctuation. ● **SEE FIGURE 32–23.**

CONVERTER-DAMAGING CONDITIONS

Since converters have no moving parts, they require no periodic service. Under federal law, catalyst effectiveness is warranted for 80,000 miles or eight years.

The three main causes of premature converter failure are:

- **Contamination.** Substances that can destroy the converter include exhaust that contains excess engine oil, antifreeze, sulfur (from poor fuel), and various other chemical substances.

- **Excessive temperatures.** Although a converter operates at high temperature, it can be destroyed by excessive temperatures. This most often occurs either when too much unburned fuel enters the converter, or with excessively lean mixtures. Excessive temperatures may be caused by long idling periods on some vehicles, since more heat develops at those times than when driving at normal highway speeds. Severe high temperatures can cause the converter to melt down, leading to the internal parts breaking apart and either clogging the converter or moving downstream to plug the muffler. In either case, the restricted exhaust flow severely reduces engine power.

- **Improper air–fuel mixtures.** Rich mixtures or raw fuel in the exhaust can be caused by engine misfiring, or an excessively rich air–fuel mixture resulting from a defective coolant temp sensor or defective fuel injectors. Lean mixtures are commonly caused by intake manifold leaks. When either of these circumstances occurs, the converter can become a catalytic furnace, causing the previously described damage.

To avoid excessive catalyst temperatures and the possibility of fuel vapors reaching the converter, follow these rules:

1. Do not try to start the engine by pushing the vehicle. Use jumper cables or a jump box to start the engine.

2. Do not crank an engine for more than 40 seconds when it is flooded or firing intermittently.

3. Do not turn off the ignition switch when the vehicle is in motion.

4. Do not disconnect a spark plug wire for more than 30 seconds.

5. Repair engine problems such as dieseling, misfiring, or stumbling as soon as possible.

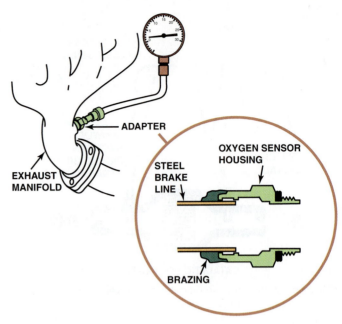

Can a Catalytic Converter Be Defective Without Being Clogged?

Yes. Catalytic converters can fail by being chemically damaged or poisoned without being mechanically clogged. Therefore, the catalytic converter should not only be tested for physical damage (clogging) by performing a backpressure or vacuum test and a rattle test but also a test for temperature rise, usually with a pyrometer, or propane test, to check the efficiency of the converter.

FIGURE 32–24 A backpressure tool can be made by using an oxygen sensor housing and using epoxy or braze to hold the tube to the housing.

DIAGNOSING CATALYTIC CONVERTERS

THE TAP TEST The simple tap test involves tapping (not pounding) on the catalytic converter using a rubber mallet. If the substrate inside the converter is broken, the converter will rattle when hit. If the converter rattles, a replacement converter is required.

TESTING BACKPRESSURE WITH A VACUUM GAUGE

A vacuum gauge can be used to measure manifold vacuum at a high idle (2000 to 2500 RPM). If the exhaust system is restricted, pressure increases in the exhaust system. This pressure is called **backpressure**. Manifold vacuum will drop gradually if the engine is kept at a constant speed if the exhaust is restricted.

The reason the vacuum will drop is that all the exhaust leaving the engine at the higher engine speed cannot get through the restriction. After a short time (within 1 minute), the exhaust tends to "pile up" above the restriction and eventually remains in the cylinder of the engine at the end of the exhaust stroke. Therefore, at the beginning of the intake stroke, when the piston traveling downward should be lowering the pressure (raising the vacuum) in the intake manifold, the extra exhaust in the cylinder *lowers* the normal vacuum. If the exhaust restriction is severe enough, the vehicle can become undriveable because cylinder filling cannot occur except at idle.

TESTING BACKPRESSURE WITH A PRESSURE GAUGE

Exhaust system backpressure can be measured directly by installing a pressure gauge in an exhaust opening. This can be accomplished in one of the following ways:

1. To test an oxygen sensor, remove the inside of an old, discarded oxygen sensor and thread in an adapter to convert it to a vacuum or pressure gauge.

   NOTE: An adapter can be easily made by inserting a metal tube or pipe. A short section of brake line works great. The pipe can be brazed to the oxygen sensor housing or it can be glued with epoxy. An 18-millimeter compression gauge adapter can also be adapted to fit into the oxygen sensor opening.
   ● **SEE FIGURE 32–24.**

2. To test an exhaust gas recirculation (EGR) valve, remove the EGR valve and fabricate a plate.

3. To test an air injection reaction (AIR) check valve, remove the check valve from the exhaust tubes leading to the exhaust manifold. Use a rubber cone with a tube inside to seal against the exhaust tube. Connect the tube to a pressure gauge.

At idle the maximum backpressure should be less than 1.5 PSI (10 kPa), and it should be less than 2.5 PSI (15 kPa) at 2500 RPM.

TESTING A CATALYTIC CONVERTER FOR TEMPERATURE RISE

A properly working catalytic converter should be able to reduce NO_x exhaust emissions into nitrogen (N) and

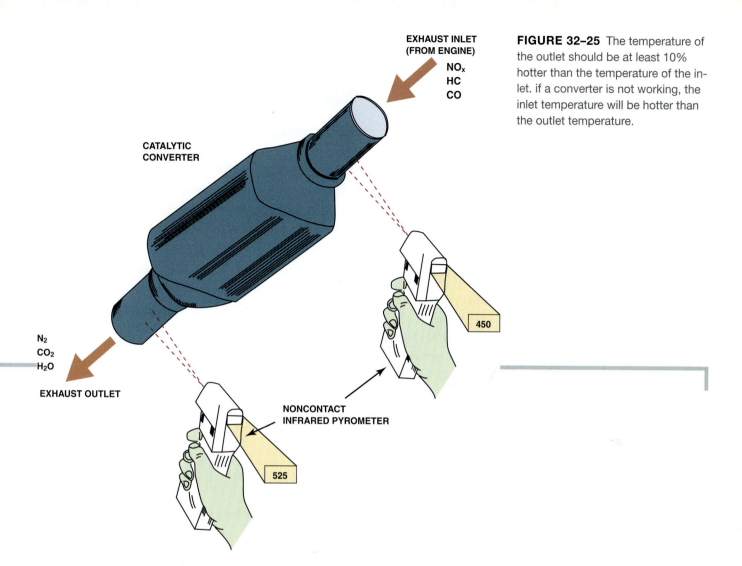

EXHAUST INLET
(FROM ENGINE)
NO$_x$
HC
CO

FIGURE 32–25 The temperature of the outlet should be at least 10% hotter than the temperature of the inlet. if a converter is not working, the inlet temperature will be hotter than the outlet temperature.

CATALYTIC
CONVERTER

450

N$_2$
CO$_2$
H$_2$O

EXHAUST OUTLET

NONCONTACT
INFRARED PYROMETER

525

oxygen (O$_2$) and oxidize unburned hydrocarbon (HC) and carbon monoxide (CO) into harmless carbon dioxide (CO$_2$) and water vapor (H$_2$O). During these chemical processes, the catalytic converter should increase in temperature at least 10% if the converter is working properly. To test the converter, operate the engine at 2500 RPM for at least 2 minutes to fully warm up the converter. Measure the inlet and the outlet temperatures using an **infrared pyrometer** as shown in ● **FIGURE 32–25.**

NOTE: If the engine is extremely efficient, the converter may not have any excessive unburned hydrocarbons or carbon monoxide to convert! In this case, a spark plug wire could be grounded out using a vacuum hose and a test light to create some unburned hydrocarbon in the exhaust. Do not ground out a cylinder for longer than 10 seconds or the excessive amount of unburned hydrocarbon could overheat and damage the converter.

CATALYTIC CONVERTER EFFICIENCY TESTS The efficiency of a catalytic converter can be determined using an exhaust gas analyzer.

OXYGEN LEVEL TEST. With the engine warm and in closed-loop, check the oxygen (O$_2$) and carbon monoxide (CO) levels.

■ If O$_2$ is zero, go to the snap-throttle test.

■ If O$_2$ is greater than zero, check the CO level.

■ If CO is greater than zero, the converter is *not* functioning correctly.

SNAP-THROTTLE TEST. With the engine warm and in closed-loop snap the throttle to wide open (WOT) in park or neutral and observe the oxygen reading.

■ O$_2$ reading should not exceed 1.2%; if it does, the converter is *not* working.

■ If the O$_2$ rises to 1.2%, the converter may have low efficiency.

■ If the O$_2$ remains below 1.2%, then the converter is okay.

OBD-II CATALYTIC CONVERTER MONITOR

The catalytic converter monitor of OBD II uses an upstream and downstream HO2S to test catalyst efficiency. When the engine combusts a lean air–fuel mixture, higher amounts of oxygen flow through the exhaust into the converter. The catalyst materials absorb this oxygen for the oxidation process, thereby removing it from the exhaust stream. If a converter cannot absorb enough oxygen, oxidation does not occur. Engineers established a correlation between the amount of oxygen absorbed and converter efficiency.

The OBD-II system monitors how much oxygen the catalyst retains. A voltage waveform from the downstream HO2S of a good catalyst should have little or no activity. A voltage waveform from the downstream HO2S of a degraded catalyst shows a lot of activity. In other words, the closer the activity of the downstream HO2S matches that of the upstream HO2S, the greater the degree of converter degradation. In operation, the OBD-II monitor compares activity between the two exhaust oxygen sensors.

TECH TIP

Aftermarket Catalytic Converters

Some replacement aftermarket (nonfactory) catalytic converters do not contain the same amount of cerium as the original part. Cerium is the element that is used in catalytic converters to store oxygen. As a result of the lack of cerium, the correlation between the oxygen storage and the conversion efficiency may be affected enough to set a false diagnostic trouble code (P0422).

CATALYTIC CONVERTER REPLACEMENT GUIDELINES

Because a catalytic converter is a major exhaust gas emission control device, the Environmental Protection Agency (EPA) has strict guidelines for its replacement, including:

- If a converter is replaced on a vehicle with less than 80,000 miles/8 years, depending on the year of the vehicle, an original equipment catalytic converter *must* be used as a replacement.

- The replacement converter must be of the same design as the original. If the original had an air pump fitting, so must the replacement.

- The old converter must be kept for possible inspection by the authorities for 60 days.

- A form must be completed and signed by both the vehicle owner and a representative from the service facility. This form must state the cause of the converter failure and must remain on file for 2 years.

TECH TIP

Catalytic Converters Are Murdered

Catalytic converters start a chemical reaction but do not enter into the chemical reaction. Therefore, catalytic converters do not wear out and they do not die of old age. If a catalytic converter is found to be defective (nonfunctioning or clogged), look for the *root* cause. Remember this:

"Catalytic converters do not commit suicide—they're murdered."

Items that should be checked when a defective catalytic converter is discovered include all components of the ignition and fuel systems. Excessive unburned fuel can cause the catalytic converter to overheat and fail. The oxygen sensor must be working and fluctuating from 0.5 to 5 Hz (times per second) to provide the necessary air–fuel mixture variations for maximum catalytic converter efficiency.

Catalytic Converter-Related Diagnostic Trouble Code

Diagnostic Trouble Code	Description	Possible Causes
P0422	Catalytic converter efficiency failure	• Engine mechanical fault • Exhaust leaks • Fuel contaminants, such as engine oil, coolant, or sulfur

FIGURE 32–26 A capless system from a Ford Flex does not use a replaceable cap and instead is spring-loaded closed.

EVAPORATIVE EMISSION CONTROL SYSTEM

The purpose of the evaporative (EVAP) emission control system is to trap and hold gasoline vapors also called volatile organic compounds, or VOCs. The charcoal canister is part of an entire system of hoses and valves called the **evaporative control system.** These vapors are instead routed into a charcoal canister, from where they go to the intake airflow so they are burned in the engine.

COMMON COMPONENTS The fuel tank filler caps used on vehicles with modern EVAP systems are a special design. Most EVAP fuel tank filler caps have pressure-vacuum relief built into them. When pressure or vacuum exceeds a calibrated value, the valve opens. Once the pressure or vacuum has been relieved, the valve closes. If a sealed cap is used on an EVAP system that requires a pressure-vacuum relief design, a vacuum lock may develop in the fuel system, or the fuel tank may be damaged by fuel expansion or contraction. ● **SEE FIGURE 32–26.**

? FREQUENTLY ASKED QUESTION

When Filling My Fuel Tank, Why Should I Stop When the Pump Clicks Off?

Every fuel tank has an upper volume chamber that allows for expansion of the fuel when hot. The volume of the chamber is between 10% and 20% of the volume of the tank. For example, if a fuel tank had a capacity of 20 gallons, the expansion chamber volume would be from 2 to 4 gallons. A hose is attached at the top of the chamber and vented to the charcoal canister. If extra fuel is forced into this expansion volume, liquid gasoline can be drawn into the charcoal canister. This liquid fuel can saturate the canister and create an overly rich air–fuel mixture when the canister purge valve is opened during normal vehicle operation. This extra-rich air–fuel mixture can cause the vehicle to fail an exhaust emissions test, reduce fuel economy, and possibly damage the catalytic converter. To avoid problems, simply add fuel to the next dime's worth after the nozzle clicks off. This will ensure that the tank is full, yet not overfilled.

FIGURE 32–27 A charcoal canister can be located under the hood or underneath the vehicle.

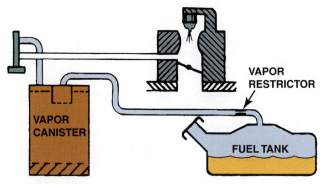

FIGURE 32–28 The evaporative emission control system includes all of the lines, hoses, and valves, plus the charcoal canister.

HOW THE EVAPORATIVE CONTROL SYSTEM WORKS

The canister is located under the hood or underneath the vehicle, and is filled with activated charcoal granules that can hold up to one-third of their own weight in fuel vapors. A vent line connects the canister to the fuel tank. ● **SEE FIGURE 32–27.**

NOTE: Some vehicles with large or dual fuel tanks may have dual canisters.

Activated charcoal is an effective vapor trap because of its great surface area. Each gram of activated charcoal has a surface area of 1,100 square meters, or more than a quarter acre. Typical canisters hold either 300 or 625 grams of charcoal *with a surface area equivalent to 80 or 165 football fields.* **Adsorption** attaches the fuel vapor molecules to the carbon surface. This attaching force is not strong, so the system purges the vapor molecules quite simply by sending a fresh airflow through the charcoal. ● **SEE FIGURE 32–28.**

VAPOR PURGING During engine operation, stored vapors are drawn from the canister into the engine through a hose connected to the throttle body or the air cleaner. This "purging" process mixes HC vapors from the canister with the existing air–fuel charge.

COMPUTER-CONTROLLED PURGE Canister purging on engines with electronic fuel management systems is regulated by the Powertrain Control Module (PCM). This is done by a microprocessor-controlled vacuum solenoid, and one or more purge valves. ● **SEE FIGURE 32–29.** Under normal conditions,

Pressure Conversions

PSI	In. Hg	In. H_2O
14.7	29.93	407.19
1.0	2.036	27.7
0.9	1.8	24.93
0.8	1.63	22.16
0.7	1.43	19.39
0.6	1.22	16.62
0.5	1.018	13.85
0.4	0.814	11.08
0.3	0.611	8.31
0.2	0.407	5.54
0.1	0.204	2.77
0.09	0.183	2.49
0.08	0.163	2.22
0.07	0.143	1.94
0.06	0.122	1.66
0.05	0.102	1.385

1 PSI = 28 inches of water; 1/4 PSI = 7 inches of water.

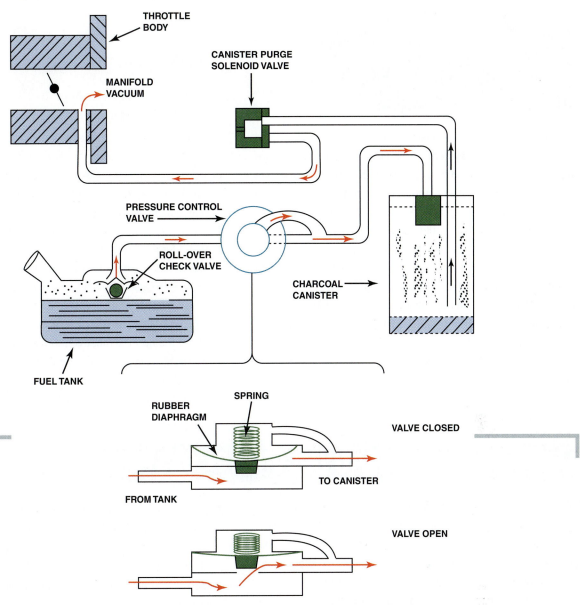

FIGURE 32–29 A typical evaporative emission control system. Note that when the computer turns on the canister purge solenoid valve, manifold vacuum draws any stored vapors from the canister into the engine. Manifold vacuum also is applied to the pressure control valve. When this valve opens, fumes from the fuel tank are drawn into the charcoal canister and eventually into the engine. When the solenoid valve is turned off (or the engine stops and there is no manifold vacuum), the pressure control valve is spring-loaded shut to keep vapors inside the fuel tank from escaping to the atmosphere.

most engine control systems permit purging only during closed-loop operation at cruising speeds. During other engine operation conditions, such as open-loop mode, idle, deceleration, or wide-open throttle, the PCM prevents canister purging.

Pressures can build inside the fuel system and are usually measured in units of inches of water, abbreviated in. H_2O (28 inches of water equals 1 PSI). Pressure buildup is a function of:

- Fuel evaporation rates (volatility)
- Gas tank size (fuel surface area and volume)
- Fuel level (liquid versus vapor)
- Fuel slosh (driving conditions)
- Temperature (ambient, in-tank, close to the tank)
- Returned fuel from the rail

NONENHANCED EVAPORATIVE CONTROL SYSTEMS

Prior to 1996, evaporative systems were referred to as evaporative (EVAP) control systems. This term refers to evaporative systems that had limited diagnostic capabilities. While they are often PCM controlled, their diagnostic capability is usually limited to their ability to detect if purge has occurred. Many systems have a diagnostic switch that could sense if purge is occurring and set a code if no purge is detected. This system does not check for leaks. On some vehicles, the PCM also has the capability of monitoring the integrity of the purge solenoid and circuit. These systems' limitations are their ability to check the integrity of the evaporative system on the vehicle. They could not detect leaks or missing or loose gas caps that could lead to excessive evaporative emissions from the vehicle. Nonenhanced evaporative systems use either a canister purge solenoid or a vapor management valve to control purge vapor.

TECH TIP

Problems After Refueling?
Check the Purge Valve

The purge valve is normally closed and open only when the PCM is commanding the system to purge. If the purge solenoid were to become stuck in the open position, gasoline fumes would be allowed to flow directly from the gas tank to the intake manifold. When refueling, this would result in a lot of fumes being forced into the intake manifold and as a result would cause a hard-to-start condition after refueling. This would also result in a rich exhaust and likely black exhaust when first starting the engine after refueling. While the purge solenoid is usually located under the hood of most vehicles and is less subject to rust and corrosion than the vent valve, it can still fail.

ENHANCED EVAPORATIVE CONTROL SYSTEM

Beginning in 1996 with OBD-II vehicles, manufacturers were required to install systems that are able to detect both purge flow and evaporative system leakage. The systems on models produced between 1996 and 2000 have to be able to detect a leak as small as .040 in. diameter. Beginning in the model year 2000, the enhanced systems started a phase-in of .020-in.-diameter leak detection.

NOTE: Chrysler says that a 0.020-in.-diameter leak in an EVAP system can yield an average of about 1.35 grams of HC per mile driven.

All vehicles built after 1995 have enhanced evaporative systems that have the ability to detect purge flow and system leakage. If either of these two functions fails, the system is required to set a diagnostic trouble code and turn on the MIL light to warn the driver of the failure.

CANISTER VENT SOLENOID VALVE The canister vent valve is a normally open valve and is only closed when commanded by the PCM during testing of the system. The vent solenoid is located under the vehicle in most cases and is exposed to the environment making this valve subject to rust and corrosion.

CANISTER PURGE SOLENOID (CPS) VALVE The purge solenoid, also called the **canister purge (CANP)** solenoid is normally closed and is pulsed open by the PCM during purging.

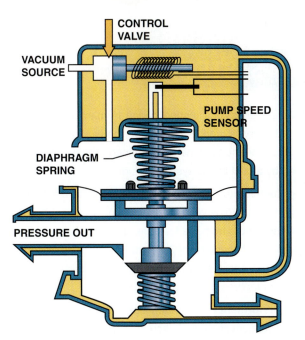

FIGURE 32–30 A leak detection pump (LDP) used on some Chrysler vehicles to pressurize (slightly) the fuel system to check for leaks.

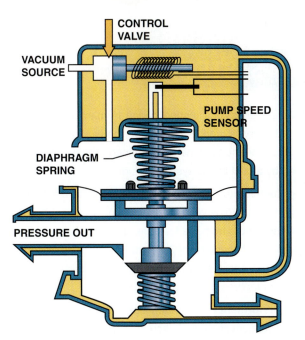

Labels on figure:
CONTROL VALVE
VACUUM SOURCE
PUMP SPEED SENSOR
DIAPHRAGM SPRING
PRESSURE OUT

LEAK DETECTION PUMP SYSTEM

Many Chrysler vehicles use a **leak detection pump (LDP)** as part of the evaporative control system diagnosis equipment. ● **SEE FIGURE 32–30.** The system works as follows:

- The purge solenoid is normally closed. The conventional purge solenoid is ground-side controlled by the PCM. The proportional purge solenoid is feed-side controlled by the PCM. The PCM will energize the solenoid to purge fuel vapors from the canister and to lower tank pressure.

- The vent valve in the LDP is normally open. Filtered fresh air is drawn through the LDP to the canister.

- The solenoid on the LDP normally blocks manifold vacuum from the engine. When grounded by the PCM, manifold vacuum is allowed to pass through the solenoid and into the upper diaphragm chamber. Vacuum will pull the diaphragm back against spring pressure (rated at 7.5 in. H_2O). As the diaphragm is pulled up, fresh air is drawn into the pressure side of the LDP diaphragm through the inlet reed valve. This is the LDP intake stroke. When the diaphragm is pulled up against spring pressure, the normally closed contacts of the LDP reed switch open. The LDP reed switch is the only input regarding EVAP system pressure for the PCM. With the switch contacts open, the PCM knows the diaphragm has been drawn upwards. When the LDP solenoid is de-energized by the PCM, fresh air is allowed to enter the top side of the diaphragm chamber displacing the vacuum that was there. Spring pressure (7.5 in. H_2O) forces the air in the lower diaphragm chamber out

through the outlet (exhaust) reed valve. This is the LDP exhaust stroke. The LDP switch contacts close once the diaphragm returns to its original at-rest position.

- The PCM checks for EVAP leaks by first de-energizing the purge solenoid (normally closed), and then rapidly cycling the LDP solenoid and watching the LDP switch. Once pressure (7.5 in. H_2O) is built up in the system, the diaphragm will be seated upwards against spring pressure. The PCM knows this since it is monitoring the LDP switch. So, the PCM compares LDP switch position against LDP solenoid cycling time to determine if leakage is present.

- When manually checking for leaks (for example, smoke machine), the vent valve must be closed. Closing of the vent valve requires that the LDP solenoid be energized and that a vacuum source be applied to the LDP solenoid. This will enable the LDP diaphragm to stroke upwards, thereby allowing the vent valve spring to close the vent valve.

PUMP PERIOD The time between LDP solenoid off and LDP switch close is called the pump period. This time period is inversely proportional to the size of the leak. The shorter the pump period, the larger the leak. The longer the pump period, the smaller the leak.

EVAP large leak ($>$0.080): less than 0.9 seconds

EVAP medium leak (0.040 to 0.080): 0.9 to 1.2 seconds

EVAP small leak (0.020 to 0.040): 1.2 to 6 seconds

ONBOARD REFUELING VAPOR RECOVERY

The onboard refueling vapor recovery (ORVR) system was first introduced on some 1998 vehicles. Previously designed EVAP systems allowed fuel vapor to escape to the atmosphere during refueling.

The primary feature of most ORVR systems is the restricted tank filler tube, which is about 1 inch (25 mm) in diameter. This reduced-size filler tube creates an aspiration effect, which tends to draw outside air into the filler tube. During refueling, the fuel tank is vented to the charcoal canister, which captures the gas fumes and with air flowing into the filler tube, no vapors can escape to the atmosphere.

STATE INSPECTION EVAP TESTS

In some states, a periodic inspection and test of the fuel system are mandated along with a dynamometer test. The emissions inspection includes tests on the vehicle before and during the dynamometer test. Before the running test, the fuel tank and cap, fuel lines, canister, and other fuel system components must be inspected and tested to ensure that they are not leaking gasoline vapors into the atmosphere.

First, the fuel tank cap is tested to ensure that it is sealing properly and holds pressure within specs. Next, the cap is installed on the vehicle, and using a special adapter, the EVAP system is pressurized to approximately 0.5 PSI and monitored for 2 minutes. Pressure in the tank and lines should not drop below approximately 0.3 PSI.

If the cap or system leaks, hydrocarbon emissions are likely being released, and the vehicle fails the test. If the system leaks, an ultrasonic leak detector may be used to find the leak.

Finally, with the engine warmed up and running at a moderate speed, the canister purge line is tested for adequate flow using a special flow meter inserted into the system. In one example, if the flow from the canister to the intake system when the system is activated is at least one liter per minute, then the vehicle passes the canister purge test.

DIAGNOSING THE EVAP SYSTEM

Before vehicle emissions testing began in many parts of the country, little service work was done on the evaporative emission system. Common engine-performance problems that can be caused by a fault in this system include:

- **Poor fuel economy.** A leak in a vacuum-valve diaphragm can result in engine vacuum drawing in a constant flow of gasoline vapors from the fuel tank. This usually results in a drop in fuel economy of 2 to 4 miles per gallon (mpg). Use a hand-operated vacuum pump to check that the vacuum diaphragm can hold vacuum.

- **Poor performance.** A vacuum leak in the manifold or ported vacuum section of vacuum hose in the system can cause the engine to run rough. Age, heat, and time all contribute to the deterioration of rubber hoses.

Enhanced exhaust emissions (I/M-240) testing tests the evaporative emission system. A leak in the system is tested by pressurizing the entire fuel system to a level below 1 pound per square inch or 1 PSI (about 14 inches of water). The system is typically pressurized with nitrogen, a nonflammable gas that makes up 78% of our atmosphere. The pressure in the system is then shut off and the pressure monitored. If the pressure drops below a set standard, then the vehicle fails the test. This test determines if there is a leak in the system.

NOTE: To help pass the evaporative section of an enhanced emissions test, arrive at the test site with less than a half-tank of fuel. This means that the rest of the volume of the fuel tank is filled with air. It takes longer for the pressure to drop from a small leak when the volume of the air is greater compared to when the tank is full and the volume of air remaining in the tank is small.

LOCATING LEAKS IN THE SYSTEM

Leaks in the evaporative emission control system will cause the malfunction check gas cap indication lamp to light on some vehicles. ● **SEE FIGURE 32–31.** A leak will also cause a gas smell, which would be most noticeable if the vehicle were parked in an enclosed garage. The first step is to determine if there is leak in the system by setting the EVAP tester to either a

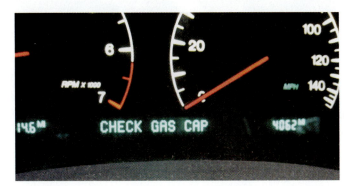

FIGURE 32–31 Some vehicles will display a message if an evaporative control system leak is detected that could be the result of a loose gas cap.

FIGURE 32–33 This unit is applying smoke to the fuel tank through an adapter and the leak was easily found to be the gas cap seal.

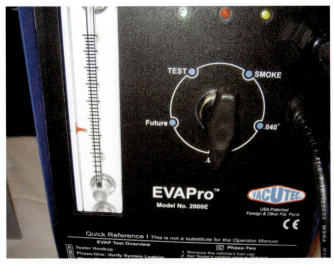

FIGURE 32–32 To test for a leak, this tester was set to the 0.020-inch hole and turned on. The ball rose in the scale on the left and the red arrow was moved to that location. If when testing the system for leaks, the ball rises higher than the arrow, then the leak is larger than 0.020. If the ball does not rise to the level of the arrow, the leak is smaller than 0.020 inch.

FIGURE 32–34 An emission tester that uses nitrogen to pressurize the fuel system.

0.040-inch or a 0.020-inch hole size leak. ● **SEE FIGURE 32–32.** After it has been determined that a leak exists and that it is larger than specified then there are two methods that can be used to check for leaks in the evaporative system.

■ **Smoke machine testing.** The most efficient method of leak detection is to introduce smoke under low pressure from a machine specifically designed for this purpose. ● **SEE FIGURE 32–33.**

■ **Nitrogen gas pressurization.** This method uses nitrogen gas under a very low pressure (lower than 1 PSI) in the fuel system. The service technician then listens for the escaping air, using amplified headphones. ● **SEE FIGURE 32–34.**

EVAPORATIVE SYSTEM MONITOR

OBD-II computer programs not only detect faults, but also *periodically test various systems* and alert the driver before emissions-related components are harmed by system faults. Serious faults cause a blinking malfunction indicator lamp (MIL) or even an engine shutdown; less serious faults may simply store a code but not illuminate the MIL.

The OBD-II requirements did not radically affect fuel system design. However, one new component, a fuel evaporative canister purge line pressure sensor, was added for monitoring purge line pressure during tests. The OBD-II requirements state that vehicle fuel systems are to be routinely tested *while underway* by the PCM management system.

All OBD-II vehicles—during normal driving cycles and under specific conditions—experience a canister purge system pressure test, as commanded by the PCM. While the vehicle is being driven, the vapor line between the canister and the purge valve is monitored for pressure changes. When the canister purge solenoid is open, the line should be under a vacuum since vapors must be drawn from the canister into the intake system. However, when the purge solenoid is closed, there should be no vacuum in the line. The pressure sensor detects if a vacuum is present or not, and the information is compared to the command given to the solenoid. If, during the canister purge cycle, no vacuum exists in the canister purge line, a code is set indicating a possible fault, which could be caused by an inoperative or clogged solenoid or a blocked or leaking canister purge fuel line. Likewise, if vacuum exists when no command for purge is given, a stuck solenoid is evident, and a code is set.

The EVAP system monitor tests for purge volume and leaks. Most applications purge the charcoal canister by venting the vapors into the intake manifold during cruise. To do this, the PCM typically opens a solenoid-operated purge valve installed in the purge line leading to the intake manifold.

A typical EVAP monitor first closes off the system to atmospheric pressure and opens the purge valve during cruise operation. A fuel tank pressure (FTP) sensor then monitors the rate with which vacuum increases in the system. The monitor uses this information to determine the purge volume flow rate. To test for leaks, the EVAP monitor closes the purge valve, creating a completely closed system. The fuel tank pressure sensor then monitors the leak down rate. If the rate exceeds PCM-stored values, a leak greater than or equal to the OBD-II standard of

FIGURE 32–35 The fuel tank pressure sensor (black unit with three wires) looks like a MAP sensor and is usually located on top of the fuel pump module (white unit).

0.040 in. (1.0 mm) or 0.020 in. (0.5 mm) exists. After two consecutive failed trips testing either purge volume or the presence of a leak, the PCM lights the MIL and sets a DTC.

The fuel tank pressure sensor is often the same part as the MAP sensor, and instead of monitoring intake manifold absolute pressure, it is used to monitor fuel tank pressure. ● **SEE FIGURE 32–35.**

ENGINE OFF NATURAL VACUUM System integrity (leakage) can also be checked after the engine is shut off. The premise is that a warm evaporative system will cool down after the engine is shut off and the vehicle is stable. A slight vacuum will be created in the gas tank during this cool down period. If a specific level of vacuum is reached and maintained, the system is said to have integrity (no leakage).

TECH TIP

Always Tighten the Cap Correctly

Many diagnostic trouble codes (DTCs) are set because the gas cap has not been properly installed. To be sure that a screw-type gas cap is properly sealed, tighten the cap until it clicks three times. The clicking is a ratchet device and the clicking does not harm the cap. Therefore, if a P0440 or similar DTC is set, check the cap. ● **SEE FIGURE 32–36.**

FIGURE 32–36 This Toyota cap has a warning—the check engine light will come on if not tightened until one click.

FIGURE 32–37 The fuel level must be above 15% and below 85% before the EVAP monitor will run on most vehicles.

TYPICAL EVAP MONITOR

The PCM will run the EVAP monitor when the following enable criteria are met. Typical enable criteria include:

- Cold start
- BARO greater than 70 kPa (20.7 in. Hg or 10.2 PSI)
- IAT between 39° and 86°F at engine start-up
- ECT between 39° and 86°F at engine start-up
- ECT and IAT within 39°F of each other at engine start-up
- Fuel level within 15% to 85%
- TP sensor between 9% and 35%

RUNNING THE EVAP MONITOR There are four tests which are performed during a typical GM EVAP monitor. A DTC is assigned to each test.

1. **Weak Vacuum Test (P0440—large leak).** This test identifies gross leaks. During the monitor, the vent solenoid is closed and the purge solenoid is duty cycled. The FTP should indicate a vacuum of approximately 6 to 10 in. H_2O.

2. **Small Leak Test (P0442—small leak).** After the large leak test passes, the PCM checks for a small leak by keeping the vent solenoid closed and closing the purge solenoid. The system is now sealed. The PCM measures the change in FTP voltage over time.

3. **Excess Vacuum Test (P0446).** This test checks for vent path restrictions. With the vent solenoid open and purge commanded, the PCM should not see excessive vacuum in the EVAP system. Typical EVAP system vacuum with the vent solenoid open is about 5 to 6 in. H_2O.

TECH TIP

Keep the Fuel Tank Properly Filled

Most evaporative system monitors will not run unless the fuel level is between 15% and 85%. In other words, if a driver always runs with close to an empty tank or always tries to keep the tank full, the EVAP monitor may not run. ● **SEE FIGURE 32–37.**

4. **Purge Solenoid Leak Test (P1442).** With the purge solenoid closed and vent solenoid closed, no vacuum should be present in the system. If there is vacuum present, the purge solenoid may be leaking.

EVAP System-Related Diagnostic Trouble Codes

Diagnostic Trouble Code	Description	Possible Causes
P0440	Evaporative system fault	• Loose gas cap • Defective EVAP vent • Cracked charcoal canister • EVAP vent or purge vapor line problems
P0442	Small leak detected	• Loose gas cap • Defective EVAP vent or purge solenoid • EVAP vent or purge line problems
P0446	EVAP canister vent blocked	• EVAP vent or purge solenoid electrical problems • Restricted EVAP canister vent line

1. Recirculating 6% to 10% inert exhaust gases back into the intake system reduces peak temperature inside the combustion chamber and reduces NO_X exhaust emissions.

2. EGR is usually not needed at idle, at wide-open throttle, or when the engine is cold.

3. Many EGR systems use a feedback potentiometer to signal the PCM the position of the EGR valve pintle.

4. OBD-II regulation requires that the flow rate be tested and then is achieved by opening the EGR valve and observing the reaction of the MAP sensor.

5. Positive crankcase ventilation (PCV) systems use a valve or a fixed orifice to transfer and control the fumes from the crankcase back into the intake system.

6. A PCV valve regulates the flow of fumes depending on engine vacuum and seals the crankcase vent in the event of a backfire.

7. As much as 30% of the air needed by the engine at idle speed flows through the PCV system.

8. The AIR system forces air at low pressure into the exhaust to reduce CO and HC exhaust emissions.

9. A catalytic converter is an after-treatment device that reduces exhaust emissions outside of the engine. A catalyst is an element that starts a chemical reaction but is not consumed in the process.

10. The catalyst material used in a catalytic converter includes rhodium, palladium, and platinum.

11. The OBD-II system monitor compares the relative activity of a rear oxygen sensor to the precatalytic oxygen sensor to determine catalytic converter efficiency.

12. The purpose of the evaporative emission (EVAP) control system is to reduce the release of volatile organic compounds (VOCs) into the atmosphere.

13. A carbon (charcoal) canister is used to trap and hold gasoline vapors until they can be purged and run into the engine to be burned.

14. OBD-II regulation requires that the evaporative emission control system be checked for leakage and proper purge flow rates.

15. External leaks can best be located by pressurizing the fuel system with low-pressure smoke.

REVIEW QUESTIONS

1. How does the use of exhaust gas reduce NO_X exhaust emission?

2. How does the DPFE sensor work?

3. What exhaust emissions does the SAI system control?

4. How does a catalytic converter reduce NO_X to nitrogen and oxygen?

5. How does the computer monitor catalytic converter performance?

6. What components are used in a typical evaporative emission control system?

7. How does the computer control the purging of the vapor canister?

CHAPTER QUIZ

1. Two technicians are discussing clogged EGR passages. Technician A says clogged EGR passages can cause excessive NO_X exhaust emission. Technician B says that clogged EGR passages can cause the engine to ping (spark knock or detonation). Which technician is correct?
   a. Technician A only
   b. Technician B only
   c. Both Technicians A and B
   d. Neither Technician A nor B

2. An EGR valve that is partially stuck open would *most likely* cause what condition?
   a. Rough idle/stalling
   b. Excessive NO_X exhaust emissions
   c. Ping (spark knock or detonation)
   d. Missing at highway speed

3. How much air flows through the PCV system when the engine is at idle speed?
   a. 1% to 3%
   b. 5% to 10%
   c. 10% to 20%
   d. Up to 30%

4. Technician A says that if a PCV valve rattles, then it is okay and does not need to be replaced. Technician B says that if a PCV valve does not rattle, it should be replaced. Which technician is correct?
   a. Technician A only
   b. Technician B only
   c. Both Technicians A and B
   d. Neither Technician A nor B

5. The switching valves on the AIR pump have failed several times. Technician A says that a defective exhaust check valve could be the cause. Technician B says that a restricted exhaust system could be the cause. Which technician is correct?
   a. Technician A only
   b. Technician B only
   c. Both Technicians A and B
   d. Neither Technician A nor B

6. Two technicians are discussing testing a catalytic converter. Technician A says that a vacuum gauge can be used and observed to see if the vacuum drops with the engine at idle for 30 seconds. Technician B says that a pressure gauge can be used to check for backpressure. Which technician is correct?
   a. Technician A only
   b. Technician B only
   c. Both Technicians A and B
   d. Neither Technician A nor B

7. At about what temperature does oxygen combine with the nitrogen in the air to form NO_x?
   a. 500°F (260°C)
   b. 750°F (400°C)
   c. 1500°F (815°C)
   d. 2500°F (1370°C)

8. A P0401 is being discussed. Technician A says that a stuck-closed EGR valve could be the cause. Technician B says that clogged EGR ports could be the cause. Which technician is correct?
   a. Technician A only
   b. Technician B only
   c. Both Technicians A and B
   d. Neither Technician A nor B

9. Which EVAP valve(s) is (are) normally closed?
   a. Canister purge valve
   b. Canister vent valve
   c. Both canister purge and canister vent valve
   d. Neither canister purge nor canister vent valve

10. Before an evaporative emission monitor will run, the fuel level must be where?
    a. At least 75% full
    b. Over 25%
    c. Between 15% and 85%
    d. The level of the fuel in the tank is not needed to run the monitor test

SCAN TOOLS AND ENGINE PERFORMANCE DIAGNOSIS

After studying Chapter 33, the reader will be able to:

1. Prepare for the ASE computerized engine controls diagnosis (A8) certification test content area "E".
2. List the steps of the diagnostic process.
3. Describe the simple preliminary tests that should be performed at the start of the diagnostic process.
4. List six items to check as part of a thorough visual inspection.
5. Explain the troubleshooting procedures to follow if a diagnostic trouble code has been set.
6. Explain the troubleshooting procedures to follow if no diagnostic trouble code has been set.
7. Discuss the type of scan tools that are used to assess vehicle components.
8. Describe the methods that can be used to reprogram (reflash) a vehicle computer.

Data link connector (DLC) 527
Drive cycle 542
Flash code retrieval 532
Key-on–engine off test (KOEO) 533
Key-on–engine running test (KOER) 533
Paper test 526
Pending code 527
Self-test automatic read-out (STAR) 533
Smoke machine 526
Technical service bulletin (TSB) 527
Trip 537

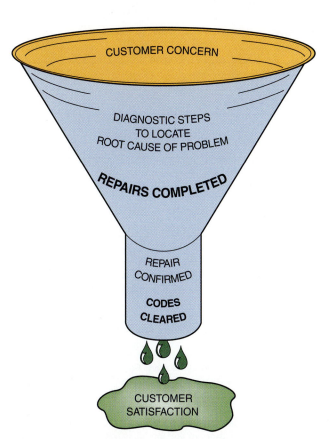

FIGURE 33–1 A funnel is one way to visualize the diagnostic process. The purpose is to narrow the possible causes of a concern until the root cause is determined and corrected.

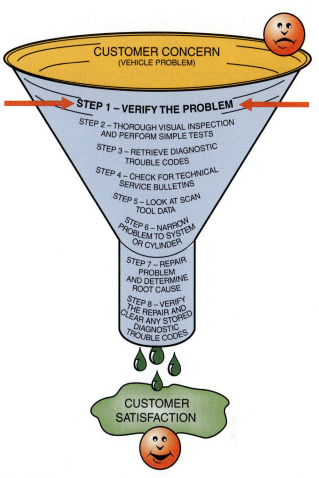

FIGURE 33–2 Step #1 is to verify the customer concern or problem. If the problem cannot be verified, then the repair cannot be verified.

THE EIGHT-STEP DIAGNOSTIC PROCEDURE

It is important that all automotive service technicians know how to diagnose and troubleshoot engine computer systems. The diagnostic process is a strategy that eliminates known-good components or systems in order to find the root cause of automotive engine performance problems. All vehicle manufacturers recommend a diagnostic procedure, and the plan suggested in this chapter combines most of the features of these plans plus additional steps developed over years of real-world problem solving.

Many different things can cause an engine performance problem or concern. The service technician has to narrow the possibilities to find the cause of the problem and correct it. A funnel is a way of visualizing a diagnostic procedure. ● **SEE FIGURE 33–1.** At the wide top are the symptoms of the problem; the funnel narrows as possible causes are eliminated until the root cause is found and corrected at the bottom of the funnel.

All problem diagnosis deals with symptoms that could be the result of many different causes. The wide range of possible solutions must be narrowed to the most likely and these must eventually be further narrowed to the actual cause. The following section describes eight steps the service technician can take to narrow the possibilities to one cause.

STEP 1 VERIFY THE PROBLEM (CONCERN)
Before a minute is spent on diagnosis, be certain that a problem exists. If the problem cannot be verified, it cannot be solved or tested to verify that the repair was complete. ● **SEE FIGURE 33–2.**

The driver of the vehicle knows much about the vehicle and how it is driven. *Before* diagnosis, always ask the following questions:

- Is the malfunction indicator light (check engine) on?
- What was the temperature outside?
- Was the engine warm or cold?

ENGINE PERFORMANCE DIAGNOSIS WORKSHEET
(To Be Filled Out By the Vehicle Owner)

Name: _____ Mileage: _____ Date: _____

Make: _____ Model: _____ Year: _____ Engine: _____

(Please Circle All That Apply in All Categories)	
Describe Problem:	
When Did the Problem First Occur?	• Just Started • Last Week • Last Month • Other _____
List Previous Repairs in the Last 6 Months:	
Starting Problems	• Will Not Crank • Cranks, but Will Not Start • Starts, but Takes a Long Time
Engine Quits or Stalls	• Right after Starting • When Put into Gear • During Steady Speed Driving • Right after Vehicle Comes to a Stop • While Idling • During Acceleration • When Parking
Poor Idling Conditions	• Is Too Slow at All Times • Is Too Fast • Intermittently Too Fast or Too Slow • Is Rough or Uneven • Fluctuates Up and Down
Poor Running Conditions	• Runs Rough • Lacks Power • Bucks and Jerks • Poor Fuel Economy • Hesitates or Stumbles on Acceleration • Backfires • Misfires or Cuts Out • Engine Knocks, Pings, Rattles • Surges • Dieseling or Run-On
Auto. Transmission Problems	• Improper Shifting (Early/Late) • Changes Gear Incorrectly • Vehicle Does Not Move when in Gear • Jerks or Bucks
Usually Occurs	• Morning • Afternoon • Anytime
Engine Temperature	• Cold • Warm • Hot
Driving Conditions During Occurrence	• Short—Less Than 2 Miles • 2–10 Miles • Long—More Than 10 Miles • Stop and Go • While Turning • While Braking • At Gear Engagement • With A/C Operating • With Headlights On • During Acceleration • During Deceleration • Mostly Downhill • Mostly Uphill • Mostly Level • Mostly Curvy • Rough Road
Driving Habits	• Mostly City Driving • Highway • Park Vehicle Inside • Park Vehicle Outside **Drive Per Day:** • Less Than 10 Miles • 10–50 • More Than 50
Gasoline Used	**Fuel Octane:** • 87 • 89 • 91 • More Than 91 **Brand:** _____
Temperature when Problem Occurs	• 32–55° F • Below Freezing (32° F) • Above 55° F
Check Engine Light/ Dash Warning Light	• Light on Sometimes • Light on Always • Light Never On
Smells	• "Hot" • Gasoline • Oil Burning • Electrical
Noises	• Rattle • Knock • Squeak • Other

FIGURE 33–3 A form that the customer should fill out if there is a driveablilty concern to help the service technician more quickly find the root cause.

- Was the problem during starting, acceleration, cruise, or some other condition?

- How far had the vehicle been driven?

- Were any dash warning lights on? If so, which one(s)?

- Has there been any service or repair work performed on the vehicle lately?

NOTE: This last question is very important. Many engine performance faults are often the result of something being knocked loose or a hose falling off during repair work. Knowing that the vehicle was just serviced before the problem began may be an indicator as to where to look for the solution to a problem.

After the nature and scope of the problem are determined, the complaint should be verified before further diagnostic tests are performed. A sample form that customers could fill out with details of the problem is shown in ● **FIGURE 33–3.**

NOTE: Because drivers differ, it is sometimes the best policy to take the customer on the test drive to verify the concern.

STEP 2 PERFORM A THOROUGH VISUAL INSPECTION AND BASIC TESTS
The visual inspection is the most important aspect of diagnosis! Most experts agree that between

FIGURE 33–4 This is what was found when removing an air filter from a vehicle that had a lack-of-power concern. Obviously the nuts were deposited by squirrels or some other animal, blocking a lot of the airflow into the engine.

10% and 30% of all engine performance problems can be found simply by performing a *thorough* visual inspection. The inspection should include the following:

- **Check for obvious problems (basics, basics, basics).**
  Fuel leaks
  Vacuum hoses that are disconnected or split
  Corroded connectors
  Unusual noises, smoke, or smell
  Check the air cleaner and air duct (squirrels and other small animals can build nests or store dog food in them). ● **SEE FIGURE 33–4.**

- **Check everything that does and does not work.** This step involves turning things on and observing that everything is working properly.

- **Look for evidence of previous repairs.** Any time work is performed on a vehicle, there is always a risk that something will be disturbed, knocked off, or left disconnected.

- **Check oil level and condition.** Another area for visual inspection is oil level and condition.
  Oil level. Oil should be to the proper level.
  Oil condition. Using a match or lighter, try to light the oil on the dipstick; if the oil flames up, gasoline is present in the engine oil. Drip some engine oil from the dipstick onto the hot exhaust manifold. If the oil bubbles or boils, coolant (water) is present in the oil. Check for grittiness by rubbing the oil between your fingers.

NOTE: Gasoline in the oil will cause the engine to run rich by drawing fuel through the positive crankcase ventilation (PCV) system.

TECH TIP

"Original Equipment" Is Not a Four-Letter Word

To many service technicians, an original-equipment part is considered to be only marginal and to get the really "good stuff" an aftermarket (renewal market) part has to be purchased. However, many problems can be traced to the use of an aftermarket part that has failed early in its service life. Technicians who work at dealerships usually go immediately to an aftermarket part that is observed during a visual inspection. It has been their experience that simply replacing the aftermarket part with the factory original-equipment (OE) part often solves the problem.

Original equipment parts are *required* to pass quality and durability standards and tests at a level not required of aftermarket parts. The technician should be aware that the presence of a new part does not necessarily mean that the part is good.

FIGURE 33–5 Using a bright light makes seeing where the smoke is coming from easier. In this case, smoke was added to the intake manifold with the inlet blocked with a yellow plastic cap and smoke was seen escaping past a gasket at the idle air control.

TECH TIP

Smoke Machine Testing

Vacuum (air) leaks can cause a variety of driveability problems and are often difficult to locate. One good method is to use a machine that generates a stream of smoke. Connecting the outlet of the **smoke machine** to the hose that was removed from the vacuum brake booster allows smoke to enter the intake manifold. Any vacuum leaks will be spotted by observing smoke coming out of the leak.
● **SEE FIGURE 33–5.**

THE EIGHT-STEP DIAGNOSTIC PROCEDURE (CONTINUED)

- **Check coolant level and condition.** Many mechanical engine problems are caused by overheating. The proper operation of the cooling system is critical to the life of any engine.

  NOTE: Check the coolant level in the radiator only if the radiator is cool. If the radiator is hot and the radiator cap is removed, the drop in pressure above the coolant will cause the coolant to boil immediately, which can cause severe burns because the coolant expands explosively upward and outward from the radiator opening.

- **Use the paper test.** A soundly running engine should produce even and steady exhaust at the tailpipe. For the **paper test,** hold a piece of paper (even a dollar bill works) or a 3-by-5-inch card within 1 inch (2.5 centimeters) of the tailpipe with the engine running at idle. The paper should blow evenly away from the end of the tailpipe without "puffing" or being drawn inward toward the end of the tailpipe. If the paper is at times drawn *toward* the tailpipe, the valves in one or more cylinders could be burned. Other reasons why the paper might be drawn toward the tailpipe include the following:

  1. The engine could be misfiring because of a lean condition that could occur normally when the engine is cold.

  2. Pulsing of the paper toward the tailpipe could also be caused by a hole in the exhaust system. If exhaust escapes through a hole in the exhaust system, air could be drawn—in the intervals between the exhaust puffs—from the tailpipe to the hole in the exhaust, causing the paper to be drawn toward the tailpipe.

- **Ensure adequate fuel level.** Make certain that the fuel tank is at least one-fourth to one-half full; if the fuel level is low it is possible that any water or alcohol at the bottom of the fuel tank is more concentrated and can be drawn into the fuel system.

- **Check the battery voltage.** The voltage of the battery should be at least 12.4 volts and the charging voltage (engine running) should be 13.5 to 15.0 volts at 2000 RPM. Low battery voltage can cause a variety of problems including reduced fuel economy and incorrect (usually too high) idle speed. Higher-than-normal battery voltage can also cause the PCM problems and could cause damage to electronic modules.

- **Check the spark using a spark tester.** Remove one spark plug wire and attach the removed plug wire to the spark tester. Attach the grounding clip of the spark tester to a good clean engine ground, start or crank the engine, and observe the spark tester. ● **SEE FIGURE 33–6.** The spark at the spark tester should be steady and consistent.

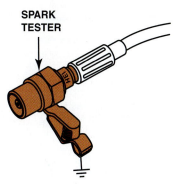

SPARK TESTER

FIGURE 33–6 A spark tester connected to a spark plug wire or coil output. A typical spark tester will only fire if at least 25,000 volts is available from the coil, making a spark tester a very useful tool. Do not use one that just lights when a spark is present, because they do not require more than about 2,000 volts to light.

CUSTOMER CONCERN
(VEHICLE PROBLEM)

STEP 1 – VERIFY THE PROBLEM
STEP 2 – THOROUGH VISUAL INSPECTION AND PERFORM SIMPLE TESTS
STEP 3 – RETRIEVE DIAGNOSTIC TROUBLE CODES
STEP 4 – CHECK FOR TECHNICAL SERVICE BULLETINS
STEP 5 – LOOK AT SCAN TOOL DATA
STEP 6 – NARROW PROBLEM TO SYSTEM OR CYLINDER
STEP 7 – REPAIR PROBLEM AND DETERMINE ROOT CAUSE
STEP 8 – VERIFY THE REPAIR AND CLEAR ANY STORED DIAGNOSTIC TROUBLE CODES

CUSTOMER SATISFACTION

FIGURE 33–7 Step 3 in the diagnostic process is to retrieve any stored diagnostic trouble codes.

If an intermittent spark occurs, then this condition should be treated as a no-spark condition. If this test does not show satisfactory spark, carefully inspect and test all components of the primary and secondary ignition systems.

NOTE: Do not use a standard spark plug to check for proper ignition system voltage. An electronic ignition spark tester is designed to force the spark to jump about 0.75 inch (19 mm). This amount of gap requires between 25,000 and 30,000 volts (25 to 30 kV) at atmospheric pressure, which is enough voltage to ensure that a spark can occur under compression inside an engine.

■ **Check the fuel-pump pressure.** Checking the fuel-pump pressure is relatively easy on many port-fuel-injected engines. Often the cause of intermittent engine performance is due to a weak electric fuel pump or clogged fuel filter. Checking fuel pump pressure early in the diagnostic process eliminates low fuel pressure as a possibility.

STEP 3 RETRIEVE THE DIAGNOSTIC TROUBLE CODES (DTCs)

If a diagnostic trouble code (DTC) is present in the computer memory, it may be signaled by illuminating a malfunction indicator lamp (MIL), commonly labeled "check engine" or "service engine soon." ● **SEE FIGURE 33–7.** Any code(s) that is displayed when the MIL is *not* on is called a **pending code.** Because the MIL is not on, this indicates that the fault has not repeated to cause the PCM to turn on the MIL. Although this pending code is helpful to the technician to know that a fault has, in the past, been detected, further testing will be needed to find the root cause of the problem.

STEP 4 CHECK FOR TECHNICAL SERVICE BULLETINS (TSBs)

Check for corrections in **technical service bulletins (TSBs)** that match the symptoms. ● **SEE FIGURE 33–8.** According to studies performed by automobile manufacturers, as many as 30% of vehicles can be repaired following the information, suggestions, or replacement parts found in a service bulletin. DTCs must be known before searching for service bulletins, because bulletins often include information on solving problems that involve a stored diagnostic trouble code.

STEP 5 LOOK CAREFULLY AT SCAN TOOL DATA

Vehicle manufacturers have been giving the technician more and more data on a scan tool connected to the **data link**

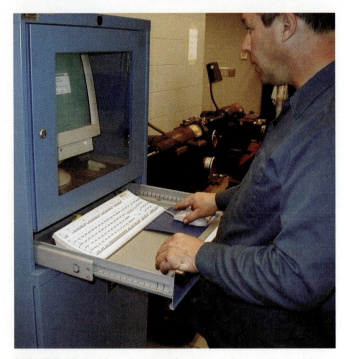

FIGURE 33–8 After checking for stored diagnostic trouble codes (DTCs), the wise technician checks service information for any technical service bulletins that may relate to the vehicle being serviced.

FIGURE 33–9 Looking carefully at the scan tool data is very helpful in locating the source of a problem.

THE EIGHT-STEP DIAGNOSTIC PROCEDURE (CONTINUED)

connector (DLC). ● SEE FIGURE 33–9. Beginning technicians are often observed scrolling through scan data without a real clue about what they are looking for. When asked, they usually reply that they are looking for something unusual, as if the screen will flash a big message "LOOK HERE—THIS IS NOT CORRECT." That statement does not appear on scan tool displays. The best way to look at scan data is in a definite sequence and with specific, selected bits of data that can tell the most about the operation of the engine, such as the following:

- Engine coolant temperature (ECT) is the same as intake air temperature (IAT) after the vehicle sits for several hours.

- Idle air control (IAC) valve is being commanded to an acceptable range.

- Oxygen sensor (O2S) is operating properly:
  1. Readings below 200 mV at times
  2. Readings above 800 mV at times
  3. Rapid transitions between rich and lean

STEP 6 NARROW THE PROBLEM TO A SYSTEM OR CYLINDER
Narrowing the focus to a system or individual cylinder is the hardest part of the entire diagnostic process.

- Perform a cylinder power balance test.
- If a weak cylinder is detected, perform a compression and a cylinder leakage test to determine the probable cause.

STEP 7 REPAIR THE PROBLEM AND DETERMINE THE ROOT CAUSE
The repair or part replacement must be performed following vehicle manufacturer's recommendations and be certain that the root cause of the problem has been found. Also follow the manufacturer's recommended repair procedures and methods.

STEP 8 VERIFY THE REPAIR AND CLEAR ANY STORED DTCs
● SEE FIGURE 33–10.

- Test drive to verify that the original problem (concern) is fixed.

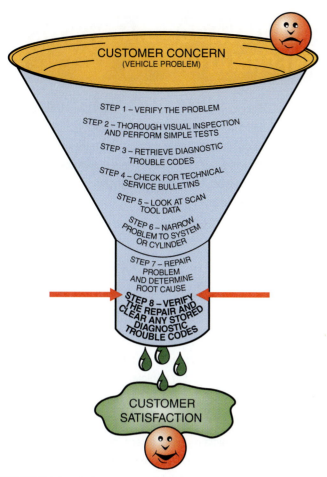

FIGURE 33–10 Step 8 is very important. Be sure that the customer's concern has been corrected.

- Verify that no additional problems have occurred during the repair process.

- Check for and then clear all diagnostic trouble codes. (This step ensures that the computer will not make any changes based on a stored DTC, but should not be performed if the vehicle is going to be tested for emissions because all of the monitors will need to be run and pass.)

- Return the vehicle to the customer and double-check the following:

  1. The vehicle is clean.
  2. The radio is turned off.
  3. The clock is set to the right time and the radio stations have been restored if the battery was disconnected during the repair procedure.

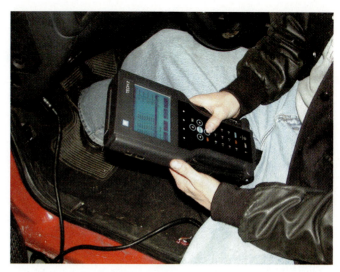

FIGURE 33–11 A TECH 2 scan tool is the factory scan tool used on General Motors vehicles.

🔧 **TECH TIP**

One Test Is Worth 1,000 "Expert" Opinions

Whenever any vehicle has an engine performance or driveability concern, certain people always say:

"Sounds like it's a bad injector."

"I'll bet you it's a bad computer."

"I had a problem just like yours yesterday and it was a bad EGR valve."

Regardless of the skills and talents of those people, it is still more accurate to perform tests on the vehicle than to rely on feelings or opinions of others who have not even seen the vehicle. Even your own opinion should not sway your thinking. Follow a plan, perform tests, and the test results will lead to the root cause.

SCAN TOOLS

Scan tools are the workhorse for any diagnostic work on all vehicles. Scan tools can be divided into two basic groups:

1. **Factory scan tools.** These are the scan tools required by all dealers that sell and service the brand of vehicle. Examples of factory scan tools include:
   - **General Motors**—Tech 2. ● **SEE FIGURE 33–11.**
   - **Ford**—New Generation Star (NGS)
   - **Chrysler**—DRB-III or Star Scan (CAN-equipped vehicles)

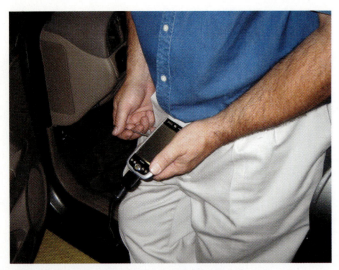

FIGURE 33–12 Some scan tools use pocket PCS which make it very convenient to use.

SCAN TOOLS (CONTINUED)

- **Honda**—HDS or Master Tech
- **Toyota**—Master Tech

All factory scan tools are designed to provide bidirectional capability which allows the service technician the opportunity to operate components using the scan tool thereby confirming that the component is able to work when commanded. Also all factory scan tools are capable of displaying all factory parameters.

2. **Aftermarket scan tools.** These scan tools are designed to function on more than one brand of vehicle. Examples of aftermarket scan tools include:

- **Snap-on** (various models including the MT2500 and Modis)
- **OTC** (various models including Genisys and Task Master)
- **AutoEnginuity** and other programs that use a laptop or handheld computer for the display

While many aftermarket scan tools can display most if not all of the parameters of the factory scan tool, there can be a difference when trying to troubleshoot some faults. ● **SEE FIGURE 33–12.**

RETRIEVAL OF DIAGNOSTIC INFORMATION

To retrieve diagnostic information from the Powertrain Control Module (PCM), a scan tool is needed. If a factory or factory-level scan tool is used, then all of the data can be retrieved. If a global (generic) only type scan tool is used, only the emissions-related data can be retrieved. To retrieve diagnostic information from the PCM, use the following steps:

STEP 1 Locate and gain access to the data link connector (DLC).

STEP 2 Connect the scan tool to the DLC and establish communication.

> **NOTE: If no communication is established, follow the vehicle manufacturer's specified instructions.**

STEP 3 Follow the on-screen instructions of the scan tool to correctly identify the vehicle.

STEP 4 Observe the scan data, as well as any diagnostic trouble codes.

STEP 5 Follow vehicle manufacturer's instructions if any DTCs are stored. If no DTCs are stored, compare all sensor values with a factory acceptable range chart to see if any sensor values are out-of-range.

Parameter Identification (PID)

Scan Tool Parameter	Units Displayed	Typical Data Value
Engine Idling/Radiator Hose Hot/Closed Throttle/ Park or Neutral/Closed Loop/Accessories Off/ Brake Pedal Released		
3X Crank Sensor	RPM	Varies
24X Crank Sensor	RPM	Varies
Actual EGR Position	Percent	0
BARO	kPa/Volts	65–110 kPa/ 3.5–4.5 Volts
CMP Sensor Signal Present	Yes/No	Yes
Commanded Fuel Pump	On/Off	On
Cycles of Misfire Data	Counts	0–99
Desired EGR Position	Percent	0

ECT	°C/°F	Varies
EGR Duty Cycle	Percent	0
Engine Run Time	Hr: Min: Sec	Varies
EVAP Canister Purge	Percent	Low and Varying
EVAP Fault History	No Fault/ Excess Vacuum/ Purge Valve Leak/ Small Leak/ Weak Vacuum	No Fault
Fuel Tank Pressure	Inches of H_2O/ Volts	Varies
HO2S Sensor 1	Ready/ Not Ready	Ready
HO2S Sensor 1	Millivolts	0–1,000 and Varying
HO2S Sensor 2	Millivolts	0–1,000 and Varying
HO2S X Counts	Counts	Varies
IAC Position	Counts	15–25 preferred
IAT	°C/°F	Varies
Knock Retard	Degrees	0
Long Term FT	Percent	0–10
MAF	Grams per second	3–7
MAF Frequency	Hz	1,200–3,000 (depends on altitude and engine load)
MAP	kPa/Volts	20–48 kPa/0.75–2 Volts (depends on altitude)
Misfire Current Cyl. 1–10	Counts	0
Misfire History Cyl. 1–10	Counts	0
Short Term FT	Percent	0–10
Start Up ECT	°C/°F	Varies
Start Up IAT	°C/°F	Varies
Total Misfire Current Count	Counts	0
Total Misfire Failures	Counts	0
Total Misfire Passes	Counts	0
TP Angle	Percent	0
TP Sensor	Volts	0.20–0.74
Vehicle Speed	MPH/Km/h	0

Note: Viewing the PID screen on the scanner is useful in determining if a problem is occurring at the present time.

TROUBLESHOOTING USING DIAGNOSTIC TROUBLE CODES

Pinning down causes of the actual problem can be accomplished by trying to set the opposite code. For example, if a code indicates an open throttle position (TP) sensor (high resistance), clear the code and create a shorted (low-resistance) condition. This can be accomplished by using a jumper wire and connecting the signal terminal to the 5-volt reference terminal. This should set a diagnostic trouble code.

- **If the opposite code sets,** this indicates that the wiring and connector for the sensor is okay and the sensor itself is defective (open).

- **If the same code sets,** this indicates that the wiring or electrical connection is open (has high resistance) and is the cause of the setting of the DTC.

METHODS FOR CLEARING DIAGNOSTIC TROUBLE CODES
Clearing diagnostic trouble codes from a vehicle computer sometimes needs to be performed. There are three methods that can be used to clear stored diagnostic trouble codes.

CAUTION: Clearing diagnostic trouble codes (DTCs) also will clear all of the noncontinuous monitors.

- **Clearing codes—Method 1.** The preferred method of clearing codes is by using a scan tool. This is the method recommended by most vehicle manufacturers if the procedure can be performed on the vehicle. The computer of some vehicles cannot be cleared with a scan tool.

- **Clearing codes—Method 2.** If a scan tool is not available or a scan tool cannot be used on the vehicle being serviced, the power to the computer can be disconnected.

  1. Disconnect the fusible link (if so equipped) that feeds the computer.

  2. Disconnect the fuse or fuses that feed the computer.

  NOTE: The fuse may not be labeled as a computer fuse. For example, many Toyotas can be cleared by disconnecting the fuel-injection fuse. Some vehicles require that two fuses be disconnected to clear any stored codes.

- **Clearing codes—Method 3.** If the other two methods cannot be used, the negative (−) battery cable can be disconnected to clear stored diagnostic trouble codes.

NOTE: Because of the adaptive learning capacity of the computer, a vehicle may fail an exhaust emissions test if the vehicle is not driven enough to allow the computer to run all of the monitors.

CAUTION: By disconnecting the battery, the radio presets and clock information will be lost. They should be reset before returning the vehicle to the customer. If the radio has a security code, the code must be entered before the radio will function. Before disconnecting the battery, always check with the vehicle owner to be sure that the code is available.

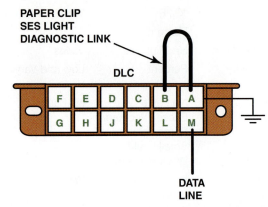

FIGURE 33–13 To retrieve flash codes from an OBD-I General Motors vehicle, connect terminals A and B with the ignition on–engine off. The M terminal is used to retrieve data from the sensors to a scan tool.

FLASH CODE RETRIEVAL ON OBD-I GENERAL MOTORS VEHICLES

The GM system uses a "check engine" or "check engine soon" MIL to notify the driver of possible system failure. Under the dash (on most GM vehicles) is a data link connector (DLC) previously called an assembly line communications link (ALCL) or assembly line diagnostic link (ALDL).

Most General Motors diagnostic trouble codes can be retrieved by using a metal tool and contacting terminals A and B of the 12-pin DLC.  **SEE FIGURE 33–13.** This method is called **flash code retrieval** because the MIL will flash to indicate diagnostic trouble codes. The steps are as follows:

1. Turn the ignition switch to on (engine off). The "check engine" light or "service engine soon" light should be on. If the amber malfunction indicator light (MIL) is not on, a problem exists within the light circuit.

2. Connect terminals A and B at the DLC.

3. Observe the MIL. A code 12 (one flash, then a pause, then two flashes) reveals that there is no engine speed indication to the computer. Because the engine is not running, this simply indicates that the computer diagnostic system is working correctly.

   NOTE: Refer to service manual diagnostic procedures if the MIL is on and does not flash a code 12 when terminals A and B are connected.

4. After code 12 is displayed three times, the MIL will flash any other stored DTCs in numeric order starting with the lowest-number code. If only code 12 is displayed another three times, the computer has not detected any other faults.

NOTE: Trouble codes can vary according to year, make, model, and engine. Always consult the service literature or service manual for the exact vehicle being serviced. Check service information for the meaning and recommended steps to follow if a diagnostic trouble code is retrieved.

🔧 **TECH TIP**

Do Not Lie to a Scan Tool!

Because computer calibration may vary from year to year, using the incorrect year for the vehicle while using a scan tool can cause the data retrieved to be incorrect or inaccurate.

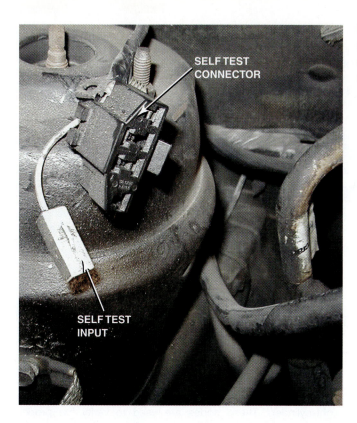

SELF TEST CONNECTOR

SELF TEST INPUT

FIGURE 33–14 A Ford OBD-I self-test connector. The location of this connector can vary with model and year of vehicle.

RETRIEVING FORD DIAGNOSTIC CODES

The best tool to use during troubleshooting of a Ford vehicle is a **self-test automatic readout (STAR)** tester, new generation STAR (NGS), WDS (Worldwide Diagnostic System), or another scan tool with Ford capabilities. If a STAR tester or scan tool is not available, a needle (analog) type of voltmeter can be used for all OBD-I (prior to 1996) systems. See the Tech Tip "Put a Wire in the Attic and a Light in the Basement!" to obtain flash codes. The test connector is usually located under the hood on the driver's side. ● **SEE FIGURE 33–14.**

KEY ON–ENGINE OFF TEST (ON-DEMAND CODES OR HARD FAULTS)

With the ignition key on (engine off), watch the voltmeter pulses, which should appear within 5 to 30 seconds. (Ignore any initial surge of voltage when the ignition is turned on.)

The computer will send a two-digit code that will cause the voltmeter to pulse or move from left to right. For example, if the voltmeter needle pulses two times, then pauses for 2 seconds, and then pulses three times, the code is 23. There is normally a 4-second pause between codes.

SEPARATOR PULSE. After all the codes have been reported, the computer will pause for about 6 to 9 seconds, then cause the voltmeter needle to pulse once, and then pause for another 6 to

9 seconds. This is the normal separation between current trouble codes and continuous memory codes (for intermittent problems). Code 11 is the normal pass code, which means that no fault has been stored in memory. Therefore, normal operation of the diagnostic procedure using a voltmeter should indicate the following if no codes are set: 1 pulse (2-second pause), 1 pulse (6- to 9-second pause), 1 pulse (6- to 9-second pause), 1 pulse (2-second pause), and finally, 1 pulse. These last two pulses that are separated by a 2-second interval represent a code 11, which is the code used between current and intermittent trouble codes.

CONTINUOUS MEMORY CODES (SOFT CODES)

Continuous memory codes are set based on information stored while the vehicle was in normal operation. These codes represent an intermittent problem and should only be used for diagnosis if the **KOEO** test results in code 11 (no faults detected). Therefore, any codes displayed after the separation pulse represent failures that have been detected but may no longer be present.

KEY ON–ENGINE RUNNING (KOER) TEST

During the **KOER** self-test, the sensors are checked by the computer under actual operating conditions and the output devices (actuators) are operated and checked for expected results. Start the

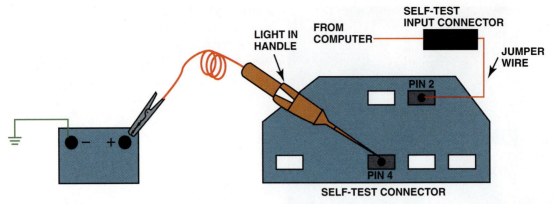

FIGURE 33–15 To retrieve Ford DTCs using a test light and a jumper wire, turn the ignition switch on (engine off) and make the connections shown. The test light will blink out the diagnostic trouble codes.

RETRIEVING FORD DIAGNOSTIC CODES (CONTINUED)

 **TECH TIP**

Put a Wire in the Attic and a Light in the Basement!

Retrieving DTCs from a Ford using low-cost test equipment is easier when you remember the following: *"Put a wire in the attic and a light in the basement."*

After warming the engine to operating temperature, perform these simple steps:

1. Locate the data link connector (DLC) under the hood. Connect a jumper wire from the single-wire pigtail called the self-test input to terminal #2 at the top (attic) of the connector.

2. To read DTCs, connect a standard 12-volt test light (not a self-powered continuity light) to the positive battery terminal and the lower (basement) terminal (#4) of the DLC. ● **SEE FIGURE 33–15.** Turn the ignition to on (engine off). The DTCs will be displayed by means of the flashes of the test light.

To clear stored Ford DTCs, simply disconnect the jumper wire from the self-test input while the codes are being flashed. This interruption is the signal to the computer to clear any stored DTCs.

engine and raise the speed to 2500 to 3000 RPM to warm the oxygen sensor within 20 seconds of starting. Hold a steady high engine speed until the initial pulses appear (2 pulses for a four-cylinder engine, 3 pulses for a six-cylinder, and 4 pulses for an eight-cylinder). These codes are used to verify the proper processor (computer) is in the vehicle and that the self-test has been entered. Continue to hold a high engine speed until the code pulses begin (10 to 14 seconds).

STEERING, BRAKE, AND OVERDRIVE SWITCH TEST

To test the power steering pressure switch, the technician must turn the steering wheel one-half turn after the ID code has been displayed. The brake pedal and the overdrive cancel switch must also be cycled after the ID code to allow the system to detect a change of state of these switches.

DYNAMIC RESPONSE CHECK. The dynamic response test checks the throttle position (TP) mass air flow (MAF) and manifold absolute pressure (MAP) sensors during a brief wide-open throttle (WOT) test performed by the technician. The signal for the technician to depress the throttle briefly to wide open is a single pulse or a code 10 on a STAR tester.

If any hard (on-demand) faults appear, these should be repaired first and then any soft (continuous) codes next. Use the factory "pinpoint tests" to trace the problem. Refer to service information for a description of Ford-specific alphanumeric DTCs.

FLASH CODE RETRIEVAL ON CHRYSLER VEHICLES

To put the computer into the self-diagnostic mode, the ignition switch must be turned on and off twice within a 5-second period (on-off-on-off-on). The computer will flash a series of fault codes. Older Chrysler brand products flash the "check engine" lamp on the dash.

NOTE: Unlike other manufacturers, most Chrysler brand vehicles equipped with OBD II will display the P-codes on the odometer display by cycling the ignition key as previously performed on older vehicles.

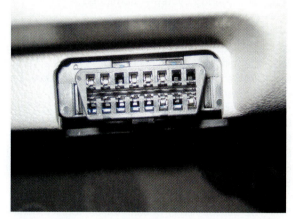

FIGURE 33–16 A typical OBD-II data link connector (DLC). The location varies with make and model and may even be covered, but a tool is not needed to gain access. Check service information for the exact location if needed.

OBD-II DIAGNOSIS

Starting with the 1996 model year, all vehicles sold in the United States must use the same type of 16-pin data link connector (DLC) and must monitor emission-related components. ● **SEE FIGURE 33–16.**

RETRIEVING OBD-II CODES A scan tool is required to retrieve diagnostic trouble codes from most OBD-II vehicles. Every OBD-II scan tool will be able to read all generic Society of Automotive Engineers (SAE) DTCs from any vehicle.

Fuel and Air Metering System

Code	Description
P0100	Mass or Volume Airflow Circuit Problem
P0101	Mass or Volume Airflow Circuit Range or Performance Problem
P0102	Mass or Volume Airflow Circuit Low Input
P0103	Mass or Volume Airflow Circuit High Input
P0105	Manifold Absolute Pressure or Barometric Pressure Circuit Problem
P0106	Manifold Absolute Pressure or Barometric Pressure Circuit Range or Performance Problem
P0107	Manifold Absolute Pressure or Barometric Pressure Circuit Low Input
P0108	Manifold Absolute Pressure or Barometric Pressure Circuit High Input
P0110	Intake Air Temperature Circuit Problem
P0111	Intake Air Temperature Circuit Range or Performance Problem
P0112	Intake Air Temperature Circuit Low Input
P0113	Intake Air Temperature Circuit High Input
P0115	Engine Coolant Temperature Circuit Problem
P0116	Engine Coolant Temperature Circuit Range or Performance Problem
P0117	Engine Coolant Temperature Circuit Low Input
P0118	Engine Coolant Temperature Circuit High Input
P0120	Throttle Position Circuit Problem
P0121	Throttle Position Circuit Range or Performance Problem
P0122	Throttle Position Circuit Low Input
P0123	Throttle Position Circuit High Input
P0125	Excessive Time to Enter Closed-Loop Fuel Control
P0128	Coolant Temperature Below Thermostat Regulating Temperature
P0130	O2 Sensor Circuit Problem (Bank 1* Sensor 1)
P0131	O2 Sensor Circuit Low Voltage (Bank 1* Sensor 1)
P0132	O2 Sensor Circuit High Voltage (Bank 1* Sensor 1)
P0133	O2 Sensor Circuit Slow Response (Bank 1* Sensor 1)
P0134	O2 Sensor Circuit No Activity Detected (Bank 1* Sensor 1)
P0135	O2 Sensor Heater Circuit Problem (Bank 1* Sensor 1)
P0136	O2 Sensor Circuit Problem (Bank 1* Sensor 2)
P0137	O2 Sensor Circuit Low Voltage (Bank 1* Sensor 2)
P0138	O2 Sensor Circuit High Voltage (Bank 1* Sensor 2)
P0139	O2 Sensor Circuit Slow Response (Bank 1* Sensor 2)
P0140	O2 Sensor Circuit No Activity Detected (Bank 1* Sensor 2)
P0141	O2 Sensor Heater Circuit Problem (Bank 1* Sensor 2)
P0142	O2 Sensor Circuit Problem (Bank 1* Sensor 3)
P0143	O2 Sensor Circuit Low Voltage (Bank 1* Sensor 3)
P0144	O2 Sensor Circuit High Voltage (Bank 1* Sensor 3)
P0145	O2 Sensor Circuit Slow Response (Bank 1* Sensor 3)
P0146	O2 Sensor Circuit No Activity Detected (Bank 1* Sensor 3)
P0147	O2 Sensor Heater Circuit Problem (Bank 1* Sensor 3)
P0150	O2 Sensor Circuit Problem (Bank 2 Sensor 1)
P0151	O2 Sensor Circuit Low Voltage (Bank 2 Sensor 1)
P0152	O2 Sensor Circuit High Voltage (Bank 2 Sensor 1)
P0153	O2 Sensor Circuit Slow Response (Bank 2 Sensor 1)
P0154	O2 Sensor Circuit No Activity Detected (Bank 2 Sensor 1)
P0155	O2 Sensor Heater Circuit Problem (Bank 2 Sensor 1)

Fuel and Air Metering System—Continued

P0156	O2 Sensor Circuit Problem (Bank 2 Sensor 2)
P0157	O2 Sensor Circuit Low Voltage (Bank 2 Sensor 2)
P0158	O2 Sensor Circuit High Voltage (Bank 2 Sensor 2)
P0159	O2 Sensor Circuit Slow Response (Bank 2 Sensor 2)
P0160	O2 Sensor Circuit No Activity Detected (Bank 2 Sensor 2)
P0161	O2 Sensor Heater Circuit Problem (Bank 2 Sensor 2)
P0162	O2 Sensor Circuit Problem (Bank 2 Sensor 3)
P0163	O2 Sensor Circuit Low Voltage (Bank 2 Sensor 3)
P0164	O2 Sensor Circuit High Voltage (Bank 2 Sensor 3)
P0165	O2 Sensor Circuit Slow Response (Bank 2 Sensor 3)
P0166	O2 Sensor Circuit No Activity Detected (Bank 2 Sensor 3)
P0167	O2 Sensor Heater Circuit Problem (Bank 2 Sensor 3)
P0170	Fuel Trim Problem (Bank 1*)
P0171	System Too Lean (Bank 1*)
P0172	System Too Rich (Bank 1*)
P0173	Fuel Trim Problem (Bank 2)
P0174	System Too Lean (Bank 2)
P0175	System Too Rich (Bank 2)
P0176	Fuel Composition Sensor Circuit Problem
P0177	Fuel Composition Sensor Circuit Range or Performance
P0178	Fuel Composition Sensor Circuit Low Input
P0179	Fuel Composition Sensor Circuit High Input
P0180	Fuel Temperature Sensor Problem
P0181	Fuel Temperature Sensor Circuit Range or Performance
P0182	Fuel Temperature Sensor Circuit Low Input
P0183	Fuel Temperature Sensor Circuit High Input

Fuel and Air Metering (Injector Circuit)

P0201	Injector Circuit Problem—Cylinder 1
P0202	Injector Circuit Problem—Cylinder 2
P0203	Injector Circuit Problem—Cylinder 3
P0204	Injector Circuit Problem—Cylinder 4
P0205	Injector Circuit Problem—Cylinder 5
P0206	Injector Circuit Problem—Cylinder 6
P0207	Injector Circuit Problem—Cylinder 7
P0208	Injector Circuit Problem—Cylinder 8
P0209	Injector Circuit Problem—Cylinder 9
P0210	Injector Circuit Problem—Cylinder 10
P0211	Injector Circuit Problem—Cylinder 11
P0212	Injector Circuit Problem—Cylinder 12
P0213	Cold Start Injector 1 Problem
P0214	Cold Start Injector 2 Problem

Ignition System or Misfire

P0300	Random Misfire Detected
P0301	Cylinder 1 Misfire Detected
P0302	Cylinder 2 Misfire Detected
P0303	Cylinder 3 Misfire Detected
P0304	Cylinder 4 Misfire Detected
P0305	Cylinder 5 Misfire Detected
P0306	Cylinder 6 Misfire Detected
P0307	Cylinder 7 Misfire Detected
P0308	Cylinder 8 Misfire Detected
P0309	Cylinder 9 Misfire Detected
P0310	Cylinder 10 Misfire Detected
P0311	Cylinder 11 Misfire Detected

P0312	Cylinder 12 Misfire Detected
P0320	Ignition or Distributor Engine Speed Input Circuit Problem
P0321	Ignition or Distributor Engine Speed Input Circuit Range or Performance
P0322	Ignition or Distributor Engine Speed Input Circuit No Signal
P0325	Knock Sensor 1 Circuit Problem
P0326	Knock Sensor 1 Circuit Range or Performance
P0327	Knock Sensor 1 Circuit Low Input
P0328	Knock Sensor 1 Circuit High Input
P0330	Knock Sensor 2 Circuit Problem
P0331	Knock Sensor 2 Circuit Range or Performance
P0332	Knock Sensor 2 Circuit Low Input
P0333	Knock Sensor 2 Circuit High Input
P0335	Crankshaft Position Sensor Circuit Problem
P0336	Crankshaft Position Sensor Circuit Range or Performance
P0337	Crankshaft Position Sensor Circuit Low Input
P0338	Crankshaft Position Sensor Circuit High Input

Auxiliary Emission Controls

P0400	Exhaust Gas Recirculation Flow Problem
P0401	Exhaust Gas Recirculation Flow Insufficient Detected
P0402	Exhaust Gas Recirculation Flow Excessive Detected
P0405	Air Conditioner Refrigerant Charge Loss
P0410	Secondary Air Injection System Problem
P0411	Secondary Air Injection System Insufficient Flow Detected
P0412	Secondary Air Injection System Switching Valve or Circuit Problem
P0413	Secondary Air Injection System Switching Valve or Circuit Open
P0414	Secondary Air Injection System Switching Valve or Circuit Shorted
P0420	Catalyst System Efficiency below Threshold (Bank 1*)
P0421	Warm Up Catalyst Efficiency below Threshold (Bank 1*)
P0422	Main Catalyst Efficiency below Threshold (Bank 1*)
P0423	Heated Catalyst Efficiency below Threshold (Bank 1*)
P0424	Heated Catalyst Temperature below Threshold (Bank 1*)
P0430	Catalyst System Efficiency below Threshold (Bank 2)
P0431	Warm Up Catalyst Efficiency below Threshold (Bank 2)
P0432	Main Catalyst Efficiency below Threshold (Bank 2)
P0433	Heated Catalyst Efficiency below Threshold (Bank 2)
P0434	Heated Catalyst Temperature below Threshold (Bank 2)
P0440	Evaporative Emission Control System Problem
P0441	Evaporative Emission Control System Insufficient Purge Flow
P0442	Evaporative Emission Control System Leak Detected
P0443	Evaporative Emission Control System Purge Control Valve Circuit Problem
P0444	Evaporative Emission Control System Purge Control Valve Circuit Open
P0445	Evaporative Emission Control System Purge Control Valve Circuit Shorted
P0446	Evaporative Emission Control System Vent Control Problem

Auxiliary Emission Controls—Continued

P0447   Evaporative Emission Control System Vent Control Open

P0448   Evaporative Emission Control System Vent Control Shorted

P0450   Evaporative Emission Control System Pressure Sensor Problem

P0451   Evaporative Emission Control System Pressure Sensor Range or Performance

P0452   Evaporative Emission Control System Pressure Sensor Low Input

P0453   Evaporative Emission Control System Pressure Sensor High Input

Vehicle Speed Control and Idle Control

P0500   Vehicle Speed Sensor Problem

P0501   Vehicle Speed Sensor Range or Performance

P0502   Vehicle Speed Sensor Low Input

P0505   Idle Control System Problem

P0506   Idle Control System RPM Lower Than Expected

P0507   Idle Control System RPM Higher Than Expected

P0510   Closed Throttle Position Switch Problem

Computer Output Circuit

P0600   Serial Communication Link Problem

P0605   Internal Control Module (Module Identification Defined by J1979)

Transmission

P0703   Brake Switch Input Problem

P0705   Transmission Range Sensor Circuit Problem (PRNDL Input)

P0706   Transmission Range Sensor Circuit Range or Performance

P0707   Transmission Range Sensor Circuit Low Input

P0708   Transmission Range Sensor Circuit High Input

P0710   Transmission Fluid Temperature Sensor Problem

P0711   Transmission Fluid Temperature Sensor Range or Performance

P0712   Transmission Fluid Temperature Sensor Low Input

P0713   Transmission Fluid Temperature Sensor High Input

P0715   Input or Turbine Speed Sensor Circuit Problem

P0716   Input or Turbine Speed Sensor Circuit Range or Performance

P0717   Input or Turbine Speed Sensor Circuit No Signal

P0720   Output Speed Sensor Circuit Problem

P0721   Output Speed Sensor Circuit Range or Performance

P0722   Output Speed Sensor Circuit No Signal

P0725   Engine Speed Input Circuit Problem

P0726   Engine Speed Input Circuit Range or Performance

P0727   Engine Speed Input Circuit No Signal

P0730   Incorrect Gear Ratio

P0731   Gear 1 Incorrect Ratio

P0732   Gear 2 Incorrect Ratio

P0733   Gear 3 Incorrect Ratio

P0734   Gear 4 Incorrect Ratio

P0735   Gear 5 Incorrect Ratio

P0736   Reverse Incorrect Ratio

P0740   Torque Converter Clutch System Problem

P0741   Torque Converter Clutch System Performance or Stuck Off

P0742   Torque Converter Clutch System Stuck On

P0743   Torque Converter Clutch System Electrical

P0745   Pressure Control Solenoid Problem

P0746   Pressure Control Solenoid Performance or Stuck Off

P0747   Pressure Control Solenoid Stuck On

P0748   Pressure Control Solenoid Electrical

P0750   Shift Solenoid A Problem

P0751   Shift Solenoid A Performance or Stuck Off

P0752   Shift Solenoid A Stuck On

P0753   Shift Solenoid A Electrical

P0755   Shift Solenoid B Problem

P0756   Shift Solenoid B Performance or Stuck Off

P0757   Shift Solenoid B Stuck On

P0758   Shift Solenoid B Electrical

P0760   Shift Solenoid C Problem

P0761   Shift Solenoid C Performance or Stuck Off

P0762   Shift Solenoid C Stuck On

P0763   Shift Solenoid C Electrical

P0765   Shift Solenoid D Problem

P0766   Shift Solenoid D Performance or Stuck Off

P0767   Shift Solenoid D Stuck On

P0768   Shift Solenoid D Electrical

P0770   Shift Solenoid E Problem

P0771   Shift Solenoid E Performance or Stuck Off

P0772   Shift Solenoid E Stuck On

P0773   Shift Solenoid E Electrical

* The side of the engine where number one cylinder is located.

OBD-II ACTIVE TESTS

The vehicle computer must run tests on the various emission-related components and turn on the malfunction indicator lamp (MIL) if faults are detected. OBD II is an *active* computer analysis system because it actually tests the operation of the oxygen sensors, exhaust gas recirculation system, and so forth whenever conditions permit. It is the purpose and function of the Powertrain Control Module (PCM) to monitor these components and perform these active tests.

For example, the PCM may open the EGR valve momentarily to check its operation while the vehicle is decelerating. A change in the manifold absolute pressure (MAP) sensor signal will indicate to the computer that the exhaust gas is, in fact, being introduced into the engine. Because these tests are active and certain conditions must be present before these tests can be run, the computer uses its internal diagnostic program to keep track of all the various conditions and to schedule active tests so that they will not interfere with each other.

OBD-II DRIVE CYCLE   The vehicle must be driven under a variety of operating conditions for all active tests to be performed. A **trip** is defined as an engine-operating drive cycle that contains the necessary conditions for a particular test to be performed. For example, for the EGR test to be performed, the engine has to be at normal operating temperature and decelerating for a minimum amount of time. Some tests are performed when the engine is cold, whereas others require that the vehicle be cruising at a steady highway speed.

TYPES OF OBD-II CODES

Not all OBD-II diagnostic trouble codes are of the same importance for exhaust emissions. Each type of DTC has different requirements for it to set, and the computer will only turn on the MIL for emissions-related DTCs.

TYPE A CODES. A type A diagnostic trouble code is emission related and will cause the MIL to be turned on at the *first trip* if the computer has detected a problem. Engine misfire or a very rich or lean air–fuel ratio, for example, would cause a type A diagnostic trouble code. These codes alert the driver to an emissions problem that may cause damage to the catalytic converter.

TYPE B CODES. A type B code will be stored and the MIL will be turned on during the *second consecutive trip*, alerting the driver to the fact that a diagnostic test was performed and failed.

NOTE: Type A and Type B codes are emission related and will cause the lighting of the malfunction indicator lamp, usually labeled "check engine" or "service engine soon."

TYPE C AND D CODES. Type C and type D codes are for use with non-emission-related diagnostic tests. They will cause the lighting of a "service" lamp (if the vehicle is so equipped).

OBD-II FREEZE-FRAME

To assist the service technician, OBD II requires the computer to take a "snapshot" or freeze-frame of all data at the instant an emission-related DTC is set. A scan tool is required to retrieve this data. CARB and EPA regulations require that the controller store specific freeze-frame (engine-related) data when the first emission related fault is detected. The data stored in freeze-frame can only be replaced by data from a trouble code with a higher priority such as a trouble related to a fuel system or misfire monitor fault.

NOTE: Although OBD II requires that just one freeze-frame of data be stored, the instant an emission-related DTC is set, vehicle manufacturers usually provide expanded data about the DTC beyond that required. However, retrieving enhanced data usually requires the use of the vehicle-specific scan tool.

The freeze-frame has to contain data values that occurred at the time the code was set (these values are provided in standard units of measurement). Freeze-frame data is recorded during the first trip on a two-trip fault. As a result, OBD-II systems record the data present at the time an emission-related code is recorded and the MIL activated. This data can be accessed and displayed on a scan tool. Freeze-frame data is one frame or one instant in time. Freeze-frame data is not updated (refreshed) if the same monitor test fails a second time.

REQUIRED FREEZE-FRAME DATA ITEMS.
- Code that triggered the freeze-frame
- A/F ratio, airflow rate, and calculated engine load
- Base fuel injector pulse width
- ECT, IAT, MAF, MAP, TP, and VS sensor data
- Engine speed and amount of ignition spark advance
- Open- or closed-loop status
- Short-term and long-term fuel trim values
- For misfire codes—identify the cylinder that misfired

NOTE: All freeze-frame data will be lost if the battery is disconnected, power to the PCM is removed, or the scan tool is used to erase or clear trouble codes.

DIAGNOSING INTERMITTENT MALFUNCTIONS

Of all the different types of conditions that you will see, the hardest to accurately diagnose and repair are intermittent malfunctions. These conditions may be temperature related (only occur when the vehicle is hot or cold), or humidity related (only occur when it is raining). Regardless of the conditions that will cause the malfunction to occur, you must diagnose and correct the condition.

When dealing with an intermittent concern, you should determine the conditions when the malfunction occurs, and then try to duplicate those conditions. If a cause is not readily apparent to you, ask the customer when the symptom occurs. Ask if there are any conditions that seem to be related to, or cause the concern.

Another consideration when working on an OBD-II-equipped vehicle is whether a concern is intermittent, or if it only occurs when a specific diagnostic test is performed by the PCM. Since OBD-II systems conduct diagnostic tests only under very precise conditions, some tests may only be run once during an ignition cycle. Additionally, if the requirements needed to perform the test are not met, the test will not run during an ignition cycle. This type of onboard diagnostics could be mistaken as "intermittent" when, in fact, the tests are only infrequent (depending on how the vehicle is driven). Examples of this type of diagnostic test are HO2S heaters, evaporative canister purge, catalyst efficiency, and EGR flow. When diagnosing intermittent concerns on an OBD-II-equipped vehicle, a logical diagnostic strategy is essential. The use of stored freeze-frame information can also be very useful when diagnosing an intermittent malfunction if a code has been stored.

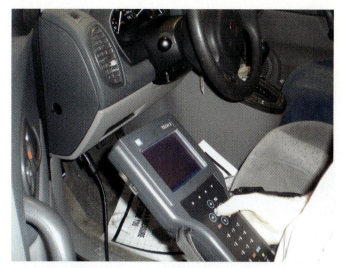

FIGURE 33–17 The first step in the reprogramming procedure is to determine the current software installed using a scan tool. Not all scan tools can be used. In most cases using the factory scan tool is needed for reprogramming unless the scan tool is equipped to handle reprogramming.

SERVICE/FLASH PROGRAMMING

Designing a program that allows an engine to meet strict air quality and fuel economy standards while providing excellent performance is no small feat. However, this is only part of the challenge facing engineers assigned with the task of developing OBD-II software. The reason for this is the countless variables involved with running the diagnostic monitors. Although programmers do their best to factor in any and all operating conditions when writing this complex code, periodic revisions are often required.

Reprogramming consists of downloading new calibration files from a scan tool, personal computer, or modem into the PCM's electronically erasable programmable read-only memory (EEPROM). This can be done on or off the vehicle using the appropriate equipment. Since reprogramming is not an OBD-II requirement however, many vehicles will need a new PCM in the event software changes become necessary. Physically removing and replacing the PROM chip is no longer possible.

The following are three industry-standard methods used to reprogram the EEPROM:

- Remote programming
- Direct programming
- Off-board programming

REMOTE PROGRAMMING. Remote programming uses the scan tool to transfer data from the manufacturer's shop PC to the vehicle's PCM. This is accomplished by performing the following steps:

- Connect the scan tool to the vehicle's DLC. ● **SEE FIGURE 33–17.**
- Enter the vehicle information into the scan tool through the programming application software incorporated in the scan tool. ● **SEE FIGURE 33–18.**
- Download VIN and current EEPROM calibration using a scan tool.
- Disconnect the scan tool from the DLC and connect the tool to the shop PC.
- Download the new calibration from the PC to the scan tool. ● **SEE FIGURE 33–19.**
- Reconnect the scan tool to the vehicle's DLC and download the new calibration into the PCM.

CAUTION: Before programming, the vehicle's battery must be between 11 and 14 volts. Do not attempt to program while charging the battery unless using a special battery charger which does not produce excessive ripple voltage such as the Midtronics PSC-300 (30 amp) or PSC-550 (55 amp) or similar as specified by the vehicle manufacturer.

FIGURE 33–18 Follow the on-screen instructions.

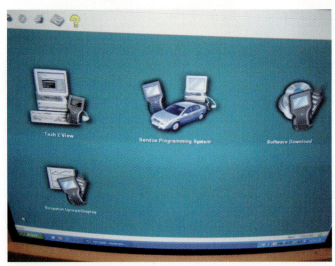

FIGURE 33–19 An Internet connection is usually needed to perform updates although some vehicle manufacturers use CDs which are updated regularly at a cost to the shop.

SERVICE/FLASH PROGRAMMING (CONTINUED)

DIRECT PROGRAMMING. Direct programming does utilize a connection between the shop PC and the vehicle DLC.

OFF-BOARD PROGRAMMING. Off-board programming is used if the PCM must be programmed away from the vehicle. This is preformed using the off-board programming adapter. ● **SEE FIGURE 33–20.**

J2534 REPROGRAMMING Legislation has mandated that vehicle manufacturers meet the SAE J2534 standards for all emissions-related systems on all new vehicles starting with model year 2004. This standard enables independent service repair operators to program or reprogram emissions-related ECMs from a wide variety of vehicle manufacturers with a single tool. ● **SEE FIGURE 33–21.** A J2534 compliant pass-through system is a standardized programming and diagnostic system. It uses a personal computer (PC) plus a standard interface to a software device driver, and a hardware vehicle communication interface. The interface connects to a PC, and to a programmable ECM on a vehicle through the J1962 data link connector (DLC). This system allows programming of all vehicle manufacturer ECMs using a single set of programming hardware. Programming software made available by the vehicle manufacturer must be functional with a J2534 compliant pass-through system.

FIGURE 33–20 Connecting cables and a computer to perform off-board programming.

The software for a typical pass-through application consists of two major components including:

■ The part delivered by the company that furnishes the hardware for J2534 enables the pass-through vehicle communication interface to communicate with the PC and provides for all Vehicle Communication Protocols as required by SAE J2534. It also provides for the software interface to work with the software applications as provided for by the vehicle manufacturers. ● **SEE FIGURE 33–22.**

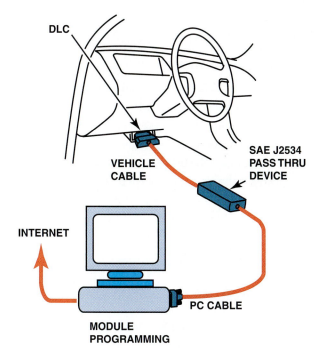

FIGURE 33–21 The J2534 pass-through reprogramming system does not need a scan tool to reflash the PCM on most 2004 and newer vehicles.

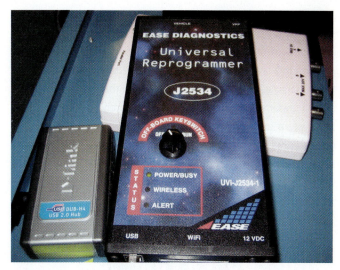

FIGURE 33–22 A typical J2534 universal reprogrammer that uses the J2534 standards.

- The second part of the pass-through enabling software is provided for by the vehicle manufacturers. This is normally a subset of the software used with their original equipment manufacturer (OEM) tools and their website will indicate how to obtain this software and under what conditions it can be used. Refer to the National Automotive Service Task Force (NASTF) website for the addresses for all vehicle manufacturers' service information and cost, *www.NASTF.org*.

Since the majority of vehicle manufacturers make this software available in downloadable form, having an Internet browser (Explorer/Netscape) and connection is a must.

MANUFACTURER'S DIAGNOSTIC ROUTINES

Each vehicle manufacturer has established their own diagnostic routines and they should be followed. Most include the following steps:

STEP 1 Retrieve diagnostic trouble codes.

STEP 2 Check for all technical service bulletins that could be related to the stored DTC.

STEP 3 If there are multiple DTCs, the diagnostic routine may include checking different components or systems instead of when only one DTC was stored.

STEP 4 Perform system checks.

STEP 5 Perform a road test matching the parameters recorded in the freeze-frame to check that the repair has corrected the malfunction.

STEP 6 Repeat the road test to cause the MIL to be extinguished.

NOTE: Do not clear codes (DTCs) unless instructed by the service information.

Following the vehicle manufacturer's specific diagnostic routines will ensure that the root cause is found and the repair verified. This is important for customer satisfaction.

COMPLETING SYSTEM REPAIRS

After the repair has been successfully completed, the vehicle should be driven under similar conditions that caused the original concern. Verify that the problem has been corrected. To perform this test drive, it is helpful to have a copy of the freeze-frame parameters that were present when the DTC was set. By driving under similar conditions, the PCM may perform a test of the system and automatically extinguish the MIL. This is the method preferred by most vehicle manufacturers. The DTC can be cleared using a scan tool, but then that means that monitors will have to be run and the vehicle may fail an emission inspection if driven directly to the testing station.

PROCEDURES FOR RESETTING THE PCM

The PCM can be reset or cleared of previously set DTCs and freeze-frame data in the following ways:

1. **Driving the Vehicle.** Drive the vehicle under similar conditions that were present when the fault occurred. If the conditions are similar and the PCM performed the noncontinuous monitor test and it passed three times, then the PCM will extinguish the MIL. This is the method preferred by most vehicle manufacturers, however, this method could be time consuming. If three passes cannot be achieved, the owner of the vehicle will have to be told that even though the check engine light (MIL) is on, the problem has been corrected and the MIL should go out in a few days of normal driving.

2. **Clear DTCs Using a Scan Tool.** A scan tool can be used to clear the diagnostic trouble code (DTC), which will also delete all of the freeze-frame data. The advantage of using a scan tool is that the check engine (MIL) will be out and the customer will be happy that the problem (MIL on) has been corrected. Do not use a scan tool to clear a DTC if the vehicle is going to be checked soon at a test station for state-mandated emission tests.

3. **Battery Disconnect.** Disconnecting the negative battery cable will clear the DTCs and freeze-frame on many vehicles but not all. Besides clearing the DTCs, disconnecting the battery for about 20 minutes will also erase radio station presets and other memory items in many cases. Most vehicle manufacturers do not recommend that the battery be disconnected to clear DTCs and it may not work on some vehicles.

TECH TIP

The Brake Pedal Trick

If the vehicle manufacturer recommends that battery power be disconnected, first disconnect the negative battery cable and then depress the brake pedal. Because the brake lights are connected to battery power, depressing the brake pedal causes all of the capacitors in the electrical system and computer(s) to discharge through the brake lights.

ROAD TEST (DRIVE CYCLE)

Use the freeze-frame data and test-drive the vehicle so that the vehicle is driven to match the conditions displayed on the freeze-frame. If the battery has been disconnected, then the vehicle may have to be driven under conditions that allow the PCM to conduct monitor tests. This drive pattern is called a **drive cycle.** The drive cycle is different for each vehicle manufacturer but a universal drive cycle may work in many cases. In many cases performing a universal drive cycle will reset most monitors in most vehicles.

UNIVERSAL DRIVE CYCLE

PRECONDITIONING: PHASE 1.

    MIL must be off.

    No DTCs present.

    Fuel fill between 15% and 85%.

    Cold start—Preferred = 8-hour soak at 68°F to 86°F.

    Alternative = ECT below 86°F.

1. With the ignition off, connect scan tool.

2. Start engine and drive between 20 and 30 mph for 22 minutes, allowing speed to vary.

3. Stop and idle for 40 seconds, gradually accelerate to 55 mph.

4. Maintain 55 mph for 4 minutes using a steady throttle input.

5. Stop and idle for 30 seconds, then accelerate to 30 mph.

6. Maintain 30 mph for 12 minutes.

7. Repeat steps 4 and 5 four times.

    Using scan tool, check readiness. If insufficient readiness set, continue to universal drive trace phase II.

    Important: (Do not shut off engine between phases).
Phase II:

1. Vehicle at a stop and idle for 45 seconds, then accelerate to 30 mph.

2. Maintain 30 mph for 22 minutes.

3. Repeat steps 1 and 2 three times.

4. Bring vehicle to a stop and idle for 45 seconds, then accelerate to 35 mph.

5. Maintain speed between 30 and 35 mph for 4 minutes.

6. Bring vehicle to a stop and idle for 45 seconds, then accelerate to 30 mph.

7. Maintain 30 mph for 22 minutes.

8. Repeat steps 6 and 7 five times.

9. Using scan tool, check readiness.

SUMMARY

1. Funnel diagnostics—Visual approach to a diagnostic procedure:
   Step 1 Verify the problem (concern)
   Step 2 Perform a thorough visual inspection and basic tests
   Step 3 Retrieve the diagnostic trouble codes (DTCs)
   Step 4 Check for technical service bulletins (TSBs)
   Step 5 Look carefully at scan tool data
   Step 6 Narrow the problem to a system or cylinder
   Step 7 Repair the problem and determine the root cause
   Step 8 Verify the repair and check for any stored DTCs

2. Care should be taken to not induce high voltage or current around any computer or computer-controlled circuit or sensor.

3. A thorough visual inspection is important during the diagnosis and troubleshooting of any engine performance problem or electrical malfunction.

4. If the MIL is on, retrieve the DTC and follow the manufacturer's recommended procedure to find the root cause of the problem.

5. OBD-II vehicles use a 16-pin DLC and common DTCs.

REVIEW QUESTIONS

1. Explain the procedure to follow when diagnosing a vehicle with stored DTCs using a scan tool.

2. Discuss what the PCM does during a drive cycle to test emission-related components.

3. Explain the difference between a type A and type B OBD-II diagnostic trouble code.

4. List three things that should be checked as part of a thorough visual inspection.

5. List the eight-step funnel diagnostic procedure.

6. Explain why a bulletin search should be performed after stored DTCs are retrieved.

7. List the three methods that can be used to reprogram a PCM.

1. Technician A says that the first step in the diagnostic process is to verify the problem (concern). Technician B says the second step is to perform a thorough visual inspection. Which technician is correct?
   a. Technician A only
   b. Technician B only
   c. Both Technicians A and B
   d. Neither Technician A nor B

2. Which item is *not* important to know before starting the diagnosis of an engine performance problem?
   a. List of previous repairs
   b. The brand of engine oil used
   c. The type of gasoline used
   d. The temperature of the engine when the problem occurs

3. A paper test can be used to check for a possible problem with _____.
   a. The ignition system (bad spark plug wire)
   b. A faulty injector on a multiport engine
   c. A burned valve
   d. All of the above

4. Which step should be performed *last* when diagnosing an engine performance problem?
   a. Checking for any stored diagnostic trouble codes
   b. Checking for any technical service bulletins (TSBs)
   c. Performing a thorough visual inspection
   d. Verify the repair

5. Technician A says that if the opposite DTC can be set, the problem is the component itself. Technician B says if the opposite DTC cannot be set, the problem is with the wiring or grounds. Which technician is correct?
   a. Technician A only
   b. Technician B only
   c. Both Technicians A and B
   d. Neither Technician A nor B

6. The preferred method to clear diagnostic trouble codes (DTCs) is to _____.
   a. Disconnect the negative battery cable for 10 seconds
   b. Use a scan tool
   c. Remove the computer (PCM) power feed fuse
   d. Cycle the ignition key on and off 40 times

7. Which is the factory scan tool for Chrysler brand vehicles equipped with CAN?
   a. Star Scan
   b. Tech 2
   c. NGS
   d. Master Tech

8. Technician A says that reprogramming a PCM using the J2534 system requires a factory scan tool. Technician B says that reprogramming a PCM using the J2534 system required Internet access. Which technician is correct?
   a. Technician A only
   b. Technician B only
   c. Both Technicians A and B
   d. Neither Technician A nor B

9. Technician A says that knowing if there are any stored diagnostic trouble codes (DTCs) may be helpful when checking for related technical service bulletins (TSBs). Technician B says that only a factory scan tool should be used to retrieve DTCs. Which technician is correct?
   a. Technician A only
   b. Technician B only
   c. Both Technicians A and B
   d. Neither Technician A nor B

10. Which method can be used to reprogram a PCM?
    a. Remote
    b. Direct
    c. Off-board
    d. All of the above

A8 ASE TEST SPECIFICATIONS

CONTENT AREA	QUESTIONS IN TEST	PERCENTAGE OF TEST	COVERED IN CHAPTER #
A. General Engine Diagnosis	12	17%	3, 4, 13, 33
B. Ignition System Diagnosis and Repair	12	17%	17
C. Fuel, Air Induction, and Exhaust Systems Diagnosis and Repair	13	19%	10, 12, 26–32
D. Emissions Control Systems Diagnosis and Repair	10	14%	31, 32
1. Positive Crankcase Ventilation (1)			
2. Exhaust Gas Recirculation (3)			
3. Exhaust Gas Treatment (3)			
4. Evaporative Emissions Controls (3)			
E. Computerized Engine Controls Diagnosis and Repair	19	27%	18–25
F. Engine Electrical Systems Diagnosis and Repair	4	6%	15
1. Battery (1)			
2. Starting System (1)			
3. Charging System (2)			
TOTAL	70	100%	

1. An injector pulse can be tested for by using a _____.
   a. Spark tester
   b. Vacuum hose and a test light
   c. NOID light
   d. DVOM on "pulse ck"

2. A starter motor is drawing too many amperes (current). Technician A says that this could be due to low battery voltage. Technician B says that it could be due to a defective starter motor. Which technician is correct?
   a. Technician A only
   b. Technician B only
   c. Both Technicians A and B
   d. Neither Technician A nor B

3. All of the following could be a cause of excessive starter ampere draw except _____.
   a. A misadjusted starter pinion gear
   b. A loose starter housing
   c. Armature wires separated from the commutator
   d. A bent armature

4. The starter motor armature has been rubbing on the pole shoes. The probable cause is _____.
   a. A bent starter shaft
   b. A worn commutator on the armature
   c. Worn starter bushing(s)
   d. Both a and c

5. A starter cranks for a while, then whines. Technician A says that the starter solenoid may be bad. Technician B says that the starter drive may be bad. Which technician is correct?
   a. Technician A only
   b. Technician B only
   c. Both Technicians A and B
   d. Neither Technician A nor B

6. On a negative ground battery system _____.
   a. Disconnect the ground cable first and reconnect the positive cable first
   b. Disconnect the ground cable first and reconnect the positive cable last
   c. Disconnect the positive cable first and reconnect the ground cable first
   d. Disconnect the positive cable first and reconnect the ground cable last

7. A technician is checking the charging system for low output. A voltage drop of 1.67 volts is found between the generator (alternator) output terminal and the battery positive terminal. Technician A says that a corroded connector could be the cause. Technician B says that a defective rectifier diode could be the cause of the voltage drop. Which technician is correct?
   a. Technician A only
   b. Technician B only
   c. Both Technicians A and B
   d. Neither Technician A nor B

8. A technician places a hand on top of a carburetor with the engine running. The engine runs better. Technician A says the choke is defective. Technician B says the engine has a vacuum leak. Which technician is correct?
   a. Technician A only
   b. Technician B only
   c. Both Technicians A and B
   d. Neither Technician A nor B

9. A driver turns the ignition switch to "start" and nothing happens (the dome light remains bright). Technician A says that dirty battery connections or a defective or discharged battery could be the cause. Technician B says that an *open* control circuit such as a defective neutral safety switch could be the cause. Which technician is correct?
   a. Technician A only
   b. Technician B only
   c. Both Technicians A and B
   d. Neither Technician A nor B

10. Engine ping during acceleration can be caused if the ignition timing is _____.
    a. Advanced   b. Retarded

11. Normal battery drain (parasitic drain) on a vehicle with many computer and electronic circuits is _____.
    a. 20 to 30 mA   c. 150 to 300 mA
    b. 2 to 3 A   d. 0.3 to 0.4 A

12. When jump starting _____.
    a. The last connection should be the positive post of the dead battery
    b. The last connection should be the engine block of the dead vehicle
    c. The generator (alternator) must be disconnected on both vehicles
    d. The bumpers should touch to provide a good ground between the vehicles

13. Technician A says that a voltage-drop test of the charging circuit should only be performed when current is flowing through the circuit. Technician B says to connect the lead of a voltmeter to the positive and negative terminals of the battery to measure the voltage drop of the charging system. Which technician is correct?
    a. Technician A only
    b. Technician B only
    c. Both Technicians A and B
    d. Neither Technician A nor B

14. A pickup coil is being measured with a digital multimeter set to the kilo ohm position. The specification for the resistance is 500 to 1,500 ohms. The digital face reads 0.826. Technician A says that the coil is okay. Technician B says that the resistance is below specifications. Which technician is correct?
    a. Technician A only
    b. Technician B only
    c. Both Technicians A and B
    d. Neither Technician A nor B

15. A blown head gasket is suspected on a 5-year-old vehicle. The service technician should perform which of the following tests to confirm the problem?
    a. Running compression test, vacuum test
    b. Leakdown test, compression test
    c. PCV test, oil pressure test
    d. Dipstick test, timing chain slack test

16. Technician A says to check for spark by connecting a spark tester to the end of a spark plug wire. Technician B says that a regular spark plug should be connected to the end of a spark plug wire to check for spark. Which technician is correct?
    a. Technician A only
    b. Technician B only
    c. Both Technicians A and B
    d. Neither Technician A nor B

17. A defective (open) spark plug wire was found in an engine that was misfiring during acceleration. Technician A says that the distributor and rotor should be carefully inspected and replaced if necessary because the defective wire could have caused a carbon track. Technician B says that the ignition coil should be replaced because the bad wire could have caused the coil to become tracked internally. Which technician is correct?
    a. Technician A only
    b. Technician B only
    c. Both Technicians A and B
    d. Neither Technician A nor B

18. Technician A says that all spark plugs should be gapped before being installed in the engine. Technician B says that platinum spark plugs should *not* be regapped after having been used in an engine. Which technician is correct?
    a. Technician A only
    b. Technician B only
    c. Both Technicians A and B
    d. Neither Technician A nor B

19. The vacuum hose to a MAP sensor became disconnected. Technician A says that the lack of vacuum to the sensor will cause the computer to provide a rich mixture to the engine. Technician B says that the computer will supply a lean mixture to the engine. Which technician is correct?
    a. Technician A only
    b. Technician B only
    c. Both Technicians A and B
    d. Neither Technician A nor B

20. The connector to the throttle position (TP) sensor became disconnected. Technician A says that the engine may not idle correctly unless it is reconnected. Technician B says that the engine may hesitate on acceleration. Which technician is correct?
    a. Technician A only
    b. Technician B only
    c. Both Technicians A and B
    d. Neither Technician A nor B

21. An oxygen sensor (O2S) is being tested. Technician A says that the O2S voltage should fluctuate from above 800 mV to below 200 mV. Technician B says the O2S has to be above 600°F (315°C) before testing can begin. Which technician is correct?
    a. Technician A only
    b. Technician B only
    c. Both Technicians A and B
    d. Neither Technician A nor B

22. Technician A says that OBD-II generic codes are the same for all OBD-II vehicles. Technician B says that the DLC is located under the hood on all OBD-II vehicles. Which technician is correct?
    a. Technician A only
    b. Technician B only
    c. Both Technicians A and B
    d. Neither Technician A nor B

23. Ignition timing on an engine equipped with computer-controlled distributor ignition (DI) is being discussed. Technician A says that the computer can only advance the timing. Technician B says that the signal from the knock sensor (KS) can cause the timing to retard. Which technician is correct?
    a. Technician A only
    b. Technician B only
    c. Both Technicians A and B
    d. Neither Technician A nor B

24. Two technicians are discussing jump starting a computer-equipped vehicle with another computer-equipped vehicle. Technician A says that the ignition of both vehicles should be in the off position while making the jumper cable connections. Technician B says that the computer-equipped vehicles should not be jump started. Which technician is correct?
    a. Technician A only
    b. Technician B only
    c. Both Technicians A and B
    d. Neither Technician A nor B

25. A fully-charged 12-volt battery should measure _____.
    a. 12.6 volts
    b. 12.4 volts
    c. 12.2 volts
    d. 12.0 volts

26. Two technicians are discussing an OBD-II diagnostic trouble code (DTC) P0301. Technician A says that this is a generic code. Technician B says that the code is a manufacturer's specific code. Which technician is correct?
    a. Technician A only
    b. Technician B only
    c. Both Technicians A and B
    d. Neither Technician A nor B

27. Battery voltage during cranking is below specifications. Technician A says that a fault in the engine may be the cause. Technician B says that the starter motor may be defective. Which technician is correct?
    a. Technician A only
    b. Technician B only
    c. Both Technicians A and B
    d. Neither Technician A nor B

28. An engine cranks but will not start. No spark is available at the end of a spark plug wire with a spark tester connected and the engine cranked. Technician A says that a defective pickup coil could be the cause. Technician B says that a defective ignition module could be the cause. Which technician is correct?
    a. Technician A only
    b. Technician B only
    c. Both Technicians A and B
    d. Neither Technician A nor B

29. An engine misfire is being diagnosed. One spark plug wire measured "OL" on a digital ohmmeter set to the K ohm scale. Technician A says that the spark plug should be replaced. Technician B says that the ignition coil may also need to be replaced because it may be *tracked* due to the high voltage created by the defective spark plug wire. Which technician is correct?
    a. Technician A only
    b. Technician B only
    c. Both Technicians A and B
    d. Neither Technician A nor B

30. An engine equipped with a turbocharger is burning oil (blue exhaust smoke all the time). Technician A says that a defective wastegate could be the cause. Technician B says that a plugged PCV system could be the cause. Which technician is correct?
    a. Technician A only
    b. Technician B only
    c. Both Technicians A and B
    d. Neither Technician A nor B

31. An engine idles roughly and stalls occasionally. Technician A says that using fuel with too high an RVP level could be the cause. Technician B says that using winter-blend gasoline during warm weather could be the cause. Which technician is correct?
    a. Technician A only
    b. Technician B only
    c. Both Technicians A and B
    d. Neither Technician A nor B

32. A compression test gave the following results:

    Cylinder 1: 155
    Cylinder 2: 140
    Cylinder 3: 110
    Cylinder 4: 105

    Technician A says that a defective (burned) valve is the most likely cause. Technician B says that a leaking intake manifold gasket could be the cause. Which technician is correct?
    a. Technician A only
    b. Technician B only
    c. Both Technicians A and B
    d. Neither Technician A nor B

33. Two technicians are discussing a compression test. Technician A says that the engine should be turned over with the pressure gauge installed for "four puffs." Technician B says that the maximum difference between the highest-reading cylinder and the lowest-reading cylinder should be 20%. Which technician is correct?
    a. Technician A only
    b. Technician B only
    c. Both Technicians A and B
    d. Neither Technician A nor B

34. Technician A says that oil should be squirted into all of the cylinders before taking a compression test. Technician B says that if the compression greatly increases when some oil is squirted into the cylinders, it indicates defective or worn piston rings. Which technician is correct?
    a. Technician A only
    b. Technician B only
    c. Both Technicians A and B
    d. Neither Technician A nor B

35. During a cylinder leakage (leak-down) test, air is noticed coming out of the oil-fill opening. Technician A says that the oil filter may be clogged. Technician B says that the piston rings may be worn or defective. Which technician is correct?
    a. Technician A only
    b. Technician B only
    c. Both Technicians A and B
    d. Neither Technician A nor B

36. A cylinder leakage (leak-down) test indicates 30% leakage, and air is heard coming out of the air inlet. Technician A says that this is a normal reading for a slightly worn engine. Technician B says that one or more intake valves are defective. Which technician is correct?
    a. Technician A only
    b. Technician B only
    c. Both Technicians A and B
    d. Neither Technician A nor B

37. Two technicians are discussing a cylinder power balance test. Technician A says the more the engine RPM drops, the weaker the cylinder. Technician B says that all cylinder RPM drops should be within 50 RPM of each other. Which technician is correct?
    a. Technician A only
    b. Technician B only
    c. Both Technicians A and B
    d. Neither Technician A nor B

38. Technician A says that cranking vacuum should be the same as idle vacuum. Technician B says that a sticking valve is indicated by a floating vacuum gauge needle reading. Which technician is correct?
    a. Technician A only
    b. Technician B only
    c. Both Technicians A and B
    d. Neither Technician A nor B

39. Technician A says that black exhaust smoke is an indication of too rich an air–fuel mixture. Technician B says that white smoke (steam) is an indication of coolant being burned in the engine. Which technician is correct?
    a. Technician A only
    b. Technician B only
    c. Both Technicians A and B
    d. Neither Technician A nor B

40. Excessive exhaust system back pressure has been measured. Technician A says that the catalytic converter may be clogged. Technician B says that the muffler may be clogged. Which technician is correct?
    a. Technician A only
    b. Technician B only
    c. Both Technicians A and B
    d. Neither Technician A nor B

41. A head gasket failure is being diagnosed. Technician A says that an exhaust analyzer can be used to check for HC when the tester probe is held above the radiator coolant. Technician B says that a chemical-coated paper changes color in the presence of combustion gases. Which technician is correct?
    a. Technician A only
    b. Technician B only
    c. Both Technicians A and B
    d. Neither Technician A nor B

42. Technician A says that catalytic converters should last the life of the vehicle unless damaged or contaminated. Technician B says that catalytic converters wear out and should be replaced every 50,000 miles (80,000 km). Which technician is correct?
    a. Technician A only
    b. Technician B only
    c. Both Technicians A and B
    d. Neither Technician A nor B

43. A technician is measuring the battery voltage while cranking the engine and observes 11.2 volts on the voltmeter. Technician A says that the starter may be defective. Technician B says that the battery or cables may be defective. Which technician is correct?
    a. Technician A only
    b. Technician B only
    c. Both Technicians A and B
    d. Neither Technician A nor B

44. The charging system voltage is found to be lower than specified by the vehicle manufacturer. Technician A says that a loose or defective drive belt could be the cause. Technician B says that a defective generator (alternator) could be the cause. Which technician is correct?
    a. Technician A only
    b. Technician B only
    c. Both Technicians A and B
    d. Neither Technician A nor B

45. The fuel pressure on a port-injected engine drops to zero in less than 20 minutes after the engine is turned off. Technician A says to pinch off the fuel return line and if the pressure stays high, the regulator is defective. Technician B says to pinch off the fuel supply line and if the pressure drops off, the problem could be a leaking fuel injector(s). Which technician is correct?
    a. Technician A only
    b. Technician B only
    c. Both Technicians A and B
    d. Neither Technician A nor B

46. Technician A says that if the thermostat is removed from the engine, the engine may overheat. Technician B says that coolant bypasses the thermostat when the thermostat is closed. Which technician is correct?
    a. Technician A only
    b. Technician B only
    c. Both Technicians A and B
    d. Neither Technician A nor B

47. Two technicians are discussing pressure testing the cooling system to check for leaks. Technician A says to pump up the radiator to 20 to 25 PSI and watch for the pressure to drop. Technician B says that the entire cooling system is being pressure checked except the cap by pressurizing the radiator. Which technician is correct?
    a. Technician A only
    b. Technician B only
    c. Both Technicians A and B
    d. Neither Technician A nor B

48. A 4-year-old pickup truck has a high CO reading. Technician A says that a hole in the exhaust downstream from the oxygen sensor could be the cause. Technician B says a defective (electrically open) injector could be the cause. Which technician is correct?
    a. Technician A only
    b. Technician B only
    c. Both Technicians A and B
    d. Neither Technician A nor B

49. A vehicle that has a higher than normal HC and CO reading is most likely running _____.
    a. Rich   b. Lean

50. A short-term fuel trim of 0% and a long-term fuel trim of +20% means _____.
    a. The engine is running lean now
    b. The engine has a history of running rich
    c. The engine has a history of running lean
    d. The engine is running rich now

51. The catalytic converter can be tested using _____.
    a. A vacuum gauge connected to the intake manifold vacuum
    b. A temperature measuring tool
    c. A pressure gauge attached in the place of the O2S
    d. All of the above

52. A four-cylinder TBI engine has a rich DTC. Technician A says that this could be caused by a faulty injector. Technician B says a faulty MAP sensor could be the cause. Which technician is correct?
    a. Technician A only
    b. Technician B only
    c. Both Technicians A and B
    d. Neither Technician A nor B

53. A pickup coil is being measured with a digital multimeter set to the ohm scale. The meter reads 0.01 ohm between the pickup coil lead and a good engine ground. Technician A says that the pickup coil is electronically open. Technician B says that the pickup coil is shorted to ground. Which technician is correct?
    a. Technician A only
    b. Technician B only
    c. Both Technicians A and B
    d. Neither Technician A nor B

54. An engine has a rough idle but runs okay above idle speed. Technician A says that the EGR valve could be partially stuck open. Technician B says that the thermostat may be stuck open. Which technician is correct?
    a. Technician A only
    b. Technician B only
    c. Both Technicians A and B
    d. Neither Technician A nor B

55. An oxygen sensor reads lower than normal. Technician A says that the engine may have a vacuum leak (intake manifold air leak). Technician B says that the exhaust manifold may be cracked. Which technician is correct?
    a. Technician A only
    b. Technician B only
    c. Both Technicians A and B
    d. Neither Technician A nor B

56. An engine has a defective spark plug. Technician A says that the O2S will read lower than normal due to the misfire. Technician B says that the O2S will read higher than normal due to the misfire. Which technician is correct?
    a. Technician A only
    b. Technician B only
    c. Both Technicians A and B
    d. Neither Technician A nor B

57. An engine with a cracked spark plug is being analyzed using an ignition scope. Technician A says that the cylinder with the defective spark plug will have a shorter than normal firing line. Technician B says that the spark line will be longer than normal for the cylinder with the cracked spark plug. Which technician is correct?
    a. Technician A only
    b. Technician B only
    c. Both Technicians A and B
    d. Neither Technician A nor B

58. The idle speed of a port fuel-injected engine is too fast. Technician A says that the PCV valve may be defective. Technician B says the EGR valve may be stuck closed. Which technician is correct?
    a. Technician A only
    b. Technician B only
    c. Both Technicians A and B
    d. Neither Technician A nor B

59. An engine starts and idles okay but it misfires above idle. Technician A says that the fuel pump may be weak. Technician B says that the secondary ignition system may have a fault. Which technician is correct?
    a. Technician A only
    b. Technician B only
    c. Both Technicians A and B
    d. Neither Technician A nor B

60. A customer comments that the engine misfires when going up a hill or on hard acceleration. When viewing the scope, the technician sees that the #5 firing line is about 5 to 6 kV higher than the rest, and the spark line slants down from the firing line to the coil oscillations. What is the most likely cause?
    a. A fuel-fouled plug on #5
    b. A plug with a worn electrode on #5
    c. A high-resistance plug wire on #5
    d. This is a normal pattern

61. A high O2S voltage could be due to _____.
    a. A rich exhaust
    b. A lean exhaust
    c. A defective spark plug wire
    d. Both a and c

62. A low O2S voltage could be due to _____.
    a. A rich exhaust
    b. A lean exhaust
    c. A defective spark plug wire
    d. Both b and c

63. A fuel-injected vehicle is tested on a four-gas exhaust analyzer.

   $HC = 102$ PPM $CO = 0.3\%$ $O_2 = 6.3\%$ $CO_2 = 6.1\%$

   Technician A says that everything is okay including the TP setting because the O_2 and CO_2 are about equal. Technician B says that the engine is running lean. Which technician is correct?
   a. Technician A only
   b. Technician B only
   c. Both Technicians A and B
   d. Neither Technician A nor B

64. A technician is working on a vehicle equipped with a port-injected engine. After connecting the vehicle to a scan tool, the technician finds it has a long-term fuel trim of $+20\%$. Technician A says that an exhaust leak in front of the oxygen sensor could cause this. Technician B says that a defective plug wire could cause this. Which technician is correct?
   a. Technician A only
   b. Technician B only
   c. Both Technicians A and B
   d. Neither Technician A nor B

65. The oil pressure warning light comes on when the oil pressure reaches about _____.
   a. 1 PSI   c. 8 PSI
   b. 4 PSI   d. 12 PSI

66. The spark line is short in duration (0.60 ms maximum), and the firing line is low on all cylinders. What is the most likely cause?
   a. The cap to rotor button has excessive resistance.
   b. The rotor to distributor air gap is too close.
   c. The secondary is shorted between its windings.
   d. The primary coil resistance is too low.

67. Two technicians are discussing catalytic converters. Technician A says that a nonworking (chemically inert) catalytic converter will test as being clogged during a vacuum or back pressure test. Technician B says that the temperature of the inlet and outlet of the converter can detect if it is working okay. Which technician is correct?
   a. Technician A only
   b. Technician B only
   c. Both Technicians A and B
   d. Neither Technician A nor B

68. HC and CO_2 are high and CO and O_2 are low. The most likely cause is _____.
   a. Too-rich conditions
   b. Fault in the secondary ignition system
   c. Stuck-open EGR
   d. Lean misfire

69. A typical O2S sensor output can be measured for changing _____.
   a. DC volts   c. Ohms (resistance)
   b. AC volts   d. Frequency (hertz)

70. Two technicians are discussing excessive HC exhaust emissions. Technician A says that a stuck-open thermostat could be the cause. Technician B says that a lean misfire could be the cause. Which technician is correct?
   a. Technician A only
   b. Technician B only
   c. Both Technicians A and B
   d. Neither Technician A nor B

ANSWERS FOR ENGINE PERFORMANCE (A8) SAMPLE ASE CERTIFICATION TEST

1. c	19. a	37. b	55. c
2. c	20. c	38. d	56. a
3. c	21. c	39. c	57. c
4. d	22. a	40. c	58. a
5. b	23. c	41. c	59. c
6. a	24. a	42. a	60. c
7. a	25. a	43. d	61. a
8. b	26. a	44. c	62. d
9. b	27. c	45. c	63. b
10. a	28. c	46. c	64. c
11. a	29. c	47. b	65. b
12. b	30. b	48. d	66. c
13. a	31. c	49. a	67. b
14. a	32. d	50. c	68. b
15. b	33. c	51. d	69. a
16. a	34. b	52. c	70. c
17. c	35. b	53. b	
18. c	36. b	54. a	

ENGINE PERFORMANCE (A8)

TASK	TEXTBOOK PAGE NO.
A. GENERAL DIAGNOSIS (12 QUESTIONS)	
1. Verify driver's complaint, perform visual inspection, and/or road test vehicle; determine needed action.	523–529
2. Research applicable vehicle and service information, such as engine management system operation, vehicle service history, service precautions, and technical service bulletins, and service campaigns/recalls.	2–4
3. Diagnose noises and/or vibration problems related to engine performance; determine needed action.	204–205
4. Diagnose the cause of unusual exhaust color, odor, and sound; determine needed action.	201–205
5. Perform engine manifold vacuum or pressure tests; determine needed action.	212–214
6. Perform cylinder power balance test; determine needed action.	211
7. Perform cylinder cranking compression test; determine needed action.	208–209
8. Perform cylinder leakage/leak-down test; determine needed action.	210
9. Diagnose engine mechanical, electrical, electronic, fuel, and ignition problems with an oscilloscope, engine analyzer, and/or scan tool; determine needed action.	298–304
10. Prepare and inspect vehicle for HC, CO, CO_2, and O_2 exhaust gas analysis; perform test and interpret exhaust gas readings.	483–488
11. Verify valve adjustment on engines with mechanical or hydraulic lifters.	227–230
12. Verify camshaft timing (including engines equipped with variable valve timing) determine needed action.	225–226
13. Verify engine operating temperature, check coolant level and condition, perform cooling system pressure test; determine needed repairs.	222
14. Inspect and test mechanical/electrical fans, fan clutch, fan shroud/ducting, and fan control devices; determine needed repairs.	144–146
15. Read and interpret electrical schematic diagrams and symbols.	–
16. Test and diagnose emissions or driveability problems, caused by battery condition, connections, or excessive key-off battery drain; determine needed repairs.	235–238
17. Perform starter current draw test; determine needed action.	245
18. Perform starter circuit voltage drop tests; determine needed action.	247
19. Inspect, test, and repair or replace components and wires in the starter control circuit.	248
20. Test and diagnose engine performance problems, resulting from an undercharge, overcharge, or a no-charge condition; determine needed action.	252–256
21. Inspect, adjust, and replace alternator (generator) drive belts, pulleys, tensioners, and fans.	253
22. Inspect, test, and repair or replace charging circuit components, connectors, and wires.	256

TASK	TEXTBOOK PAGE NO.

B. IGNITION SYSTEM DIAGNOSIS AND REPAIR (8 QUESTIONS)

	TASK	TEXTBOOK PAGE NO.
1.	Diagnose ignition system related problems such as no-starting, hard starting, engine misfire, poor driveability, spark knock, power loss, poor mileage, and emissions problems; determine root cause; determine needed repairs.	281–286
2.	Interpret ignition system related diagnostic trouble codes (DTC); determine needed repairs.	527
3.	Inspect, test, repair, or replace ignition primary circuit wiring and components.	282–286
4.	Inspect, test, service, repair or replace ignition system secondary circuit wiring and components.	286–289
5.	Inspect, test, service, and replace ignition coil(s).	282–283
6.	Inspect, test, and replace ignition system sensors; adjust as necessary.	283–285
7.	Inspect, test, and/or replace ignition control module (ICM)/powertrain/engine control module (PCM/ECM); reprogram as needed.	286

C. FUEL, AIR INDUCTION, AND EXHAUST SYSTEM DIAGNOSIS AND REPAIR (9 QUESTIONS)

	TASK	TEXTBOOK PAGE NO.
1.	Diagnose fuel system related problems, including hot or cold no-starting, hard starting, poor driveability, incorrect idle speed, poor idle, flooding, hesitation, surging, engine misfire, power loss, stalling, poor mileage, and emissions problems; determine root cause; determine needed action.	455–462
2.	Interpret fuel or induction system related diagnostic trouble codes (DTCs); analyze fuel trim and other scan tool data; determine needed repairs.	470
3.	Inspect fuel tank, filler neck, and gas cap; inspect and replace fuel lines, fittings, and hoses, check fuel for contaminants and quality.	99–102; 402–406
4.	Inspect, test, and replace fuel pump(s) and/or fuel pump assembly; inspect, service, and replace fuel filters.	412–418
5.	Inspect and electrical fuel pump control circuits and components; determine needed repairs.	410
6.	Inspect, test, and repair or replace fuel pressure regulation system and components of fuel injection systems; perform fuel pressure/volume test.	412–418
7.	Inspect, remove, service, or replace throttle assembly; make related adjustments.	469
8.	Inspect, test, clean, and replace fuel injectors and fuel rails.	467–470
9.	Inspect, service, and repair or replace air filtration system components.	525
10.	Inspect throttle assembly, air induction system, intake manifold and gaskets for air/vacuum leaks and/or unmetered air.	367
11.	Remove, clean, inspect, test, and repair or replace fuel system vacuum and electrical components and connections.	455
12.	Inspect, service, and replace exhaust manifold, exhaust pipes, oxygen sensors, mufflers, catalytic converters, resonators, tailpipes, and heat shields.	171; 375–380; 396–398; 508
13.	Test for exhaust system restriction or leaks; determine needed action.	508
14.	Inspect, test, clean, and repair or replace turbocharger or supercharger and system components.	192; 198

D. EMISSIONS CONTROL SYSTEMS DIAGNOSIS AND REPAIR (INCLUDING OBD II) (8 QUESTIONS)
1. POSITIVE CRANKCASE VENTILATION (1 QUESTION)

	TASK	TEXTBOOK PAGE NO.
1.	Test and diagnose emissions or driveability problems caused by positive crankcase ventilation (PCV) system.	499–500
2.	Inspect, service, and replace positive crankcase ventilation (PCV) filter/breather cap, valve, tubes, orifice/metering device, and hoses.	500–501

For every task in Engine Performance the following safety requirement must be strictly enforced:
Comply with personal and environmental safety practices associated with clothing; eye protection; hand tools; power equipment; proper ventilation; and the handling, storage, and disposal of chemicals/materials in accordance with local, state, and federal safety and environmental regulations.

ENGINE PERFORMANCE (A8)

TASK	TEXTBOOK PAGE NO.	WORKTEXT PAGE NO.
A. GENERAL ENGINE DIAGNOSIS		
1. Complete work order to include customer information, vehicle identifying information, customer concern, related service history, cause, and correction. (P-1)	2–4	9
2. Identify and interpret engine performance concern; determine necessary action. (P-1)	523–528	40, 198–201
3. Research applicable vehicle and service information, such as engine management system operation, vehicle service history, service precautions, and technical service bulletins. (P-1)	2–4	6, 7, 8, 15, 23, 81, 82, 105, 107, 145, 150, 151,173
4. Locate and interpret vehicle and major component identification numbers. (P-1)	2–4	4, 5, 12, 13, 100, 101
5. Inspect engine assembly for fuel, oil, coolant, and other leaks; determine necessary action. (P-2)	202–204	24, 43–46
6. Diagnose abnormal engine noise or vibration concerns; determine necessary action. (P-3)	204–205	47, 49
7. Diagnose abnormal exhaust color, odor, and sound; determine necessary action. (P-2)	202–205	48, 50
8. Perform engine absolute (vacuum/boost) manifold pressure tests; determine necessary action. (P-1)	212–214	51
9. Perform cylinder power balance test; determine necessary action. (P-2)	211	51
10. Perform cylinder cranking and running compression tests; determine necessary action. (P-1)	208–209	54–56
11. Perform cylinder leakage test; determine necessary action. (P-1)	210	57
12. Diagnose engine mechanical, electrical, electronic, fuel, and ignition concerns; determine necessary action. (P-1)	298–304	58–60
13. Prepare 4 or 5 gas analyzer; inspect and prepare vehicle for test, and obtain exhaust readings; interpret readings, and determine necessary action. (P-3)	483–488	174
14. Verify engine operating temperature; determine necessary action. (P-1)	134, 222	26, 61
15. Perform cooling system pressure tests; check coolant condition; inspect and test radiator, pressure cap, coolant recovery tank, and hoses; perform necessary action. (P-1)	137–143	27, 28
16. Verify correct camshaft timing. (P-1)	225–226	69
B. COMPUTERIZED ENGINE CONTROLS DIAGNOSIS AND REPAIR		
1. Retrieve and record diagnostic trouble codes, OBD monitor status, and freeze frame data; clear codes when applicable. (P-1)	529–535	202
2. Diagnose the causes of emissions or driveability concerns with stored or active diagnostic trouble codes; obtain, graph, and interpret scan tool data. (P-1)	538	62, 102–104, 203, 204

TASK	TEXTBOOK PAGE NO.	WORKTEXT PAGE NO.
3. Diagnose emissions or driveability concerns without stored diagnostic trouble codes; determine necessary action. (P-1)	527–528	63, 175
4. Check for module communication (including CAN/BUS systems) errors using a scan tool. (P-2)	314–318	99
5. Inspect and test computerized engine control system sensors, powertrain/engine control module (PCM/ECM), actuators, and circuits using a graphing multimeter (GMM)/digital storage oscilloscope (DSO); perform necessary action. (P-1)	334–341; 348–350; 359–360; 375–379; 396–398	108–137; 147–149; 152–155; 171
6. Access and use service information to perform step-by-step diagnosis. (P-1)	4–5; 541	207
7. Diagnose driveability and emissions problems resulting from malfunctions of interrelated systems (cruise control, security alarms, suspension controls, traction controls, A/C, automatic transmissions, non-OEM-installed accessories, or similar systems); determine necessary action. (P-3)	523–542	19, 106, 146, 157, 206, 210
8. Perform active tests of actuators using a scan tool; determine necessary action. (P-1)	433; 450	156, 209
9. Describe the importance of running all OBDII monitors for repair verification. (P-1)	542	158, 205, 208

C. IGNITION SYSTEM DIAGNOSIS AND REPAIR

TASK	TEXTBOOK PAGE NO.	WORKTEXT PAGE NO.
1. Diagnose ignition system related problems such as no-starting, hard starting, engine misfire, poor driveability, spark knock, power loss, poor mileage, and emissions concerns; determine necessary action. (P-1)	281–286	83, 84, 88, 93–96
2. Inspect and test ignition primary and secondary circuit wiring and solid state components; test ignition coil(s); perform necessary action. (P-1)	282–286	85–87; 89, 90, 97
3. Inspect and test crankshaft and camshaft position sensor(s); perform necessary action. (P-1)	283–285	91, 98
4. Inspect, test, and/or replace ignition control module, powertrain/engine control module; reprogram as necessary. (P-2)	286	92

D. FUEL, AIR INDUCTION, AND EXHAUST SYSTEMS DIAGNOSIS AND REPAIR

TASK	TEXTBOOK PAGE NO.	WORKTEXT PAGE NO.
1. Diagnose hot or cold no-starting, hard starting, poor driveability, incorrect idle speed, poor idle, flooding, hesitation, surging, engine misfire, power loss, stalling, poor mileage, dieseling, and emissions problems; determine necessary action. (P-1)	455–462	159–162
2. Check fuel for contaminants and quality; determine necessary action. (P-2)	99–102	16–18
3. Inspect and test fuel pumps and pump control systems for pressure, regulation, and volume; perform necessary action. (P-1)	412–418	139–143
4. Replace fuel filters. (P-2)	411	144
5. Inspect throttle body, air induction system, intake manifold, and gaskets for vacuum leaks and/or unmetered air. (P-2)	455; 469	68, 172
6. Inspect and test fuel injectors. (P-1)	467–470	163–169
7. Verify idle control operation. (P-1)	450–451; 469	170
8. Inspect the integrity of the exhaust manifold, exhaust pipes, muffler(s), catalytic converter(s), resonator(s), tail pipe(s), and heat shield(s); perform necessary action. (P-1)	171; 375–380; 396–398	36–37
9. Perform exhaust system back-pressure test; determine necessary action. (P-1)	508	191
10. Test the operation of turbocharger/supercharger systems; determine necessary action. (P-3)	192–198	41

E. EMISSIONS CONTROL SYSTEMS DIAGNOSIS AND REPAIR

TASK	TEXTBOOK PAGE NO.	WORKTEXT PAGE NO.
1. Diagnose oil leaks, emissions, and driveability concerns caused by the positive crankcase ventilation (PCV) system; determine necessary action. (P-2)	499–500	182

TASK	TEXTBOOK PAGE NO.	WORKTEXT PAGE NO.
2. Inspect, test, and service positive crankcase ventilation (PCV) filter/breather cap, valve, tubes, orifices, and hoses; perform necessary action. (P-2)	500–501	183–184
3. Diagnose emissions and driveability concerns caused by the exhaust gas recirculation (EGR) system; determine necessary action. (P-1)	494–495	176
4. Inspect, test, service, and replace components of the EGR system, including EGR tubing, exhaust passages, vacuum/pressure controls, filters, and hoses; perform necessary action. (P-1)	497	177–179
5. Inspect and test electrical/electronic sensors, controls, and wiring of exhaust gas recirculation (EGR) systems; perform necessary action. (P-2)	496	180–181
6. Diagnose emissions and driveability concerns caused by the secondary air injection and catalytic converter systems; determine necessary action. (P-2)	503–504	185
7. Inspect and test mechanical components of secondary air injection systems; perform necessary action. (P-3)	504	186
8. Inspect and test electrical/electronically-operated components and circuits of air injection systems; perform necessary action. (P-3)	503	187
9. Inspect and test catalytic converter efficiency. (P-1)	508–510	188–190
10. Diagnose emissions and driveability concerns caused by the evaporative emissions control system; determine necessary action. (P-1)	516–517	192–194
11. Inspect and test components and hoses of the evaporative emissions control system; perform necessary action. (P-1)	517–518	195–196
12. Interpret diagnostic trouble codes (DTCs) and scan tool data related to the emissions control systems; determine necessary action. (P-1)	538	197

F. ENGINE RELATED SERVICE

TASK	TEXTBOOK PAGE NO.	WORKTEXT PAGE NO.
1. Adjust valves on engines with mechanical or hydraulic lifters. (P-1)	227–230	71
2. Remove and replace timing belt; verify correct camshaft timing. (P-1)	225–226	70
3. Remove and replace thermostat and gasket/seal. (P-1)	222	30
4. Inspect and test mechanical/electrical fans, fan clutch, fan shroud/ducting, air dams, and fan control devices; perform necessary action. (P-1)	144–146	31
5. Perform common fastener and thread repairs, to include: remove broken bolt, restore internal and external threads, and repair internal threads with a threaded insert. (P-1)	–	64
6. Perform engine oil and filter change. (P-1)	–	34
7. Identify hybrid vehicle internal combustion engine service precautions. (P-3)	226	72

ENGLISH GLOSSARY

Above ground storage tank (ABST) A storage tank that stores used oil and is located above ground.

AC coupling A selection that can be made to observe a waveform.

AC/DC clamp-on DMM A type of meter that has a clamp that is placed around the wire to measure current.

AC Ripple Voltage An alternating current voltage that rides on top of a DC charging current output from an AC generator (alternator).

Acceleration simulation mode Uses a dynamometer that applies a heavy load on the vehicle at a steady-state speed.

Accelerator pedal position (APP) sensor A sensor that is used to monitor the position and rate of change of the accelerator pedal.

Accumulator A temporary location for fluid under pressure.

Actuator An electrical or mechanical device that converts electrical energy into a mechanical action, such as adjusting engine idle speed, altering suspension height, or regulating fuel metering.

Adjustable wrench A wrench that has a movable jaw to allow it to fit many sizes of fasteners.

Adsorption Attaches the fuel vapor molecules to the carbon surface.

AFV Alternative-fuel vehicle.

AGST Aboveground storage tank, used to store used oil.

Air–fuel ratio The ratio of air to fuel in an intake charge as measured by weight.

Ampere hour A battery rating that combines the amperage output times the amount of time in hours that a battery is able to supply.

Analog-to-digital (AD) converter An electronic circuit that converts analog signals into digital signals that can then be used by a computer.

Anhydrous ethanol A type of ethanol that has almost zero absorbed water.

Annealing A heat-treating process that takes out the brittle hardening of the casting to reduce the chance of cracking from the temperature changes.

ANSI American National Standards Institute.

Antiknock Index (AKI) The pump octane.

API gravity An arbitrary scale expressing the gravity or density of liquid petroleum products devised jointly by the American Petroleum Institute and the National Bureau of Standards.

Asbestosis A health condition where asbestos causes scar tissue to form in the lungs causing shortness of breath.

ASD Automatic Shutdown Relay.

ASM 50/15 test Places a load of 50% on the vehicle at a steady 15 mph. This load represents 50% of the horsepower required to simulate the FTP acceleration rate of 3.3 mph/sec.

ASM 25/25 test Places a 25% load on the vehicle while it is driven at a steady 25 mph. This represents 25% of the load required to simulate the FTP acceleration rate of 3.3 mph/sec.

ASTM American Society for Testing Materials.

B5 A blend of 5% biodiesel with 95% petroleum diesel.

B20 A blend of 20% biodiesel with 80% petroleum diesel.

Back pressure The exhaust system's resistance to flow. Measured in pounds per square inch (PSI).

Baffle A plate or shield used to direct the flow of a liquid or gas.

Bar When air is pumped into the cylinder, the combustion chamber receives an increase of air pressure known as boost and is measured in pounds per square inch (PSI), atmospheres (ATM), or bar.

BARO sensor A sensor used to measure barometric pressure.

Barometric manifold absoluter pressure (BMAP) sensor A sensor that measures both the barometric pressure and the absolute pressure in the intake manifold.

Barometric pressure The pressure of the atmosphere which changes due to atmospheric conditions and altitude.

Base timing The timing of the spark before the computer advances the timing.

Baud rate The speed at which bits of computer information are transmitted on a serial data stream. Measured in bits per second (bps).

BCI Battery Council International.

Bench grinder An electric-powered grinding stone usually combined with a wire wheel and mounted to a bench.

Bias voltage a weak signal voltage applies to an oxygen sensor by the PCM. This weak signal voltage is used by the PCM to detect when the oxygen sensor has created a changing voltage and for diagnosis of the oxygen senor circuit.

Binary system A computer system that uses a series of zeros and ones to represent information.

Biodiesel A renewable fuel manufactured from vegetable oils, animal fats, or recycled restaurant grease.

Biomass Non-edible farm products, such as cornstalks, cereal straws, and plant wastes from industrial processes, such as sawdust and paper pulp, used in making ethanol.

Block The foundation of any engine. All other parts are either directly or indirectly attached to the block of an engine.

BMAP sensor A sensor that has individual circuits to measure barometric and manifold pressure. This input not only allows the computer to adjust for changes in atmospheric pressure due to weather, but also is the primary sensor used to determine altitude.

BNC connector A miniature standard coaxial cable connector.

BOB Break-out box.

Bolts A threaded fastener use to attach two parts. The threaded end can be installed into a casting such as an engine block or a nut used to join two parts.

Boost An increase in air pressure above atmospheric. Measured in pounds per square inch (PSI).

Bore The inside diameter of the cylinder in an engine.

Boxer A type of engine design that is flat and has opposing cylinders. Called a boxer because the pistons on one side resemble a boxer during engine operation. Also called a pancake engine.

Breaker bar A handle used to rotate a socket; also called a flex handle.

British thermal unit (BTU) A unit of heat measurement.

Bump cap A hat that is plastic and hard to protect the head from bumps.

Burn kV Spark line voltage.

BUS A term used to describe a communication network.

Bypass ignition Commonly used on General Motors engines equipped with distributor ignition (DI), as well as those equipped with waste-spark ignition.

Bypass valve Allows intake air to flow directly into the intake manifold bypassing the supercharger.

CA Cranking amperes. A rating for batteries.

CAA Clean Air Act. Federal legislation passed in 1970 that established national air quality standards.

Calibration codes Codes used on many Powertrain Control Modules (PCM).

California Air Resources Board A state of California agency that regulates the air quality standards for the state.

Cam-in-block design An engine where the crankshaft is located in the block rather than in the cylinder head.

Camshaft A shaft in an engine that is rotated by the crankshaft by a belt or chain and used to open valves.

Campaign A recall where vehicle owners are contacted to return a vehicle to a dealer for corrective action.

CAN A type of serial data transmission.

Cap screw A bolt that is threaded into a casting.

Capacity test A battery test that tests a battery by applying an electric load.

Casting number An identification code cast into an engine block or other large cast part of a vehicle.

CAT III An electrical measurement equipment rating created by the International Electrotechnical Commission (IEC). CAT III indicates the lowest level of instrument protection that should be in place when performing electrical measurements on hybrid electric vehicles.

Catalysts Platinum and palladium used in the catalytic converter to combine oxygen (O_2) with hydrocarbons (HC) and carbon monoxide (CO) to form nonharmful tailpipe emissions of water (H_2O) and carbon dioxide (CO_2).

Catalytic converter An emission control device located in the exhaust system that changes HC and CO into harmless H_2O and CO_2. If a three-way catalyst, NOx is also separated into harmless, separate N and O.

Catalytic cracking Breaking hydrocarbon chains using heat in the presence of a catalyst.

CCM Comprehensive Component Monitor.

Cellulose ethanol Ethanol produced from biomass feedstock such as agricultural and industrial plant wastes.

Cellulosic biomass Composed of cellulose and lignin, with smaller amounts of proteins, lipids (fats, waxes, and oils), and ash.

Cerium An element that can store oxygen.

Cetane number A measure of the ease with which the fuel can be ignited.

CFR Code of Federal Regulations.

Cheater bar A pipe or other object used to lengthen the handle of a ratchet or breaker bar. Not recommended to be used as the extra force can cause the socket or ratchet to break.

Chisels A type of hand tool used to mark or cut strong material such as steel.

CID Component Identification.

CKP Crankshaft position sensor.

Class 2 A type of BUS communication used in General Motors vehicles.

Clock generator A crystal that determines the speed of computer circuits.

Close end wrench A type of hand tool that has an end that surrounds the head of a bolt or nut.

Closed-loop operation A phase of computer-controlled engine operation in which oxygen sensor feedback is used to calculate air–fuel mixture.

Cloud point The low-temperature point at which the waxes present in most diesel fuel tend to form wax crystals that clog the fuel filter.

CMP Camshaft position sensor.

CNG Compressed natural gas.

Coal-to-liquid A refining process in which coal is converted to liquid fuel.

Coast-down stall A condition that results in the engine stalling when coasting to a stop .

Coil-on-plug ignition An ignition system without a distributor, where each spark plug has an ignition coil.

Combination wrench A wrench that is open ended at one end and has a box end at the other end.

Combustion The rapid burning of the air–fuel mixture in the engine cylinders, creating heat and pressure

Combustion chamber The space left within the cylinder when the piston is at the top of its combustion chamber.

Companion cylinders Two cylinders that share an ignition coil on a waste-spark-type ignition system.

Compressed natural gas (CNG) An alternative fuel that uses natural gas compressed at high pressures and used as a vehicle fuel.

Compression ratio The ratio of the volume in the engine cylinder with the piston at bottom dead center (BDC) to the volume at top dead center (TDC).

Compression-sensing ignition A type of waste-spark ignition system that does not require the use of a camshaft position sensor to determine cylinder number.

Compression test An engine test that helps determine the condition of an engine based on how well each cylinder is able to compress the air on the compression stroke.

Compressor bypass valve This type of relief valve routes the pressurized air to the inlet side of the turbocharger for reuse and is quiet during operation.

Conductance testing A type of electronic battery tester that determines the condition and capacity of a battery by measuring the conductance of the cells.

Connecting rod A metal rod that connects the piston to the crankshaft.

Continuity light A test light that has a battery and lights if there is continuity (electrical connection) between the two points that are connected to the tester.

Controller A term that is usually used to refer to a computer or an electronic control unit (ECU).

CPS Canister purge solenoid.

CPU Central processor unit.

Cracking A refinery process in which hydrocarbons with high boiling points are broken into hydrocarbons with low boiling points.

Cranking vacuum test Measuring the amount of manifold vacuum during cranking.

Crankshaft The part of an engine that transfers the up and down motion of the pistons to rotary motion.

Crest The outside diameter of a bolt measured across the threads.

Cross counts The number of times an oxygen sensor changes voltage from high to low (from low to high voltage is not counted) in 1 second (or 1.25 second, depending on scan tool and computer speed).

CRT Cathode ray tube.

Cycle A series of events such as the operation of the four strokes of an engine that repeats.

Cycle life The number of times a battery can be charged and discharged without suffering significant degradation in its performance.

Cylinder The part of an engine that is round and houses the piston.

Cylinder head temperature (CHT) sensor- A temperature sensor mounted on the cylinder head and used by the PCM to determine fuel delivery.

Cylinder leakage test A test that involves injecting air under pressure into the cylinders one at a time. The amount and location of any escaping air helps the technician determine the condition of the engine.

DC coupling A selection that can be made to observe a waveform.

DDS Demand delivery system.

DE The abbreviation for the drive end housing of a starter or generator (alternator).

Default position The position of the throttle plate in an electronic throttle control without any signals from the controller.

Delta Pressure Feedback EGR sensor This sensor measures the pressure differential between two sides of a metered orifice positioned just below the EGR valve's exhaust side.

Demand delivery system (DDS) A type of electronic fuel injection system.

Detonation A violent explosion in the combustion chamber created by uncontrolled burning of the air–fuel mixture; often causes a loud, audible knock. Also known as spark knock or ping.

DI Distributor ignition.

Diagnostic executive Software program designed to manage the operation of all OBD-II monitors by controlling the sequence of steps necessary to execute the diagnostic tests and monitors.

Diesel oxidation catalyst Consists of a flow-through honeycomb style substrate structure that is washcoated with a layer of catalyst materials, similar to those used in a gasoline engine catalytic converter.

Differential pressure sensor (DPS) A sensor used in the exhaust system of a diesel engine to detect when regeneration of the PM trap is needed.

Diesohol Standard #2 diesel fuel combined with up to 15% ethanol.

Digital computer A computer that uses on and off signals only. Uses an A to D converter to change analog signals to digital before processing.

Direct injection A fuel-injection system design in which gasoline is injected directly into the combustion chamber.

DIS Distributorless ignition system. Also called direct-fire ignition system.

Displacement The total volume displaced or swept by the cylinders in an internal combustion engine.

Distillation The process of purification through evaporation and then condensation of the desired liquid.

Distillation curve A graph that plots the temperatures at which the various fractions of a fuel evaporate.

Distributor cap Provides additional space between the spark plug connections to help prevent crossfire.

Division A block.

Divorced coil   Used by most waste-spark ignition coils to keep both the primary and secondary winding separated.

DMM   Digital multimeter. A digital multimeter is capable of measuring electrical current, resistance, and voltage.

Double-layer technology   The process used to build ultra-capacitors which involve the use of two carbon electrodes separated by a membrane.

Double overhead camshaft (DOHC)   An engine design that has two overhead camshafts. One camshaft operates the intake valves and the other for the exhaust valves.

DPS   Differential pressure sensor.

Drive-by-wire   A term used to describe an engine equipped with an electronic throttle control (ETC) system.

Drive size   The size in fractions of an inch of the square drive for sockets.

Driveability Index   A calculation of the various boiling temperatures of gasoline that once complied can indicate the fuels ability to perform well at low temperatures.

DSO   Digital storage oscilloscope, takes samples of the signals that can be stopped or stored.

Dual overhead camshaft   An engine design with two camshafts above each line of cylinders—one for the exhaust valves and one for the intake valves.

Dump valve   Features an adjustable spring design that keeps the valve closed until a sudden release of the throttle. The resulting pressure increase opens the valve and vents the pressurized air directly into the atmosphere.

Duty cycle   Refers to the percentage of on-time of the signal during one complete cycle.

DVOM   Digital volt-ohm-millimeter.

Dwell section   The amount of time that the current is charging the coil from the transistor-on point to the transistor-off point.

Dwell   The number of degrees of distributor cam rotation that the points are closed.

Dynamic compression test   A compression test done with the engine running rather than during engine cranking as is done in a regular compression test.

E & C   Entertainment and comfort.

E10   A fuel blend of 10% ethanol and 90% gasoline.

E2PROM   Electrically erasable programmable read-only memory.

E85   A fuel blend of 85% ethanol and 15% gasoline.

ECA   Electronic Control Module. The name used by Ford to describe the computer used to control spark and fuel on older-model vehicles.

ECM   Electronic control module on a vehicle.

ECT   Engine coolant temperature.

ECU   Electronic control unit on a vehicle.

E-diesel   Standard #2 diesel fuel combined with up to 15% ethanol. Also known as diesohol.

EECS   Evaporative Emission Control System.

EEPROM   Electronically erasable programmable read-only memory.

EGR valve position   A linear potentiometer on the top of the EGR valve stem indicates valve position for the computer.

ELD   The abbreviation for electrical load detection, a circuit used in the charging system to allow the system to work only when needed thereby improving fuel economy.

Electrolysis   The process in which electric current is passed through water in order to break it into hydrogen and oxygen gas.

Electromagnetic interference   An undesirable electronic signal. It is caused by a magnetic field building up and collapsing, creating unwanted electrical interference on a nearby circuit.

Electronic air control (EAC)   The idle air control valve.

Electronic Ignition System (EIS)   A term used to describe the type of Chrysler ignition system.

Electronic returnless fuel system (ERFS)   A fuel delivery system that does not return fuel to the tank.

Electronic spark timing   The computer controls spark timing advance.

Electronic throttle control (ETC)   A system that moves the throttle plate using an electric motor instead of a mechanical linkage from the accelerator pedal.

Enable criteria   Operating condition requirements.

Energy carrier   Any medium that is utilized to store or transport energy. Hydrogen is an energy carrier because energy must be used to generate hydrogen gas that is used as a fuel.

Energy density   A measure of the amount of energy that can be stored in a battery relative to the volume of the battery container. Energy density is measured in terms of watt-hours per liter (Wh/L).

Engine fuel temperature (EFT)   sensor- A temperature sensor located on the fuel rail that measures the temperature of the fuel entering the engine.

Engine mapping   A computer program that uses engine test data to determine the best fuel–air ratio and spark advance to use at each speed of the engine for best performance.

EPA   Environmental Protection Agency.

EREV   Abbreviation for extended range electric vehicles.

Ethanol   Grain alcohol that is blended with gasoline to produce motor fuel. Also known as ethyl alcohol.

Ethyl alcohol   See *ethanol*.

Ethyl tertiary butyl ether   An octane enhancer for gasoline. It is also a fuel oxygenate that is manufactured by reacting isobutylene with ethanol. The resulting ether is high octane and low volatility. ETBE can be added to gasoline up to a level of approximately 13%.

Exhaust gas recirculation   An emission control device to reduce NOx (oxides of nitrogen).

Exhaust valve   The valve in an engine that opens to allow the exhaust to escape into the exhaust manifold.

Extension   A socket wrench tool used between a ratchet or breaker bar and a socket.

External combustion engine   A type of engine that burns fuel from outside the engine itself such as a steam engine.

External trigger   Occurs when the trace starts when a signal is received from another (external) source.

Eye wash station   A water fountain designed to rinse the eyes with a large volume of water.

Fail safe position   A term used to describe the default position for the throttle plate in an electronic throttle control (ETC) system.

False air   A term used to describe air that enters the engine without being measured by the mass air flow sensor.

False lean indication   Occurs when an oxygen sensor reads low as a result of a factor besides a lean mixture.

False rich indication   A high oxygen sensor voltage reading that is not the result of a rich exhaust. Some common causes for this false rich indication include a contaminated oxygen sensor and having the signal wire close to a high voltage source such as a spark plug wire.

FCHV   Fuel-cell hybrid vehicle.

FCV   Fuel-cell vehicle.

FFV   Flexible fuel vehicle.

Files   A hand tool that is used to smooth rough or sharp edges from metal.

Filter basket   Final filter.

Fire blanket   A fireproof wool blanket used to cover a person who is on fire and smother the fire.

Fire extinguisher classes   The types of fires that a fire extinguisher is designed to handle are referred to as fire classes.

Firing line   The leftmost vertical (upward) line.

Firing order   The order that the spark is distributed to the correct spark plug at the right time.

Fisher-Tropsch   A method to create synthetic liquid fuel from coal.

Flare   An increase and then decrease in engine speed.

Flare-nut wrench   A type of wrench used to remove fuel, brake, or air-conditioning lines.

Flash point   The temperature at which the vapors on the surface of the fuel will ignite if exposed to an open flame.

Flex fuel   Flex-fuel vehicles are capable of running on straight gasoline or gasoline/ethanol blends.

Flow gauge   Tests for proper airflow in the EVAP system.

Flyback voltage   The inductive kick created when the primary field collapses is used by the PCM to monitor secondary ignition performance.

Formaldehyde   Formed when RFG is burned, and the vehicle exhaust has a unique smell when reformulated gasoline is used.

Four stroke cycle An engine design that requires four stokes to complete one cycle with each stroke requiring 180 degrees of crankshaft rotation.

Freeze-frame A snapshot of all of the engine data at the time the DTC was set.

Frequency The number of times a waveform repeats in one second, measured in hertz (Hz), frequency band.

Fretting A term used to describe the shedding of a gasket caused by the expansion and contraction of the two surfaces on the sides of the gasket.

FTD Fischer-Tropsch diesel.

FTP Federal Test Procedure.

Fuel cell An electrochemical device that converts the energy stored in hydrogen gas into electricity, water, and heat.

Fuel rail A term used to describe the tube that delivers the fuel from the fuel line to the individual fuel injectors.

Fuel compensation sensor A sensor used in flex-fuel vehicles that provides information to the PCM on the ethanol content and temperature of the fuel as it is flowing through the fuel delivery system.

Fuel-cell stack A collection of individual fuel cells, which are stacked end-to-end into one compact package.

Functionality Refers to PCM inputs checking the operation of the outputs.

Fungible A term used to describe a product that has the same grade or meets the same specifications, such as oil, that can be interchanged with another product without any affect.

Gang fired Pulsing injectors in groups.

Gasoline Refined petroleum product that is used primarily as a motor fuel. Gasoline is made up of many different hydrocarbons and also contains additives for enhancing its performance in an ICE.

Gasoline direct injection (GDI) A fuel-injection system design in which gasoline is injected directly into the combustion chamber.

Gas-to-liquid A refining process in which natural gas is converted into liquid fuel.

GAWR Gross axle weight rating. A rating of the load capacity of a vehicle and included on placards on the vehicle and in the owner's manual.

Gerotor A type of positive displacement pump that is often used in engine oil pumps. It uses the meshing of internal and external gear teeth to pressurize the fuel.

Glow plug A heating element that uses 12 volts from the battery and aids in the starting of a cold engine.

GMLAN GM local area network. A type of serial data transmission by General Motors.

GMM Graphing multimeter. A cross between a digital meter and a digital storage oscilloscope.

Grade The strength rating of a bolt.

Grain alcohol See *ethanol*.

Graticule The grid lines on the scope screen.

GVWR Gross vehicle weight rating. The total weight of the vehicle including the maximum cargo.

Hacksaws A type of hand tool that is used to cut metal or other hard materials.

Hall-effect switch A semiconductor moving relative to a magnetic field, creating a variable voltage output. A type of electromagnetic sensor used in electronic ignition and other systems and used to determine position. Named for Edwin H. Hall, who discovered the Hall effect in 1879.

Hammers A hand tool that is used to apply force by swinging.

Hangers Made of rubberized fabric with metal ends that hold the muffler and tailpipe in position so that they do not touch any metal part. This helps to isolate the exhaust noise from the rest of the vehicle.

Hazardous waste materials A classification of materials that can cause harm to people or the environment.

Heat of compression Air is compressed until its temperature reaches about 1000°F.

Helmholtz resonator Used on the intake duct between the air filter and the throttle body to reduce air intake noise during engine acceleration.

HEPA vacuum High-efficiency particulate air filter vacuum used to clean brake dust.

Hertz The measurement of frequency.

HEUI Hydraulic Electronic Unit Injection, a type of diesel injector system.

HEV an abbreviation for hybrid electric vehicle.

High Energy Ignition General Motors' name for their electronic ignition.

High-impedance meter Measures the total internal resistance of the meter circuit due to internal coils, capacitors, and resistors.

High-pressure common rail Diesel fuel under high pressure, over 20,000 PSI (138,000 kPa), is applied to the injectors, which are opened by a solenoid controlled by the computer. Because the injectors are computer controlled, the combustion process can be precisely controlled to provide maximum engine efficiency with the lowest possible noise and exhaust emissions.

Homogeneous charge compression ignition A low-temperature combustion process that involves air–fuel mixtures being burned without the use of spark ignition.

HV cables Vehicle cables that carry high voltage.

HV High voltage. Applies to any voltage above 50 volts.

Hydraulic electronic unit injection (HEUI) A type of diesel fuel injector that uses high pressure engine oil to operate the injector.

Hydraulic power assist A hybrid vehicle configuration that utilizes hydraulic pumps and accumulators for energy regeneration.

Hydrocracking A refinery process that converts hydrocarbons with a high boiling point into ones with low boiling points.

Hydrokinetic pump This design of pump rapidly moves the fuel to create pressure.

I/M 240 test It is a portion of the 505-second FTP test used by the manufacturers to certify their new vehicles. The "240" stands for 240 seconds of drive time on a dynamometer.

IAC Idle air control.

Idle speed control motor A motor, usually a stepper motor used to move a pintle that allows more or less air past the throttle plate thereby controlling idle speed.

Idle stop A block or screw that stops the throttle plate from closing all of the way which could cause it to stick in the housing.

Idle vacuum test A test performed using a vacuum gauge attached to the intake manifold of an engine running at idle speed.

ICE Internal combustion engine.

IEC International Electrotechnical Commission.

Initial timing Ignition timing set at base timing.

Igniter Ignition Control Module.

Ignition coil An electrical device that consists of two separate coils of wire: a primary and a secondary winding. The purpose of an ignition coil is to produce a high-voltage (20,000 to 40,000 volts), low-amperage (about 80 mA) current necessary for spark ignition.

Ignition control module (ICM) Controls (turns on and off) the primary ignition current of an electronic ignition system.

Ignition control Igniter Another name for an ignition control module (ICM).

Ignition timing The exact point of ignition in relation to piston position.

Inches of Mercury (in. Hg.) A measurement of vacuum; pressure below atmospheric pressure.

Indirect injection (IDI) Fuel is injected into a small prechamber, which is connected to the cylinder by a narrow opening. The initial combustion takes place in this prechamber. This has the effect of slowing the rate of combustion, which tends to reduce noise.

Inductive ammeter A type of ammeter that is used a Hall-effect sensor in a clamp that surrounds a conductor carrying a current.

Inductive reactance An opposing current created in a conductor whenever there is a charging current flow in a conductor.

Inert Chemically inactive.

Inertia switch Turns off the electric fuel pump in an accident.

Initial timing Where the spark plug fires at idle speed. The computer then advances the timing based off engine speed and other factors.

Injection pump Delivers fuel to the injectors at a high pressure and at timed intervals. Each injector sprays fuel into the combustion chamber at the precise moment required for efficient combustion.

Input conditioning What the computer does to the input signals to make them useful; usually includes an analog to digital converter and other electronic circuits that eliminate electrical noise.

Input Information on data from sensors to an electronic controller is called input. Sensors and switches provide the input signals.

Intake valve A valve in an engine used to allow air or air and fuel into the combustion chamber.

IOD Ignition off draw. Another name used to describe battery electrical drain.

Intercooler Similar to a radiator, wherein outside air can pass through, which cools the pressurized heated air.

Intermediate oscillations Also called the "ringing" of the coil as it is pulsed as viewed on a scope.

Internal combustion engine A term used to describe a normal engine used in vehicles where the fuel is consumed inside the engine itself.

Inverter An electronic device used to convert DC (direct current) into AC (alternating current).

Ion-sensing ignition A type of coil-on-plug ignition that uses a signal voltage across the spark plug gap after the plug has fired to determine the air-fuel mixture and if spark knock occurred.

Iridium spark plugs Use a small amount of iridium welded onto the tip of a small center electrode 0.0015 to 0.002 inch (0.4 to 0.6 mm) in diameter. The small diameter reduces the voltage required to jump the gap between the center and the side electrode, thereby reducing possible misfires. The ground or side electrode is usually tipped with platinum to help reduce electrode sap wear.

ISC Idle speed control motor.

KAM Keep-alive memory.

Keyword A type of network communications used in many General Motors vehicles.

Kilo Means 1,000; abbreviated k or K.

Knock sensor A sensor that can detect engine spark knock.

Leak defection pump Chrysler uses an electric pump that pressurizes the fuel system to check for leaks by having the PCM monitor the fuel tank pressure sensor.

Lean indicator The higher the oxygen O_2 levels in the exhaust the leaner the air–fuel mixture.

LED Abbreviation for light emitting diode.

LED test light Uses an LED instead of a standard automotive bulb for a visual indication of voltage.

Lift pump The diesel fuel is drawn from the fuel tank by the lift pump and delivers the fuel to the injection pump.

Linear air–fuel ratio sensor Another name for a wide band oxygen sensor.

Linear EGR Contains a stepper motor to precisely regulate exhaust gas flow and a feedback potentiometer that signals to the computer the actual position of the valve.

Linesman's gloves Type of gloves worn by technicians when working around high-voltage circuits. Usually includes a rubber inner glove rated at 1,000 volts and a protective leather outer glove when used for hybrid electric vehicle service.

Liquefied petroleum gas (LPG) Sold as compressed liquid propane that is often mixed with about 10% of other gases such as butane, propylene, butylenes, and mercaptan to give the colorless and odorless propane a smell.

Load test A type of battery test where the battery is placed under an electrical load.

Logic probe A type of tester that can detect either power or ground. Most testers can detect voltage but some cannot detect if a ground is present without further testing.

Low-grade heat Cooling system temperatures that are very close to the temperature of the ambient air, resulting in lowered heat transfer efficiency.

LP-gas See *liquefied petroleum gas*.

LRC Abbreviation for load response control also known as electronic load detection. A system used in many charging systems that activate the generator (alternator) when an electrical load is detected and not all of the time to help improve fuel economy.

M85 Internal combustion engine fuel containing 85% methanol and 15% gasoline.

Magnetic pulse generator The pulse generator consists of a trigger wheel (reluctor) and a pickup coil. The pickup coil consists of an iron core wrapped with fine wire, in a coil at one end and attached to a permanent magnet at the other end. The center of the coil is called the pole piece.

Magnetic sensor Uses a permanent magnet surrounded by a coil of wire. The notches of the crankshaft (or camshaft) create a variable magnetic field strength around the coil. When a metallic section is close to the sensor, the magnetic field is stronger because metal is a better conductor of magnetic lines of force than air.

Magnetic-resistive sensor A sensor that is similar to a magnetic sensor but, instead of producing an analog voltage signal, the electronics inside the sensor itself generate a digital on/off signal or an output.

Malfunction indicator lamp This amber, dashboard warning light may be labeled check engine or service engine soon.

MAP sensor A sensor used to measure the pressure inside the intake manifold compared to a perfect vacuum.

Married coil Also called a tapped transformer.

Mass air flow sensor Measures the density and amount of air flowing into the engine, which results in accurate engine control.

MCA An abbreviation for marine cranking amperes battery rating.

Mechanical force A force applied to an object.

Mechanical power A force applied to an object which results in movement or motion.

Mechanical returnless fuel system (MRFS) A returnless fuel delivery system design that uses a mechanical pressure regulator located in the fuel tank.

Mega Million. Used when writing larger numbers or measuring a large amount of resistance.

Membrane electrode assembly The part of the PEM fuel cell that contains the membrane, catalyst coatings, and electrodes.

Mercury A heavy metal.

Meter accuracy The accuracy of a meter measured in percent.

Meter resolution The specification of a meter that indicates how small or fine a measurement the meter can detect and display.

Methanol Typically manufactured from natural gas. Methanol content, including co-solvents, in unleaded gasoline is limited by law to 5%.

Methanol-to-gasoline (MTG) A refining process in which methanol is converted into liquid gasoline.

Methyl alcohol See *methanol*.

Methyl tertiary butyl ether A fuel oxygenate that is permitted in unleaded gasoline up to a level of 15%.

Metric bolts Bolts manufactured and sized in the metric system of measurement.

Micro (μ) One millionth of a volt or ampere.

Micron Equal to 0.000039 in.

Milli (m) One thousandth of a volt or ampere.

Millisecond sweep The scope will sweep only that portion of the pattern that can be shown during a 5- or 25-ms setting.

MSDS Material safety data sheet.

MTHF Methyltetrahydrofuron. A component of P-series nonpetroleum-based fuels.

Multiplexing A process of sending multiple signals of information at the same time over a signal wire.

Mutual induction The generation of an electric current due to a changing magnetic field of an adjacent coil.

Naturally (normally) aspirated An engine that uses atmospheric pressure for intake.

NEDRA National Electric Drag Racing Association.

Negative back pressure An EGR valve that reacts to a low pressure area by closing a small internal valve, which allows the EGR valve to be opened by vacuum.

Negative temperature coefficient Usually used in reference to a temperature sensor (coolant or air temperature). As the temperature increases, the resistance of the sensor decreases.

Network A communications system used to link multiple computers or modules.

Neutral position A term used to describe the home or the default position of the throttle plate in an electronic throttle control system.

NGV Natural gas vehicle.

NiMH Nickel-metal hydride. A battery design used for the high voltage batteries in most hybrid electric vehicles.

Node A module and computer that is part of a communications network.

Noid light Designed to electrically replace the injector in the circuit and to flash if the injector circuit is working correctly.

Nonchecking Some General Motors throttle-body units that do not hold pressure.

Non-methane hydrocarbon The standard by which exhaust emission testing for hydrocarbons is evaluated.

Nonprincipal end Opposite the principal end and is generally referred to as the front of the engine, where the accessory belts are used.

Nonvolatile RAM Computer memory capability that is not lost when power is removed. See also *read-only memory (ROM)*.

Nuts A female threaded fastener that is used with a bolt to hold two parts together.

OBD On-board diagnostic.

Octane rating The measurement of a gasoline's ability to resist engine knock. The higher the octane rating, the less prone the gasoline is to cause engine knock (detonation).

Oil galleries An oil pump, which is driven by the engine, forces the oil through the oil filter and then into passages in the crankshaft and block.

OL Open circuit.

Opacity The percentage of light that is blocked by the exhaust smoke.

Open-circuit battery voltage test A test of battery condition that is performed without a load on the battery.

Open-end wrench A type of wrench that allows access to the flats of a bolt or nut from the side.

Open-loop operation A phase of computer-controlled engine operation where air–fuel mixture is calculated in the absence of oxygen sensor signals. During open loop, calculations are based primarily on throttle position, engine RPM, and engine coolant temperature.

Optical sensors Use light from a LED and a phototransistor to signal the computer.

Organic A term used to describe anything that was alive at onetime.

ORVR Onboard refueling vapor recovery.

OSC Oxygen storage capacity.

Oscilloscope (scope) A visual volt meter.

OSHA Occupational Safety and Health Administration.

Oxygen sensor A sensor in the exhaust system to measure the oxygen content of the exhaust.

Oxygenated fuels Fuels such as ETBE or MTBE that contain extra oxygen molecules to promote cleaner burning. Oxygenated fuels are used as gasoline additives to reduce CO emissions.

Ozone Oxygen-rich (O3) gas created by sunlight reaction with unburned hydrocarbons (HC) and oxides of nitrogen (NOx); also calledsmog.

Palladium A catalyst that starts a chemical reaction without becoming a part of, or being consumed in, the process.

Pancake engine See *boxer*.

Paper test Hold a piece of paper or a 3 _ 5 index card (even a dollar bill works) within 1 inch (2.5 centimeters) of the tailpipe with the engine running at idle. The paper should blow out evenly without "puffing." If the paper is drawn toward the tailpipe at times, the exhaust valves in one or more cylinders could be burned.

Paired cylinders Another name used to describe companion cylinders in a waste-spark-type ignition system.

Parasitic load A term used to describe a battery drain with all circuits off. Also called battery electrical drain or ignition off draw.

Parameter identification The information found in the vehicle data stream as viewed on a scan tool.

PCM The onboard computer that controls both the engine management and transmission functions of the vehicle.

PCV Pressure control valve.

Peripheral pump Turbine pump.

Petrodiesel Another term for petroleum diesel, which is ordinary diesel fuel refined from crude oil.

Petroleum Another term for crude oil. The literal meaning of petroleum is "rock oil."

PFE sensor Pressure feedback EGR sensor.

PHEV Plug-in hybrid electric vehicle.

Pickup coil An ignition electronic triggering device in the magnetic pulse generator system.

Piezoresistivity Change in resistance due to strain.

Pinch weld seam A strong section under a vehicle where two body panels are welded together.

Ping Secondary rapid burning of the last 3% to 5% of the air–fuel mixture in the combustion chamber causes a second flame front that collides with the first flame front causing a knock noise. Also called detonation or spark knock.

Piston stroke A one-way piston movement between the top and bottom of the cylinder.

Pitch The pitch of a threaded fastener refers to the number of threads per inch.

Platinum spark plug A spark plug that has a small amount of the precious metal platinum welded onto the end of the center electrode, as well as on the ground or side electrode. Platinum is a grayish-white metal that does not react with oxygen and therefore, will not erode away as can occur with conventional nickel alloy spark plug electrodes.

Platinum A catalyst that starts a chemical reaction without becoming a part of, or being consumed in, the process.

Plenum A chamber, located between the throttle body and the runners of the intake manifold, used to distribute the intake charge more evenly and efficiently.

Pliers A hand tool with two jaws used to grasp or turn a part.

Polarity The condition of being positive or negative in relation to a magnetic pole.

Polymer electrolyte fuel cell Another term for PEM fuel cell.

Pop tester A device used for checking a diesel injector nozzle for proper spray pattern. The handle is depressed and pop off pressure is displayed on the gauge.

Port fuel-injection Uses a nozzle for each cylinder and the fuel is squirted into the intake manifold about 2 to 3 inches (70 to 100 mm) from the intake valve.

Positive back pressure An EGR valve that is designed with a small valve inside that bleeds off any applied vacuum and prevents the valve from opening unless there is exhaust backpressure applies to the valve.

Positive displacement All of the air that enters is forced through the roots-type supercharger.

Power balance test Determines if all cylinders are contributing power equally. It determines this by shorting out one cylinder at a time.

PPE Abbreviation for personal protective equipment.

PPO Pure plant oil.

Preconverter A small, quick heating oxidation converter.

Pressure control valve (PCV) A valve used to control the fuel system pressure on a demand delivery-type fuel system.

Pressure differential A difference in pressure from one brake circuit to another.

Pressure relief valve A valve located in a power steering pump that uses a check ball, which unseats and allows fluid to return to the reservoir if pressure exceeds a certain volume.

Pressure vent valve (PVV) A valve located in the fuel tank to prevent overpressure due to the thermal expansion of the fuel.

Prevailing torque nut A special design of nut fastener that is deformed slightly or has other properties that permit the nut to remain attached to the fastener without loosening.

Primary ignition circuit The ignition components that regulate the current in the coil primary winding by turning it on and off.

Primary winding The coil winding that is controlled by the electronic ignition control module or PCM.

Principal end The end of the engine that the flywheel is attached to.

Programmable controller interface (PCI) A type of serial data transmission used by Chrysler.

PROM Programmable read-only memory.

Propane See *liquified petroleum gas*.

Proton exchange membrane (PEM) A low-temperature fuel cell known for fast starts and relatively simple construction.

Pulse generator A sensor used in distributor ignitions used to trigger the ignition module.

Pulse train A DC voltage that turns on and off in a series of pulses.

Pulse width A measure of the actual on-time measured in milliseconds.

Punches A type of hand tool used to drive roll pins.

Pup converter See *preconverter*.

Purge flow sensor Checks for adequate purge flow.

Pushrod engine Uses one camshaft for the intake valves and a separate camshaft for the exhaust valves. When the camshaft is located in the block, the valves are operated by lifters, pushrods, and rocker arms.

PWM Pulse-width modulation.

R & R Remove and replace.

RAM Random-access memory.

Range The distance a vehicle can travel on a full charge or full-fuel tank without recharging or refueling. Range is measured in miles or kilometers.

Raster Stacked.

Rationality Refers to a PCM comparison of input value to values.

Ratchet A type of hand tool that is used to rotate a socket and is reversible.

RCRA Resource Conservation and Recovery Act.

Recall A notification to the owner of a vehicle that a safety issue needs to be corrected.

Reformulated gasoline (RFG) has oxygenated additives and is refined to reduce both the lightest and heaviest hydrocarbon content from gasoline in order to promote cleaner burning.

Regeneration A process of taking the kinetic energy of a moving vehicle and converting it to electrical energy and storing it in a battery.

Reid vapor pressure A method of determining vapor pressure of gasoline and other petroleum products. Widely used in the petroleum industry as an indicator of the volatility of gasoline.

Reluctor A notched metal wheel used with a magnetic sensor to trigger crankshaft or camshaft position.

Residual check valve A valve in the outlet end of the master cylinder to keep the hydraulic system under a light pressure on drum brakes only.

Residual or rest pressure Prevents vapor lock and hot-start problems on these systems.

Restricted exhaust The engine will be low on power, yet smooth.

Rhodium A catalyst that starts a chemical reaction without becoming a part of, or being consumed in, the process.

Right-to-know laws Laws that state that employees have a right to know when the materials they use at work are hazardous.

Ripple current The unwanted AC current from a generator (alternator).

RMS A method of calculating surface roughness using the square root of the average readings squared.

Roller cell Vane pump.

ROM Read-only memory.

Roots-type Named for Philander and Francis Roots, two brothers from Connersville, Indiana, who patented the design in 1860 as a type of water pump to be used in mines. Later it was used to move air and is used today on two-stroke cycle Detroit diesel engines and other supercharged engines. The roots-type supercharger is called a positive displacement design because all of the air that enters is forced through the unit.

Rotary engine Operates on the four-stroke cycle but uses a rotor instead of a piston and crankshaft to achieve intake, compression, power, and exhaust stroke.

Rotary vane pump The pump consists of a central impeller disk, several rollers or vanes that ride in notches in the impeller, and a pump housing that is offset from the impeller centerline.

Rotor gap Measures the voltage required to jump the gap (0.030 to 0.050 in. or 0.8 to 1.3 mm) between the rotor and the inserts (segments) of the distributor cap.

Running compression test A test that can inform a technician of the relative compression of all the cylinders.

RVP Abbreviation for Reid Vapor Pressure.

SAE Society of Automotive Engineers.

Saturation The point of maximum magnetic field strength of a coil.

Schmitt trigger Converts the analog signal into a digital signal.

Screwdrivers A type of hand tool used to install or remove screws.

Secondary ignition circuit The components necessary to create and distribute the high voltage produced in the secondary windings of the coil.

Secondary winding A winding that has about 100 times the number of turns of the primary winding, referred to as the turns ratio (approximately 100:1).

Self-induction The generation of an electric current in the wires of a coil created when the current is first connected or disconnected.

Sequential fuel injection (SFI) A fuel injection system in which injectors are pulsed individually in sequence with the firing order.

Serial communications interface (SCI) A type of serial data transmission used by Chrysler.

Serial data Data that is transmitted by a series of rapidly changing voltage signals.

Servomotor An electric motor that moves an actuator such as the throttle plate in an electronic throttle control system.

Side-channel pump Turbine pump.

Single overhead camshaft (SOHC) When one overhead camshaft is used.

SIP State Implementation Plan.

Skewed An output from a sensor that moves in the correct direction but does not accurately measure condition it is designed to measure.

Smog The term used to describe a combination of smoke and fog. Formed by NOx and HC with sunlight.

Snips A type of hand tool used to cut sheet metal and other thin materials.

Socket A tool that fits over the head of a bolt or nut and is rotated by a ratchet or breaker bar.

Socket adapter An adapter that allows the use of one size of driver (ratchet or breaker bar) to rotate another drive size of socket.

Solvent Usually colorless liquids that are used to remove grease and oil.

Spark ignition direct injection (SIDI) GM's name for gasoline direct injection system.

Spark knock See *Detonation*.

Spark line A short horizontal line immediately after the firing line.

Spark output The term that Ford used to describe the OBD-II terminology for the output signal from the PCM to the ignition system that controls engine timing.

Spark tester Looks like a spark plug except it has a recessed center electrode and no side electrode. The tester commonly has an alligator clip attached to the shell so that it can be clamped on a good ground connection on the engine.

Specific energy The energy content of a battery relative to the mass of the battery. Specific energy is measured in watt-hours per kilogram (Wh/kg).

Speed density The method of calculating the amount of fuel needed by the engine.

Splice pack A central point where many serial data lines jam together, often abbreviated SP.

Spontaneous combustion A condition that can cause some materials, such as oily rags, to catch fire without a source of ignition.

SST The abbreviation for special service tools.

SPOUT The term used by Ford to describe the "spark out" signal from the ICM to the PCM.

SRE The abbreviation for slip ring end part of a generator (alternator).

SST The abbreviation for special service tool.

Standard corporate protocol (SCP) A network communications protocol used by Ford.

State of health (SOH) A signal sent by a module to all of the other modules in the network indicating that it is well and able to transmit.

Stoichiometric ratio The ideal mixture or ratio at which all of the fuel combines with all of the oxygen in the air and burns completely.

Straight vegetable oil Vegetable oil, a triglyceride with a glycerin component joining three hydrocarbon chains of 16 to 18 carbon atoms each.

Stroke The distance the piston travels in the cylinder of an engine.

Stud A short rod with threads on both ends.

Supercharger Forces the air–fuel mixture into the cylinder for even greater power.

Superimposed A position used to look at differences in patterns between cylinders in all areas except the firing line.

Supercharger An engine driven device that forces air under pressure into the intake manifold to increase engine power.

Surface charge A charge on a battery that just on the surface of the plates and does not indicate the true state of charge of the battery.

SWCAN An abbreviation for single wire CAN (Controller Area Network).

Switchgrass A feedstock for ethanol production that requires very little energy or fertilizer to cultivate.

Switching   Turning on and off of the primary circuit.

Syncrude   A product of a process where coal is broken down to create liquid products. First the coal is reacted with hydrogen (H_2) at high temperatures and pressure with a catalyst.

Syn-gas   Synthesis gas generated by a reaction between coal and steam. Syn-gas is made up of mostly hydrogen and carbon monoxide and is used to make methanol. Syn-gas is also known as town gas.

Synthetic fuel   Fuels generated through synthetic processes such as Fischer-Tropsch.

Tap test   Involves tapping (not pounding) on the catalytic converter using a rubber mallet.

Tapped transformer   See *married coil*.

Task manager   A term Chrysler uses to describe the software program that is designed to manage the operation of all OBD-II monitors by controlling the sequence of steps necessary to execute the diagnostic tests and monitors.

TBI   Throttle-body injection.

Tensile strength   The maximum stress used under tension (lengthwise force) without causing failure.

Terminating resistors   Resistors placed at the end of a high-speed serial data circuit to help reduce electromagnetic interference.

Tertiary-amyl methyl ether   An oxygenate added to gasoline that is flammable and can form explosive mixtures with air. It is slightly soluble in water, very soluble in ethers and alcohol, and soluble in most organic solvents including hydrocarbons.

Test light   A light used to test for voltage. Contains a light bulb with a ground wire at one end and a pointed tip at the other end.

Tetraethyl lead   A liquid added to gasoline in the early 1920s to reduce the tendency to knock.

Throttle body temperature (TBT)   sensor- A temperature sensor that is mounted on the throttle body and measures the temperature of the air entering the engine.

Throttle position sensor   The sensor that provides feedback concerning the position of the throttle plate.

TID   Test Identification.

Time base   Setting how much time will be displayed in each block.

Top dead center (TDC)   The highest point in the cylinder that the piston can travel. The measurement from bottom dead center (BDC) to TDC determines the stroke length of the crankshaft.

Transistor   A semiconductor device that can operate as an amplifier or an electrical switch.

Transmission fluid temperature (TFT)   sensor- A sensor located inside an automatic transmission/transaxle that measures the temperature of the fluid.

Trigger level   The start of the display.

Trigger slope   The voltage direction that a waveform must have in order to start the display.

Triggering   The action of a sensor that turns on or off the current through an ignition coil at the ignition control module or PCM.

Trouble light   A light designed to help service technicians see while working on a vehicle.

True transformer   See *divorced coil*.

TSB   Technical service bulletin.

Turbine pump   Turns at higher speeds and is quieter than the other electric pumps.

Turbo lag   The delay between acceleration and turbo boost.

Turbocharger   An exhaust-powered supercharger.

Turn ratio   The number of times that the secondary windings in an ignition coil exceed that of the primary winding.

TWC   Three-way converter.

Twisted pair   A pair of wires that are twisted together from 9 to 16 turns per foot of length. Most are twisted once every inch (12 per foot) to help reduce electromagnetic interference from being induced in the wires as one wire would tend to cancel out any interference pickup up by the other wire.

UART   Universal Asynchronous Receive/Transmit, a type of serial data transmission.

UBP   UART-based protocol.

UCG   Underground coal gasification.

Ultracapacitor   A specialized capacitor technology with increased storage capacity for a given volume.

UNC   Unified national coarse. A type of thread used on fasteners.

Underground coal gasification (UCG)   A process performed underground where coal is turned into a liquid fuel.

Underground storage tank   A type of oil tank that is located underground.

UNF   Unified national fine. A type of thread used on fasteners.

Universal joint   A joint in a steering or drive shaft that allows torque to be transmitted at an angle.

Up-integrated ignition   Ignition control where all timing functions are performed in the PCM, rather than being split between the ignition control module and the PCM.

Used cooking oil   A term used when the oil may or may not be pure vegetable oil.

Used oil   Any petroleum-based or synthetic oil that has been used.

Vacuum   Any pressure less than atmospheric pressure (14.7 PSI).

Vacuum test   Testing the engine for cranking vacuum, idle vacuum, and vacuum at 2,500 RPM.

VAF   Vane air flow.

Vapor lock   A lean condition caused by vaporized fuel in the fuel system.

Variable fuel sensor   See *fuel compensation sensor*.

Variable reluctance sensor   Magnetic sensor.

VECI   Vehicle emission control information. This sticker is located under the hood on all vehicles and includes emission-related information that is important to the service technician.

V-FFV   An abbreviation for a virtual flexible fuel vehicle. This type of vehicle does not use a fuel sensor and instead uses the oxygen sensor(s) to detect the amount of alcohol being used in the system.

VIN   Vehicle identification number.

Virtual-flexible fuel vehicle   The virtual-flexible fuel vehicle can operate on pure gasoline, E10, E85, or any combination.

VOC   Volatile organic compound.

Volatility   A measurement of the tendency of a liquid to change to vapor. Volatility is measured using RVP, or Reid vapor pressure.

Voltage drop test   An electrical test performed with current flowing through the circuit to determine what voltage is lost to resistance.

Volumetric efficiency   The ratio between the amount of air–fuel mixture that actually enters the cylinder and the amount that could enter under ideal conditions expressed in percent.

Wankel engine   Rotary engine.

Washcoat   A porous aluminum material which makes the surface rough.

Washers   Flat metal discs with a hole in the center used under threaded fasteners to help spread the clamping force over a wider area.

Waste vegetable oil   This oil could include animal or fish oils from cooking.

Wastegate   A valve similar to a door that can open and close. The wastegate is a bypass valve at the exhaust inlet to the turbine. It allows all of the exhaust into the turbine, or it can route part of the exhaust past the turbine to the exhaust system.

Waste-spark ignition   Introduced in the mid-1980s, it uses the onboard computer to fire the ignition coils.

Water-fuel separator   Separates water and fuel in a diesel engine.

Wet compression test   A test that uses oil to help seal around the piston rings.

WHMIS   Workplace Hazardous Materials Information Systems.

Wide-band oxygen sensor   An oxygen sensor design that is capable of detecting actual air–fuel ratios. This is in contrast to a conventional oxygen sensor that only changes voltage when richer or leaner than stoichiometric air–fuel ratio.

Wind farms   A group of windmills in one area.

Wood alcohol   See *methanol*.

World wide fuel charter   A fuel quality standard developed by vehicle and engine manufacturers in 2002.

Wrench   A hand tool used to grasp and rotate a threaded fastener.

WWFC   The abbreviation for world wide fuel charter.

Por encima de tanque molido (ABST) de almacenamiento Un tanque de almacenamiento que almacena aceite usado y está localizado por encima de tierra.

La corriente alterna acoplándose Una selección que puede ser hecha para observar un waveform.

/ la CD de corriente alterna DMM que se sujeta adelante Un tipo de metro que tiene una abrazadera que se colocó alrededor del alambre para medir corriente.

El voltaje de la Onda de corriente alterna Un voltaje alternante de la corriente que va montado sobre parte superior de una CD cargando a la cuenta salida actual de un generador de corriente alterna (el alternador)

El modo de simulación de aceleración Usa un dinamómetro que le aplica una carga pesada en el vehículo en una velocidad estatal en novio.

El sensor de la posición del pedal acelerador (la APLICACIÓN) Un sensor que se usa para monitorear la posición y tasa de cambio del pedal acelerador

El acumulador Una posición temporal para fluido a presión.

El accionador Un dispositivo eléctrico o mecánico que convierte energía eléctrica en una acción mecánica, como el motor ajustador la velocidad sin valor, alterando altura de suspensión, o regulando combustible midiendo.

La llave inglesa Una torcedura que tiene una mandíbula móvil para permitir que eso equipe muchos dimensiona de sujetadores.

La adsorción Agregados las moléculas de vapor de combustible para el carbón salen a la superficie.

AFV El vehículo de combustible alternativo.

AGST El tanque de almacenamiento Aboveground, usado para almacenar usó aceite.

El aire – dele pábulo a la proporción La proporción de aire a echarle combustible a en un cargo de la toma tan medido por peso.

El amperio-hora Una batería evaluando eso se combina la salida de amperaje por la cantidad de tiempo en las horas que una batería puede dar abasto.

Convertidor digital analógico (el Año de Cristo) Un circuito electrónico que muta señales analógicas en señales digitales que luego pueden ser usadas por una computadora.

El etanol anhidro Un tipo de etanol que tiene casi cero amortiguó agua.

Endureciendo por calor Uno endureciendo por calor que el proceso que remueve el endurecimiento quebradizo de la fundición para reducir el acaso de chasquear de la temperatura cambia.

ANSI El Instituto Nacional Americano de Estándares.

El índice de antidetonante (AKI) El octano de la bomba.

La gravedad API Una escala arbitraria expresando la gravedad o la densidad de líquidos productos petroleros ideados conjuntamente por el Instituto Petrolero Americano y la Agencia Nacional de Estándares.

La asbestosis Una condición de salud donde las causas de asbesto dejen una cicatriz en tejido fino para formar en los pulmones causando dificultad para respirar.

ASD El Relevador Automático de Cierre.

ASM 50/15 experimente Coloca una carga de 50 % en el vehículo en un novio 15 millas por hora. Esta carga representa 50 % del caballo de fuerza requerido para simular la tasa de aceleración FTP de / sec de 3.3 millas por hora.

ASM La prueba del 25/25 Coloca una carga de 25 % en el vehículo mientras es conducida en unas constantes 25 millas por hora. Esto representa 25 % de la carga requerida para simular la tasa de aceleración FTP de / sec de 3.3 millas por hora.

ASTM La Sociedad Americana para Probar Materiales.

B5 Un preparado de biodiesel de 5 % con diesel de 95 % de petrolero.

B20 Un preparado de biodiesel de 20 % con diesel de 80 % de petrolero.

La contrapresión La resistencia del sistema eductor a fluir. Medido en las libras por la pulgada cuadrada (PSI).

El deflector Un plato o un escudo acostumbró dirigir el flujo de un líquido o un gas.

La barra Cuando el aire es bombeado al cilindro, la cámara de combustión recibe un incremento de presión atmosférica conocido como el estímulo y está medida en libras por la pulgada cuadrada (PSI), atmósferas (el cajero automático), o barra.

El sensor BARO Un sensor acostumbró medir presión barométrica.

El sensor múltiple barométrico de presión del absoluter (BMAP) Un sensor que mide ambos la presión barométrica y la presión absoluta en el tubo múltiple de la toma

La presión barométrica La presión de la atmósfera que cambia debido a la altitud y condiciones atmosféricas.

Base oportunidad del momento La oportunidad del momento de la chispa antes de la computadora propone la oportunidad del momento.

La tasa de baudio La velocidad en la cual los pedacitos de información de la a computadora está transmitida en una corriente serial de datos. Medido a pedazos por segundo (bps).

BCI El Concejo de la Batería Internacional.

La trituradora del banco Un esmeril de poder eléctrico usualmente combinado con una rueda de rayos de alambre y montado para un banco.

Influencie voltaje Un voltaje débil de la señal se aplica a un sensor de oxígeno por el PCM. Este voltaje débil de la señal es usado por el PCM para detectar cuándo creó el sensor de tiene, oxígeno un voltaje cambiante y para el diagnóstico del circuito del senor de oxígeno.

El sistema binario Un sistema de la computadora que usa una serie de ceros y Los unos para representar información.

Biodiesel Un combustible renovable confeccionó de aceites vegetales, mantecas animales, o grasa reciclada del restaurante.

La biomasa Los productos de campo incomestibles, como tallos del maíz, las pajas del cereal, y los desperdicios de la planta de procesos, como el serrín y el periódico despulpan, acostumbraron haciendo etanol.

El bloque La fundación de cualquier motor. Todos los demás partes están uno u otro directamente o indirectamente adjunto para el bloque de un motor.

El sensor BMAP Un sensor que tiene al individuo circunvala para medir presión barométrica y múltiple. Este aporte no sólo deja la computadora ajustarse para los cambios en el presión atmosférica debido al clima, sino que también es el sensor primario usado para determinar altitud.

El conector BNC Un conector cablegráfico coaxial estándar en miniatura.

La SACUDIDA La caja de escape forzado.

Los pernos Un uso roscado del sujetador para pegar dos divide. El fin roscado puede ser instalado en una fundición como un bloque del motor o una nuez acostumbró unir dos partes.

El estímulo Un incremento en la presión atmosférica por encima de atmosférico. Medido en las libras por la pulgada cuadrada (PSI).

El aburrido El diámetro interior cilindro en un motor.

El boxeador Un tipo de diseño del motor que es plano y tiene oponerse a los cilindros. Designado un boxeador porque los pistones a un lado se parezcan a un boxeador durante la operación del motor. También designado un motor del panqueque.

La barra del interruptor Una agarradera acostumbró rotar un conector; También designado una agarradera del doblez.

La unidad térmica británica (el BTU) Una medida de unidad de calor.

La gorra de golpe Un sombrero que es plástico y duro para proteger la cabeza de golpes.

El kV de la quemadura El voltaje de la línea de la chispa.

El AUTOBÚS Un término acostumbró describir una red de comunicación.

La ignición de la carretera de circunvalación Comúnmente usada en General Motors que los motores equiparon con que la ignición distribuidora (DI), así como también esos equipó con desaprovecha la ignición de la chispa.

La válvula desviadora Deja aire de la toma desembocar directamente en el tubo múltiple de la toma bordeando el supercargador.

CA Haciendo girar amperios. Una valuación para baterías.

CAA Limpie Acto de Aire. La legislación federal pasó en 1970 que establecieron Los estándares nacionales de calidad de aire.

Los códigos de calibración Los códigos usados en muchos Powertrain Control Los módulos (PCM).

Los Recursos de Aire de California Se Embarcan Un estado de agencia de California que regula los estándares de calidad de aire para el estado.

La leva en diseño del bloque Un motor donde el cigüeñal está ubicado en el bloque en vez de en la culata de cilindro.

El árbol de levas Un eje en un motor que se rotó por el cigüeñal por un cinturón o una cadena y usado para abrir válvulas.

La campaña Una retentiva donde los dueños del vehículo son contactados para devolverle un vehículo a un distribuidor para la acción correctiva.

La LATA Un tipo de transmisión de datos serial.

El tornillo de cabeza Un perno que se ensartó en una fundición.

La prueba de aptitud Una prueba de la batería que prueba una batería aplicándole una carga eléctrica.

Lanzando número Un código de la identificación emitido en un bloque del motor u otro molde grande divide de un vehículo.

La CAT III Una valuación del equipo de medida eléctrica creada por la Comisión Electrotécnica Internacional (IEC). CAT III indica el nivel mínimo de protección del instrumento que debería estar en lugar al realizar medidas eléctricas en vehículos eléctricos híbridos.

Los catalizadores El platino y palladium utilizado en el convertidor catalítico para combinar oxígeno (O2) con hidrocarburos (HC) y monóxido de carbono (Colorado) para formar emisiones poco dañinas del tubo de escape de agua (H2O) y dióxido de carbono (CO2).

El convertidor catalítico Un dispositivo de control de la emisión localizó en el sistema eductor que cambia a HC y Colorado en el inofensivo H2O y CO2. Si un catalizador de tres formas, NOx es también separado en N inofensiva, separada y O.

El agrietamiento catalítico Rompiendo cadenas de hidrocarburo usando calor en presencia de un catalizador.

CCM El Monitor Componente Asimilativo.

El etanol de celulosa El etanol produjo de feedstock de la biomasa como desperdicios agrícolas de la planta industrial y.

La biomasa Cellulosic Compuesto de celulosa y lignin, con cantidades más pequeñas de proteínas, los lípidos (las grasas, las ceras, y los aceites), y la ceniza.

El cerio Un elemento que puede almacenar oxígeno.

El número Cetane Una medida de la facilidad con la cual el combustible puede estar en llamas.

CFR El Código de Reglas Federales.

La barra del embaucador Una tubería u otro objeto acostumbró alargar la agarradera de un trinquete o la barra del interruptor. No recomendable para ser utilizado como la fuerza adicional puede causar que el conector o el trinquete se quiebre.

Los cinceles Un tipo de herramienta de la mano acostumbró marca o hirió fuertemente material como acero

El Departamento de Investigación Criminal La Identificación Componente.

CKP El sensor de la posición del cigüeñal.

Clase 2 Un tipo de comunicación del AUTOBÚS usada en vehículos Generales de Motores.

El generador del reloj Un cristal que determina la velocidad de circuitos de la computadora.

La llave mecánica cercana de fin Un tipo de herramienta de la mano que tiene un fin que rodea la cabeza de un perno o un tipo de nuez.

La operación de circuito cerrado Una fase de operación del motor controlado por computadora en la cual la información retroactiva del sensor de oxígeno se usa para calcular apariencia – la mezcla de combustible.

El punto de oscuridad El punto de baja temperatura en el cual las ceras presentan en la mayoría de aceite pesado tienda a formar cristales de cera que atascan el filtro de combustible.

CMP El sensor de la posición del árbol de levas.

CNG El gas natural comprimido.

El carbón para líquido Un proceso refinador en el cual el carbón es convertido al combustible líquido.

El puesto que se se desliza por una pendiente abajo Una condición que resulta en el motor atollándose al deslizarse por una pendiente para un alto.

La bobina en ignición del tapón Un sistema de ignición sin un distribuidor, donde cada bujía del motor tiene una bobina de ignición.

La llave de combinación Una llave mecánica que está abierta fenecó en un extremo y tiene un fin de la caja en el otro extremo.

La combustión El ardor rápido del aire – échele combustible a la mezcla en los cilindros del motor, creando calor y presión

La cámara de combustión El espacio salió dentro del cilindro cuando el pistón está en la cima de su cámara de combustión.

Los cilindros del compañero Dos cilindros que comparten una ignición se enrolla en un sistema de ignición de tipo de chispa residual.

El gas natural comprimido (CNG) Un combustible alternativo que usa gas natural comprimió en las presiones altas y acostumbró como un combustible del vehículo.

El índice de compresión La proporción del volumen en el cilindro del motor con el pistón en el punto muerto inferior para el (TDC) volumen en el punto muerto superior (BDC).

Ignición que detecta compresión Un tipo de sistema de ignición de la chispa residual que no requiere que el uso de un sensor de la posición del árbol de levas determine número del cilindro.

La prueba de compresión Una prueba del motor que ayuda a determinar la condición de un motor basó adelante qué tan sano cada cilindro puede comprimir el aire en el golpe de compresión.

La válvula desviadora del compresor Este tipo de válvula de seguridad encamina el aire presurizado a la ensenada lateral de la turbina alimentadora para el aprovechamiento y está quieto durante la operación.

La conductancia experimentando Un tipo de probador electrónico de la batería que determina la condición y aptitud de una batería midiendo la conductancia de las celdas.

La barra de conexión Una barra de metal que conecta el pistón para el cigüeñal.

La luz de continuidad Una luz experimental que tiene una batería y luces si hay continuidad (la conexión eléctrica) entre los dos puntos que están relacionados al probador.

El controlador Un término que se usa usualmente para referirse a una computadora o una unidad electrónica (ECU) de control.

CPS El solenoide de purga de la lata.

CPU La unidad del procesador central.

El agrietamiento Un proceso de la refinería en el cual los hidrocarburos con puntos de ebullición altos son cortados en los hidrocarburos con puntos de ebullición bajos.

Haciendo girar examen de vacío Midiendo la cantidad de vacío múltiple Durante hacer girar.

El cigüeñal La parte de un motor que transfiere el movimiento levantado y detenido de los pistones para el movimiento de rotación.

La cresta El diámetro exterior de un perno medido a través de los hilos.

Cruce cuentas El número de por un sensor de oxígeno cambia voltaje de a gran altura para mugir (de punto bajo para el alto voltaje no es contado) en 1 segundo (o 1.25 secundan, según que la herramienta de tomografía y la computadora aceleren).

CRT El tubo de rayos catódicos.

El ciclo Una serie de acontecimientos como la operación de los cuatro golpes de un motor que repite.

Recicle vida El número de por una batería puede ser cargado a la cuenta y muerto sin sufrir degradación significativa en su función.

El cilindro La parte de un motor que está alrededor y aloja el pistón.

El sensor de temperatura de la culata de cilindro (CHT) Un sensor de temperatura se montó en la culata de cilindro y acostumbró por el PCM para determinar entrega de combustible.

La prueba de la fuga del cilindro Una prueba que implica inyectar aire bajo presión en los cilindros uno de cada vez. La cantidad y la posición de cualquier librándose de ayudas de aire el técnico determinan la condición del motor.

La CD acoplándose Una selección que puede ser hecha para observar un waveform.

DDS El sistema de la entrega de demanda.

Delaware La abreviación para la vivienda de fin de paseo en coche de un arrancador o el generador (el alternador)

Deje incumplida posición La posición del plato del obturador en un control electrónico del obturador sin cualquier señales del controlador.

El sensor del delta Pressure Feedback EGR Estas medidas del sensor que el diferencial de presión entre dos lados de un orificio medido situó simplemente debajo del lado eductor de la válvula EGR.

El sistema de la entrega de demanda (DDS) Un tipo de sistema electrónico de la inyección de combustible.

La detonación Una explosión violenta en la cámara de combustión creada por el ardor no dominado del aire – la mezcla de combustible; A menudo las causas un golpe fuerte, audible. También conocido como el golpe de la chispa o el sonido corto y metálico.

DI La ignición distribuidora.

El ejecutivo diagnóstico El programa del software diseñado para manejar la operación de todo OBD-II monitorea controlando la secuencia de pasos necesarios para ejecutar los monitores y pruebas diagnósticas.

El catalizador de oxidación de diesel Consta de un flujo a través de la estructura del substrate de estilo del panel que es washcoated con un estrato de materiales de catalizador, parecido a esos usó en un motor de gasolina convertidor catalítico.

El sensor de presión diferencial (los tratamientos de datos) Un sensor usado en el sistema eductor de un motor Diesel a detectar cuándo es necesaria la regeneración de la trampa de la noche.

Diesohol El aceite pesado del #2 estándar combinado con hasta etanol de 15 %.

La computadora digital Una computadora la que acostumbra adelante completamente hace señales sólo. Usa una A para convertidor de la D para cambiar señales analógicas para digital antes de ir en procesión.

Dirija inyección Un diseño de sistema de la inyección de combustible en el cual la gasolina es inyectada directamente en la cámara de combustión.

DIS El sistema de ignición Distributorless. También la ignición de tiro directo designada El sistema.

El desplazamiento El volumen total desplazado o se barre por los cilindros en un motor de explosión.

La destilación El proceso de purificación a través de la evaporación y luego la condensación del líquido deseado.

La curva de destilación Una gráfica que representa gráficamente las temperaturas en las cuales las fracciones diversas de un combustible se evapora.

La gorra distribuidora Provee espacio adicional entre las conexiones de la bujía del motor para ayudar a impedir fuego cruzado.

La división Un bloque.

La bobina divorciada Usado por la mayoría de chispa desperdiciada que las bobinas de ignición para alojar ambos el serpenteo primario y secundario separó.

DMM El multímetro digital. Un multímetro digital es capaz de medir corriente eléctrica, resistencia, y voltaje.

La tecnología del estrato doble El proceso acostumbró construir ultracondensadores que implican el uso de dos electrodos de carbón separados por una membrana.

Duplique árbol de levas aéreo (DOHC) Un diseño del motor que tiene dos árboles de levas aéreos. Un árbol de levas dirige las válvulas de admisión y el otro para las válvulas de escape.

Los tratamientos de datos El sensor de presión diferencial.

El paseo en coche por alambre Un término usado describir un motor equipado con un sistema electrónico de control del obturador (ETC).

Conduzca tamaño El tamaño en fracciones de una pulgada del paseo en coche cuadrado para conectores.

Driveability Index Un cálculo de las temperaturas de ebullición diversas de gasolina esa vez accedida puede indicar la habilidad de combustibles para desenvolverse en las bajas temperaturas.

DSO El almacenamiento digital oscilloscope, tomas toma muestras de las señales que pueden estar bloqueadas o almacenadas.

El árbol de levas aéreo dual Un diseño del motor con dos árboles de levas por encima de cada línea de cilindros – uno para las válvulas de escape y uno para las válvulas de admisión.

La válvula de descarga Características un diseño primaveral regulable que mantiene la válvula cerrada hasta una liberación repentina del obturador. El incremento resultante de presión abre la válvula y despresuriza el aire presurizado directamente en la atmósfera.

El ciclo arancelario Se refiere al porcentaje de adelante cronometra de la señal durante un ciclo completo.

DVOM El milímetro digital de ohm de voltio.

More sección La cantidad de tiempo que la corriente cargue a la cuenta la bobina del transistor en punto para el punto feriado en transistor.

More El número de grados de rotación distribuidora de la leva que los puntos están cerrados.

La prueba dinámica de compresión Una prueba de compresión hecha con el motor corriendo en vez de durante motor haciendo girar tal cual hecho en una prueba normal de compresión.

La E y C El entretenimiento y la comodidad.

E10 Un preparado de combustible de etanol de 10 gasolina % y de 90 %.

E2PROM La memoria eléctricamente que se lee sólo programable borrable.

E85 Un preparado de combustible de etanol de 85 gasolina % y de 15 %.

ECA El Módulo Electrónico de Control. El nombre usado por Ford para describir la computadora solió controlar chispa y nutrirse de modelo mayor Los vehículos.

ECM El módulo electrónico de control en un vehículo.

ECT La temperatura de líquido de refrigeración del motor.

ECU La unidad electrónica de control en un vehículo.

E-diesel El aceite pesado del #2 estándar combinado con hasta etanol de 15 %. También conocido como diesohol.

EECS El Controlador Evaporatorio de la Emisión.

EEPROM La memoria electrónicamente que se lee sólo programable borrable.

La posición de la válvula EGR Un potenciómetro lineal en lo alto del vástago de válvula EGR indica posición de la válvula para la computadora.

ELD La abreviación para la detección de carga eléctrica, un circuito usada en el sistema embestidor dejar el sistema trabajo sólo cuando se necesita por consiguiente mejorando economía de combustible.

La electrólisis El proceso en el cual la corriente eléctrica es hecha pasar pora el agua para cortarla en hidrógeno y el gas de oxígeno.

La interferencia electromagnética Una señal electrónica indeseable. Se debe a un campo magnético aumentándose y derrumbándose, creando interferencia eléctrica no deseada en un circuito cercano.

El control electrónico (EAC) de aire La válvula de control desocupada de aire.

El sistema electrónico (EIS) de Ignición Un término acostumbró describir el tipo de sistema de ignición del Chrysler.

Los returnless electrónicos le dan pábulo al sistema (ERFS) Un sistema de la entrega de combustible que no le devuelve el combustible al tanque.

La oportunidad del momento electrónica de la chispa La computadora controla avance de oportunidad del momento de la chispa.

El control electrónico (ETC) del obturador Un sistema que mueve el plato del obturador usando un motor eléctrico en lugar de una vinculación mecánica del pedal acelerador.

Posibilite criterios Los requisitos operativos de condición.

El trasportador de energía Cualquier medio que es utilizado para almacenar o transportar energía. El hidrógeno es un trasportador de energía porque la energía debe usarse para generar gases de hidrógeno que es utilizado como un combustible.

La densidad de energía Una medida de la cantidad de energía que se almacenó en una batería relativo al volumen del envase de la batería. La densidad de energía es medida en términos de vatio-horas por el litro (Wh / L).

El sensor de temperatura de combustible del motor (EFT) Un sensor de temperatura halló en el riel de combustible que mide la temperatura del combustible entrando en el motor.

El motor haciendo mapas Un programa de computadora que usa datos de prueba del motor para determinar el mejor combustible – la proporción de aire y la chispa avanzan al uso en cada velocidad del motor para la mejor función.

EPA La Agencia Medioambiental de Protección.

EREV La abreviación para el rango extendido los vehículos eléctricos

El etanol El alcohol de grano que se hizo juego con gasolina para producir combustible motor. También conocido como alcohol etílico.

El alcohol etílico Vea *etanol*.

El etilo el éter terciario de butilo Un realzador del octano para gasolina. Es también un combustible oxigena eso sale a la luz reaccionando isobutylene con etanol. El éter resultante es octano alto y volatilidad baja. ETBE puede ser añadido a gasolina hasta un nivel de aproximadamente 13 %.

Agote recirculación del gas   Un dispositivo de control de la emisión para reducir a NOx (los óxidos de nitrógeno).

La válvula de escape   La válvula en un motor que abre dejar el tubo de escape escapar en el tubo múltiple eductor.

La extensión   Una herramienta de la llave de tubo usada entre un trinquete o el interruptor atranca y un conector.

El motor de combustión externa   Un tipo de motor que quema combustible de exterior el motor mismo como una máquina de vapor.

El gatillo externo   Ocurre cuando la huella empieza cuando una señal es recibida de otra (el parte exterior) fuente.

La estación de lavado del ojo   Una fuente de agua diseñada para enjuagar los ojos con un volumen grande de agua.

Yerre posición segura   Un término acostumbró describir la posición predeterminada para el plato del obturador en un sistema electrónico de control del obturador (ETC)

El aire falso   Un término acostumbró describir aire que entra en el motor sin ser comedido por el sensor masivo de flujo de aire.

La indicación parca falsa   Ocurre cuando un sensor de oxígeno lee el punto bajo como resultado de un factor además de una mezcla delgada.

La indicación enriquecedora falsa   Un voltaje alto del sensor de oxígeno leyendo eso no es el resultado de un tubo de escape sustancioso. Algunas causas comunes para esta indicación enriquecedora falsa incluyen un sensor contaminado de oxígeno y a hacer el alambre de la señal cerca de una fuente alta de voltaje como una chispa taponar alambre.

FCHV   El vehículo híbrido de la célula en combustible.

FCV   El vehículo de la célula en combustible.

FFV   El vehículo flexible de combustible.

Los archivos   Una herramienta de la mano que se usa para alisar al grosero o bordes cortantes de metal

La canasta del filtro   El filtro final localizado en la ensenada para el inyector de combustible.

La manta apagafuegos   Una manta lanera a prueba de fuego acostumbró abrigar a una persona que está en fuego y humareda el fuego.

Las clases del extintor de fuego   Los tipos de fuegos que un extintor de fuego es diseñado para manipular son llamadas clases de fuego.

La línea de fuego   La línea de vertical del leftmost (hacia arriba).

La orden de encendido   La orden que la chispa es distribuida para la bujía del motor correcta a buena hora.

Fisher-Tropsch   Un método para crear combustible líquido sintético de carbón.

La llamarada   Un incremento y luego disminuya en la velocidad del motor.

La llave mecánica de la nuez de llamarada   Un tipo de llave mecánica acostumbró quitar combustible, frenar, o acondicionando el aire de líneas.

El punto de inflamación   La temperatura en la cual los vapores en la superficie del combustible comenzarán a arder si expuesto para una llama abierta.

Flexione combustible   Los vehículos de combustible de doblez son capaces de funcionar con gasolina derecha o gasolina /etanol se mezcla.

El calibre de flujo   Las pruebas para corriente de aire correcta en el sistema EVAP.

El voltaje Flyback   La patada inductiva creada cuando el campo primario colapsa es usado por el PCM para monitorear función secundaria de ignición.

Formaldehyde   RFG cuándo forjado está quemado, y el tubo de escape del vehículo tiene un olor único cuándo la gasolina reformulada es usado.

Cuatro acarician ciclo   Un diseño del motor que requiere cuatro ceba para completar un ciclo con cada golpe requiriendo 180 grados de rotación del cigüeñal.

El fotograma   Una foto de todo el datos del motor en el tiempo lo DTC estaba listo.

La frecuencia   El número de por un waveform repite en el un segundo, midió en banda de hertz (Hz), de frecuencia.

Apurándose   Un término usado para describir el derramamiento de un empaque dio lugar a que por la expansión y la contracción de las dos superficies en los lados del empaque.

FTD   El diesel de Fischer-Tropsch.

FTP   El Método Experimental Federal.

La celda de combustible   Un dispositivo electroquímico que convierte la energía almacenó en gas de hidrógeno en electricidad, agua, y calor.

El riel de combustible   Un tem acostumbró describir el tubo que entrega el combustible de la línea de combustible para los inyectores individuales de combustible.

Échele combustible al sensor de compensación   Un sensor usado en vehículos de combustible de doblez que le provee la información al PCM en el contenido de etanol y temperatura del combustible en su estado actual a través del sistema de la entrega de combustible.'

La pila de la célula en combustible   Una colección de celdas individuales de combustible, cuáles son apilado unidos por los extremos en un paquete compacto.

La funcionabilidad   Se refiere a los aportes PCM comprobando la operación de las salidas.

Fungible   Un término acostumbró describir un producto que tiene el mismo grado o se encuentra las mismas especificaciones, como aceite, eso puede ser intercambiado con otro producto sin cualquier afecto.

La pandilla despedida   Pulsando inyectores en grupos.

La gasolina   El producto petrolero refinado que es usado primordialmente como un combustible motor. La gasolina está hecha de muchos hidrocarburos diferentes y también contiene aditivos para realzar su función en un HIELO.

La gasolina la inyección directa (GDI)   Un diseño de sistema de la inyección de combustible en el cual la gasolina es inyectada directamente en la cámara de combustión.

El gas para líquido   Un proceso refinador en el cual el gas natural es convertido en combustible líquido.

GAWR   La valuación vulgar del peso del eje. Una valuación de la aptitud de carga de un vehículo e incluido en pancartas en el vehículo y en el manual del dueño.

Gerotor   Un tipo de bomba positiva de desplazamiento que es a menudo usada en bombas de aceite de motor. Acostumbra lo engranando de dientes internos y externos del engranaje presurizar el combustible.

El tapón encendedor   Un elemento calentador que usa 12 voltios de la batería y ayudas en la puesta en marcha de un motor frío.

GMLAN   La General Motors la red local del área. Un tipo de transmisión de datos serial por General Motors.

GMM   Haciendo un gráfico de multimetro. Una cruz entre un metro digital y un osciloscope digital de almacenamiento.

El grado   La valuación de fuerza de un perno.

El alcohol de grano   Vea *etanol*.

La retícula   Las líneas cuadriculadas en el alcance filtran.

GVWR   La valuación vulgar del peso del vehículo. El peso total del vehículo incluyendo el máximo cargamento.

Las sierras para metales   Un tipo de herramienta de la mano que se usa para cortar metal u otros materiales duros.

El interruptor de efecto de vestíbulo   Un traslado semiconductor relativo a un campo magnético, creando una salida variable de voltaje. Un tipo de sensor electromagnético usado en ignición electrónica y otros sistemas y usado para determinar posición. Denominado para Edwin H. Hall, quién descubierto el efecto del Vestíbulo en 1879.

Los martillos   Una herramienta de la mano que se usa para aplicarle fuerza meciéndose.

Las perchas   Hecho de tela recubierta de hule con metal acaba ese agarre el silenciador y el tubo de escape en posición correcta a fin de que no toquen cualquier parte de metal. Esto ayuda a aislar el ruido eductor del resto de vehículo.

Los materiales de desecho arriesgados   Una clasificación de materiales que pueden causar que el daño pueble o el ambiente.

El calor de compresión   El aire es comprimido hasta su temperatura alcanza acerca de 1000 °F.

El resonador Helmholtz   Usados en la toma el ducto entre el filtro de aire y el cuerpo humano del obturador para reducir toma de aire divulgan durante la aceleración del motor.

HEPA pase la aspiradora   El vacío del filtro de aire del particulate de eficiencia alta acostumbró por completo frenar polvo.

El hertz   La medida de frecuencia.

HEUI La inyección Electrónica hidráulica de la Unidad, un tipo de sistema del inyector de diesel.

HEV Una abreviación para vehículo eléctrico híbrido.

La Ignición Alta de Energía El nombre de la General Motors para su ignición electrónica.

El metro de impedancia alta Mide la resistencia interna total del circuito de metro debido a bobinas internas, condensadores, y reostatos.

El riel común de presión alta El aceite pesado bajo la presión alta, sobre 20,000 PSI (138,000 kPa), es aplicado a los inyectores, cuáles son abiertos por un solenoide controlado por la computadora. Porque los inyectores son computadora controlada, el proceso de combustión puede controlarse precisamente a proveer máxima eficiencia del motor del ruido posible mínimo y agotar emisiones.

El encendido por compresión homogéneo de cargo Un proceso de combustión de baja temperatura que requiere aire – las mezclas de combustible estando quemado sin el uso de encendido de chispa.

HV cablegrafía Los cables del vehículo que conllevan alto voltaje.

HV El alto voltaje. Se aplica a cualquier voltaje por encima de 50 voltios.

La inyección electrónica hidráulica (HEUI) de la unidad Un tipo de inyector de aceite pesado que usa aceite de motor alto de presión para dirigir el inyector.

La asistencia de fuerza hidráulica Una configuración híbrida del vehículo que utiliza bombas hidráulicas y acumuladores para la regeneración de energía.

Hydrocracking Un proceso de la refinería que convierte hidrocarburos con un punto de ebullición alto en los unos con puntos de ebullición bajos.

La bomba Hydrokinetic Este diseño de bomba rápidamente mueve el combustible a crear presión.

Yo M 240 experimento Es una porción de la prueba FTP de 505 segundos usada por los fabricantes para certificar sus vehículos nuevos. Las "240" posiciones para 240 segundos de paseo en coche cronometran en un dinamómetro.

IAC El control de aire sin valor.

El motor desocupado de control de velocidad Un motor, usualmente un motor del stepper usado para mover un perno que permite más o menos aire después del plato del obturador por consiguiente controlando velocidad sin valor.

El alto sin valor Un bloque o un tornillo que detiene el plato del obturador de cerrar todo el muy que podría causar que eso meta la vivienda.

La prueba de vacío sin valor Una prueba realizado que usando un calibre de vacío pegó para la toma múltiple de un motor corriendo a velocidad sin valor.

El HIELO El motor de explosión.

IEC La Comisión Electrotécnica Internacional.

La oportunidad del momento inicial La oportunidad del momento de ignición acometió contra oportunidad del momento de la base.

El deflagrador El Módulo de Control de Ignición.

La bobina de ignición Un dispositivo eléctrico que consta de dos bobinas separadas de alambre: Un primario y un serpenteo secundario. El propósito de una bobina de ignición es producir una corriente–amperaje (acerca de 80 mA del amperaje bajo de alto voltaje (20,000 para 40,000 voltios), necesaria para el encendido de chispa.

El módulo de control de ignición (ICM) Controla (las vueltas de vez en cuando) la corriente primaria de ignición de un sistema electrónico de ignición.

El deflagrador de control de ignición Otro nombre para un módulo de control de ignición (ICM).

La oportunidad del momento de ignición El punto exacto de ignición en relación a pistón La posición.

Las Pulgadas de Mercurio (Adentro. Hg.) Una medida de vacío; Ejerza presión sobre debajo de la presión atmosférica.

La inyección indirecta (IDI) El combustible es inyectado en una precámara pequeña, lo cual está relacionado al cilindro por una abertura estrecha. La combustión inicial tiene lugar en esta precámara. Esto tiene como consecuencia desacelerar la tasa de combustión, lo cual tiende a reducir ruido.

El amperímetro inductivo Un tipo de amperímetro que está usado un sensor de Hall-Effect en una abrazadera que rodea a un conductor llevando una corriente.

La reactancia inductiva Una corriente contraria creada en un conductor cuandoquiera hay un flujo actual embestidor en un conductor.

Inerte Químicamente inactivo.

El interruptor de inercia Apaga el surtidor de gasolina eléctrico en un accidente.

La oportunidad del momento inicial Donde la bujía del motor despide en la velocidad sin valor. La computadora luego propone la oportunidad del momento basada fuera de la velocidad del motor y otros factores.

La bomba de inyección Le da el combustible a los inyectores en una presión alta y en los intervalos regulares. Cada inyector rocía combustible en la cámara de combustión en el momento preciso requerido para la combustión eficiente.

Introduzca en la computadora condicionamiento Lo que la computadora hace para el aporte señala para hacerlos útiles; Usualmente incluye uno analógico a convertidor digital y otros circuitos electrónicos que eliminan ruido eléctrico.

El aporte La información en datos de sensores para un controlador electrónico es llamada aporte. Los sensores y los interruptores proveen las señales de aporte.

La válvula de admisión Una válvula en un motor acostumbró permitir aire o aire y combustible en la cámara de combustión.

IOD La ignición fuera del empate. Otro nombre acostumbró describir batería tubo de desagüe eléctrico.

Intercooler Parecido a un radiador, en donde fuera de aire puede estar de paso, que enfríe lo presurizado calentó el aire.

Intermedie oscilaciones También designado el "campaneo" de la bobina en su estado actual pulsó tan mirado en un alcance.

El motor de explosión Un término usado para describir un motor normal usó en vehículos donde el combustible es interior consumido el motor mismo.

El invertidor Un dispositivo electrónico acostumbró convertir CD (la CD) en corriente alterna (alternando corriente).

Ignición que detecta ion Un tipo de bobina en ignición del tapón que usa un voltaje de la señal a través de la abertura de la bujía del motor después del tapón ha despedido para determinar la mezcla de combustible de aire y si golpe de la chispa ocurrieron.

Iridium dele inicio a los tapones Use un poco de iridium soldado encima del consejo de un electrodo central pequeño 0.0015 para 0.002 pulgada (0.4 para 0.6 mm) en el diámetro. El diámetro pequeño reduce el voltaje requerido para saltar sobre la abertura entre el centro y el electrodo lateral, por consiguiente reduciendo fallos de encendido posibles. El electrodo molido o lateral es usualmente aboquillado con platino para ayudar a reducir desgaste de savia del electrodo.

ISC El motor desocupado de control de velocidad.

KAM Conserve memoria viva.

La palabra clave Un tipo de comunicaciones de la red usadas en muchos vehículos Generales de Motores.

El kilo Quiere decir 1,000; la k o k abreviada.

El sensor de golpe Un sensor que puede detectar golpe de la chispa del motor.

La bomba de deserción de la fuga El Chrysler usa una bomba eléctrica que presuriza el sistema de combustible del que revisar en busca se filtra haciendo al PCM monitorear el sensor de presión del tanque de combustible.

Recueste señalizador Mientras más alto el oxígeno O2 nivela en el tubo de escape más parco la mezcla de combustible de aire.

GUIADO La abreviación para diodo ligero que emite.

La luz experimental CONDUCIDA Utiliza a un LED en lugar de una bombilla automotora estándar para una indicación visual de voltaje.

La bomba aspirante El aceite pesado es sacado del tanque de combustible por la bomba aspirante y le da el combustible a la bomba de inyección.

El aire lineal – échele combustible al sensor de proporción Otro nombre para un sensor ancho de oxígeno de la banda.

EGR lineal Contiene un stepper motor para precisamente regular flujo eductor del gas y un potenciómetro de información retroactiva que señala para la computadora la posición real de la válvula.

Los guantes del juez de línea El tipo de guantes llevados puestos por técnicos al circunvenir circuitos de alto voltaje. Usualmente incluye un guante interior cauchero evaluado en 1,000 voltios y un cuero protector guante exterior cuándo usado para el servicio eléctrico híbrido del vehículo.

El gas licuado de petróleo (LPG) Vendido tan comprimido propano líquido que está a menudo con el que se relacionó bien aproximadamente 10 % de otros gases como butano, propylene, butilenos, y mercaptan para darlos el propano incoloro e inodoro un olor.

La prueba de carga Un tipo de prueba de la batería donde la batería es clasificada bajo el rubro de una carga eléctrica.

La sonda lógica Un tipo de probador que puede detectar ya sea puede energizar o puede poner en tierra. La mayoría de probadores pueden detectar voltaje pero algunos no puede detectar si una tierra es presente sin más allá la experimentación.

El calor de baja calidad Las temperaturas del sistema de enfriamiento que están muy cerca para la temperatura del aire ambiental, resultantes la eficiencia de reembarque de calor adentro aminorada.

El gas de LP La sede *licuó gas petrolero.*

LRC La abreviación para el control de respuesta de carga también conocido como la detección electrónica de carga. Un sistema usado en muchos sistemas embestidores que activan el generador (el alternador) cuando una carga eléctrica es detectada y no todo el tiempo a ayudar a mejorar le dan pábulo a la economía.

M85 El combustible del motor de explosión conteniendo methanol de 85 gasolina % y de 15 %.

El generador magnético de pulso El generador de pulso consta de una rueda del gatillo (reluctor) y una bobina de arresto. La bobina de arresto consta de un corazón de hierro envuelto con alambre fino, en una bobina en un extremo y adjunto a la presente para un imán permanente en el otro extremo. El centro de la bobina es llamado el pedazo del polo.

El sensor magnético Usa un imán permanente rodeado por una bobina de alambre. Las muescas del cigüeñal (o el árbol de levas) crean una fuerza magnética variable del campo alrededor de la bobina. Cuando una sección metálica está próxima al sensor, el campo magnético es más fuerte porque el metal es un mejor conductor de líneas magnéticas de fuerza que aire.

El sensor resistente a Magnetic Un sensor que es similar a un sensor magnético pero, en lugar de producir una señal analógica de voltaje, la electrónica dentro del sensor mismo genere uno digital en señal/feriada o una salida.

La lámpara del señalizador de funcionamiento defectuoso Este ámbar, luz de advertencia de la consola puede ser motor del cheque de etiquetado motor o de servicio pronto.

El sensor del MAPA Un sensor usado para medir la presión dentro del tubo múltiple de la toma se comparó a un vacío perfecto.

La bobina casada También designado uno transformador golpeado ligeramente.

El sensor masivo de flujo de aire Mide la densidad y cantidad de aire desembocando en el motor, lo cual da como resultado control preciso del motor.

MCA Una abreviación para valuación de la batería de amperios marina que hace girar.

La fuerza mecánica Una fuerza se aplicó a un objeto.

El poder mecánico Una fuerza se aplicó a un objeto que da como resultado movimiento o movimiento.

Los returnless mecánicos le dan pábulo al sistema (MRFS) Un diseño de sistema de la entrega de combustible de returnless que usa un regulador de presión mecánico localizó en el tanque de combustible.

Mega El millón. Usado al escribir mayores números o medir una cantidad grande de resistencia.

La asamblea del electrodo de la membrana La parte de la celda de combustible PEM que contiene la membrana, los recubrimientos de catalizador, y los electrodos.

Mercurio Un metal líquido pesado.

La exactitud de metro La exactitud de un metro medido en el por ciento.

La resolución de metro La especificación de un metro que indica qué tan en trozos pequeños o muy bien una medida que el metro puede detectar y puede exhibir.

Methanol Típicamente manufacturado de gas natural. Methanol contente, incluyendo co-solvent, en gasolina sin plomo está limitado por ley para 5 %.

Methanol-to-gasoline (MTG) Un proceso refinador en el cual el methanol es convertido En gasolina líquida.

El alcohol metílico Vea *methanol.*

El metilo el éter terciario de butilo Un combustible oxigena eso está permitido adentro La gasolina sin plomo hasta un nivel de 15 %.

Los pernos métricos Los pernos manufacturados y dimensionado en el sistema métrico de La medida.

Micro (ó) Una millonésima parte de un voltio o el amperio.

El micrón El Igual para 0.000039 Adentro.

Milli (m) Una milésima de un voltio o un amperio.

El barrido de milisegundo El alcance barrerá sólo esa porción de al patrón que puede estar mostrada durante un 5 o trasfondo de 25 señoras.

MSDS La hoja material de datos de seguridad.

MTHF Methyltetrahydrofuron. Un componente de poco petróleo de P-Series basó combustibles.

Multiplexing Un proceso de señales remitentes de múltiplo de información al mismo tiempo sobre un alambre de la señal.

La conscripción mutual La generación de una corriente eléctrica debido a un campo magnético cambiante de una bobina adyacente.

Naturalmente (normalmente) aspirado Un motor que acostumbra atmosférico La presión para toma.

NEDRA Asociación Que Pone a Competir Obstáculo Nacional Y Eléctrico.

Niegue contrapresión Una válvula EGR que reacciona para un área de baja presión barométrica cerrando una válvula interna pequeña, que deja la válvula EGR ser abierta por vacío.

Niegue coeficiente de temperatura Usualmente usado con atención a un sensor de temperatura (la temperatura de líquido de refrigeración o de aire). Como la temperatura aumenta, la resistencia del sensor decrece.

La red Un sistema de comunicaciones acostumbró conectar módulos o computadoras múltiples.

La posición neutral Un término acostumbró describir la casa o la posición predeterminada del plato del obturador en un controlador electrónico del obturador.

NGV El vehículo natural del gas.

NiMH El hidruro de metal de níquel. Un diseño de la batería destinado para las baterías altas de voltaje en la mayoría de vehículos eléctricos híbridos.

El nodo Un módulo y computadora que es de una red de comunicaciones.

La luz Noid Diseñado para eléctricamente reemplazar el inyector en el circuito y brillar intermitentemente si el circuito del inyector está en marcha correctamente.

Nonchecking Algunas unidades Generales del cuerpo humano de obturador de Motores que no mantienen ejercen presión sobre.

El hidrocarburo de poco metano El estándar por el cual la experimentación eductor de la emisión para hidrocarburos es evaluada.

Nonprincipal fenezca Al frente del fin principal y es generalmente llamada la parte delantera del motor, donde los cinturones accesorios son usados.

La RAM no volátil La capacidad de memoria de la computadora que no está perdida cuando poder está distante. Vea también *memoria que se lee sólo (ROM).*

Los frutos secos Una hembra ensartó sujetador que es usado con un perno para sujetar dos las partes juntos.

OBD En la diagnosis del pizarrón.

El número de octano La medida de habilidad de una gasolina para resistir golpe del motor. Mientras más alto el octano evaluando, lo menos propenso la gasolina debe causar golpe del motor (la detonación).

Aceite galerías Una bomba de aceite, cuál es conducida por el motor, hace el aceite pasar a la fuerza a través del filtro de aceite y luego en pasajes en el cigüeñal y el bloque.

OL Abra circuito.

La opacidad El porcentaje de luz que se bloqueó por el tubo de escape Fume.

La prueba de voltaje de la batería del circuito manifiesto Una prueba de condición de la batería que se realizó sin una carga en la batería.

La llave mecánica de fin abierto Un tipo de llave mecánica que permite acceso para los reventones de un perno o una nuez de lado.

La operación del lazo manifiesto Una fase de operación del motor controlado por computadora donde el aire – la mezcla de combustible está calculada a falta de oxígeno que el sensor señala. Durante lazo abierto, los cálculos se basan primordialmente en posición del obturador, equipan con una máquina a RPM, y temperatura de líquido de refrigeración del motor.

Los sensores ópticos El uso ligero de un LED y un phototransistor a señalar La computadora.

Orgánico Un término usado para describir cualquier cosa que estaba viva en una vez.

ORVR Onboard poniéndole combustible a recuperación de vapor.

OSC La aptitud de almacenamiento de oxígeno.

Oscilloscope (el alcance) Un metro visual de voltio.

OSHA La Gerencia de Seguridad Ocupacional y de Salud.

El sensor de oxígeno Un sensor en el sistema eductor a medir lo El oxígeno contento del tubo de escape.

Los combustibles oxigenados Los combustibles como ETBE o MTBE que contiene moléculas adicionales de oxígeno para promover al limpiador quemándose. Los combustibles oxigenados son utilizados como aditivos de gasolina para reducir emisiones de Colorado.

El ozono El gas sustancioso en oxígeno (O3) creado por la reacción de la luz del sol con óxidos e hidrocarburos que no está quemado (HC) de nitrógeno (NOx); También el calledsmog.

Palladium Un catalizador que inicia una reacción química sin ponerse una parte de, o sea consumido adentro, el proceso.

El motor del panqueque Vea al *boxeador*.

La prueba del periódico Sujete una hoja de papel o una 3 _ 5 ficha (aun una cuenta del dólar surte efecto) dentro de 1 pulgada (2.5 centí metros) del tubo de escape con el motor corriendo en desocupado. El periódico debería apagarse con el viento uniformemente sin "dar resoplidos". Si el periódico se traza hacia el tubo de escape a veces, lo Las válvulas de escape en uno o más cilindros pudieron estar quemadas.

Los cilindros arreglados en pares Otro nombre acostumbró describir cilindros del compañero en un sistema de ignición de tipo de chispa residual.

La carga parásita Un término acostumbró describir un tubo de desagüe de la batería con todo circuitos completamente. También la batería designada la ignición o tubo de desagüe eléctrico de completamente dibuja.

La identificación de parámetro La información encontró en la corriente de datos del vehículo tan mirado en una herramienta de tomografía.

PCM La computadora del onboard que controla ambos la gerencia del motor y funciones de transmisión del vehículo.

PCV Ejerza presión sobre válvula de control.

La bomba periférica La bomba de la turbina.

Petrodiesel Otro término para diesel petrolero, el aceite pesado cuál es común refinado de petróleo crudo.

El petróleo Otro término para petróleo crudo. El significado literal de petróleo es petróleo.

El sensor PFE El sensor de información retroactiva de presión EGR.

PHEV El vehículo eléctrico híbrido con enchufe.

La bobina de arresto Una ignición dispositivo provocante electrónico en el sistema magnético del generador de pulso.

Piezoresistivity Cambie en la resistencia debido a la tensión.

La costura de la soldadura de la pizca Una sección fuerte bajo un vehículo donde dos paneles del cuerpo humano son soldados juntos.

El sonido corto y metálico El ardor rápido secundario del el último 3 % para 5% del aire – la mezcla de combustible en la cámara de combustión causa unas segundas apariencias de la llama que chocan con la primera parte delantera de la llama causando un ruido de golpe. También la detonación designada o el encendido llama a la puerta.

La carrera del émbolo Un movimiento del pistón de ida pero no regreso entre la parte superior y el fondo del cilindro.

El tono El tono de un sujetador roscado se refiere al número de hilos por la pulgada.

La bujía del motor de platino Una bujía del motor que tiene un poquito del platino de metal precioso se soldó encima del fin del electrodo central, así como también en el electrodo molido o lateral. El platino es un metal de blanco grisáceo que no reacciona con oxígeno y por consiguiente, no se erosionará fuera como podrá cursar con chispa convencional de la aleación de níquel Tapone electrodos.

El platino Un catalizador que inicia una reacción química sin ponerse una parte de, o sea consumido adentro, el proceso.

La asamblea plenaria Una cámara, localizado entre el cuerpo humano del obturador y los corredores de la toma múltiple, usada para distribuir la toma carga a la cuenta más uniformemente y eficazmente.

Los alicates Una herramienta de la mano con dos mandíbulas acostumbró agarre o vuelta una parte.

La polaridad La condición de ser positivo o negativo en relación a un polo magnético.

La celda de combustible de electrólito de polímero Otro término para celda de combustible PEM.

Haga estallar probador Un dispositivo destinado para comprobar una boquilla del inyector de diesel para patrón en aerosol correcto. La agarradera es oprimida y la gaseosa fuera de la presión es exhibida en el calibre.

Ponga a babor inyección de combustible Usos una boquilla para cada cilindro y el combustible es lanzado con jeringa en la toma múltiple acerca de 2 para 3 pulgadas (70 para 100 mm) de la válvula de admisión.

La contrapresión positiva Una válvula EGR que es diseñada con una válvula pequeña interior que sangra fuera de cualquier vacío aplicado e impide la válvula de abrirse a menos que ha el backpressure eductor se aplica a la válvula.

El desplazamiento positivo Todo el aire que entra es hecho pasar a la fuerza a través del supercargador de tipo de raíces.

La prueba de balance de poder Determina si todos los cilindros son contribuir poder igualmente. Determina esto poniendo en cortocircuito fuera de un cilindro a la vez.

PPE La abreviación para equipo protector personal.

PPO El aceite puro de la planta.

Preconverter Un convertidor pequeño, rápido de oxidación de calefacción.

Ejerza presión sobre válvula de control (PCV) Una válvula acostumbró controlar la presión de sistema de combustible en un sistema de combustible de tipo de entrega de demanda.

El diferencial de presión Una diferencia en la presión de un circuito del freno para otro.

La válvula de seguridad de presión Una válvula localizada en un poder timoneando bomba que usa una pelota del cheque, que derroca y deja fluido devolverle al estanque si presión excede un cierto volumen.

La válvula del respiradero de presión (PVV) Una válvula localizada en el tanque de combustible para impedir superpresión debido a la expansión termal del combustible.

Prevaleciendo nuez de fuerza de torsión Un diseño especial de sujetador de la nuez que es deforme ligeramente o tiene otras propiedades que permiso la nuez a quedar adjunto a la presente para el sujetador fuera aflojándose.

El circuito primario de ignición Los componentes de ignición que regulan la corriente en la bobina serpenteo primario revolviéndolo de vez en cuando.

El serpenteo primario La bobina bobinando eso es controlada por el módulo electrónico de control de ignición o PCM.

El fin principal El fin del motor al que el volante está pegado.

La interfaz programable (PCI) del controlador Un tipo de transmisión de datos serial usada por Chrysler.

El BAILE DE GRADUACIÓN La memoria que se lee sólo programable.

El propano Vea *gas de petróleo del liquified*.

La membrana de cambio del protón (PEM) Una celda de combustible de baja temperatura conocida para el ayuno empieza y construcción relativamente simple.

El generador de pulso Un sensor usado en igniciones distribuidoras acostumbró provocar el módulo de ignición.

El tren de pulso Un voltaje de CD que cambia de dirección de vez en cuando en una serie de pulsos.

La anchura de pulso Una medida de lo real en el tiempo medido adentro Los milisegundos.

Los punzones Un tipo de herramienta de la mano acostumbró conducir alfileres del rollo.

El convertidor del cachorro Vea *preconvertidor*.

El sensor de flujo de purga Revisa en busca de flujo adecuado de purga.

El motor Pushrod Destina un árbol de levas para las válvulas de admisión y un árbol de levas separado para las válvulas de escape. Cuando el árbol de levas está ubicado en el bloque, las válvulas son dirigidas por arrancadoras, pushrods, y balancines.

PWM La modulación de anchura de pulso.

La R y R Cambie de dirección y reemplace.

La RAM La memoria de acceso al azar.

El rango La distancia de la que un vehículo puede viajar a través en un cargo completo o tanque de combustible lleno sin recargar o reaprovisionarse. El rango es medido en millas o kilómetros.

Raster Apilado.

La racionalidad Se refiere a una comparación PCM de valor de aporte para los valores.

El trinquete Un tipo de herramienta de la mano que se usa para rotar un conector y es reversible.

RCRA Recurso Conservation y Recovery Actúan.

La retentiva Una notificación para el dueño de un vehículo que un asunto de seguridad necesita a corregirse.

La gasolina Reformulated (RFG) Ha oxigenado aditivos y están refinados para reducir ambos el contenido más ligero y más pesado de hidrocarburo de gasolina para promover al limpiador quemándose.

La regeneración Un proceso de tomar la energía cinética de un vehículo en movimiento y convertirlo a energía eléctrica y almacenarlo en una batería.

La presión de vapor Reid Un método de presión de vapor determinante de gasolina y otros productos petroleros. Ampliamente usado en la industria petrolera como un señalizador de la volatilidad de gasolina.

Reluctor Una rueda de metal mellada usada con un sensor magnético para detonar cigüeñal o la posición del árbol de levas.

La válvula de retención residual Una válvula en el fin de la conexión de salida del cilindro maestro para mantener el sistema hidráulico bajo una presión ligera en tambor Frena sólo.

El residuo o la presión de descanso Impide bolsa de vapor y problemas de principio caliente en estos sistemas.

El tubo de escape restringido El motor estará bajo en el poder, pero el alisado.

El rodio Un catalizador que inicia una reacción química sin ponerse una parte de, o sea consumido adentro, el proceso.

Bien para saber leyes Las leyes que manifiestan que los empleados tienen derecho a saber cuándo los materiales que acostumbran en el trabajo es arriesgado.

La corriente de la onda La corriente no deseada de corriente alterna de un generador (el alternador).

RMS Un método de aspereza calculadora de la superficie usando la raíz cuadrada de las lecturas promedias cuadradas.

La celda del rodillo La bomba de la veleta.

ROM La memoria que se lee sólo.

El tipo de raíces Denominados para Don Juan y Francis Roots, dos hermanos de Connersville, Indiana, quien patentaron el diseño en 1860 como un tipo de bomba de agua para ser usados en minas. Más tarde se usó para mover aire y es usado hoy en motores Dieseles ciclistas Detroit de dos tiempos y otros motores supercargados a la cuenta. El supercargador de tipo de raíces es llamado un diseño positivo de desplazamiento porque todo el aire que entra es hecho pasar a la fuerza a través de la unidad.

El motor rotativo Interviene quirúrgicamente el ciclo de cuatro tiempos pero usa un rotor en lugar de un pistón y el cigüeñal para lograr toma, compresión, poder, y golpe eductor.

La bomba rotativa de la veleta La bomba consta de un disco central del impeller, varios rodillos o veletas que andan en muescas en el impeller, y una bomba alojando eso es deducido de la línea divisoria central de la carretera del impeller.

La abertura del rotor Medidas el voltaje requerido para saltar sobre la abertura (0.030 para 0.050 adentro. o 0.8 para 1.3 mm) entre el rotor y los insertos (los segmentos) del distribuidor sellan con una tapa.

Corriendo prueba de compresión Una prueba que le puede dar a un técnico cuenta de la compresión relativa de todos los cilindros.

RVP La Abreviación para Reid Vapor Pressure

SAE La Sociedad de Ingenieros Automotores.

La saturación El punto de máxima fuerza magnética del campo de una bobina.

Schmitt provoque Convierte la señal analógica en una señal digital.

Los destornilladores Un tipo de herramienta de la mano acostumbró instalar o quitar tornillos.

El circuito secundario de ignición Los componentes necesarios para crear y distribuir el alto voltaje producido en los serpenteos secundarios de la bobina.

El serpenteo secundario Un serpenteo que tiene aproximadamente 100 cronometra el número de vueltas del serpenteo primario, referido como la proporción de vueltas (aproximadamente 100:1).

La autoinducción La generación de una corriente eléctrica en los alambres de una bobina creada cuándo la corriente es primera conectada o sometida a la eutanasia.

La inyección secuencial (SFI) de combustible Un sistema de la inyección de combustible en el cual los inyectores son pulsados individualmente consecutivamente con la orden de encendido.

Las comunicaciones seriales interactúan (SCI) Un tipo de transmisión de datos serial usada por Chrysler.

Los datos seriales Los datos que es transmitido por una serie de señales de voltaje rápidamente cambiantes.

El servomotor Un motor eléctrico que mueve un accionador como el plato del obturador en un controlador electrónico del obturador.

La bomba del canal lateral La bomba de la turbina.

Singularice árbol de levas aéreo (SOHC) Cuando un árbol de levas aéreo es usado.

El SORBO Indique Plan de Implementación.

Torcido Una salida de un sensor que se mueve entre la dirección correcta pero exactamente no mide condición es diseñada a la medida.

El humo y niebla El término acostumbró describir una combinación de humo y niebla. Formado por NOx y HC con luz del sol.

Los recortes Un tipo de herramienta de la mano acostumbró cortar metal en chapa y otros materiales delgados.

El conector Una herramienta que calza sobre la cabeza de un perno o una nuez y es rotada por un trinquete o la barra del interruptor.

El adaptador del conector Un adaptador que deja el uso de un tamaño de conductor (el trinquete o el interruptor atranca) rotar otro tamaño de paseo en coche de conector.

El solvente Los líquidos usualmente incoloros que se usan para quitar engrasan y aceitan.

El encendido de chispa la inyección directa (SIDI) El nombre de la General Motors para gasolina el sistema directo de la inyección.

El golpe de la chispa Vea *Detonación*.

La línea de la chispa Una línea horizontal pequeña inmediatamente después de la línea de fuego.

La salida de la chispa El término que los Fordes usaron para describir la terminología OBD-II para la señal de salida del PCM para el sistema de ignición que los controles equipan con una máquina la oportunidad del momento.

El probador de la chispa Se parece a una bujía del motor pero tiene un electrodo central diferido y ningún electrodo lateral. El probador comúnmente tiene un clip del lagarto adjuntado a la concha a fin de que puede ser sujetado en una buena toma de tierra en el motor.

La energía específica La energía contenta de una batería relativo a populacho de la batería. La energía específica es medida en vatio-horas por el kilogramo (Wh/kg).

La densidad de velocidad El método de calcular la cantidad de combustible necesitado por el motor.

Empalme paquete Uno punto céntrico donde muchas líneas seriales de datos se apiñan, a menudo abrevió a SP.

La combustión espontánea Una condición que puede causar algunos materiales, como los harapos aceitosos, para comenzar a arder sin una fuente de ignición.

El avión supersónico de transporte La abreviación para herramientas de servicio discrecional.

El PICO El término usado por Ford para describir la "chispa fuera de" señal del ICM para el PCM.

SRE La abreviación para parte de fin del anillo de desliz de un generador (el alternador).

El avión supersónico de transporte La abreviación para herramienta de servicio discrecional.

El protocolo corporativo estándar (SCP) Un protocolo de comunicaciones de la red usado por Ford.

El estado de salud (SOH) Una señal envió por un módulo a todos los demás módulos en la red señalando que está sana y capaz transmitir.

La proporción Stoichiometric La proporción o mezcla ideal en la cual todo el combustible se combina con todo el oxígeno en el aire y quema completamente.

El aceite directamente vegetal El aceite vegetal, un triglicérido con una unión del componente de glicerina tres las cadenas de hidrocarburo del 16 al 18 los átomos de carbón cada uno.

El golpe La distancia los recorridos del émbolo en el cilindro de un motor.

El semental Una barra pequeña con hilos en ambos fenece.

Supercharger Le fuerza el aire – la mezcla de combustible en el cilindro para aun el mayor poder.

Superpuesto Una posición usada para considerar diferencias en patrones entre cilindros en todas las áreas excepta la línea de fuego.

Supercharger Un motor dispositivo conducido que le fuerza aire bajo presión en la toma múltiple para aumentar poder del motor.

El cargo de la superficie Un cargo en una batería que simplemente en la superficie de los platos y no indica el estado verdadero de cargo de la batería.

SWCAN Una abreviación para alambre solo PUEDE (la Red del área del Controlador).

Switchgrass Un feedstock para la producción de etanol que requiere muy poca energía o el fertilizante a cultivar.

La alternación Encendiéndose intermitentemente del circuito primario.

Syncrude Un producto de un proceso donde el carbón sea abatido para crear productos líquidos. Primero el carbón es reaccionado con hidrógeno (H2) en altas temperaturas y presión con un catalizador.

Syn-gas El gas de síntesis generado por una reacción entre carbón y vapor. Syn-gas está hecho en su mayor parte hidrógeno y monóxido de carbono y se usa para hacer methanol. Syn-gas está también conocido como gas del pueblo.

El combustible sintético Los combustibles generaron procesos sintéticos directos como Fischer-Tropsch.

La prueba de golpe ligero Implica taconear (no golpeando) en el convertidor catalítico usando un mazo cauchero.

El transformador golpeado ligeramente Vea *bobina casada.*

El gerente de tarea Un Chrysler de término acostumbra describir el programa de el software que es diseñado para manejar la operación de todos los monitores OBD-II controlando la secuencia de pasos necesarios para ejecutar los monitores y pruebas diagnósticas.

TBI La inyección del cuerpo humano de obturador.

La fuerza de tensión El máximo estrés usado bajo la tensión (la fuerza colocada a lo largo) sin causar fracaso.

Terminando reostatos Los reostatos acomodados al final de un circuito serial de datos de alta velocidad a ayudar a reducir interferencia electromagnética.

El éter de metilo de tertiary-amyl Uno oxigena sumado para gasolina que es inflamable y puede formar mezclas explosivas con aire. Es ligeramente soluble en agua, muy soluble en éteres y alcohol, y soluble en la mayoría de solventes orgánicos incluyendo hidrocarburos.

Pruebe luz Una luz acostumbró experimentar para el voltaje. Contiene una bombilla con un alambre molido en un extremo y un consejo enseñado con el dedo en el otro extremo.

Tetraethyl lleve la delantera Un líquido agrandó gasolina en los inicios de 1920s para reducir la tendencia para golpear.

El sensor de temperatura del cuerpo humano del obturador (TBT) Un sensor de temperatura que se montó en el cuerpo humano del obturador y medidas la temperatura del aire entrando en el motor.

El sensor de la posición del obturador El sensor que provee información retroactiva concirniéndole la posición del plato del obturador.

TID Pruebe Identificación.

Cronometre base El trasfondo cuánto tiempo será exhibido en cada bloque.

El punto muerto superior (TDC) El punto más alto en el cilindro del que el pistón puede viajar a través. La medida de punto muerto inferior (BDC) para TDC determina la longitud de golpe del cigüeñal.

El transistor Un dispositivo semiconductor que puede operar como un amplificador o un interruptor eléctrico.

El sensor de temperatura de fluido de transmisión (TFT) Un sensor halló dentro de un transeje automático de transmisión que mide la temperatura de la fluido.

Provoque ras con ras El principio del despliegue.

La cuesta del gatillo La dirección de voltaje que un waveform debe tener para iniciar el despliegue.

Desencadenándose La acción de un sensor que se enciende o fuera de la corriente a través de una bobina de ignición en la ignición controla módulo o PCM.

La luz de emergencia Una luz diseñada para ayudar a reparar a técnicos la sede al trabajar en un vehículo.

El transformador verdadero Vea *bobina divorciada.*

TSB El boletín técnico de servicio.

La bomba de la turbina Las vueltas en las velocidades superiores y están más quietas que las otras bombas eléctricas.

El atraso del turbo El retraso entre la aceleración y el estímulo del turbo.

La turbina alimentadora Un supercargador de poder eductor.

La proporción de vuelta El número de veces que los serpenteos secundarios en una bobina de ignición excedan eso del serpenteo primario.

TWC El convertidor de tres formas.

El par torcido Un par de alambres que son retorcidos juntos del 9 al 16 cambia de dirección por pie de longitud. La mayoría es retorcida una vez en todas formas (12 por pie) para ayudar a reducir interferencia electromagnética en los alambres como un alambre tendría tendencia a cancelar fuera cualquier El arresto de interferencia levantado por el otro alambre.

UART Receive Asincrónico universal/Transmit, un tipo de transmisión de datos serial.

UBP El protocolo basado a UART.

UCG La gasificación clandestina de carbón.

Ultracapacitor Una tecnología especializada del condensador con aptitud aumentada de almacenamiento para un volumen dado.

UNC El nacional unificado grueso. Un tipo de hilo usado en sujetadores.

La gasificación clandestina (UCG) de carbón Un proceso funcionó clandestinamente donde el carbón es convertido en un combustible líquido.

El tanque subterráneo de almacenamiento Un tipo de depósito de petróleo que está ubicado subterráneo.

UNF La multa nacional unificada. Un tipo de hilo usado en sujetadores.

El acoplamiento universal Una juntura en una dirección o el árbol propulsor que deja a fuerza de torsión serle transmitidas en ángulo.

La ignición integrada a Up El control de ignición donde toda oportunidad del momento que funciones son realizadas en el PCM, en vez de ser hendidura entre el módulo de control de ignición y el PCM.

El aceite de cocinar usado Un término usado cuando el aceite puede o no puede ser aceite vegetal puro.

El aceite usado Cualquier aceite basado en petróleos o sintético que ha sido usado.

El vacío Cualquier presión menos de la presión atmosférica (14.7 PSI).

La prueba de vacío Probando el motor para hacer girar vacío, vacío sin valor, y vacío en 2,500 RPM.

VAF El flujo de aire de la veleta.

La bolsa de vapor Una condición parca y causada por ahí vaporizada combustible en el sistema de combustible.

El sensor variable de combustible Vea *sensor de compensación de combustible.*

El sensor variable de renuencia El sensor magnético.

VECI La información de control de la emisión del vehículo. Esta etiqueta adhesiva está ubicada bajo la capucha en todos los vehículos e incluye información relatada en emisión que es importante para el técnico de servicio.

V-FFV Una abreviación para un vehículo flexible virtual de combustible. Este tipo de vehículo no usa un sensor de combustible y en lugar de eso usa el sensor de oxígeno (s) para detectar la cantidad de ser alcoholes acostumbró en el sistema.

VIN El número de la identificación del vehículo.

El vehículo flexible a Virtual de combustible El vehículo flexible de combustible virtual puede intervenir quirúrgicamente gasolina pura, E10, E85, o cualquier combinación.

VOC El compuesto orgánico volátil.

La volatilidad Una medida de la tendencia de un líquido a convertirse en vapor. La volatilidad es medida utilizando a RVP, o presión de vapor Reid.

La prueba de caída de voltaje Una prueba eléctrica funcionó con corriente fluyendo a través del circuito para determinar qué voltaje está perdido para la resistencia.

La eficiencia volumétrica La proporción entre la cantidad de aire – échele combustible a la mezcla que realmente entra en el cilindro y la cantidad que podría entrar bajo las condiciones ideales expresadas en el por ciento.

El motor Wankel Un motor rotativo.

Washcoat Un material poroso de aluminio que hace la superficie áspera.

Las máquinas de lavar Los discos planos de metal con un hueco en medio usado bajo sujetadores roscados para ayudar a lo que esparcir sujeta fuerza sobre un área más ancho.

Desaproveche aceite vegetal Este aceite podría incluir al animal o los aceites de pescado de cocinar.

La válvula de expulsión Una válvula parecido a una puerta que puede abrir y el final. La válvula de expulsión es una válvula desviadora en la ensenada eductor para la turbina. Permite todo el tubo de escape en la turbina, o puede encaminar parte del pasado eductor la turbina al sistema eductor.

La ignición de la chispa desperdiciada Introducido en lo mid-1980s, usa el onboard La computadora para pegarle fuego a la ignición arrolla.

El separador de combustible de agua Las separatas lagrimean y le echan combustible a en un motor Diesel.

Moje examen de compresión Una prueba que usa aceite para ayudar a la foca alrededor de lo Los anillos de pistón.

WHMIS El Lugar De Trabajo los Sistemas Arriesgados de Información de Materiales.

El sensor de abolición ancho de oxígeno Un diseño del sensor de oxígeno que es capaz de detectar aire real – dele pábulo a las proporciones. Esto está en contraste para un sensor convencional de oxígeno que sólo cambia voltaje cuándo más rico o más parco que aire del stoichiometric – dele pábulo a la proporción.

Los parques eólicos Un grupo de molinos en un área.

El alcohol de madera Vea *methanol*.

La carta constitucional ancha mundial de combustible Un estándar de calidad de combustible desarrollado por fabricantes del vehículo y del motor en 2002.

La llave mecánica Una herramienta de la mano acostumbró agarre y rotáceo uno sujetador roscado.

WWFC La abreviación para carta constitucional ancha mundial de combustible.

INDEX